TWENTIETH-CENTURY
RHETORICS AND RHETORICIANS

215
431
21119

TWENTIETH-CENTURY RHETORICS AND RHETORICIANS

Critical Studies and Sources

Edited by
Michael G. Moran
and
Michelle Ballif

GREENWOOD PRESS
Westport, Connecticut • London

Library of Congress Cataloging-in-Publication Data

Twentieth-century rhetorics and rhetoricians : critical studies and sources / edited by
Michael G. Moran and Michelle Ballif.
    p. cm.
    Includes bibliographical references and index.
    ISBN 0–313–30391–6 (alk. paper)
    1. Rhetoric—History—20th century. I. Moran, Michael G. II. Ballif, Michelle, 1964–
P301.T89   2000
808'.009'04—dc21   99–059559

British Library Cataloguing in Publication Data is available.

Library of Congress Catalog Card Number: 99–059559
ISBN: 0–313–30391–6

First published in 2000

Greenwood Press, 88 Post Road West, Westport, CT 06881
An imprint of Greenwood Publishing Group, Inc.
www.greenwood.com

Printed in the United States of America

The paper used in this book complies with the
Permanent Paper Standard issued by the National
Information Standards Organization (Z39.48–1984).

10 9 8 7 6 5 4 3 2 1

P
301
T89
2000

To

Elizabeth Jennings Moran

and

B. Arcy

CONTENTS

INTRODUCTION

The twentieth century could be characterized as having been a rhetorical century. Although at the beginning of the century, rhetoric, despite its rich heritage, lacked intellectual vigor, after midcentury rhetoric became a key concept, a key term, not only within its own home disciplines of English and Speech Communications Departments but also within nearly every social science. The twentieth century has witnessed "the linguistic turn" as evidenced by work in language philosophy and linguistics (Ludwig Wittgenstein and C. S. Peirce); speech-act theory (J. L. Austin and J. Searle); semiotics (Ferdinand de Saussure and Umberto Eco); hermeneutics (Martin Heidegger and Hans-Georg Gadamer); neo-pragmatism (Richard Rorty and Stanley Fish); argumentation theory (Stephen Toulmin and Chaïm Perelman); as well as literary studies, cultural studies, anthropology, and even the so-called hard sciences. Rhetoric, having found itself disparaged for centuries, now finds itself as the center of attention, as scientists Thomas S. Kuhn and Paul Feyerabend discussed the rhetoricity of the scientific method and as philosophers Jacques Derrida and Michel Foucault discussed the rhetoricity of the metaphysical tradition. Rhetoric seems to have found a welcome embrace in the twentieth century.

Of course, all of this attention has begged the centuries-old question of the *definition* of rhetoric. Twentieth-century rhetoric, in fact, defies definition. Indeed, at the groundbreaking Wingspread Conference, which produced *The Prospect of Rhetoric* (Bitzer and Black 1971), participant Larry Rosenfield remarked, " 'So far as I can tell,' the notion of rhetorical phenomena 'includes everything but tidal waves.' Richard McKeon responded, 'Why not tidal waves?' " (qtd. in Bitzer 20). Although some, including Lloyd Bitzer himself, now argue for a more delimiting definition of rhetoric and rhetorical phenomena, this volume, *Twentieth-Century Rhetorics and Rhetoricians*, does not. Rather this volume desires to represent the multiple ways in which rhetoric has been conceived, theorized, and practiced by rhetoricians during the last 100 years. However, due to space constraints, the editors have had to, by including some, exclude others. For the purposes of this volume we have limited the figures and movements to those who most notably impacted rhetoric within the realm of English studies, particularly as they inform writing theory, and hence we have excluded contributions made by those in the disciplines of speech communications and sociolinguistics, for example. Also, we have included major figures who may not consider themselves to be rhetoricians but who have, nevertheless, made significant contributions to rhetorical theory and who have informed other rhetoric scholars and movements within the field.

The purpose of this reference volume is to provide introductory entries on many major and minor twentieth-century rhetoricians. The book is intended to be used not only by the expert but also by students entering the field and scholars in related fields who need an introduction to the rhetoric and rhetoricians of the period. Each entry offers a brief biography of the rhetoricians, followed by an analysis of the figure's rhetorical theory and an up-to-date bibliography of the figure's primary works as well as critical responses to that work. Although the figures are arranged alphabetically for easy reference, users can also read the volume through from beginning to end to get a sense of the major statements in rhetoric of the period. While not every minor rhetorician appears in the volume, the editors have attempted to offer a broad survey of representative figures of the period. The editors have also attempted to include representatives of most major schools of rhetorical theory from the century, including current-traditionalists, expressivists, cognitivists, neoclassicists, social-epistemicists, poststructuralists and postmodernists, and scholars of the new technologies. While these categories overlap and some theorists can fit into more than one, the categories do offer a useful overview of the directions that rhetoric took during the century, and a few words about each will provide an intellectual context for the figures in the book.

The editors are aware of the irony of producing a book of individual rhetoricians, 80 percent of whom are male, all of whom are white. The radical rhetoricity of the last part of this century has called into question issues of canonicity, of Great-Men histories, of solitary authorship, and has made a call for difference. We concur with the editors of *Professing the New Rhetorics* that "this lack [of difference] be seen as [a] reminder that, until recently, the rhetorical canon has been dominated by white, male contributors. But rather than view this as an exclusion or reification, we might more constructively use this knowledge as a call for future inquiry . . . [a call] to find new voices, new contributions, and even more new rhetorics" (Enos and Brown xiii). We are confident that these newer-than-new rhetorics created at the end of the previous century will compose a subsequent volume, *Rhetorics and Rhetoricians of the Twenty-first Century*.

CURRENT-TRADITIONAL RHETORIC

Current-traditional rhetoric was the dominant teaching rhetoric of the century up through the 1960s when other rhetorics, especially expressive and neoclassic systems, challenged its supremacy. Current-traditionalism grew to full strength during the late nineteenth century, especially at Harvard, where rhetoricians such as Adams Sherman Hill and Barrett Wendell produced their influential texts that outlined the approach. Current-traditional rhetoric was committed to the positivism of nineteenth-century science that assumed that reality existed apart from language used to express it. Hence, language is useful only to the extent that it is clear and does not distort reality. Good writing, the current-traditionalists assumed, should function as a windowpane through which the reader can see the truth that the writer presents. Current-traditionalists therefore emphasized the plain, unadorned style that was most closely identified with early science of the British Royal Society.

Current-traditional rhetoric was a truncated system that largely ignored the central canon of the Aristotelian rhetoric. In Aristotle's *Rhetoric*, invention, the system of *topoi* designed to help the rhetor discover arguments, was centrally important, as Aristotle's famous definition suggests: "So let Rhetoric be defined as *the faculty of discovering* in the particular case what are the available means of persuasion" (1.2; emphasis added). Invention, the art of discovering arguments that suit the occasion, is at the heart of Aristotelian rhetoric. Current-traditional rhetoric, on the other hand, assumed that student writers already had ideas to communicate. What they needed was a system to help them manage those ideas. Consequently, rhetoricians of this school emphasized various strategies for organizing into essays the ideas and insights that the writer brought to the writing process. Most current-traditional rhetorics therefore provided strategies for paragraphing and organizing longer pieces of discourse by means of the modes of discourse, which usually consisted of some combination of description, narration, exposition, and argumentation/persuasion. As Sharon Crowley argues in *The Methodical Memory*, invention, limited to the results of individual introspection, was largely reduced to a concern for establishing spatial relationships among ideas on a page (13).

Although current-traditional rhetoric dominated school rhetorics for the first 60 years of the past century (and continues as a reactionary force, especially in conservative textbooks), it was not an innovative movement during this century. It represents the stultification of rhetoric at a time when composition was considered by many as an intellectually stagnant element of English studies. Consequently, this volume contains no entries on the current-traditionalists, to a large extent because most of the innovators of this system, including Hill and Wendell, did their important work in the previous century. In the current volume, we do include entries on innovative rhetoricians who questioned the hegemony of this dominant rhetoric, including Frank Aydelotte, one of the founders of the thought approach to composition, and Fred Newton Scott and Gertrude Buck, two early-century theorists sometimes considered epistemicists. Even in Scott's work, however, the power of current-traditional rhetoric manifests itself. Although he was an innovative theorist and developed one of the most important rhetoric programs in the country at the University of Michigan, his textbooks were clearly in the current-traditionalist camp and often advocated methods of rhetoric at odds with his theory stated elsewhere.

EXPRESSIVE RHETORIC

The first sustained challenge to current-traditional orthodoxy came in the form of expressive rhetoric. Expressivism rejected the scientism of current-traditionalism with its emphasis on correctness, clarity, and form and emphasized instead personal writing that reflected the autonomous writer's individual experience, reactions, and beliefs. Meaning, the expressivists assumed, resulted from a private search in which the writer drew on both intellect and emotion to discover a personally significant truth. The writing that expressivists valued was often the personal narrative that explored a student's experience and relayed it to a sympathetic audience. Most expressivists also emphasized the writing process, advocating the processes of prewriting, drafting, and editing as important stages in the discovery of written meaning. They therefore placed the discovery process at the heart of the act of writing, but this discovery was largely limited to personal significance. Critics of expressivism have pointed out the romantic, even solipsistic, assumptions of much expressive pedagogy, especially its rejection of writing's social context. More recent work, however, especially Sherrie L. Gradin's *Romancing Rhetorics*, has pointed out the implicit concern in much expressionist thought for "the dialectical interaction among writer, community, and social, political, and economic conditions of existence" (108). Gradin identifies many sites in expressive pedagogy that value social interaction in the form of conferencing, collaboration, and empathy with a reader. Gradin identifies Ann Berthoff as a "pioneer" of social expressivism because of her emphasis in books such as *The Making of Meaning* (1981) and *Reclaiming the Imagination* (1984) on personal language being meaningful only within social contexts (115–16).

While not a formal school, expressivists formed a loose-knit group of practitioners and theorists who changed the landscape of writing instruction beginning in the late 1960s and 1970s, when they enjoyed their widest influence. The practitioners, who developed pedagogies based on expressive principles, included Ken Macrorie, Donald Murray, Ann Berthoff, and Peter Elbow, among others, all of whom produced important books during the 1960s and 1970s. Macrorie's *Uptaught* (1970), which was influenced by the student dissent of the 1960s, introduced the notion of "Engfish," that voiceless prose typical of many freshman writers, to point to the major problem of student prose: It is boring, canned, and dead. In its place he called for writing that was fresh, original, and personal. Macrorie went on to produce textbooks such as *Telling Writing* (3rd ed. 1980), *Writing to Be Read* (3rd ed. 1984), and *Searching Writing* (1980), designed to elicit the kind of interesting personal writing that he valued. A professional writer himself, Don Murray attempted to bring to college writing instruction the techniques that professional writers use. In *A Writer Teaches Writing* (1968) and his textbook *Write to Learn* (1984), Murray advocated that student writers discover subjects for writing within their own experiences and develop them using the writing process. He also pioneered the writing conference in which student writers discuss their drafts with a teacher functioning as a coach. Finally, perhaps the best known of the expressionists, Peter Elbow produced a series of important books on expressive pedagogy beginning with *Writing without Teachers* (1973) and continuing with *Writing with Power* (1981) and *Embracing Contraries* (1986). Elbow has remained a powerful advocate for expressivism even as the profession has more recently embraced the principles of social construction and postmodernism. Unlike these later movements, which have advocated the writer's voice as a product of social, cultural, and political forces, Elbow has remained committed to the individual as an autonomous entity capable of exploring his or her thoughts and feelings and writing about them. He has also argued against the recent emphasis on academic writing, which he claims devalues the student's personal voice.

In addition to the practitioners, discourse theorists have established expressivism as a distinct kind of discourse. Perhaps the most influential theorist is James Britton. With colleagues Tony Burgess, Nancy Martin, Alex McLeod, and Harold Rosen in *The Development of Writing Abilities (11–18)* (1975), he researched the kind of writing that children produced in British schools during the 1960s and early 1970s. Based on the analysis of student scripts, Britton and his coauthors developed their influential taxonomy of discourse based on the function categories of transactional, expressive, and poetic. Most school writing, he discovered, was transactional, which included informative and conative (regulative and persuasive) writing. Students had little chance to produce expressive writing, the kind of writing, Britton and his colleagues argued, that was the relatively unstructured, not highly explicit writing that reveals the writer's self and personality to a sympathetic audience. Because of these qualities, expressive writing, Britton concluded, is the most important kind of writing for young students to practice. Developmentally, it is the type from which the two other functions differentiate themselves as students develop cognitively and gain experience with written language. Students, Britton concluded, should begin reading and writing expressive prose and then advance to transactional and poetic functions as their language abilities mature. The second major theorist is James Kinneavy, who in his important *A Theory of Discourse* (1971) identified expressive discourse as one of the four major aims of discourse, along with reference, persuasive, and literary. While Kinneavy does not argue with Britton that students should learn to write expressive discourse before turning to other forms, he does view expressive discourse as "psychologically prior" to the other aims. Expressive discourse, which is a component in all other kinds of discourse,

Kinneavy argues, "gives all discourse a personal significance to the speaker and listener" (396).

COGNITIVE RHETORIC

If expressivists such as Murray and Emig began sustained work on the writing process, cognitive rhetoric has extended that work by developing cognitive models that attempt to model the writing process. Unlike the expressivists, who valued a kind of intuition very much in the romantic tradition, the cognitivist attempted to develop a rhetoric based on the workings of the human mind as understood by cognitive scientists. Cognitive theories draw on the findings of cognitive science, an interdisciplinary conglomeration of fields that includes elements of psychology, artificial intelligence, linguistics, anthropology, philosophy, and neuroscience (Miller, Polson, and Kintsch 1). Over the past several decades, as Andrea A. Lunsford notes in "Cognitive Studies and Teaching Writing," cognitive science has built bridges "between disciplines in order to work toward a general theory of cognition and communication" (146). Perhaps the most important contribution of cognitive science to composition theory has been the models of the writing process developed by Linda Flower and John R. Hayes in a series of articles (see the entry on Flower) and by Carl Bereiter and Marlene Scardamalia in *The Psychology of Written Composition* (1987), one of the most thorough statements of the cognitivist position.

Flower and Hayes's model, outlined in "A Cognitive Process Theory of Writing," was developed through their controversial thinking-aloud protocols in which they recorded writers as they explained out loud what they think and do during all stages of a writing task. While they have been criticized for distorting the writing process, the protocol scripts, once analyzed, have provided data from which Flower and Hayes constructed their famous model of the writing process. The model, based largely on the principles of Aristotelian rhetoric, emphasizes the recursive interactions among various cognitive functions that writers use when producing a document. These functions include activities such as analyzing the writing assignment (including evaluating the topic and audience); planning the discourse, which includes generating information, setting goals, and organizing; translating thought into language; and reviewing the written material by means of reading and editing. All of these stages of the process are recursive in that the writer can return to earlier stages anywhere in the process. In addition to the many scholarly essays that present various parts of the model, Flower has written *Problem Solving Strategies*, a textbook based on her research, now in its fifth edition.

Cognitive rhetoric, especially the Flower and Hayes version, has been criticized on a number of grounds ranging from (1) weaknesses in protocol analysis, (2) a confusion of what their model means, and (3) the theory's tendency to ignore social context. Since the entire model grew out of writers' protocols, these deserve special attention. In a classic analysis, Marilyn Cooper and Michael Holzman attack protocols on the grounds that they are suspect as a method of data collection because few people are trained well enough to talk about something that they are at the same time doing. Cooper and Holzman also claim that while the protocol scripts that Flower and Hayes provided are suspiciously coherent, most protocols are partial, elliptical, a mere trace of the subject's thoughts. Flower and Hayes argue in response that it is true that protocol analysis presents only a partial picture of the complexity of composition. But the method is one of the few ways to discover what writers think and experience during all steps of the writing process. Analyzing the protocols helps researchers in the cognitive school achieve their goals, to explore the planning and generation of ideas in writing. A second criticism of Flower and Hayes focuses on their model of the composing process. Cooper and Holzman, and Stephen North, criticize Flower and Hayes for confusing their model with empirical reality by claiming that it is "an actual description of mental processes" rather than an ideal model that is an abstraction designed to encourage further research (Cooper and Holzman 285). The danger occurs when teachers, taking the model literally, instruct students to follow it as if it described how actual people behave (285). Perhaps the strongest criticism has come from social constructionists such as Patricia Bizzell in "Cognition, Convention, and Certainty," who argues that the Flower and Hayes model is flawed because it assumes that writing is a psychological process that takes place free from meaningful social and political contexts. Thinking, the social constructivists assume, is conditioned by social forces, a fact that the early work of Flower and Hayes did not emphasize. Flower has answered her critics by producing *The Construction of Negotiated Meaning*, which proposes a social cognitive theory of writing. She admits that social knowledge and conventions of thinking provide both options and constraints; but within those constraints, individual writers produce unique constructions and these "individual differences in making meaning [in writing] are the reason we read one another" (110).

RECLAMATION OF THE CLASSICAL TRADITION/ HISTORIOGRAPHIES OF RHETORIC

The long reign of current-traditional rhetoric was deposed by a renewed interest in the rhetorical tradition, in classical rhetoric, specifically. Current-traditional rhetoric—as has been noted—was relatively uninformed by rhetorical practices and principles, particularly in its neglect of the canon of invention. By the beginning of the twentieth century, rhetoric bore little resemblance to its progenitor, the classical rhetoric of Athens, Greece. Although scholars continued to study classical texts, this work was conducted outside of English departments: in classics and speech communication departments. The reintroduction of classical rhetoric to English departments, as detailed in "The Revival of Rhetoric

in America" by Robert J. Connors, Lisa S. Ede, and Andrea Lunsford, was
begun in the late 1930s and early 1940s when scholars such as Kenneth Burke
infused literary criticism with neo-Aristotelian principles (8).

This revival began in earnest by the 1963 Conference on College Composition
and Communication (CCCC), the meeting "that most historians of rhetoric point
to as the first gathering of the 'modern' profession of composition studies. During that year's meeting, Wayne Booth gave his paper on 'The Rhetorical
Stance,' Francis Christensen delivered his 'Generative Rhetoric of the Sentence,'
and, most important for classical studies, Edward P. J. Corbett spoke on 'The
Usefulness of Classical Rhetoric' " (Connors, Ede, and Lunsford 10). Corbett's
landmark presentation, which was subsequently published in *College Composition and Communication*, "was but the first of a whole series of articles he
would write on the application of classical rhetoric to writing. Corbett's work
culminated in his important textbook, *Classical Rhetoric for the Modern Student*,
which appeared in 1965" (10).

Renewed research in classical studies led English scholars to turn to their
counterparts in speech communications departments, who had long since been
engaged in recovery work, thereby bridging the historical severance between
the two departments. The Rhetoric Society of America, founded in 1968, facilitated this cooperation.

Thus, the reclamation of classical rhetoric served to join rhetoricians in English and speech communication departments, to endow compositionists with a
professional legitimacy unknown in American institutions, and to attack current-
traditional rhetoric's theoretical and pedagogical sterility. In short, the rediscovery of classical rhetoric in the latter half of the century, the rediscovery of
Aristotelian principles such as invention, provided teachers of writing with a
historically respected and tested body of knowledge and a theory and vocabulary
with which to discuss writing concerns.

Although most compositionists perceived the embrace of classical rhetoric to
be a welcome answer to the arhetorical nature of current-traditional rhetoric,
there was increasing uneasiness in the face of the "uneasy," indeed violent,
social conditions of the 1960s and early 1970s, prompting a questioning of
whether classical rhetoric (particularly Aristotelian rhetoric) was capable or even
appropriate to answer to the democratic ills of the time. S. Michael Halloran in
an essay entitled "On the End of Rhetoric, Classical and Modern" argues that
texts that "resurrect the classical tradition more or less intact . . . have a musty,
antiquarian air about them, as if their authors had succeeded in blotting out a
hundred years or so of modern history" (335). The problem with classical rhetorical theory, such as Aristotle's, according to Halloran and others, is that it
assumes that ancient and modern worlds are identical, which they are not. Contemporary appropriations of classical rhetoric were also challenged by poststructuralist thought, which in effect questioned the stability of the rhetorical
situation, of the speaker (as a unified agent of discourse), of the audience, and
indeed of *logos* itself.

The attention to classical rhetoric flowered into a general interest in the history of rhetoric and the history of writing instruction. Innumerable histories or sections of histories have subsequently enriched the discipline, including the work of George Kennedy, Richard Enos, Nan Johnson, James Berlin, Winifred Bryan Horner, Robert Connors, Miriam Brody, Sharon Crowley, to name a few historians who have worked toward fulfilling James J. Murphy's claim of 1983. Publishing "The Historiography of Rhetoric: Challenges and Opportunities," Murphy claimed that "one of the very oldest and most truly international human disciplines, Rhetoric, is at long last beginning to achieve its own history" (1), is at long last being "mapped out" (3).

The 1980s witnessed this "mapping" out of the rhetorical tradition but questioned (in the spirit of the new rhetorics, prompted by poststructuralist thought) not only the desire for a "universal" history but also the methodology of writing *any* history of rhetoric. Sharon Crowley's "Let Me Get This Straight" traces the publication of these various challenges, which came fast and furiously. The discipline was, indeed, caught up in the fervor of historiography. In 1988, in a packed hall, demonstrative of the discipline's interest in and enthusiasm for the topic, eight scholars, constituting an "octalog," presented a CCCC panel, facilitated by James J. Murphy. The scholars James Berlin, Robert Connors, Sharon Crowley, Richard Leo Enos, Victor J. Vitanza, Susan C. Jarratt, Nan Johnson, and Jan Swearingen discussed—in brief position statements and dialogue—"The Politics of Historiography." That is, as Berlin argued: "The difficulty for the historian is that, even when evidence is available and extensive, the writing of history is itself a rhetorical act. The historian is herself underwriting a version of the normal, of the proper arrangement of classes, races, and genders. History does not write itself, having in itself no inherent pattern of development. Historians cannot escape this play of power, inherent in all signifying practices" (11).

Perhaps the two most prolific groups of rhetoric historiographers are those that challenge the rhetorical tradition for its exclusions of women and of sophistry. Feminists ask questions such as, How has the rhetorical tradition excluded the contributions of women? and How has the rhetorical tradition defined rhetoric as a practice from which women were de facto excluded from participating (i.e., as "public" discourse)? Patricia Bizzell, in response to her anthologizing efforts (with Bruce Herzberg, *The Rhetorical Tradition*), suggests that there are at least three approaches that feminist research could take in examining the history of rhetoric. The first she borrows from Judith Fetterley: to be a "resisting reader," to "notice aspects of the canonical texts that the reader is not supposed to notice, but that disturb, when the reader is a woman, and create resistance to the view of reality the work seems to want to purvey" (51). The second is to recover women who were practicing rhetoric as traditionally defined, to include them alongside the already canonized male rhetors. The third is to redefine what rhetoric is by including in the history of rhetoric discursive practices of women ("Opportunities" 51). Historians such as Karlyn Kohrs Campbell, Andrea Lunsford, Krista Ratcliffe, and Cheryl Glenn, for example, have written feminist, revisionary histories. Those scholars interested in challenging the rhetorical tradition for its exclusions based on race face the same "opportunities for research."

Critics of the history of rhetoric, as it has previously been canonized, also look to the tradition's exclusion of sophistry. Just as Corbett and others have recovered Aristotelian rhetoric to infuse rhetorical pedagogy with substance and relevance, current historians, including Jarratt, Vitanza, John Poulakos, Jasper Neel, Takis Poulakos, and Steven Mailloux, have recovered the sophists and their practices as a counterrhetoric and a counterpedagogy to Platonic and Aristotelian rhetorics (with their classicist and racist underpinnings), as a new democratic rhetoric for the people. John Poulakos writes: "Contrary to what some of their critics have said, the sophists' motto was not the survival of the fittest but fitting as many as possible for survival. In this sense, the sophists can be said to have helped strengthen the recently instituted democracy by forging a mentality aware of the centrality of persuasion in the coordination of sociopolitical action and the resolution of human conflicts" (14). Likewise Jarratt, in *Rereading the Sophists*, identifies sophistic rhetoric with liberatory pedagogy; Sharon Crowley makes "A Plea for the Revival of Sophistry" to encourage a more sociopolitically oriented writing pedagogy. Further, Jarratt and Victor Vitanza have identified our contemporary postmodern world as a "Third Sophistic."

SOCIAL-EPISTEMIC RHETORIC

In reaction to current-traditional rhetoric, various "new" rhetorics appeared, including expressivist, cognitive, and neo-Aristotelian rhetorics, as detailed above. The term *new rhetorics* eludes definition (in fact, the book *Defining the New Rhetorics* [Enos and Brown] refuses to do so), as it refers, apparently, to any rhetorical practice and pedagogy *other* than current-traditional rhetoric. There are, however, basic predilections of new rhetorics, which could be characterized as social-epistemic.

In 1970, Chaïm Perelman defined the new rhetoric as a "theory of argumentation" that "aims at somehow modifying an existing state of affairs" ("The New Rhetoric" 153, 154). Unlike current-traditional rhetoric, then, the new rhetoric conceives of rhetoric as *doing* something, specifically constructing and modifying reality and social conditions and relations. Further, unlike classical rhetoric, the new rhetoric does not, in Richard Ohmann's estimation, set as its aim "overcoming resistance to a course of action, an idea, a judgment" (300). Rather, "[m]odern rhetoric lowers the barrier between speaker or writer and audience. It shifts the emphasis toward cooperation, mutuality, social harmony" (300). Indeed, according to Kenneth Burke, the "key term for the 'new' rhetoric would be *'identification'*" rather than persuasion (qtd. in Ohmann 203). In addition to Perelman and Olbrechts-Tyteca, other early advocates of a new rhetoric include I. A. Richards, Walter Ong, Richard Weaver, and Stephen Toulmin.

Proponents of a new rhetoric maintained, contrary to the positivism of current-traditionalists, that rhetoric is, in the words of Robert Scott, "epistemic," that is, as Ohmann suggests, "Truth is not a lump of matter, decorated and disguised, but finally delivered intact" (300), but rather is a "web of shifting complexities" constructed *rhetorically*. Additionally, rhetoric is, for the new rhetoricians, a *social* act. Hence, advocate James Berlin calls the new rhetoric "social-epistemic" to argue that rhetoric is indeed epistemic—it constructs knowledge—but to stress that it constructs *social* knowledge, which is situated materially and historically. In *Rhetoric and Reality*, Berlin writes: "In epistemic rhetoric there is never a division between experience and language, whether the experience involves the subject, the subject and other subjects, or the subject and the material world. . . . Rhetoric then becomes implicated in all human behavior. . . . [Truth] emerges only as the three—the material, the social, and the personal—interact, and the agent of mediation is language" (17).

In a 1982 essay, "Contemporary Composition," Berlin identifies Ann Berthoff and Andrea Lunsford as early practitioners of social-epistemic rhetoric. According to his criteria there, we could also include Janet Emig. Since that time, social-epistemic rhetoric has proliferated, giving rise to social constructivist, critical race, feminist, and neo-Marxist liberatory rhetorics and pedagogies.

Social constructivists, working from the insights of Thomas S. Kuhn (*The Structure of Scientific Revolutions*) and of Richard Rorty (*Philosophy and the Mirror of Nature*), hold that knowledge is, in the words of Rorty, "*socially justified belief*." According to this definition, knowledge is a function of social discourse about beliefs through which meaning is generated, not on personal reflections of an a priori reality. Knowledge is, then, truly "a collaborative artifact" that results from "intellectual negotiations" (Bruffee, "Liberal Education" 103, 107). The key terms are "collaboration," "consensus," "community," and "conversation." Kenneth Bruffee ("Collaborative Learning and 'The Conversation of Mankind' ") and Karen Burke LeFevre (*Invention as a Social Act*) were early advocates, as were Andrea Lunsford and Lisa Ede, who maintained that writing is a social act. Lunsford continues to advance social constructivist practices, as evidenced by her latest reader (coedited by John Ruszkiewicz) entitled *The Presence of Others*.

Social constructivist practice has received criticism, notably by John Trimbur and Greg Myers, who argue, separately, that consensus-seeking pedagogies have a dangerous potential to glorify the discursive production of knowledge while ignoring how that production sustains hierarchical systems of power. Myers writes: "The ideas of *consensus* and *reality* . . . though they seem so progressive, are part of the structure of ideology. . . . [For to have consensus] must mean that some interests have been suppressed or excluded" ("Reality, Consensus, and Reform" 156). Trimbur concurs in "Consensus and Difference in Collaborative Learning," arguing that intellectual negotiation and discourse should aim at revealing differences, rather than solidifying identifications.

This emphasis on identifying *difference*—certainly informed by poststructuralist thought—has focused attention on issues of race and gender and the differences such factors make in rhetorical practice, as well as how such differences are, themselves, rhetorically constructed. Scholars in feminist rhetoric, working out of social-epistemic principles, seek to identify how the world has been rhetorically constructed to guarantee male privilege. One of the functions of a feminist rhetoric, then, is "criticizing and reshaping the official male language and, through it, male manners and male power" (Marks and de Courtivron 6). Scholars of the rhetoric of race, likewise, seek to examine how "whiteness" or "blackness," for example, has been rhetorically figured and maintained.

Social-epistemic pedagogy advocates that the composition classroom should be a site of creating "critical consciousness." Susan Jarratt claims that critical pedagogy, most heavily influenced by Paulo Freire (*Pedagogy of the Oppressed*), Ira Shor (*Critical Teaching and Everyday Life*), and Stanley Aronowitz and Henry Giroux (*Education under Siege*), "places the project of human emancipation—a liberatory democratic practice—at the center of the educational process" (*Rereading the Sophists* 107). By so doing, she, as well as Berlin and others, endeavors to make the class a course in cultural studies, that is, a course in the ideological critique of culture in order to reveal how culture reifies and propagates injustices.

Although it currently continues to have many practitioners, critical pedagogy does have its detractors. Maxine Hairston, for one, in her 1985 chair of CCCC address, warned that "[w]riting courses, especially required freshman courses, should not be *for* anything or *about* anything other than writing itself" ("Diversity, Ideology, and Teaching Writing" 659). Seven years later, she attacked critical pedagogy practices, accusing them of providing a pedagogy that "puts dogma before diversity, politics before craft, ideology before critical thinking, and the social goals before the educational needs of the student" (660). "The new model," she argues, "envisions required writing courses as vehicles for social reform rather than as student-centered workshops designed to build students' confidence and competence as writers" (660).

Because of space limitations, we are unable to address all the ways social-epistemic rhetoric has enriched twentieth-century rhetorical practice, including fostering literacy studies, reenvisioning basic writing, spawning writing across the curriculum and writing in the discipline programs, and generating studies in the rhetoric of science.

The rhetoric of the new rhetoric expresses a hope that rhetoric can address and remedy social ills and injustices. Patricia Bizzell, for example, speculates that new rhetorics offer us "the opportunity now to collaborate on forging a more collective, pluralistic, inclusive national discourse." She further states: "I certainly believe that such a democratic shared language is needed in view of the political problems that confront us: racial injustice, economic inequality, environmental destruction, and the prospect of nuclear war" ("Beyond Anti-Foundationalism" 259).

POSTSTRUCTURALIST AND POSTMODERN RHETORICS

The so-called linguistic turn of the twentieth century manifested itself in the structuralist and semiotic thought of linguists such as Roman Jakobson and Ferdinand de Saussure, who argued that culture could be analyzed as a networked system of signs. A sign, which is composed of two parts—a signifier (the "sound-image" or lexical unit) and a signified (the concept referent)—is characterized by its diacritical and arbitrary nature. That is, its identity is established negatively, not positively, based on its difference from all other signs in the system, and further, the relationship between a signifier and its signified is not necessary or motivated but purely conventional.

Poststructuralism is a critique or "deconstruction" of structuralism, as evidenced by the work of the latter Roland Barthes, Paul de Man, Jacques Derrida, Jacques Lacan, and Michel Foucault, for example. Derrida, in his infamous address of 1966 "Structure, Sign and Play in the Discourse of the Human Sciences," demonstrated how the supposed self-referential unity of any sign system is dependent on a privileged, transcendental signified (e.g., God) that is seen to be exterior to and independent of that system. He further argues that Saussure must have, in Kenneth Burke's terms, such a "god term" in order to make the distinction between signifier and signified. For Derrida, there is no term that can stand outside the system; thus, there is no distinction between signifier and signified, for every signified functions as a signifier in endless "free play" of signification. Derrida also claims that due to this free play or slippage of signification, no stable or present meaning exists but rather only difference and deferral (*différance*). In this way, every term is a "supplement" trying to make up for the lack of a stable sign.

Derrida, pointing to this instability of signification, thereby deconstructs the Western tradition's metaphysical foundations of presence and logocentrism, demonstrating how so-called stable constructs such as Truth are made "present" but always in deferral and thus are always already absent. Derrida also reveals how the binaries of the metaphysical tradition—given as opposing terms (e.g., Truth/Falsehood)—are dependent on each other, in fact cohabit each other, demonstrating again that identity is a function of nonidentity (a thing is only that which it is not). The poststructuralist critique, then, challenges the efficacy of language to "represent" or to make present ideas, as well as challenging the very stability and foundation of any given idea and additionally challenging the supposed, self-present, sovereign, knowing and speaking subject.

Postmodernism is a very flexible term referring to late twentieth-century art and architecture (Linda Hutcheon, *The Poetics of Postmodernism*) as well as to the historical moment of postindustrial capitalism (Fredric Jameson, *Postmodernism, or, The Cultural Logic of Late Capitalism*). Here we use the term as Jean-François Lyotard defines it in *The Postmodern Condition* as the loss of faith in the grand narratives that have heretofore sustained the Enlightenment project, specifically the ideal of emancipation through total identity (of self and community) and through rational thought. The poststructuralist critique revealed an epistemological and legitimation crisis by radically questioning all foundations of Western thought and by demonstrating the impossibility of stabilizing those foundations. In addition, theorists such as Hélène Cixous, Gilles Deleuze, and Felix Guattari have demonstrated the complicity of Enlightenment foundations or grand narratives with systems of oppression and have revealed the phallogocentric construction of subjectivity.

Postmodernism could be seen as the fulfillment of this critique, a realization of a world that is radically antifoundational. Jean Baudrillard writes in *Simulations*: "All of Western faith [was] engaged in this wager on representation: that a sign could refer to the depth of meaning, that a sign could *exchange* for meaning and that something could guarantee this exchange—God, of course. But what if God himself can be simulated . . . ? Then the whole system becomes weightless . . . never again exchanging for what is real, but exchanging in itself" without any reference, without any principle of the real (10).

Poststructuralists and postmodernists challenge the conception of rhetoric as essentially communicative in purpose. Indeed, they question the very efficacy or possibility of communication: For if language operates as a free play of signifiers rather than as a conveyor of clear and distinct ideas, what of classical systems of rhetoric? And if subjects of language are subject to language (that is constituted in and through language), what of the classical rhetor as agent of discourse? These presuppositions and challenges seriously problematize traditional notions of the rhetor, of the text, of the rhetorical situation.

Composition theorists who have taken on this set of problematics include Susan Miller (*Rescuing the Subject*), Lester Faigley (*Fragments of Rationality*), James Berlin (*Rhetoric, Poetics, and Culture*), John Schilb ("Cultural Studies, Postmodernism, and Composition"), and Victor J. Vitanza ("Three Countertheses"), to name a few. The majority of composition theorists prefer, however, to figure poststructuralist rhetorics as "cultural critique" or "ideology critique" and hence are continuing the tradition of social-epistemic rhetoric. An example is John Trimbur's "Composition Studies: Postmodern or Popular?" He writes: "Cultural studies . . . portrays spectators and consumers not only as subject positions created by the discursive apparatus of the state, the media, and the culture industry but also as active interpreters of their own experience, who use the cultural practices and productions they encounter differentially and for their own purposes" (127). Although the kind of rhetorical practice advocated by Trimbur and Berlin, for example, engages a poststructuralist deconstruction of the practices of everyday life, its methodology is ultimately not postmodern, although it often goes by this name.

A postmodernist would challenge the principles of the "real" presupposed in social-epistemic rhetorics, namely, its beliefs in ideology, in neo-Marxist tenets, in critical subjectivity, and in emancipatory possibilities. Further, a postmodernist would radically challenge the conceptions of rhetoric as *persuasion* and as *epistemic* because both of these conceptions emanate from a belief in the primacy of the speaking and knowing subject. A postmodernist rhetoric, then, is a challenge to the new rhetorics and its very foundations. Victor J. Vitanza writes: "Such a discourse would place in post-Cartesian doubt the very (supposed) foundations of the field of composition" by placing "in doubt humanistic and conventional ways of thinking about authorship, the self, and gender" as well as "the modes/aims of exposition (valued as perspicuity) and argumentation (valued as consensus)." Additionally, it places in doubt "the revealed wisdom of even teaching students to write. In general, such a discourse can (if allowed) place in aporia the very value, or even possibility, of community itself, which traditionally has been the end of rhetoric" ("Three Countertheses" 140).

This radical antifoundationalism and call for perpetual doubt is countered by many, particularly feminist and other traditionally disenfranchised groups, such as people of color, who claim that radical postmodernist rhetorics deny rhetorical and political agency—the very agency that these groups have (due to race, class, or gender discrimination) been historically denied. Further, postmodern rhetorics have been accused of being, therefore, apolitical due to their antipathy for any kind of programmatic politics. Postmodernism's radical antifoundationalism and emphasis on radical alterity question political formations based on identity (e.g., feminism congregating under the name *Woman*).

Patricia Bizzell concurs with the postmodern and poststructuralist critique of the subject and agrees that we can no longer think of rhetoric as "communication taking place among internally unified, rational individuals who can more or less freely choose among available means of persuasion" ("Prospect" 37). But she finds the postmodern subject as "an entity with little or no agency" (38). Therefore, "not entirely happy" with this situation, echoing the sentiments of many, she makes a call for the "Prospect of Rhetorical Agency."

Susan Jarratt and Nedra Reynolds argue for a situated agency, a rhetorically and materially constituted agency, which would avoid reifying the transcendental subject as a disembodied, unified cogito. They demonstrate how subjects, while situated within social structures such as gender, class, and race, still provide political agency. Jürgen Habermas, similarly, refuses to locate subjectivity in the autonomous individual and attempts to provide agency through "communicative action," through a rhetorical process of "mutual understanding between subjects capable of speech and action" (295–96). The aim of such theorists is to deconstruct the transcendental subject but to offer new, possible subjectivities that can create meaning and construct communities. Thus, even sympathetic critics of poststructuralist and postmodern rhetorics argue that we need to move beyond antifoundationalism. Bizzell writes: "We have not yet acknowledged that if no unimpeachable authority and transcendent truth exist, this does not mean that no respectable authority and no usable truth exist. Our nostalgia for the self-evident and absolute prevents us from accepting as legitimate the authority created by collective discursive exhange and its truth as provisionally binding" ("Beyond Anti-Foundationalism" 261).

ELECTRONIC AND COMPUTER-ASSISTED RHETORICS

Richard Lanham, in *The Electronic Word*, proudly announces that the "long reign of black-and-white textual truth has ended" (x). Indeed, the electronic age has challenged the traditional conception of composition as putting pen to paper, as well as challenging conceptions of literacy and of texts. The adoption of computer technology in writing instruction in the latter part of the century seemed a natural extension of the shifting paradigms of rhetorical theory—for example, the shift from current-traditional rhetoric's focus on the product to the new rhetorics' emphasis on the process (marked by Janet Emig's *The Composing Processes of Twelfth Graders* and Linda Flower and John Hayes's protocol research). The first usages of computer technology, accordingly, focused mainly on ways to help the writer with the writing process, such as aiding the student in invention by providing preprogrammed heuristic prompts. The discipline's growing interest in collaborative learning during the early 1980s generated an interest in developing "networked" classrooms. Lester Faigley's *Fragments of Rationality* is one such account of a locally networked pedagogy. Before long, the further development of the Internet and various user-friendly email clients and Web browsers spawned another wave of research in electronic and computer-assisted composition and promised the advent of a "global" citizenry and a literacy to support it. Researchers and theorists riding this wave foresaw that the technological revolution had several far-reaching effects for reading and for writing practices.

The greater claim is that the technological revolution stands to alter how we think. That is, according to literacy theorists such as Eric Havelock and Walter Ong, our communication technologies affect the consciousness of their users. For example, in *Preface to Plato*, Havelock argues that the invention of alphabetic writing made possible the higher-order analytic thinking. Now a more powerful revolution is occurring. As Dennis Baron argues: "Historians of print are fond of pointing to the invention of the printing press in Europe as the second great cognitive revolution. . . . Computer gurus offer us a brave new world of communications where we will experience cognitive changes of a magnitude never before known ("From Pencils to Pixels" 19).

In what ways electronic rhetorics will transform future cognitive habits is now a topic of great speculation. Indeed, proponents of poststructuralist and postmodern rhetorics, including Michael Joyce, George Landow, Jay Bolter, Victor Vitanza, Cynthia Haynes, and D. Diane Davis, hope that electronic rhetorics, such as hypertext, and electronic spaces, such as MOOs (Multi User Domain Object Oriented), will subvert the tradition of phallocentric discourse and the institutions it supports. Donna Haraway's infamous "A Manifesto for Cyborgs" states the case of a "struggle for language and the struggle against perfect communication, against the one code that translates all meaning perfectly, the central dogma of phallogocentrism" (218). Jay Bolter similarly claims that the "electronic medium . . . complicates our understanding of [texts] as either mimesis or expression, [because] it denies the fixity of the text, and it questions the authority of the author" (*Writing Space* 153).

Many advocates suggest this is the means for securing global literacy as well as guaranteeing a liberatory writing space characterized by equality and free from the cultural limitations of race, class, and gender. Susan Romano characterizes this vision, of which she is suspicious, as a "redistribution of control over language and knowledge via temporal and spatial reconfigurations and via idiom itself. Not only do students in general benefit from this reconfiguration; those students most effectively silenced by the traditional learning format—those we call marginalized—stand to gain the most" ("The Egalitarianism Narrative" 5).

Despite the claims of an egalitarian offspring, there are critics of the marriage between composition studies and technology. These critics do not espouse, however, that the marriage not take place but that all parties recognize the potential enslavement and oppression that results from such a relationship. Eugene Provenzo, for example, warns against an institutionalized electronic panopticon ("The Electronic Panopticon"), a technopaideia resulting from microsurveillance. Provenzo tells us that young students, in an effort to ensure their good behavior, are currently told that there is a "big" computer downtown that records everything they do. Joseph Janangelo tells a similar Orwellian tale as he describes the ways in which teachers surveil students and likewise the ways in which a student is electronically harassed by other students ("Technopower and Technoppression"). This technopower, argue Cynthia Selfe and Richard J. Selfe, despite its claims to egalitarianism, merely reinscribes existing borders of power ("The Politics of the Interface" 481).

Additionally, what the egalitarian narrative hides is the fact that there is no equal access to technological resources. Lester Faigley presents us with some "hard facts": "Even though the student-to-computer ratio in American schools has risen to about 9-to-1, over half of those machines are so obsolete that they cannot be connected to the Internet" ("Beyond Imagination" 131). Charles Moran states the case, baldly, arguing that "scholarship in computers and composition studies has not addressed the fact that access to emerging technologies, like access to other goods and services in America, is a function of wealth and social class" ("Access" 205).

Research in electronic rhetorics and computer-assisted composition has begun, in earnest, to address these criticisms as well as to ask harder and harder questions of the technology and its implications. Because, as Richard Lanham argues, "electronic information seems to resist ownership" (*Electronic Word* 19), one such unresolved issue for twentieth-century rhetorics is the issue of intellectual property and authorship. The "romantic-author-and-the-expression-of-his-unique-ideas-in-fixed-works paradigm that has evolved over the last 300 years," Andrea Lunsford notes in "Intellectual Property in an Age of Information," "is not adequate to the needs of . . . a global information economy," and therefore "what is at stake for us includes literally everything, from the way we get accepted into and rewarded in the academy, to the research we conduct, to the way we conduct our classes" (271).

The twentieth century was one of the important ages in the history of rhetoric. While it began—in English departments at least—with the poverty of current-traditional theory and practice that largely ignored invention and emphasized conventional form and clarity of style, as the century progressed rhetoricians developed more sophisticated and complex theories and applications. Classical rhetoric, including sophistic practice, was revived and enriched the field's understanding of the breadth of rhetorical function. Other theorists developed expressive rhetoric, which emphasized, among other things, the writing process, which revolutionized the teaching of writing. Cognitive rhetoric, with its emphasis on the connection between writing and thought, elaborated more complex views of the writing process emphasizing the writer's ability to identify a rhetorical problem and respond to it using cognitive strategies. These four approaches, however, share a belief in a unified self, a transcendent knower who acts on other similar individuals. Social-epistemic rhetoric, on the other hand, questions the transcendent self and views writers as subjects constructed through social processes and according to ideological motivations. Postmodern rhetorics, furthermore, view writing subjects as noncentered, as effects of language, of conflicting and libidinally motivated discourses.

The following essays expand on the theories that we have outlined here, and we hope that this reference book, by providing accessible essays on many of the major rhetoricians of the past century, encourages others to examine critically our vibrant rhetorical tradition that we take with us into the twenty-first century.

BIBLIOGRAPHY

Aristotle. *The Rhetoric of Aristotle*. Ed. Lane Cooper. Englewood Cliffs, NJ: Prentice-Hall, 1932.

Aronowitz, Stanley, and Henry A. Giroux. *Education under Siege: The Conservative, Liberal, and Radical Debate over Schooling*. South Hadley, MA: Bergin & Garvey, 1985.

Baron, Dennis. "From Pencils to Pixels: The Stages of Literacy Technologies." *Passions, Pedagogies, and 21st Century Technologies*. Ed. Gail E. Hawisher and Cynthia L. Selfe. Logan: Utah State University Press, 1999. 15–33.

Baudrillard, Jean. *Simulations*. Trans. Paul Foss, Paul Patton, and Philip Beitchman. New York: Semiotext(e), 1983.

Bereiter, Carl, and Marlene Scardamalia. *The Psychology of Written Composition*. Hillsdale, NJ: Erlbaum, 1987.

Berlin, James A. "Contemporary Composition: The Major Pedagogical Theories." *College English* 44.8 (December 1982):765–77.

———. *Rhetoric and Reality: Writing Instruction in American Colleges, 1900–1985*. Carbondale: Southern Illinois University Press, 1987.

————. *Rhetorics, Poetics, and Cultures*. Urbana, IL: NCTE, 1996.

Berlin, James A., Robert J. Connors, Sharon Crowley, Richard Leo Enos, Victor J. Vitanza, Susan C. Jarratt, Nan Johnson, and Jan Swearingen, with James J. Murphy. "The Politics of Historiography." *Rhetoric Review* 7.1 (Fall 1988): 5–49.

Berthoff, Ann E. *The Making of Meaning: Metaphors, Models, and Maxims for Writing Teachers*. Portsmouth, NH: Boynton/Cook, 1981.

————. *Reclaiming the Imagination: Philosophical Perspectives for Writers and Teachers of Writing*. Portsmouth, NH: Boynton/Cook, 1984.

Bitzer, Lloyd. "Rhetoric's Prospects: Past and Future." *Making and Unmaking the Prospects for Rhetoric*. Ed. Theresa Enos. Mahwah, NJ: Lawrence Erlbaum, 1997. 15–20.

Bitzer, Lloyd F., and Edwin Black, eds. *The Prospect of Rhetoric: Report of the National Developmental Project*. Englewood Cliffs, NJ: Prentice, 1971.

Bizzell, Patricia. "Beyond Anti-Foundationalism to Rhetorical Authority: Problems Defining 'Cultural Literacy.' " *Academic Discourse and Critical Consciousness*. Pittsburgh: University of Pittsburgh Press, 1992. 256–76.

————. "Cognition, Convention, and Certainty." *PRE/TEXT* 3.3 (1982): 213–43.

————. "Opportunities for Feminist Research in the History of Rhetoric." *Rhetoric Review* 11.1 (1992–1993): 50–58.

————. "The Prospect of Rhetorical Agency." *Making and Unmaking the Prospects for Rhetoric*. Ed. Theresa Enos. Mahwah, NJ: Lawrence Erlbaum, 1997. 37–42.

Bizzell, Patricia, and Bruce Herzberg, eds. *The Rhetorical Tradition*. Boston: Bedford/St. Martin's, 1990.

Bolter, Jay David. *Writing Space: The Computer, Hypertext, and the History of Writing*. Hillsdale, NJ: Lawrence Erlbaum, 1991.

Britton, James, Tony Burgess, Nancy Martin, Alex McLeod, and Harold Rosen. *The Development of Writing Abilities (11–18)*. London: Macmillan Education, 1975.

Bruffee, Kenneth A. "Collaborative Learning and 'The Conversation of Mankind.' " *College English* 46.7 (November 1984): 635–52.

————. "Liberal Education and the Social Justification of Belief." *Liberal Education* 68.2 (1982): 95–114.

Connors, Robert J., Lisa S. Ede, and Andrea Lunsford. "The Revival of Rhetoric in America." *Essays on Classical Rhetoric and Modern Discourse*. Ed. Robert J. Connors, Lisa S. Ede, and Andrea Lunsford. Carbondale: Southern Illinois University Press, 1984. 1–15.

Cooper, Marilyn, and Michael Holzman. "Talking about Protocols." *College Composition and Communication* 34.3 (1983): 284–93.

Crowley, Sharon. "Let Me Get This Straight." *Writing Histories of Rhetoric*. Ed. Victor Vitanza. Carbondale: Southern Illinois University Press, 1994. 1–19.

————. *The Methodical Memory: Invention in Current-Traditional Rhetoric*. Carbondale: Southern Illinois University Press, 1992.

————. "A Plea for the Revival of Sophistry." *Rhetoric Review* 7.2 (1989): 318–34.

Derrida, Jacques. "Structure, Sign, and Play in the Discourse of the Human Sciences." *Writing and Difference*. Trans. Alan Bass. Chicago: University of Chicago Press, 1978.

Elbow, Peter. *Embracing Contraries: Explorations in Learning and Teaching*. New York: Oxford University Press, 1986.

————. *Writing without Teachers*. New York: Oxford University Press, 1973.

————. *Writing with Power: Techniques for Mastering the Writing Process*. New York: Oxford University Press, 1981.

Emig, Janet. *The Composing Processes of Twelfth Graders*. Urbana, IL: NCTE, 1971.

Enos, Theresa, and Stuart C. Brown. *Defining the New Rhetorics*. Newbury Park, CA: Sage, 1993.

————. *Professing the New Rhetorics*. Englewood Cliffs, NJ: Blair, 1994.

Faigley, Lester. "Beyond Imagination: The Internet and Global Digital Literacy." *Passions, Pedagogies, and 21st Century Technologies*. Ed. Gail E. Hawisher and Cynthia L. Selfe. Logan: Utah State University Press, 1999. 129–39.

————. *Fragments of Rationality: Postmodernity and the Subject of Composition*. Pittsburgh: University of Pittsburgh Press, 1993.

Flower, Linda. *The Construction of Negotiated Meaning: A Social Cognitive Theory of Writing*. Carbondale: Southern Illinois University Press, 1994.

————. *Problem Solving Strategies*. 5th ed. Fort Worth, TX: Harcourt Brace, 1999.

Flower, Linda, and John R. Hayes. "A Cognitive Process Theory of Writing." *College Composition and Communication* 32.4 (1981): 365–87.

————. "Response to Marilyn Cooper and Michael Holzman, 'Talking about Protocols.' " *College Composition and Communication* 34.1 (1983): 284–93.

Freire, Paulo. *Pedagogy of the Oppressed*. Trans. Myra Bergman Ramos. New York: Continuum, 1989.

Gradin, Sherrie L. *Romancing Rhetorics: Social Expressivist Perspectives on the Teaching of Writing*. Portsmouth, NH: Boynton/Cook, 1995.

Habermas, Jürgen. *The Philosophical Discourse of Modernity: Twelve Lectures*. Trans. Frederick Lawrence. Cambridge, MA: MIT Press, 1987.

Hairston, Maxine. "Diversity, Ideology, and Teaching Writing." *Cross-Talk in Comp Theory*. Ed. Victor Villanueva, Jr. Urbana, IL: NCTE, 1997. 659–75.

Halloran, S. Michael. "On the End of Rhetoric, Classical and Modern." *Professing the New Rhetorics*. Ed. Theresa Enos and Stuart C. Brown. Englewood Cliffs, NJ: Blair, 1994. 331–43.

Haraway, Donna. "A Manifesto for Cyborgs." *Feminism/Postmodernism*. Ed. Linda Nicholson. New York: Routledge, 1990. 190–233.

Havelock, Eric A. *Preface to Plato*. Cambridge, MA: Belknap Press of Harvard University Press, 1963.

Hutcheon, Linda. *A Poetics of Postmodernism: History, Theory, Fiction*. New York: Routledge, 1988.

Jameson, Fredric. *Postmodernism, or, The Cultural Logic of Late Capitalism*. Durham: Duke University Press, 1991.

Janangelo, Joseph. "Technopower and Technoppression: Some Abuses of Power and Control in Computer-Assisted Writing Environments." *Computers and Composition* 9.1 (1991): 47–64.

Jarratt, Susan C. *Rereading the Sophists: Classical Rhetoric Refigured*. Carbondale: Southern Illinois University Press, 1991.

Jarratt, Susan C., and Nedra Reynolds. "The Splitting Image: Contemporary Feminisms and the Ethics of *ethos*." *Ethos: New Essays in Rhetorical and Critical Theory*. Ed. James S. Baumlin and Tita French Baumlin. Dallas: Southern Methodist University Press, 1994. 37–63.

Kinneavy, James L. *A Theory of Discourse*. New York: Norton, 1971.

Kuhn, Thomas S. *The Structure of Scientific Revolutions*. 2nd ed. Chicago: University of Chicago Press, 1970.

Lanham, Richard A. *The Electronic Word*. Chicago: University of Chicago Press, 1993.

LeFevre, Karen Burke. *Invention as a Social Act*. Carbondale: Southern Illinois University Press, 1987.

Lunsford, Andrea A. "Cognitive Studies and Teaching Writing." *Perspectives on Research and Scholarship in Composition*. Ed. Ben W. McClelland and Timothy R. Donovan. New York: MLA, 1985. 145–61.

———. "Intellectual Property in an Age of Information: What Is at Stake for Composition Studies?" *Composition in the Twenty-first Century: Crisis and Change*. Ed. Lynn Z. Bloom, Donald A. Daiker, and Edward M. White. Carbondale: Southern Illinois University Press, 1996.

Lunsford, Andrea A., and John J. Ruszkiewicz, eds. *The Presence of Others*. 2nd ed. New York: St. Martin's Press, 1997.

Lyotard, Jean-François. *The Postmodern Condition*. Trans. Geoff Bennington and Brian Massumi. Minneapolis: University of Minnesota Press, 1988.

Macrorie, Ken. *Searching Writing: A Contextbook*. Rochelle Park, NJ: Hayden, 1980.

———. *Telling Writing*. 3rd ed. Rochelle Park, NJ: Hayden, 1980.

———. *Uptaught*. New York: Hayden, 1970.

———. *Writing to Be Read*. 3rd ed. Upper Montclair, NJ: Boynton/Cook, 1984.

Marks, Elaine, and Isabelle de Courtivron. *New French Feminisms*. New York: Schocken Books, 1980.

Miller, J., P. Polson, and W. Kintsch. "Problems of Methodology in Cognitive Science." *Method and Tactics in Cognitive Science*. Ed. W. Kintsch, J. Miller, and P. Polson. Hillsdale, NJ: Erlbaum, 1984. 1–20.

Miller, Susan. *Rescuing the Subject*. Carbondale: Southern Illinois University Press, 1989.

Moran, Charles. "Access: The A-Word in Technology Studies." *Passions, Pedagogies, and 21st Century Technologies*. Ed. Gail E. Hawisher and Cynthia L. Selfe. Logan: Utah State University Press, 1999. 205–20.

Murphy, James J. "The Historiography of Rhetoric: Challenges and Opportunities." *Rhetorica* 1.1 (1983): 1–8.

Murray, Donald M. *A Writer Teaches Writing: A Practical Method of Teaching Composition*. Boston: Houghton Mifflin, 1968.

———. *Write to Learn*. New York: Holt, Rinehart and Winston, 1984.

Myers, Greg. "Reality, Consensus, and Reform in the Rhetoric of Composition Teaching." *College English* 48.2 (1986): 154–73.

North, Stephen M. *The Making of Knowledge in Composition: Portrait of an Emerging Field*. Upper Montclair, NJ: Boynton/Cook, 1987.

Ohmann, Richard. "In Lieu of a New Rhetoric." *Professing the New Rhetorics*. Ed. Theresa Enos and Stuart C. Brown. Englewood Cliffs, NJ: Blair, 1994. 298–306.

Perelman, Chaïm. "The New Rhetoric: A Theory of Practical Reasoning." *Professing the New Rhetorics*. Ed. Theresa Enos and Stuart C. Brown. Englewood Cliffs, NJ: Blair, 1994. 145–77.

Poulakos, John. *Sophistical Rhetoric in Classical Greece*. Columbia: University of South Carolina Press, 1995.

Provenzo, Eugene. "The Electronic Panopticon." *Literacy Online*. Ed. Myron C. Tuman. Pittsburgh: University of Pittsburgh Press, 1992. 163–81.

Romano, Susan. "The Egalitarianism Narrative: Whose Story? Which Yardstick?" *Computers and Composition* 10.1 (1993): 5–28.

Rorty, Richard. *Philosophy and the Mirror of Nature*. Princeton, NJ: Princeton University Press, 1979.

Schilb, John. "Cultural Studies, Postmodernism, and Composition." *Contending with Words*. Ed. Patricia Harkin and John Schilb. New York: MLA, 1991. 173–88.

Selfe, Cynthia L., and Richard J. Selfe. "The Politics of the Interface: Power and Its Exercise in Electronic Contact Zones." *College Composition and Communication* 45.4 (1994): 480–504.

Shor, Ira. *Critical Teaching and Everyday Life*. Boston: South End Press, 1980.

Trimbur, John. "Composition Studies: Postmodern or Popular?" *Into the Field: Sites of Composition Studies*. Ed. Anne Ruggles Gere. New York: MLA, 1993. 117–32.

———. "Consensus and Difference in Collaborative Learning." *College English* 51.6 (1989): 602–16.

Vitanza, Victor J. "Three Countertheses: Or, A Critical In(ter)vention into Composition Theories and Pedagogies." *Contending with Words*. Ed. Patricia Harkin and John Schilb. New York: MLA, 1991. 139–72.

FRANK AYDELOTTE
(1880–1956)

Michael G. Moran

The father of the thought approach in composition studies, Frank Aydelotte was born in Sullivan, Indiana, in 1880, the son of William E. Aydelotte and Matilda Brunger Aydelotte. The elder Aydelotte was half owner and operator of a woolen mill famous regionally for the quality of its finished goods. During the summer, young Aydelotte worked in the mill from 6:30 A.M. to 6:30 P.M. (Blanshard 9). From his father he learned the importance of hard work and striving for excellence. From his mother he developed intellectual interests through her love of books.

After graduating from high school in Sullivan, Aydelotte matriculated at Indiana University (IU) in 1896, where he majored in English. After graduating in 1900, he taught school and worked as a journalist before entering Harvard to take an M.A. in 1903. While at Harvard, he worked as Charles Townsend Copeland's assistant for English A, then the most influential freshman English course in the nation. It emphasized the formal elements of writing and taught students the modes of discourse and mechanical correctness. Students wrote the famous daily essays invented by Barrett Wendell and Dean Le Baron Briggs. Six days a week, students would produce an essay of a single page on a personal subject. The purpose of this writing was to help students develop a sense of correctness and form, and the papers were graded with these goals in mind. A good percentage of Aydelotte's duties as Copeland's assistant was to read and comment on those dailies. The work exhausted Aydelotte, encouraging him to reject the Harvard approach in favor of less frequent, more thoughtful essays.

In 1904, Aydelotte attended Oxford University as a member of the second class of American Rhodes Scholars. At Oxford, Aydelotte experienced an educational system that he believed had solved many of the problems that bedeviled American higher education. He was taken with the Oxford tutorials because they placed the responsibility of learning on the student, not the teacher. The tutors did not teach a course; instead, they outlined a body of reading that the student needed to master to prepare for a set of comprehensive examinations. Unlike American course examinations, which encouraged cramming and forgetting, the Oxford comprehensives required students to master the reading thoroughly over several years. Aydelotte also found the Oxford social life valuable. Oxford students, unlike their American counterparts, spent a good deal of time discussing significant issues. Aydelotte found this discussion fruitful because it encouraged students to test ideas in debate. Finally, and most important, Aydelotte became enamored of the Oxford honor schools. While the average student could take a pass degree, which required about the same effort as the American B.A., the ambitious student enrolled in one of the honor schools, which demanded work on a higher level and required students to read in several related disciplines. The honor school of English Language and Literature, for instance, combined the study of English literature, language, history, and philosophy.

In terms of writing instruction, Aydelotte approved of the British system of tutors working individually with students to improve their reading, writing, research, and thinking skills. Rather than taking a writing course, students met with their tutors once a week to read a paper they had written on a topic assigned from the reading list. How to approach the topic and how much ground to cover were left to the student. The tutor would then critique the paper for content and rhetorical effectiveness. This kind of personal, individualized instruction, Aydelotte concluded, led to rapid improvement of thinking and writing skills.

Aydelotte's main contribution to American education in general and English studies in particular was to incorporate elements of the Oxford system into the American college and university. He first developed the thought approach in freshman English at IU; next, he modified the approach for teaching engineering writing at the Massachusetts Institute of Technology (MIT); finally, and most significantly, he modified the approach to develop Swarthmore's nationally influential Honors Program, which placed writing in the disciplines at the center of the learning process. While the first two programs were interesting failures, Aydelotte's work at Swarthmore established the national model for honors education in this country.

AYDELOTTE'S RHETORICAL THEORY

When Aydelotte returned to IU in 1908 as a visiting associate professor, he was determined to implement a series of reforms of freshman English. He found himself in a department that modeled its writing program on Harvard's. Professor Will B. Howe was chair, and he had taken his B.A., M.A., and Ph.D. at Harvard when men like Adams Sherman Hill, Wendell, Briggs, and Copeland were developing English A. The IU freshman writing course was based on Harvard formalism, emphasizing the modes of discourse, the paragraph, and mechanical correctness. Writing courses were separated from literature courses. Aydelotte began his reforms in an inhospitable environment.

While developing his freshman course, English 2A, Aydelotte wrote a series of essays and books that articulated the theory of the thought course. His first two were *College English* (1913) and *The Oxford Stamp* (1917/1967), an essay collection that indicated the Oxford influence on his educational reforms. *College English* explained to both students and teachers the specifics of the approach. In these two books, Aydelotte articulated one of the few alternatives to Harvard's formalism.

The thought approach began with a simple assumption: In order to write well, students must think clearly, and writing is a tool used to work out thought on the page. A second assumption was that for students to think, they must have written material to think about. Hence, the thought approach combined reading and writing. During the first quarter of the three-quarter course, students read essays by eminent Victorians on a series of issues central to modern life: the nature of education, the connections between science and the humanities, and the relationship between morality and business, among others. These essayists included Matthew Arnold, John Henry, Cardinal Newman, Thomas Carlisle, and John Ruskin. During the second two quarters, students read selections of literature from significant authors, including John Milton, William Shakespeare, Alexander Pope, William Wordsworth, and Alfred Lord Tennyson. These authors were to be read neither for their aesthetic qualities nor for their historical significance. Instead, they were to be read for their thoughtful criticisms of life. By reading them, Aydelotte assumed, students would clarify their personal beliefs. The purpose of writing was to help students work out their individual worldviews.

In practical terms, Aydelotte combined two courses in IU's curriculum to create English 2A. The first of these was the freshman writing course, English 7; the second, English 2, the introductory survey to English literature. English 2A focused on a limited number of works that students were to read critically and write on. When English 2A began to draw more students than the other two courses, hostility toward it and Aydelotte heightened. When Aydelotte returned to Oxford in 1912 to revise his B.Litt. thesis, *Elizabethan Rogues and Vagabonds*, for publication by Oxford's Clarendon Press in 1913, English 2A disappeared from the catalog.

The thought approach, however, developed a small national following and participated in a movement to make writing instruction more intellectual and less rule governed. Aydelotte's work appeared about the same time Harrison Ross Steeves of Columbia developed the idea course. This course introduced students to a series of significant modern ideas in the anthology *Representative Essays in Modern Thought* (1913) to provide students with subjects for their essays (see Steeves's "The Cultivation of Ideas" [1912]). Aydelotte, however, did not approve of this approach on the grounds that the collection of essays took students too far afield from English literature, the subject English teachers were trained to teach.

The thought approach was not without its weaknesses, two of which were pointed out at the time. The main problem was that the course assumed that American students had a strong educational background. The general approach worked well at Oxford, which was an elitist institution accepting only the best British students. These students had years of language training and were prepared to read and write independently. Students coming from the farms and towns of Indiana often had checkered backgrounds and could not work at the level Aydelotte expected. Many needed work on form and mechanics before taking 2A. Second, Aydelotte privileges thought over rhetoric and assumes that clear thinking will automatically lead to clear writing. Therefore, when students have an important point to make, they will magically find the necessary rhetorical strategy. As one of Aydelotte's contemporary critics, Ada Snell, argued, content and form are not as distinct as Aydelotte claims. To write in a genre, students must understand the conventions of that genre, and Aydelotte was not interested in teaching such conventions.

In 1915, anxious to leave the hostility of IU, Aydelotte took a professorship of English at MIT. The president of the institute, Richard Maclauren, was anxious to hire an English professor to reinvigorate English instruction. Being a New Zealander trained in the British tradition, Maclauren was attracted to Aydelotte's Oxford views. Although Aydelotte went to MIT primarily to gain access to the Boston libraries' collections of Renaissance literature, his research became secondary as he grew fascinated with the problem of teaching engineers to write.

While at MIT Aydelotte edited the first anthology of readings for technical communication, *English and Engineering* (1917; 2nd ed. 1923). Like *Materials*, the anthology for English 2A, this book collects thoughtful readings. In this case, the readings address engineering issues. These included the nature of good writing, engineering as a profession rather than a trade, science and its place in the modern world, and the role of liberal studies in engineering education. Unlike most engineering writing courses developing at the time, Aydelotte's did not emphasize workplace writing. He considered such practical courses limiting. He believed that students who learned to write well in his philosophical course would be able to write well in any context. This position, however, is not unassailable. Students would leave his course with little sense of the kind of daily writing that future employers would expect.

In 1921, Aydelotte's stature within the educational community was such that he was offered the presidency of Swarthmore College. Aydelotte had had limited success modifying the Oxford approach at IU and MIT. The students he worked with were mostly average college students. At Swarthmore, he saw an opportunity to develop a true Oxford-style honors college. Before he took the position, he had announced his plans to the Board of Managers and the faculty. Soon after arriving, a group of faculty informed him that they wanted to implement his program. Aydelotte oversaw the change in Swarthmore from a sleepy Quaker college more interested in athletics and social life than in academics to one of the premier academic institutions in the nation (see Aydelotte's *Breaking* for a full discussion).

Central to the Swarthmore honors course was the honors seminar, and central to the seminar was writing. After being admitted to the Honors Program as rising juniors, students reading for honors took eight coordinated seminars during their last two years. Four of those seminars were in their major subject; four were in related, or cognate, areas. For instance, English majors would take four seminars in English literature and two in philosophy and two in English history. If the literature course was in Renaissance literature, the history and philosophy courses would be in related areas. In all seminars, students wrote and delivered papers on topics usually assigned by the professor. Both the professor and the other students critiqued the papers for form and content. Students did not receive course grades; instead, like the Oxford student, they took comprehensive examinations at the end of their Honors Program.

Aydelotte's contributions to rhetoric are historically important. The thought approach to freshman English was one of the few alternatives to Harvard formalism, and Aydelotte's liberal approach to technical communication was one of the early attempts to formulate a teaching method in that field. His work in honors education remains seminal, providing a working model for integrating writing into the undergraduate honors seminar.

BIBLIOGRAPHY

Primary Sources

Aydelotte, Frank. *Breaking the Academic Lockstep: The Development of Honors Work in American Colleges and Universities.* 2nd ed. New York: Harper Brothers, 1944.

———. *College English: A Manual for the Study of English Literature and Composition.* New York: Oxford University Press, 1913.

———. *Elizabethan Rogues and Vagabonds.* Oxford: Clarendon Press, 1913.

———. *English and Engineering.* 1917. 2nd ed. New York: McGraw-Hill, 1923.

———. *The Oxford Stamp, and Other Essays: Articles from the Educational Creed of an American Oxonian.* New York: Oxford University Press, 1917. Freeport, NY: Books for Libraries Press, 1967.

———, ed. *Materials for the Study of English Literature and Composition.* 2nd ed. New York: Oxford University Press, 1916.

Steeves, Harrison Ross. "The Cultivation of Ideas in the College Writing Course." *Educational Review* 44 (1912): 45–54.

Steeves, Harrison Ross, and Frank Humphrey Ristine, eds. *Representative Essays in Modern Thought: A Basis for Composition.* New York: American Book, 1913.

Biography

Blanshard, Frances. *Frank Aydelotte of Swarthmore*. Ed. Brand Blanshard. Middletown, CT: Wesleyan University Press, 1970.

Criticism

Moran, Michael G. "Frank Aydelotte: AT&T's First Outside Writing Consultant, 1917–1918." *Journal of Technical Writing and Communication* 25.3 (1995): 231–41.
———. "Frank Aydelotte, Social Criticism, and Freshman English." *Notes on Teaching English* 18.2 (1991): 13–19.
———. "The Road Not Taken: Frank Aydelotte and the Thought Approach to Engineering Writing." *Technical Communication Quarterly* 2.2 (1993): 161–75.
Moran, Michael G., and Maureen Byrnes Hardegree. "Frank Aydelotte (1880–1956): A Bibliography." *Bulletin of Bibliography* 50.1 (1993): 19–28.
Snell, Ada L. F. "Freshman Composition." *Nation* 5 (January 1911): 9.

MIKHAIL BAKHTIN
(1895–1975)

James P. Zappen

Mikhail Mikhailovich Bakhtin was born in Orel, south of Moscow, in 1895 and grew up in Vilnius and Odessa, cosmopolitan border towns that offered an unusually heterogeneous mix of disparate languages and cultures.[1] He studied classics and philology at St. Petersburg (later Petrograd) University, then moved to the country, first to Nevel and then to Vitebsk, in the wake of the revolutions of 1917. There he maintained an association with other intellectuals, the so-called Bakhtin circle, among them Valentin Voloshinov and Pavel Medvedev. Bakhtin shared with members of this circle a variety of interests, most especially Kant and contemporary German philosophy and the new physics of Planck, Einstein, and Bohr.

During this period, he completed several works on ethics and aesthetics, among them *Toward a Philosophy of the Act*, published long after his death. From 1924 to 1929, Bakhtin lived in Leningrad (formerly Petrograd), supported by his wife, Elena Alexandrovna, while unemployed due to suspicions arising from his religious activities and to a bone disease, which necessitated the amputation of his right leg in 1938. During the late 1920s, he wrote *Problems of Dostoevsky's Art*, published in 1929 and partially translated in "Three Fragments from the 1929 Edition." He may or may not have written several books published in others' names but sometimes attributed to him, including Voloshinov's *Freudianism: A Critical Sketch* and *Marxism and the Philosophy of Language* and Medvedev and Bakhtin's *The Formal Method in Literary Scholarship*.[2] Bakhtin was arrested in 1929, probably as a result of his religious activities, and exiled in Kazakhstan, where he stayed until 1936, when he accepted a professorship at the Mordovian Pedagogical Institute in Saransk. During the 1930s and early 1940s, he completed some of his most important studies of the novel, including "Discourse in the Novel," "Forms of Time and of the Chronotope in the Novel," and "Epic and Novel." He also completed his major work on Rabelais, submitted as his doctoral dissertation to the Gorky Institute of World Literature in Moscow in 1941 (he was later awarded the lower degree of Candidate). Forced to move from Saransk to Savelovo to escape the great purge of 1937, Bakhtin returned after World War II, his relative obscurity during the Stalinist years perhaps saving his life.

A successful teacher in Saransk during the 1950s, Bakhtin was discovered in the early 1960s by a group of Moscow graduate students who had read his Dostoevsky book. He wrote notes titled "Toward a Reworking of the Dostoevsky Book" in 1961; published a second edition of the book, *Problems of Dostoevsky's Poetics*, in 1963; published the Rabelais book, *Rabelais and His World*, in 1965; and published a collection of his most important essays on the novel, *The Dialogic Imagination*, in the year of his death, 1975. During the last 25 years of his life, he also wrote several essays later published under the title *Speech Genres and Other Late Essays*. His work spread throughout the West in the 1980s and is the subject of vigorous debate and reassessment in Russia in the mid-1990s (Emerson, *First Hundred Years*).

Bakhtin's interests in his early years apparently shaped his thinking throughout his career. His experience in Vilnius and Odessa exposed him to a rich and complex mix of different language groups, cultures, and classes, illustrative of the mix of languages that he would later call *heteroglossia* (Clark and Holquist 21 ff.). His reading in contemporary German philosophy and recent developments in physics introduced him to the problem of unity amid differences that would persist throughout his work and its reception in Russia and the West. Bakhtin resisted the neo-Kantian emphasis upon an all-embracing unity: "The original Kantian concept of the heterogeneity of ends is much closer to Bakhtin's work than the later Neo-Kantian lust for unity" (Holquist 6). But he was receptive to Einstein's revelation of a complex unity of differences—his demonstration that "one body's motion has meaning only in relation to another body"—from which Bakhtin seems to have inferred that all meaning is relational, the result of a "dialogue" between and among bodies—physical, political, conceptual (Holquist 20–21). Finally, Bakhtin's religious activities as an intellectual from the Orthodox tradition introduced him to the communal ideal of the early church, transformed into a new social order characterized by "the concept of *sobornost'*, 'togetherness' or 'true sense of community' " (Clark and Holquist 129 ff.).

BAKHTIN AND DIALOGICAL RHETORIC

Bakhtin's concept of dialogue has potential to expand and enrich the rhetorical tradition. Contemporary rhetorical theory contrasts Bakhtinian dialogue with Aristotelian rhetoric, construed as persuasion (Bialostosky, "Dialogics" 789; Dentith 321; Farrell 63, 233–41) but differs on whether dialogue and rhetoric are distinct forms of discourse (Bialostosky, "Dialogics" 789–90); whether dialogue, construed as conversation, sets the larger context within which rhetoric occurs (Farrell 241–47); or whether dialogue is a subset of rhetoric, all discourse being "suasive," "*interested*," hence rhetorical (Dentith 311–12, 321–22). Contemporary composition theory, in contrast, reads Bakhtinian dialogue as a communicative interaction between speaker and listener (rather than a persuasion directed by the speaker to the listener) and thus as a fundamental challenge to traditional rhetoric (Kent 34–35; Schuster 2–4). Composition theorists find in Bakhtinian dialogue a multiplicity and diversity of voices (Bialostosky, "Liberal Education" 194–96), a "hierarchical inversion" of traditional student/teacher roles (Ewald 238), and a relationship of collaboration among participants in dialogic discourse (Kent 35–36).

Bakhtin's scattered and inconsistent statements about rhetoric are largely negative, but they nonetheless admit and encourage a reinterpretation of rhetoric as dialogue and hence a recognition of forms of discourse such as the expression, juxtaposition, or negotiation of differences that are only marginally persuasive, if at all, but are nonetheless potentially enriching for contemporary rhetorical theory and criticism. Bakhtin distinguishes Socratic dialogue from Platonic monologue, the early and middle Platonic dialogues being dialogic, the late dialogues monologic (*Problems of Dostoevsky's Poetics* 109–12, 132–33). He identifies rhetoric with Aristotelian forensic, deliberative, and epideictic speeches and claims that this rhetoric becomes shallow and inauthentic when torn from reality and from the context in which it is framed ("Discourse in the Novel" 353–54). His reading of the rhetorical tradition is not necessarily an indictment of this tradition, however, but a caution against its tendency to become a merely abstract, formal, logical mode of analysis. The larger context in which Bakhtin situates his discussion of rhetoric suggests the possibility of a dialogized or dialogical rhetoric that views all human activity and all human discourse as a complex unity of differences. This dialogized or dialogical rhetoric is not only a multiplicity and diversity of voices, a "heteroglossia," but an act of (and an active) listening to each voice from the perspective of the others, a "dialogized heteroglossia." Its purpose is to test our own and others' ideas and ourselves and thus to determine together what we should think and how we should live. Its characteristic forms are the expression, juxtaposition, or negotiation of our individual and our cultural differences. This dialogical rhetoric follows a line of development from Socrates rather than Plato and Aristotle through Bakhtin's reading of Rabelais and Dostoevsky to contemporary African American, feminist, and postcolonial theory. This rhetoric would bring to the rhetorical tradition several concepts developed in Bakhtin's work and in contemporary cultural theory: context, utterance, and dialogue as a broad concept applicable to all human discourse; polyphony, heteroglossia, and carnival; and dialogue as a subset of human discourse distinct from monologue and from traditional rhetorical theory and criticism.[3]

CONTEXT, UTTERANCE, DIALOGUE

Bakhtin's early ethical work is concerned with the act rather than the word but is formative for his later work on communication and rhetoric (Morson and Emerson 25–27, 68–71). In *Toward a Philosophy of the Act*, Bakhtin rejects the "theoreticism" of traditional ethics—its construction of universal concepts, propositions, and laws—in favor of a description or phenomenology of the world that situates each actually performed act or deed within its unique, concrete context (22–28). Embracing relativity theory but not relativism (Holquist 20–23; Morson and Emerson 26), Bakhtin claims that each "I" who performs an act or deed holds a unique place within the architectonic whole of Being (*Toward a Philosophy of the Act* 40–41, 53–54). Because I hold such a unique place, and because my uniqueness is both given and yet to be achieved, I must actualize my uniqueness (41–42). In doing so, I join in communion with a unity, or rather a uniqueness, of an actual, once-occurrent, and never-repeatable whole (37–40). This ethical imperative (Bakhtin calls it *"my non-alibi in Being"*), which requires that I act out my unique place within a complex unity, remains implicit in Bakhtin's later works on communication and helps to explain the persistent theme of unity amid differences in contemporary appropriations of Bakhtin (40).

Bakhtin brings to his study of communication the same strong sense of context that he had brought, via relativity theory, to his ethical work. At some point he had come to realize that the act is equivalent to the word, that the unique act in communion with the whole is an act of communication (Morson and Emerson 49–52, 59–62). As he reflects in "Toward a Reworking of the Dostoevsky Book," *"To be means to communicate"* and "Life by its very nature is dialogic" ("Toward a Reworking of the Dostoevsky Book" 287, 293). As he had rejected theoreticism in ethics, Bakhtin rejects abstract and systematic thinking in communication in favor of a contextual understanding of the word (Holquist 59–66; Morson and Emerson 123–30). Whereas traditional disciplines such as the philosophy of language, stylistics, and linguistics had studied *language* as an abstract system—sentences as decontextualized lexical and grammatical forms—Bakhtin proposes to study *communication*, that is, language as extra-linguistic or metalinguistic—utterances situated within the framing context of their dialogic interrelations with other utterances.[4] In "The Problem of Speech Genres," Bakhtin claims that the sentence, considered as a unit of language in traditional disciplines, has only the context of the speech of one speaking (or writing) subject (72–73). The utterance, in contrast, considered as a unit of spoken (or written) communication, is situated within the framing context of an exchange of speaking (or writing) subjects (73–74). Thus, the utterance, unlike the sentence, correlates directly with "the extraverbal context of reality (situation, setting, prehistory)" and with the utterances of other speakers (73). As "a link in the chain of speech communication," the utterance has several distinguishing characteristics: a referentially semantic element (its theme), an expressive element (the speaker's or writer's attitude toward the theme), and, most important, an element of responsiveness or *"addressivity"* (its relation to other utterances) (84, 90–91, 95).

The framing context of the utterance includes both the author of the utterance (as speaker or writer) and the persons to whom the author responds and from whom the author expects a response (Morson and Emerson 133–35, 136–39). The author of the utterance takes an active position "in one referentially semantic sphere or another," that is, a position in relation to its subject or theme ("Speech Genres" 84, 90). In addition, the author of the utterance also expresses an evaluative attitude toward the subject or theme of the utterance, a "subjective emotional evaluation of the referentially semantic content" (84). The referentially semantic content of the utterance captures its *meaning* and is accessible to traditional studies of language as system, such as linguistics (84–86). The evaluative attitude captures the *specific sense* of the utterance and is discernible only in the context of "a particular actual reality and particular real conditions," which are extralinguistic or metalinguistic (85–86).

The persons to whom the author responds and from whom the author expects a response are the authors of other utterances preceding and succeeding the author's own—the other links in the chain of speech communication. These persons can have a variety of relationships to the author, but typically the person or persons to whom the author responds are authors of other utterances on the author's subject or theme (91–92). The author "is not the biblical Adam, dealing only with virgin and still unnamed objects, giving them names for the first time" (93). Therefore, the author constructs each utterance not only in response to a theme and with an expressive attitude toward that theme but also as a response to "other viewpoints, world views, trends, theories, and so forth" (94). The person or persons from whom the author expects a response—"the addressee"— is an active participant in the chain of speech communication, for whom the entire utterance is constructed in anticipation of the response (94–95).

The framing context of the utterance also includes the author as creator and the "superaddressee" or ideal addressee (Morson and Emerson 135–36). In "The Problem of the Text," Bakhtin explains that the author as creator (of a literary work) makes from heterogeneous, alien utterances a unified and whole utterance in which the author is a constitutive element (115). In a traditional literary work, the author creates and interprets the world depicted in the work from a position that is higher and qualitatively different from that of the characters (116). In Dostoevsky's works, the author occupies a position on the same plane with the characters and in dialogue with them. The superaddressee is the ideal addressee "whose absolutely just responsive understanding is presumed, either in some metaphysical distance or in distant historical time" (126).

These constituents of the utterance are situated within the framing context of the utterance not in isolation from each other—as components in an abstract system of language—but in their dialogic interrelations, which shape both individual utterances and whole cultures. In Bakhtin's broad concept of dialogue,

all human discourse is a complex web of dialogic interrelations with other utterances (Holquist 40–44; Morson and Emerson 49–52, 130–33). In "Discourse
in the Novel," Bakhtin explains how these dialogic interrelations preexist and
shape each individual utterance: "The living utterance, having taken meaning
and shape at a particular historical moment in a socially specific environment,
cannot fail to brush up against thousands of living dialogic threads, woven by
socio-ideological consciousness around the given object of an utterance; it cannot fail to become an active participant in social dialogue" (276). In *Problems
of Dostoevsky's Poetics*, he illustrates these dialogic interrelationships with reference to two judgments: "Life is good." "Life is good." (183). From the point
of view of logic, these are absolutely identical judgments (183–84). Each expresses the same semantic orientation toward its referential object. Considered
as a dialogic interrelationship, as the utterances of two successive speaking subjects, however, these two judgments express affirmation or agreement between
the two speaking subjects (184). Thus, they express not only a referentially
semantic content but also an expressive attitude of affirmation or agreement,
each with the other—a dialogic interrelation accessible only to an extralinguistic
or metalinguistic understanding of the context of the actual historical and social
conditions in which they were produced.

In "Response to a Question from the *Novy Mir* Editorial Staff," Bakhtin explains how the dialogic interrelations that shape individual utterances also shape
whole cultures (Emerson, "Keeping the Self Intact" 109–14; Morson and Emerson 54–56). From a cultural and intercultural perspective, these interrelations
are a viewing of each culture from the standpoint of another: "In the realm of
culture, outsideness is a most powerful factor in understanding. It is only in the
eyes of *another* culture that foreign culture reveals itself fully and profoundly"
("Response" 7). These dialogic interrelations take place on the boundaries between cultures and are the sites of "the most intense and productive life of
culture" (2).

POLYPHONY, HETEROGLOSSIA, CARNIVAL

Bakhtin describes these dialogic interrelations in different terms in different
works: *polyphony* in *Problems of Dostoevsky's Poetics; heteroglossia* in "Discourse in the Novel"; and *carnival* in *Rabelais and His World* and the Dostoevsky book. Each of these terms captures, though each with a different
emphasis, the dialogic interrelationship of utterances as a complex unity of differences. Polyphony is the distinguishing characteristic of a particular kind of
novel, the polyphonic novel. In *Problems of Dostoevsky's Poetics*, Bakhtin explains how Dostoevsky creates the polyphonic novel by repositioning the idea
of the novel, its truth, within multiple and various consciousnesses rather than
a single consciousness and by repositioning the author of the novel alongside
the characters as one of these consciousnesses, creator of the characters but also
their equal (Clark and Holquist 239–52; Morson and Emerson 231–68). Bakhtin

claims that this new kind of novel is no longer a direct expression of the author's truth but an active creation of the truth in the consciousnesses of the author, the characters, and the reader, in which all participate as equals (Morson and Emerson 234–37, 251–59). This truth is a unified truth that nonetheless requires a plurality of consciousnesses: "It is quite possible to imagine and postulate a unified truth that requires a plurality of consciousnesses, one that cannot in principle be fitted into the bounds of a single consciousness, one that is, so to speak, by its very nature *full of event potential* and is born at a point of contact among various consciousnesses" (*Problems* 81). Such a unified truth, the unified truth of the polyphonic novel, combines several autonomous consciousnesses into "a higher unity, a unity, so to speak, of the second order," which Bakhtin explains only by analogy with "the complex unity of an Einsteinian universe" (16).

The author of the polyphonic novel, the characters, and the reader participate as equals in the creation of this truth. Thus, the author occupies a new position in relation to the characters and exercises a new creative process (Morson and Emerson 237–41, 243–46). The authorial position is "a *fully realized and thoroughly consistent dialogic position,*" in which the author speaks with, not about, a character as someone who is actually present (*Problems* 63–64). The author's dialogic position in relation to the characters requires a new creative process, occurring "in the *real present*," as an ongoing activity, not as a stenographer's report of a finished dialogue, from which the author has already withdrawn and over which the author presides as a higher authority (63). The characters participate in this ongoing dialogue not as objects of the author's consciousness but as "*free* people, capable of standing *alongside*," agreeing or disagreeing with, even rebelling against, their creator (6). These characters are "*not only objects of authorial discourse but also subjects of their own directly signifying discourse,*" and together they become "*a genuine polyphony of fully valid voices*" (6–7). In the polyphonic novel, the reader, too, participates in the dialogue (Morson and Emerson 247–51). Indeed, the reader must participate since the dialogic interaction "provides no support for the viewer who would objectify an entire event according to some ordinary monologic category (thematically, lyrically or cognitively)—and this consequently makes the viewer also a participant" (*Problems* 18).

Heteroglossia is a broader concept than polyphony, a description of speech styles in a language, especially characteristic of the novel but apparent in languages generally (Clark and Holquist 268–70, 290–94; Holquist 69–70; Morson and Emerson 139–45, 232, 309–17). In "Discourse in the Novel," Bakhtin describes heteroglossia as a complex mixture of languages and worldviews that is always, except in some imagined ideal condition, dialogized, as each language is viewed from the perspective of the others. This dialogization of languages, dialogized heteroglossia, creates a complex unity, for whatever meaning language has resides neither in the intention of the speaker nor in the text but at a point between speaker or writer, listener or reader (Morson and Emerson 284–

90). Such a dialogization of languages is always occurring, and language is always changing, as a result of what Bakhtin calls *hybridization*, the mixture of two different languages within a single utterance (Morson and Emerson 325–44).

While traditional disciplines such as linguistics emphasize the centripetal forces that centralize and unify a language, Bakhtin emphasizes the centrifugal forces that decentralize and disunify: "Every utterance participates in the 'unitary language' (in its centripetal forces and tendencies) and at the same time partakes of social and historical heteroglossia (the centrifugal, stratifying forces)" ("Discourse" 272). These centrifugal, stratifying forces of heterglossia produce a complex mixture of languages that is also, and equally, a mixture of attitudes or points of view about the world: "For any individual consciousness living in it, language is not an abstract system of normative forms but rather a concrete heteroglot conception of the world. All words have the 'taste' of a profession, a genre, a tendency, a party, a particular work, a particular person, a generation, an age group, the day and hour" (293). This complex mixture of languages is not merely a mixture, however, but a dialogized heteroglossia, a viewing of each language from the perspective of another (273, 295–96).

Such a dialogization of languages creates a complex unity of oneself with the other, for meaning in a language resides neither in my intention nor in what I speak or write but at a point between my intention and that of another. On the one hand, the word that I speak is already "half someone else's" (293). It becomes my own only when I populate it with my own intention (293–94). On the other hand, the word that I speak becomes populated in turn with the intention of another, for in the active life of the word my intention is always directed toward the active understanding of the other, which is itself populated with its own intentions (282). This dialogization of languages, dialogized heteroglossia, occurs constantly through a process of hybridization, both intentional and unintentional. Hybridization "is a mixture of two social languages within the limits of a single utterance, an encounter, within the arena of an utterance, between two different linguistic consciousnesses, separated from one another by an epoch, by social differentiation or by some other factor" (358). Hybridization is intentional as an artistic device in the novel (358). It is also unintentional and as such is the primary means of change in a language, "a mixing of various 'languages' co-existing within the boundaries of a single dialect, a single national language, a single branch, a single group of different branches or different groups of such branches, in the historical as well as paleontological past of languages" (358–59).

Carnival is both a general sense of the world and of language and a specific literary form (Clark and Holquist 295–320; Holquist 89–90; Morson and Emerson 443–69). In *Rabelais and His World*, carnival is a way of life and a mode of language opposed to the official norms of church and state and as a binary opposition is perhaps at odds with concepts such as polyphony and heteroglossia (Morson and Emerson 443–56).[5] As a way of life, it is an expression of universal freedom: "Carnival is not a spectacle seen by the people; they live in it, and everyone participates because its very idea embraces all the people. While carnival lasts, there is no other life outside it. During carnival time life is subject only to its laws, that is, the laws of its own freedom" (*Rabelais* 7). As a mode of language, carnival is specifically an expression of freedom from official norms and values, "a special type of communication impossible in everyday life," with "special forms of marketplace speech and gesture, frank and free, permitting no distance between those who came in contact with each other and liberating from norms of etiquette and decency imposed at other times" (10). Best characterized as a general tone of laughter, this carnivalesque language is an expression of freedom from official norms and as such stands in binary opposition to the authority of church and state (Clark and Holquist 299–302; Morson and Emerson 445–46). This language of laughter "builds its own world versus the official world, its own church versus the official church, its own state versus the official state" (*Rabelais* 88). But carnival is not simply an invitation to individual freedom (Clark and Holquist 302). Rather, it is an invitation to become a part of a complex unity, a bodily collectivity: "In this whole the individual body ceases to a certain extent to be itself; it is possible, so to say, to exchange bodies, to be renewed (through change of costume and mask). At the same time the people become aware of their sensual, material bodily unity and community" (*Rabelais* 255).

In *Problems of Dostoevsky's Poetics*, carnival is a specific literary form with origins in Socratic dialogue (Kristeva 78–81; Morson and Emerson 456–69). In this context, carnival perhaps more closely resembles Bakhtin's concepts of dialogue, polyphony, and heteroglossia. As explained in the Dostoevsky book, the carnivalistic line of development in the novel that leads to Dostoevsky has its origins in the seriocomical genres, the most important of which is the Socratic dialogue (109). The seriocomical genres capture "a specific *carnival sense of the world*" best characterized by an "atmosphere of *joyful relativity*" (107). The Socratic dialogues in particular have their basis in "the dialogic nature of truth" created by way of two basic stylistic devices: anacrisis, the "means for eliciting and provoking the words of one's interlocutor"; and syncrisis, "the juxtaposition of various points of view on a specific object" (110–11). The dialogues engage these two devices not to persuade but to test both the ideas and the persons and lives of the various participants—Socrates, the sophists, and other historical figures—by presenting their ideas and their persons "in their free and creative development against a dialogizing background of other ideas" (112).

DIALOGUE, MONOLOGUE, RHETORIC

The Socratic dialogues provide a historical precedent for Bakhtin's rereading of the rhetorical tradition. Bakhtin distinguishes dialogue from monologue, and he sometimes (disparagingly) associates rhetoric with monologue, but he also seems to encourage a rethinking of the rhetorical tradition that would admit dialogue, polyphony, heteroglossia, and carnival: a dialogized or dialogical rhetoric. In *Problems of Dostoevsky's Poetics*, Bakhtin explains dialogue in its narrow or limited sense as a subset of human discourse, distinct from monologue and including several specific types of dialogue, among them stylization, parody, and hidden polemic (Morson 63–74; Morson and Emerson 146–59). He distinguishes monologue from dialogue as single-voiced and double-voiced discourse, respectively. Monologic, single-voiced discourse is discourse that recognizes only itself and its object, discourse that does not recognize other people's words (*Problems* 185–87). Such discourse "is directed toward its referential object and constitutes the ultimate semantic authority within the limits of a given context" (189). Dialogic, double-voiced discourse is discourse that contains a deliberate reference to someone else's words (185–87). Such discourse inserts "a new semantic intention into a discourse which already has, and which retains, an intention of its own" (189). Of the several specific types of double-voiced discourse, parody and hidden polemic have received special attention in contemporary cultural theory. Unlike stylization, which follows another's thought in the same direction, merely making it conventional, parody adopts someone else's discourse but "introduces into that discourse a semantic intention that is directly opposed to the original one," the second voice clashing with the first and creating "an arena of battle between two voices" (193). Unlike both stylization and parody, each of which adapts another's words to its own intention, hidden polemic does not reproduce another's words with a new intention but rather, directing itself toward its own referential object, strikes a polemical blow at another's discourse on the same theme, the same referential object: "A word, directed toward its referential object, clashes with another's word within the very object itself" (195).

In his discussion of Socratic dialogue earlier in the Dostoevsky book, reading the rhetorical tradition from the perspective of Socrates and Plato, Bakhtin distinguishes Socratic dialogue from Platonic monologue—the early and middle from the late Platonic dialogues—and (with obvious hostility) from the monologic single-voicedness of the rhetorical tradition (Zappen 71–74). In the early and middle Platonic dialogues, "the dialogic nature of truth" that lay at the carnivalistic base of Socratic dialogue determined its form, though not necessarily the content of individual dialogues (*Problems* 110). In the late Platonic dialogues, "the monologism of the content" begins to destroy the form, so that Socratic dialogue "entered the service of the established, dogmatic worldviews of various philosophical schools and religious doctrines" and "lost all connection with a carnival sense of the world and was transformed into a simple form for expounding already found, ready-made irrefutable truth" (110). Like the late Platonic dialogues and worse, the rhetorical tradition is monologic in its rationality and dogmatism, its "one sided seriousness," its "stupid fetish for definition," its "singleness of meaning" (107, 132).

In "Discourse in the Novel," reading the rhetorical tradition from the perspective of Aristotle's *Rhetoric*, Bakhtin criticizes rhetoric's practice and its analytical power but apparently admits the possibility of a dialogized or dialogical rhetoric. The rhetorical genres—the rhetoric of the courts, political rhetoric, and publicist rhetoric (Aristotle's forensic, deliberative, and epideictic rhetoric)—are inherently dialogic and double-voiced (353–54). They "possess the most varied forms for transmitting another's speech, and for the most part these are intensely dialogized forms" (354). As dialogized and double-voiced, these genres "provide rich material for studying a variety of forms for transmitting another's speech, the most varied means for formulating and framing such speech" (354). Nonetheless, in practice, rhetoric often degenerates into merely formal wordplay: "Rhetoric is often limited to purely verbal victories over the word; when this happens, rhetoric degenerates into a formalistic verbal play" (353). As a result, its double-voicedness is shallow, its analytical power also merely formal (354). Though rhetoric tends toward the abstract, the formal, the purely logical, it is of its nature intensely dialogized and thus seems amenable to Bakhtin's concept of dialogue, as indeed it proves to be in contemporary cultural theory.

DIALOGICAL RHETORIC AND CONTEMPORARY CULTURAL THEORY

Given its Socratic origins, Bakhtin's dialogized or dialogical rhetoric is less a means of persuasion than a means of testing our own and others' ideas and ourselves and a testing especially of our individual and our cultural differences. As developed in contemporary cultural theory, this rhetoric takes forms such as the expression, juxtaposition, and negotiation of these differences. Dale Peterson observes that contemporary literary theorists have turned to Bakhtin to explain "the expressive power of marginalized and uncanonical forms of articulation" (89). African American literary theorist Henry Louis Gates, Jr., for example, explains this expressive power as a complex process of signifying akin to Bakhtinian parody and hidden polemic. Gates emphasizes that the African American literary tradition is expressive of the Black Experience; it is, in Ralph Ellison's phrase, "a sharing of that 'concord of sensibilities' which the group *expresses*" (124, 128). Gates explains, however, that this expressiveness is indirect, a kind of Signifyin(g)/signifying that has its roots in tales of the Signifying Monkey, whose rhetorical strategy "ever punning, ever troping, ever embodying the ambiguities of language," dupes the ever-literal Lion into tangling with the Elephant, who invariably trounces him (52, 56). Gates argues that African American writers, like the Signifying Monkey, "Signify upon each other's texts by rewriting the received textual tradition" (124). Their texts may be either parody or hidden polemic (or sometimes both), parody when they "configure into relationships based on . . . repetition and revision," hidden polemic when they clash " 'on the grounds of the referent itself' . . . the so-called Black Experience" (110–12).

Peterson argues that African American literary theorists such as Gates have given Bakhtin a "selective hearing . . . a hearing that has been particularly sensitive to the empowering and emancipatory implications of the Russian's polyphonic discourse analysis, but only gradually and reluctantly attentive to the problematic and double-edged aspects of Bakhtin's theory of the utterance as a site of unavoidable semantic contestation" (93–94). Peterson acknowledges that the ongoing African American dialogue with Bakhtin has contested "the production and enunciation of canon-forming narratives about a singular tradition or language essence" (96). Nonetheless, Peterson's criticism appears to question, on Bakhtin's authority, the empowering and emancipatory function of expressive discourse. From the perspective of Bakhtin's early ethical work, however, this expressive function is essential to any meaningful dialogue, for if I must actualize my uniqueness, lest "the whole of Being" be somehow incomplete, and if *"To be* means *to communicate"* (*Toward a Philosophy of the Act* 41–42; "Toward a Reworking of the Dostoevsky Book" 287), then the expression of each individual's, and each culture's, ideas is a necessary prologue to the dialogical testing of those ideas and of the persons who hold them.

Some feminist theorists engage Bakhtin's notion of carnival as a juxtaposition of marginalized and official discourses for the purpose of testing—and challenging—official discourses. Clair Wills draws an analogy between Bakhtinian carnival, hysteria, and women's texts, noting that "both carnival and hysteria are excluded from official public norms" and seeking "to dialogise the public realm by bringing the excluded and 'non-official' into juxtaposition with the official" for the purpose of disrupting and remaking official norms and discourses (130–31). Wills notes the power of literature, demonstrated by Bakhtin's reading of Rabelais, to dialogize popular and official discourses within particular texts and institutional contexts (131–33). She argues by analogy that women's texts can challenge literary norms and thereby challenge the cultural authority embedded within the literary canon—especially if this literary protest is conducted not only within individual texts but also within the context of the dominant literary institutions, such as publishing houses (140–41, 149). Such a notion of carnival as a juxtaposition of marginalized and official discourses sets these discourses in a dialogic interrelationship with each other, not, however, "in their free and creative development" but with opposition and even antagonism toward each other (*Problems* 112). Noting Wills's analogy between Bakhtinian carnival and women's texts, Elizabeth Butler Cullingford observes that "only to the extent that it enters into antagonistic dialogue with 'official' discourse, hybridizing it, can the energies of carnival become politically transformative" (26).

Other cultural theorists, in contrast, read Bakhtin's notion of hybridization as a form of cultural negotiation, a viewing of one culture from the perspective of another, testing what is best in each, not one in opposition to the other, however, but each in negotiation with the other. Recalling Bakhtin's observation that we understand our own culture only from the standpoint of another ("Response" 7), Mikhail Epstein contrasts American multiculturalism, which emphasizes the rights and dignity of individuals as "the ultimate minority," with Russian trans-culturalism, which posits "a free multidimensional totality" and assumes that each of us is incomplete without the other: "No human is a full entity, so all of us are called to restore, through our cultural perceptions and occupations, the full totality that nature does not give us" (301–2, 304). From a Russian trans-cultural perspective, therefore, the American multicultural ideal of difference means, paradoxically, that we must differ not only from others but also from our own (previous) selves, as we outgrow our own identity and become "an integral personality that can include the qualities and possibilities of other people's experience" (305–6). Russian cultural theorists Anesa Miller-Pogacar and Marina Timchenko label this unifying process *hybridization* and explain that from a cultural perspective "this principle implies that when one nation or ethnic group borrows from another, the new cultural expression that results will enhance aspects of both sources and expand the universal repertoire of human creativity" (Miller-Pogacar 18; see also Timchenko 139).

Postcolonial theorist Homi Bhabha transforms Bakhtinian hybridization into a rhetorical process of cultural negotiation. Bhabha's agenda for postcolonial theory is to undermine the binary opposition between colonizer and colonized and to emphasize rather "the mutualities and negotiations across the colonial divide" (Moore-Gilbert 116). Bhabha infers from Bakhtin's notion of the utterance as a link in the chain of speech communication a broader concept of human solidarity that transcends cultural boundaries (Bhabha 188–92; see also Moore-Gilbert 136–37). Such forms of human solidarity are "hybrid forms," developed via a "*public rhetoric*," construed as "the symbolic process of political negotiation" (Bhabha 22–25). Bhabha's agenda for postcolonial theory turns on an unresolved tension between the postcolonial as an individual agent with its own self-identity and the postcolonial as a hybrid, mixed and impure—the site of political negotiation (Moore-Gilbert 129–30).

Contemporary cultural theory, in particular its Russian and postcolonial artic-ulations, thus reflects the theme of unity amid difference so persistent in Bakhtin's work. It also suggests something of the range of discursive forms that concepts such as dialogue, polyphony, heteroglossia, and carnival might bring to the rhetorical tradition.[6]

NOTES

1. Clark and Holquist (16–62, 95–145, 253–74, 321–45, 353–58), Holquist (1–13, 190–95), and Morson and Emerson (xiii–xv, xvii–xx, 63–100) survey Bakhtin's life and works.

2. Clark and Holquist (146–70) and Morson and Emerson (101–19) review some of the arguments for and against Bakhtin's authorship of these works.

3. Morson and Emerson (130–31) find at least three distinct senses of the term *dialogue* in Bakhtin's work: "dialogue as a global concept, as a view of truth and the world"; dialogue as a general concept applicable to "*every* utterance"; and dialogue as a specific concept that distinguishes dialogic from monologic discourse.

4. The critique of traditional linguistics and related disciplines appears in "Discourse in the Novel" (260–75) and "The Problem of Speech Genres" (63 ff); the explication of the utterance in "The Problem of Speech Genres" (73 ff.) and "The Problem of the Text" (104 ff.); the exposition on the dialogic relationship as extralinguistic or metalinguistic in *Problems of Dostoevsky's Poetics* (182–85).

5. Morson and Emerson (445–46) find this kind of binary opposition to be quite at odds with Bakhtin's more characteristic concepts of dialogue and heteroglossia, which "see in every utterance the crossing of numerous intentions, worldviews, and evaluations at intricate dialogic angles."

6. I am grateful to Jerry Blitefield, Beth Britt, Lee Honeycutt, Kevin Hunt, Mike Jackson, Terese Monberg, and Filipp Sapienza for fruitful discussions about Bakhtin and contemporary cultural theory.

BIBLIOGRAPHY

Primary Sources

Bakhtin, M[ikhail] M. "Discourse in the Novel." *The Dialogic Imagination: Four Essays.* Ed. Michael Holquist. Trans. Caryl Emerson and Michael Holquist. 1975. Austin: University of Texas Press, 1981. 259–422.

———. "The Problem of Speech Genres." *Speech Genres and Other Late Essays.* Ed. Caryl Emerson and Michael Holquist. Trans. Vern W. McGee. 1979. Austin: University of Texas Press, 1986. 60–102.

———. "The Problem of the Text in Linguistics, Philology, and the Human Sciences: An Experiment in Philosophical Analysis." *Speech Genres and Other Late Essays.* Ed. Caryl Emerson and Michael Holquist. Trans. Vern W. McGee. 1979. Austin: University of Texas Press, 1986. 103–31.

———. *Problems of Dostoevsky's Poetics.* Ed. and trans. Caryl Emerson. 1963. Minneapolis: University of Minnesota Press, 1984.

———. *Rabelais and His World.* Trans. Hélène Iswolsky. 1965. Bloomington: Midland/ Indiana University Press, 1984.

———. "Response to a Question from the *Novy Mir* Editorial Staff." *Speech Genres and Other Late Essays.* Ed. Caryl Emerson and Michael Holquist. Trans. Vern W. McGee. 1979. Austin: University of Texas Press, 1986. 1–7.

———. *Speech Genres and Other Late Essays.* Ed. Caryl Emerson and Michael Holquist. Trans. Vern W. McGee. 1979. Austin: University of Texas Press, 1986.

———. "Three Fragments from the 1929 Edition *Problems of Dostoevsky's Art.*" *Problems of Dostoevsky's Poetics,* "Appendix I." Ed. and trans. Caryl Emerson. 1929. Minneapolis: University of Minnesota Press, 1984. 275–82.

———. *Toward a Philosophy of the Act.* Ed. Vadim Liapunov and Michael Holquist. Trans. Vadim Liapunov. 1986. Austin: University of Texas Press, 1993.

———. " 'Toward a Reworking of the Dostoevsky Book' (1961)." *Problems of Dostoevsky's Poetics,* "Appendix II." Ed. and trans. Caryl Emerson. 1976. Minneapolis: University of Minnesota Press, 1984. 283–302.

Biography

Clark, Katerina, and Michael Holquist. *Mikhail Bakhtin*. Cambridge: Belknap/Harvard University Press, 1984.

Criticism

Bhabha, Homi K. *The Location of Culture*. London: Routledge, 1994.
Bialostosky, Don H. "Dialogics as an Art of Discourse in Literary Criticism." *Publications of the Modern Language Association* 101 (1986): 788–97.
———. "Liberal Education, Writing, and the Dialogic Self." *Landmark Essays on Bakhtin, Rhetoric, and Writing*. Ed. Frank Farmer. Mahwah, NJ: Hermagoras/Erlbaum, 1998. 187–96.
Cullingford, Elizabeth Butler. "The Historical Poetics of Excrement: Yeats's Crazy Jane and the Irish Bishops." *A Dialogue of Voices: Feminist Literary Theory and Bakhtin*. Ed. Karen Hohne and Helen Wussow. Minneapolis: University of Minnesota Press, 1994. 20–41.
Dentith, Simon. "Bakhtin versus Rhetoric?" *Face to Face: Bakhtin in Russia and the West*. Ed. Carol Adlam, Rachel Falconer, Vitalii Makhlin, and Alastair Renfrew. Sheffield, England: Sheffield Academic Press, 1997. 311–25.
Emerson, Caryl. *The First Hundred Years of Mikhail Bakhtin*. Princeton, NJ: Princeton University Press, 1997.
———. "Keeping the Self Intact during the Culture Wars: A Centennial Essay for Mikhail Bakhtin." *New Literary History* 27 (1996): 107–26.
Epstein, Mikhail N. *After the Future: The Paradoxes of Postmodernism and Contemporary Russian Culture*. Trans. Anesa Miller-Pogacar. Amherst: University of Massachusetts Press, 1995.
Ewald, Helen Rothschild. "Waiting for Answerability: Bakhtin and Composition Studies." *Landmark Essays on Bakhtin, Rhetoric, and Writing*. Ed. Frank Farmer. Mahwah, NJ: Hermagoras/Erlbaum, 1998. 225–41.
Farrell, Thomas B. *Norms of Rhetorical Culture*. New Haven, CT: Yale University Press, 1993.
Gates, Henry Louis, Jr. *The Signifying Monkey: A Theory of African-American Literary Criticism*. New York: Oxford University Press, 1988.
Holquist, Michael. *Dialogism: Bakhtin and His World*. London: Routledge, 1990.
Kent, Thomas. "Hermeneutics and Genre: Bakhtin and the Problem of Communicative Interaction." *Landmark Essays on Bakhtin, Rhetoric, and Writing*. Ed. Frank Farmer. Mahwah, NJ: Hermagoras/Erlbaum, 1998. 33–49.
Kristeva, Julia. *Desire in Language: A Semiotic Approach to Literature and Art*. Ed. Leon S. Roudiez. Trans. Thomas Gora, Alice Jardine, and Leon S. Roudiez. New York: Columbia University Press, 1980.
Miller-Pogacar, Anesa. "Introduction: Recovering Traditions for a New Cultural Era." *Re-entering the Sign: Articulating New Russian Culture*. Ed. Ellen E. Berry and Anesa Miller-Pogacar. Ann Arbor: University of Michigan Press, 1995. 1–22.
Moore-Gilbert, Bart. *Postcolonial Theory: Contexts, Practices, Politics*. London: Verso, 1997.
Morson, Gary Saul. "Parody, History, and Metaparody." *Rethinking Bakhtin: Extensions*

and Challenges. Ed. Gary Saul Morson and Caryl Emerson. Evanston, IL: North-western University Press, 1989. 63–86, 271–74.

Morson, Gary Saul, and Caryl Emerson. *Mikhail Bakhtin: Creation of a Prosaics*. Stanford: Stanford University Press, 1990.

Peterson, Dale E. "Response and Call: The African American Dialogue with Bakhtin and What It Signifies." *Bakhtin in Contexts: Across the Disciplines*. Ed. Amy Mandelker. Evanston, IL: Northwestern University Press, 1995. 89–98, 200–204.

Schuster, Charles I. "Mikhail Bakhtin as Rhetorical Theorist." *Landmark Essays on Bakhtin, Rhetoric, and Writing*. Ed. Frank Farmer. Mahwah, NJ: Hermagoras/Erlbaum, 1998. 1–14.

Timchenko, Marina. "Transition: The State of Contemporary Artistic Culture." *Re-entering the Sign: Articulating New Russian Culture*. Ed. Ellen E. Berry and Anesa Miller-Pogacar. Ann Arbor: University of Michigan Press, 1995. 129–43.

Wills, Clair. "Upsetting the Public: Carnival, Hysteria and Women's Texts." *Bakhtin and Cultural Theory*. Ed. Ken Hirschkop and David Shepherd. Manchester, England: Manchester University Press, 1989. 130–51.

Zappen, James P. "Bakhtin's Socrates." *Rhetoric Review* 15 (1996): 66–83.

ROLAND GÉRARD BARTHES
(1915–1980)

Hans Kellner

Roland Gérard Barthes was born in Cherbourg, France, on November 12, 1915. His father, Louis Barthes, was killed in a naval battle in 1916. Roland was raised by his mother, Henriette Binger Barthes, with whom he lived with few interruptions until her death in 1977. His early years were spent in Bayonne. In 1924 the family moved to Paris because of his academic promise. His *license* and *diplôme* were in classical studies; the final *license* (1943), in grammar and philology. Recurring bouts of tuberculosis prevented Barthes from winning the doctorate and a conventional university career. Most of World War II was spent in sanatoria. In addition to a brief stint as a lycée instructor, he spent various periods teaching abroad (Hungary, Romania, Egypt). After a difficult time of minor research posts and extensive freelance critical writing, Barthes joined the École pratique des Hautes Études, where he worked from 1960 until his ascension to the chair of Literary Semiology at the Collège de France in 1978. His working life as a writer, which produced over a dozen books and a vast number of essays, was one of extraordinary discipline and productivity. By the 1960s Barthes had become, with Claude Lévi-Strauss, the head of the structuralist movement and an intellectual figure of international renown. In the last decade of his life, he turned more to matters of the uncodifiable, the body, and the personal. On February 25, 1980, after a luncheon party with President-elect François Mitterand, Barthes was struck by a truck. He died on March 26 at age 64.

Roland Barthes was an ambiguous figure who found postmodern indeterminacies in traditional texts and archaic roots in poststructural theory, who championed personal desire and freedom while at times writing the most strictly formal of descriptions, who often wrote in the leftist lingua franca of French intellectuals while dismissing all versions of political discourse as oppressive, who turned his most personal desire into textual theory yet in principle favored all theories that denied the identity of the subject. He was, as he put it, more classical than the theory of the text that he defended. The protean appearance of his oeuvre led him to explain the inconsistencies by noting that he was always following his desires and that his body changed from time to time. Because intellectual things resemble erotic things, binary structuralism, for example, was an erotic object for him. Finally, however, the reader of Barthes must recognize that the writer shows such a depth of craft and craftiness that he is always elusive, even in the most personal revelations. The subtlety of his verbal imagination led him to produce sensibilities about language that broadened the vocabulary of linguistic and personal discussion, creating a new set of objects to be described and a sense of unexplored possibilities. One might say that Barthes did for language what Rousseau did for feelings. Although Barthes began to write explicitly about his own sexuality only late in life, many of his themes and devices question the process of social categorization that excluded the homosexual man from the mythic narratives of culture.

BARTHES'S RHETORICAL THEORY

Barthes maintained that language itself is an alien force that compels obedience to its vision of the world, forcing us to say what it wants. One is forced, for example, to suppose oneself a subject before speaking of an action that then becomes simply an attribute, so that what one does must follow from what one is. Neuter or complex gendering is forbidden to the speaker of French, who must choose between masculine and feminine. And one cannot escape social relations in a language that requires address to be either familiar or formal. Each use of language, however intimate, serves power: Assertions create authority; repetitions invoke the social. Thus, every sign is gregarious to the extent that a stereotype is called forth. At once master and slave, the speaker comfortably affirms what he repeats. Power and servility are intertwined. Although Barthes used the term "fascist" to describe language, he despised political discourse, in which one correct word always followed another. The stereotypes of political language lead to myths, where dominant social stereotypes are embodied to become a second nature, part of the given background of life. The study of myth, the falsely natural, occupied Barthes in one form or another throughout his career.

For science (the model of political language), knowledge is an utterance; for letters, it is the act of speech that exposes the force, position, condition, and effects of the speaker. Thus, his dream, and utopia, was a permanent revolution of language that Barthes called *literature*. From his essays of the late 1940s to *Writer Sollers* (1979), Barthes was seeking and supporting new forms of writing, while acknowledging that these often bored, irritated, and disturbed him. The value of such writing, for Barthes, was its resistance to any definitive naming that placed the subject in the world and fixed its possibilities. Calling such writing *writerly*, and the texts thus produced *écriture*, Barthes foresaw the emergence of a certain practice of writing that could counteract the immense social pressures built into language. In his own practice of writing, Barthes continually changed his approaches and methods, moving from the phenomenological thematics of his *Michelet*, to the binary semiotics of *The Fashion System*, the reading codes spelled out in *S/Z*, the topical analysis of *A Lover's Discourse*, the personal self-reflection of *Roland Barthes*, and the bodily awareness of *Camera Lucida*. Because he preferred beginnings and grew bored with applications of existing programs, Barthes often offered sketches of concepts and methods that he promptly dropped. Few, if any, writers about language have been more fertile and varied. Although many critics imitated Barthesian techniques, he was impossible to follow because the idea of "following" was anathema, an impermissible restriction. Words that must follow other words (political discourse), ideas that must follow other ideas (ideology), events that must follow other events (narrative) are all part of a mythic structure that drenches the world with *meaning*, while policing the creation of new meanings.

The obvious influences on Barthes are major figures in French thought after the war. From Claude Lévi-Strauss, Roman Jakobson, and Algirdas Greimas, Barthes took the structural devices that he deployed in his individual ways. Jacques Lacan, Jacques Derrida, and Michel Foucault provided the sort of fashionable terms and topics that Barthes used and discarded as he pleased. Philippe Sollers remained the model of the modernist writer Barthes praised (even if he did not personally enjoy the work). More important, perhaps, are the figures that Barthes had read in his younger years. His first important work, *Writing Degree Zero*, was a response to Jean-Paul Sartre's *Situation of the Writer in 1947*. Sartre (who would die two months after Barthes) established the role of the postwar intellectual as above all a relation to political writing; from the start, Barthes turned away from Sartrean polemicism and toward a poetic individualism of the word. Bertolt Brecht's influence shows in Barthes's aversion to theatricality and expressive show. In Mallarmé, Barthes found the theorist of a modern poetic that would liberate the word from its surroundings.

Barthes's work begins with Saussure's sign, the creation of an arbitrary signifier and signified. To this he adds connotation and metalanguage, which open and destabilize the sign by turning it into a new process; the signifier (connotation) and the signified (metalanguage) become new signs, endlessly proliferating and saturating the world with signification. Connotation and metalanguages are social; their products at a cultural level Barthes called *myth*.

In his discussion *Mythologies*, Barthes broadened immeasurably both the realm of rhetoric and its formal procedures. He defined myth as the addition of social usage to the meaningless material world; whenever something is spoken about (or written or represented), it becomes filled with meaning, part of a signifying field that must be read or deciphered. The subject of Barthes's best-known "mythology," professional wrestling, spells out through its excess and spectacle a complete intelligibility: As in ancient tragedy, the struggle for Justice is made manifest by the suffering, defeat, and humiliation of the wrestlers, the misdeeds of the "bastard," and the heavily underlined morality of it all. Myth, as Barthes presents it, is too rich in meaning, nauseating in Sartre's sense. It is like the singer who emphasizes expressiveness rather than simply presenting the corporeality of his voice. Myth turns history, a contingent state of events, into nature. The consumer of myth takes it as a system of fact, but it remains a semiological system. In his writing of the 1950s, Barthes attributed social myths primarily (but not exclusively) to the political Right; later, after 1968, he noted that the mythical is present wherever sentences are written or stories are told.

Barthes's semiological mythology is intended as a decoding process that will reveal the secrets of discourse above the level of the sentence. As such, it will become a new rhetoric. Barthes describes the "old" rhetoric as an empire greater than any empire in Western history. A "super-civilization," rhetoric is the only practice through which the sovereignty of language has been recognized. It is hardly surprising, therefore, that "the world is incredibly full of old Rhetoric" (*Semiotic Challenge* 11). Barthes's discussion of the "old rhetoric" emphasizes its obsession with classification, and the ideological force behind taxonomy. To classify is to give and enforce an identity, a stable place in a system. With the tropes and figures, however, a "taxonomic frenzy" breaks out, in which the naming and classification of figures is in effect the creation of new ones. The breakdown of this endless proliferation was inevitable because it is here that rhetoric in Barthes's account attempts to code speech, which is impossible. Following Saussure's definitions, the code ends where language ends; speech, the system of language where connotation and metalanguage presides, cannot be meaningfully coded, so the rhetorical attempt to master the unmasterable led to a mirage. Obviously, to speak of an "old" rhetoric (the French *ancienne* can mean "ancient" or "former") implies some new, modern, or subsequent rhetoric. It was such a new rhetoric that Barthes sought continuously to invent throughout his life. The classificatory powers of rhetoric are still usable, Barthes notes (and he used them powerfully), but the "ideology" of the old rhetoric has been made clear by the "other thing" that has replaced it. This observation on the fate of rhetoric in the contemporary world parallels Barthes's turn from structuralist binary taxonomy (*The Fashion System*) to the unclassifiable passions of *Camera Lucida*.

In narrative prose, Barthes saw the epitome of what he feared and desired, the domination of meaning. Narrative is likened to cross-country walking, a long, laborious progress, step by relentless step, broken only by the sudden "euphoria" of a panorama. This view of narrative, which Barthes attributes to Jules Michelet, throws light on many of Barthes's later positions. He advocated and practiced a form of reading that fetishized parts of the text, pulling from it items of personal interest, unconstrained by the pressure of the whole and its meaning. In *The Empire of Signs*, Barthes described aspects of Japanese culture as a sort of free signification, a play of surfaces that is not captured by the Western emphasis on meaning. Thus, Bunraku theater offers the spectator nothing to "read," an exemption from meaning that reveals the void at the heart of theater, unlike the space of Western theater, which reveals the truth of feeling and situation by drawing away a curtain of stage or character. Haiku, in a similar way, illustrates this exemption from meaning by excluding description and definition so as to say, simply, "That!" The Japan that Barthes creates in *The Empire of Signs* is a version of his utopia where signs are uncontrolled by the weight of social mythologies and spectacle.

Barthes frequently posed antitheses in a classical manner, promoting a new term against the traditional one. Thus, the concept of *text*, a plural unfinished, indeterminate process that resists any clear, final description. Opposed to text is the *work*, an object that can be formally described and historically explained. The work can be read, but the text is unreadable in the sense that it can never be grasped. The text is thus a blissful, utopian space where no one language or code rules over another. The emergence of the text corresponds to the death of the author in the sense of a ruling origin for writing, the figure whose intention must prevail. Once the text is assumed to be indecipherable and subject to play, the author has no function; the scriptor, a vast, impersonal system of available codes, emerges. In effect, Barthes announces the victory of the reader over the writer.

To free the text from the tyranny of its meaning was his goal; reading was his strategy. The fruit of Barthes's research on reading was *S/Z*, a testimony to his penchant for fragmentation. Beginning from a distinction between the classic, *readerly* work, with a distinct message, and the *writerly* text, which obligates a reader continually to write it because it lacks a fixed meaning, Barthes upholds the writerly because "the goal of literary work (of literature as work) is to make the reader no longer a consumer, but a producer of the text" (*S/Z* 4). In *S/Z* Barthes took "Sarrasine," a Balzac story that would apparently fit in the readerly category, and demonstrated that even this tale possesses plural senses, is a writerly text, an infinite galaxy of signifiers, not a structure of signifieds. After dividing the text into 561 segments, or *lexia*, he uses five codes (the Hermeneutic, Semiotic, Action, Symbolic, and Referential) to analyze how reading takes place. Instead of decoding a message built into "Sarrasine," however, the codes proliferate meanings into a cosmos of expanding connotations and discourses, leading in many diverse directions and allowing no authoritative conclusion. The dream of a structural grammar of the text, of the sort foreshadowed by Vladimir Propp and sketched by Algirdas Greimas is gone, and a poststructural vision emerges. The codes are the voice of what has already been seen, read, done, experienced; they open up a vast network of possible meanings and references beside every utterance. *S/Z* represented a new and scandalous kind of literary criticism. By exploding the text and refusing to reassemble the shards of meaning into a master thematics, Barthes indicates a multiplicity of voices and signs, all of which must be heard and noted. The thematics of a classic text like "Sarrasine" is infinite, but since this is impossible, the meaning of such a work in any given reading is arbitrary, settled by a throw of the dice.

Barthes's last book, *Camera Lucida*, offers a new vocabulary and a new perspective on his obsession with freeing the poetic word. He describes the *studium* in a photograph, that which is interesting, admirable, capable of being examined and enjoyed; against this, he places the *punctum*, an element that wounds him. The punctum disturbs the studium by refusing to respect the general sense of the photograph; its theme or subject means nothing to one who has been "pricked" by a detail that has no discernible meaning or even relevance to the photo but has an overwhelming impact on an individual. One of the terms Barthes uses to describe the punctum is "a cast of the dice," indicating its chance nature. There can, of course, be a science of the studium in the sense of what makes a photograph successful, how it signifies, what structures it. But the punctum is an absolute particularity and can never form the basis of a science within our discourse of meaning. Yet such a new science is again what Barthes desires and sketches in *Camera Lucida*, where he notes his own responses to a series of photos. The most important photograph, a very personal image of his deceased mother, he does not place in the book, which becomes a meditation on death, loss, and memory. The science he desires, in fact, is a literature that mediates between the inconsistency of life and the indeterminacy of reading. *Camera Lucida*, which appeared just before the accident that ended Barthes's life, may be seen as a prologue to the Proustian novel that Barthes had been preparing to write.

Barthes's embrace of inconsistency took the form of a fluid movement from method to method and from topic to topic. He loved beginnings but hated to finish his work. As a result, his oeuvre seems a collection of fragments, projects, sketches. Much of Barthes's neologistic terminology found favor with critics, but he could have no real disciples because his topic and his method were really Roland Barthes. Writing the self has a ring of autobiographical reportage about it, a capturing in language of the substance and story of a life. Barthes, however, reconceived both terms—"writing" and "self"—making the self a product of a certain writing process, rather than the reverse. Because the writing he desired, an unattainable *écriture*, had no centered theme and vertically liberated the word (as Mallarmé had wanted), Barthes describes for us a reading and writing self that obeys the impulses of the body (especially pleasure and boredom) while resisting the constraining syntax and grammar of society. That this free desire was limited to writing (and an almost unspoken sexuality) made of writing the locus of utopia, dreamed of and practiced but never held fast.

In *Writing Degree Zero*, Barthes insists, "Writing is in no way an instrument for communication" (*Writing* 19). It is placed between two given systems, language and style, which map out a version of nature between them. Language is (as Saussure maintained) a social product. Style, for Barthes, is the personal and carnal relationship of a fleshly body and language. As we can choose neither our bodies (or their desires) nor our society (and its demands), they serve as inescapable natural forces. "Writing" emerges as a complex reflection of relations of power and language; our writing is never ours alone but rather the product of a history yet to be written. This history, of which Barthes offers only a few samples, would explain why, while Balzac and Flaubert may have the same social and political thoughts, between their writing there is an essential break.

One pole of writing is the purely axiological writing characteristic of politics and struggle. Here definitions prevail, and tautologies represent a preconceived world. By adopting this sort of writing, a new sort of scriptor (Barthes is writing in the late 1940s) assumes a history, the history that accompanies the chosen mode of writing. To assume this mode of writing is a blind alley, Barthes asserts; it offers the intellectual only the choice of becoming a hack or veering back toward the instability of literature. It is alienated writing either way. Realism, the ideology of political writing of all sorts, was Barthes's frequent target. Historical discourse claims to be the representation of reality, but in Barthes's view the real was only a vague notion hiding behind the almighty referent and privileged through repeated assertions that "this happened." The details that seem to denote reality actually create it, producing an effect of the real.

For Barthes, invention often consisted of "stealing a language," appropriating one discourse and applying it to something entirely different, as he does when he uses structural linguistics to describe the fashion system. Because he was always beginning again, Barthes has given his readers an array of antitheses (the "very spectacle of meaning"): readerly/writerly, pleasure/bliss, studium/punctum, author/scriptor, text/work, denotation/connotation, truth/criticism. The five codes of reading, the reality effect, the death of the author, the image repertoire, the grain of the voice, and *écriture* are but a few of the vast number of concepts that Barthes invents and moves beyond. It is the adjective and the definition that he resists; he does not want to be named.

His imaginary utopia would realize the notion of a world of writing: "Taken aslant by language, the world is written through and through; signs, endlessly deferring their foundations, transforming their signifieds into new signifiers, infinitely citing one another, nowhere coming to a halt: writing is generalized" (*Image* 167–68).

BIBLIOGRAPHY

Primary Sources

Barthes, Roland. *Oeuvres complètes*. 3 vols. Paris: Seuil, 1993, 1994, 1995.

Books in English Include

Barthes, Roland. *Camera Lucida*. Trans. Richard Howard. 1979. New York: Farrar, Straus & Giroux, 1982.
———. *Criticism and Truth*. Trans. Kathleen Pilcher Keuneman. 1966. Minneapolis: University of Minnesota Press, 1987.

————. *Elements of Semiology*. Trans. Annette Lavers and Colin Smith. 1965. New York: Farrar, Straus & Giroux, 1977.

————. *The Empire of Signs*. Trans. Richard Howard. 1980. New York: Hill and Wang, 1982.

————. *The Fashion System*. Trans. Matthew Ward and Richard Howard. 1967. Berkeley: University of California Press, 1990.

————. *Incidents*. 1987. Berkeley: University of California Press, 1992.

————. *A Lover's Discourse: Fragments*. Trans. Richard Howard. 1977. New York: Farrar, Straus & Giroux, 1989.

————. *Michelet*. Trans. Richard Howard. 1954. Berkeley: University of California Press, 1987.

————. *Mythologies*. Trans. Annette Lavers. 1957. New York: Farrar, Straus & Giroux, 1972.

————. *On Racine*. Trans. Richard Howard. 1963. Berkeley: University of California Press, 1992.

————. *The Pleasure of the Text*. Trans. Richard Miller. 1973. New York: Farrar, Straus & Giroux, 1975.

————. *Roland Barthes*. Trans. Richard Howard. 1975. Berkeley: University of California Press, 1994.

————. *Sade, Fourier, Loyola*. Trans. Richard Miller. 1971. Baltimore: Johns Hopkins University Press, 1997.

————. *S/Z*. Trans. Richard Miller. 1970. New York: Farrar, Straus & Giroux, 1975.

————. *Writer Sollers*. Trans. Philip Thody. 1979. Minneapolis: University of Minnesota Press, 1987.

————. *Writing Degree Zero*. Trans. Annette Lavers and Colin Smith. 1953. New York: Farrar, Straus & Giroux, 1977.

Collected Essays in English Include

————. *Critical Essays*. Trans. Richard Howard. 1964. Evanston, IL: Northwestern University Press, 1972.

————. *The Grain of the Voice: Interviews, 1972–1980*. Trans. Linda Coverdale. Berkeley: University of California Press, 1991.

————. *Image—Music—Text*. Trans. Stephen Heath. New York: Farrar, Straus & Giroux, 1978.

————. *The Responsibility of Forms: Critical Essays on Art, Music, and Representation*. Trans. Richard Howard. Berkeley: University of California Press, 1991.

————. *The Rustle of Language*. Trans. Richard Howard. Berkeley: University of California Press, 1989.

————. *The Semiotic Challenge*. Trans. Richard Howard. 1985. Berkeley: University of California Press, 1994.

Biography

Calvet, Louis-Jean. *Roland Barthes: A Biography*. Trans. Sarah Wykes. 1990. Bloomington and Indianapolis: Indiana University Press, 1994.

Criticism

Bensmaïa, Réda. *The Barthes Effect: The Essay as Reflective Text*. Minneapolis: University of Minnesota Press, 1987.

Culler, Jonathan. *Roland Barthes*. New York: Oxford University Press, 1983.

Johnson, Barbara. "The Critical Difference." *Diacritics* 8.2 (1978):2–9.

Miller, D. A. *Bringing Out Roland Barthes*. Berkeley: University of California Press, 1992.

Moriarty, Michael. *Roland Barthes*. Stanford: Stanford University Press, 1991.

JAMES A. BERLIN
(1942–1994)

Victor J. Vitanza

James A. Berlin attended Central Michigan University between 1960 and 1964, receiving his B.A. in English, graduating summa cum laude. He was an elementary school teacher in Flint and Detroit, Michigan, between 1965 and 1970. He attended the University of Michigan beginning in 1969, receiving his M.A. in English in 1970 and his Ph.D. in English in 1975. His dissertation was on the relation of German idealism to Tennyson, Browning, and Arnold. Upon graduation and until 1981, he was an assistant professor of composition at Wichita State University. Between 1981 and 1985 and during 1986–1987, he was associate professor and full professor of English at the University of Cincinnati. In 1987, he moved to Purdue University.

Berlin was visiting professor at Pennsylvania State University (summer term, 1986) and at the University of Texas at Austin (1985–1986). His administrative experience included serving as assistant director of composition at Wichita State; director of the Kansas Writing Project; and director of freshman English at Cincinnati. Berlin was a National Endowment for the Humanities (NEH) Fellow, 1978–1979, with Richard Young at Carnegie-Mellon University, which proved to be the impetus for much of his later thinking and work. The fellowship topic was rhetorical invention and the composing process. He attended an NEH summer seminar at the University of California at Berkeley with Sheldon Rothblatt. The topic was High Victorian culture. His academic awards included Honorable Mention, Modern Language Association (MLA) Mina Shaughnessy Award, for *Rhetoric and Reality*, 1988; and posthumously the Outstanding Book Award, Conference on College Composition and Communication (CCCC), for *Rhetorics, Poetics, and Cultures*, 1998.

He was not only an academic but also a family man. He was married to Sandy Berlin and had two sons, "Dan the Man" and "Captain Christopher." He coached his sons' soccer team. He was the organizer of the annual get-together of his extended family. He had a wonderful sense of humor and of social justice. He mentored many of the now-notable teachers in the field of composition. In many ways, as one person said, "he [was] the field of composition." He died of a heart attack on February 2, 1994, after attempting his daily five-mile jog.

In a period of 15 years—beginning in 1980—Berlin published articles and books at a time of immense change in the field of composition (written communication) and rhetoric. His typologies of composition theories and pedagogies, which were constantly in revision, became the primary terministic screens through which theorists and practitioners would think, talk, and write about the field. He applied these screens not only to mapping composition studies but also to rhetorical theory, to the histories of writing instructions and rhetorics, and to cultural studies. An understanding of Berlin's work, therefore, will give any new person to the field a set of maps to traverse a rather difficult terrain—with many twists and turns—that often baffles the uninitiated. Berlin's is a unified vision of the field, yet always in a state of revision. His two constants are the classroom as a political site and justice as a political goal.

BERLIN'S RHETORICAL THEORY: TOPOLOGIES AND THEORIES OF COMPOSITION STUDIES

When working as an NEH Fellow in 1978–1979, Berlin, along with Robert Inkster, wrote and published "Current-Traditional Rhetoric: Paradigm and Practice" (1980), which is greatly indebted to, yet extends, the previous work of Daniel Fogarty (*Roots for a New Rhetoric*) and Richard Young. Fogarty states that current-traditional rhetoric (CTR) is a commonsense realist epistemological and metaphysical view put forth by authors of popular eighteenth- and nineteenth-century textbooks (e.g., George Campbell, Hugh Blair, Richard Whately, and John Genung). CTR presumes "writing" primarily to be algorithmic and solely concerned with stylistic correctness (grammar, syntax, punctuation, usage, and so on) at the expense of inventional procedures. (In CTR, reality is not problematic, and writing is a managerial art and not one of discovery. A writer must simply know the right word for the right thing. In this view, only "correctness" of product can be taught, whereas the processes can but remain elusive.)

To determine whether CTR still informs the field of composition, Berlin and Inkster analyzed four popular textbooks semiotically across the communications triangle of *encoder* (writer), *decoder* (reader), *reality*, and *code* (language). They concluded that the texts are based primarily on an epistemological view of reality as nonproblematic and of language as a mere tool to describe reality. In their own words, they warn that "the current-traditional paradigm is even more powerfully and profoundly entrenched than has been supposed" and "represents a danger to teachers, students, the wider purposes of our educational enterprise, and even our social and human fabric" (13).

Strongly suggested in this conclusion are an ethics and a politics—an ethical politics—which Berlin would even more strongly state as he refines his thinking about composition theory and instruction, and most notably, in his "Contemporary Composition: The Major Pedagogical Theories" (1982). Berlin claims that "to teach writing is to argue for a version of reality, and the best way of knowing and communicating it" and "in teaching writing we are tacitly teaching a version of reality and the student's place and mode of operation in it. Yet many teachers . . . look upon their vocations as the imparting of a largely mechanical skill" (766).

In this by now canonized article, Berlin identifies four groups of composition theorists:

- Neo-Aristotelians or classicists (reality can be known through sense experience);
- Positivists or current-traditionalists (commonsense reality is determined inductively);
- Neo-Platonists or expressionists (reality is only appearance, but "truth" can be known through a "private vision" that is "inexpressible"); and
- New rhetoricians, or social-epistemics (the realities of the material world are socially constructed) (766).

Each group has its tacit rules for "discovering and communicating knowledge" (766). Berlin, of course, favors the new rhetoricians, which we will return to in the second section of this discussion.

In his first book-length study, *Writing Instruction in Nineteenth-Century American Colleges* (1984), Berlin more fully expresses and exemplifies his view that "every rhetoric . . . is grounded in a noetic field: a closed system defining what can, and cannot, be known; the nature of the knower; the nature of the relationship between the knower, the known, and the audience; and the nature of language" (2). Because the book examines writing instruction in nineteenth-century American colleges, Berlin's noetic fields slightly change to

- Classical (from Aristotle and others),
- Psychological-epistemological (from eighteenth-century rhetoric), and
- Romantic (from the American Transcendental movement).

Berlin becomes more political in purpose: "In the composition or communications class, the student is being indoctrinated in a basic epistemology, usually the one held by society's dominant class, the group with the most power" (2).

It should be more clear now that incrementally Berlin is mapping/remapping (reterritorializing, rehistoricizing) composition studies so as to determine for the profession its ethicopolitical weaknesses and possible strengths. In mapping, for Berlin, there is a eutopian revisionary aim at work.

In his second book, *Rhetoric and Reality: Writing Instruction in American*

Colleges. 1900–1985 (1987), Berlin establishes more generic terms with specific categories subsumed in each:

- Objective theories (CTR, behaviorist, semanticist, and linguistic rhetorics)
- Subjective theories (romantic and liberal rhetorics; American Freudian and post-Freudian psychologies, with nondirective therapists)
- Transactional theories (classical, cognitive, and epistemic)

The terms become much richer and thicker in their descriptive value, covering more conceptual territory and allowing for more distinctions. These wide variations are owing to the constant and rapid ideological redevelopments of writing instruction in the twentieth century.

In "Rhetoric and Ideology in the Writing Class" (1988), Berlin puts forth his most sharply political and highly contested taxonomy and refers to specific, representative theorists and practitioners, who could not but respond to the charges against them. Selecting from his previous revisions of his taxonomy, Berlin points his finger this time at

- "cognitive rhetoric" (480–84) and
- "expressionistic rhetoric" (384–87)

His third category, in which he invests full faith, is

- "social-epistemic rhetoric" (488–93)

Because this article is best discussed in terms of ideology and composition-cultural studies, I will take it up under the appropriate rubric below.

HISTORIES/HISTORIOGRAPHIES OF RHETORIC AND COMPOSITION

While an NEH Fellow (1978–1979), Berlin spent much time reading eighteenth- and nineteenth-century British historians of rhetoric. In the early 1980s until his death, he similarly spent time reading Marx, Marxists, post-Marxists, and socialist theorists and critics such as Paulo Freire, Henry Giroux, Ira Shor, Stuart Hall, Richard Ohmann, Fredric Jameson, and Goran Therborn. As he read these social critics, he began to reinterpret the early British historians and began to see how they contributed an impoverished and at times a pernicious methodology to the writing of histories for the field(s) of composition and rhetoric. These old histories are important, for they determine the basis and legitimation for what is acceptable—thinkable and practical—in the teaching of writing.

When Berlin began writing histories, there were no contemporary book-length

histories of written communication, with the exception of work done in dissertation form by, say, Albert Kitzhaber in 1953. The histories that were available,
in brief article or chapter form, followed the basic tenets of writing history
according to CTR and some vague, nostalgic notion of what "the" grand narrative of history in the oral or written traditions might be. Therefore, Berlin not
only had to write history but also had to develop a historiography, a rhetoric
for writing history, and had to do so in the face of much contestation (see Berlin
et al., "The Politics").

Berlin best summarizes his methodology in "Revisionary History: The Dialectical Method" (1987), in which he distinguishes "previous histories" from
"the new histories." Previous historians have assumed "that there are moments
of time in which the essential features of the one true rhetoric can be directly
observed. For the classicist, this moment is in the past, in the rhetoric of ancient
Greece or Rome" (49). And "for the modern . . . the essence of rhetoric is to be
found in the here and now, at the end of a long succession of historical progress"
(49). What would be new in the writings of the histories of written communication—beyond the classicist and modernist—is "to see the formal statements
of this discipline [of written communication] as a study that is at the center of
social activity" (52). Again, Berlin interjects the topos of the social (or dialectics) as the ground for revision. The dialectical method that is to be employed
on "the center" is a rhetoric, or rhetorics, that would mediate between the "material and social conditions of society" and "the political and cultural" conditions
(52). Berlin explains:

The ability to read, write, and speak in accordance with the code sanctioned by a culture's
ruling class is the main work of education, and this is true whether we are discussing
ancient Athens or modern Detroit. These rules are of course inscribed in a rhetoric, a
systematic designation of who can speak, when and where they can speak, and how they
can and must speak. Educational institutions inculcate these rules, determining who is
fit to learn them and who has finally done so—in other words, who is authorized to be
heard. A rhetoric codifies these rules for the members of a society. It is therefore never
simply a set of disembodied principles that discuss the way language is used for purposes
of persuasion or communication. It is a set of strictures regarding the way language is
used in the service of power. It designates who may have access to power and who may
not, doing so in a way even more effective than legal sanctions with all of their punitive
devices. To use Althusser's terms a rhetoric serves as an important ideological state
apparatus. It affirms economic, social, political, and cultural arrangements, doing so in
the name of passing on to the young the "natural" rules that govern discursive and, more
important, non-discursive practices. (52)[1]

Berlin would, therefore, have us study dialectically the ideological structures of
how to speak, how to write, and in general, *how to communicate,* which are
used to determine the business of the polis. We must also study dialectically,
however, the oppositional, discounted ideological ways to produce a revolutionary discourse that, Berlin says, calls "into question the social and political

formulations of its rivals" (54). He reminds us, "There are always competing rhetorics at any historical moment because there are always competing ideologies, and this is demonstrable despite the fact that our rhetorical histories have attempted to ignore this conflict" (54–55). At this moment, Berlin draws a bridge between writing and having these histories and using them in education: *It is the cultural, ideological conflicts that are to be taught in the schools.* Hence, Berlin would want us to employ a plurality of approaches, but always for ethicopolitical purposes (56–58). He would have us rebegin a revision of history by understanding that "our only hope in not being able to know everything . . . is to know as many versions of the whole as we can, as many conceptual systems in their concrete application as possible" (59).

The many versions and conceptual systems are precisely what Berlin locates in his taxonomies of nineteenth- and twentieth-century histories of writing instruction. Would he claim that his taxonomies are *the* taxonomies? Of course not! He would, instead, have us locate yet other versions and systems and bring them into conflict with his. This exchange, then, would be the realization of the dialectical principle at work, with the hope of including minoritarian voices in the discussion.

COMPOSITION STUDIES, IDEOLOGY, AND CULTURAL STUDIES (THE SOCIAL-EPISTEMIC PATHS)

Let us return now to "Rhetoric and Ideology in the Writing Class" and then extend Berlin's discussion of ideology to his discussions of cultural studies. It's a brief stretch. Let us recall that Berlin locates three rhetorics: *cognitive psychology* (Flower and Hayes), *expressionism* (Murray and Elbow), and *social-epistemic* (his own). Psychology, in general, and cognitive psychology, in particular, claim to be nonideological, since they aspire to a scientistic-objective view of the world. Expressionism claims to be in an ideological struggle with the scientistic-objective view. The weakness of expressionism, Berlin claims, is that it is "open to appropriation by the very forces it opposes" (478). In place of these two rhetorics, Berlin once again proposes social-epistemic. To be sure, the term *ideology* is by now a loose term. Berlin consequently defines the term by way of Goran Therborn, a Marxist sociologist who employs Althusser's notions of ideology and Foucault's notions of power (a micropolitics of power). Berlin quotes Therborn: "The operation of ideology in human life basically involves the constitution and patterning of how human beings live their lives as conscious, reflecting initiators of acts in a structured, meaningful world. Ideology operates as discourse [rhetoric], addressing or, as Althusser puts it, interpellating [hailing, calling] human beings as subjects" (479; in Therborn 15).

Ideology is "inscribed" in language and rhetoric (discourse formations). There is a point of stasis ("constitution") and a habit ("patterning") to each person's life. A person's identity and subjectivity are determined by ideological structures. Berlin writes: "[I]deology provides the language to define the subject (the self), other subjects, the material world, and the relation of all of these to each other" (479). Therefore, any attempt to claim that there is an outside to ideology simply would not hold. Could not be possible! And yet, as Therborn and Berlin claim, there is nonetheless a set of standards that ideology provides to determine "What exists?" "What is good?" and "What is possible?" (479; in Therborn 18). In other words, though "we" are hailed by ideology, we can still work for the common good in an ethical and political way within ideology. To be a subject is to be subjected; however, the subject is nonetheless capable of becoming an agent of change.

At this point it is easier to see the connection between *ideology* and *rhetoric*, for these questions concerning ideology are the parallel questions concerning ancient-through-modern rhetorical propositions often associated with deliberative discourse: respectively, the proposition of *fact*, of *value*, and of *policy* (cf. Eagleton).

The connection between ideology (rhetoric) and power is inextricably intertwined. Berlin gives the example of poverty: "The desire for its change will go for nothing if [the prevailing, dominant] ideology indicates that a change is simply not possible (the poor we have always with us). In other words, the last mode of interpellation is especially implicated in power relationships in a group or society, in deciding who has power and in determining what power can be expected to achieve" (479). With social-epistemic rhetoric, it is *possible* to see the competing means of arguing against the ideology of the dominant discourse. These competing means are important, for they can help disclose the ideological structures as not determinant and can help offer viable solutions and counter-solutions.

The rest of Berlin's discussion in this article is an ideological critique of the works of Flower and Hayes and Murray and Elbow. It might be easier to see now at this point that what Berlin practices is a kind of academic-ideological "cognitive mapping"[2] (or cartographic inquiry) of the teaching of writing, locating, and critiquing where the various "We"s are and then asking his various readers if *this* or *this* or *this* is where they want their teaching and their students to be located in power relationships. (The not-so-subtle question, of course, is, What is it that you want—ideologically—for your profession and for student writers?) As was expected, some of those critiqued and others who felt critiqued as holding unfavorable ideological locations in Berlin's map of the profession responded to Berlin in *College English*, and he in return to them again—all of which brings into play the kind of dialectical-ideological clash that Berlin believed the profession needed to correct its overreliance on the dominant discourse and ideology (see Flower; Schilb; Scriben).

Berlin contributed immensely to the development of cultural studies in the teaching and thinking about writing instruction. Perhaps his most important work is "Composition Studies and Cultural Studies: Collapsing Boundaries." Described briefly, Berlin greatly extends his discussion in "Rhetoric and Ideology," focusing this time on *two* rhetorics within English departments as having pro-

ing them historically through the ages. He also makes an important distinction between "pedagogy" (in school) and "education" (out of school/*scholé*).

2. The phrase "cognitive mapping" is used by many writers. I have in mind Fredric Jameson's article by the same title in *Marxism and the Interpretation of Culture*, ed. Cary Nelson and Lawrence Grossberg (Urbana: University of Illinois Press, 1988), 347–57.

BIBLIOGRAPHY

Primary Sources

Berlin, James A. "Composition and Cultural Studies." *Composition and Resistance*. Ed. C. Mark Hurlbert and Michael Blitz. Portsmouth, NH: Boynton/Cook, 1991.

———. "Composition Studies and Cultural Studies: Collapsing Boundaries." *Into the Field: Sites of Composition Studies*. Ed. Anne Ruggles Gere. New York: MLA, 1993. 99–116.

———. "Contemporary Composition: The Major Pedagogical Theories." *College English* 44.8 (1982): 765–77.

———. "Cultural Studies." *Encyclopedia of Rhetoric and Composition*. Ed. Theresa Enos. New York: Garland, 1996. 154–56.

———. "Freirean Pedagogy in the U.S.: A Response." *Journal of Advanced Composition* 12.2 (1992): 414–21.

———. "James Berlin Responds. 'Rhetoric and Ideology in the Writing Class.' " *College English* 51.7 (1989): 770–77.

———. "Postmodernism, Politics, and Histories of Rhetorics." *PRE/TEXT* 11.3–4 (1990): 169–87.

———. "Poststructuralism, Cultural Studies, and the Composition Classroom." *Rhetoric Review* 11.1 (1992): 16–33. Rpt. *Professing the New Rhetoric*. Ed. Theresa Enos and Stuart C. Brown. Englewood Cliffs, NJ: Prentice-Hall, 1994. 461–80.

———. "Revisionary Histories of Rhetoric: Politics, Power, and Plurality." *Writing Histories of Rhetoric*. Ed. Victor J. Vitanza. Carbondale: Southern Illinois University Press, 1994. 112–27.

———. "Revisionary History: The Dialectical Method." *PRE/TEXT* 8.1–2 (1987): 47–61.

———. "Rhetoric and Ideology in the Writing Class." *College English* 50.5 (1988): 477–94.

———. "Rhetoric and Poetics in the English Department: Our Nineteenth-Century Inheritance." *College English* 47.5 (1985): 531–33.

———. *Rhetoric and Reality: Writing Instruction in American Colleges. 1900–1985*. Carbondale: Southern Illinois University Press, 1987.

———. *Rhetorics, Poetics, and Cultures: Refiguring College English Studies*. Urbana, IL: NCTE, 1996.

———. "Richard Whately and Current-Traditional Rhetoric." *College English* 42.1 (1980): 10–17.

———. *Writing Instruction in Nineteenth-Century American Colleges*. Carbondale: Southern Illinois University Press, 1984.

Berlin, James A., Robert J. Connors, Sharon Crowley, Richard Leo Enos, Victor J. Vi-

tanza, Susan C. Jarratt, Nan Johnson, and Jan Swearingen, with James J. Murphy.
"The Politics of Historiography." *Rhetoric Review* 7.1 (Fall 1988): 5–49.

Berlin, James A., and Robert P. Inkster. "Current-Traditional Rhetoric: Paradigm and
Practice." *Freshman English News* 8.3 (1980): 1–4, 13–14.

Berlin, James A., and John Trimbur, guest eds. Special Issue: "Marxism and Rhetoric."
PRE/TEXT 13.1–2 (1992).

Berlin, James A., and Michael Vivion, eds. *Cultural Studies in the English Classroom.*
Portsmouth, NH: Boynton/Cook, 1992.

Material Used by Berlin

Eagleton, Terry. *Literary Theory: An Introduction.* Minneapolis: University of Minnesota
Press, 1983.

Fogarty, Daniel. *Roots for a New Rhetoric.* New York: Teachers College, Columbia
University, 1959.

Freire, Paulo. *Pedagogy of the Oppressed.* New York: Continuum, 1970.

Kitzhaber, Albert R. "Rhetoric in American Colleges, 1850–1900." Diss., Washington
University, 1953; in published form, *Rhetoric in American Colleges, 1850–1900.*
Dallas: Southern Methodist University Press, 1990.

Ohmann, Richard. *English in America: A Radical View of the Profession.* New York:
Oxford University Press, 1976.

Shor, Ira. *Critical Teaching and Everyday Life.* Chicago: University of Chicago Press,
1987.

Therborn, Goran. *The Ideology of Power and the Power of Ideology.* London: Verso,
1980.

Criticism

Alcorn, Marshall W., Jr. "Changing the Subject of Postmodernist Theory: Discourse,
Ideology, and Therapy in the Classroom." *Rhetoric Review* 13.2 (Spring 1995):
331–49.

Bizzell, Patricia. "Beyond Anti-Foundationalism to Rhetorical Authority: Problems Defining 'Cultural Literacy.' " *College English* 52.6 (1990): 661–75.

Connors, Robert J. Rev. of *Writing Instruction in Nineteenth-Century American Colleges,*
by James A. Berlin. *College Composition and Communications* 37.2 (1986): 247–
49.

Crowley, Sharon. Rev. of *Rhetoric and Reality: Writing Instruction in American Colleges
1900–1985,* by James A. Berlin. *College Composition and Communications* 39.2
(1988): 245–47.

Downing, David B., James J. Sosnoski, with Keith Dorwick, eds. "Cultural Studies and
Composition: Conversations in Honor of James Berlin." *Works and Days*
14.1–2 (1996).

Faigley, Lester. *Fragments of Rationality: Postmodernity and the Subject of Composition.*
Pittsburgh: University of Pittsburgh Press, 1992.

Flower, Linda. "Comments on James Berlin. 'Rhetoric and Ideology in the Writing
Class.' " *College English* 51.7 (1989): 765–69.

"Jim Berlin's Last Work: Future Perfect, Tense" (A collection of articles by Linda Brodkey, Patricia Harkin, Susan Miller, John Trimbur, and Victor J. Vitanza on *Rhetorics, Poetics, Cultures*). *Journal of Advanced Composition* 17.3 (1997): 489–505.

Schilb, John. "Comments on James Berlin. 'Rhetoric and Ideology in the Writing Class.' " *College English* 51.7 (1989): 769–70.

Scriben, Karen. "Comments on James Berlin. 'Rhetoric and Ideology in the Writing Class.' " *College English* 51.7 (1989): 764–65.

Vitanza, Victor J. "Seminar on James A. Berlin." Available at: http://www.uta.edu/english/V/berlin/ (Taught at University of TX, Arlington, Fall 1998. Of special value are the notes for each seminar meeting—explaining and responding in detail to each major work by Berlin—and the discussions on the BERLIN–L.)

ANN E. BERTHOFF
(1924–   )

Rex L. Veeder

In *Audits of Meaning: A Festchrift in Honor of Ann E. Berthoff*, Paulo Freire describes his experiences reading Ann E. Berthoff, saying she "deeply impacted his way of thinking." He continues: "What became clear to me is that *Forming/ Thinking/Writing* is not merely a text about composition theory, or reading and writing, but much more. In this book, Ann Berthoff evaluates the discourse of composition theory to a philosophical level with which I completely identify" (xi–xii). It might be said that, like Freire, many of those who admire Berthoff's work often have a philosophical view of rhetoric.

Berthoff once said that she has at times been intimidated by rhetoric. It could be said as well that at times she has intimidated rhetoricians. Her more than 50 years of scholarship, writing, and teaching have been punctuated with disciplinary arguments that have added to our understanding of the role of language, thinking, and the imagination in rhetorical studies. She began her teaching career in 1948, and she said in her acceptance speech for the 1998 CCCC (Conference on College Composition and Communication) Exemplar Award that her career has not been "paradigmatic." Berthoff declined opportunities to earn a Ph.D., choosing instead to focus her time and energy upon her teaching and writing. She has taught at Bryn Mawr College and was a professor at the University of Massachusetts, Boston. She has served as a friendly but aggressive agitator, advocating for philosophical views of rhetoric that have been at times less popular but most often necessary because of their practical implications.

Her contributions to rhetoric orbit around a center of gravity created by hard thinking and reflection. As she once put it, "I like almost everything the begins with 're' " (In conversation). Berthoff's work is a testimony to the necessity of the role of discovery, invention, and metacognition in rhetorical studies. At the same time, her work with Paulo Freire is an indication of her strong commitment to social and spiritual principles in pedagogy. Understanding Berthoff's relationship to rhetoric, then, involves understanding her ability and desire to see rhetoric in the context of a variety of disciplines including philosophy, language, literature, composition, history, and pedagogy.

BERTHOFF'S RHETORICAL THEORY

Berthoff is a teacher's rhetorician—someone who is passionately dedicated to the interrelatedness of rhetoric and teaching. Much of her work, such as *The Making of Meaning, Forming/Thinking/Writing*, and *Reclaiming the Imagination*, is dedicated to teachers and their understanding of rhetoric as the composing act. Thus, recognizing Berthoff's rhetoric involves understanding what kind of a teacher she is. In her edition of *Richards on Rhetoric*, she includes a selection of Richards's writings on Mencius and Richards's description of Mencius informs our understanding of Berthoff. Like Mencius, Berthoff is not often "presenting a view to be discussed and criticized" but offering pragmatic instruments for thinking with rhetoric. Also, like Mencius's teachings, Berthoff's approach to rhetoric is to be "lived with" for a time to "see what it does to you thereafter" (*Richards on Rhetoric* 53).

Ann Berthoff has sometimes been called an expressionist, but her methods indicate that she is not easily defined as an expressionist. Instead, she is a "reflectionist" and a pragmatist interested in helping others learn to compose. She is a practical romantic, someone who sees the imagination as an instrument for composing and composing as a form of hard thinking. One of her consistent messages is that metacognition is a central instrument in the art of teaching writing. As she puts it, metacognition is "species-specific," and the "capacity for thinking about thinking, for interpreting interpretations, for knowing our knowledge, is, I think, the chief resource for any teacher and the ground of hope in the enterprise of teaching reading and writing" ("Is Teaching Still Possible?" 11).

Understanding Berthoff's rhetorical theory involves recognizing that much of her work is dedicated to helping composers, as rhetoricians, engage complexity and manage it in order to, as she puts it, "control their becoming" (26). Berthoff most often invites readers to begin with a philosophical view of rhetoric and then to follow that philosophical view to approaches that stem from it. In her own experience as a teacher, she finds the rhetoric of composition most useful when applied through the instruments of observation, triadicity, imagination, and language.

Observation is a matter of looking and then looking again at things and ideas. Her insistence that metacognition is at the heart of learning leads her to suggest the use of "dialogical notebooks," in which writers first record their observations and then reconsider them. This approach allows students to "learn to transform things into questions" and to "develop perspectives and contexts" in ways that help them see composing as dealing with relationships among those things observed, whether those "things" are physical things or ideas (*The Sense of Learning* 23).

Triadicity, a way of thinking that rejects simple dualities and focuses instead upon the relationship among three ideas, is her way of talking about the pragmatic approaches to thinking where monolithic perspectives and dualistic perspectives are replaced by a triadic approach as a matter of course. Her readings of Charles Sanders Peirce are influential here, but even without his influence, triadicity is consistent with her argument that all composing is a matter of paying attention to multiple perspectives rather than closing down the possibilities in order to achieve a quick but stilted closure. In her view, triadicity is not a transcendent act but rather the fundamental act of thinking and, thus, composing.

Berthoff's theory of imagination focuses upon the imagination as an instrument for thinking rather than as a tool for escaping reality. Imagination is an active force that is involved in shaping our rational interpretations of the world. Her call to "reclaim" the imagination is a call for rhetoricians to come to grips with the interesting possibilities of active composition rather than to define rhetoric in terms of communicating something already thought. Her emphasis on the imagination is, therefore, an emphasis upon the way the mind works to make meaning through forming and reforming our perceptions. This is not so much a psychological approach to writing as it is a practical look at the act of composition as an art wherein our associations and observations are rewoven into the text to create and re-create perspectives while we compose. As she puts it in *Forming/Thinking/Writing*:

Rhetoric is only superficially a matter of evaluating audience and adjusting tone; it has deeper foundations that we can discover only insofar as we develop a philosophy of knowledge, a theory of imagination. A "rhetoric" should, therefore, be concerned not just with sorting out topics and places but with exploring the dialectic of names and purposes, images and concepts, thinking and forming. (6)

Rather than say Berthoff has a theory of language, it might be better to say that she has a philosophy of language from which a number of interrelated theories grow. Her philosophy is defined by her commitment to the active role of language as an instrument of our becoming. The mistake, linguistically, she argues, is to assume that words are merely signs pointing to predetermined or assured meanings. What happens in our rhetorical acts, she points out, is that composers use language as an instrument to make meanings, and those meanings depend upon a triadic exchange among signifier, sign, and context. Also, language, by naming and fixing concepts, is a nucleus around which meanings form. This forming, conceptualizing, or meaning making is all the more significant because language is at once conversant with others and with itself. Thus, Berthoff's theory of language grows from a clear sense of how language itself works to change our meanings as we use it to make meaning. Because of this, she argues that our understanding of language must be first philosophic—or, more directly, it must be based upon a constant audit of how it effects our meanings.

Ann E. Berthoff's rhetorical legacy may be in her defense of rhetoric and in her critique of shallow definitions of it. She is important to rhetoricians because she so well takes them to task when they limit rhetoric. When we see rhetoric through her eyes, we see it in interanimation with philosophy, composition, and teaching.

Berthoff's synoptic view of rhetoric is an invitation to focus on the essential role of rhetoric in rigorous thinking and learning. Communication and public oratory may be essential elements of her view of rhetoric, but her emphasis is upon the idea that we must use the instruments of knowing in order to understand what we think clearly enough to communicate. Her vision of rhetoric is that it has much to do with what makes us human, including a spiritual dimension that many overlook—as when scholars focus on Freire's Marxism but fail to recognize his intense religious convictions. Finally, her love for teaching and students illuminates her writing in such a way that she will be remembered as the teacher's rhetorician.

As the writings in *Audits of Meaning* suggest, one measure of her enduring legacy is that articles written about her are not about her so much as applications of what she has been teaching. Rhetoricians refer to her theories in writing about genre theory, academic discourse, hermeneutics, the uses of the imagination, and criticism. Her love of literature and her work with I. A. Richards and Samuel Taylor Coleridge offer rhetoricians a bridge to discussions of literature, and her work with journals has had an influence upon those interested in writing across the curriculum. For a rhetor, someone who teaches rhetoric, this is high praise because her readers are challenged to pick up her rhetorical instruments and use them.

BIBLIOGRAPHY

Primary Sources

Berthoff, Ann E. *Forming/Thinking/Writing: The Composing Imagination.* Rochelle Park, NJ: Hayden Book Company, 1978.
———. "Is Teaching Still Possible? Writing, Meaning, and Higher Order Reasoning." *College English* 46.6 (1984): 743–55.
———. *The Making of Meaning: Metaphors, Models, and Maxims for Writing Teachers.* Montclair, NJ: Boynton/Cook, 1981.
———. *The Mysterious Barricades: Language and Its Limits.* Toronto: University of Toronto Press, 2000.
———. "Paulo Freire's Liberation Pedagogy." *Language Arts* 67.4 (1990): 362–69.
———. "Problem-Dissolving by Triadic Means." *College English* 58.1 (1996): 9–21.
———. "The Problem of Problem-solving." *College Composition and Communication* 22.3 (1971): 237–42.
———. "Reading the World, Reading the Word: Paulo Freire's Pedagogy of Knowing."

Only Connect. Ed. Thomas Newkirk. Upper Montclair, NJ: Boynton/Cook, 1986. 119–30.

———. *Reclaiming the Imagination: Philosophical Perspectives for Writers and Teachers of Writing.* Upper Monclair, NJ: Boynton/Cook, 1983.

———. "Rhetoric as Hermeneutic." *College Composition and Communication* 42.3 (1991): 279–87.

———. "Semiotics and Edward Sapir." *The Semiotic Web 1990.* Ed. Thomas A. Sebeok. New York: Mouton de Gruyter, 1991. 47–59.

———. *The Sense of Learning.* Upper Monclair, NJ: Boynton/Cook, 1990.

———, ed. *Richards on Rhetoric: I. A. Richards Selected Essays (1929–1974).* New York: Oxford University Press, 1991.

Criticism

Lassner, Phillis. "Bridging Composition and Women's Studies: The Work of Ann. E. Berthoff and Susan K. Langer." *Journal of Teaching Writing* 10.1 (1991): 21–37.

Lynn, Steven. "Reading the Writing Process: Toward a Theory of Current Pedagogies." *College English* 49.8 (1987): 902–10.

Smith, Louise Z., ed. *Audits of Meaning: A Festschrift in Honor of Ann E. Berthoff.* Foreword by Paulo Freire. Portsmouth, NH: Boynton/Cook, 1988.

WAYNE C. BOOTH
(1921–   )

Gregory Clark

Wayne Booth is a rhetorical critic and theorist who has anchored his work in literary studies. His project, sustained throughout his career, has been to teach students of life as well as of letters to understand how communication can function as a process of mutual inquiry—enacting influence and requiring choice—and is thus inherently of ethical consequence. Booth's body of work can be read as asserting and explaining his belief that to live well requires individuals to commit themselves deliberately to careful and critical communication of this sort—that, as he once put it, "talking together critically, really trying to be open and honest, is your best defense against misjudgment" ("Art and the Church" 25). His persistent concern throughout his work is to understand and explain how communicative encounters in general, and the encounter of writer and reader in particular, can be sustained in ways that enable people to progress. And Booth means *progress* in an ethical sense, for he does believe that living well requires people to learn to live well *together*. That is why, for him, ethical progress is necessarily a collaborative act.

This concern is sufficiently prominent throughout Booth's work to prompt one summary, in *Contemporary Literary Critics*, to observe that his concept of the aesthetic experience is located not in the individual act of perception but in the moment of interaction described as a "meeting of minds" (Borklund 86). Locating it there renders the category of the aesthetic inseparable from the category of the ethical—for Booth, inseparable from the act of establishing and maintaining cooperative human connection. Indeed, Booth himself suggests that all of his work in rhetoric and criticism can be read as following an admonition given him long ago by one of his undergraduate mentors: "You shouldn't be looking for reasons to do a rebellion," he was told. "You should be looking only for reasons *not to*" ("Three Unfinished Projects" 41). And in his mature

major statement on rhetorical criticism, *The Company We Keep*, he locates the
aesthetic experience in the sense of "happiness" that "is found in a pursuit of
friendship"—in the kind of essentially ethical act of engaging "something more
than our limited selves" (172). Whether it takes the form of literary criticism,
rhetorical theory, or even pedagogical philosophy, all of Booth's work advocates
and praises acts of writing and, particularly, of reading that enable people to
establish and maintain the kind of common understandings that provide places
where they can, for a time, live and work together. In doing so, Booth's work
expresses his insistent hope that through their discourse people can invent shar-
able reasons to sustain cooperation and connection.

ORIGINS

This hope is at least partially a product of Booth's personal history. Although
his birth year is 1921, he has described himself as "born into the heart of the
nineteenth century" ("Three Unfinished Projects" 36). With deep roots in an
agricultural Mormon village in central Utah, Booth inherited the living legacy
of an important communal experiment. In the nineteenth century, Mormonism
was more than a religion: It was a utopian movement in ways that were essentially American. Collectively, early Mormons self-consciously reenacted aspirations that had been fundamental in the new nation's Puritan history. Like the
young men of Massachusetts Bay, Booth learned early to understand himself as
an integral element of an enlightened community that believed itself charged
with the task of enabling the eventual progress of humankind through an interweaving of individual and collective actions. And though his own family
claimed a certain independence from the local culture, and though he acquired
from them habits of thinking critically around the religion it expressed, Booth
carried out of his childhood a full share of this sense of responsibility to work
hard to bring God's children together. By early manhood he was calling particulars of both culture and doctrine into hard question, but he seems never to
have questioned this native hope that people should be and could be brought
together, nor to have rejected his inherited sense of personal responsibility to
bring about that hope's realization.

Between 1938 and 1944, Booth entered adulthood through two of the traditional gateways available to his generation of male Mormons: He went to college
at the nearby Brigham Young University, and he went on a proselytizing mission
for his church. College complicated his home world with exposure to the critical
minds of influential teachers, as well as to documents of the history and literature
of the wider world. He embraced the complexity he found there and its conse-
quent confusion and immersed himself in the life of the intellect. But it was
after college, while working for two years as a missionary in Chicago, that he
discovered his particular intellectual vocation. Daily he found himself trying to
talk his way onto common ground with people whose worlds seemed incommensurable with his. That required, in his words, "having to 'translate,' hour

by hour, what *I wanted to say* into *what I presumed could be heard*" (emphasis in original). And because of his own doubts about aspects of the doctrine he was teaching, the necessity of this constant translation engaged him in what he came later to understand as the practice of rhetoric—experienced then and defined now as "the art of mediating between your own views and the world, the art of discovering in your circumstances what the possibilities for transformation are—including the possibilities for your own increased understanding" ("Three Unfinished Projects" 48). It was, then, the ethical dilemma Booth encountered in the act of proselytizing his world to others who did not share it that introduced him to the centrality of rhetoric to the development of the individual and to maintenance and improvement of social life.

In 1946, after two years in the army in Europe, Booth returned to the city where he first fully confronted the ethical problems inherent in this project of bringing disparate people together and began intensive graduate study at the University of Chicago. There he engaged the formidable minds of what has been called the "Chicago School" of neo-Aristotelian critics: notably, in his own education, Richard McKeon, Elder Olson, and Ronald Crane. Booth completed his Ph.D. there in 1950 with a dissertation on *Tristram Shandy* and took his first job teaching English at Haverford College. Still grappling with the problematical relationship of ethics and rhetoric, he took a year off in 1952 to educate himself by reading the major philosophers on "value theory," and following that year, he returned to teaching, now at Earlham College, where he remained for the next nine years. Booth describes himself during these years as devoted wholeheartedly to the project of teaching and gradually beginning to write. In 1962, after publishing his first book of rhetorical criticism, *The Rhetoric of Fiction*, he found himself back at the University of Chicago as the George M. Pullman Professor of English, and he has remained at Chicago ever since. That book was followed by a series of statements developing his "pluralist" vision of literary criticism in particular and, more generally, his notion of the centrality of open and mutually constructive rhetorical exchange to an ethical human life. Most prominent among these are *A Rhetoric of Irony* and *Modern Dogma and the Rhetoric of Assent*, both published in 1974; *Critical Understanding: The Powers and Limits of Pluralism* (1979); and *The Company We Keep* (1988). Since 1970 he has been Distinguished Service Professor at Chicago and is now Emeritus.

In Booth's own assessment, all of his writing—whether on literature, rhetoric, or education—has been "about how we manage to get together, sometimes, in our efforts to reach a human truth, and why we so often fail to," and all of it argues some version of his native conviction that "it is better for two people to understand each other, even in joint error, than for one of them to hold the truth unwilling or unable to share it with the other" ("Three Unfinished Projects" 51). This assessment defines Booth's conception of rhetoric and describes the essentially pedagogical mandate that has shaped his career as a practitioner and theorist of its practice. That is why his work—pursued now for almost half a century—is less about literature and literary criticism than it is about living and learning together. Like Cicero's Crassus in *De Oratore*, Booth is an accomplished rhetorician whose project is not so much to explain rhetorical theory and practice it effectively as it is to prompt people to understand rhetorical exchange as a method for living a better and more mutually satisfying life. Regardless of its particular focus, his published work presents this notion of rhetoric not just as a concept but as an admonition. And in his most prominent writings, Booth's voice is thoughtfully and respectfully but thoroughly admonitory.

BOOTH'S RHETORIC

A useful way to survey Booth's work may be to examine it through the lens provided by his own central dilemma—a need to justify and explain his belief in the inherent interdependence of two human capacities for knowledge that seem incommensurable. These are, essentially, faith and reason. His work addresses this dilemma as his career develops by examining the intimate connections of their disciplinary expressions: religion and rhetoric. In tracing that project through his major books, readers can identify not so much a resolution of the conflict that structures this dilemma as an intensifying critique of the dichotomy that defines it, and an increasing tendency to defer in his judgments to his own carefully reasoned and more or less secular sense of what constitutes faith.

In his 1991 essay "Rhetorics and Religion: Are They Essentially Wedded?" Booth poses a question central to his concept of rhetoric that combines the aesthetic and the ethical: "Why will the student of rhetoric be led, inescapably led—provided that he or she pushes the inquiry with full vigor—to religion?" (63). As he develops it in this essay, his general answer to that question is that a careful study of rhetoric leads to a recognition that "*some* religious questions, and even *some* religious answers, can be cognitively meaningful" (63–64). This is an answer that enacts that advice his own undergraduate teacher once gave him—to look not for reasons to rebel but for reasons not to, advice that he first systematized in *Modern Dogma and the Rhetoric of Assent* (1974). Our inherited and learned notions of reason, and especially of reasoned rhetoric, Booth argued succinctly in 1991, require that we "subject each suspected truth to a systematic effort to 'falsify' it, to doubt it with every conceivable means of doubt." The problem with the practice of that sort of rhetoric is that its discipline deprives us

of the rhetorical resources of shared emotion and commitment, the resources of metaphor and analogy, and all other forms of eloquence, [as well as] of a notion of rhetoric as inquiry, rhetoric as an art of invention through exploration of shared commonplaces. (70)

If, however, we conceive of the role of reason in rhetoric differently, and come to understand rhetoric as "the whole art that attempts to provide reasons for changing our minds, reasons no matter how 'unreasonable,' " then its practice requires us to abandon our dependence on our capacities for rational critique alone and take something very like a leap of faith into the perceptions and ideas of people whose worlds we don't fully understand but with whom we must, and want to, live. Making that leap of faith requires, in Booth's words, that we "agree to assent to what we cannot in good faith seriously doubt. . . . Here we will doubt only those propositions for which we have good specific reasons for doubt" rather than "undertake to doubt everything we cannot demonstrate scientifically or logically" (73).

Making that leap is a kind of interaction—indeed, it is a mode of relation—that requires us "to listen to one another, to attend to the other party's arguments *as if* they might make better sense than our own" (75). Here is Booth's description of that social interaction and the kind of individual transformation it prompts:

You enter your opponent's mind; your opponent's mind enters yours, and, before you know it, your mind has been forced either to reject your former precious truth or, now that you see it deeper, you must embrace both your old truth and your opponent's new one. (75)

For him, this is the way that "genuine progress is made"—progress that is as much ethical as epistemological—"even though the final, full truth remains forever elusive" (76). Indeed, pursued within the sort of communicative interaction that Booth is describing, purposes of knowing truth and of doing good are fully interwoven. And to engage in such a relationship requires of each participant a generous measure of humility and of what amounts to faith that this process of genuine exchange with another will afford both the benefits of progress.

For Booth, this sort of communicative interaction enacts what is, more or less, religion. That is why he can argue that the full study of rhetoric leads to issues of religion. As he ends his essay on "Rhetorics and Religion," Booth shares his hope (and his admonition) that more scholars in rhetoric and criticism will, very consciously,

undertake studies of how we might improve our ways of talking together . . . not just how we might do it better technically, but how we might improve it *really*. Such scholars would be marked by their radical critique of the divorce of rhetoric and reality—of the notion that we get in touch with reality with some method that is untainted by rhetoric and then sell our results *with* rhetoric. (79)

Booth is one such scholar who replaces as the object of his study that familiar notion of rational and objective discursive reality with interactions of practical rhetorical exchange that enact this secularized notion of religion. *Experienced* reality—the reality people work within and maintain together from day to day—is a dynamic social situation where what individuals know is rendered volatile in exchanges with others with whom they find themselves necessarily connected, exchanges within which individual beliefs and values are continually called into question and consequently reshaped.

It is in this place that Booth's first book, *The Rhetoric of Fiction* (1961), locates the experience of literary reading. By describing how an author projects an identity through a fictional text, and how that identity works—at least at that moment—to reconstruct the reader's own identity, this book renders the act of reading fiction an instance of the rhetorical, and thus relational, interaction. Within this textual relationship, the author influences the reader in the same ways that physical companions engaged in conversation shape each other's experience of their present shared reality. Soon after *The Rhetoric of Fiction*, Booth began articulating this notion of a relational reality (one in which epistemological desires and ethical accountabilities are inseparably embedded) in terms of rhetorical theory. His essay "The Rhetorical Stance" (1963) offered the methodological reminder that a rhetorical assertion can effectively influence others as its originator intends only if its substance is made to accommodate their needs and desires, and doing that requires the rhetor himself or herself to present as inherent in the message an identity he or she can recognize as a person to whom they can connect and attend. And his subsequent "The Revival of Rhetoric" (1965) encompassed this method in a seemingly simple definition of the rhetorical that presents to people working in English studies in general his redefinition of their common project: What people do, need to do, and need to learn to do—and what "English" needs to teach them to do—is engage together "in acts of mutual persuasion" that enact nothing more and nothing less than "mutual inquiry" (12).

In 1974 Booth published two more books. One, *A Rhetoric of Irony*, continued the literary project begun in *The Rhetoric of Fiction*: to explain the rhetorical effects of literary texts on those who read them and in doing so to admonish readers to respond to texts as wary rhetorical—and thus ethical—critics. Here he described irony functioning in fiction as an assertion by an author of an intimacy that claims the reader's trust. Booth's purpose in this book is to alert readers to the relational claims enacted by the ironies they encounter in a text and to admonish them to assess the consequences of the trust demanded. In doing so, he identified himself frankly as an advocate of what might be described as rhetorical humility and discursive faith: *A Rhetoric of Irony* is, in his words, "unabashedly in a tradition of evangelical attempts to save the world or at least a piece of it, through critical attention to language" (xii). The other book, *Modern Dogma and the Rhetoric of Assent*, expands the project that emerged in his articles on rhetorical theory of the early 1960s and that he reiterated in his 1991 essay on the connection of rhetoric and religion: to redefine rhetoric as the communicative interaction of people who must use reasoned discourse to structure the ethical interactions that enable them to find and maintain common ground for their cooperation. Also "evangelical" in its attempt to save us through critical attention to the ways that we address and respond to each other *Modern Dogma* argues in these terms:

> The rhetoric that concerns us here will be the art of probing what men believe they ought to believe, rather than proving what is true according to abstract methods. It is thus always dirtying its hands in mere opinion, offering its services to both sides of a controversy, and producing results that are at best rather messy. And rhetoric is always tainted, in the view of purer disciplines, by concern for audiences. (xiii)

Consequently, people participating in such a discourse tend to, and ought to, draw upon all available resources—rational and non-—in a collaborative attempt to identify together some aspects of what is good and true. In doing so they enact "the belief that the primary act of man is to assent to truth rather than to detect error" (xvi)—a belief that enables ethical obligations to constrain epistemological desires.

Booth notes that he wrote *Modern Dogma* as a reflection on his experience as a dean at Chicago during the campus unrest of the late 1960s, when he witnessed the practice of a rhetoric that guaranteed the breakdown of cooperative interaction and, consequently, made ethical failure inevitable. Each side in the conflict between student activists and university administrators used strictly logical criteria as grounds to reject the other side's positions and claims (what was at issue between them was who had the truth) and thus designate the opposing side unreasonable and wrong. What Booth recognized in that impasse is the need for a rhetoric that seeks something other than *the* truth and in doing so provides more complex and humane criteria for judgment. Specifically, he wrote that "the rules for good discourse or clear thinking can no longer be confined to logical prose—we must take in the proofs of personal appeal and commitment, of art and myth and ritual." In coming to that conclusion, Booth located rhetoric on the boundary between epistemological and ethical realms—or, rather, he suggested the possibility that rhetorical interaction eliminates the distinction that separates those realms. This location enables the hope that despite seemingly irreconcilable differences in their positions, people can still use discourse to construct and maintain "a community that every man can assent to: as old as Adam and as new as the morning newscast, it is the community of those who want to discover good reasons together." The common project of people who constitute this community is not so much to disprove the beliefs of differing others as it is to improve their own (viii). Here, rhetorical interaction functions as an act of faith that discourse will lead to moments of shared belief and cooperation as people who, though differing in their destinations, encounter each other as fellow travelers.

Booth applied this concept of rhetoric directly to the practice of literary criticism in his next major book, *Critical Understanding: The Powers and Limits of Pluralism* (1979). Here he brings his literary and rhetorical projects together, advocating and enacting his rhetoric of assent in the method he describes as a "critical pluralism" that might enable literary critics to interact in ways that are mutually transformative. Like *Modern Dogma, Critical Understanding* was written in direct response to the discursive impasse of sectarian adversaries—this time among literary theorists and critics. Here Booth proposes critical pluralism as a rhetoric that offers an ecumenical alternative to that impasse that could, nonetheless, further the work of discriminating the relative quality and validity of opposing readings:

A full critical pluralism would be a kind of methodological perspectivism that credited not only accuracy and validity but some degree of adequacy to at least two critical modes, though it would no doubt find many others either false or invalid or grossly reductive. It would take seriously the notion . . . that every inquirer is inherently limited by his language, that we can see only what our equipment allows us to see; but it would take with equal seriousness the task of discriminating kinds and qualities of equipment. (32–33)

This last sentence describes one founding principle of this method—one that is something like humility. And the following statement describes another—one that is something like faith:

Would you not agree, friends of truth that you are, that reality, though it appears to us in diverse forms, is all *somehow* unified? Discriminate realities as you will, you must finally admit that everything is related to everything else, *really* related, in some important sense, and that it is thus more important to work on recognizing new similarities beneath differences than to make distinctions where none were before. (94)

Here, again, Booth's concept of the unifying project of religion—at least his secularized conception of it—is interwoven with his concept of the critical work of rhetoric: "Our goal is . . . the reduction of meaningless controversy, of unjustified critical killing—which is to say an *increase* in the kind of debate that yields critical understanding" (344).

Indeed, at one point in this book Booth described "understanding" as "the goal, process, and result whenever one mind succeeds in entering another mind" (262). In his next major book, *The Company We Keep: An Ethics of Fiction* (1988), he examines how readers might enact such understanding critically—in his sense of a humble and faithful act of critique. *The Company We Keep*, like most statements of critical method, is concerned with discerning and determining quality in literature. However, the critical process that Booth recommends here goes well beyond that goal: It enlists the individual judgment of readers in the service of collective, as well as individual, transformation. Given his assumption that "each work of art or artifice . . . determines to some degree, for the viewer or reader, *how at least this one moment will be lived*" and that "we can even say that the proffered work shows us how our moments *should* be lived" (17; emphasis in original), Booth works in this book to develop among readers in general and critics in particular a more or less systematic and disciplined "way of sharing knowledge, not just opinions about why some stories we tell each other are pearls of great price while others are dangerous drugs or even poisons" (26).

This is an ethically inflected epistemological method—he labels it "coduction" (70)—that acknowledges that one reader's judgment of value in a literary text is necessarily embedded in the web of particular influences and experiences that reader brings to the text. But it also relies on a reader's awareness of his or her present affiliation with a collectivity of readers of that text—of "the past experiences of many judges who do not even have a roughly codified set of precedents to guide them." Coduction is a kind of displaced discourse in which readers together determine a judgment of a text's value. As a method, it contextualizes that process within a community of some sort and thus renders any critical judgment "a communal enterprise rather than a private, 'personal' calculation logically coercive on all who hear it" (72). Here individuals consent to allow their own judgments to be transformed by a set of beliefs they establish together with other readers about literary meaning and quality. The judgment that follows is as much ethical as it is epistemological—for what drives aesthetic judgment for Booth is the two interwoven. Such judgment is enacted by asking and then answering, together with people with whom one at least momentarily identifies and to whom one is at least presently accountable, this question: "Should I believe this narrator and thus join him? Am I willing to be the kind of person that this storyteller is asking me to be?" (39). The goal of this sort of judgment—of this criticism—is not to identify "the best that has been thought and said" so much as it is "to find forms of critical talk that will improve the range or depth or precision of our appreciation" (113)—an appreciation of matters that are initially literary but extend well beyond that realm. This enhanced appreciation is not so much aesthetic, or even philosophical, as it is ethical in a simple relational sense: "[W]hat makes life human, and what makes human life worth living," Booth writes, "are our relations of trust and affection" (173). To establish and strengthen these relationships is the purpose served by this sort of critical work.

RHETORIC AND ETHICS

Booth's project is not to displace judgment of aesthetic value with judgment of ethical value. Rather, it is to enable readers to understand that in its rhetorical function aesthetic form embodies an inherently ethical and, thus, socially epistemological act. And in working out this project, Booth can be read as completing an important aspect of Kenneth Burke's, a project with which Booth's often self-consciously interacts. Well known, for example, is Booth's interchange with Burke, initially published in *Critical Inquiry* ("Kenneth Burke's Way of Knowing") in 1974 and then recontextualized and explored by Booth in *Critical Understanding* (1979). And in recent work ("Kenneth Burke's Religious Rhetoric," for example), Booth continues to grapple with the relationship of his ideas to Burke's, particularly as he tries to locate for himself places where his own attempts to interweave reason and faith, and Burke's work—in which Burke claims to avoid interweaving the two—might intersect. Essentially, Booth remains convinced that Burke's project, like his own, involves articulating a discursive ethics that enacts both modes of knowing. This entry on Booth concludes, then, with an attempt to sketch out that place of intersection—a place where Booth's contribution to rhetorical theory might be understood to reside.

Burke's innovative rhetorical concept of form has significant ethical implications that Burke himself does not develop. What he does provide is a technical description of how the formal expression of a writer's intention can affect the judgments of the people who read it. Specifically, it enables readers to trace the effects a text has on them and thus to monitor changes in their perceptions that a text can prompt. But Burke's theory of form does not provide a way to adjudicate the *value* of such encounters. The closest Burke comes in his theoretical discussion of form to enabling the ethical project of valuing that is at the core of both rhetoric and literary criticism is his description, in *Counter-Statement*, of eloquence as the effect that follows when discursive form and function fully blend. But, given his definition of eloquence, that isn't very close: "Eloquence is not showiness; it is, rather, the result of the desire in the artist to make a work perfect by adapting it in every minute detail to the racial appetites" (41). His choice of the opaque term "racial appetites" to describe what it is that enables people to engage with others in mutually transformative interactions suggests how far he had to reach to give an intrinsically ethical theory of form the appearance of being value neutral. Indeed, Burke's own *The Rhetoric of Religion* (1961) avoids the matters of value addressed by religion by focusing technically, and in exhaustive detail, on "the nature of religion as a rhetoric"—on "the *terminology* of religion" (iv; emphasis in original). And it is Burke's insistent habit of neutralizing such matters of value for the sake of scientizing his system that Booth's work, particularly in *Company*, can be read as correcting.

Burke's theory of form demonstrates persuasively that the function of discursive form is, in Booth's terms, "to implant and reinforce patterns of desire" and that this function has considerable rhetorical power whether a writer intends to manipulate readers or to interact with them as respected equals. In *Company*, Booth articulates the ethical dilemma that rhetorical reality presents to readers: "If we do not surrender to those patterns, we cannot really be said to have 'taken in' a given [text]; yet if we do surrender, we find ourselves to some degree shaped into those patterns" (272). But what Booth offers, not only here but throughout his work, is a way out of that dilemma. The rhetoric Booth envisions and describes is one of critical response. Centered not in the needs of the *rhetor*—as is most rhetorical theory—but in the needs of those to whom rhetoric is addressed, this rhetoric teaches a reader to acknowledge the fallibility of both the rhetor—who has the power to shape the judgments of the reader addressed—

and of the reader himself or herself as a person who might have something to gain by allowing the self to be transformed in some way by the rhetoric. In doing so, Booth lets readers out of the ethical squeeze between a response that would render readers passive—and made over in the rhetor's intended image—or arrogantly resistent to influence and transformation altogether.

Booth's work asserts his belief that people do share both an "irresistible urge to improve life" *and* a desire to act on that urge together. Inherent in that urge and desire is a dangerous tendency toward misjudgment as well as the hope that misjudgment might be avoided by "talking together critically, really trying to be open and honest" ("Art and the Church" 25). The work of maintaining a rhetorical exchange that progresses toward that hopeful end, he seems to suggest, is primarily the responsibility of those to whom rhetoric is addressed. A primary social obligation, then, is to act and interact as a rhetorical critic. For Booth, doing that requires a deliberate (and *deliberative*) leap of what amounts to faith—faith in the ability of people to accomplish together greater good than they can separately. This faith is founded upon a belief that both self and society can be transformed for the better, but only through an interdependent process in which, as *Modern Dogma* describes it, we learn "to listen to one another, to attend to the other party's arguments *as if* they might make better sense than our own" (75). Such interaction is a humble leap of faith that renders rhetoric more or less a religious act. What enables the moment of ethical choice that is at the core of the act of criticism, then, is the imaginative trying out of the way of life that this leap of faith enables. Having deliberately given ourselves over, imaginatively, to someone else's way of life, we can then choose whether to make it our own. Religion and rhetoric come together, then—encompassing epistemology, ethics, and aesthetics—as readers allow themselves to experience, in Booth's terms, "the patterns of desires and fulfillments" that are inherent in the texts that address them while attending fully to "the shaping power of the work" as they do so (*The Company We Keep* 427).

Late in his career, Kenneth Burke identified the options of reactive "motion" and purposeful "action" as "the basic polarity" ("[Nonsymbolic] Motion/ [Symbolic] Action" 809). And believing as he did in the human necessity of connection and relationship, Burke wrote throughout his long life about distinguishing choices of actions that enable connection and relationship from choices of motion that constitute retreats from it. Booth believes, with Burke, in the ethical necessity of human collectivity. But his work goes well beyond Burke's description of that to admonition. Burke identifies action—purposeful response in interaction—as the proper human choice, and then Booth explores what the project of making those choices entails. Burke identifies the power inherent in the utterances of others to render us creatures of motion, and then Booth explains how we can respond to that power in ways that release the transformative potential of our interactions. Simply put, Burke shows us that, though separate in our bodies, we use language to bridge the gaps that separate us and, in doing so, remake our reality imaginatively in collective terms. Then Booth shows us how to do that in ways that might render the reality we remake together a better one for us all.

CONCLUSION

Wayne Booth continues to be an important voice in both literary and rhetorical studies—one that persistently addresses the rhetoricity of literature and, further, the issues of collective valuing that are at the center of any discursive act. In his persistent refusal to isolate literary criticism from public discourse, and matters of technique and aesthetics from matters of politics and ethics, Booth reminds his readers of the artificiality of disciplinary boundaries and renders rhetorical expertise a necessity for every citizen of a literate culture. Indeed, he presents rhetoric to his readers as the way of ethical life.

BIBLIOGRAPHY

Primary Sources

Booth, Wayne C. "Art and the Church: Question and Answer Sessions with Wayne C. Booth." *Literature and Belief* (1981): 19–26.
———. *The Company We Keep: An Ethics of Fiction.* Berkeley: University of California Press, 1988.
———. *Critical Understanding: The Powers and Limits of Pluralism.* Chicago: University of Chicago Press, 1979.
———. "The Idea of a *Uni*versity as Seen by a Rhetorician." The 1987 Ryerson Lecture. Chicago: University of Chicago Press, 1987. Reprinted in his *The Vocation of a Teacher: Rhetorical Occasions, 1967–1988.* Chicago: University of Chicago Press, 1989.
———. "Kenneth Burke's Religious Rhetoric: 'God-Terms' and the Ontological Proof." Unpublished.
———. "Kenneth Burke's Way of Knowing." *Critical Inquiry* 1 (1974): 1–22.
———. "Let Us All Mount Our Good Chargers, Whatever Their Names, and Gallop Off Joyfully in All Directions, a Mysteriously United Company Serving the Empress of All the Sciences, Rhetoric." Afterword. *Rhetoric and Pluralism: Legacies of Wayne Booth.* Ed. Frederick J. Antczak. Columbus: Ohio State University Press, 1995. 279–307.
———. " 'LITCOMP': Some Rhetoric Addressed to Cryptorhetoricians about a Rhetorical Solution to a Rhetorical Problem." *Composition and Literature: Bridging the Gap.* Ed. Winifred B. Horner. Chicago: University of Chicago Press, 1983. 57–80.
———. "Mere Rhetoric, Rhetoric, and the Search for Common Learning." *Common Learning: A Carnegie Colloquium on General Education.* Washington, DC: Carnegie Foundation for the Advancement of Teaching, 1981. 22–55.
———. *Modern Dogma and the Rhetoric of Assent.* Chicago: University of Chicago Press, 1974.
———. "The Revival of Rhetoric." *PMLA* 80.2 (1965): 8–12.

————. "The Rhetorical Stance." *College Composition and Communication* 14.3 (1963): 139–45.

————. *The Rhetoric of Fiction.* Chicago: University of Chicago Press, 1961.

————. *A Rhetoric of Irony.* Chicago: University of Chicago Press, 1974.

————. "Rhetorics and Religion: Are They Essentially Wedded?" *Radical Pluralism and Truth: David Tracy and the Hermeneutics of Truth.* Ed. Werner G. Jenrod and Jennifer L. Rike. New York: Crossroad, 1991. 62–80.

————. "The Scope of Rhetoric Today: A Polemical Excursion." *The Prospect of Rhetoric.* Ed. Lloyd Bitzer and Edwin Black. Englewood Cliffs, NJ: Prentice-Hall, 1971. 93–114.

Burke, Kenneth. *Counter-Statement.* 1931. Berkeley: University of California Press, 1968.

————. "(Nonsymbolic) Motion/(Symbolic) Action." *Critical Inquiry* 4.4 (1978): 809–38.

————. *The Rhetoric of Religion: Studies in Logology.* 1961. Berkeley: University of California Press, 1970.

Biography

"Art and the Church: Question and Answer Sessions with Wayne C. Booth." *Literature and Belief* 1.1 (1981): 19–26.

"Three Unfinished Projects." *Contemporary Authors Autobiography Series.* Vol. 5. Ed. Adele Sarkissian. Detroit: Gale Research, 1987. 31–51.

Criticism

Antczak, Frederick J., ed. *Rhetoric and Pluralism: Legacies of Wayne Booth.* Columbus: Ohio State University Press, 1995.

Bator, Paul G. "The 'Good Reasons Movement': A 'Confounding' of Dialectic and Rhetoric?" *Philosophy and Rhetoric* 21.1 (1988): 38–47.

Bialostosky, Donald H. "Booth's Rhetoric, Bakhtin's Dialogics, and the Future of Novel Criticism." *Novel* 18.3 (1985): 209–16, 223–36.

Borklund, Elmer. *Contemporary Literary Critics.* 2nd ed. New York: Macmillan, 1982.

Chatman, Seymour. "The 'Rhetoric' 'of' 'Fiction.' " *Reading Narrative: Form, Ethics, Ideology.* Ed. James Phelan. Columbus: Ohio State University Press, 1989. 40–56.

Kaufer, David S., and Christine M. Neuwirth. "Contrasts between Ironic and Metaphoric Understanding: An Elaboration of Booth's Observations." *Western Journal of Speech Communication* 47.1 (1983): 75–83.

Weiler, Michael. "Arguments in Fiction." *Argumentation Theory and the Rhetoric of Assent.* Ed. David Cratis Williams and Michael Hazen. Tuscaloosa: University of Alabama Press, 1990. 103–16.

JAMES BRITTON
(1908–1994)

Christopher C. Burnham

Born on May 18, 1908, in Scarborough, England, James Britton took both his B.A. and M.A. from the University of London. He taught in state secondary schools for eight years, publishing an antitextbook, *English on the Anvil* (1934), to counter the rule-mongering drill-based grammar manuals that then dominated the schools. More important, it forecast the person- and purpose-centered approach to language learning he would develop through his career. He left school teaching in 1938 to become education editor for the powerful John Murray Publishers of London. His editorial career was interrupted by service with the Royal Air Force during World War II. His autobiographical *Record and Recall: A Cretan Memoir* (1988) memorializes a German paratrooper attack on a British radar station in 1941 in which he and a small group of countrymen barely escaped capture. He returned to editing, only to leave John Murray for graduate studies in 1948. He completed his M.A. in 1952 and then settled into a distinguished career of teaching and research. His major concerns were language acquisition, the functions of writing and literature, and how school curricula can aid or frustrate student growth. In 1954, he joined the English Education Department at the University of London Institute of Education. He served a long term as head of the English Department and was ultimately appointed Goldsmiths Professor. Retiring in 1975, he remained active as a scholar, teacher, and consultant working throughout the English-speaking world. With his last books, *Flight-path of My Words: Poems 1940–1992*, published just before his death, and *Literature in Its Place* (1993), he returned to the ideas that anchored all his work: Through language individuals come to understand experience; literature preserves and consolidates that understanding as the art of collective human experience. He died in 1994.

Britton's work weaves sources from such diverse disciplines as cognitive psychology, aesthetic and language philosophy, literary theory, and cultural history. As an educator he ranged unbound, placing emerging theories in relation to one another and ignoring controversies within disciplines to derive useful applications. He draws on such various sources as D. W. Harding, George Kelly, A. R. Luria, M. M. Bakhtin, Martin Buber, Louise Rosenblatt, M. Polanyi, and Georges Gusdorf, in addition to those mentioned elsewhere in this entry. His intellect is synthetic and dialogic; rather than setting up oppositions, he establishes continua where seeming opposites support each other in synergistic relations.

BRITTON'S RHETORICAL THEORY

Britton's development is not marked by disjunct and redirection but by elaboration. He generally works by identifying contradictions and anomalies in current theory and then developing alternative approaches derived from diverse theories, empirical analyses, and his own close observation. Following John Dewey, he argues that knowledge is social and that humans learn by articulating their experiences. Language, learning, and literature make us most human. He continuously asserts the responsibility of public education to respect and develop each person's potential, arguing that schools are a powerful agent for offsetting class inequities.

The shape of Britton's career afforded him regular opportunities to revisit and expand his original thinking on his central concern: language and learning, especially expressive language (talking and writing for self and among informed intimates). *Language and Learning* (1970) theorizes language development and the relation between language and learning. Comprehensive in his purview, he traces the process from when a child first learns to talk at home, through her schooling, and ultimately to her fully mature use of language to create and maintain relations with people, to transact the business of life, and to participate in intellectual and cultural life. *The Development of Writing Abilities (11–18)* (1975), with Tony Burgess, Nancy Martin, Alex McLeod, and Harold Rosen, tests the theory in the context of school instruction. Using empirical analysis as well as observational studies, the Project represents an early but paradigmatic example of teacher research. The book critiques then-current British school curricula, offering extensive suggestions for change. Analyzing scripts collected systematically through various grade levels, the research team found that, in the higher levels, students wrote predominantly to one audience in one mode for one purpose. Students wrote information provided them by the curriculum into prescribed forms for teachers who read as evaluators. The researchers recommend shifting emphasis from writing for evaluation to using writing to support collaboration and cooperative learning, as well as for reflecting upon personal and cultural experience. In short, they argue, school uses of language should more closely reflect and support the actual uses of language in life.

"Shaping at the Point of Utterance" appears in *Reinventing the Rhetorical*

Tradition (1980), an important collection of essays offering radical syntheses of then-current rhetorical theory. Britton's contribution speculates on how internalized linguistic and semantic patterns at once enable but also determine composition. Through "retrospective structuring," writers shuttle back and forth from discovering and shaping concepts and experience—rhetorical invention—to communicating those discoveries using already available patterns and structures. "Shaping at the point of utterance" involves balancing tensions between the conflicting elements of a rhetorical act. Through the process writers mediate their own individual need to discover, shape, and share experience with their socially developed, internalized sense of a reader's need for structures and meanings that are both congruent with but different from previous ones. Previous patterns learned through reading and other language activities at once initiate and determine invention. Shaping meaning from the writer's experience according to the writer's purpose and his or her sense of a reader's needs and expectations maps the transformation of language from its expressive origins within the writer to its ultimate position along a continuum bounded by transactional (informational, regulative, or persuasive) and poetic (literary) categories (62–65). The essay anticipates much of the theoretical controversy James Berlin raises, especially in *Rhetoric and Reality* (1987), surrounding the seeming conflict between subjective rhetorics and objective and transactional (social-epistemic) rhetorics. Britton's approach holds that the elements of the rhetorical field are interdependent rather than exclusionary.

Another essay, "Spectator Role and the Beginnings of Writing" (1982), reopens the discussion of expressive language, confirming earlier findings about the instrumental role it plays in developing other kinds of writing but ending with a speculation about the relation between gossip and literature and how language, like art, helps humans to shape and understand experience. Adding a chapter and postscript to the second edition of *Language and Learning* (1993), he turns full circle to his original concern, in the process questioning and correcting some of Jean Piaget's assertions about children's inability to reason and, invoking Jerome Bruner's theory of two human modes of thinking, the logico-scientific or paradigmatic and the narrative posited in *Actual Minds, Possible Worlds* (1986). Bruner's energy goes to relegitimizing the narrative mode or consciousness, making it equal in value to the paradigmatic. Similarly, Britton argues the centrality of literature, especially narrative and story, in shaping human understanding and culture.

"English Teaching: Prospect and Retrospect" (1982) offers some of Britton's most powerful conclusions about language, learning, and teaching. In schools, language serves three purposes. First, through language we establish and maintain human relationships that create the possibility for learning. When students question, summarize, sympathize, and instruct through language, they venture into and through Vygotsky's zone of proximal development. Learning comes through cooperative social interaction between the learner and a knowledgeable teacher or peer. Second, language supports learning through providing the means to understand and use information and to organize the objective elements of experience. Third, language allows individuals to explore and shape subjective experience, in the process creating and preserving a picture of the world and the learner in that world (205–7). Schools nurture and preserve individual understanding and control. In the process, schools strengthen and develop culture. Britton's theory systematizes formal and informal language use, from high literature and the regularized communication of factual information in stock forms to simple social talk and gossip, into a comprehensive theory of learning.

BRITTON'S INFLUENCE ON RHETORIC AND COMPOSITION

In the discipline, Britton exerts most influence through the developmental taxonomy of writing that he derived from close observation of the process through which children learn language. With origins in linguistics and cognitive and developmental psychology, the taxonomy emphasizes the expressive function of language, providing a wealth of linguistic and pedagogical insights that can be developed for a variety of purposes. His theory has clear implications for teaching of writing, for understanding relations between writing and learning, and for writing across the curriculum.

In *Language and Learning* (1970), Britton invokes Edward Sapir's distinction between the referential and expressive functions of language. Britton emphasizes the expressive function. It opposes the referential whose purpose is to represent and transcribe material reality. For Britton, the expressive function makes language personal and idiosyncratic. It provides a means for individuals to connect abstract concepts with personal experience and to negotiate public and private significance. The result is concrete understanding and learning. Additional sources for Britton's theory include Vygotsky's "inner speech," Bruner's cognitive psychology, with its emphasis on the instrumental relationship between language and learning, and Noam Chomsky's generative transformational theory of language. In *Discourse: A Critique and Synthesis of Major Theories* (1989), Timothy Crusius credits Britton's important contribution to discourse theory. In comparison to the theories of James Moffett, James Kinneavy, and Frank D'Angelo, Britton's is the most comprehensive. It is the only theory to attend to the regulative function of language and to include a developmental matrix that considers both mature and immature uses of language.

In *Development of Writing Abilities (11–18)* (1975), an observational and empirical analysis of the writing students do in school, Britton and his colleagues focus on the two primary roles writers can play when producing language: the participant role, in which writers use language to get things done, and the spectator role, in which writers use language to relive the past. As participants, writers shape reality to an end. As spectators, writers re-create reality.

Locating participant and spectator roles at either end of a continuum, he introduces a third mediating role, the expressive, in which the writer functions as both participant and spectator. From each role he derives a category of writing. In the participant role, writers produce *transactional* writing, in which language is used to accomplish the business of the world. Transactional writing is divided further into informative and conative writing, roughly corresponding to the traditional classifications of exposition and persuasion. In material added to the second edition of *Language and Learning* (1993), Britton adjusts these categories slightly to include informative, regulative, and persuasive writing. Informative writing makes information available; regulative writing impels or commands action, and persuasive writing moves readers from inaction or ambivalence to specific action. In each instance the writing involves a transaction between writer and reader—hence, its name.

On the other end of the continuum, writers acting in the spectator role produce *poetic* writing. Poetic writing is language used as an art medium, as a verbal icon, whose purpose is to be an object that pleases or satisfies the writer. The reader's response is to share that satisfaction. In traditional terms, poetic writing is literary discourse, language that "exists for *its own sake* and not as a means of achieving something else" ([1975] 91).

With transactional and poetic writing constituting the opposing boundaries of the participant/spectator continuum, Britton establishes a third category, expressive writing, that mediates the two. As a functional category, expressive writing represents a mode rather than a form. More important than its existence as a text, expressive writing achieves its purpose through allowing the text to come to existence. Examples include "thinking out loud on paper" (89); notes and drafts intended for the personal and private use of writers and their collaborators; journal writing documenting or exploring immediate thoughts, feelings, and moods; and personal letters.

In the expressive mode, writers shuttle back and forth between participant and spectator roles, generating ideas, then shaping them into language that can stand on its own. With its generative function, expressive writing plays an obvious role in learning to write: "Thus, in developmental terms, the expressive is a kind of matrix from which differentiated forms of mature writing are developed" (83). In addition, as a link between the private and personal and the public and social, as the language of association and connection, expressive language is the language of learning.

From its inception, Britton's taxonomy has influenced process-based approaches to teaching writing. The approaches developed by Peter Elbow and Donald Murray, among others, implicitly or explicitly use Britton's developmental taxonomy to help students and teachers navigate the journey through which personal and private insights and sensations become coherent, publicly accessible writing. From a theoretical perspective, Christopher Burnham, in "Expressive Rhetoric: A Source Study" (1993), argues that Britton's taxonomy creates common space that contains the seeming oppositions between expressive, cognitive and social approaches to rhetoric, providing a coherent model for understanding writing as the result of interactions among individually and culturally defined forces. In *Romancing Rhetorics* (1995), Sherrie Gradin, though indirectly, examines the theoretical debt expressivist, social-expressivist, and collaborative pedagogies owe to Britton. Writing-across-the-curriculum commentators, especially Toby Fulwiler and Art Young in *Language Connections* (1982), have long proposed using Britton-based expressive writing systematically in class journals in all disciplines as a powerful tool for improving learning. More recently, the write-to-learn pedagogy presented by Stephen Fishman and Lucille McCarthy in *John Dewey and the Challenge of Classroom Practice* (1998) owes an obvious debt to Britton's work. In short, Britton's work so pervades contemporary writing pedagogy that he has become part of our tacit tradition.

BIBLIOGRAPHY

Primary Sources

Britton, James N. *English on the Anvil: A Language and Composition Course for Secondary Schools*. London: Foyles Educational, 1934; Eighth printing, London: John Murray, 1952.
———. "English Teaching: Prospect and Retrospect." *Prospect and Retrospect: Selected Essays of James Britton*. Ed. Gordon Pradl. Montclair, NJ: Boynton/Cook, 1982.
———. *Flight-path of My Words: Poems 1940–1992*. London: Loxwood, Stoneleigh, 1993.
———. *Language and Learning*. London: Allen Lane, 1970.
———. *Language and Learning*. 2nd ed. Portsmouth, NH: Boynton/Cook, 1993.
———. *Literature in Its Place*. London: Cassell, 1993.
———. "Shaping at the Point of Utterance." *Reinventing the Rhetorical Tradition*. Ed. Aviva Freedman and Ian Pringle. Conway, AR: L & S, 1980. 61–67.
———. "Spectator Role and the Beginnings of Writing." *Prospect and Retrospect: Selected Essays of James Britton*. Ed. Gordon Pradl. Montclair, NJ: Boynton/Cook, 1982.
Britton, James, Tony Burgess, Nancy Martin, Alex McLeod, and Harold Rosen. *The Development of Writing Abilities (11–18)*. London: Macmillan Education, 1975.

Biography

Britton, James N. *Record and Recall: A Cretan Memoir*. London: Lightfoot, 1988.

Criticism

Berlin, James. *Rhetoric and Reality: Writing Instruction in American Colleges, 1900–1985*. Carbondale: Southern Illinois University Press, 1987.
Bruner, Jerome. *Actual Minds, Possible Worlds*. Cambridge, MA: Harvard University Press, 1986.
Burnham, Christopher C. "Expressive Rhetoric: A Source Study." *Defining the New*

Rhetorics. Ed. Theresa Enos and Stuart C. Brown. Newbury Park, CA: Sage, 1993.

Crusius, Timothy. *Discourse: A Critique and Synthesis of Major Theories*. New York: MLA, 1989.

Fishman, Stephen, and Lucille McCarthy. *John Dewey and the Challenge of Classroom Practice*. New York: Teachers College Press, 1998.

Fulwiler, Toby, and Art Young, eds. *Language Connections: Writing and Reading across the Curriculum*. Urbana, IL: NCTE, 1982.

Gradin, Sherrie L. *Romancing Rhetorics: Social Expressivist Perspectives on the Teaching of Writing*. Portsmouth, NH: Boynton/Cook, 1995.

GERTRUDE BUCK
(1871–1922)

Gerald P. Mulderig

Gertrude Buck was born on July 14, 1871, in Kalamazoo, Michigan, the daughter of George M. and Annie Bradford Buck. After earning her bachelor's degree in English at the University of Michigan in 1894, she pursued graduate work at the university under the direction of Fred Newton Scott, Michigan's rising star in rhetoric at the time. Buck's master's thesis, *Figures of Rhetoric: A Psychological Study*, was the first of nine volumes of his students' work that Scott edited and published as monographs between 1895 and 1918 under the series title Contributions to Rhetorical Theory. In 1898, Buck became the first of Scott's students to earn a Ph.D. in the program that in 1903 would become the University of Michigan's distinguished Department of Rhetoric, headed by Scott from its inception until his retirement in 1926. Her dissertation, *The Metaphor: A Study in the Psychology of Rhetoric*, was published as the fifth of Scott's Contributions to Rhetorical Theory monographs.

In 1897, as she was completing her Ph.D., Buck was recruited to the faculty of Vassar College by Laura Johnson Wylie, the newly appointed chair of Vassar's Department of English and herself the first woman to have received a Ph.D. from Yale University. Buck assumed responsibility for the department's rhetoric and composition courses and was promoted from instructor to associate professor in 1901 and to professor in 1907. For most of her career at Vassar, Buck shared a house in Poughkeepsie with Wylie, where the two often hosted discussions and receptions for Vassar students and faculty and for members of the community. In August 1921, Buck suffered a stroke, remaining incapacitated until her death on January 8, 1922. At her own death 10 years later, Wylie left the bulk of her estate to the Gertrude Buck Fund of Vassar College and directed in her will that her body be cremated and her ashes buried with Buck in Philadelphia's Woodlands Cemetery.

Buck's major articles on English grammar, rhetorical theory, and the teaching of writing appeared during the first half of her tenure at Vassar. In addition to her dissertation and a monograph on argumentation and debate, she also published five books between 1897 and 1906—a treatise on educational theory (with Harriet Scott); textbooks on argumentative writing, expository writing (with Vassar colleague Elisabeth Woodbridge), and narrative writing (also with Woodbridge); and an English grammar (with Fred Newton Scott).

On leave in 1915–1916, Buck enrolled in George Pierce Baker's playwriting workshop, English 47, at Harvard and completed work on another book, *The Social Criticism of Literature*, published in 1916 by Yale University Press. Returning to Vassar, she established and taught a workshop based on Baker's model. In 1919, she took this playwriting course and its accompanying dramatic productions beyond the college and founded the Poughkeepsie Community Theatre, in which she remained active until her death. Buck's own plays and poetry were published in a collection edited by Wylie in 1922 (*Poems and Plays*).

BUCK'S RHETORICAL THEORY

Buck's approach to language, rhetoric, and writing was influenced by the post-Darwinian psychological theory of the late nineteenth century, which described the mind in organic rather than mechanical terms, depicting it as constantly growing, developing, and adapting to its environment. For Buck, theories of language use that ignored this psychological premise had little validity or value, and her books and articles constitute a single-minded critique of mechanistic models of grammar and rules for writing. In their place, she stressed "the social function and the organic structure of language" (*Brief English Grammar* 3) and proposed ways of teaching and learning writing that anticipated modern theories of composition by more than half a century.

Buck's dissertation on metaphor introduced many of the themes that she would draw on throughout her career. Rejecting the centuries-old conception of metaphors and other figures of speech as devices that a writer assembles and wields to produce rhetorical effects, she located the origins of metaphor in unconscious psychological processes and defined its function in terms of communication rather than persuasion. The child, she proposed, unknowingly creates metaphors by confusing different things, applying the term "moon," for example, to other round, glowing objects, such as lamps. The adult may also experience this momentary perception of different things as the same, though unlike a child, an adult immediately distinguishes between the two objects in question. Metaphor comes into being, that is, through the growth of a single perception into dual elements rather than through the mechanical conjoining of two disparate entities into one. In Buck's view, the poetic metaphor represents a writer's re-creation of the unconscious, fleeting perception of different things as identical, and the function of metaphor in her theory is linked to this account of its origins: Metaphor seeks "to communicate to another person the maker's vision of an object as it appeared to him at the moment of expression, not at all to carry out a dark design of persuading the reader that this object is something which the writer knows it is not" (*Metaphor* 35).

In a series of articles published between 1897 and 1909 and in the English grammar that she coauthored with Fred Scott in 1905, Buck articulated a theory of grammar similarly grounded in the organic nature of thought and the communicative function of language. Like metaphor, the sentence, she argued, originates in a single embryonic perception that grows and divides, first into a clearer expression of actor and act and then into a succession of smaller elements. "As the two main limbs of the tree keep dividing into smaller branches, then into twigs and leaves," she wrote, "so does the sentence. The subject and the predicate divide and subdivide into clauses, phrases, and finally into words" ("Sentence-Diagram" 258). With her theory of the sentence as an organism, Buck sought to discredit prevailing mechanical conceptions of the sentence as a unit assembled from individual words and held together with the glue of conjunctions and linking verbs. If thought, she argued, is "not a heap of shreds and patches . . . but a single, differentiating organic process," and if language is the living expression of this mental activity, then language structures such as sentences cannot properly be regarded as "the mechanical aggregation of originally separate parts" ("Foundations of English Grammar Teaching" 484–86). What most disturbed Buck about such mechanistic theories of grammar—theories popularized in English classrooms by sentence diagramming and similar exercises in sentence analysis—was the way they privileged word manipulation over true communication. "[S]entences are not mere puzzles, combinations of words in a certain pattern," she insisted. "They exist to convey thought" ("Make-Believe Grammar" 28). Grammatical study not grounded in language's social function was bankrupt, Buck believed, for it ignored "that great process of communication by language . . . through which alone society can profit by the achievements of its members" (33).

This Platonic conception of language's potential to improve society was also at the heart of Buck's theories of rhetoric and writing. Buck regarded discourse whose primary end is mere persuasion as the aggressive imposition of one individual's will upon another's, an antisocial use of language that she associated with sophistic rhetoric. In its place, she endorsed a Platonic model of discourse according to which the speaker seeks to communicate truth, thereby benefitting rather than dominating his or her audience. Although she conceded that we are "not now-a-days on such joyfully intimate terms with the absolute truth as was Plato," Buck nonetheless felt that the essential element in Platonic rhetoric—"a real communication between speaker and hearer, to the equal advantage of both"—should also be the central feature of modern writing instruction ("Present Status of Rhetorical Theory" 86–87). If it were, she believed, composition courses would properly focus on "a genuine occasion for writing" rather than on the "formal rhetorical precepts" and contrived essay topics that characterized writing instruction at the time. Freed from the notion of composition as an "artificial rule-regarding process," motivated by "having something to say which another person wishes or needs to hear," students would learn to discover subjects of value in their own experiences and to frame them for a real audience of readers ("Recent Tendencies" 371, 373–74, 379).

In her innovative textbooks, Buck characteristically addressed the concept of audience in psychological terms. *A Course in Argumentative Writing*, for example, defines argumentation as "the act of establishing in the mind of another person a conclusion which has become fixed in your own, by means of setting up in the other person's mind the train of thought or reasoning which has previously led you to this conclusion" (3). Induction and deduction consequently appear in the book not as logical machinery but as mental processes that students learn to observe in themselves and then to establish in their readers. Logic, in Buck's terms, is thus changed from a "dead tool" of persuasion into a "living expression of thought" (v). In her analysis of description in *A Course in Expository Writing* (Buck and Woodbridge), Buck similarly grounded rhetorical strategies in cognitive theory. Just as she had proposed that sentences begin as inchoate thoughts, gradually branching into linguistic structures, here she argued that our awareness of physical things begins with only a general sense of their features, out of which grow perceptions of finer and finer details. Details in a written description, she suggested, ought therefore to be arranged in the order in which they are perceived rather than spatially so that the description will recreate for the reader the experience of perception. An effective rhetorical structure, in other words, is "the outer expression of thought-groups as they exist in the mind" (25).

Buck's enlightened ideas about writing were far ahead of her time, but they were no match for the forces that entrenched current-traditional rhetoric in American schools and colleges in the early and middle decades of the twentieth century. Her interest in the cognitive dimensions of writing, her insistence that writing be taught and learned in the context of a true rhetorical situation, and her call for an end to the arbitrary rules and conventions perpetuated in composition textbooks would find few other champions until the so-called revival of rhetoric in the 1960s.

BIBLIOGRAPHY

Primary Sources

Buck, Gertrude. *A Course in Argumentative Writing*. New York: Holt, 1899.
———. *Figures of Rhetoric: A Psychological Study*. Contributions to Rhetorical Theory
    1. Ann Arbor: n.p., 1895.
———. "The Foundations of English Grammar Teaching." *Elementary School Teacher*
    3.6 (1903): 480–87.
———. "Make-Believe Grammar." *School Review* 17.1 (1909): 21–33.
———. *The Metaphor: A Study in the Psychology of Rhetoric*. Contributions to Rhetorical Theory 5. Ann Arbor: Inland [1899].

———. *Poems and Plays*. Ed. Laura Johnson Wylie. New York: Duffield, 1922.

———. "The Present Status of Rhetorical Theory." *Modern Language Notes* 15.3 (1900): 84–87.

———. "The Psychological Significance of the Parts of Speech." *Education* 18.5 (1898): 269–77.

———. "The Psychology of the Diagram." *The School Review* 5.7 (1897): 470–72.

———. "Recent Tendencies in the Teaching of English Composition." *Educational Review* 22 (November 1901): 371–82.

———. "The Sentence-Diagram." *Educational Review* 13 (March 1897): 250–60.

———. *The Social Criticism of Literature*. New Haven: Yale University Press, 1916.

———. "Some Preliminary Considerations in Planning the Revision of Grammatical Terminology." *English Journal* 2.1 (1913): 11–17.

———. "What Does 'Rhetoric' Mean?" *Educational Review* 22 (June 1901): 197–200.

Buck, Gertrude, and Kristine Mann. *A Handbook of Argumentation and Debating*. Orange, NJ: Orange Chronicle, 1906.

Buck, Gertrude, and Elisabeth Woodbridge Morris. *A Course in Narrative Writing*. New York: Holt, 1906.

Buck, Gertrude, and Fred Newton Scott. *A Brief English Grammar*. Chicago: Scott, Foresman, 1905.

Buck, Gertrude, and Harriet M. Scott. *Organic Education: A Manual for Teachers in Primary and Grammar Grades*. Ann Arbor, MI: Sheehan, 1897. Heath's Pedagogical Lib. 35. Boston: Heath, 1899.

Buck, Gertrude, and Elisabeth Woodbridge. *A Course in Expository Writing*. New York: Holt, 1899.

Biography

"Gertrude Buck, 1871–1922." Biographical Card File. Special Collections. Vassar College Libraries, Poughkeepsie.

Gertrude Buck Memorial Number. Spec. issue of *Vassar Miscellany Monthly* 9.5 (1923): 1–28.

"Miss Wylie's Will Probated." *Poughkeepsie Sunday Courier*, April 17, 1932: 13.

Morris, Elisabeth Woodbridge, ed. *Miss Wylie of Vassar*. New Haven, CT: Yale University Press, 1934.

Paton, Lucy A. "Gertrude Buck: Graduate Student 1915–16." *Memorial Biographies of Deceased Former Students of Radcliffe College*. Radcliffe College Archives, Cambridge, 1943.

"Professor Buck of Vassar Dies." *Poughkeepsie Eagle-News*, January 9, 1922: 5.

Criticism

Allen, Virginia. "Gertrude Buck and the Emergence of Composition in the United States." *Vitae Scholasticae: The Bulletin of Educational Biography* 5.1–2 (1986): 141–59.

Burke, Rebecca J. *Gertrude Buck's Rhetorical Theory*. Occasional Papers in Composition History and Theory. Manhattan: Dept. of English, Kansas State University, n.d.

Campbell, JoAnn, ed. *Toward a Feminist Rhetoric: The Writing of Gertrude Buck*. Pitt

Series in Composition, Literacy, and Culture. Pittsburgh: University of Pittsburgh Press, 1996.

Mulderig, Gerald P. "Gertrude Buck's Rhetorical Theory and Modern Composition Teaching." *Rhetoric Society Quarterly* 14.3–4 (1984): 95–104.

KENNETH DUVA BURKE
(1897–1993)

Tilly Warnock

Kenneth Burke was a man of life and of letters whose career as a rhetorician, literary and cultural critic, fiction writer, poet, editor, and translator extended from the 1920s into the 1990s. He redefined "literature" as "equipment for living" and considered "human life as a project in 'composition' " (*Attitudes* 173). As his theories and practices demonstrate, Burke's personal and professional biographies are interrelated.

He was born on May 5, 1897 in Pittsburgh, Pennsylvania, the son of James Leslie Burke and Lillyan Duva Burke. He graduated from Peabody High School in Pittsburgh in 1915, where he formed lifelong friendships with several classmates, Malcolm Cowley, Susan Jenkins, and James Light.

In 1916, Burke went to Ohio State University for a semester. He then attended Columbia University in 1917 but decided in early 1918 to quit because he became "horrified at the realization of what college can do to a man of promise" and because he wanted to begin his "existence as a Flaubert" in Greenwich Village (Paul, *Correspondence* 256).

In 1919 he married Lily Batterham, and in 1920 they bought a farm on Amity Road in Andover, New Jersey, although Burke continued to work in New York. He and his family of three daughters lived in New York and in Andover.

In 1920 he published four stories in *The Dial*, and in 1924 he published his first book, a collection of short stories, *The White Oxen, and Other Stories*. In 1925 he published in *The Dial* his first critical essay, "Psychology of Form," which he later included in *Counter-Statement*. Burke also published stories, essays, reviews, and translations in magazines such as *Broom, Secession, The Freeman, Vanity Fair, The Bookman*, and *The Dial*.

He worked at *The Dial* from 1923 until 1929 in various editorial positions and was music critic there from 1927 to 1929. In 1928 he received the *Dial*

Prize for distinguished service to American letters. From 1926 to 1929 Burke researched drug addiction for the Laura Spelman Rockefeller Memorial Trust and worked as a staff member for the Bureau of Hygiene.

In 1931 he published his first book of criticism, *Counter-Statement*, reprinted in 1960. He published in 1932 his novel, *Towards a Better Life: Being a Series of Epistles, or Declamations*, revised in 1966. Burke and Lily divorced in 1933; he married her sister, Elizabeth (Libby) Batterham, with whom he had two sons.

In 1935 Burke won a Guggenheim Fellowship and spoke at the American Writers Congress on the subject of "Revolutionary Symbolism in America." He argued that "people" would be a more effective term than "workers" to persuade Americans after the Great Depression to join the Communist Party. His focus on the rhetoric of the symbol failed to persuade a critical audience.

Burke had a distinguished career as a teacher, although he never finished college nor held a tenured position at a university. In 1937 he began teaching at the New School for Social Research as a lecturer in the practice and theory of literary criticism. He lectured at the University of Chicago in 1938, and from 1943 to 1961 he taught at Bennington College. He held visiting professorships at several universities, including Harvard University, the University of Washington, the University of San Diego, Princeton University, and Emory University.

Between 1933 and 1969 Burke published his other major critical works: *Permanence and Change: An Anatomy of Purpose*, published in 1935 and revised in 1954; *Attitudes toward History*, published in 1937 and revised in 1959; *The Philosophy of Literary Form*, published in 1941 and revised in 1967; *A Grammar of Motives*, published in 1945; *A Rhetoric of Motives*, published in 1950; *The Rhetoric of Religion: Studies in Logology*, published in 1961; and *Language as Symbolic Action: Essays on Life, Literature, and Method*, published in 1966.

In later editions of his major works, Burke framed and thus revised earlier versions by adding prefaces, introductions, afterwards, and appendices, all of which provided "perspective by incongruity" and insight from "retrospective arrangement."

Throughout his career, Burke wrote poetry, fiction, and music, as well as criticism. In 1955 he published a collection of poems, *Book of Moments; Poems, 1915–1954*, and in 1968 he published *Collected Poems, 1915–1967*, the augmented version of *The Complete White Oxen: Collected Short Fiction*, and "Dramatism," which appeared in *The International Encyclopedia of the Social Sciences*. He published a series of lectures, *Dramatism and Development*, in 1972 and "Dramatism and Logology" in 1985.

Throughout his life, Burke worked with major writers, critics, and visual artists who became his friends, including William Carlos Williams, Matthew Josephson, Theodore Roethke, Marianne Moore, Jean Toomer, R. P. Blackmur, Alfred Stiegletz, Georgia O'Keefe, Allen Tate, Katherine Anne Porter, Hart Crane, Stanley Edgar Hyman, Ralph Ellison, and others. He exchanged letters, articles, and poems that record Burke's role as friend, editor, and critic and his ways of thinking through issues about art, language, literature, and life.

In recognition of his influence, Burke was given honorary degrees by Dartmouth College, Fairfield University, Northwestern University, Kenyon College, and Emory University, among others. In 1967 the American Academy of Arts and Sciences invited him to be a member, and Brandeis University gave him the Special Award for Notable Achievement in the Arts. The New Jersey Association of Teachers of English gave him the Poet of the Year Award in 1968, and the American Academy of Arts and Sciences presented him the Award for Contribution to the Humanities in 1977. He received the National Medal for Literature and the Gold Medal for Eminence in Belles Lettres in 1981 and the George Herbert Mead Award from the Society for the Study of Interaction in 1982.

Burke maintained his humility and his humor, referring to his works as "boikwoiks" and to himself as the "word man," "we," "logologist," and "Burke." Using the "comic corrective," Burke continued throughout his life to imagine things "other than they are," as a way of assessing what is and what might be and as a means of figuring out what might convince *animal symbolicum* to use language wisely.

Burke's wife Libby died in 1969. When he died at 96 at his home on Amity Road in Andover in 1993, he was survived by two daughters, two sons, and twelve grandchildren.

BURKE'S RHETORICAL THEORY OF LANGUAGE AS SYMBOLIC ACTION

Kenneth Burke's criticism, developed over seven decades, was initially his counterstatement to ideas about art and literature flourishing in the 1920s, particularly symbolist aesthetics and formalist criticism. He continued to widen the scope and circumference of his rhetoric to critique cultural and technological forces that led to the series of wars through which he lived: World War I, the Great Depression, World War II, the Korean War, civil rights violence, the Vietnam War, the Cold War, Star wars, drug wars, the Gulf War, and many more.

Burke did not fight in physical battles, but the primary aim of his rhetoric is to combat attitudes and actions that prevent people from "getting along" with each other (*Attitudes* 256) and to demonstrate how people can fight verbally rather than physically. His rhetoric is dedicated on the title page of *A Grammar of Motives* to the proposition that *animal symbolicum* has the means—language—to replace war and the kill with persuasive uses of language: "*ad bellum purificandum.*"

This overall motive leads Burke to select "rhetoric" as his key term because it is the "terministic screen" that most directly addresses how people understand and misunderstand each other and how they might learn more effectively to come to terms rather than to war. Burke maintains "rhetoric" as his key term, subordinating other perspectives, such as "poetics," "politics," "economics," and "religion," because he believed that "rhetoric" would most likely yield the consequences he sought, and other terministic screens could be used to achieve his rhetorical aims.

The development of Burke's rhetoric from this motive can be tracked in many ways, each of which, as he shows us, is motivated and consequential. Terms, theories, attitudes, and approaches are never neutral.

My primary motive for selecting a developmental approach to Burke's rhetoric in the following discussion is that it emphasizes how Burke continued to revise his terms, theories, and attitudes throughout his career to make them work for his own purposes and to persuade his readers. Approaching Burke's rhetoric as recursive and revisionary also follows one of Burke's leads as to how to read his rhetoric.

In his "Preface to the Second Edition" of *Counter-Statement*, written in 1932, Burke says that the "gist" of the book is in the theory of form and the summary of it on page 124 in "Lexicon Rhetoricae." He adds that this theory and the summary may also be the gist "of the books by me that grew out of it" (2nd ed. *Counter-Statement* xi).

Like any perspective, this one is both a reflection and a deflection. A "gain" of this angle is that it emphasizes revision; a "loss" is that it minimizes difference. It suggests a coherent linear and recursive progress but obscures the digressive movement of his criticism. And while it dramatizes Burke's mind at work, it does not stress how Burke's writing responds to others and to world situations, except in the argument that Burke's rhetoric is a counterstatement to ideas that lead to war and the kill.

Further, a developmental approach to Burke's rhetoric allows attention to each work, but it allows only a little attention to any single work. As it stresses revision, it is in part a foundational approach, one that conflicts with Burke's view that rhetoric deals with matters of doubt and uncertainty.

Aware of the limitations of this approach that presents identification, dramatism, logology, and the comic corrective as outgrowths of his theory of form, I attempt to follow another of Burke's leads, expressed in *how he writes* rather than in *what he advocates*. I blur clear-cut distinctions by taking his "roundabout" approach, by resisting the (rotten) perfectionist tendency to make matters "crystal clear" (*Attitudes* 86), by providing "perspective by incongruity," and by refusing to make "final decisions" (*Grammar* 117). I admit that "a direct hit is not likely here" and that the "best [I] can do is to try different approaches towards the same center, whenever the opportunity offers" (*Rhetoric* 137).

THE THEORY OF FORM IN *COUNTER-STATEMENT* AND ITS RAMIFICATIONS

In opposition to the aesthetics of symbolism and the pure art movement that claimed to remove art from life, Burke defines "form" in his first book as action, specifically as the arousing and fulfilling of desires and appetites, and he presents art as persuasive action in the world. From his perspective, a work of literature addresses readers and aims to be read and accepted; in other words, art is rhetoric.

In "Lexicon Rhetoricae," he explains that "[a] work has form in so far as one part of it leads a reader to anticipate another part, to be gratified by the sequence" (2nd ed. *Counter-Statement* 124). Form as action has five aspects: progressive, including syllogistic and qualitative progression; repetitive; conventional; and minor or incidental form. Progressive and repetitive form are obviously active, but Burke demonstrates how all of the forms are active in that they engage readers in the creation of meaning. He argues that the motive of all art is to communicate, and the consequence of all effective art is change in the audience.

Counter to understanding in the 1930s of the symbol as removed from reality, Burke grounds the symbol by redefining the word *symbol* as an "abstraction from a situation," a "strategy for encompassing a situation," and as a "pattern of experience." Symbols, from words to works of art, are means of titling or summarizing complex situations, so that they can be dealt with. Our language is a "terministic screen" that constructs the world, as the world, in turn, constructs us. For him, forms of the world, text, and mind are dialectically interrelated, and human agents act by using these forms purposefully.

Throughout *Counter-Statement* Burke builds toward his definition of a theory in "Lexicon" by examining literary texts, by Flaubert, Gide, Mann, De Gourmont, and others, that move readers to participate in the creation of meaning. He builds his theory also in "Psychology and Form" when he distinguishes between a psychology of information and the psychology of form by demonstrating how texts weigh form and information differently. He also builds toward his theory by outlining the poetic process by which a writer attempts to discover what will probably lead readers to an attitude of acceptance of a work of art.

The process, as Burke defines it, presents writing and reading as dialectically interrelated actions that are personally and culturally situated. Writing and reading are actions by people for specific motives, in particular contexts, using language. More specifically in Burke's terms, poets "channel" their emotions into symbols that are common to the culture but that poets "individuate" for their purposes. Audiences respond by reindividuating the symbols, because of their nature as *animal symbolicum* and because of their personal and collective motives and contexts. For the writer and reader to communicate, there must be a division between them but also a shared "margin of overlap."

In *Counter-Statement*, then, Burke revises "symbol" and "form" into actions, "literature" and "art" into communication, and poetics into rhetoric. From this work on, he continues to use these terms, but he does so assuming that his revisions have been accepted by readers as they have been by him. Recognition of Burke's redefinitions questions the familiar claim that Burke moves from aesthetic concerns in the 1920s to social concerns in the 1930s and that he broadened the circumference of his analysis from self-expression and literature to communication in general and discourse of all forms. From a developmental perspective, Burke argued in his first book of criticism that literature is social and cultural action, self-expression is communication through cultural forms, and aesthetics is rhetoric. Instead of replacing "aesthetics" with "action," Burke redefines "aesthetics" as action. Instead of replacing literature with communication in general, he revises the definition of literature into "equipment for living." What Burke shows readers is how to revise words and change attitudes and actions.

Implicit in Burke's theory of form in 1931 is his "Definition of Man," sketched in *A Rhetoric of Religion* and articulated more fully in *Language as Symbolic Action* in 1966. By his definition, human beings are the "symbol-using (symbol-making, symbol-misusing) animal" (*Language* 3). While "all living organisms interpret many of the signs about them," *animal symbolicum* can "extend the scope of the critical process" (*Permanence* 5). Unlike our animal counterparts, people can "interpret our interpretations" (*Permanence* 6).

Burke later revises his definition of man into a definition of human beings and modifies "symbol-using animal" into "Bodies That Learn Language," in keeping with his growing awareness of the extent to which language uses people and abuses people. In early works he emphasizes how people are agents who choose language symbols for particular reasons, but he also demonstrates how people are constructed by language, by scenic constraints, and by their biologies. Throughout, Burke makes clear that linguistic choices are ethical decisions that are motivated by and consequential in the world. Choices, therefore, are not free; nevertheless, people must act.

He constantly reminds readers that "[l]anguage, to be used properly, must be 'discounted' ": "We must remind ourselves that, whatever *correspondence* there is between a *word* and the *thing* it names, the word is *not* the thing" (*Rhetoric of Religion* 18). The correspondences people create between words and things are not, however, inconsequential. In addition, Burke demonstrates the discounting within language in his discussions of the linguistic marvel, the negative. A word means one thing because it does not mean another, and a word means one thing in one context and something else in another. Words imply their opposites, as the stated evokes the unstated. Rhetorically, the hortatory negative or the "thou shalt not" exists along with every command, law, and attempt to order and reorder. Any assertion carries with it an assertion to the contrary, or there would be no motive to assert.

In later works, Burke circles back to critique and builds on some of his terms, assumptions, and arguments in *Counter-Statement*, so that they work in new contexts. In *Philosophy of Literary Form*, in 1941, Burke extends his early argument that art is communication when he says that "there is no 'pure' literature" and that "[e]verything is medicine" (3rd ed. *Philosophy* 293). All art attempts to *do* something to, or have an effect on, someone. The critic's role is to counter and correct, if not cure.

Similarly, Burke expands his theory of form into a rhetoric of history in

Attitudes toward History, into rhetorics of science, education, and religion in *Permanence and Change*, into a rhetoric of literature in *The Philosophy of Literary Form*, into a rhetoric of philosophy in *A Rhetoric of Motives*, and into a rhetoric of religion in *The Rhetoric of Religion*. In each, he analyzes the motives and persuasiveness of progressive, repetitive, conventional, and minor or incidental forms, as well as the revisionary force of symbolic action.

Because of the range of his rhetoric, scholars in many disciplines acknowledge Burke's influence and recognize his contributions to literary, cultural, and rhetorical studies through his theory of language as symbolic action. More specifically, rhetoricians praise him for what is considered his major contribution to contemporary rhetoric and to the rhetorical tradition—Burke's revision of Aristotle's persuasion by his notion of identification.

IDENTIFICATION

Burke's image of "margin of overlap" in *Counter-Statement* becomes his theory of identification in *A Rhetoric of Motives* by way of his discussion of the universal paradox of substance in *A Grammar of Motives*. In this case, as elsewhere, Burke revises terms by using them in different scenes, and he demonstrates how terms, like motives and consequences, change according to the context.

Identification is a key term in Burke's rhetoric because it names the cooperation between writer and reader that for him is essential for persuasion. Communication is the "dancing of attitudes" and a "courtship ritual"; for Burke, communication is "a generalized form of love" (*Rhetoric of Motives* 37). The distance between people, between their individual bodies, motivates them to seek a "margin of overlap" so that they can communicate.

In *Counter-Statement* he defines symbols as "abstractions from situations" and "strategies for encompassing situations" and shows a dialectical relationship between words and worlds. In *A Grammar of Motives*, Burke goes further to argue that word symbols are not only drawn from specific contexts but that they are meaningful within the contexts for which they are adapted. For example, he revises accepted notions of substance as essence into substance as *that which is* because of *that which it is not*. He discusses the words with "stance" as their root in general, whose etymological root denotes place or placement, to argue that we must understand all terms contextually and understand our terms as acts in the process of revision.

After cataloging types of substance, Burke incorporates all under "dialectical substance," which he says is the "over-all category of dramatism" (*Grammar* 33). Later he develops his theory of Dramatism more broadly, but here he defines "dramatism" as the dialectical relationships among terms and between terms and contexts. He explains that "symbolic communication is not a merely external instrument, but also intrinsic to men as agents": "Its motivational prop-

erties characterize both 'the human situation' and what men are 'in themselves' "
(*Grammar* 33). Here he anticipates his later redefinition of human beings as
"Bodies That Learn Language."

Burke explores the ambiguities of substance in an attempt to explain his
concept of identification. Having revised the term "substance," by dissociating
it from "essence" and realigning it with "place," "position," and "scene," he
revises self and identity through "identification": "In being identified with B, A
is 'substantially one' with a person other than himself. Yet at the same time he
remains unique, an individual locus of motives. Thus he is both joined and
separate, at once a distinct substance and consubstantial with another" (*Rhetoric*
21). For Burke, writers and readers must identify with each other if persuasion
is to occur: "You persuade a man only insofar as you can talk his language by
speech, gesture, tonality, order, attitude, idea, *identifying* your ways with his"
(*Rhetoric* 55).

Burke develops terms not to fix people and ideas once and for all but to
suggest the "active nature" of categories, terms, and perspectives (*Philosophy*
296). He resists the reduction of forms to formulas and formulations because
he believes in the usefulness of their active and generative possibilities. His aim
is seldom to resolve contradictions and ambiguities. Instead, he says his task is
"to study and clarify the *resources* of ambiguity" (*Grammar* xix).

Because his overall motive is to help people bridge differences and transcend
conflicts, he must be both realistic and idealistic. He therefore acknowledges the
contradictions in *animal symbolicum*, in language, and in culture. He deals with
matters at hand and chooses the "lightning rod" approach of Aristotle, which
takes in and reforms forces, as opposed to the "censorship" principle of Plato,
which excludes or suppresses (2nd ed. *Counter-Statement* xii).

Burke is perhaps best known as the rhetorician who replaced Aristotle's persuasion with identification. An important qualification of this claim, one in keeping with this developmental approach to his rhetoric, is that Burke understood
identification as essential for persuasion to occur: Instead of replacing persuasion, he argues that identification is prior to persuasion. A more subtle modification to the claim that Burke replaced persuasion by identification is necessary
because for him identification *is* persuasion, in that it requires that people—both
writer and reader—revise themselves to some extent. Therefore, identification
is already persuasion.

More specifically, as he argues in *Counter-Statement*, the appeal of forms is
that they create and gratify needs and, in this sense, "form *is* the appeal" (2nd
ed. *Counter-Statement* 138). Formal identification relies on collaboration between writer and reader, both of whom participate in the making of meaning.
But identification is even more complicated. The killer, for example, identifies
with the killed in an act of murder, and soldiers on opposing sides "cooperate"
in war. As terms define each other, they are implicit in their opposites. Burke
uses *identification* synonymously with *consubstantiation* at times, but he also

presents identification often as partial, temporary, and externally motivated, as well as formal.

His dialectical view of the individual and society also informs his concept of identification. He says that "there *is* the individual" and that each person "is a unique combination of experiences, a unique set of situations, a unique aggregate of mutually re-enforcing and conflicting 'corporate we's' " (*Attitudes* 289). He draws on the work of George Herbert Mead on social interaction to develop his representative anecdote of the parlor room, in which people express themselves and are revised in conversational give-and-take that long preceded them and that will continue long after they are gone. Burke warns that, however social the nature of symbolic action is, individuals are also defined by their own central nervous systems.

Through symbolic action, the individual builds "his symbolic bridges between his own unique combination and the social pattern" (*Attitudes* 289). Through symbolic pontifications, mergers, and extensions, people form and implement their individual roles by "utilizing the bureaucratic body" of society. In all acts of identification, writers and readers are to varying degrees revised, and their identities are transformed through interaction with others. Burke shows how people, in acts of communication, "must 'die' and be 'reborn' " as they come to terms with each other (289). Courtship rituals, the dancing of attitudes, conversations in the parlor, disturbances in the Human Barnyard, and the Wars of Nerves all rely on identification of some sort and have the potential for death and rebirth.

Having established the dialectic and dialogic relationship between the individual and society through common language, Burke can shift his emphasis according to his specific purposes, audiences, and situations, and he can use "identification" with flexibility. He can also expand the notion of identification to include the dramatic interactions among various elements within any act of communication.

DRAMATISM AND LOGOLOGY

Burke thus revises his theory of forms into his theory of identification and then into his theory of Dramatism. Language for Burke is action and performance. He explains that the "Dramatistic screen involves a methodic tracking down of the implications in the idea of symbolic action, and of man as the kind of being that is particularly distinguished by an aptitude for such action" (*Language* 54). He builds Dramatism on the metaphorical claim that "All the world's a stage" but denies that Dramatism is a metaphor. He also builds Dramatism on human biology and the desire to communicate and on his belief that rhetoric is "an approach to specially human motivation" (54).

He distinguishes between "action" and "motion" to differentiate between symbolicity and animality and between conscious acts and unconscious motions.

The act/motion distinction defines action as a matter of choice and of ethics, within given contexts, and, as with Burke's other sets of differences, he demonstrates how the categories result from rhetorical purposes rather than ontological differences.

What follows from "action" as his key term is drama, then conflict, then victimage and scapegoating, and then the kill. In his "Definition of Man," people become "rotten with perfection." But what follows from action may also take the "Upward Way" to perfection and transcending, but only temporarily before the negative sets in. For Burke, language itself tends toward absolutes and hierarchies, but upward and downward ways may be countered by "ways in," "ways out," and "ways roundabout" and by "rebirth rituals," whereby one must "die" and be "reborn" (*Attitudes* 289).

Burke summarizes Dramatism in his Pentad, his five terms with ratios for possible interrelationships among the terms. The Pentad is a form for analyzing language as action, human motives, and human relations—"act," "scene," "agent," "agency," and "purpose." Once again, the Pentad is meant to generate rather than contain or constrain. The agent who uses the Pentad, for example, can change the scope and circumference of each of the terms and select among the possible ratios among the terms, depending on the agent's purposes and on scenic constraints. Although "audience" is not a separate term in the Pentad, it is implicit in "scene," "purpose," "act," "agency," and even in "agent."

Because of its apparent simplicity and efficiency, the Pentad is often extracted from Burke's rhetoric and treated as a formula for the analysis of motives and acts. But Burke's own use of the terms of the Pentad presents them as forms of action. The Pentad is a heuristic with a generative power that can be multiplied by using the ratios among terms or that can be eliminated when the terms and ratios are misused. As with his other terms, the terms of the Pentad are general and changing, until they are applied in specific contexts. Burke always aims to reduce complexities without being reductive.

Although "attitude" is also not a term of the Pentad, he defines "attitude" as an "incipient action," and in a sense, "act" entails attitude. Since acts arise from situations, the term "attitude" is also implicit in "scene." And since attitudes also motivate agents and purposes and affect the selection of agencies, the term "attitude" informs all terms of the Pentad, as attitude informs human actions in general. Burke undercuts a strictly formal interpretation of the Pentad when he adds a sixth term and explains he would have included "attitude" and developed a hexad if he had six instead of five children.

The terminological orientation of Dramatism and the Pentad extends in *The Rhetoric of Religion* into "Studies in Logology" or "studies in words-about-words" (vi). His "logological thesis" argues that "since the theological use of language is thorough, the close study of theology and its forms will provide us with good insight into the nature of language itself as a motive" (vi).

Logology thus extends the range of Burke's rhetoric as developed in earlier works as he focuses more closely on how words define words and how language constructs people and worlds. "God" is a "god-term" that unifies actions, attitudes, and other terms as it transcends and revises them. Any symbol is "an abstraction from a situation" and a "strategy for encompassing a situation." As logologist, Burke examines the implications of how language works, particularly to create technology that has the power to threaten, create, and destroy human life.

Because of logology's emphasis on how words define words and how the relationships between words and things are arbitrary, recent critics align Burke with poststructuralism. Burke's discussions of "discounting" and of the paradox of the negative—in which words for the nonverbal discuss the nonverbal in terms of "what it is not" (*Rhetoric of Religion* 18)—anticipate Derrida and his notion of *différance*. Identifying Burke with deconstruction and poststructuralism yields interesting results, but such alignments, like all alignments according to Burke's rhetoric, must be first understood as rhetorically motivated.

For example, Cary Nelson, in "Writing as the Accomplice of Language: Kenneth Burke and Poststructuralism," offers a "counter-Burke" to the "humanistic Burke." He defines the issue as "whether one sees the symbol-using animal in Burke as an independent agent or as a figure occupying the role of agency within a verbal drama that is in a sense already written for us" (158).

In Burke's terms, the issue might be which view of symbol-using animal—as agent or agency—is more useful for specific purposes in particular contexts. Further, Burke would probably extend the question to ask whether symbol-using animal might be profitably seen at times also as "scene," "act," "purpose," or a combination of these and other terms of the Pentad. Issues of agency, identity, positionality, and subjectivity are central to Burke, but the rhetorical usefulness of such terms remains primary. For him an assertion is not a claim of certainty or truth but of what might work in a particular scene. Rhetoric stands the test of the collective.

Because Burke selected "rhetoric" as his key term and worked persistently yet playfully with it for seven decades, his "main ideal of criticism" is "to use all that is there to use" (*Philosophy* 23). Critics choose among the available kinds of criticism, based on their purposes, the texts and context that they read and participate in, and the probable consequences of their selections, in order to be persuasive in given contexts. Burke's motive for criticism is commonplace yet not conventional in literary criticism: to help people get along and avoid war and to provide "equipment for living" and "strategies for living." Essential equipment includes his action theories of form, identification, dramatism, and logology but also the comic corrective.

THE COMIC CORRECTIVE

Burke practices what he advocates in order to persuade his readers. He does so by questioning his own assertions, gaining perspective by incongruity, and inviting his readers to collaborate in the construction of meaning. His rhetoric is a system that resists systematization and final answers because the "attitude of attitudes" for Burke is the "Comic Corrective" that sees people as mistaken, not vicious, and perceives the world as it is and as it might be.

The comic frame or corrective is the resource that helps people imagine revisions of the way things are. The comic attitude, which entails attitudes of doubt and uncertainty, accounts in large part for how Burke gets along with his readers and encourages them to accept what he says and does. When he asks himself and his readers, "Now, where are we?" he asks for help, for cooperation, for shared meaning-making. When he admits that the "reader need not have followed these random 'radiations' too closely" and that he "could just have well have taken countless other zigzag paths," he undermines his own authority and encourages readers to identify with him. He shares authority with readers when he explains he can touch upon matters "in hardly more than a headline manner" (*Attitudes* 400) and that, "where problems of terminology are concerned," he "must always keep on the move" (*Language* 73–74).

Similarly, Burke plays with all of his terms and theories to gain "liquidity," "dissociation," and "pliancy" and to resist rigidity. He reduces international and interpersonal motives and conflicts to his image of the universe as "something like a piece of cheese" that can be "sliced in an infinite number of ways," so that one person's cuts often conflict with another's cuts (*Permanence* 103). With the comic perspective, he offers attitudes, terms, and actions that will probably, he calculates, help people avoid war and death:

The progress of humane enlightenment can go no further than in picturing people not as *vicious*, but as *mistaken*. When you add that people are *necessarily* mistaken, that *all* people are exposed to situations in which they must act as fools, that *every* insight contains its own special kind of blindness, you complete the comic circle, returning again to the lesson of humility that underlies great tragedy. The audience, from its vantage point, sees the operation of errors that the characters of the play cannot see; thus seeing from two angles at once, it is chastened by dramatic irony; it is admonished to remember that when intelligence means *wisdom* (in contrast with the modern tendency to look upon intelligence as merely *coefficient of power* for heightening our ability to get things, be they good things or bad), it requires fear, resignation, the sense of limits, as an important ingredient. (*Attitudes* 41–42)

According to Burke, the comic frame makes a person a "student of himself" and makes "it possible for him to 'transcend' occasions when he has been tricked or cheated, since he can readily put such discouragements in his 'assets' column, under the head of 'experience' " (171). This frame "considers human life as a project in 'composition' " (173) and provides the "*charitable* attitude towards people that is required for the purposes of persuasion and co-operation" (166).

Burke's rhetoric teaches us how to revise our terms and attitudes by what he says but also by what he does. He demonstrates throughout his writing how to analyze what is and what was, in order to imagine what might be and to assess the probable consequences of our symbolic actions.

BIBLIOGRAPHY

Primary Sources

Burke, Kenneth. *Attitudes toward History.* 3rd ed. 1937; 1959. Berkeley: University of California Press, 1984.

———. *Book of Moments: Poems, 1915–1954.* Los Altos, CA: Hermes Publications, 1955.

———. *Collected Poems, 1915–1967.* Berkeley: University of California Press, 1968.

———. *The Complete White Oxen: Collected Short Fiction of Kenneth Burke.* Berkeley: University of California Press, 1968.

———. *Counter-Statement.* Berkeley: University of California Press, 1931.

———. *Counter-Statement.* 2nd ed. Berkeley: University of California Press, 1968.

———. "Dramatism." *The International Encyclopedia of Social Sciences.* Ed. D. L. Sills. New York: MacMillan/Free Press, 1968. 445–52.

———. *Dramatism and Development.* Barre, MA: Clark University Press, 1972.

———. "Dramatism and Logology." *Communication Quarterly* 33 (1985): 89–93.

———. *A Grammar of Motives.* Berkeley: University of California Press, 1945.

———. *Language as Symbolic Action: Essays on Life, Literature, and Method.* Berkeley: University of California Press, 1966.

———. "Methodological Repression and/or Strategies of Containment." *Critical Inquiry* 5 (1978): 401–16.

———. "(Nonsymbolic) Motion/(Symbolic) Action." *Critical Inquiry* 4 (1978): 809–38.

———. *Permanence and Change: An Anatomy of Purpose.* 3rd ed. 1935; 1954. Berkeley: University of California Press, 1984.

———. *The Philosophy of Literary Form: Studies in Symbolic Action.* 3rd ed. 1941; 1967. Berkeley: University of California Press, 1973.

———. *A Rhetoric of Motives.* 1950. Berkeley: University of California Press, 1969.

———. *The Rhetoric of Religion: Studies in Logology.* 1961. Berkeley: University of California Press, 1970.

———. *Towards a Better Life: Being a Series of Epistles, or Declamations.* 1932. Berkeley: University of California Press, 1966.

———. *The White Oxen, and Other Stories.* 1924. Berkeley: University of California Press, 1968.

Criticism

Alcorn, Marshall W., Jr. *Narcissism and the Literary Libido: Rhetoric, Text, and Subjectivity.* New York: New York University Press, 1994.

Allen, Virginia. "Some Implications of Burke's 'Ways of Knowing' for Composition Theory." *Journal of Advanced Composition* 3.1–2 (1982): 10–21.

Biesecker, Barbara A. *Addressing Postmodernity: Kenneth Burke, Rhetoric, and a Theory of Social Change.* Tuscaloosa: University of Alabama Press, 1997.

Booth, Wayne. *Critical Understanding: The Powers and Limits of Pluralism.* Chicago: University of Chicago Press, 1979.

———. *A Rhetoric of Irony.* Chicago: University of Chicago Press, 1974.

Brock, Bernard L. *Kenneth Burke and Contemporary European Thought: Rhetoric in Transition.* Tuscaloosa: University of Alabama Press, 1995.

Brummett, Barry, ed. *Landmark Essays on Kenneth Burke.* Davis, CA: Hermagoras Press, 1993.

Burks, Don M., ed. *Rhetoric, Philosophy, and Literature: An Exploration.* West Lafayette, IN: Purdue University Press, 1978.

Bygrave, Stephen. *Kenneth Burke: Rhetoric and Ideology.* New York: Routledge, 1993.

Carter, C. Allen. *Kenneth Burke and the Scapegoat Process.* Norman: University of Oklahoma Press, 1996.

Chesebro, James W., ed. *Extensions of the Burkeian System.* Tuscaloosa: University of Alabama Press, 1993.

Clifford, John. "Burke and the Tradition of Democratic Schooling: Festschrift in Honor of Ann E. Berthoff." *Audits of Meaning.* Ed. Louise Z. Smith. Portsmouth, NH: Boynton/Cook, 1988. 29–40.

Coe, Richard M. "Beyond Diction: Using Burke to Empower Words—and Wordlings." *Rhetoric Review* 11.2 (1993): 368–77.

———. "Defining Rhetoric—and Us." *Journal of Advanced Composition* 10.1 (1990): 39–52.

———. *Form and Substance: An Advanced Rhetoric.* New York: John Wiley and Sons, 1981.

Comprone, Joseph. "Kenneth Burke and the Teaching of Writing." *College Composition and Communication* 29.4 (1978): 336–40.

Condit, Celeste Michelle. "Post-Burke: Transcending the Substance of Dramatism." *Quarterly Journal of Speech* 78.3 (1992): 349–55.

Covino, William A. *The Art of Wondering: A Revisionist Return to the History of Rhetoric.* Portsmouth, NH: Boynton/Cook, 1988.

Crusius, Timothy W. "A Case for Kenneth Burke's Dialectic and Rhetoric." *Philosophy and Rhetoric* 19.1 (1986): 23–37.

———. "Kenneth Burke's *Auscultation*: A 'De-Struction' of Marxist Dialectic and Rhetoric." *Rhetorica* 6.4 (1988): 355–79.

———. "Orality in Kenneth Burke's Dialectic." *Philosophy and Rhetoric* 21.2 (1988): 116–30.

Frank, Armin Paul. *Kenneth Burke.* New York: Twayne, 1969.

Hassett, Michael. "Constructing an Ethical Writer for the Postmodern Scene." *Rhetoric Society Quarterly* (Annual Edition) 25 (1995): 179–96.

———. "Sophisticated Burke: Kenneth Burke as Neosophistic Rhetorician." *Rhetoric Review* 13.2 (1995): 371–90.

Heath, Robert L. "Kenneth Burke's Break with Formalism." *Quarterly Journal of Speech* 70 (1984): 132–43.

———. *Realism and Relativism: A Perspective on Kenneth Burke.* Macon, GA: Mercer University Press, 1986.

Henderson, Greig E. *Kenneth Burke: Literature and Language as Symbolic Action.* Athens: University of Georgia Press, 1988.

Holland, Virginia. *Counterpoint: Kenneth Burke and Aristotle's Theories of Rhetoric.* New York: Philosophical Library, 1959.

Hyman, Stanley Edgar. *The Armed Vision: A Study in the Methods of Literary Criticism*. New York: Knopf, 1948.

Hyman, S. E., and Barbara Karmillers, eds. *Perspectives by Incongruity*. Bloomington: University of Indiana Press, 1964.

———. *Terms for Order*. Bloomington: University of Indiana Press, 1964.

Jameson, Fredric. "Ideology and Symbolic Action." *Critical Inquiry* 5.2 (1978–1979): 417–22.

———. "The Symbolic Inference: Or, Kenneth Burke and Ideological Analysis." *Critical Inquiry* 4.3 (1977–1978): 507–23.

Jay, Paul. "Kenneth Burke and the Motives of Eloquence." *American Literary History* 1.3 (1989): 535–53.

———. "Modernism, Postmodernism, and Critical Style: The Case of Burke and Derrida." *Genre* 21.3 (1988): 339–58.

———, ed. *The Selected Correspondence of Kenneth Burke and Malcolm Cowley 1915–1981*. New York: Viking, 1988.

Lentricchia, Frank. *Criticism and Social Change*. Chicago: University of Chicago Press, 1983.

Lewis, Clayton W. "Burke's Act in *A Rhetoric of Motives*." *College English* 46.4 (1984): 368–76.

McMahon, Robert. "Kenneth Burke's Divine Comedy: The Literary Form of *The Rhetoric of Religion*." *Publications of the Modern Language Association* 104.1 (1989): 53–63.

Nelson, Cary. "Writing as the Accomplice of Language: Kenneth Burke and Poststructuralism." *The Legacy of Kenneth Burke*. Ed. Herbert W. Simons and Trevor Melia. Madison: University of Wisconsin Press, 1989. 156–73.

Payne, David. *Coping with Failure: The Therapeutic Uses of Rhetoric*. Columbia: University of South Carolina Press, 1989.

Rueckert, William H., ed. *Critical Responses to Kenneth Burke*. Minneapolis: University of Minnesota Press, 1969.

———. *Encounters with Kenneth Burke*. Urbana: University of Illinois Press, 1994.

———. *Kenneth Burke and the Drama of Human Relations*. Berkeley: University of California Press, 1963.

Sheard, Cynthia Miecznikowski. "*Kairos* and Kenneth Burke's Psychology of Political and Social Communication." *College English* 55.3 (1993): 291–310.

Simons, Herbert W., and Trevor Melia, eds. *The Legacy of Kenneth Burke*. Madison: University of Wisconsin Press, 1989.

Southwell, S. B. *Kenneth Burke and Martin Heidegger: With a Note against Deconstruction*. Gainesville: University of Florida Press, 1987.

"Special Issue on Kenneth Burke." *PRE/TEXT* 6.3–4 (1985).

White, Hayden, and Margaret Brose, eds. *Representing Kenneth Burke*. Baltimore: Johns Hopkins University Press, 1982. 119–49.

Winterowd, W. Ross. "Kenneth Burke: An Annotated Glossary of His Terministic Screen and a 'Statistical' Survey of His Major Concepts." *Rhetoric Society Quarterly* 15.3–4 (1985): 145–77.

FRANCIS CHRISTENSEN
(1902–1970)

Russell Greer and Michael G. Moran

Francis Christensen was born in 1902 in Salt Lake City, Utah, the son of Lorenzo and Hilma Christensen. He studied English and philosophy at the University of Utah, graduating with his bachelor's degree in English in 1927 from the University of California at Berkeley before attending Harvard University. There he earned a second master's degree in English in 1931 and a doctorate in 1934. He taught English as an instructor at the University of Wisconsin–Madison from 1934 to 1937 and at DePauw University in Greencastle, Indiana, in 1938. In 1939 he accepted a faculty position at the University of Southern California (USC), Los Angeles, where he taught for 30 years, retiring as a full professor in 1969. After leaving USC, he was associated briefly with Northern Illinois University in DeCalb, Illinois. He died in July 1970.

While teaching at USC, Christensen established himself as a leading figure in composition studies by publishing a series of articles in *College English* and *College Composition and Communication* between 1963 and 1965. These articles stimulated interest in and enthusiasm for Christensen's structural approach to composition, which he called *generative rhetoric*. In 1967 he published *Notes toward a New Rhetoric: Six Essays for Teachers*, a collection of his essays (a posthumous second edition in 1978, coauthored with his second wife Bonnijean, included three additional essays). Collectively these essays put forward Christensen's theory of generative rhetoric. Rhetorician Lester Faigley calls *Notes* "the most important work on written language during this period" (*Fragments* 81).

CHRISTENSEN'S RHETORICAL THEORY

Francis Christensen was deeply influenced by the increasing importance of linguistics in composition studies in the late 1950s and early 1960s. He developed generative rhetoric in reaction to a disagreement during this period between proponents of "correctness" and those of "usage." As Faigley has described, this split developed largely because of the emergence of sociolinguistics, which challenged traditional judgments about acceptable and unacceptable English. The controversy peaked in September 1961 with the publication of *Webster's Third International Dictionary*, which based its entries on descriptive rather than prescriptive principles. This shift in perspective set off a public debate between those who wanted the dictionary to describe the usage of actual writers and those who wanted it to prescribe what experts consider the correct usage. From this debate, Christensen developed generative rhetoric to defend usage as an important criterion for teaching writing.

He first outlined the basic tenets of this theory in the presidential address given at the opening general session of the California Association of Teachers of English in San Diego in February 1962 (later published in the *Conference Report* and in the first chapter of the second edition of *Notes*). In this address, Christensen rejected following formal rules for their own sake if those rules are out of touch with the living language. He said, "The worst book I ever used in class was a grammar written by a man I know who must have tested every sentence by diagraming it" (Christensen and Christensen 18). Christensen's solution was to begin an inductive study of contemporary American prose writers to discover the underlying structures of the living language. From this study, he learned that professional writers rely on "an astounding use of sentence modifiers, especially appositives and absolute constructions" (18). One particular professional writer, novelist John Erskine, provided a key concept for Christensen's theory with this quotation:

When you write, you make a point, not by subtracting as though you sharpened a pencil, but by adding. . . . What you say is found not in the noun but in what you add to qualify the noun. . . . The noun, the verb, and the main clause serve merely as the base on which meaning will rise. . . . The modifier is the essential part of any sentence. (qtd. in *Notes* 4)

This principle of addition became the cornerstone of Christensen's theory of generative rhetoric.

His theory gives teachers and students a clear, easily understood, formal method for improving writing by teaching how to add layers of complexity: "The teacher can use the idea of levels of structure to urge students to add further levels to what he has already produced, so that the structure itself becomes an aid to discovery" (*Notes* 2).

Christensen applied this understanding of structure first to the sentence and then to the paragraph. He never, however, applied the concept of generative rhetoric to portions of texts longer than the paragraph, although followers of his method would expand his work in that direction. In generative rhetoric, four essential principles apply to both the sentence and the paragraph: (1) addition; (2) direction of movement; (3) levels of abstraction; and (4) texture.

His first principle, addition, is an extension of Erskine's comments and soundly rejects the periodic sentence in favor of what had previously been called the "loose sentence." Christensen renamed this structure "the cumulative sentence" and declared it to be the hallmark of good contemporary writing:

The cumulative sentence is the opposite of the periodic sentence. It does not represent the idea as conceived, pondered over, reshaped, packaged, and delivered cold. It is dynamic rather than static, representing the mind thinking. The main clause . . . exhausts the mere fact of the idea; logically there is nothing more to say. The additions stay with the same idea, probing its bearings and implications, exemplifying it or seeing an analogy or metaphor for it, or reducing it to details. Thus the mere form of the sentence generates ideas. (*Notes* 6)

Examples of the cumulative sentence appear in the second, third, and fifth sentences of this quotation by Christensen.

Closely linked to this principle of "addition" is "direction of movement," by which Christensen accounts for the reading effect of those additions to the sentence and paragraph. Adding modifiers before the words they affect creates a direction of modification in the reading process that can be indicated by "an arrow pointing forward" (*Notes* 5). Adding modifiers after the words they modify creates a different reading experience that can be indicated "by an arrow pointing backward" (5). Generative rhetoric makes writers aware of how modifiers change the reading process. It also urges writers to take advantage of this give-and-take between the main clause and its modifiers to create textual complexity, a sign of mature writers.

Christensen's third principle, "levels of generality" or "levels of abstraction," is a grammatical concept that subdivides the meaning of a sentence among various levels. These levels begin with the main clause, where the main idea is stated in "general or abstract or plural terms" (*Notes* 7). After that main clause appears, the sentence moves to a lower level of generality, or abstraction, or to singular terms, restating the information in the main clause more specifically. The movement to a lower level of generality Christensen calls *subordination*. The presentation of modification on the same level of generality he calls *coordination*. These concepts work in a similar way in paragraphs. In paragraphs the subsequent sentences after the "top" or first sentence expand the idea in concrete terms. Such sentences are subordinated to the top sentence. Christensen notes that there is "no theoretical limit to the number of structural layers or levels, each at a lower level of generality, any or all of them compounded, that a speaker or writer may use" (7). Both sentences and paragraphs can combine coordinated and subordinated structural relations to create complex elements of discourse.

His fourth principle, "texture," is the least developed. He defines it as a descriptive term to account for the effect of additions to the sentence and paragraph. Weak writers who fail to add modifiers create a "thin" or "plain and bare" texture. Strong writers who add modifiers frequently create a "dense or rich" texture (*Notes* 8).

Christensen has enjoyed widespread influence. Part of that influence can be attributed to the curriculum materials that he developed for the Nebraska Curriculum Demonstration Center and made available as *The Christensen Rhetoric Program* to English teachers. These workbooks and teaching materials provided practical instruction in generative rhetoric and inspired numerous research projects to test the validity of the approach.

Other researchers have qualified, modified, or expanded Christensen's work on the paragraph. David H. Karrfalt and Willis J. Pitkin have independently critiqued various elements of Christensen's theory, especially the notion that only two major relationships, coordination and subordination, exist between discourse elements. Both theorists have suggested that other kinds of structural relationships must be introduced to understand the structure of actual prose. Other researchers have developed matrices based on Christensen's approach to analyzing texts. These include Nold and Davis's discourse matrix and Richard M. Coe's *Toward a Grammar of Passages*, which develops a simple numerical system to suggest the subordinate and coordinate relationship between sentences in paragraphs. Other theorists, most notably Michael Grady, Frank D'Angelo, and Richard L. Larson, applied Christensen paragraph principles to the entire essay.

The influence of Christensen's work is still strong 30 years after the publication of the first edition of *Notes*. Many textbooks continue to discuss the cumulative sentence as an important stylistic device and the Christensen paragraph as a useful tool for teaching this unit. The method itself, however, has severe limitations. By emphasizing a single sentence type, Christensen de-emphasizes the range of stylistic options that writers of English regularly use, and his structural approach to the paragraph lacks the flexibility and wide explanatory power that Paul C. Rodgers's notion of the stadium of discourse offers. Christensen's claim that he developed a new rhetoric is too strong. More accurately, he created a few parts that can be used in a new rhetoric.

BIBLIOGRAPHY

Primary Sources

Christensen, Bonnijean. *The Christensen Method: Text and Workbook*. New York: Harper & Row, 1979.

Christensen, Francis. *The Christensen Rhetoric Program: The Sentence and the Paragraph: The Student Workbook*. New York: Harper & Row, 1968.

———. *Notes toward a New Rhetoric: Six Essays for Teachers*. New York: Harper & Row, 1967.

———, ed. *The Sentence and the Paragraph*. Champaign, IL: National Council of Teachers of English, 1963.

Christensen, Francis, and Bonnijean Christensen. *Notes toward a New Rhetoric: Nine Essays for Teachers*. 2nd ed. New York: Harper & Row, 1978.

Biography

Nasso, Christine, ed. "Francis Christensen." *Contemporary Authors: Permanent Series*. Vol. 2. Detroit: Gale Research Company, 1978.

Criticism

Coe, Richard M. *Toward a Grammar of Passages*. Carbondale: Southern Illinois University Press, 1988.

D'Angelo, Frank. "A Generative Rhetoric of the Essay." *College Composition and Communication* 25.5 (1974): 388–96.

Faigley, Lester. *Fragments of Rationality: Postmodernity and the Subject of Composition*. Pittsburg: University of Pittsburgh Press, 1992.

———. "The Influence of Generative Rhetoric on the Syntactic Fluency and Writing Effectiveness of College Freshmen." *Research in the Teaching of English* 13.3 (1979): 197–206.

Grady, Michael. "A Conceptual Rhetoric of the Composition." *College Composition and Communication* 22.5 (1971): 348–54.

Karrfalt, David H. "The Generation of Paragraphs and Larger Units." *College Composition and Communication* 19.3 (1968): 211–17.

Larson, Richard L. "Toward a Linear Rhetoric of the Essay." *College Composition and Communication* 22.2 (1971): 140–46.

Nold, Ellen W., and Brent E. Davis. "The Discourse Matrix." *College Composition and Communication* 31.2 (1980): 141–52.

Pitkin, Willis L., Jr. "Hierarchies and the Discourse Hierarchy." *College English* 38.7 (1977): 648–59.

Rodgers, Paul C., Jr. "A Discourse-Centered Rhetoric of the Paragraph." *College Composition and Communication* 17.1 (1962): 2–11.

HÉLÈNE CIXOUS
(1937–   )

D. Diane Davis

Born in Oran, Algeria, on June 5, 1937 (just two years prior to World War II), to a French-Jewish father (Georges) and a German mother (Eve), Hélène Cixous began life under the signs of exclusion and repudiation. And yet this French-German-Jew counts herself lucky to "have [had] foreignness, exile, war, the phantom memory of peace, mourning and pain, as the place and time of [her] birth" ("From the Scene" 2). For, despite the anti-Jewish climate, Cixous remembers having "a very strong feeling of paradise" in Oran, a family life full of "dreams and creation" ("Albums" 196). Given that her father, who died when she was only 11, "loved music, drawing, words, books," that he engaged the family in "word games" for entertainment, it's no surprise that Cixous developed an early love for language and poetry (196). Her native tongue was not French— rather, she, along with her mother, "sang in German" ("From the Scene" 2). She was, however, fluent in French, and in 1955, Cixous married, moved to Paris, and enrolled at Lycée Lakanal (her second all boys' school). There she says she encountered for the first time "the odour of misogyny" ("Albums" 204) and "felt the true torments of exile" (205). Her firsthand experiences with anti-Semitism and misogyny, which hurled her into the place of "the other," left her acutely aware of the need for an/other way of thinking, one that would rigorously oppose all forms of oppression and attend to "the other" without appropriation or annihilation. This other way of thinking would be tied intricately to the radically creative force of writing, poetry, and music.

Cixous continued her studies in France, and within a few years, she had passed her teaching exams (*agrégation*) (1959) in English, borne two children (Anne-Emmanuelle [1955] and Pierre-François [1961]), and accepted her first *assistante* at the University of Bordeaux (1962). Cixous began her thesis on James Joyce in 1960 but became a full professor and chair of English literature at the University of Nanterre (1967) before she had earned her doctorate. In May 1968, in answer to student uprisings against the conservative French university structure, and at the behest of the Minister of Education, Cixous established the then-experimental Université de Paris VIII–Vincennes, which she staffed with Latin American writers and edge-pushing new philosophers, such as Michel Foucault, Gilles Deleuze, and Michel Serres (Jean-François Lyotard would join the faculty in 1970). That same year, Cixous received her *Doctorat d'État*—becoming, at age 31, France's youngest "Doctor"—and, along with Tzvetan Todorov and Gérard Genette, founded *Poétique*, an experimental review that performed/promoted a different way of reading. Cixous published both her thesis on Joyce and her first novel, *Dedans*, in 1969, and since then, she has published more than 45 novels and plays and 7 books of theory/criticism. In 1974, she created Europe's first doctoral program in Women's Studies, which conservative legislators have attempted to abolish several times. Thanks in each instance, however, to overwhelming international protests, Cixous's doctoral program in *Études Féminines*, which she still chairs, continues to thrive.[1]

"SEXUAL DIFFERENCE" AND *ÉCRITURE FÉMININE*

Although Cixous's fictional works far outnumber her explicitly theoretical/critical pieces, most American scholars know her better for the latter. "The Laugh of the Medusa" and "Sorties" are probably the most influential of her works in this country, both of which perform and invite *écriture féminine*, a writing style that is said to be "feminine." But, and this is crucial to Cixous's project, neither "sexual difference" nor *écriture féminine* has anything inherently to do with anatomy: Cixous is no biological essentialist. On the contrary, sexual difference is, for Cixous, multiple, intractable; it refers to a wild web of differences, which are effaced by the either/or mentality: Most of us, she says, "are not strong enough, not agile enough" to cope with the "confusion, torment, or bewilderment" that the sexual "identity card" covers over (*Three* 50–51). However, it is precisely our belief in this illusion of a "simplified and clear-cut" identity (be it sexual, ethnic, national, or whatever) that becomes the condition of possibility for systematic exclusions. And, according to Cixous, "only writing" can shatter this illusion and reveal the other-in-me that rustles beneath the cover. Cixous—a *woman* with a *man*'s education, a Jew with a German heritage—celebrates and engages this shattering writing, this *écriture féminine*.

The feminine, for Cixous, is not opposed to the masculine (the easy way out) but something else altogether; it's a postgendered way of responding that flies the binary coup. *Écriture féminine* is a style of writing that embraces "the feminine," revealing this line of flight, this "elsewhere" that overflows the either/or choice. It is most often performed by those coded "female," but "women's" edge in this arena is not biological—it's cultural: it's often easier for women because their gender socialization leaves them more open to otherness. "It is much harder," Cixous says, "for man to let the other come through him" ("Sorties" 85). And yet Cixous observes that being coded female does not necessarily leave one less interested in mastery nor more capable of *écriture féminine*— even "females" will have to become *féminine* in this sense; she also celebrates the works of Genet, Kleist, Shakespeare, Joyce, and other male writers as moving examples of *écriture féminine*. In fact, in "Sorties," she tells us: "I owed my life to Kleist," to his writing, a feminine writing that inspired her "to be more than one feminine one or masculine one" (112).

CIXOUS AND WRITING/RHETORICAL THEORY

Cixous's brand of *écriture féminine* issues a direct challenge not only to rhetoric and composition but to rhetorical studies in general because it's not codifiable, not reducible to a set of transferable skills—it is not a *technē*; it has more to do with *tuchē* and *kairos*. As Cixous has noted, "this practice [*écriture féminine*] will never be able to be *theorized*, enclosed, coded" ("Sorties" 92); one "can't make a recipe of it, for as soon as we begin to inscribe signs, to attract attention, we destroy" (*Three* 50). "This writing cannot be taught . . . but it can be learned, cannot be generalized, but it can be shared" (*Three* 7). Furthermore, this writing is not about getting to "the point": "Writing is not arriving," Cixous says; it's about departing—"One has to get going. This is what writing is, starting off" (*Three* 65), getting onboard to take the ride. And in contradistinction to both expressivist and social-epistemic rhetorics of composing, this writing is neither about discovering/expressing one's so-called inner self nor about accounting for one's socially constituted self. In fact, to write, according to Cixous, is to put one's "proper" identity (whether inherent or constructed) *on the line*: "Coming to writing" requires the affirmative decision to let everything go, to allow the writing itself to *crack one's shell*, shatter one's *topoi*, "hurl [one] off into foreign countries" (*Three* 59). Writing, Cixous says, is about "learning to die" (*Three* 10), to shed one's identity terms long enough to experience what they silence, to "seek out the shattered, the multiple I" (*"Coming to Writing"* 40).

It's tempting to believe and to teach that "we are the ones writing," but Cixous says "clearly this isn't true" (*Three* 98): We are taken (over) by writing in the way we are taken (over) by dreams, and the "genuine text" is the one "whose brilliance upsets the scribe" (*Three* 156). "Good writing," then, requires more than effective invention, organization, and delivery; it requires a straining to receive, the patience to let "the other" approach without hurrying or silencing, to let "the other" come close without knocking it over ("Clarice Lispector" 62). "Good writing" is transgressive inasmuch as it calls into and embraces what Clarice Lispector, one of Cixous's most important influences, calls "the imund": the improper, the unaccountable, the overflow—that which one's own identity card designates as "beyond the good side of the law, the proper, the world of order" (*Three* 119). For Cixous, this is writing, avowing the *unavowable*, which necessarily will shatter "the eggshell [that] we are" (63), necessarily will cost us a life but then also will grant us another. This is why Cixous suggests that "[t]he only [text] worth writing is the one we don't have the courage or the strength to write. The [text] that hurts us (we who are writing), that makes us tremble, redden, bleed" (32).

This description of writing obviously flies in the face of the rhetorical tradition, which celebrates the political power of rhetoric, the capacity of a speaker/ writer to argue well enough to move an audience toward a predetermined action or attitude. *Écriture féminine* could not be less interested in arguing well within either/or structures of thought, and yet Cixous is quick to note the ethicopolitical force of this writing: From it, she says, springs "the very possibility for change" ("Laugh" 879), for an/Other way of thinking altogether, one that overflows phallogocentric thought habits and heads for "what-is-not-the-same," for an "elsewhere," a place that "is not obliged to reproduce the system." Because, "[i]f there is a somewhere else that can escape the infernal repetition," the very either/ or mentality that sets us up for systematic exclusions, that manages, unbelievably, to give the nod to genocide/gynocide[2]/genus-cide,[3] Cixous assures us that this escape "lies in that direction," beyond simple argument, beyond mastery— "where [this 'elsewhere'] writes itself, where it dreams, where it invents new worlds" ("Sorties" 72).

NOTES

1. Most of the dates and events listed here were gathered and published by Mireille Calle-Gruber in "Chronicle," a chapter from Calle-Gruber and Cixous's *Rootprints: Memory and Life Writing* (209–13).

2. "Gynocide" is Cixous's term. See "Laugh of the Medusa": "There will have been a long history of gynocide" (888).

3. "Genus-cide" is Victor Vitanza's term. See his *Negation, Subjectivity, and the History of Rhetoric* (46).

BIBLIOGRAPHY

Primary Sources

Cixous, Hélène. "Castration or Decapitation?" Trans. Annette Kuhn. *Signs* 7.1 (1981): 41–55. Trans. of "Le sexe ou la tête?" (1976).

————. "Clarice Lispector: The Approach." *"Coming to Writing" and Other Essays*. Ed. Deborah Jenson. Trans. Sarah Cornell, Deborah Jenson, Ann Liddle, and Susan Sellers. Cambridge: Harvard University Press, 1991. 59–77.

————. *"Coming to Writing" and Other Essays*. Ed. Deborah Jenson. Trans. Sarah Cornell, Deborah Jenson, Ann Liddle, and Susan Sellers. Cambridge: Harvard University Press, 1991.

————. "Extreme Fidelity." Trans Ann Liddle and Susan Sellers. *Writing Differences: Readings from the Seminar of Héléne Cixous*. Ed. Susan Sellers. New York: St. Martin's Press, 1988. 9–36.

―――. "From the Scene of the Unconscious to the Scene of History." Trans. Deborah Carpenter. *The Future of Literary Theory*. Ed. Ralph Cohen. New York: Routledge, 1989. 1–18.

―――. *Hélène Cixous Reader*. Ed. Susan Sellers. New York: Routledge, 1994.

―――. "The Laugh of the Medusa." Trans. Keith Cohen. *Signs* 1.4 (1976): 875–93. Trans. of "Le rire de la Médusa" (1975).

―――. *Readings: The Poetics of Blanchot, Joyce, Kafka, Lispector, Tsvetaeva*. (Seminars 1982–1984). Trans. Verena Conley. London: Harvester Wheatsheaf, 1992.

―――. *Reading with Clarice Lispector*. Trans. Verena Andermatt Conley. Minneapolis: Minnesota University Press, 1990. Trans. of *L'heure de Clarice Lispector* (1989).

―――. "Sorties: Out and Out: Attacks/Ways Out/Forays." *The Newly Born Woman*. With Catherine Clement. Trans. Betsy Wing. *Literature* 24. Minneapolis: University of Minnesota Press, 1986. 63–132. Trans. of *La jeune née*. (1975).

―――. *Three Steps on the Ladder of Writing*. Welleck Library Lectures, Irvine (June 1990). Trans. Sarah Cornell and Susan Sellers. New York: Columbia University Press, 1993.

Cixous, Hélène, and Mereille Calle-Gruber. "Albums and Legends." *Rootprints: Memory and Life Writing*. New York: Routledge, 1997. 179–206.

Biography

Cixous, Hélène, and Mireille Calle-Gruber. *Rootprints: Memory and Life Writing*. New York: Routledge, 1997.

Conley, Verena Andermatt. *Hélène Cixous*. Buffalo: University of Toronto Press, 1992.

Sellers, Susan. *Hélène Cixous: Authorship, Autobiography, and Love*. Cambridge, MA: Blackwell Publishers, 1996.

Criticism

Conley, Verena Andermatt. *Hélène Cixous: Writing the Feminine*. Lincoln: Nebraska University Press, 1984.

Gallop, Jane. "Keys to Dora." *The Daughter's Seduction: Feminism and Psychoanalysis*. New York: Cornell University Press, 1982. 132–150.

Jarratt, Susan. "The First Sophists and Feminism: Discourses of the 'Other'." *Rereading the Sophists: Classical Rhetoric Refigured*. Carbondale: Southern Illinois University Press, 1991. 63–80.

Jones, Ann. "Writing the Body: Toward an Understanding of l'*Écriture Féminine*." *Feminist Studies* 7.2 (1981): 247–63.

Junker, Clara. "Writing with Cixous." *College English* 50.4 (1988): 424–36.

Kogan, Vivian. "I Want Vulva? Hélène Cixous and the Poetics of the Body." *L'Espirit créateur* 25.2 (1985): 73–85.

Sellers, Susan. *Hélène Cixous: A Politics of Writing*. London: Routledge, 1991.

―――. "Writing Woman: Hélène Cixous' Political 'Sexts.' " *Women's Studies International Forum* 9.4 (1986) 443–47.

Vitanza, Victor. "A Feminist Sophistic?" *Negation, Subjectivity, and the History of Rhetoric*. New York: State University of New York Press, 1997. 207–34.

Wilcox, Helen, Keith Mcwatters, Ann Thompson, and Linda R. Williams, eds. *The Body and the Text: Hélène Cixous, Reading and Teaching.* Hemel Hempstead: Harvester Wheatsheaf, 1990.

Worsham, Lynn. "Writing against Writing: The Predicament of *Écriture Féminine* in Composition Studies." *Contending with Words: Composition and Rhetoric in a Postmodern Age.* Ed. Patricia Harkin and John Schilb. New York: MLA, 1991. 82–104.

ROBERT J. CONNORS
(1951–)

Patricia J. McAlexander

Robert J. Connors was born in Springfield, Massachusetts, received his B.A. from the University of Massachusetts in 1973, and attended graduate school in English at Ohio State. In 1980 he received his Ph.D. with a major in rhetoric and composition theory; his particular mentor there was Edward P. J. Corbett. Connors taught first at Louisiana State University as an assistant professor of English and director of the English Writing Laboratory; he moved in 1984 to the University of New Hampshire, where he is presently a professor of English and director of its writing center. His many publications have established his reputation as a major historian and critic of college composition in America.

Connors revealed a 1960s idealism during graduate school: He was, he said, "galvanized" by the "moral charge" of teaching writing in order to give students a chance at the good life ("Rhetorical History" 238). His ambitious 554-page dissertation grew out of his interest in both rhetoric and teaching; it describes the history of theories on invention, arrangement, style, the sentence, and the paragraph; evaluates those theories; and provides classroom applications. Because Connors felt that the "new" discipline of composition, which he sees as beginning with the Harvard writing classes in 1885, lacked a sense of history, he attempted in his early publications (1981–1987) to establish such a sense. To do so he drew on his training in classical rhetoric and on secondary sources such as Albert Kitzhaber's 1953 dissertation "Rhetoric in American Colleges, 1850–1900"; but mainly, as he later states, he relied on his own vast reading of one type of source: nineteenth- and twentieth-century rhetoric and composition textbooks.

In most of these early articles, Connors takes a history-of-ideas approach: He traces the ways nineteenth- and twentieth-century composition was taught and accounts for the pedagogical patterns he finds in terms of one or two historical factors. Although this approach now may seem oversimplified (Connors himself later wished he had looked into "larger" cultural questions and examined more diverse sources ["Rhetorical History" 238]), his articles do provide the discipline with valuable historical background. At the same time, they go beyond mere history, for, like his model Kitzhaber, Connors charged his historical research with moral purpose. A strong advocate of the product-to-process paradigm shift originating in the 1960s, Connors sharply criticizes the composition classes and texts he describes because they were based on the product-based, error-focused, formulaic "current-traditional" rhetoric.

A number of articles can illustrate this period of Connors's work. "The Rise and Fall of the Modes of Discourse," which won the Richard C. Braddock Award for the best article in the 1981 volume of *College Composition and Communication*, criticizes composition texts from approximately 1895 to the 1950s for repeatedly classifying essays into four types: exposition, description, narration, and argument. Connors argues that these modes were popularized only because they "fit into the abstract, mechanical nature of writing instruction" so convenient to teachers (453); in actuality, according to Connors, they are irrelevant to the process of writing (455). Connors's criticism continues in a discussion of one specific text: "Current-Traditional Rhetoric: Thirty Years of [James McCrimmon's] *Writing with a Purpose*" (1981) flagellates author McCrimmon because, throughout the seven editions of his popular book (1950–1980), he did not make sufficient use of recent composition research, particularly that research that advocated the process approach. Connors next takes a specific textbook type to task: In "Handbooks: History of a Genre" (1983), he traces the development of the nineteenth century's little manuals of rules into prescriptive, exercise-filled "tomes" of "reductive rhetoric" (95–96) used by ill-trained and overworked composition teachers in the twentieth century to "get rid of the pain of being . . . genuine reader[s]" (97). Similarly, in "Textbooks and the Evolution of the Discipline" (1986) Connors points out that when teacher training is poor, texts meet instructors' needs by including many exercises and drills; but he goes on to argue that the rigid pedagogy of such texts rather than liberating teachers enslaves them. Finally, Connors attacks the composition discipline itself in "Mechanical Correctness as a Focus in Composition Instruction" (1985); here he describes how historical forces like Harvard's 1874 writing exam turned the noble discipline of Aristotle and Cicero into a "stultifying error-hunt" (61). Clearly Connors's historical approach provided him with a convenient tool for criticizing modern composition practices, particularly the use of the current-traditional approach.

And yet, in spite of Connors's strong stand against this approach, some of the articles of this period express a sense that perhaps the paradigm had, after all, some value. At the end of the article on *Writing with a Purpose*, for example, Connors admits that he had developed "more sympathy" for McCrimmon, that he now sees current-traditional rhetoric not as "an occupying foe" but as "an ailing friend" ("Current-Traditional Rhetoric" 219–20). And in "Mechanical

Correctness" he concludes that we must strike a balance between "theorists, rhetoricians, proponents of writing as discovery or communication" and "traditionalists, the front-line teachers, the proponents of writing as a vocational skill," who stress rules of grammar (70).

Connors's mellowing attitude is most apparent in "Frequency of Formal Errors in Current College Writing" (1988), coauthored with former Ohio State colleague Andrea Lunsford. Examining the history of error-frequency studies over the past 80 years and then presenting an analysis of errors based on 3,000 contemporary teacher-marked college themes, Connors and Lunsford refer not to an external battle of values but to their own internal conflict between "our more traditional pedagogical selves" who want error-free writing and our "process-oriented" selves who ignore student errors (396). Further, their discovery that, contrary to the prevailing view, today's students are *not* making a greater number of errors than they used to, led Connors to recognize the limitations of his own historical context. He later wrote, "Our [his and Lunsford's] pre-existing ideas [about error] were shown to be simple and sometimes wrong. ... We were as prejudiced and historically constrained as all the authors we had read" ("Rhetorical History" 239–40).

Connors, then, seemed to have come to terms with the product-process conflict. His 1990s historical studies, though still often campaigns to improve present-day composition, focus on two other issues: labor and gender. "Overwork/Underpay: Labor and Status of Composition Teachers since 1880" (1990) details the low status of composition teachers in the early 1900s—much the same status, he suggests, as composition teachers hold today. The teaching of introductory writing courses is still an apprenticeship for teaching literature once the Ph.D. is earned; permanent instructors are still often women or "surplus Ph.Ds"; grading themes still involves a tremendous amount of work. Indeed, Connors dramatically describes the teaching of composition in terms of "nightmares," "hells," and "academic sweatshop[s]" (110–11).

Connors turns to his most controversial topic, gender, in "Women's Reclamation of Rhetoric in the Nineteenth Century" (1995) and "Teaching and Learning as a Man" (1996). Earlier, Connors had argued that the change from rhetorical debate to written composition and from abstract to personal topics arose from the influence of romanticism and democracy. Now he argues that the major reason for these changes was the growing numbers of women in American colleges. Indeed, he claims that composition as we know it today is "probably the most feminized discipline outside of women's studies" ("Women's Reclamation" 87). Almost a companion piece to this article, "Teaching and Learning as a Man" argues that today's feminized composition pedagogy is inappropriate for males. Not only do male instructors distrust their abilities to mentor male students, but the curriculum, employing collaboration, personal essay topics, and nurturing student-teacher relationships, does not suit men: They prefer individual work, impersonal essay topics, and hierarchical relationships.

Since most of his publications include explorations of the past, Connors has come to be regarded as an expert not only in composition history but also in historiography, and he is often asked to write or speak on that subject. In these talks and articles, Connors gives reasons for historical research that reflect his own practice. He sees the study of the past as a way to more clearly understand, and thus improve, the present. History, he contends, is the discipline's "memory," without which "we are shackled to a narrow presentism" ("Rhetorical History" 231); his tracing of the history of problems in the teaching of writing has been mainly "to find out whether or not we can do anything about [those problems] today" (Murphy et al. 12–13). Connors's advice to young scholars grows out of his own research experience: He tells them to explore many types of sources—old journals, professional books, and unpublished primary materials in archives—and to read studies of class, social structure, economics, and gender so that they can understand their own cultural/historical biases ("Dreams and Play" 20–21).

Connors's latest work, *Composition-Rhetoric* (1997), is a compilation, expansion, and update of his past research. This book traces the evolution in the United States of the paradigm for teaching composition that Connors now terms "composition-rhetoric"—a more accurate name, he says, than "current-traditional rhetoric." Of course, he pays particular attention to textbooks, grammar, teacher workloads, and gender influences.

Perhaps Connors's most influential publications, however, are two of his pedagogical books. He coauthored *The St. Martin's Handbook* with Andrea Lunsford through four editions—1988, 1992, 1995, and 1999 (the latest under the title *The New St. Martin's Handbook*). This text applies process theory to composition while maintaining updated but basically traditional lessons on "correctness." *The St. Martin's Guide to Teaching Writing*, coauthored with Cheryl Glenn, has been a companion volume to the *Handbook*. (Its fourth edition also has "New" in the title.) Designed to liberate inexperienced teachers from insecurity and textbook dependence, this book combines the theoretical and practical with its discussions of teaching techniques, sample syllabi, and reprints of articles vital to the development of modern composition theory.

As a scholar who has published prolifically, Connors has throughout the 1980s and 1990s been an important figure on the composition scene. But given the "moral charge" he felt even as a graduate student, he may be most gratified with his role in writing the two pedagogical books. They have drawn on his research and his resulting insights to advance those groups he has always been most interested in—the students and the teacher—practitioners in the composition classroom.

BIBLIOGRAPHY

Primary Sources

Connors, Robert J. "Basic Writing Texts: History and Current Avatars." *A Sourcebook for Basic Writers*. Ed. Theresa Enos. New York: Random House, 1987. 259–74.

————. *Composition-Rhetoric: Background, Theory, and Pedagogy*. Pittsburgh: University of Pittsburgh Press, 1997.

————. "Current-Traditional Rhetoric: Thirty Years of *Writing with a Purpose*." *Rhetoric Society Quarterly* 11.4 (1981): 208–21.

————. "Dreams and Play: Historical Method and Methodology." *Methods and Methodology in Composition Research*. Ed. Gesa Kirsch and Patricia A. Sullivan. Carbondale: Southern Illinois University Press, 1992. 15–36.

————. "Handbooks: History of a Genre." *Rhetoric Society Quarterly* 13.2 (1983): 87–98.

————. "Mechanical Correctness as a Focus in Composition Instruction." *College Composition and Communication* 36.1 (1985): 61–72.

————. "Overwork/Underpay: Labor and Status of Composition Teachers since 1880." *Rhetoric Review* 9.1 (1990): 108–25.

————. "Personal Writing Assignments." *College Composition and Communication* 38.2 (1987): 166–83.

————. "Rhetorical History as a Component of Composition Studies." *Rhetoric Review* 7.2 (1989): 230–40.

————. "Rhetoric in the Modern University: The Creation of an Underclass." *The Politics of Writing Instruction: Postsecondary*. Ed. Richard Bullock and John Trimbur. Portsmouth, NH: Boynton/Cook, 1991. 55–84.

————. "The Rise and Fall of the Modes of Discourse." *College Composition and Communication* 32.4 (1981): 444–55.

————. "A Study of Rhetorical Theories for College Writing Teachers." Diss., Ohio State University, 1980.

————. "Teaching and Learning as a Man." *College English* 58.2 (1996): 137–57.

————. "Textbooks and the Evolution of the Discipline." *College Composition and Communication* 37.2 (1986): 178–94.

————. "Women's Reclamation of Rhetoric in the Nineteenth Century." *Feminine Principles and Women's Experience in American Composition and Rhetoric*. Ed. Louise Wetherbee Phelps and Janet Emig. Pittsburgh: University of Pittsburgh Press, 1995. 67–90.

————. "Writing the History of Our Discipline." *An Introduction to Composition Studies*. Ed. Erika Lindemann and Gary Tate. New York: Oxford University Press, 1991. 49–71.

Connors, Robert, and Cheryl Glenn. *The New St. Martin's Guide to Teaching Writing*. 4th ed. Boston: Bedford/St. Martin's, 1999.

Connors, Robert J., and Andrea A. Lunsford. "Frequency of Formal Errors in Current College Writing, or Ma and Pa Kettle Do Research." *College Composition and Communication* 39.4 (1988): 395–409.

Lunsford, Andrea, and Robert Connors. *The New St. Martin's Handbook*. 4th ed. Boston: Bedford/St. Martin's, 1999.

Murphy, James J., James Berlin, Robert J. Connors, Sharon Crowley, Richard Leo Enos, Victor J. Vitanza, Susan C. Jarratt, Nan Johnson, and Jan Swearingen. "Octalog: The Politics of Historiography." *Rhetoric Review* 7.1 (1988): 5–49.

Criticism

Breidenback, Cathleen. "Comment on 'Teaching and Learning as a Man.' " *College English* 59.4 (1997): 470–72.

Crowley, Sharon. "Response to Robert J. Connors, 'The Rise and Fall of the Modes of Discourse,' *CCC*, 32 (December, 1981), 444–455." *College Composition and Communication* 35.1 (1984): 88–91.

———. Review of *Composition-Rhetoric: Backgrounds, Theory, and Pedagogy* by Robert J. Connors. *Rhetoric Review* 16.2 (1998): 340–43.

Kitzhaber, Albert R. "Rhetoric in American Colleges, 1850–1900." Diss., Washington University, 1953.

Mountford, Roxanne. "The Feminization of Rhetoric?" Review of *Composition-Rhetoric: Backgrounds, Theory, and Pedagogy* by Robert J. Connors. *JAC: A Journal of Composition Theory* 19.3 (1999): 485–92.

EDWARD P. J. CORBETT
(1919–1998)

Shannon Zimmerman

Edward P. J. Corbett, the man most responsible for the revival of classical rhetoric during the 1960s, was born on October 29, 1919, in Jamestown, North Dakota. When Corbett was eight years old, he and his family settled in Milwaukee, Wisconsin, where Corbett received a scholarship to attend Marquette University High School. "The tuition was $150 a year," Corbett once stated. "Without the scholarship, my family could never have afforded to send me to Marquette" (Corbett, Telephone Interview). Corbett focused on languages at the prestigious school, taking a special interest in both Latin and Greek.

The son of John Corbett, a railroad dispatcher and Works Project Administration laborer, and Adrienne Beaupre, a homemaker, Corbett took an undergraduate degree in liberal education from Venard College in Clark's Summit, Pennsylvania, in 1942. After a tour of duty as a radar technician during World War II, Corbett entered the graduate program in English language and literature at the University of Chicago, earning an M.A. in 1948. As a doctoral candidate at Loyola University of Chicago, Corbett wrote a wide-ranging study of the Scottish rhetorician Hugh Blair that examined the ways in which Blair modified and expanded the classical tradition by using it to address the concerns of belles lettres, the Enlightenment-inspired attempt to identify the underlying rules of verbal communication. Corbett completed the dissertation, "Hugh Blair: A Study of His Rhetorical Theory," in 1956 and subsequently began his distinguished career as rhetorical theorist, historian, and practitioner.

Corbett's teaching career has included positions at the University of Chicago, Creighton University, and Ohio State University, where he served as the director of Freshman Composition from 1966 to 1971. Corbett founded the Rhetoric Society of America in 1968, and in 1971 he was elected president of the Conference on College Composition and Communication, the field's leading professional organization. From 1974 to 1979, Corbett edited the Conference's journal, *College Composition and Communication*, shaping the field of composition studies in its nascent stage through the careful selection of important scholarship and timely essays of his own.

CLASSICAL RHETORIC AND MODERNITY

Without question, Corbett's persuasive insistence on the continuing relevance of classical rhetoric during modern times represents his most important contribution to the field of rhetorical study. Corbett asserts in his seminal textbook *Classical Rhetoric for the Modern Student* (currently entering a fourth edition) that his rhetorical theory is "so much indebted to Aristotle . . . that it can be regarded as a mere restatement, with some modifications and extensions, of the *Rhetoric*" (540). This impulse to modify and extend the classical tradition informs virtually all of Corbett's work.

For Corbett, classical rhetoric offers a rich resource for contemporary students for two primary reasons. First, the classical tradition addresses "the whole man" in its insistence on the three modes of appeal—the appeal to reason (*logos*), the appeal to emotion (*pathos*), and the appeal of the speaker's character (*ethos*). Second, unlike the anonymous theme writing taught in many composition classrooms, classical rhetoric encourages students to write toward the end of persuading a specific audience. By emphasizing these two points, and by recounting the history of classical rhetoric, Corbett revitalized the tradition, showing it to be a subtle and powerful tool for contemporary writers.

Importantly, Corbett's suggestions for the uses of classical rhetoric are never rigid. Corbett, in fact, seems acutely aware of the need for flexibility in the contemporary composition classroom, an awareness borne of many years of pedagogical experience and of an eminently pragmatic view of the discipline. In short, Corbett's work attempts to find a useful symmetry between the canons of classicism, which, as he shows, are more flexible than many contemporary teachers may suppose, and the diverse demands of modernity. In terms of its impact on contemporary rhetorical theory and practice, this achievement cannot be overstated.

THE PEDAGOGICAL STANCE

Like that of Hugh Blair, Corbett's work reveals the mind of a gifted synthesizer, a curious and wide-ranging intellectual, and perhaps most significantly, a thoughtful teacher. This last quality may account for Corbett's considerable influence among teachers of composition, for his prose is marked by both scholarly erudition and an intimate understanding of the day-to-day work of writing instructors. For Corbett, rhetoric is an eminently practical art, an art decidedly at odds with what he terms the "cult of self-expression" that had come into vogue during the 1960s. Corbett, in fact, cautions teachers against prolonged

journal and personal narrative exercises, citing a concern for adolescent solipsism and self-consciousness. Corbett instead emphasizes the moral and civic
dimensions of rhetoric, contending that the precepts of the classical tradition,
particularly those of Cicero and Quintillian, can foster ethical as well as intellectual development. In this regard, Corbett recommends that teachers adopt the
classical pedagogical technique of imitation or role-playing. Such role-playing,
he says, cultivates a sensitive understanding of the members of one's audience,
allowing simultaneously for more effective persuasion and empathy for one's
fellow humans.

According to Corbett, then, rhetoric attends not only to the acquisition of
knowledge but also to the processes of learning and living, simultaneously preparing students for both the composition of essays and interaction with others
in the public sphere. In an essay from 1963, "The Usefulness of Classical Rhetoric," Corbett begins by asking, "What does classical rhetoric have to offer
composition teachers?" (162). This question of usefulness clearly has broad implications for Corbett, and it underlies the vast majority of his work.

THE HISTORICAL VIEW

Several of Corbett's most important essays review the tenets and history of
the classical tradition and speak directly to how teachers might use this rhetoric
in the contemporary classroom. The overview of the rhetorical tradition presented in *Classical Rhetoric for the Modern Student* is one of the most expansive
of these. Arguing that rhetoric as a discipline emerged inductively from the
practice of many teachers and orators, Corbett surveys the field's documented
history, tracing rhetoric from its forensic origins in fifth-century Sicily, through
the Attic sophists and Aristotle, to its virtual dissolution during the first third of
the twentieth century when handbooks distilled rhetorical principles to mere sets
of rules covering correct grammar, usage, and spelling. He also traces the resurgence of interest in rhetoric, describing the role of speech departments and
journals as well as the work of such "new rhetoricians" as I. A. Richards, Kenneth Burke, and Chaïm Perelman.

In "What Is Being Revived?" (1967), Corbett presents another overview of
the rhetorical tradition, one designed for those teachers who had become in-
trigued by the resurgence of rhetoric in academic journals and conferences.
Rhetoric had become virtually synonymous with vacuous, overheated speech,
and, in the essay, Corbett seeks to redeem the term by surveying the classical
tradition and by forecasting how such a rhetoric might be used in the contemporary classroom. While agreeing that definitions of rhetoric from Aristotle to
Kenneth Burke have differed significantly in terms of emphasis, Corbett contends that the object of that emphasis—effective, strategic communication—has
remained constant. "Rhetoric," as Corbett defines it, constitutes the "art governing the choice of strategies that a speaker or writer must make in order to
communicate most effectively with an audience" (166). Importantly, this art

consists not only of an awareness of audience but also of a knowledge about that audience, its passions, and motivations. Consequently, Corbett frequently refers teachers and students to Book Two of Aristotle's *Rhetoric*, admonishing them not to shrink from emotional appeals. Though such appeals should be used judiciously, knowledge about one's audience must begin with the understanding that human beings are creatures of intellect *and* passion.

After rehearsing the tenets of Aristotelian rhetoric, Corbett concedes that, as it was employed by some teachers, this elaborate system "got lost in its own labyrinth or became enamored of the sound of its own words" (167). But Corbett also insists that Aristotle's schema is a practical, cohesive, and intellectually charged system, one that has provided the underlying principles for most of the "rhetorics" that have emerged in its wake. The use of the plural is significant here, for Corbett insists that the classical tradition is hardly monolithic.

To support his contention, Corbett traces the various strands of the rhetorical tradition from the classical period to the first third of the twentieth century, noting particularly the points at which the various rhetorics diverge. This pluralist view of classical rhetoric and its diverse legacy deeply informs Corbett's own appropriation of the tradition for the contemporary classroom. Since his overarching goal is the "fashioning of a rhetoric that is relevant to our age" (172), Corbett suggests that those concerned with the development of the field look to other disciplines for additional insight. "The rhetorics of the past," Corbett contends, "have all been concerned with the composition of a discursive, uninterrupted monologue. What we need now is a rhetoric of the process rather than the product" (172).

PROCESS RATHER THAN PRODUCT

In "A New Look at Old Rhetoric," Corbett surveys the field of composition and discovers two camps of instructors whose interests converge upon a single yet potentially diffuse objective: "a variety of rhetorics, which if they cannot teach our students to write better can at least teach them something needful to know about the art of prose discourse" (16). Corbett discerns one group of teachers committed to what he calls the "new rhetoric," a broad term encompassing rhetorical approaches informed by psychology, semantics, and behavioral science. But he also finds fervent followers of the classical tradition. Characterizing himself as one who has "been burning incense at the ancient shrine" (16), Corbett undertakes an examination of the classical tradition toward the end of learning whether this "ancient—maybe antiquated"—rhetoric includes anything of value for the contemporary classroom (16).

Corbett contends that cohesion is one reason classical rhetoric has attracted so many contemporary adherents. The new rhetoric, he suggests, exists for now only in parts, requiring a scholar–tailor to stitch it into a whole coat. Conversely, classical rhetoric, while a bit frayed around the edges and out of style, is a "substantial coat," one that "with some judicious cutting and plucking, might be [rendered] fashionable again" (17). Corbett argues that classical rhetoric addresses "all the processes involved in composing a discourse" (17), whereas the new rhetorics tend to focus more discretely upon individual aspects of composition. Corbett anticipates a breakthrough for the newer rhetorics when the *psychology* of composition is more fully understood. He also suggests, however, that when it occurs, this breakthrough will merely provide extensions and modifications of the insights provided by the classical tradition. After all, Book Two of Aristotle's *Rhetoric*, according to Corbett, "was the beginning, admittedly primitive but amazingly perceptive, of psychology" (*Classical* 540).

Corbett also turns to Aristotle for a discussion of the single biggest obstacle facing contemporary student writers: the inability to find enough to say on a given subject. The *Rhetoric*, he points out, addresses the problem through the *topoi*, classical rhetoric's formulaic tools for generating arguments. But Corbett's enthusiasm for what he terms "pump primers" is not without qualification. While contending that the nearly mechanical approach to invention the topics provide can offer struggling students a tremendous resource, he acknowledges that he himself never writes in anything like a systematic way. The topics, therefore, have for Corbett an air of "unreality" ("New Look" 18). However, this air does not diminish the usefulness of the topics in the contemporary classroom. "A system that succeeded in making Tudor schoolboys remarkably articulate and expansive," Corbett suggests, "might help to banish the two-sentence paragraph from our own student's themes" ("New Look" 18).

THE RHETORICAL TRIANGLE

Corbett frequently emphasizes classical rhetoric's sensitive treatment of the triadic relationship that exists within any rhetorical situation—the relationship among speaker, speech, and audience. In his view, any useful "new rhetoric" that might emerge would disregard the classical triad at its own peril. Even Marshall McLuhan's electronic rhetoric, for example, can ill afford to lose sight of Aristotle's pragmatic insistence on the overarching significance of audience.

The various appeals with which rhetors negotiate a rhetorical situation are similarly significant. With regard to *pathos*, Corbett acknowledges a potential for abuse, yet he also argues that teachers fail their students if they forego an in-depth consideration of emotions for fear of misuse. Aristotle, he says, took man as he is; not as he should be; contemporary teachers should do no less. In any case, the ethical appeal checks the power of *pathos*, for a speaker who exploits the emotions of his audience will soon diminish the power of his character, the rhetor's most powerful resource.

In this regard, Corbett once again takes his lead from Aristotle. Since rhetoric navigates the murky waters of contingency—what *may* be true as opposed to what is verifiably true—a speaker or writer succeeds or fails based largely upon his ability to inspire trust in his audience. Aristotle cautions, however, that when preparing a speech, a rhetor must not rely on a previously established reputation;

the ethical appeal must be imbedded within the speech itself. Corbett notes sympathetically that many readers of Aristotle are troubled by the Machiavellian edge of this precept, for it seems to suggest that a rhetor should craft his speech in such a way that it will elicit trust regardless of the speaker's true character.

But Corbett points out that neither Aristotle nor he denies that a speaker's prior reputation will, in fact, inform an audience's reaction. One's reputation can and should influence a speech's reception, but it is sloppy rhetorical practice to rely upon that influence. The ideal rhetor, says Corbett, is indeed Quintillian's "good man skilled in speaking," and as teachers, we should help students cultivate moral character by stressing the importance of values like honesty, integrity, and tolerance. Nonetheless, rhetoric remains the art of finding all the available means of persuasion, and the ethical appeal is perhaps the most pivotal of these means. There is no denying that using character as part of a rhetorical strategy offers opportunity for abuse. But, following Aristotle once more, Corbett argues that if it is abused, we should attribute the abuse not to the art but to the artist.

Regarding *logos*, Corbett suggests that a new rhetoric might expand or modify the classical tradition by supplementing the Aristotelian precepts about logical appeals through the resources of cultural anthropology, behavioral science, and linguistics. Though Aristotle's analysis was essentially correct, Corbett argues, we now know more about the makeup of human nature. If we intend to be successful, contemporary rhetors, we must avail ourselves of this knowledge. Yet Corbett claims that the classical tradition anticipates even this impulse. Responding to the charge that classical rhetoric is not useful in modern classrooms because it focuses almost exclusively upon argumentation, Corbett points to Cicero's description of the three offices of rhetoric: to teach, to please, and to incite. For Corbett, this indicates that rhetoric is a "means-end art" ("New Look" 20), one that animates all modes of discourse, and one that simply must absorb new knowledge about human nature if it is to continue as a technique for finding the available means of persuasion. Corbett singles out stylistics as an area where contemporary researchers are making great strides that should inform any new rhetoric.

But in addition to drawing on the insights of modern scholars, we should also return to the classical tradition's discussion of style. While classical notions about the rhythm of effective prose are probably not applicable in a noninflected language like English, Corbett says, modern teachers and students would do well to revisit the ancients' cataloging of figures. With characteristic good humor, Corbett states, "I refuse to believe that our students would suffer a permanent trauma if we were to expose them to such common schemes and tropes as anaphora, antimetabole, polyptoton, antanaclasis, paronomasia, anthimeria" ("New Look" 21).

With these terms in mind, Corbett rejects the argument that reviving the classical tradition for the contemporary classroom would entail learning an entirely new vocabulary. Teachers of English, of all people, should know that new knowledge frequently comes with new language, and in any case, there are very often contemporary terms that would serve just as well. If "understatement" is less threatening that the classical "litotes," Corbett says, then teachers should by all means use the more familiar term. Showing his eminent practicality yet again, Corbett maintains that vocabulary is only a means to the end of more effective prose and persuasion.

POLITICAL RHETORIC

In the ambitious and widely reprinted "The Rhetoric of the Open Hand and the Closed Fist," Corbett offers an example of the expansion and modification of the classical tradition that he has been urging his follow teachers to attempt. The essay grafts the ancient philosopher Zeno's well-known metaphor—which draws a distinction between the expansive discourse of orators and the more laconic, tightly structured discourse of philosophers—onto rhetoricians of the 1960s. Corbett argues that Zeno's open hand might now represent that rhetoric committed to a rational and conciliatory form of discourse, whereas the closed fist has become the rhetoric of 1960s-style political protest, which Corbett characterizes as "non-rationale, non-sequential, often non-verbal, [and] frequently provocative" (288). For Corbett, the "black-power militant" provides the foremost example of "closed fist" rhetoric. The essay is largely comparative, with Corbett commenting upon the evolution of rhetoric from the Renaissance to modern times. Toward that end, Corbett reviews the main precepts and proponents of "open hand" rhetoric during the Renaissance, suggesting that the period's rhetoric amounts to an extension and revision of the classical tradition.

"Closed fist" rhetoric, conversely, seems to Corbett almost completely uninformed by the tenets of classical rhetoric. Featuring marches, boycotts, sit-ins, and other forms of public protest, this variety of rhetoric is largely nonverbal. Language plays a role, of course, but that role is ancillary; demonstration is the hallmark of closed fist rhetoric, at least until the "final confrontation comes, and we are [taken] back to the strategies of traditional rhetoric" (292). The impetus for this "body rhetoric" also has much to do with the dramatic diversity of contemporary cultural experience, which has problematized the capacity of language to represent reality as well as the capacity of traditional rhetorical strategies to affect change. The notion of the solitary speaker holding forth from behind the lectern, for instance, is hopelessly outdated. In its place, we find new rhetorical strategies deployed in the context of a group, the contemporary rhetor realizing that in such complex times the sustained attention of an audience is a limited resource. "*Vox populi*," Corbett claims, "can be heard in the back benches of the executive and legislative assemblies" (293).

But the voice of the people can have an abrasive, coercive edge, especially when it limits the choices available to the receiver of the communication. The rhetoric of the closed fist begins when those who would deploy it perceive that the traditional means of communication have left them without choices. For

Corbett, however, choice is "the key concept of rhetoric" (293). Consequently, he fears that the "new rhetoric" may paradoxically signal the elimination of rhetoric itself, particularly of the logical arguments that should underlie every attempt at persuasion. As Corbett sees it, the rhetoric of the closed fist has little patience with rational discourse, preferring action over contemplation, protest over conciliation. While Corbett sympathizes with the disenfranchised for whom the rhetoric of the closed fist may indeed be the only available means of persuasion, he laments its use at institutions of higher learning whose members can hardly claim to be disenfranchised. "This retreat from reason may be part of the shift to the primacy of the emotional appeal," Corbett observes presciently. "God help us all" (294).

Given Corbett's obvious enthusiasm for the classical tradition, it is tempting to interpret his remarks as a nostalgic gesture, as an argument for a return to order during a period of historic upheaval. But Corbett once again displays his talent and propensity for synthesis in the conclusion of his discussion. Acknowledging that the rhetoric of the open hand has frequently provided seemingly benign cover for established institutions and their ideologies, Corbett concedes that there are times when closed fist rhetoric is appropriate, perhaps even occasions when it overlaps with the rhetoric of the open hand. "The open hand and the closed fist," as he says, "have the same basic skeletal structure. If rhetoric is, as Aristotle defined it, 'a discovery of *all* the available means of persuasion,' let us be prepared to open and close that hand as the occasion demands. Then maybe the hand-me-down from the dim past can lend a hand-up to us poor mortals in this humming present" (296).

CORBETT'S PLACE IN HISTORY

Corbett will likely be remembered primarily for the substantial contribution he made to composition studies during the 1970s, the decade during which that field began to take shape. As president of the Conference on College Composition and Communication and, especially, as editor of *College Composition and Communication*, Corbett nurtured the field in its early days, shaping its origin and framing the terms of its evolution. Corbett also helped to establish the important graduate program in rhetoric at Ohio State University, a program that served as a laboratory for many of the ideas he promotes in his own scholarship. Corbett is also an enthusiastic historian, committed to imparting the history of the classical tradition to teachers who might then employ it in their classrooms.

This historical impulse animates much of Corbett's work, and in this regard, his strengths are of a piece with his weaknesses. What seems dubious about Corbett's work, for instance, is the totalizing insistence upon classical rhetoric's capacity to address "the *whole* man" ("Usefulness" 162; emphasis added), or "*all* the processes involved in composing a discourse" ("New Look" 17; emphasis added), or the way the classical topics "accurately categorize the mental processes involved in *any* kind of inquiry" ("New Look" 18; emphasis added). But these remarks must be gauged in relation to Corbett's rather broad understanding of classical rhetoric. The system proposed by Aristotle and expanded by Cicero, Quintillian, and many others is no monolith. Rather, it is a flexible model for discovering the available means of persuasion *within a given rhetorical situation*. For Corbett, then, classical rhetoric is context sensitive, a "means-end" art that, if it is to retain its usefulness, must be improved upon and refined as we acquire more information about ourselves and our audiences.

This pedagogical imperative touches as well upon the admirable moral dimension of Corbett's work. In his view, teachers of composition should assist students in developing moral character by drawing upon classical rhetoric's capacity to teach empathy. We cannot hope to persuade our audiences, after all, if we do not on some level identify with them. According to Corbett, this makes rhetoric a fundamentally political or civic art, an art with important ramifications for the quality of society. "Rhetoric," Corbett says, "will have a future in the continuing struggle for freedom only if we cultivate it. If we do not cultivate rhetoric, we will inherit the alternatives of babble or silence" ("Rhetoric, the Enabling Discipline" 208).

BIBLIOGRAPHY

Primary Sources

Corbett, Edward P. J. *Classical Rhetoric for the Modern Student*. New York: Oxford University Press, 1965.

————. "Hugh Blair: A Study of His Rhetorical Theory." Diss. Loyola University, 1956.

————. "A New Look at Old Rhetoric." *Rhetoric: Theories for Application*. Ed. Robert M. Gorrell. Champaign, IL: National Council of Teachers of English, 1967. 16–22.

————. "Rhetoric, the Enabling Discipline." *Selected Essays of Edward P. J. Corbett*. Ed. Robert J. Connors. Dallas: Southern Methodist University Press, 1989. 194–208.

————. "The Rhetoric of the Open Hand and the Closed Fist." *College Composition and Communication* 20.5 (1969): 288–296.

————. "A Survey of Rhetoric." *Classical Rhetoric for the Modern Student*. New York: Oxford University Press, 1965.

————. "The Usefulness of Classical Rhetoric." *College Composition and Communication* 14.3 (1963): 162–64.

————. "What Is Being Revived?" *College Composition and Communication* 18.3 (1967): 166–72.

Biography

Connors, Robert J. "Edward P. J. Corbett." *Encyclopedia of Rhetoric and Composition: Communication from Ancient Times to the Information Age*. Ed. Theresa Enos. New York: Garland, 1996. 150–51.

————. "Introduction." *Selected Essays of Edward P. J. Corbett*. Ed. Robert J. Connors. Dallas: Southern Methodist University Press, 1989. xi–xxii.

Corbett, Edward P. J. Telephone Interview. March 8, 1998.

FRANK J. D'ANGELO
(1928–   )

Theresa Enos

Frank J. D'Angelo was born and raised in New Orleans, the son of immigrants Francesco D'Angelo and Mariana Grisaffi. From an early age D'Angelo was exposed to the city's and his Italian parents' rich linguistic environment. His father loved opera, played in a local band, and performed on the stage; his mother was a storyteller, drawing on maxims and proverbs that taught by example, and entertained with Sicilian folk songs. Part of young D'Angelo's linguistic heritage were the early morning rhyming songs of street vendors selling watermelons and crawfish, as well as the music of Mardi Gras parades, blues, and New Orleans jazz.

D'Angelo's interests in rhetoric and composition have been heavily influenced by this linguistic mixture of his early life in New Orleans. His parents encouraged him to follow the American Dream, with education as the key. In parochial school he excelled in reading, spelling, grammar, geography, and penmanship. At age 12 he entered New Orleans' Jesuit High School, a college preparatory school, on an academic scholarship, excelling in English, Latin, and public speaking. After graduation, now being the sole support of his widowed mother and younger brother, he worked for the Veteran's Administration; then, after serving two years in Korea, D'Angelo returned to the federal government, married, and enrolled at Loyola University on the GI Bill. Planning to take a business degree, he switched to English, recognizing his lifelong love of reading and language, and upon graduation in 1960, he taught high school in New Orleans. During this period, in order to improve his teaching, he started reading professional journals like *College Composition and Communication* and attended his first National Council of Teachers of English (NCTE) meeting, which led to his decision to work toward an advanced degree in English at Tulane.

With his M.A. (1963) and, by now, a family of his own, he continued to teach high school. In 1966 he began to participate in workshops and summer institutes that provided training in linguistics, rhetoric and composition, and literary theory. He continued to attend NCTE conferences and delved deeper into structural and transformational linguistics. During this period of intense study and outreach, he helped put together a book of essays on the teaching of English, *The Growing Edges of Secondary English*, published by NCTE. These experiences inspired D'Angelo to become a college English teacher. He went on to receive an Advanced Certificate from the University of Illinois in 1967 and his Ph.D. from the University of Nebraska in 1970—and with Ph.D. in hand, he took a position with Arizona State University. In 1995 he became professor emeritus of English at Arizona State University.

D'Angelo's scholarly and professional career has brought him recognition and honors. He is a former chair of the Conference on College Composition and Communication (CCCC), a former member of the Executive Committee of the NCTE, a former chair of the Modern Language Association's Writing Division, and a former member of the board of directors of the Rhetoric Society of America. He has served as advisory editor for *Rhetoric Review*, the *Journal of Advanced Composition*, and *Focuses*. While at Arizona State, he developed one of the first graduate programs that offered a specialization in rhetoric and composition. In 1977 he won the Richard Braddock Award, given by the CCCC to the author of the outstanding article on the theory and/or practice of composition. In 1993 he won the Edward P. J. Corbett Award, given by the journal *Focuses* for the best article that year. His most recent scholarly contributions include "Rhetorical Criticism" in the *Encyclopedia of Rhetoric and Composition*, his work as advisory editor of that encyclopedia, and a scholarly textbook titled *Composition in the Classical Tradition*.

D'ANGELO'S RHETORICAL THEORY

Almost all of D'Angelo's research and publications have been influenced by classical traditions; his concern with the classics represents a vital substrand in the new rhetorics. His scholarly contributions to the new rhetorics range from connecting the classical *topoi* to the nineteenth-century methods of developing paragraphs, to adding his own taxonomy to the Kinneavian concept of the modes of discourse, to working with schema theory and literary structuralism—all leading to methods of organizing texts. Much of his important later work focuses on the four master tropes of Giambattista Vico and Hayden White; using the master tropes as a conceptual framework for producing texts, D'Angelo developed a rhetoric of tropes.

The 1970s and early 1980s were for D'Angelo an initiatory period, much like rhetoric itself at this point in its modern history. During this time, composition teachers began a strong movement to claim rhetoric and composition as a field of study in English departments. Teachers who were required to teach first-year writing in increasing numbers found little published on the teaching of composition, and there was hardly any guidance concerning writing pedagogy in graduate school. The formal and informal symposia these teachers organized during this time gave them a forum where they could talk about their research interests, deliver papers, and develop professionally. These groups of teachers and scholars drawn together by their interest in rhetoric gave writing teachers, who at this time had no identity or status in their own departments, not only a place to gather and exchange ideas but also a forum to chart future direction. In this environment, D'Angelo began his work in the new rhetorics, publishing on generative rhetoric ("A Generative Rhetoric of the Essay"), theories of discourse ("Modes of Discourse" and "Paradigms as Structural Counterparts of *Topoi*"), classical rhetoric ("Imitation and the Teaching of Style" and "The Evolution of the Analytic *Topoi*: A Speculative Inquiry"), and linguistic stylistics ("Paradigms as Structural Counterparts of *Topoi*"). D'Angelo's body of work during this period strongly influenced a fledgling field by application of classical rhetoric to linguistics and to the teaching of writing.

A Conceptual Theory of Rhetoric led the way into the new rhetorical theory-building and especially to the explosive interest in a new area, cognitive rhetoric. The book is an important taxonomy of theory because it reexamines rhetorical history with precise descriptions and analyses of discourse. Offering a comprehensive theory and building, in part, on James Kinneavy's *A Theory of Discourse* (Norton, 1980), D'Angelo provides yet a different theoretical approach to rhetoric that draws heavily from the classical *topoi* and modern psycholinguistics. Out of D'Angelo's work in the new rhetorics came one of the 1970s more important scholarly textbooks, *Process and Thought in Composition*. This rhetoric is important because it presented the classical modes as processes of thought, as levels of cognition, rather than subscribing to the nineteenth and early twentieth centuries' legacy of formalistic product-oriented modes. D'Angelo's work in the 1970s and early 1980s paralleled the fledgling discipline's in that this period gave direction and method to the teaching of composition with rhetoric at its center.

From the mid-1980s to the early 1990s, D'Angelo continued to draw on classical rhetoric to advance new rhetorical theory, and he continued to play a major part in the drive to professionalize the field. From the classical art of arrangement, he historicized the topic sentence ("The Topic Sentence Revisited") and traced arrangement's relationship to the four master tropes—metaphor, metonymy, synecdoche, and irony. In "Prolegomena to a Rhetoric of Tropes," he explores his theories of arrangement, and in "Tropics of Arrangement: A Theory of *Dispositio*," he shows how they are embedded and work in nonfiction. In "The Four Master Tropes: Analogues of Development," he relates the master tropes to theories of human psychological development.

D'Angelo was one of the first new rhetoricians to connect rhetoric and cultural studies. In various articles he has demonstrated how the rhetoric of advertising seduces ("Advertising and the Modes of Discourse" and "Subliminal Seduction: An Essay on the Rhetoric of the Unconscious"), how greeting cards persuade

("The Rhetoric of Sentimental Greeting Card Verse"), and how grafitti with its puns, alliteration, and rhyme draws on classical rhetorical strategies ("Sacred Cows Make Great Hamburgers: The Rhetoric of Graffiti").

Frank D'Angelo's importance to rhetoric and composition is that he has been a major figure in the twentieth-century revival of classical rhetoric in English Studies and the teaching of writing. His career paralleled rhetoric and composition's new directions in the early 1970s and the theory building of the 1980s that helped situate rhetoric and composition as a metadiscipline in the 1990s. D'Angelo's conceptual theories of rhetoric make him one of the century's more important new rhetoricians. But his place in the new rhetorics is made secure by the praxis he has constructed out of his modern theory building. His innovative and creative work on the use of dialogue, the *progymnasmata*, proverbs, sentence paradigms, invention and arrangement, his groundbreaking 1970s textbook, and his current work on narrative and argument all demonstrate that, like the ancients, D'Angelo's new rhetoric has as its very basis practice.

Part of our living history, D'Angelo is a twentieth-century rhetorician who has devoted his career to restoring rhetoric to its former central role in education; his work enables us to see rhetoric's truly interdisciplinary nature.

BIBLIOGRAPHY

Primary Sources

D'Angelo, Frank J. "Advertising and the Modes of Discourse." *College Composition and Communication* 29.4 (1978): 356–61.

———. "Aims, Modes, and Forms of Discourse." *Teaching Composition: 12 Bibliographical Essays*. Rev. ed. Ed. Gary Tate. Fort Worth: Texas Christian University Press, 1987. 131–54.

———. *Composition in the Classical Tradition*. Needham Heights, MA: Allyn & Bacon, 2000.

———. *A Conceptual Theory of Rhetoric*. Cambridge, MA: Winthrop, 1975.

———. "The Evolution of the Analytic *Topoi*: A Speculative Inquiry." *Classical Rhetoric and Modern Discourse*. Ed. Robert Connors, Lisa Ede, and Andrea Lunsford. Carbondale: Southern Illinois University Press, 1984. 50–68.

———. "The Four Master Tropes: Analogues of Development." *Rhetoric Review* 11.1 (1992): 91–107.

———. "A Generative Rhetoric of the Essay." *College Composition and Communication* 25.3 (1974): 338–96.

———. "A Generative Rhetoric of the Essay." *Rhetoric and Composition: A Sourcebook for Teachers*. Ed. Richard Graves. New York: Hayden, 1976. 201–11.

———. "Imitation and Style." *College Composition and Communication* 24.3 (1973): 283–90.

———. "Imitation and the Teaching of Style." *forum: Essays on Theory and Practice in the Teaching of Writing*. Ed. Patricia L. Stock. Montclair, NJ: Boynton/Cook, 1983. 173–88.

———. "Modes of Discourse." *Teaching Composition: Ten Bibliographical Essays*. Ed. Gary Tate. Fort Worth: Texas Christian University Press, 1976. 111–35.

———. "19th Century Forms/Modes of Discourse." *College Composition and Communication* 35.1 (1984): 31–42.

———. "Paradigms as Structural Counterparts of *Topoi*." *Linguistics, Stylistics, and the Teaching of Composition*. Ed. Donald McQuade. Akron, OH: Language and Style, 1979. 41–51.

———. *Process and Thought in Composition*. Cambridge, MA: Winthrop, 1977. 2nd ed. 1980. 3rd ed. Boston: Little, Brown, 1985.

———. "Prolegomena to a Rhetoric of Tropes." *Rhetoric Review* 6.1 (1987): 32–40.

———. "Rhetorical Criticism." *Encyclopedia of Rhetoric and Composition: Communication from Ancient Times to the Information Age*. Ed. Theresa Enos. New York: Garland, 1996. 604–8.

———. "Rhetoric and Cognition: Toward a Metatheory of Discourse." *PRE/TEXT* 3.2 (1982): 105–17.

———. "The Rhetoric of Sentimental Greeting Card Verse." *Rhetoric Review* 10.2 (1992): 337–45.

———. "Sacred Cows Make Great Hamburgers: The Rhetoric of Graffiti." *College Composition and Communication* 25.2 (1974): 173–80.

———. "The Sentence." *Research in Composition and Rhetoric*. Ed. Michael G. Moran and Ronald F. Lunsford. Westport, CT: Greenwood Press, 1984. 303–17.

———. "Subliminal Seduction: An Essay on the Rhetoric of the Unconscious." *Rhetoric Review* 4.2 (1986): 160–71.

———. "Style as Structure." *Style* 8.1 (1974): 322–64.

———. "The Topic Sentence Revisited." *College Composition and Communication* 37.2 (1986): 431–41.

———. "Tropics of Arrangement: A Theory of *Dispositio*." *Journal of Advanced Composition* 10.1 (1990): 101–9.

———. "Up Against the Wall, Mother: The Rhetoric of Slogans, Catch Phrases, and Graffiti." *A Symposium in Rhetoric*. Ed. William E. Tanner, J. Dean Bishop, and Turner S. Kobler. Denton: Texas Woman's University Press, 1976. 104–14.

Suhor, Charles, John Sawyer, and Frank J. D'Angelo, eds. *The Growing Edges of Secondary English*. Champaign, IL: NCTE, 1968.

Biography

Dupont, Leslie. "Frank J. D'Angelo." *Encyclopedia of Rhetoric and Composition: Communication from Ancient Times to the Information Age*. Ed. Theresa Enos. New York: Garland, 1996.

Criticism

Crusius, Timothy W. *Discourse: A Critique and a Synthesis of Major Theories*. New York: MLA, 1989. 80–101.

PAUL DE MAN
(1919–1983)

Jo Suzuki

Paul de Man was born on December 6, 1919, in Antwerp, one of the largest seaports in Europe and the largest Flemish-speaking city in Belgium. He entered the Free University of Brussels in 1937 to study science and philosophy and earned the degree called Candidature in 1940. After an unsuccessful attempt to leave Belgium to escape the German occupying forces, he got a job writing a column entitled "Chronique littéraire" for the collaborationist daily newspaper *Le Soir* because of the influence of his uncle Hendrik de Man, a prominent socialist thinker and government minister in Belgium at that time. Paul de Man resigned from this position in protest against the German control of the newspaper in November 1942. His writings for *Le Soir* and for the Flemish journal *Het Vlaamsche Land* during this period were not discovered until 1987, four years after his death, when they drew a sensationalistic response in and out of academia.[1]

De Man left Belgium in 1948 for America, planning to start a publishing firm. Arriving in New York, he first worked as a clerk in the Doubleday bookshop in Grand Central Station. Then he obtained a job teaching French literature at Bard College during the academic years of 1949 to 1951. After leaving Bard, he went on to Boston to teach French at the Berlitz School in the fall of 1951. There he attended the informal gathering of graduate students at Harvard and met the professors of comparative literature, Harry Levin and Renato Poggioli. With their encouragement, de Man was accepted for a position as a junior fellow of the Society of Fellows at Harvard. From Harvard, de Man earned an M.A. in 1958 and a Ph.D. in 1960. His Ph.D. dissertation title was "Mallarmé, Yeats, and the Post-Romantic Predicament."

Leaving Harvard, de Man taught at Cornell from 1960 to 1969 and Johns Hopkins from 1968 to 1970 while alternating the appointment as Ordinarius for

Comparative Literature at the University of Zurich from 1963 to 1970.[2] In 1966, at the colloquium on "The Languages of Criticism and the Sciences of Man" held at Johns Hopkins, de Man met Jacques Derrida for the first time; this marked the beginning of their long-lasting friendship and intellectual alliance.[3] In 1970, de Man moved to Yale. While he was there, the group of scholars including him, Derrida (who came at his invitation), Harold Bloom, Geoffrey Hartman, and J. Hillis Miller became known as the "Yale School." De Man was made Sterling Professor of Comparative Literature and French in 1979 and continued his productive teaching and writing career at Yale until his death. Paul de Man died of cancer on December 21, 1983.

DE MAN'S RHETORICAL THEORY

Paul de Man is one of the most influential and most controversial rhetorical theorists of this century. De Man was the main force behind the introduction, development, and popularization of what is called "deconstruction" or "deconstructive criticism," which became prevalent in American academia during the late 1970s and the early 1980s. He introduced rhetorical concepts and terminologies to the criticisms of literary and philosophical texts and generated renewal of interest in rhetoric. Moreover, his epistemological view of rhetoric raised controversy and rekindled the ancient sophistic debate between philosophy and rhetoric in contemporary academia. De Man saw rhetoric as an epistemological position that privileged multiplicity and indeterminacy in opposition to philosophy, which privileged an epistemology of certainty, singularity, and totalization. He says, "Rhetoric as I understand it, for which irony is the concept of limit, is not only multiple. The multiple is also totalized—it's the disruption of the single" (Moynihan 587). Thus his work can be placed in the age-long conflict between philosophy and rhetoric, taking the side of rhetoricians over philosophers (cf. Norris 65–101). The extent of his influence, not only through his writing but also through his teaching, can be evidenced in the special issue of *Yale French Studies* in his tribute titled "The Lesson of Paul de Man." A decade and a half after his death, his works are still collected and published. As previously mentioned, the posthumous discovery of his early journalistic writings raised sensational responses in and out of academia and called for the publication of two volumes, one a collection of his "wartime journalism" articles (*Wartime Journalism, 1939–43*) and the other a collection of articles by various scholars in response to this discovery (*Responses: On Paul de Man's Wartime Journalism*). Both his supporters and detractors still continue to generate discussions regarding his work. If the energy spent by one's detractors is any indication of one's historical importance (in the tradition of Plato and Gorgias of Leontini), we can see one such indication of de Man's importance in Brian Vickers's acclaimed *In Defence of Rhetoric*, where Vickers considers de Man's work so great a threat as to spend a considerable space (10 pages!) attacking it as the "example of the reduction, fragmentation, and misapplication of rhetoric in modern literary discourse" in the chapter titled "The Future of Rhetoric" (453).

As he preferred to write essays on diverse topics to writing books throughout the three decades of his academic career, de Man's works show his multifarious interests. Some, however, recognize two or three discernible phases in his works (cf. Miller, *Times Literary Supplement* 685; Wlad Godzich, "Foreword: The Tiger on the Paper Mat," in *The Resistance to Theory* ix–xii). These phases can be called the existential/phenomenological, the rhetorical, and the politico-ideological phases. As discussed below, these phases are not distinct and periodic but cumulative and dependent, as the themes and concepts developed in the earlier ones flow into and form an inseparable base of the latter ones.

The initial existential/phenomenological phases of de Man's works are collected in his first book *Blindness and Insight* and in the posthumously published collection *Critical Writings, 1953–1978*. In the works in these volumes, we can observe remarkable convergence of the two main threads of his intellectual upbringing: One is his interest in and concern for such existential and phenomenological notions as self, consciousness, and temporality, which he developed while he was still on the Continent; the other is his characteristic style of close reading and critical linguistic analysis, which he acquired through his training in the New Criticism after his crossing of the Atlantic. In his interview with Robert Moynihan in 1980, de Man notes that the New Criticism gave him linguistic terminologies that allowed him to escape from what he called the "existential philosophical mode of discourse" characterized by its "ontological language or the language of the subject, the language of the self" (Moynihan 589): The New Criticism, by its rejection of the external mode of criticisms (such as biographical and historical criticism) and adherence to "close reading" and rigorous rhetorical exegesis, made him shift his focus away from person (i.e., writer) to text, from subjectivity to language.

Yet while the New Critics, following the Romantic tradition, delve in organicism and discovery of the "totalities of meaning," de Man utilizes the same exegetical procedure to accomplish just the opposite. In "Form and Intent in the American New Criticism," he writes:

As it refines its interpretations more and more, American criticism does not discover a single meaning, but a plurality of significations that can be radically opposed to each other. Instead of revealing a continuity affiliated with the coherence of the natural world, it takes us into a discontinuous world of reflective irony and ambiguity. Almost in spite of itself, it pushes the interpretative process so far that the analogy between the organic world and the language of poetry finally explodes. This unitarian criticism finally becomes a criticism of ambiguity, an ironic reflection on the absence of the unity it had postulated. (*Blindness and Insight* 28)

We can observe in this passage two of his seminal thoughts to be further developed in his subsequent works, namely, the critique of the ideology of the

Romantic aesthetics and the linguistic resistence of the unitarian or totalizing interpretation, which he later calls "deconstruction."

Regarding the phenomenological topics in this phase of his work, de Man particularly preoccupies himself with the notion of "self" in relation to the act of reading. In *Blindness and Insight*, he dedicates three articles to investigate this topic. In all three articles, "self" appears not as a singular and stable entity but as something that becomes highly problematic: In his critique of Ludwig Binswanger, he describes "self" as something to be sublimated; in his critique of Maurice Blanchot, it becomes estranged; and finally, in his critique of Georges Poulet, it even becomes immolated.

Although the subtitle of *Blindness and Insight* reads *Essays in the Rhetoric of Contemporary Criticism*, the majority of the essays in it have little to do with rhetoric. In his interview, de Man admits that his earlier works did not utilize rhetorical concepts: "I have by no means always used that [rhetorical] terminology. It is not at all present in *Blindness and Insight*, for instance" (589). However, with the 1969 essay titled "Rhetoric of Temporality" (which was added later to the second edition of *Blindness and Insight*), de Man makes his "rhetorical turn." In his foreword to the revised second edition of *Blindness and Insight*, he writes, "With the deliberate emphasis on rhetorical terminology, ["Rhetoric of Temporality"] argues what seemed to me to be a change, not only in terminology and in tone but in substance. This terminology is still uncomfortably intertwined with the thematic vocabulary of consciousness and of temporality that was current at the time, but it signals a turn that, at least for me, has proven to be productive" (xii). This "new" approach culminates in the publication of his second book, *Allegories of Reading*, in 1979.

In the opening essay of *Allegories of Reading* titled "Semiology and Rhetoric," de Man explicates his notion of rhetoric. Rhetoric to him is not just a linguistic analysis of tropes and figures (6) but an epistemological approach to a text that stands in opposition to the other two members of the trivium, namely, grammar and logic. Both grammar and logic seek universalization (or "totalization") of linguistic phenomena, logic dealing with prepositions and grammar with syntactic formations. As such, logic and grammar "stand to each other in a dyadic relationship of unsubverted support" (7). Rhetoric, in contrast, disrupts this universalization as it "radically suspends logic [and grammar] and opens up vertiginous possibilities of referential aberration" (10).

De Man's grammar–logic/rhetoric couplet does not form a binary opposition (in the structuralist sense) since they are not mutually exclusive but exist simultaneously in a given reading of a text (12). As the logical-grammatical and the rhetorical possibilities are ever copresent in a given text, every reading has a tendency either to unify and totalize its mode of experience through the "grammaticization" of rhetoric or to suspend its multiplicity of possibilities in indeterminacy through the "rhetoricization" of grammar (16). De Man sees that, in the "semiological" approaches to literature taken by such critics as Roman Jakobson, Roland Barthes, Gérard Genette, Tzvetan Todorov, and A. J. Greimas, the fundamental and irreducible difference between grammar and rhetoric is ignored by "letting grammar and rhetoric function in perfect continuity, and in passing from grammatical to rhetorical structure without difficulty or interruption" (6). These approaches privilege grammar over rhetoric and "grammatize" rhetoric by reducing tropes and figures to a predictable pattern of paradigmatic substitution. De Man opposes this trend by emphasizing "rhetoricization of grammar" so as to revive the interplay between the two, and this interplay between rhetoric and grammar/logic is behind the very concept for which de Man is most widely known, that is, the critical reading procedure known as "deconstruction." In his answer to the question, How would you define the term *deconstruction?* de Man says, "It's possible, within a text, to frame a question or to undo assertions made in the text by means of elements which are in the text, which frequently would be precisely structures that play off rhetorical against grammatical elements" (Moynihan 599).

The term *deconstruction*, however, is not original to de Man. He credits Derrida for its invention and acknowledges that he first encountered it in reading his *Of Grammatology:* "I consciously came across 'deconstruction' for the first time in the writings of Jacques Derrida, which means that it is associated with a power of inventive rigor to which I lay no claim but which I certainly do not wish to erase" (*Allegories of Reading* x; see also Moynihan 600). It is interesting to note that of all the unique concepts and terminologies that he employed in his works (such as his application of rhetoric and rhetorical terminologies to literary criticism, the notion of the duality of blindness/insight and of reading/ misreading, textual lacunae, aberrations and aporia, etc.), it was this "borrowed term" that became the focal point of academic controversy and brought him notoriety. In his preface to *Allegories of Reading*, we see de Man consciously noting the notoriousness of the term "deconstruction": "Deconstruction, as was easily predictable, has been much misrepresented, dismissed as a harmless academic game or denounced as a terrorist weapon" (x). Rather than giving in to the natural inclination once and for all to "straighten out" these misrepresentations, he counters this tendency in a characteristically de Manian fashion: "[A]nd I have all the fewer illusions about the possibility of countering these aberrations since such an expectation would go against the drift of my own readings" (x).

Although de Man, Derrida, and others who follow their conceptual mode and style are often grouped as "deconstructionists" and their views as "deconstructionism" (mostly by their popular and/or academic detractors), it is important to note that this popular label is erroneous and misleading. Deconstruction is not some methodology to be embraced and followed, as it does not claim to bring in any external framework to the act of reading. De Man writes, "The deconstruction is not something we have added to the text but it constituted the text in the first place. A literary text simultaneously asserts and denies the authority of its own rhetorical mode, and by reading the text as we did we were only trying to come closer to being as rigorous a reader as the author had to be in order to write the sentence in the first place" (17). Furthermore, deconstruction is not something we consciously do to a text: "[D]econstruction is not something we can decide to do or not to do at will. It is co-extensive with any use of language, and this use is compulsive or . . . imperative" (125). Deconstruction is thus inherent in the very nature of language, or, as de Man formulates it, " 'the text deconstructs itself, is self-deconstructive' rather than being deconstructed by a philosophical intervention from the outside of the text" (*Resistance to Theory* 118).

The autonomy, and primacy of language, as seen in its self-deconstructive nature, is one of the main characteristics of the de Manian rhetorical theory and sets his deconstruction apart from Derrida's. De Man himself notes this as he contrasts his and Derrida's work: "I have a tendency to put upon texts an inherent authority, which is stronger, I think, than Derrida is willing to put on them. I assume as a working hypothesis . . . that the text *knows* in an absolute way what it's doing" (118). This emphasis on the autonomous and self-deconstructive nature of language carries on to the final politico-ideological phase of his work.

In the works of the politico-ideological phase, which are collected in the posthumous volumes *The Resistance to Theory* and *Aesthetic Ideology*, de Man makes an overt and conscious turn to the issues of history, ideology, and politics. Although he claims that he never ignored these issues early in his career, he admits that he was reluctant to tackle them because he believed that he was not ready to handle them until the preparatory works were done to equip him with necessary conceptual and linguistic tools: "I have always maintained that one could approach the problems of ideology and by extension the problems of politics only on the basis of critical-linguistic analysis, which had to be done in its own terms, in the medium of language, and I felt I could approach those problems only after having achieved a certain control over those questions" (*Resistance to Theory* 121).

De Man's critical-linguistic procedure to analyze the problem of ideology is evident in the titular essay of *The Resistance to Theory*. This essay, which was originally commissioned by the Modern Language Association to be included in *Introduction to Scholarship in Modern Languages and Literature* but was subsequently rejected, most immediately deals with the issue of contemporary academics' aversion and resistance to literary theory. The argument that de Man uses in it, however, covers the same familiar ground as "Semiology and Rhetoric": It revisits the trivium and sets rhetoric in opposition to grammar and logic. What is new in the argument of "The Resistance to Theory" is the added element of referential reality. De Man defines the trivium and relates it to contemporary literary theory as follows: "The most familiar and general of all linguistic models, the classical *trivium*, . . . is in fact a set of unresolved tensions powerful enough to have generated an infinitely prolonged discourse of endless frustration of which contemporary literary theory, even at its most self assured, is one more chapter" (13). The argument in "Semiology and Rhetoric" explicates this "unresolved tension" (i.e., between rhetoric and grammar-logic) in terms of their internal relationship; the argument in "The Resistance to Theory" explicates it in terms of their respective relationship to the reality outside linguistic construct: Whereas logic and grammar present language as having an immediate access to referential reality ("Grammar stands in the service of logic which, in turn, allows for the passage to the knowledge of the world"), rhetoric halts this access (14–15). The contemporary resistance to "theory" is therefore one's resistance to be painfully reminded of this epistemological volatility (17).

This language-reality connection and/or disjunction is crucial to understanding de Man's notion of "ideology." He defines ideology as "the confusion of linguistic with natural reality, of reference with phenomenalism" (11). One is taken by ideology when a linguistic construct appears to him/her as a natural and immediate property of the referential reality. De Man goes on to claim that "more than any other mode of inquiry . . . the linguistics of literariness is a powerful and indispensable tool in the unmasking of ideological aberrations, as well as determining factor in accounting for their occurrence" (11). Unmasking ideology involves, therefore, deconstructing what is considered "natural" to show that it indeed is a linguistic construct disjoined from reality.

Another form of the notion of the linguistic-referential disjunction is seen in "Conclusions: Walter Benjamin's 'The Task of the Translator' " (*Resistance to Theory* 73–93). In this article, de Man uses Benjamin's text to show that translation by definition is a failure to translate:

The translator can never do what the original text did. Any translation is always second in relation to the original, and the translator as such is lost from the very beginning. He is per definition underpaid, he is per definition overworked, he is per definition the one history will not really retain as an equal. (80)

This is because in the process of translation, the original lexical forms, grammatical structures, and symbols must be disjoined from the source language as it is translated into the target language.

What is most remarkable about this view of translation is that de Man goes on to extend it to other activities that are derived from original activities. For example, philosophy is a translation of original perception, criticism is a translation of original works of art, and history is a translation of original actions. As a translation, these activities have failed to accomplish what they set out to accomplish from the very beginning and are subject to being deconstructed. Thus, de Man's ideology critique extends every area of linguistic activity. This is a far cry from the common charge raised against deconstruction as being a mere academicism and political quietism. De Man's reply to this charge is that "[t]hose who reproach literary theory for being oblivious to social and historical (that is to say ideological) reality are merely stating their fear at having their own ideological mystifications exposed by the tool they are trying to discredit" (11).

Paul de Man's rhetorical theory is a product of a rare combination of the vastness of his Continental philosophical background, the linguistic subtlety that comes from his New Critical training, and the personal political sensitivity that undoubtedly came from tasting the forbidden fruit and acquiring the experiential knowledge of the danger of totalitarian nationalism. Despite his tainted past and the notoriety that the term *deconstruction* acquired, de Man must be recognized as one of the most important rhetorical theorists of our time, and his works must be appreciated as one of the finest examples of scholarship.

NOTES

1. For the most comprehensive chronological account of the discovery of de Man's early writings, as well as the defense of de Man, see Jacques Derrida's "Like the Sound of the Sea Deep within a Shell: Paul de Man's War" (in *Responses: On Paul de Man's Wartime Journalism*; originally in the spring 1988 issue of *Critical Inquiry*).

2. See Stefano Rosso's "An Interview with Paul de Man" in *The Resistance to Theory* (116–17) for de Man's view on the differences between European and American scholarship.

3. See Derrida's *Mémoires: For Paul de Man*. For the relationship between de Man's and Derrida's work in de Man's own words, see Stefano Rosso's "An Interview with Paul de Man" in *The Resistance to Theory* (116–18); for the difference between them, see J. Hillis Miller's " 'Reading' Part of a Paragraph in *Allegories of Reading*" in *Reading de Man Reading* (Waters and Godzich).

BIBLIOGRAPHY

Primary Sources

De Man, Paul. *Aesthetic Ideology*. Ed. Andrzej Warminski. Minneapolis: University of Minnesota Press, 1996.
———. *Allegories of Reading: Figural Language in Rousseau, Nietzsche, Rilke and Proust*. New Haven, CT: Yale University Press, 1979.
———. *Blindness and Insight: Essays in the Rhetoric of Contemporary Criticism*. 2nd ed. Minneapolis: University of Minnesota Press, 1983.
———. *Critical Writings, 1953–1978*. Ed. Lindsay Waters. Minneapolis: University of Minnesota Press, 1989.
———. "Mallarmé, Yeats, and the Post-Romantic Predicament." Diss. Harvard University, May 1960.
———. *The Resistance to Theory*. Minneapolis: University of Minnesota Press, 1986.
———. *The Rhetoric of Romanticism*. New York: Columbia University Press, 1984.
———. *Wartime Journalism, 1939–43*. Ed. Werner Hamacher, Neil Hertz, and Thomas Keenan. Lincoln: University of Nebraska Press, 1988.
Moynihan, Robert. "Interview with Paul de Man." *The Yale Review* 73.4 (1984): 576–602.

Biography

Culler, Jonathan. "Paul de Man." *Modern American Critics since 1955. Dictionary of Literary Biography*. Vol. 67. Ed. Gregory S. Jay. Detroit: Gale Research, 1988. 74–89.

Hamacher, Werner, Neil Hertz, and Thomas Keenan, eds. *Responses: On Paul de Man's Wartime Journalism*. Lincoln: University of Nebraska Press, 1989.

Norris, Christopher. *Paul de Man: Deconstruction and the Critique of Aesthetic Ideology*. New York: Routledge, 1988.

Waters, Lindsay. "Introduction, Paul de Man: Life and Works." *Critical Writings, 1953–1978*. Ed. Lindsay Waters. Minneapolis: University of Minnesota Press, 1989. ix–lxxiv.

Criticism

Brooks, Peter, Shoshana Felman, and J. Hillis Miller, eds. "The Lesson of Paul de Man." *Yale French Studies*. No. 69. New Haven, CT: Yale University Press, 1985.

Culler, Jonathan. "Paul de Man." *Modern American Critics since 1955. Dictionary of Literary Biography*. Vol. 67. Ed. Gregory S. Jay. Detroit: Gale Research, 1988. 74–89.

De Graef, Ortwin. *Serenity in Crisis: A Preface to Paul de Man 1939–1960*. Lincoln: University of Nebraska Press, 1993.

Derrida, Jacques. *Of Grammatology*. Trans. Gayatri Chakravorty Spivak. Baltimore: Johns Hopkins University Press, 1976.

———. *Mémoires: For Paul de Man*. Trans. Cecile Lindsay, Jonathan Culler, and Eduardo Cadava. New York: Columbia University Press, 1986.

Miller, J. Hillis. "Untitled." *The Times Literary Supplement* 17–23 June 1988: 676, 685.

Norris, Christopher. *Paul de Man: Deconstruction and the Critique of Aesthetic Ideology*. New York: Routledge, 1988.

Vickers, Brian. *In Defense of Rhetoric*. New York: Oxford University Press, 1988.

Waters, Lindsay, and Wlad Godzich, eds. *Reading de Man Reading*. Minneapolis: University of Minnesota Press, 1989.

JACQUES DERRIDA
(1930–   )

Cynthia Haynes

Jacques Derrida was born in El-Biar, Algeria, of Sephardic Jewish parents on July 15, 1930. As a young man he studied philosophy in Paris at the École Normale Supérieure (1952–1956) and at the Sorbonne (1953–1954). Derrida eventually taught at both the Sorbonne (1960–1964) and the École (1965–1984), hitting the scene in the United States in the mid-1960s with several teaching stints at Harvard, Johns Hopkins, and Yale University. Today, Derrida divides his time between Paris, where he is Director d'Études at the École des Hautes Études en Science Sociales, and the United States, where he holds a teaching appointment at the University of California at Irvine in philosophy, French, and comparative literature.

In a remarkable burst of publications in 1967, Derrida's entrance into philosophical and literary history was secured with the publication of three major works: *Of Grammatology, Writing and Difference*, and *Speech and Phenomena*. But controversy and confusion surrounded Derrida's arrival due to both the highly difficult language he employs and the fact that his work seeks to examine sacred philosophical and literary assumptions. When English translations of his work began to appear in the early 1970s, the effect on English studies in general was profoundly revolutionary. As for rhetoric, Derrida's work provided a serious validation of the field's historical affinity for sophistic counterprinciples to philosophy's definitions of "truth," "reality," "knowledge," "self," and "language" (cf. Vitanza). During the 1970s, Derrida came to represent an intellectual counterculture bent on questioning the academic status quo.

Interestingly, it was not until 1980, following an illustrious and prolific decade during which he published *Dissemination, Margins of Philosophy, Positions*, and numerous other articles, that Derrida earned his Doctorate d'État (see Yeghiayan; Spivak's "Translator's Preface" ix). The occasion prompted him to write on the process of having written and published so much prior to receiving the degree in an essay entitled "The Time of a Thesis: Punctuations" (1983). In his characteristic manner, Derrida situates himself at odds with the "academy" and in some ways offers us a telling glimpse into his most significant contribution to twentieth-century rhetoric. In that essay he acknowledges the binding force of *legitimate* scholarship. He writes that "[t]he reproductive force of authority can get along more comfortably with declarations or theses whose content presents itself as revolutionary, provided that they respect the rites of legitimation, the rhetoric and the institutional symbolism which defuses and neutralizes whatever comes from outside the system" (44). Derrida understands how threatening his work is and why. He warns that when one's politics or ethics is questioned, it is often because "the first defensive and reactionary reflex is to accuse of ethico-political irresponsibility, even of 'nihilism,' the very one who comes like this to question and disturb the *doxa* in its slumber" ("Canons" 202–3). Just what comes to disturb, and thus prompts Derrida to carve his work into the sedimentation of geophilosophical bedrock, is something that early on he describes as the birth of a "formless, mute, infant, and terrifying form of monstrosity" ("Structure" 293). These incisive comments describe Derrida's most important contribution to rhetoric, *deconstruction*, a theory of writing and a strategy of reading that threatens the "received traditions" of the production and interpretation of meaning.

   To chronicle and evaluate Derrida's contribution to rhetoric requires waiving much of his work that falls beyond a synoptic rhetorical scope, even though twentieth-century rhetoric is a kaleidoscope of crystalline forces that shape patterns of meaning, pedagogy, and scholarship viewed from many perspectives and projected through multiple refractions of light. We cannot, for example, do justice to how Derrida's thinking has influenced theology, Eastern philosophies, feminist theory, ethicopolitics, architecture, and other critical and aesthetic domains. That said, Derrida's work is part of a serious confluence of radical changes that occurred in both Europe and the United States during the 1960s and whose lasting influences continue to reverberate even today. As a writer for the avant-garde journal *Tel Quel* in France, Derrida aligned himself with intellectual and political student movements against the "establishment" even though he was, and still is, clearly among the academic elite. But then that is part of Derrida's project of *deconstruction*, working from within and acknowledging (always) that he inhabits the very structures he aims to critique. In that sense, deconstruction does not come from the "outside," as its critics believe. Philosophically speaking, Derrida's work is most widely recognized for its role in a massive critique of Western metaphysics begun in the late nineteenth century. Thus, while Derrida's rereadings of Plato, Aristotle, and countless others serve to break free from "limited" realms of classical rhetorical inquiry, *deconstruction* has without a doubt changed what we think of as philosophy and rhetoric, and it has done so from within the very structure of their historical conflict.

THE ORIGINS OF DECONSTRUCTION

Deconstruction can be situated at the apex of a history of the critique of Western metaphysics that has been under way since Nietzsche questioned the nature of truth, morals, language, and subjectivity in the late nineteenth century. With the publication of *Being and Time* in 1927, Martin Heidegger took Nietzsche further than we imagined was possible, initiating the next phase in the "destructive hermeneutics" that Nietzsche had begun. The critique begun by Nietzsche and Heidegger, as well as the paradigm of critique itself, took a radical turn in the work of Derrida.

In many ways, Derrida has uprooted the foundations of Western philosophical assumptions more than any other single writer. Derrida's thinking shook the foundations near an epicenter where Heideggerian hermeneutics was already at work on the *destruction* of Western metaphysics with respect to the question of Being and the hegemonic relation of Being to *logos* (what Derrida would come to call *logocentrism*). However, even though he is indebted to Heidegger, Derrida's reliance on him only goes so far. The key points of contention between Heidegger's hermeneutics of destruction and Derrida's deconstruction rest primarily with logocentrism. To begin with, although Heidegger calls for the destruction of Western metaphysics, Derrida claims that Heidegger is a metaphysician thoroughly entrenched in a logocentric tradition grounded in the notion of being as pure presence. One way Heidegger attempts to overturn the metaphysical tradition is through redefining *logos* according to a pre-Socratic sense of preverbal revelation or disclosure. But Derrida suggests Heidegger is a victim of the very tradition he tries to overturn.

According to Derrida, Heidegger is caught in logocentrism by virtue of his deconstruction of the term *logos*. Heidegger's excavation of *logos* by way of a Heraclitean metaphor of lightning, the revealing and concealing illumination of truth, is problematic for several reasons. The problem of "illumination" in Heidegger's reading of the pre-Socratic thought found in "The Anaximander Fragment" prevents him from moving beyond the threshold of metaphysical presencing to the "excess of difference" that Derrida considers the key to deconstruction. In Heidegger's lecture on the fragment, he identifies difference as the "illumination of the distinction" between Beings and beings as a "trace which remains preserved in the language to which Being comes" (*Early* 51). The concepts of *difference* and *trace* become something else in Derrida. Heidegger's trace is a signifier for presence. But in *"Ousia et grammé"* Derrida emphasizes difference rather than presence: "Beyond Beings and beings, this difference, ceaselessly differing from and deferring (itself), would trace (itself) (by itself)— this *différance* would be the first or last trace if one could still speak, here, of origin and end" (*Margins* 67). Ultimately, Derrida thinks Heidegger did not go far enough in his turn away from truth and Being to language.

In other words, the second problem Derrida points to is that Heidegger could not abandon the primacy of the "Subject." Spivak explains that "[t]o be sure, when Heidegger sets Being before all concepts, he is attempting to free language from the fallacy of a fixed origin, which is also a fixed end. But, *in a certain way*, he also sets up Being as what Derrida calls the 'transcendental signified' " ("Translators" xvi). As Derrida argues, the question of Being (that Heidegger translates as *Dasein*) "cannot be reduced to a subjectivity, certainly, but the existential analytic still retains the formal traits of every transcendental analytic" (" 'Eating Well' " 98). *Dasein* harbors essential traits like "freedom, resolute-decision . . . the 'call' [*Ruf*] toward a moral conscience, responsibility, primordial imputability or guilt [*Schuldigsein*], etc." (98). In contrast, Derrida turns to Nietzsche's critique of consciousness and the ethics of Emmanuel Levinas to reconceive the "subject" in different terms.

Nietzsche understood that any notion of a subject necessitates a fixed "unified concept" that is no more than "the result of 'interpretation.' " Nietzsche often stresses that it is a specifically linguistic figurative habit of immemorial standing: 'that when it is thought [*wenn gedacht wird*] there must be something "that thinks" is simply a formulation of our grammatical custom that adds a doer to every deed.' . . . The *'insertion of a subject' is 'fictitious'* " (qtd. in Spivak, "Translators" xxiv). Derrida also relies on Levinas because he speaks of subjectivity "in a new, forceful, and unusual way" (112). For Levinas, the subject is constituted as the "subjectivity of the *hostage* . . . the one who is delivered to the other in the sacred openness of ethics, to the origin of sacredness itself" (112). In essence, we are responsible for (or hostage to) the other *before* being responsible for ourselves. To understand this shift necessitates a deconstruction not only of classical subjectivity and Aristotelian ethics but of what constitutes the "other" (*pathos*) as well. Herman Rapaport explains that for Derrida a subject is "reunited with a pre-history that occurs 'outside' of Greek logocentrism where the Other as radically Other, cannot be thought, an 'outside' where the self is divested of that ontology which precludes the ethical understanding of its responsibilities before the alterity of the Other" (*Heidegger and Derrida* 221).

Whether Derrida's critique of Heidegger is on or off the mark, one thing is clear: Hermeneutics and deconstruction are fundamentally opposed on the issue of reading and subjectivity. If hermeneutics is linked to the possibility of decidability, deconstruction is a demonstration of the inevitability of undecidability. Deconstruction is an attempt to mark the nonlimits of a text and of interpretation in general. Furthermore, subjectivity is problematized, as questions of authority, intention, truth, and knowledge become objects of deconstruction instead of the a priori absolutes that hermeneutics guards in its economy of metaphysical presence. Meaning is built of traces, and traces are nothing but structures of differences. Derrida calls this "unfolding of difference" *différance* (*Positions* 10). Deconstruction suggests that only through *persistent* negation (the play of revealing and concealing) are we capable of interpretation at all. In other words, the hermeneutic notion of reading celebrates identity and presence; a deconstructive reading celebrates difference and absence.

The question of reading, then, contains an aggregation of differential structures and a history of resistance to those structures. If reading presupposes the relation of ethics and the subject, deconstructive reading rejects that it is a relation *necessarily* linked by *logos*. In fact, according to Derrida, the subject resists our attempts both to represent (write) it and to decode (read) it. In his essay "Freud and the Scene of Writing," Derrida announces: "The 'subject' of writing does not exist if we mean by that some sovereign solitude of the author. The subject of writing is a *system* of relations between strata: the Mystic Pad, the psyche, society, the world" (226–27). In short, he claims, subjectivity is "inscribed in a system of *différance*" (*Positions* 28).

Noting the irony of subjects deconstructing subjectivity (e.g., "[I]f the 'subject' is thus put in question, it is clear that the philosopher creating his system must distrust himself as none other" [Spivak, "Translators" xxvii]), Derrida similarly acknowledges that it is difficult to order reading protocols to perform according to a system whose goal is to intervene in reading processes of all kinds. Thus, Derrida confesses that a certain frustration accompanies reading that opposes "a hermeneutical or exegetical method which would seek out a finished signified beneath a textual surface" (*Positions* 63). For Derrida, reading is transformational, but "this transformation cannot be executed however one wishes. It requires protocols of reading . . . [and, he says] I have not yet found any that satisfy me" (63).

DECONSTRUCTION AND READING

Derrida has become synonymous with deconstruction and with certain key terms that seem to defy interpretation. But these terms are invaluable capacitors of the energy conducting the latest revival of rhetoric. To view deconstruction within a constellation of concepts whose orbit is also rhetorical, it is necessary to understand that Derrida would resist marking any "key" concepts as such, though some critics call them "concept-metaphors" for convenience's sake. If pressed, Derrida defines deconstruction as marking the limits of certain "ways" of *reading* and of all systems that privilege those readings. Consequently, the extreme case of discussing key Derridean concepts must be bracketed and identified as *one* reading of concepts that Derrida himself alternately places in upper and lower case. For Derrida, there are no neutral terms. That is, when we apply one term to a second term as a way of controlling or defining the second term, the first term cannot be neutral.

As a result, *deconstruction* is by no means a term we all define in the same way. For the sake of specifying what Derrida means, then, consider this brief description as he outlines it in *Positions*. Deconstruction is not a destruction of binary structures but a general strategy to avoid "both simply *neutralizing* the binary oppositions of metaphysics and simply *residing* within the closed field of oppositions, thereby confirming it" (41). In other words, deconstruction involves a double gesture; it is a *double science*. The double gesture consists in overturning a violent hierarchy (in which one term governs the other) at a "given moment" and marking the interval between the inversion of the two terms, releasing the emergence of a new concept not "included in the previous regime" (41–42). Put simply, the deconstructive gesture can only be marked in a "grouped textual field" (42). By imploding this field, deconstruction threatens several centers of "perceived" freedom, the author and the reader.

In her essay "Reading the World," Gayatri Spivak suggests that the question of freedom is at the heart of the dispute about reading that exists between rhetoric and composition theorists and literary critics. Spivak claims that the "fear of a critical reading that would question the writer's direct access to his or her meaning is related to the received dogma of the illusion of freedom" (30). If, as Spivak argues, the illusion of freedom is at the heart of our desire for access to meaning, then we are no longer in a *fundamental* position to *theorize* interpretation, epistemology, literacy, ontology, rhetoric, composition, reading, and so forth. In other words, a strategy like deconstruction reveals that systemic thinking and the structures that enable it are always subject to a blindness that prevents us from seeing the fragility of all fundamentalisms. Thus, we learn from deconstructive readings of such systems that they are suspended in space and time, not grounded in solid concepts, and they are suspended from tenuous threads, not rooted in conceptual soil. By implication, then, "reading" and the "subject" are poised/suspended (precariously) at the points of tension that sustain binary systems like: reading/writing, theory/praxis, aesthetics/politics, knowledge/opinion, nature/culture, masculine/feminine, teacher/student, analyst/analysand, and other dichotomies that serve as critical coordinates in rhetoric and composition research. In other words, "the structure of binary oppositions in general is questioned by grammatology. Différance invites us to undo the need for balanced equations, to see if each term in an opposition is not after all an accomplice of the other" (Spivak, "Translators" lix).

DECONSTRUCTION AND WRITING

What makes Derrida's work significantly different (and vitally important) to research in rhetoric is its ability to put such binary thinking into question by deconstructing any master narrative (e.g., freedom, history, science, ethics, philosophy) that grounds itself in Western metaphysics. In *Dissemination*, Derrida's critique of logocentrism, he begins with the Platonic privileging of speech over writing in the *Phaedrus*. Simply stated, Derrida reveals a tendency in post-Platonic philosophy to authorize presence and to reward the reification of structures that privilege re-presentations of presence. In a system designed to exclude and repress inferior structures, a secondary system sets itself up as a gatekeeper to guard the position of privilege. What makes the gatekeeper so powerful is that while it closes off any number of possible scenarios, perspectives, or counterpoints, it operates as a lacuna within the primary system of privilege. That is, it hides its true function behind a *scapegoat* mechanism.

By revealing Plato's blindness to the chain of signification at work in language, Derrida reads *writing* as a *pharmakon* (i.e., as both poison and remedy) and introduces a whole matrix of terms that unravel the effects of *reading* under Platonism. For example, in Derrida's deconstruction of the speech/writing opposition in Plato's *Phaedrus*, Spivak notes that writing has the "negative privilege of being the scapegoat whose exclusion represents the definition of the metaphysical enclosure" ("Translators" lxix). Derrida discloses that by describing writing as a *pharmakon* (poison, medicine) and Socrates as the *pharmakeus* (poisoner, medicine man), Plato neglects to use the related word *pharmakos* (scapegoat) (lxxi). According to Spivak, it is "[a]round this lacuna . . . [that] Derrida recounts the fable of writing (and Socrates) as scapegoat and welcomes *pharmakon* into this chain of substitutions for 'écriture' " (lxxi–xxii). Thus, we must not assume the *pharmakon* is a simple opposition. It is "neither remedy nor poison, neither good nor evil" (*Positions* 43). Derrida defines the economy of the *pharmakon* as, among other things, "the movement, the locus, and the play: (the production of) difference" (*Dissemination* 127).[1]

In other words, deconstruction is a *movement*, not a position. According to Simon Critchley, it works by ethical discourse, which "is confined to the movement of *traversing* the philosophical *logos* between two points of tension: between belonging and the breakthrough, philosophy and non-philosophy" (70). Critchley explains that for Derrida "deconstruction takes place (*a lieu*), and it does so wherever there 'is' something (*ou il y a quelque chose*)" (22). The figure (trope) that Derrida uses to describe the "double gesture" of deconstructive reading is the *chiasmus* (χ). In *Positions*, Derrida explains that he is interested in the form of the *chiasmus* "not as the symbol of the unknown, but because there is in it . . . a kind of fork (the series *crossroads, quadrifurcum, grid, trellis, key*, etc.) that is, moreover, unequal, one of the points extending its range further than the other: this is the figure of the double gesture, the intersection" (70).

DECONSTRUCTION AND RHETORIC

Given the plethora of concepts and traversals that deconstruction inaugurates, it is crucial to rhetoricians to view Derrida's project as an ally to their own attempts to dismantle the tradition that conceives language founded upon logic instead of rhetoric. This tradition assumes that signs represent ideas and that language serves as an instrument for the production and conveyance of ideas. In addition, this tradition is grounded in the fundamental principle that human consciousness represents ideas through language. To understand the significance of Derrida's role in this dismantling, readers should refer to his first book, *Speech and Phenomena and Other Essays on Husserl's Theory of Signs* (1967), which followed his translation of Husserl's *Origin of Geometry* ("Introduction" 1962) and in which he first introduces the notion of *différance*.

In the context of his critique of Husserl's theory of meaning, Derrida argues that Husserl's attempt to rehabilitate metaphysics pivots upon two distinctions:

expression and indication, and retention and representation. Husserl argues that expression alone is endowed with meaning, while indication is simply a token of communication. The second distinction he makes is between retention (immediate, sensory traces) and representational experiences (recalled over time). Both of these distinctions are grounded in the temporality of presence, according to Derrida. Husserl's emphasis on time as presence neglects to account for the fact that time is an endless deferring of presence. The play Derrida makes upon *differing* and *deferring* constitutes one way to interpret his concept of *différance*. For Derrida, expressive self-presence always takes on an indicative character, and retention and representation are both involved in the ceaseless movement of temporal distancing.

In Derrida's strategy of deconstruction, *différance* is neither a word nor a concept. It refers to the origin of the production of differences but also (and more specifically) to the *play* of differences. Derrida's concept-metaphor *différance* is rooted in Saussure's *Course in General Linguistics*, in which Saussure claimed that language is a system of signs whose identity is the effect of difference and not of essence. Derrida departs from Saussure when he designates *différance* as the movement of these differences, or the trace-structure of the sign. In short, *différance* describes the possibility of meaning, of distinguishing between what something is and what something is not. For example, the word *tree* has meaning only insofar as it differs from the word *cat*. In other words, it belongs to a sequential system of language whose members are related "differentially." In *A Teacher's Introduction to Deconstruction*, Sharon Crowley suggests that another way to think of *différance* is in terms of the "inter-textual or interrelational aspects of knowing" in general (10). She explains that what "a culture, or an individual, 'knows' at any given moment is available only because its configurations differ from, and yet depend on, what preceded it" (10). If you try to take something like the American Civil War, for example, out of a "contextual aspect of inquiry," where does it begin and end? she asks (11). *Différance* reminds us of the futility of removing any "text" (like the Civil War) not only from its context but from all differential meanings produced by reconfiguring the "text" in relation to other permutations of perspective. Inasmuch as *différance* works to prevent us from isolating a text for study, it foregrounds the rhetorical situation of texts (cf. Biesecker) and the rhetoricity of language (cf. de Man).

Derrida's concept-metaphor of *trace*, closely associated with the term *différance*, binds yet another aspect of deconstruction to rhetoric: invention. The *trace* is most simply understood as Derrida's name for what is never there. But the simplicity is deceiving. For example, grammatology requires an understanding of writing as one representation of the *trace* but not the *trace* itself. Derrida claims that the *trace* itself does not exist. The *trace* calls identity into question and also reveals the futility of revealing origins. According to Derrida, the question "where does writing begin," like all questions of origin, can benefit from what the *trace* teaches us: Questions of origin carry with them a metaphysics of presence. The *trace* can only operate through examples. Writing (inscription) is one such example.

Writing, however, in its broadest sense means much more than inscription, as shown earlier in Derrida's reading of Freud's mystic writing pad, that is, as a system of relations between strata. The "scene of writing" is roughly analogous to the composing process. In *Applied Grammatology*, Gregory Ulmer characterizes Derrida's grammatology (the production of texts) as a pedagogy in itself. In fact, for Ulmer, Derrida's deconstructive method of text analysis makes of writing not a method of criticism but of invention. What distinguishes Derrida's writing as invention from invention in classical rhetoric hinges on the fact that Derrida locates invention within the movement of language itself, rather than in the individual writer. As central as invention is to the canon of rhetoric, its continued focus on the writer still dominates contemporary methods of teaching rhetoric, regardless of the fact that deconstruction derails Aristotle's tri-part system of rhetorical proofs: *ethos, pathos*, and *logos*. The focus on Aristotle's system is directly related to the constituent elements of the twentieth-century version often called the "communication triangle," translated as sender, receiver, and message. Rhetoricians James Kinneavy, Wayne Booth, Lloyd Bitzer, and Kenneth Burke (among others) rendered the triangle in variations that added a fourth (language or signal) and fifth element (Burke's pentad: agent, action, scene, purpose, and agency).

The common thread among these inventional schema is an Aristotelian focus on the writer rather than on the complex network of signifying relations radicalized in Derrida's concept of the trace-structure as the name for a movement of differences not dependent on an instrumental model of language (as a "tool" of invention). As Jasper Neel points out, "[m]ost Western writers assume that writing serves as a vehicle to carry thought" (*Plato* 162). Neel shows precisely how dangerous Derrida's grammatology is in its constant depiction of writing as "some sort of supplement" (*Grammatology* 144–45; qtd. in Neel, *Plato* 161). Neel writes that the "process of supplementation endangers thought because writing, rather than merely serving as an empty vehicle waiting to transport and then discharge thought whole, adds itself to and then substitutes itself for thought" (162). The danger, according to Neel, "amounts to a profound threat to reason" (163). Herein lies the dilemma of deconstruction: It is consistently represented as what tears down, destroys, negates, effaces, and otherwise obliterates any possibility of meaning. Seen this way, it is no surprise that Derrida and those who support his project find themselves having to define deconstruction by what it is "not," that is to say, by arguing against the negative by using negation. That irony led Derrida to begin characterizing deconstruction as affirmative.

AFFIRMATIVE DECONSTRUCTION

In *Spurs: Nietzsche's Styles*, Derrida gives various readings of Nietzsche's master concept-metaphors such as "woman," distance, veils, truth, "history of an error," and so forth. According to Spivak, with *Spurs*, Derrida launches a new phase in the evolving history of deconstruction. In his first phase, Derrida works to "keep the question alive" through deconstructive readings of various major writers and texts. By taking a text apart, or watching a text unravel itself (as he prefers to call it), deconstruction took on the appearance of a negative gesture. While Derrida has consistently maintained that we always already inhabit the structures we deconstruct, "affirmative deconstruction" allows a critic to acknowledge that such structures contain social, ethical, and political violence. As he explains in *Of Grammatology*, deconstruction does not destroy structures from the outside; it is a movement from within that borrows all the strategies of subversion from the old structure. Much of the credit for his move to affirmation can be traced to his preference for Nietzsche's "joyous affirmation of the play of the world and of the innocence of becoming, the affirmation of a world of signs without fault, without truth, without origin" versus Rousseau's melancholy, which he characterizes as "sad, negative, *nostalgic*, [and] guilty" (qtd. in Spivak, "Translator's Preface" xiii).

Spivak claims that the difference between the two phases of deconstruction is in the attitude toward the object of critique, that we give assent without excuse, that we inhabit the discourse completely. She calls this "negotiating with structures of violence" ("Feminism"). Using deconstruction as a kind of lever to enter a violent text (such as Heidegger's complicity with Nazism, or Nietzsche's definition of truth as "woman"), affirmative deconstruction enables the critic to negotiate, to accuse the text responsibly, then lift the lever and use the text, rather than not use it at all. In Spivak's estimation, affirmative deconstruction demands that we see complicity but not that we necessarily see it oppositionally.

Following *Spurs* (1978), Derrida's next variation on the theme of affirmation occurs in *The Ear of the Other* (1982) and later in *Of Spirit* (1987). Spivak describes *The Ear of the Other* as a discourse on the politics of reading. By reading Nietzsche's most autobiographical work, *Ecce Homo*, Derrida opens up our notions of the closed text of an author, which is closed only by the proper name we call a signature. In Derrida's view, just because Nietzsche is dead, the future of the Nietzsche text is not closed. That is, the discourse bearing his name lives on in society and serves as a legitimating reference for ideologues. It is no secret that Nietzsche's work did serve the Nazis in ways that even Nietzsche predicted (and lamented). Such an appropriation invites an affirmative deconstruction because, as Derrida suggests, we should not ignore that there exists in Nietzsche thought that lent itself precisely to fascism. This is where Spivak steps in to urge that such an appropriation allows us to "use" the text without "excusing" it.

In the past 10 years, Derrida has taken up the question of politics and responsibility more and more as his critics continue to misunderstand and misrepresent deconstruction as negative and apolitical. In an interview with Gary Olson on the topic of rhetoric published in 1991, Derrida is eager to set the record straight, so to speak. Even if his supporters do not always see it, Derrida suspects that "[m]isunderstanding is always significant; it's not simply a mistake, or just an absurdity. It's something that is motivated by some interest and some understanding" (Olson 140). He also says that some people react vehemently *because* they understand more than supporters do, because they know what is at stake (140). In one instance he broadened the context for deconstruction to include questioning the authority and hard structures of institutions as well as literary texts. He explains that deconstruction is "not only a way of reading texts in the trivial sense; it's also a way of dealing with institutions" (Olson 128). In other words, at the university, where much depends upon one's position, Derrida wants to "consider all the devices and interests presiding over the establishment of 'assured values' " (Rand 198). Thus, among other things, deconstruction means "the questioning of what synthesis is, what thesis is, what a position is, what composition is, not only in terms of rhetoric, but what *position* is, what *positing* means" (Olson 128). So while Derrida "guards the question" of rhetoric and the so-called tradition, he continues to wield the philosophical hammer of Nietzsche. In response to teachers who oppose deconstruction because (they say) its effects are disorder, and who say this just to exclude deconstruction, Derrida says: "That's what I call bad faith in the service of conservative politics" (131). In an even stronger passage, Derrida deplores these kinds of deliberate attacks on deconstruction:

When people try to confine deconstruction in negative models as something nonpolitical, noninstitutional or as something confined to books, to speculative speeches, to what is in the library, when they interpret text as something which is written down and not in the generalized concept that I've tried to elaborate, I think it's a very serious misrepresentation. But it's the symptom of a resistance; it's not simply a mistake. . . . They didn't want to understand. (141)

RHETORIC AS/AND DECONSTRUCTION

One of the most frequently voiced problems about deconstruction is that it is self-destructive. That is, if given enough rope, a deconstructive reading eventually deconstructs itself. After all, is that not the ultimate deconstructive task, to put itself out of business? Yes and no. Jacques Derrida writes again and again that deconstruction is not about origins and ends. It is not about mapping a territory so much as it is about finding the edge of a dangerous precipice and realizing that there are more edges than we can know and deeper canyons into which we can descend without giving ourselves over to the groundlessness of the abyss—which is not necessarily a bad thing. So when Jasper Neel laments the fact that in Derrida's interview with Olson he sides more with philosophy than rhetoric, rhetoricians should be cautious about finding this problematic. Neel faults Derrida for saying that there are concepts outside of "rhetoric," that everything is not rhetoric (Neel, "Where" 149). This is a question of reading. Derrida argues that we should be suspicious of "rhetoricism," not rhetoric per se (Olson 138). In Derrida's mind, they are two different things. He is marking the affinity of rhetoric with its classical Greek sense of "speaking" in general. He maintains that to "give absolute privilege to rhetoric you fall into what I call logocentrism or phonocentrism . . . [and] the hegemony of speaking over anything else—writing, acting, and so on—is a kind of rhetoricism" (139).

Neel, it seems, falls into the same mire of misunderstanding that many do who attempt to derail Derrida on the grounds that his argument (his *logos*) is flawed. For that, we need a rhetoric informed by deconstruction to expose how reading irresponsibly limits rhetoric by keeping it in its place—safe at home in the gilded halls of academic scholarly argument. Rhetoric should be at home with Derrida, who (like rhetoric) lives in a world of metaphysical homelessness; he is "someone who admits that he does not know where he is going" ("Time of a Thesis" 50). Rhetoric on any other path may not be rhetoric at all.

NOTE

1. Portions of this section are drawn from a larger project of mine, "In the Name of *Ethos*: Derrida and the Promise of Reading," in *In the Name of Writing* (1994).

BIBLIOGRAPHY

Primary Sources

Derrida, Jacques. "Canons and Metonymies: An Interview with Jacques Derrida." *Logomachia: The Conflict of the Faculties*. Ed. Richard Rand. Lincoln: University of Nebraska Press, 1992. 195–218.

———. *Dissemination*. Trans. Barbara Johnson. Chicago: University of Chicago Press, 1981.

———. *The Ear of the Other: Otobiography, Transference, Translation: Texts and Discussions with Jacques Derrida*. Ed. Christie V. McDonald. Trans. Peggy Kamuf and Avital Ronell. Lincoln: University of Nebraska Press, 1988.

———. " 'Eating Well,' or the Calculation of the Subject: An Interview with Jacques Derrida." With Jean-Luc Nancy. Trans. Peter Conner and Avital Ronell. *Who Comes after the Subject?* Ed. Eduardo Cadava, Peter Conner, and Jean-Luc Nancy. New York: Routledge, 1991. 96–119.

———. "Freud and the Scene of Writing." *Writing and Difference*. Trans. Alan Bass. Chicago: University of Chicago Press, 1978. 196–231.

———. "Introduction à *L'Origine de la géométrie* par Edmund Husserl." Paris: Presses Universitaires de France, 1962. Edmund Husserl's "Origin of Geometry": An Introduction. Trans. with an introduction and afterword by John P. Leavey, Jr. Lincoln: University of Nebraska Press, 1989.

———. *Margins of Philosophy*. Trans. Alan Bass. Chicago: University of Chicago Press, 1982.

———. "Mochlos; or, The Conflict of the Faculties." *Logomachia: The Conflict of the Faculties*. Ed. Richard Rand. Lincoln: University of Nebraska Press, 1992. 1–34.

————. *Of Grammatology.* Trans. Gayatri Chakravorty Spivak. Baltimore: Johns Hopkins University Press, 1976.

————. *Of Spirit: Heidegger and the Question.* Trans. Geoffrey Bennington and Rachel Bowlby. Chicago: University of Chicago Press, 1989.

————. *Positions.* Trans. Alan Bass. Chicago: University of Chicago Press, 1981.

————. *Speech and Phenomena and Other Essays on Husserl's Theory of Signs.* Trans. David B. Allison. Evanston, IL: Northwestern University Press, 1973.

————. *Spurs: Nietzsche's Styles.* Chicago: University of Chicago Press, 1978.

————. "Structure, Sign, and Play in the Discourse of the Human Sciences." *Writing and Difference.* Trans. Alan Bass. Chicago: University of Chicago Press, 1978. 278–93.

————. "The Time of a Thesis: Punctuations." *Philosophy in France Today.* Ed. Alan Montefiore. Cambridge: Cambridge University Press, 1983. 34–50.

————. *Writing and Difference.* Trans. Alan Bass. Chicago: University of Chicago Press, 1978.

Biography

Neel, Jasper. " 'Where Have You Come From, Reb Derissa, and Where Are You Going?': Gary Olson's Interview with Jacques Derrida." *(Inter)views: Cross-Disciplinary Perspectives on Rhetoric and Literacy.* Ed. Gary A. Olson and Irene Gale. Carbondale: Southern Illinois University Press, 1991. 145–51.

Olson, Gary A. "Jacques Derrida on Rhetoric and Composition: A Conversation." *(Inter)views: Cross-Disciplinary Perspectives on Rhetoric and Literacy.* Ed. Gary A. Olson and Irene Gale. Carbondale: Southern Illinois University Press, 1991. 121–41.

Rand, Richard. "Canons and Metonymies: An Interview with Jacques Derrida." *The Conflict of the Faculties.* Ed. Richard Rand. Lincoln: University of Nebraska Press, 1992. 195–218.

Criticism

Behler, Ernest. *Confrontations: Derrida/Heidegger/Nietzsche.* Trans. Steven Taubeneck. Stanford: Stanford University Press, 1991.

Biesecker, Barbara A. "Rethinking the Rhetorical Situation from within the Thematic of *Différance.*" *Philosophy and Rhetoric* 22.2 (1989): 110–30.

Critchley, Simon. *The Ethics of Deconstruction: Derrida and Levinas.* Oxford: Blackwell, 1992.

Crowley, Sharon. *A Teacher's Introduction to Deconstruction.* Urbana, IL: NCTE, 1989.

de Man, Paul. *Allegories of Reading: Figural Language in Rousseau, Nietzsche, Rilke, and Proust.* New Haven, CT: Yale University Press, 1979.

Gasche, Rodolphe. *Inventions of Difference: On Jacques Derrida.* Cambridge, MA: Harvard University Press, 1994.

Haynes, Cynthia. "In the Name of Writing: Rhetoric and the Politics of Ethos." Diss., University of Texas at Arlington, 1994.

Heidegger, Martin. *Early Greek Thinking: The Dawn of Western Philosophy.* Trans. David Farrell Krell and Frank A. Capuzzi. San Francisco: Harper & Row, 1984.

Neel, Jasper. *Plato, Derrida, and Writing*. Carbondale: Southern Illinois University Press, 1988.

Rapaport, Herman. *Heidegger and Derrida: Reflections on Time and Language*. Lincoln: University of Nebraska Press, 1989.

Saussure, Ferdinand de. *Course in General Linguistics*. Ed. Charles Bally and Albert Sechehaye with the collaboration of Albert Riedlinger. Trans. Roy Harris. La Salle, IL: Open Court, 1986.

Spivak, Gayatri Chakravorty. "Feminism and Deconstruction, Again: Negotiating with Unacknowledged Masculinism." *Between Feminism and Psychoanalysis*. Ed. Teresa Brennan. London: Routledge, 1989. 206–23.

———. "Reading the World: Literary Studies in the 1980s." *Writing and Reading Differently: Deconstruction and the Teaching of Composition and Literature*. Ed. G. Douglas Atkins and Michael L. Johnson. Lawrence: University Press of Kansas, 1985. 27–37.

———. "Translator's Preface." *Of Grammatology*, by Jacques Derrida. Baltimore: Johns Hopkins University Press, 1974. ix–xxxvii.

Ulmer, Gregory L. *Applied Grammatology: Post(e)-Pedagogy from Jacques Derrida to Joseph Beuys*. Baltimore: Johns Hopkins University Press, 1985.

Vitanza, Victor J. "Concerning a Post-Classical *Ethos* as Para/Rhetorical Ethics, the 'Selphs,' and the Excluded Third." *Ethos: New Essays in Rhetorical and Critical Theory*. Ed. James S. Baumlin and Tita French Baumlin. Dallas: Southern Methodist University Press, 1994. 389–431.

Yeghiayan, Eddie. Bibliography of Jacques Derrida (November 11, 1998). Critical Theory Institute at the University of California at Irvine. Available at: http://sun3.lib.uci.edu/~scctr/Wellek/jacques.html

PETER ELBOW
(1935–   )

Nedra Reynolds and Claire Roche

Peter Elbow was born in 1935 in New York, New York, and raised in New Jersey. He attended Proctor Academy in Andover, New Hampshire, then earned B.A. degrees from Williams College (1957) and Exeter College, Oxford. After a year of graduate study at Harvard (1959–1960), Elbow taught at the Massachusetts Institute of Technology (MIT) and then became a founding faculty member at Franconia College (1963–1965). He completed a Ph.D. from Brandeis University in 1969, specializing in Chaucer, and has held faculty positions at MIT (1968–1972), Evergreen College (1972–1981), and the State University of New York (SUNY) at Stony Brook (1982–1987). Elbow is currently full professor of English at the University of Massachusetts at Amherst.

Many of Elbow's earliest intellectual commitments and his evolving theories about knowledge, learning, and the power of language can be traced to the events and milieu of 1968. Coming of age intellectually and politically in the 1960s, Elbow identified himself as a conscientious objector, became committed to group therapy, and discovered the excitement of teaching interdisciplinary courses. His first publication, in 1968, was an article for *Christian Century* titled "Who Is a Conscientious Objector." Also in 1968, Elbow began teaching evening writing classes in Roxbury, Massachusetts, where he began to experiment with the teacherless method. By this time, Elbow had considerable teaching experience from MIT and elsewhere, which he brought to bear on his opportunities to design courses at the newly founded Franconia College (New Hampshire). Here Elbow served as chair of the core curriculum and planned and taught interdisciplinary courses for general education that were informed by his in-depth reading into psychology. These commitments from the 1960s—protesting injustice, working with writers, learning from group therapy, and teaching rich interdisciplinary courses—have shaped much of Elbow's work.

Upon completing his dissertation, Elbow was offered a position at Berkeley as a Chaucer specialist, but he remained in the Boston area, where he continued to record and analyze his own writing processes and to pursue his interest in metaphor and the power of language. Elbow's first book, *Oppositions in Chaucer*, marks his interest in irony, tensions, ambiguities, and contraries—and he pursues these figures, for decades to come, in the context of teaching and writing and through a variety of English studies topics. In 1970, his career began as one of the country's foremost authorities on writing and the teaching of writing when he signed a contract with Oxford University Press for *Writing without Teachers*. Originally named "Writing without Tears," the book evolved from his scattered notes about his struggles with writing through graduate school and the demands of academic readers. From some of his earliest published articles on teaching (*College English* in 1968), to his most recent publications on assessment and grading ("Grading Student Writing" [1997]), Elbow has remained committed to pedagogical innovation and to responsible teaching.

Peter Elbow's pedagogical contributions and presence in the profession are immeasurable, and his work has had a significant impact on contemporary theories of composing processes, "voice," empowerment, and the writing self. For Elbow, the self develops within a social context, but self-expression and individual belief are often difficult to cultivate in the midst of oppressive social environments; thus, writers need strategies in order to develop their own voices and to find their own truths. Elbow's rhetorical theories focus on the affirmative qualities of oppositions, contraries, and tensions, and the connections between feeling and thinking. Rooted in Gestalt and Freudian psychology and alternative epistemologies, Elbow's ideas resist categorical or absolute theories of language or subjectivity. His arguments have challenged many of the academy's traditional approaches to writing and thinking, but they can also be traced through traditions both neo-Platonic and romantic. Through his engagement in collaborative projects and public dialogue with many of his colleagues, Elbow contributes to the field of rhetoric and composition in a variety of ways.

ELBOW'S RHETORICAL THEORY

Because of his prolific career and his tendency to be self-reflective, it is not difficult to trace the evolution of Elbow's key ideas or to recognize those who have influenced his thought. Elbow credits Michael Polanyi and Carl Rogers, in particular, for the seeds of the believing game, and Ken Macrorie for introducing him to freewriting. Readers will also find obvious debts—some acknowledged and others not—to Plato and the organic nature of discourse; to Freud and psychotherapy; to Piaget and others on growth.

His most popular work, *Writing without Teachers*, published in 1973 by Oxford University Press, is, arguably, one of the most significant texts on English studies pedagogy of the last three decades. Like Janet Emig, Elbow is concerned with the harm that has been done to generations of potential writers through educational practices and attitudes about writing that stifle self-expression and inhibit the development of one's own voice. Written from his own experiences with struggling to write, Elbow outlines methods of a teacherless writing class, dependent on drafting, revising, and sharing. While writing response groups were not new in 1973, Elbow revived the concept of writing groups by promising self-empowerment to those who were willing to try new methods, take risks, and meet the responsibilities of cooperative learning. In part a response to the times, teacherless classes offered freedom from rigid school-sponsored writing in exchange for more confidence and more control over language. But they also demanded that members be committed and dependable and willing to share, guidelines for success that Elbow emphasized repeatedly.

Uncensored writing, or freewriting, was another method that Elbow elaborated upon through his experiences with therapy. Although he credits Ken Macrorie for introducing him to freewriting, Elbow's *Writing without Teachers* probably did more to promote it than any other source, and freewriting is predictably included in the invention section of every process writing textbook. Freewriting encourages writers to write nonstop, without censorship or editing, creating a flow of words that may contain a "nugget" worth mining in later drafts. Chapter 1 of *Writing without Teachers* introduces freewriting because so many of Elbow's ideas depend on these exercises and the concept of "freeing" one's own voice from the confinements of sloppy thinking, premature editing, or demanding audiences. Believing that writing should be nurtured more than codified, Elbow relies on organic metaphors—most memorably, growing and cooking—for his discussion of writing processes.

The most important contribution of *Writing without Teachers* to rhetorical theory appears in the appendix essay, "The Doubting Game and the Believing Game." This essay explores concepts that Elbow has continued to wrestle with for 30 years with slight variations (e.g., "The Uses of Binary Thinking" [1993]). By attempting to reverse the traditional binary opposition of Western intellectual thought, which privileges doubt over belief, Elbow stakes out territory from which most of his ideas originate. "Belief" has been undervalued and disprivileged in the academy, in intellectual circles, and in the culture at large. Critical and analytical thinking teach people to doubt and disprove or to approach every claim skeptically. However, Elbow argues that our thinking processes would be enhanced and enriched by our ability to "embrace" every claim, to defer doubt until we have tried just as hard to believe—to see the issue from all sides or to anticipate all possibilities. Although he does not advocate being uncritical or anti-intellectual (the believing game requires muscle), Elbow opposes pursuing one truth, in one way, and has very little use for closure, consensus, or resolution that truncates thinking or shuts down further exploration. Running counter to most methods of academic or scientific thinking, Elbow advocates affirming two sides of an argument as equally valid or important.

Many of Elbow's aims in "The Doubting Game and the Believing Game" are exploratory, even celebratory, and not an attempt to argue vehemently for one position. One of his characteristic rhetorical goals is to make dichotomies explicit without attempting to reconcile them—to discover them, forward them, but finally to just leave them hanging. In fact, he would rather leave arguments unreconciled, unresolved. Similarly, he resists any type of packaged thinking or prescribed problem-solving approaches, a tendency of cognitive researchers that diminishes the autonomy and individuality of the self.

Elbow's ideas about the self stem largely from his knowledge of Freud and from his attraction to metaphor as a means to truth. Labeled by James Berlin as one of "the leading expressionists of the sixties and seventies" (151), Elbow is perhaps best known for his emphasis on authentic voice and on writing as personal expression. Voice can develop only from an individual's own struggles and play with language and from an organic approach to the creative process.

Elbow has defined and defended expressive writing on a number of occasions: On Conference on College Composition and Communication (CCCC) panels in 1989 and 1991, and again in *College Composition and Communication* (*CCC*) in 1995, he and David Bartholomae took opposing sides in a conversation about personal and academic writing. Elbow's dilemma of being both a writer and an academic is well known to his readers, and he believes that students are put into the same fundamental conflict. Academic discourse, "the discourse that academics use when they publish for other academics," is a significant site of conflict for Elbow because, he argues, it is an artificial form of student writing and has a limited role in a writer's development ("Reflecting" 135). Elbow defines "generic" academic discourse as "giving reasons and evidence, yes, but doing so as a person speaking with acknowledged interests to others—whose interest and position one acknowledges and tries to understand" (142). Although he recognizes the validity of the need to instruct students in academic discourse, Elbow has argued for years that coaching students in only one form of discourse is to do them a disservice.

Elbow's alternatives to academic discourse can generally be classified as personal or private writing, essential for coming to know. Being able to write one's reality—to represent it clearly and forcefully—results in empowerment, and empowerment grows largely from the relationship between a self and her language. The influence of social or cultural forces is more incidental than constructive, and more inhibiting than defining. Elbow's rhetorical theory exists where self and reality come together: The reality of the self and the ability to represent that self to a reader make up the rhetorical transaction.

Perhaps Elbow's most direct contributions to rhetorical theory occur in two related articles, "The Shifting Relationships between Speech and Writing" (which won the 1986 Braddock Award) and his 1987 article "Closing My Eyes as I Speak: An Argument for Ignoring Audience." In both articles, Elbow challenges assumptions about relationships between speech and writing or between a writer and her audience. The first article argues against the popular notions that speech and writing are entirely distinct; while admitting their differences, Elbow concentrates on their similarities. Through identifying the shared features of speech and writing, Elbow is also able to define good writing; for example, good writing works on readers not through the dimension of space but through the dimension of time ("Shifting Relationships" 294). Elbow wants to give writers more options, particularly ways to make writing more like speech since the best writing, according to Elbow, has such qualities of speech as a "lively or heightened semantic presence" (299). However, the advantage of writing over speech is its ability to enhance "the play of mentalities"; the technology of writing encourages cognitive movement or back and forth processes that speech cannot accomplish.

In "Closing My Eyes as I Speak," Elbow analyzes the effects of audience awareness on writers in the act of composing and argues that ignoring audience can lead to better writing. Sometimes writers need to silence the imagined judgments of others in order to make the move from discourse as communication to discourse as "poiesis" or play. Elbow recommends more emphasis on private writing, which teaches a "crucial cognitive capacity to engage in extended and productive thinking that doesn't depend on audience prompts or social stimuli" (62). In both of these articles, Elbow's goal is to empower writers—to give them more options as they try to discover their own voices or truths—and offers definitions of good writing that depend on "voice."

Elbow wants to resist theories of writing that rely on steps or patterns; for example, he questions the cognitive research that suggests adolescent writers have trouble "decentering"; and, in a related point, he questions whether writer-based prose, or that written with an eye toward readers, is truly "better" than reader-based prose, that which is done for the writer's own understanding or without an audience firmly in mind. Elbow generally distrusts cognitive research on writing processes and models because of its overgeneralizations and inability to make fine distinctions for individual writers. Mostly, Elbow distrusts cognitive research because it cannot make room for "magic."

In each of Elbow's major works, *Writing without Teachers*, *Writing with Power*, and *Embracing Contraries*, the magic and mystery of linguistics and symbols are present in some form. In the rituals, habits, and play of writing Elbow finds something akin to the magic of chant and incantation. The authentic voice of the writer is magical and mysterious, and writing is just as ephemeral as it is permanent. And it is here that the influence of Kenneth Burke can be seen in Elbow's corpus. A powerful and magical use of voice allows for the transcending of differences between the writer and her audience; thus the audience can identify with or, in Burkean terms, share substance with, the writer.

Regardless of the pedagogical or rhetorical topic, Elbow's rhetorical position is always to question the status quo, challenge traditional notions, and ask his readers to consider ideas' slant. In recent years, Elbow has published a number of articles about assessment, grades, and evaluation of writing. Because assessment is an area defined by bottom-line numbers and unimaginative approaches to the complexities of writing, Elbow finds it an appealing area in which to advocate his beliefs about writing and language. For assessment, this means questioning typical grading practices and advocating "messier" procedures, including portfolios. One of the first to integrate portfolio assessment into a writing program (along with Pat Belanoff), Elbow has used portfolios to highlight problems with assessment, to encourage collaboration in writing programs, and to help teachers enrich their classroom practices.

References to Elbow's work appear—although often quite briefly—in a wide variety of publications within modern composition studies, usually in the context of discussions of teaching, the process approach, freewriting, or voice (see, for example, Villanueva). More extensive or critical engagements with Elbow occur in the work of Berlin, Bartholomae, Susan Jarratt, and Joseph Harris, all of whom object to Elbow's belief in the personal as the center of truth or reality. Each of these critiques is a result of composition's turn to social construction and cultural theories of language, discourse, and the self. Berlin focuses on expressionistic rhetoric; Bartholomae, on academic discourse; Jarratt, on conflict and relations of power; and Harris, on the rhetoric of authenticity; but they have in common a concern with Elbow's celebration of individualistic epistemologies.

Feminists have argued that Elbow's power of the personal can put women students at greater disadvantage—for reproducing stereotypical views of women's epistemologies (Jarratt; Malinowitz). Similarly, others argue that personal writing (to be shared) happens only when a writer is already operating from a position of some power in relation to her peers and, as a result, has little or nothing to risk (Malinowitz). The more a writer has at stake personally, the less likely that writer is to benefit from the kinds of writing Elbow encourages teachers to pursue with their students.

Elbow's contribution to twentieth-century rhetorical theory begins with his insistence that binary oppositions are artificial, unnecessary, and detrimental to thinking or to the pursuit of "trustworthy knowledge." Reversing them is not a solution; embracing the tension—a more difficult intellectual feat—might be. Over his 30-year career, Elbow's ideas—and the strong reactions to them as the field has evolved—served to push the field into new directions.

For most readers in rhetoric and composition studies, Elbow's appeal stems from his commitment to teaching and from his sincere and accessible writing style: He routinely asks for help in solving problems or asks for more dialogue and engagement about issues that concern him. As John Schilb writes, "Elbow's work remains especially influential, probably because he writes clearly and makes concrete, sensible recommendations for teaching: Form peer review groups, have classes write a lot, let them freewrite, evaluate them through portfolios, don't push them to mimic academic discourse" (214). Through such strategies as self-disclosure and a conversational style for hard questions about thinking and learning, Elbow's scholarship draws a huge readership, a testament to his voice and passion.

BIBLIOGRAPHY

Primary Sources

Books

Elbow, Peter. *Embracing Contraries: Explorations in Learning and Teaching*. New York: Oxford University Press, 1986.

———. *Oppositions in Chaucer*. Middletown, CT: Wesleyan University Press, 1975.

———. *What Is English?* New York: MLA, 1990.

———. *The Writer's Craft*. Consulting Author. Evanston, IL: McDougal, Littell, 1995.

———. *Writing without Teachers*. New York: Oxford University Press, 1973.

———. *Writing with Power: Techniques for Mastering the Writing Process*. New York: Oxford University Press, 1981.

———. ed. *Landmark Essays on Voice and Writing*. Landmark Essay Series. Vol. 4. Davis, CA: Hermagoras Press, 1994.

Elbow, Peter, and Mary Deane Corcinelli, eds. *Writing to Learn: Strategies for Assigning and Responding to Writing across the Disciplines*. San Francisco: Jossey-Bass, 1997.

Elbow, Peter, and Sheryl I. Fontaine, eds. *Nothing Begins with N: New Investigations of Freewriting*. Carbondale: Southern Illinois University Press, 1991.

Articles and Chapters

Elbow, Peter. "Being a Writer vs. Being an Academic: A Conflict in Goals." *College Composition and Communication* 46.1 (1995): 72–83.

———. "Closing My Eyes as I Speak: An Argument for Ignoring Audience." *College English* 49.1 (1987): 50–69.

———. "Complex Irony in Chaucer." *Dissertation Abstracts International* (1969): 30/06, 2480.

———. "The Definition of Teaching." *College English* 30.3 (1968): 187–201.

———. Foreword. *Portfolios: Process and Product*. Ed. Pat Belanoff and Marcia Dickson. Portsmouth, NH: Heinemann, 1991. ix–xvi.

———. "Forward: About Personal Experience in Academic Writing." PRE/TEXT 11.1 (1990): 7–20.

———. "Grading Student Writing: Making It Simpler, Fairer, Clearer." *New Directions for Teaching and Learning* 69.1 (1997): 127–40.

———. "High Stakes and Low Stakes in Assigning and Responding to Writing." *New Directions for Teaching and Learning* 69.1 (1997): 5–13.

———. "How Chaucer Transcends Oppositions in the 'Knight's Tale.'" *The Chaucer Review: A Journal of Medieval Studies and Literary Criticism* 7.2 (1972): 97–112.

———. "Making Better Use of Student Evaluations of Teachers." *ADE Bulletin* 101.1 (1992): 2–8.

———. "A Method for Teaching Writing." *College English* 30.2 (1968): 115–25.

———. "On the Nature of Holistic Scoring: An Inquiry Composed on E-mail." *Assessing Writing* 1.1 (1994): 91–107.

———. "The Pleasures of Voice in the Literary Essay: Explorations in Prose of Gretel Ehrlich and Richard Selzer." *Literary Nonfiction: Theory, Criticism, Pedagogy*.

Ed. Chris Anderson. Carbondale: Southern Illinois University Press, 1989. 211–34.

———. "Ranking, Evaluating, and Liking: Sorting Out Three Forms of Judgment." *College English* 55.2 (1993): 187–206.

———. "Real Learning and Interdisciplinary Courses." *Journal of General Education* 23.2 (1971): 111–41.

———. "Reflecting on Academic Discourse: How It Relates to Freshmen and Colleagues." *College English* 53.2 (1991): 135–55.

———. "The Shifting Relationships between Speech and Writing." *College Composition and Communication* 36.3 (1985): 283–303.

———. "Some Thoughts on Expressive Discourse: A Review Essay." *Journal of Advanced Composition* 11.1 (1991): 83–93.

———. "Toward a Phenomenology of Freewriting." *Journal of Basic Writing* 8.1 (1989): 42–71.

———. "Two Boethian Speeches in 'Troilus and Criseyde' and Chauserian Irony." *Literary Criticism and Historical Understanding: Selected Papers from the English Institute*. Ed. Phillip Damon. New York: Columbia University Press, 1967. 85–107.

———. "The Uses of Binary Thinking." *Journal of Advanced Composition* 13.1 (1993): 51–78.

———. "The War between Reading and Writing—And How to End It." *Rhetoric Review* 12.1 (1993): 5–24.

———. "Who Is a Conscientious Objector: An Explication of the Law Under Which a Draft Age Man May Say No." *Christian Century* (7 August 1968): 989–93.

———. "Will the Virtues of Portfolios Blind Us to Their Potential Dangers?" *New Directions in Portfolio Assessment: Reflective Practice, Critical Theory, and Large-Scale Scoring*. Ed. Laurel Black, Donald A. Daiker, Jeffrey Sommers, and Gail Stygall. Portsmouth, NH: Heinemann, 1994. 40–55.

———. "Writing Assessment in the 21st Century: A Utopian View." *Composition in the Twenty-first Century: Crisis and Change*. Ed. Lynn Z. Bloom, Donald A. Daiker, and Edward M. White. Carbondale: Southern Illinois University Press, 1996. 83–100.

Biography

"Elbow, Peter." *Contemporary Authors*. New Revision Series. Vol. 28. Detroit: Gale Research, 1981. 153–54.

Enos, Theresa, ed. "Elbow, Peter." *Encyclopedia of Rhetoric and Composition: Communication from Ancient Times to the Information Age*. New York: Garland Publishing, 1996. 208–9.

Criticism

Bartholomae, David. "Writing with Teachers: A Conversation with Peter Elbow." *College Composition and Communication* 46.1 (1995): 62–71.

Berlin, James A. *Rhetoric and Reality: Writing Instruction in American Colleges, 1900–1985*. Carbondale: Southern Illinois University Press, 1987.

Briggs, John. "Peter Elbow, Kenneth Burke, and the Idea of Magic." *Journal of Advanced Composition* 11.2 (1991): 363–75.

Harris, Joseph. *A Teaching Subject: Composition since 1966.* Upper Saddle River, NJ: Prentice-Hall, 1997.

Huot, Brian. "The Need for a Theory of Writing Assessment." *Composition in the Twenty-first Century: Crisis and Change.* Ed. Lynn Z. Bloom, Donald A. Daiker, and Edward M. White. Carbondale: Southern Illinois University Press, 1996. 112–15.

Jarratt, Susan C. "Feminism and Composition: The Case for Conflict." *Contending with Words: Composition and Rhetoric in a Postmodern Age.* Ed. Patricia Harkin and John Schilb. New York: MLA, 1991. 105–23.

Malinowitz, Harriet. *Textual Orientations: Lesbian and Gay Studies and the Making of Discourse Communities.* Portsmouth, NH: Boynton/Cook, 1995.

Perry, Patricia Harris. "Transformation of Consciousness and Knowledge-Making about Writing: The Philosophies and Praxes of Paulo Freire and Peter Elbow." *Dissertation Abstracts International* 52 (1991): 1251A–52A.

Schilb, John. *Between the Lines: Relating Composition Theory and Literary Theory.* Portsmouth, NH: Boynton/Cook, 1996.

Smith, Elizabeth Overman. "Peter Elbow and the Networked Computer Classroom: Doubting and Believing to Negotiate Knowledge." *Conference of College Teachers of English Studies* 57.1 (1992): 51–56.

Villanueva, Victor, Jr., ed. *Cross-Talk in Comp Theory: A Reader.* Urbana, IL: NCTE, 1997.

JANET EMIG
(1928–   )

Deborah A. Noel

Janet Emig was born on October 12, 1928, in Cincinnati, Ohio. She recalls her early schooling as creative and inspirational, a series of encounters with "particularly active artists" who sought careers in education when depression-era opportunities were limited (Nelms 173). Emig entered Mt. Holyoke College with a four-year scholarship from Westinghouse and a plan to pursue medicine. Her interest in science continued until her literary talents began to overshadow other academic strengths. During her years in college, she devoted much of her time to writing poetry and fiction (completing a novel before graduating), and after winning both the Phi Kappa Delta Poetry Prize in 1949 and the Kathryn McFarland Prose Prize in 1950, she became an English major. Her transition into composition studies was enabled by the Mt. Holyoke English Department, which was one of the few that offered a composition major during the time. Emig graduated from Mt. Holyoke magna cum laude in 1950 and proceeded directly to the University of Michigan to pursue an M.A. with a focus on writing.

After Michigan, Emig took her first teaching jobs in the Cincinnati Public Schools, the Hillsdale School for Girls in Cincinnati, and Wyoming High School in Wyoming, Ohio. Inspired by her talented colleagues at Wyoming, Emig became interested in pedagogy and conceived her first publication, "We Are Trying Conferences" (1960). The significance of this early work can be measured by its articulation of themes that would persist in Emig's later thought: her focus on composition pedagogy and her interest in verbalizing the writing process. During this period, Emig was nominated to the National Council of Teachers of English Committee on the Reading and Teaching of Poetry. These positive experiences spurred her return to graduate school at Harvard University.

Persisting through the loss of her mentor, Priscilla Tyler (who left Harvard after Emig's first year), the disintegration of the already bare-bones English

Education composition program at Harvard, and the high dropout rate of her colleagues, Emig engaged in a unique, diverse program of study, attending classes in linguistics at the Massachusetts Institute of Technology and lectures by the likes of Noam Chomsky, Kenneth Lynn, and Perry Miller. The work that would eventually become her most famous monograph, *The Composing Processes of Twelfth Graders* (1971), had its genesis in her dissertation, which was completed in 1969 after Emig had been working as an assistant professor at the University of Chicago's School of Education for four years. For reasons related to the lack of respect afforded her work, her gender, and her nationality, Emig was denied tenure at both Chicago and Lethbridge University in Alberta, Canada, where she had taken a job for both professional and political reasons (like many faculty, Emig left the United States during this period to protest the Vietnam War).

Revised during her stay at Lethbridge, *The Composing Processes of Twelfth Graders* was published in 1971, the same year in which Emig was finally offered a tenure-track associate professorship at Rutgers, the State University of New Jersey, in Brunswick. There she stayed until her retirement, though initially the climate at Rutgers was not as welcoming as she had hoped. In "Journal of a Pessimist" (1980) and in interviews with Gerald Nelms, Emig reveals that pervasive sexism at Rutgers "delayed her promotions" and "cost her thousands of dollars in salary" (Nelms 189).

Despite these obstacles, Emig found the interdisciplinary nature of her department at Rutgers conducive to her own eclectic interests. She published widely during these years, earning the Mina Shaughnessy Award for her collection of essays *The Web of Meaning* and the Exemplar Award of the Conference on College Composition and Communication. In her continued work with the National Council of Teachers of English (NCTE), she has served as president and chaired various committees, including the NCTE Committee on the Role and Status of Women in the Council and in the Profession. In addition, she helped initiate and finally directed the New Jersey Writing Project and participated in the English Coalition Conference in 1987, an ambitious assemblage of 60 teachers from eight academic organizations and all levels of American education. As professor emerita of Rutgers University, Emig continues to write and consult from her home in Washington State, devoting much of her time to her poetry.

EMIG'S WORK IN COMPOSITION THEORY

Sharing the burden of defining a discipline with a mere handful of other scholars, Emig early on assumed the responsibility of "trying to suggest all the avenues of research" available to researchers in composition (Nelms 166). Informed by rhetorical theory and literary studies as well as linguistics, psychology, philosophy, and biology, her work has been influenced by such diverse figures as Thomas Kuhn, George Kelly, Michael Polyani, Eric Lenneberg, Jean Piaget, Lev Vygotsky, Jerome Bruner, and Howard Gardner. Despite institutionalized schisms, she frequently brings all of these spheres of influence to bear in her various projects.

Perhaps the most important of Emig's contributions to her field has been her work on process composition pedagogy. Starting with "The Relation of Thought and Language Implicit in Some Early American Rhetoric and Composition Texts" (1963), Emig established herself as a formidable thinker interested in sweeping changes for the composition field. Fixing her critical eye on the likes of Hugh Blair, George Campbell, and others, Emig exposes what she considers to be an "oversimplification of the writing process and a focus on product" (*Web* 1). What lies at the heart of their texts, she finds, is the idea that fully formed thought precedes any actual writing, which serves only a limited, supportive role in language. Emig would spend the rest of her career undoing this oversimplification, arguing instead that writing is a meaning-making process. The crucial element missing from early American and modern American composition texts, Emig argues, is what came to be known as "pre-writing," the stage or stages during the composing process when drafting involves invention.

Reiterating this thesis in "The Uses of the Unconscious in Composing" (1963), Emig argues that by excluding prewriting, writers and teachers fail to make even "a small obeisance in the direction of the untidy, of the convoluted, of the not-wholly-known, of a more intricate self and process" (*Web* 48). Their focus on fully formed thought does not at all jibe with advice given by professional writers, she argues. By implementing a prewriting stage, teachers could allow students to make better use of their unconscious thought (or what she would later call "preconscious" thought, following psychologist Lawrence S. Kubie). All of this suggests that composition teachers need to provide the proper environment and, above all, the right amount of time in order to expect students to produce even remotely inspired work.

At this point in her career, Emig's work begins to reveal a burgeoning interest in developmental psychology or what she calls "developmental rhetoric." In "Origins of Rhetoric: A Developmental View" (1969), Emig argues that since rhetorical skills begin to emerge in early childhood as a natural stage of development, composition teachers may arrive too late and apply ineffectual strategies. "Perhaps rhetorical behaviors," she writes, "will not yield to the kinds of interventions we have classically called teaching composition—giving assignments, reading products, and requesting or demanding major or minor reformulations and revisions" (*Web* 58). An approach that focuses on the earlier stages of the composition process, rather, may mimic more closely the sort of developmental clues children get from their mothers in early language acquisition. Building on the mothering model of teaching, Emig later depicted both learning and teaching as gendered ("Non-Magical Thinking" [1979]), suggesting that female writing teachers are more adept at enabling writing because they teach from less egocentric positions, creating an environment conducive to natural development rather than leading students in various writing tasks.

Emig continued to focus on the early stages of rhetorical and cognitive development in other works during the early 1970s, though her most significant publication in 1971, *The Composing Processes of Twelfth Graders*, takes a different tack. Here Emig uses a case study approach (one that had not previously been attempted in composition studies), working closely with students through interviews, writing journals, and observation. Her most significant finding involves the designation of two principal modes of writing: Writing done in school as a response to an assignment is primarily *extensive*, whereas personal writing done independent of the writing classroom is *reflexive*. Emig argues that these modes involve completely different emotional and intellectual approaches and thus require different criteria for evaluation; the extensive is often formulaic, less inspired, whereas the reflexive "is a longer process with more portions; students writing reflexively often engage in quite long pre-writing activities; they reformulate more; starting and stopping are more discernible moments in the process; and the aesthetic contemplation of their own product of writing sometimes occurs" (*Composing Processes* 4). Based on her survey of eight twelfth-grade writers, Emig concludes that composition teachers failed to meet the challenges new process-oriented theories were posing. They focused on the superficial characteristics of their school-sponsored products (spelling, penmanship, and grammar) rather than the quality or evolution of thought expressed. Emig recommends teachers employ a wider range of writing styles in both modes and take advantage of composing aloud, one of the most significant strategies explored in the study.

In another of her most famous works during the 1970s, "Hand, Eye, Brain: Some 'Basics' in the Writing Process" (1974), Emig adds a biological component to the writing process. Most significant in this essay is her research into the relationship between physical impairment and composing. Drawing on Piaget, she notes that his three basic modes of learning hinge on the motoric, the iconic, and the representational, all of which come into play during the composing process. Emig investigates whether these basic modes take another or altered form for the blind writer or a writer without the use of her hands. Equally significant is her discussion of left versus right brain activity and studies of language abilities in split-brained patients. Research suggests that both hemispheres play a part in the activities taking place during composing (reading, writing, memory, fine motor coordination). These studies, Emig argues, have implications for rhetoric and composition theory in their relationship to the modes of discourse: "To put the matter declaratively, if hypothetically, modes of discourse may represent measurably different profiles of brain activity" (*Web* 119). Emig suggests that researchers and teachers in composition form ties with those in biological sciences.

Toward the end of the 1970s and into the 1980s, Emig continued to push for interdisciplinary writing research and practice, and her thought took a constructivist turn. In an essay that has proven crucial to the writing across the curriculum movement, "Writing as a Mode of Learning" (1977), Emig argues that writing and talking "may emanate from different organic sources and represent quite different, possibly distinct language functions" and that only writing involves "the fullest possible [bispheral] functioning of the brain" (124, 126). Although reading, listening, talking, and writing are constructive activities, only writing is both creative and originating; and since learning must be active and personal to be meaningful, writing may be the most unique and effective pedagogical tool. In essays such as "The Tacit Tradition: The Inevitability of a Multi-Disciplinary Approach to Writing Research" (1980) and "Inquiry Paradigms and Writing" (1981) (*The Web of Meaning* 157–70), Emig further articulates her transactional constructivist position, depicting writing as epistemic and crucial to all learning. But this new constructivist bent should not be construed as a departure from earlier interests in cognitive development. In "Our Missing Theory" (1990), she suggests that constructivist and developmental theories should inform one another so teachers can avoid the sort of relativism she believes early exposure to poststructuralist and postmodern theories of language can engender in younger students.

Emig's contributions to composition studies have been many and varied. In his history of the composition field, Stephen North calls *The Composing Processes of Twelfth Graders* "the single most influential piece of Researcher inquiry—and maybe *any* kind of inquiry—in Composition's short history" (North 197). But the study has not always been so well received. Critics of Emig's work (see Berlin, Voss) chiefly fault her methods, suggesting that empirical modes of research are often naive and outdated and that broad generalizations drawn from limited cases studies tend to oversimplify elements of the writing and research processes. Yet it should be no mystery why a scholar burdened with the double challenge of proving both her own capability as a woman and the legitimacy of composition as a field would turn to hard empirical data. Furthermore, given the relative absence of composition research precedents in 1971, the study must be valued for its pioneering efforts to establish the field. While some of Emig's work may seem limited by its place in composition history, her thought continues to evolve, and it is unlikely that the full scope of her wide-ranging ideas has yet been measured.

BIBLIOGRAPHY

Primary Sources

Emig, Janet. "The Biology of Writing: Another View of the Process." *The Writing Processes of Students*. Ed. W. T. Petty and P. J. Finn. Buffalo: State University of New York, Department of Elementary and Remedial Education, 1975. 11–20.
———. "Components of the Composing Process among Twelfth-Grade Writers." Diss., Harvard University, 1969.
———. *The Composing Processes of Twelfth Graders*. Urbana, IL: National Council of Teachers of English, 1971.
———. "Hand, Eye, Brain: Some 'Basics' in the Writing Process." *Research on Com-*

posing: Points of Departure. Ed. Charles Cooper and Lee Odell. Urbana, IL: National Council of Teachers of English, 1974. 59–71.

———. "Journal of a Pessimist: Prospects for Academic Women in the Eighties." *Journal of Education* 162.3 (1980): 50–56.

———. "Language Learning and the Teaching Process." *Elementary English* 44.6 (1967): 602–709.

———. "On Teaching Composition: Some Hypotheses as Definitions." *Research in the Teaching of English* 1.2 (1967): 127–35.

———. "Origins of Rhetoric: A Developmental View." *The Web of Meaning.* Upper Montclair; NJ: Boynton Cook, 1983. 55–60.

———. "Our Missing Theory." *Conversations: Contemporary Critical Theory and the Teaching of Literature.* Ed. Charles Moran and Elizabeth F. Penfield. Urbana, IL: National Council of Teachers of English, 1990.

———. "The Relation of Thought and Language Implicit in Some Early American Rhetoric and Composition Texts." Qualifying Paper. Harvard Graduate School of Education; 1963.

———. "The Tacit Tradition: The Inevitability of a Multi-Disciplinary Approach to Writing Research." *Reinventing the Rhetorical Tradition.* Ed. Aviva Freedman and Ian Pringle. Ottawa: Canadian Council of Teachers of English, 1980. 9–17.

———. "The Uses of the Unconscious in Composing." *College Composition and Communication* 15 (1964): 6–11. Reprinted in *Web of Meaning*, 46–53.

———. "We Are Trying Conferences." *English Journal* 49.4 (1960): 223–28.

———. *The Web of Meaning: Essays on Writing, Teaching, Learning, and Thinking.* Upper Montclair, NJ: Boynton/Cook, 1983.

———. "Writing as a Mode of Learning." *College Composition and Communication* 28.2 (1977): 122–28.

———. "Writing, Composition, and Rhetoric." *Encyclopedia of Educational Research.* 5th ed. 1982. New York: Free Press, 2021–35.

Emig, Janet, and June Birnbaum. "Case Study." *Handbook of Research in the English/ Language Arts.* Ed. James Squire and Julie Jensen. New York: Macmillan, 1989.

———. "Creating Minds, Created Texts: Writing and Reading." *Developing Literacy: Young Children's Use of Language.* Ed. Robert P. Parker and Francis A. Davis. Newark, DE: International Reading Association, 1983. 87–104.

Biography

Nelms, Ralph Gerald. "A Case History Approach to Composition Studies: Edward P. J. Corbett and Janet Emig." Diss., Ohio State University, 1990.

Criticism

Berlin, James A. *Rhetoric and Reality: Writing Instruction in American Colleges, 1900–1985.* Carbondale: Southern Illinois University Press, 1987.

North, Stephen M. *The Making of Knowledge in Composition: Portrait of an Emerging Field.* Upper Montclair, NJ: Boynton/Cook, 1987.

Voss, Ralph F. "Janet Emig's *The Composing Processes of Twelfth Graders*: A Reassessment." *College Composition and Communication* 34.3 (1983): 278–83.

LINDA FLOWER
(1944–   )

Ronda Leathers Dively and Gerald Nelms

Linda S. Flower, who was born on March 3, 1944, in Witchita, Kansas, began her postsecondary education at Simpson College in Indianola, Iowa. She spent three years at Simpson, but after reading works by nineteenth-century American Transcendentalists, she got "itchy feet to be in Boston" and spent her last year of college at Boston University, where she took her B.A. in English and French in 1965 (Flower, "Re: book chapter"). After graduation, Flower became a text-book production assistant with Houghton Mifflin Company in Boston and worked in publishing until 1969, when she returned to graduate school and received her Ph.D in English from Rutgers in 1972. That same year she was hired as a lecturer at the University of Pittsburgh. In 1973, she became an assistant professor at Carnegie-Mellon University, teaching in the Business and Professional Communications Program for the Graduate School of Industrial Administration (GSIA). She directed this program from 1974 through 1980. Flower describes her work there as "an attempt to create a widening program of self-help. The test was whether I could show the students strategies that made a difference—the sort of things I would want to learn too" ("An Interview" 3). It was this developing interest in writing instruction as problem solving that led Flower into her earliest research—and her collaborations with John R. Hayes.

"Dick" Hayes, a psychology professor at Carnegie-Mellon, brought to the study of writing "the tools and questions of cognitive psychology" (Flower, Letter). He had completed numerous studies using talk-aloud protocol analysis. This research method involves tape recording subjects verbalizing their thinking as they perform some action, such as reading or problem solving or, in Flower and Hayes's work, writing. The researcher then codes the transcript of the pro-tocol for variables. Flower and Hayes's desire to understand writing as a problem-solving process led to a decade of fruitful collaborations on research that continues to shape how we think about composing processes.

Another important influence on Flower's work and career was Richard Young. In the fall of 1977, he invited Flower to teach in the Humanities Department of the College of Engineering at the University of Michigan while he was on leave. Young became the chair of the English Department at Carnegie-Mellon soon afterward, and Flower moved from GSIA to English. Flower refers to Young as "a wonderful mentor" and identifies his 1970 textbook *Rhetoric: Discovery and Change*, coauthored with Alton Becker and Kenneth Pike, as an influence on her thinking about writing. As Flower notes, Young, Becker and Pike reconceptualized rhetoric as problem solving, "a research agenda made famous at CMU by Simon and one [she] was already well launched into with Dick [Hayes]" (Flower, Letter). Flower states that once she began her research on writing, "suddenly, I couldn't get to my office fast enough in the morning; it was a real revelation" ("An Interview" 4). That energy and enthusiasm seem not to have waned in over two decades. Linda Flower has authored, edited, coauthored, and coedited 10 books, more than 70 articles, 25 technical reports, 2 computer programs, and more than 30 grant and funding proposals.

Flower's immense body of scholarship draws much of its persuasive strength from the fact that it is based on empirical research. She refers to her theory as "observation-based." Theory, she says, can have a variety of sources: historical scholarship—that is, extrapolations from prior theories; what Janice Lauer and J. William Asher call "rhetorical inquiry"—a deductive process of arguing for a particular conclusion; and, finally, research—"a process in which one's orienting premises enter into dialogue with a set of close, systematic observations of writers at work" ("Observation-Based Theory Building" 171; "Cognition, Context, and Theory Building" 296). Looking at theory from this perspective— as a consequence as well as a source of knowledge—points up limitations of nonobservation-based theory, especially within rhetoric and composition, whose close historical ties to teaching lead inevitably to theories being tested in practice. Empirical research can be used not only to test or confirm hypotheses but also more importantly as a heuristic involved in theory generation. Observation-based theory building, then, is a constructive, rhetorical act. Research is a tool of such construction.

A COGNITIVE PROCESS MODEL OF COMPOSING

Much of Flower's early research sought to characterize the various and distinct cognitive processes involved in composing. Flower and Hayes's seminal article "A Cognitive Process Theory of Writing," published in 1981, introduces a succinct model of composing that portrays the act as a set of goal-directed thinking processes that are hierarchically organized and profoundly recursive. Their vision was a significant departure from the prominent stage-process model that depicted a linear progression through several composing behaviors (e.g., planning, drafting, revising, editing) and that failed to acknowledge the inner processes of decision making and choice and the links between the various subprocesses and behaviors.

The Flower and Hayes model asserts that the act of composing involves three primary, interconnected elements. One is *long-term memory*, which encompasses knowledge of topic, audience, and writing conventions and processes. Another is the *task environment*, which includes (1) the *rhetorical problem* consisting of attention to the specific problem being addressed, its context or exigency, and the representation of the audience to be addressed and (2) any *text produced so far*. A third primary element in the act of composing is the set of *writing processes*, identified as (1) *planning* (goal setting, idea generating, and organizing), (2) *translating* (taking knowledge that exists in different forms, some verbal but most nonverbal, and turning it into prose), and (3) *reviewing* (evaluating and revising). All of these processes are overseen by the writer's *monitor*, a "writing strategist" that governs movement between the processes ("A Cognitive Process Theory" 369–74; see also "Images, Plans, and Prose"). In the description of their model, Flower and Hayes make clear that writers don't simply translate knowledge in memory into prose. Instead, the writer *navigates* the composing act by means of a self-generated network of goals. These goals dictate what content to use, what to say about it, and the process of document production, and they are continually being recast in accordance with what knowledge and meaning emerge as the writing process as a whole unfolds ("A Cognitive Process Theory" 377).

Flower and Hayes's model of the mind's activity during composing is a richly conceived global representation that naturally invites elaboration of its many components. The *writing processes* in particular have received special attention from Flower and her various collaborators throughout the 1980s and early 1990s. Planning and translating, for example, are clarified in Flower and Hayes's "Multiple Representation Thesis," which asserts that invention depends on the complex interplay of the mind's multiplicity of ways of representing knowledge and meaning: visually, conceptually, schematically, verbally, and so on. Given this multiplicity, we can see that meaning cannot be conceived as a "logical, fully explicit or even necessarily verbal journey" ("Images, Plans, and Prose" 129).

The Multiple Representation Thesis rests on four premises. First, as mentioned above, knowledge and meaning are represented in multiple ways, verbally and nonverbally. Second, certain alternative modes of representation exist on a continuum that can be said—in terms of composing—to move from nonverbal and abstract knowledge networks, toward text-based and formally textual modes of knowing, and eventually, toward increasingly linguistic representations and an increasing number of prose constraints ("Images, Plans, and Prose" 129–30). Third, then, linguistic representations differ considerably with regard to the number of prose constraints that define them. And fourth, the capacity of the writer for transforming nonverbal representations into verbal prose is both a source of difficulty and a testament to the writer's prowess. One important thrust of these four premises is their challenge to two still-popular views of the writing process—the romantic blind leap experience, wherein the writer is mysteriously inspired toward an effortless outpouring of text, and the assumption that writing is simply the translation of ideas into words through a linear process of isolated steps.

Flower and colleague's elaborations of *reviewing* processes indicate the remarkable distance between Flower's cognitive model of composing and the dominant earlier stage process models. Rather than viewing these processes and behaviors as simply a later stage in the monolithic writing process, Flower reconceptualizes them as the cognitive processes used in evaluating the written text, something that goes on during planning, translating, and sentence generation and after sentences have been generated, including the time after a draft of a text has been completed. The genesis of this reviewing is *task representation*—that is, an image of the revision task as, for instance, either global or local in nature. The writer, then, moves toward *evaluation*, a constructive, generative activity dependent on the act of reading for comprehension, which leads to "a progressive enlargement of goals and constraints" (Flower et al. 25). The product of evaluation is *problem representation*, a concept that may best be understood as a spectrum marked at one end by "ill-defined problems" and at the other end by "extremely well-defined problems." Ill-defined problems require mere *detections*. They simply acknowledge the presence of a problem. Well-defined problems, however, involve *diagnosis*, or the ability to categorize problems and to imagine solutions. The distinction between detection and diagnosis is crucial in accounting for the two categories of *strategy selection*, or behavioral and cognitive response to evaluation: *rewriting* and *revising*. Detection alone results simply in rewriting, a mere "from scratch" rerendering of the gist driving the original plan for generating text. Although this strategy may result in a different product, it seldom results in a better one. Diagnosis, on the other hand, results in revision, a substantial reworking of existing text with the intention of effecting changes in content, structure, voice, and so on, that hopefully lead to improved quality (Flower et al. 26). The success of the review process is determined in large part by two key variables: knowledge and intention. Knowledge can be both "declarative," which refers to texts and their features, and "procedural," which refers to "how-to" understanding enabling the writer to make changes in the text. Intention enters into the process as part of *task representation*, with regard to the goals and criteria that influence evaluation (Flower et al. 20).

It is important at this point to emphasize the recursive nature of writing as described by Flower's model. Earlier Janet Emig and Sondra Perl had argued that the notion of discrete stages in composing misrepresents how writers actually write. Flower's research and model of composing elaborate this belief. As writers compose, they create goals, criteria, and plans that guide meaning-making. But as the process proceeds, goals, criteria, plans, and text are continuously reevaluated and regenerated. The writer's attention moves back and forth within the text—and within the writer's thinking about the text.

LITERACY AS THE CONSTRUCTION OF NEGOTIATED MEANING

The recursive nature of composing is further explained by recognizing that composing is always socially situated. This situatedness works at multiple levels of cognition in Flower's theorizing. The writer always writes for an other, even if that other is the writer himself or herself. Composing is never simply composing per se; it always involves a reader or readers, an audience, or a trans-perspective imagining of the response of readers to the writing. Moreover, cognition "does not exist in a vacuum" (*Construction* 31). Thinking is always contextualized—learned through social interactions with parents, teachers, friends, television, films, music. Flower writes, "The interpretations and the knowledge [people] construct is their own, but it is built out of and in response to other voices, prior texts, social expectations, and ideological alternatives" (31). These multiple "voices"—which may not be voices at all but images, concepts, schemas, and the like—create a complicated "web of meaning," to use Emig's phrase. Webs do not allow for linear progression. Flower describes such webs of meaning as a "network of words, images, sounds, emotions, and ideas, linked by verbal, spatial, affective, or visceral relations" (39).

The inclusion of social, contextual considerations in describing literate action represents an important move on Flower's part, merging the sharply divided cognitivist and social constructionist perspectives on composing. Cognitivists have tended to focus on individual cognition, whereas social constructionists have argued that writing is best viewed as a reproduction of social conventions or a conversation involving multiple, socially engendered voices. According to Flower, on the other hand, social, cultural, and individual forces interpenetrate one another. Texts *are* shaped by social and cultural values and forces, but such shaping goes on within the context of the individual *negotiating* among these various forces and his or her own goals, criteria, and plans. This negotiation Flower says is "an internal process by which writers construct (rather than merely defend) personal, but socially situated meanings" (*Construction* 66). Flower believes that "there is no way to isolate a social process from the minds that carry it out" (31). Social conventions and discourse exist as agreements among individual minds, not disconnected entities, and as such they are situated within and among individuals. Flower explains, "[M]eaning and the work of construction are still located in the minds of individual agents, not in the reified construct of 'conversation' itself" (63).

[T]he agent in even a socially extended process of making meaning . . . is not society, community, or a discourse; that is, meanings are not made by an abstract, theoretical construct but by individual writers, readers, speakers, and listeners who are interpreting inferred meanings around them, constructing their own, and attempting to share those meanings with or impose them on other members of their social or cultural collective.

Individual meaning is not *sui generis*, but it is nonetheless a cognitive construction, created out of prior knowledge in response to the multiple layers of a writer's social, rhetorical, and cultural context. (89)

The basis for this social cognitive understanding of literacy is the human condition itself. We exist as physically separate minds that have developed ways of making connections, of achieving at least a tenuous, temporary identification with each other. Literate acts, then, are "sites of construction, tension, divergence, and conflict. They happen at the intersection of diverse goals, values, and assumptions, where social roles interact with personal images of one's self and one's situation" (19). Literate acts are "sites of negotiation where the meaning that emerges may reflect resolution, abiding contradiction, or perhaps just a temporary stay against uncertainty" (19).

READING AND THE CONSTRUCTION OF MEANING

Within this broad social cognitive theory of literate acts, Flower's explanation of the manner in which social forces and individual cognition interpenetrate each other serves to elucidate the constructive nature of not only writing but also *reading*. Traditionally, reading has been viewed as a largely passive, receptive activity, wherein *the* meaning deposited by the author into the text readily displays itself to the enlightened, capable reader. Contemporary theorists, however, view reading as a *transaction* among the text, the reader, and the context. Meaning does not exist monolithically in the text alone; rather, it emerges from the complex of influences that text, reader, and context exert upon one another. Flower has helped to show that many of the processes involved in this expanded act of reading mirror those involved in writing (see "Interpretive Acts"), particularly those processes by which readers and writers represent meaning to themselves.

Importantly, Flower and Hayes's Multiple Representation Thesis reveals as much about the nature of reading as it does about the nature of writing in its depiction of the various verbal and nonverbal representations that constitute the intricate, dynamic web of meaning an individual assigns to a given text at a given time. The web of meaning constructed during the act of reading is a response to cues in the text itself and within the social/cultural context of the reading (Haas and Flower 169). Specific components of that web might include beliefs about the subject matter, the author, and the reader's own intentions, as well as representations regarding propositional or content information, the structure of that information, and the particular functions of various textual elements (168). Depending on the manner in which a reader mediates this ever-changing web, interwoven as it is with myriad social and cultural influences, it could potentially yield diverse interpretations, just as the web created during the composing act could potentially result in multiple textual renderings. Any single interpretation represents but one possible instantiation of the web—the individual's provisional negotiation of its various components at a given point in time.

As is the case with writing, many of the subprocesses involved in the act of reading are tacit or automated. Perceived difficulties in creating a coherent or otherwise satisfying interpretation of the text, however, will send the reader into a more highly conscious, even metacognitive, mode of meaning-making. This heightened mode of textual processing may include (1) using prior knowledge to interpret certain aspects of the text or to solve certain problems that arise, (2) actively searching the text for specific information, (3) monitoring, testing, or elaborating one's current understanding of the text; and (4) reading rhetorically, which involves the realization that texts are purposeful acts composed within definite contexts and designed to incite certain reactions (Haas and Flower 170; Flower, "Construction of Purpose" 54).

In the throes of constructive activities such as rhetorical reading, readers are said to be *writing* the texts they are processing insofar as they are *actively making meaning* based on these texts. But perhaps the inevitable interconnectedness of reading and writing is most apparent in the act of composing, in that recursivity born from the situatedness of all literate acts, where it is nearly impossible to isolate these processes for separate consideration. At the very outset of the composing process, writers become *readers* of the content of their own long-term memories and the rhetorical situation in which they find themselves. A web of meaning begins to form, and gradually, as goals, criteria, and plans are set and reset, as words are produced and then sentences and then whole chunks of text are generated, writers, forced by the limitations of human memory *and* by the increasing complexity of the textual production, must read and reread their own writing, evaluating the effectiveness at meeting their writing goals. At this juncture, reading may prompt editing, revision, changes in writing goals or plans, and/or a continuation of sentence generation or drafting. As writers continue reading their unfolding texts, they return again and again to aspects of the composing act that they have already visited and perhaps revisited. In the context of composing, then, the inevitable interconnectedness of reading and writing processes provides yet another means of accounting for the profoundly recursive nature of the mind's activity.

COMMUNITY LITERACY: FLOWER'S SOCIAL COGNITIVE THEORY IN PRACTICE

Since the mid-1990s, Flower has expended considerable scholarly energy observing the tenets of her social cognitive theory of literacy as they play themselves out in the context of a community literacy project spearheaded by Carnegie-Mellon's Center for the Study of Writing and Literacy and Pittsburgh's Community House, an institution devoted primarily to providing recreational, spiritual, and social programs for residents of Pittsburgh's north side. This literacy project, known as the Community Literacy Center (CLC), has extended the mission of the Community House by involving inner-city youth and adults in collaborative problem solving through literate action based in part on Flower's social cognitive theory of writing. By consciously engaging in the process of constructing negotiated meaning, participants in the CLC—including Flower, college students acting as partners in literacy, inner-city teens, and adult literacy mentors from the neighborhood—strive to build intercultural relationships and to effect productive change within the community.

Inner-city youth and adults who become involved in the CLC commit themselves to a brand of inquiry that will enable them to assert their voices effectively in community conversations that historically have excluded them. In the spirit of constructing negotiated meaning, while reading, talking, and writing about issues that concern them, participants in the CLC rise to "greater reflective awareness of the multiple voices and sometimes conflicting forces their meaning needs to entertain" (Peck, Flower, and Higgins 215). More specifically, as they collaborate in producing documents that will become the catalysts for larger community conversations about problems such as street violence, drug abuse, excessive school suspension rates for African American males, and so on, they learn to negotiate generative conflict between multiple, competing voices, with the goal of constructing new understandings—new possibilities for action (Flower, "Negotiating" 86).

The central business of the CLC, then, is to move multicultural interaction beyond mere conversation, "beyond the celebration of difference and the examination of conflicting assumptions and beliefs," to a place where genuine *intercultural collaboration* can occur, to a place where diverse individuals "can take rhetorical action together, across differences" (214). Flower and her collaborators, Wayne C. Peck, director of Pittsburgh's Community House, and Lorraine Higgins, director of the Community Literacy Center, have characterized the subprocesses of negotiation that will lead to rhetorical action in this specific context as follows:

Writers negotiate (in the sense of arbitrate) the power relations among competing voices as well as negotiate (in the sense of navigate) the best path that tries to embrace multiple, conflicting goods. Such negotiation is not "giving in" or settling for less, but reaching for a more complex version of best. Against a backdrop of face-to-face negotiations of social and cultural difference, writers at the center are also learning to conduct internal negotiations with voices in their own minds to construct new, more responsive meanings that support a desperately needed, working community conversation. (215)

Negotiation of this kind calls for "assertive literate practices" that enable writers to identify and analyze problems, establish goals, anticipate readers' reactions, generate specific writing plans, and assess alternatives to those plans. It also requires an aptitude for collaborative planning, rival hypothesis thinking, revising, and decision making, as well as the opportunity for evaluating and adapting these strategies (214).

The style of collaboration driving the CLC involves literate exchanges that foreground race and culture and that find all participants speaking from numerous and overlapping subject positions, conditions that provide "heated and hilarious opportunities for mutual incomprehensibility" (Flower, "Negotiating" 47). Within this setting, patterns of power and authority are constantly in flux, the "teachers" frequently and necessarily becoming students of the inner-city residents' expertise regarding urban realities (48). As everyone at the CLC works to understand the various interpretations, assumptions, strategies, and literate styles that become part of the exchange, the "academic" is no longer protected from the conflict and uncertainty that facilitates intellectual growth (52). Entrenched in this often volatile but always stimulating environment, Flower continues to interrogate, elucidate, and refine her social cognitive theory of literate action through close, systematic observation from the perspective of both teacher and learner.

BIBLIOGRAPHY

Primary Sources

Emig, Janet. *The Composing Processes of Twelfth Graders*. Urbana, IL: National Council of Teachers of English, 1971.

Flower, Linda. "Cognition, Context, and Theory Building." *College Composition and Communication* 40.3 (1989): 282–311.

———. *The Construction of Negotiated Meaning: A Social Cognitive Theory of Writing*. Carbondale: Southern Illinois University Press, 1994.

———. "The Construction of Purpose in Writing and Reading." *College English* 50.5 (1988): 42–60.

———. "Interpretive Acts: Cognition and the Construction of Discourse." *Poetics* 16.2 (1987): 109–30.

———. "Negotiating the Meaning of Difference." *Written Communication* 13.1 (1996): 44–96.

———. "Observation-Based Theory Building." *Publishing in Rhetoric and Composition*. Ed. Gary A. Olson and Todd W. Taylor. Albany: State University of New York Press, 1997. 163–85.

———. *Problem-solving Strategies for Writers*. New York: Harcourt, 1980.

———. "Taking Thought: The Role of Conscious Processing in the Making of Meaning." *Thinking, Reasoning and Writing*. Ed. Elaine Maimon, Barbara Nodine, and Finnbarr O'Connor. New York: Longman, 1989. 185–212.

Flower, Linda, and John R. Hayes. "A Cognitive Process Theory of Writing." *College Composition and Communication* 32.4 (1981): 365–87.

———. "Images, Plans, and Prose: The Representation of Meaning in Writing." *Written Communication* 1.1 (1984): 120–60.

Flower, Linda, John R. Hayes, Linda Carey, Karen Schriver, and James Stratman. "Detection, Diagnosis, and the Strategies of Revision." *College Composition and Communication* 37.1 (1986): 16–55.

Haas, Christina, and Linda Flower. "Rhetorical Reading Strategies and the Construction of Meaning." *College Composition and Communication* 39.2 (1988): 167–83.

Hayes, John R., and Linda S. Flower. "Uncovering Cognitive Processes in Writing: An Introduction to Protocol Analysis." *Research on Writing: Principles and Methods.* Ed. P. Mosenthal, L. Tamor, and S. Walmsley. New York: Longman, 1983. 207–20.

Lauer, Janice M., and J. William Asher. *Composition Research: Empirical Designs.* New York: Oxford University Press, 1988.

Peck, Wayne Campbell, Linda Flower, and Lorraine Higgins. "Community Literacy." *College Composition and Communication* 46.2 (1995): 199–222.

Perl, Sondra. "Understanding Composing." *College Composition and Communication* 31.4 (1980): 363–69.

Young, Richard, Alton Becker, and Kenneth Pike. *Rhetoric: Discovery and Change.* San Diego: Harcourt Brace Jovanovich, 1970.

Biography

Flower, Linda. "An Interview with Linda Flower." With Carol Heller. *Quarterly of the National Writing Project and the Center for the Study of Writing and Literacy* 13.1 (1991): 3–5, 28–30.

———. Letter to Gerald Nelms. December 18, 1997.

———. "Re: book chapter." Email to Gerald Nelms. October 4, 1998.

Criticism

Berlin, James. "Rhetoric and Ideology in the Writing Class." *College English* 50.5 (1988): 477–94.

———. *Rhetoric and Reality: Writing Instruction in American Colleges, 1900–1985.* Carbondale: Southern Illinois University Press, 1987.

Cooper, Marilyn, and Michael Holzman. "Talking about Protocols." *College Composition and Communication* 34.3 (1983): 284–93.

Harris, Joseph. *A Teaching Subject: Composition since 1966.* Upper Saddle River, NJ: Prentice-Hall, 1997.

MICHEL FOUCAULT
(1926–1984)

Luanne Frank

Born Paul-Michel Foucault on October 15, 1926, at Poitiers, France, Michel Foucault was the second of three children of Dr. Paul Foucault, a surgeon and professor at Poitiers University's medical school, and Ann Malapert, daughter of a surgeon. He grew up in well-to-do circumstances. To remain with his sister, he began informally attending the Lycée Henri-IV in 1930 at age four. An excellent student, he remained there until 1939, then transferred to the Collège Saint-Stanislas in 1940, finishing there, and remaining in Poitiers for the two-year preparation for entrance exams for Paris's École Normale Supérieure (ENS). He was not admitted. To prepare again, he entered a Paris Lycée Henri-IV; studied under Jean Hippolyte, among others; and was fourth among admittees for 1946. At ENS, conflict characterized his life with other students, and difficulty accepting his homosexuality may have prompted an apparent suicide attempt in 1948 and possibly others. He failed the *agrégation* in 1950. In 1951, he tied for third place, the topic for his oral examination, sexuality, having been chosen by Georges Canguilhem, who had examined him for admission. Rather than request a lycée post, for which he was now qualified, Foucault spent the 1951–1952 school year as 1 of 10 recipients of a three-year research stipend at the Centre National de la Recherche Scientifique (a subject he proposed for research: "the problem of human sciences in post-Cartesian philosophers"). Leaving after one year, but continuing to live in Paris, he became an assistant lecturer in psychology at the University of Lille in 1952.

Interested in psychology since his first year at ENS, he began studying for a degree immediately after receiving his *licence* in philosophy from the Sorbonne in 1948. From the Sorbonne he then received a *licence*, and from the Institut de Psychologie de Paris a diploma, in psychology in 1949. In 1952 he received a diploma in pathological psychology from the same institute. In 1952 and 1953 he assisted a family friend, Jacqueline Verdeaux, with a translation of a small book by Ludwig Binswanger, Swiss developer of existential psychoanalysis via Martin Heidegger's *Being and Time*, and friend of Carl Gustav Jung, Sigmund Freud, Karl Jaspers, and Heidegger. Foucault and Verdeaux visited the analyst several times and talked with him of Heidegger, phenomenology, and psycho-analysis. Such was Foucault's interest in the translation, and in Binswanger's method as an antidote to the psychiatry Foucault saw practiced as he assisted Verdeaux with encephalographic work in asylum and prison venues, that Ver-deaux suggested he do a preface for the book. It appeared in 1954 as the intro-duction to Binswanger's *Dream and Existence*.

In 1955, Foucault was appointed director of the French (cultural) Institute in Uppsala, where he taught French literature and language, and availed himself of unmatched special collections in Uppsala's great library, the *Carolina redi-viva*, to do research for his doctoral thesis, begun in Sweden and destined to become *Madness and Civilization* (1961), the work with which he first became known on the French intellectual scene. In 1958 and 1959 he took similar ap-pointments in Warsaw—seeing communism at first hand—and in Hamburg.

In 1960, he taught psychology at the University of Clermont-Ferand, received his *doctorat d'etat*, the highest French degree, in 1961, and received tenure in 1962. In 1963 he published both *Death and the Labyrinth: The World of Ray-mond Roussel* and *The Birth of the Clinic*. Encouraged by Canguilhem, recently his thesis director, Foucault took administrative leave after the academic year 1965–1966 to teach philosophy at the University of Tunis. He had published *The Order of Things* in the spring of 1966 to great acclaim. He remained in Tunis for two and one-half years, political unrest prompting his accepting an August 1968 position in psychology at Nanterre, invited by Didier Anzieu. Be-fore beginning to teach, he resigned to become director of the philosophy de-partment at the new University of Vincennes, where the campus was disrupted by student actions of solidarity with revolutionary events in Paris, and Foucault's own radicalization, developed over a long period, accelerated. For now, it ex-pressed itself in demonstrations and manifestos. His academic work remained unpoliticized.

In 1969 he published *The Archaeology of Knowledge*, a hyperstructuralist theoretical treatise clarifying the methodology behind *Order*. In 1970, nominated and presented by Jules Vuillemin, and supported by Hippolyte, Georges Du-mézil, and Fernand Braudel, he was elected to the Collège de France, the most prestigious French academic institution. The title of his chair, proposed by him-self, was The History of Systems of Thought. He would be required to offer new courses annually. Five years later, in 1975, after a radical shift in meth-odology—a return to the general modality of *Madness*—he published his most influential work, *Discipline and Punish*. In 1976 there followed the first volume of *The History of Sexuality* and, in 1984, the second and third volumes: *The Use of Pleasure* and *The Care of the Self*. A fourth, "Les Aveux de la Chair," was close to final form at the time of his death. From 1966 Foucault was in increasing demand for lectures, articles, and interviews. He was in the United States often, drawing increasingly large crowds, from 1970 through 1993. He lectured for the French department at Buffalo in 1970 and 1972, visited Attica prison, lectured in New York, at Berkeley, and again in New York (for *Semiotext[e]*), in 1973. He gave the Tanner Lectures at Stanford in 1979, met and worked with Berkeley professors Hubert Dreyfus and Paul Rabinow, who were writing a book about him, and was visiting professor there in French in 1980, also giving the Howison Lectures, entitled "Truth and Subjectivity." He lectured to the Humanities Institute at New York University in 1980, at University of California in Los Angeles in 1981, the University of Vermont in 1982, and Berkeley again in spring and fall 1983. Foucault's courses at the Collège de France in his final years were "Subjectivity and Truth" (1981); "The Hermeneutics of the Subject" (1982); "The Government of Self and Others" (1983); and "Parrhesia, the Practice of Truth-Telling" (1984).

Foucault died of AIDS at age fifty-seven in the Salpetrière—the Paris hospital whose numerous roles he had described in his first major work—on June 25, 1984. In a group of testimonials published by *Le Monde*, Paul Veyne called his work "the most important event of thought in our century"; Braudel, in *Le Nouvel Observateur*, called his mind "one of the most dazzling . . . of the epoch" (Eribon 328).

FOUCAULT'S RHETORICAL THEORY

The canonic philosophers of the West, from the pre-Socratics forward, are the foundation for Foucault's thought. He rigorously grounded himself in their writings. But he was always adding to his foundations, and they came to include much else, in history, literature, art, and especially psychology. It has been said—it was thought by his fellow ENS students—that he read everything. By his own acknowledgment at the end of his life, two influences were paramount: "My entire philosophical development was determined by my reading of Heidegger. . . . It is possible that if I had not read Heidegger, I would not have read Nietzsche." "These are the two fundamental experiences I have had" (qtd. in Eribon 30). Still, among other masters of truth, Immanuel Kant, Friedrich Hegel, Karl Marx, and Freud are indispensable to his development; among professors, Maurice Merleau-Ponty; among professor–mentors, Hippolyte, Canguilhem, Louis Althusser, and Dumézil; among contemporary movements of thought, phenomenology, Heideggerian hermeneutics, and structuralism. Gaston Bachelard, Georges Bataille, Maurice Blanchot, and Pierre Klossowski are also important in later years.

The work of Foucault is part of that great surge in twentieth-century Western thought, said to stem from Ferdinand de Saussure and now called "the linguistic turn," that suddenly sees in language the foundation of the analyzable world. The idea is not new to the twentieth century, but rendered newly apprehendable via Saussure, it enjoys there an efflorescence unparalleled by its earlier emergences. By the century's second half it has become the new cultural truth through which other such truths are filtered and from which they take their comprehensibility. Fostered at first by the flourishing young sciences of linguistics and anthropology, this suddenly revised awareness of language spreads rapidly to humanistic thought in general, setting it alight with new insights, rendering it newly transparent, filling it with a new urgency, endowing it with a mighty, new legitimacy. New movements, or modes of understanding, evolving out of the turn come to be known as structuralism, semiotics, and in a succession rapid for cultural evolution, poststructuralism. Even inert corners of humanistic studies are vivified at the sight of the new vistas of understanding these movements open up.

With the linguistic turn, humanistic thought advances to within a step of recognizing itself as through and through rhetorical thought. It will be Foucault who, after rigorous demonstrations that the step is avoidable, reverses himself and closes the gap—between humanism's assumption that its discourses are pure and the Nietzschean recognition, which Foucault recovers, that such purity is a ruse. The new age's new masters of truth become "masters of discursivity." The phrase is Foucault's, and inadvertently or not, with it he describes himself: All of his major works, whatever they seem to do, uncover the development of rhetorical systems as historical forces. They describe the burgeoning of rhetorics in the human sciences and in related discourses and practices as these constitute, shape, and control the social world—and the natural world as well in its availability to consciousness. From the point of view of the turn, though again via Foucault's phraseology, there are no natural objects. This explains in large part his famous refusals to discuss given entities except across what has been said of them, that is, except as they have been rhetoricized. It may explain as well his well-known indifference to nature.

Foucault is not himself partial to the term *rhetoric*. Perhaps because he is a philosopher–historian. Perhaps because the word already shelters, and thus gives away, one of his grounding assumptions, which on methodological grounds he avoids thematizing, preferring to let it dawn gradually: the Nietzschean insight that no humanistic discourse wears but one face, that each masks another, a will to power. Again speaking Foucauldian, one could thus say: Rhetoric makes Foucault possible. For both Foucault and rhetoric understand that the less value-laden a humanistic discourse seems, the more value-laden it is.

That Foucault's grounding emphasis in his works is, in fact, rhetorical may be less than immediately apparent, not because attention to an agendaed discursivity is absent but because he fails to thematize, as such, the rhetoricity of the discourses whose emergence and efficacy he traces, instead leaving the truths he is uncovering—the nondisinterestedness of "objective" discourses, their manipulativeness and coerciveness—to make this point about themselves through his vast accumulations of historical detail. Though agendaed discursivity is characteristically a chief object of his thought, only two of his works, *Order* and *Archaeology*, make discourse their almost single-minded concern.

TRAJECTORY OF THOUGHT

Foucault's great, overriding theme throughout his work, less than apparent as the oeuvre begins to unfold, is power. Whatever the names of his well-known interests as his thought evolves—dividing practices, knowledge in the human sciences, *épistèmes*, discursive formations, truth, games of truth, individualization, normalization, identity, the subject, technologies of the self, surface discourses, nondiscursive social practices, institutions, disciplines and disciplinary spaces, governmentality—they are forms and effects of power. His concerns lie early with certain obvious, unrecognized, and thus clandestine forms power takes and the ways it is deployed, exercised, visited upon human subjects—the guises in which it dominates, represses, "subjects" them, typically without their knowledge, only sometimes against their will.

Upon these follow concerns with power's also unrecognized but generally unrecognizable epistemic forms, in which it shapes the thought of entire periods—thought exemplified for Foucault by knowledge in the human sciences—and thus shapes all human subjects. Then, to the earlier concern with power as repression, is added explicit, thematized recognition of power's productive, self-proliferating aspect and an awareness of the ubiquity of points of resistance to it. Eventually, there are added concerns with the personal measures a demystified contemporary subject—a subject steeped in Foucauldian thought—might take in anticipation of a certain sort of freedom, a freedom achievable in the face of power but also by means of it, and not alone in the given subject's name.

In his earliest thought, before the Foucauldian voice is yet full throated, the pessimism unyielding, the immaculate distancing achieved, an explicit Foucauldian theme is in fact freedom, the human's immutable desire for it. But the word's meaning is not divulged. This theme fades to implicitness in the major works, where freedom is an almost unspoken luminescence, an inadmissible yearning behind their darkness, the unidentified and shifting place from which Foucault speaks (and perhaps an explanation for what some observers call his optimism). But freedom in its Foucauldian form, if it yet exists in the early, middle, and late major works, remains indescribable, unknown—a word no longer or not yet able to speak its name. The form in which it at first knew itself now seems unsuitable, if not unseemly—naive. A quasi-Heideggerian freedom, it hangs baggy on Foucault, not yet cut to fit. Then, unexpectedly, after three decades of near silence, of yielding pride of place to power, Foucauldian freedom, power's opposite but also one of its forms, finds a voice. After 30 years, it knows itself. It reemerges as a focus of the late courses and a final interview. This is the general trajectory of Foucault's thought. Clearly, it is a circular one, ending approximately where it began but freighted with what lies between its beginnings and its final stages—and much altered.

The question of what to do about power that subjects, a question everywhere implicit in his work, is never answered: Foucault prescribes no solutions. More typically, he questions them. Still, his own understanding of power as primarily monolithic no longer, now capillary-like in its modern pervasiveness, every-where existent and exercised in the most minute remotenesses of the social, spiritual, and physical body; his understanding that resistance is likewise every-where ("wherever there is power, there is resistance" [*Sexuality* 95]); the im-probable load of specific detail in his works, suggesting each site of power's deployment as a potential point of resistance; and his own much publicized involvements in local struggles—all point a direction: Disciplinary power is resistable; it is resistable locally; and the agents of resistance are human subjects, however implacably disciplinary practices and discourses (the human sciences and their close relatives) have limited these subjects' possibilities for action.

Initially optimistic, devoting himself (in *Dream*) to uncovering the dreaming subject's deepest desires, Foucault is moved to pessimism by his encounters with mental patients during his psychological studies. He comes to recognize these subjects as thoroughly and abjectly subjected, specifically by the dis-courses and practices of psychiatry and medicine. Thence he moves (in *Mad-ness*) to an understanding of the modern subject in general as a function of these and other discourses, notably the knowledges making up the burgeoning dis-courses of the human sciences. Assuming (in *Order* and *Archaeology*) he has found in structuralism a benign discourse that can be used to describe without dominating, Foucault eventually becomes aware that the very knowledge he is developing out of it (a structuralism more radical than Levi Strauss's via a phenomenology more radical than Husserl's, both practiced in the name of a radical objectivity) is itself subjecting—objectifying, disciplinary. Long able to see himself as one of the abject he describes in *Madness* and *Birth*, he must now identify himself as, worse yet, an archdisciplinarian.

With this he abandons a rigorous structuralism. From the human sciences narrowly defined he then expands his focus (in *Discipline*) to a broader, still related range of discourses and practices, those of prisons, asylums, hospitals, workhouses, schools, and the military, recognizing contemporary Western so-ciety in general as disciplinary and carceral. From here he focuses (in *Sexuality*) on a set of predominant discourses of the present, those proliferating around sexuality, and the disciplines deriving from them, eventually tracing these to Christian practices of confession and, (in *Care*) farther back, to ancient tech-nologies of the self. In these latter he finds self-practices—training and govern-ment of self, care of self—long trivialized, forgotten, and thus preserved, that contain suggestions fruitful for present-day subjects' possible self-production.

But these practices, developed as means of governing others, are lacking in what Foucault now sees as a necessity if the exercise of power as domination is to be avoided. Partly on the basis of what he finds in these ancient techniques, partly on what he fails to find, Foucault in a final interview ("The Ethic of Care for the Self as a Practice of Freedom" ["Freedom"]) hazards a description of how power, exercisable by the long-subjected Western subject and now spoken of as freedom, might be claimed. This "practice of freedom" would not do away with power: It would include two forms of it rather than one—care of the self, care for the other. Retaining power as an inevitable component of social practice, Foucault nonetheless suggests something between its poles (the poles of self and other) that the forms of power he has genealogized did not know and failed to find: reciprocity. In engaging in power relationships in a reciprocal way, the self's practice of its own freedom—its power—becomes a form of ethics. As ethics, power becomes eligible for another name: freedom.

In summary: Foucault achieves a brief dream of freedom (*Dream*), then constructs historicizations (*Madness, Birth, Discipline, Sexuality*) and rigorously structural, layered orderings (*Order, Archaeology*) of the forms power has taken in exercising itself upon human subjects in the modern West, often in the name of "humanity"; finally (in *Care* and *Use*), via ancient forms of self-production linked historically to the contemporary self, he catches a brief glimpse (in "Freedom") of how one form of freedom might be claimed (through care *of* the self), to which another form (care of the other) could be added.

In working out his ideas, Foucault avails himself of the most powerful intellectual tools of his age: cause-effect history, phenomenology, hermeneutics, and structuralism. Each is indispensable, each unsatisfactory. Foucault rings significant changes on each, coming to practice a Nietzschean form of history—"genealogy"—and a phenomenologically rigorized form of structuralism—"archaeology"—and even a structuralist hermeneutics. He eschews a history that explains rather than describes, a phenomenology that transcendentalizes the subject (eventually he abandons his own transcendentalizing of discourse), a hermeneutics that seeks deep meaning beneath discourse and practice. Nonetheless, Foucault ongoingly employs aspects of all these methodologies. Much ink has been spilled over whether Foucault was a structuralist. Certainly structuralism, in its recognition of the sovereignty of language in producing the subject and society, remains one of the pervasive methodological influences on Foucault.

It explains his onetime, nearly single-minded focus on discourse and his retention of it as one of the two poles of his own developing methodology after his hyperstructuralist phase. The other pole is made up of social practices other than the discursive. An important part of his methodology is to divide the innumerable concrete forms he shows power taking into these two macroforms: serious discourses—those of authorities, especially in the human sciences, and nondiscursive practices, also of a serious sort. Rarely explaining his methodology or thematizing its categories, he places more or less emphasis on discourse or on nondiscursive practice in every major work, sometimes achieving a nearly balanced mix. With the exception of a period in the mid-1960s, when (in *Order* and *Archaeology*) his focus is primarily discourse, he recognizes a tight mutual dependence between discourse and practice, occasionally envisioning explanations of their relation as eventual goals of his work. An indefatigable researcher into discourses as his means of laying practices bare, he is acutely aware that discourses lay down, lay out, express, order, categorize, and preserve social practices, and his partiality appears to rest with them.

His attention focuses on discourses of two types: those known or knowable to their practitioners, and that describe, prescribe, order, rationalize, render comprehensible, and preserve knowledge-based social practices (his late work devotes itself exclusively to these); and conceivable discourses (*épistèmes* or discursive formations) unknown and unknowable by their practitioners that nonetheless determine the forms their knowing takes and, especially when that knowledge has to do with human subjects, determines these, including the knowers themselves. At the point that Foucault emphasizes discourse almost exclusively, he does so implacably, making it the a priori, the sine qua non, of social practice.

Although it is clear that a discourse/nondiscursive-social-practice binary is inevitably circular (discourse becomes practice, becomes discourse), clear also that practice is possessed of its own rhetoric, it is Foucault's characteristic attentiveness to discourse itself as a primary—sometimes as the ultimate—social fact (not necessarily an isolated one) that in part explains his significance for rhetoric. He knows that the role of language is incommensurable (1) as the figure of what one can know *in itself* ("saying" is the only form in which a truth is knowable); (2) as the figure of what one can know *about* (truth in its objective form—truth once removed from itself); (3) as the figure of what one can *be*, ongoingly (an identity, an individual, a "subject"); (4) or as the figure of what one can be but fleetingly ("I am doubtless not the only one who writes in order to have no face" [*Archaeology* 17]). But only when these insights turn Nietzschean, when Foucault exposes the ruses of truth, does his significance for rhetoric become incalculable. (Such revelations explain in part what will later become an emphasis on "telling the truth.")

With Nietzsche, Foucault sees the incorrigible rhetoricity of all humanistic discourses, their inevitable nonobjectivity and nondisinterestedness, and focuses his attention on some whose power is equaled by their deleteriousness—discourses conventionally regarded as pure, objective, humane. He has decided that, except possibly in the pure sciences, pure discourse is nonexistent, is "*das Tier, dass es nicht gibt*" (the animal that doesn't exist [Rilke, "Das Einhorn," in *Sonnets to Orpheus*]). Foucault has become the rhetorician's rhetorician.

Although his work challenges the reader, Foucault's significance—decided by his usefulness—is not restricted to scholar–theorists and others willing to move with him through his often tortuously dense, complex, multileveled, switching, folding, often confusing, sometimes repetititive or contradictory, often exhilarating works, which, like the discourses and practices he studies, typically withhold their underlying intent (his interviews reveal that what he was after was sometimes unclear to him). His thought is relevant to the multiple levels at which the discipline of rhetoric functions, especially wherever it is concerned with what drives discourses—the subject? a discourse speaking through the subject? one that is speaking through *that* one? an authority? a society's monolithic value systems? an economy's drive to productivity?—or with discourses' effects on human subjects, or with innumerable other possible permutations of the subject-discourse relation.

It is typically across the so-called problem of the subject that rhetoric encounters Foucault, and not incorrectly, since late in his life he notes the subject's having been his project all along. Also typically, his dazzling *Order* and stunning *Archaeology*, but also his revelatory *Discipline* and breathtaking *Sexuality*, are presumed the measure of his thought on the question of the subject, and his dark vision in these works is regarded as disempowering, a threat to a subject's vision of itself as potentially self-determining (whether student of composition or teacher–theorist). Although outside of rhetoric it has been said that Foucault took his deconstructions of neither the subject nor power far enough, the charge of the subject's disempowerment is a serious one in a rhetoric traditionally conceived.

But, perhaps fortunately, it is also a false charge, as Foucault's latest works and courses, as well as the interview noted above, indicate. Thus, his influence on rhetoric enlarges as rhetoricians become able to see themselves in Foucault. In doing so, they come to see him not narrowly, as an intractable personage much of whose work in identifying them as but functives implicitly denies them being, self-definition, and autonomy—and predicts their dissolution—but broadly, as a teacher-by-example. His teaching: a sort of radical mutability, evolving and writing in the name of its own and social change, and suitable for the closest study. Again and again this mutability focuses its gaze on sets of established, subject-constituting discourses and social practices; seeks, finds or constructs, describes, and follows routes to their undoing; contributes its insights to the ends of knowledge or social change; itself changes, aligning itself with its own latest discoveries; disabuses itself of the accuracy of the truths it has just espoused; subjects them to deconstruction; and begins again.

Some late twentieth-century rhetoricians recognize themselves here and their discipline as well. It remains to be seen how many spirals through deconstructions of its own myths of itself rhetoric will be willing to trace if being Foucauldian points it beyond these immutable visions. (Thus far, rhetoric has sometimes sought to wrench Foucault into forms of itself, or, by limiting itself to a single segment of his thought, refute him, who so often refutes himself.) Then again, having become Foucauldian, rhetoric may be able to go beyond Foucault, in a Foucauldian way and at his direction, to expose the potential dangers to self and other in his most advanced rhetorics—in his formulas for harnessing power as a form of freedom in the service of self *and* other and thus as an ethics. Foucault emphasized that every solution to a social problem carried its own dangers, which would have to be resisted as they became evident. It is possible that the sorts of power relationships to which his late suggestions point with tentative approval must themselves be unmasked, as he himself might soon have discovered, as new forms of disciplinary practice, and that all such solutions, developed in a regime of thought constructed across a subject/object binary, will necessarily resolve themselves into a version of it. Rhetoric is a child of such a regime.

Finding in Foucault innumerable revelations of its own necessarily disciplinary nature, rhetoric is prompted to put this rhetoricians' rhetorician's thought to work to identify dangers to the subject (as subject *and* object) inherent in its operating modes and to develop its own solutions. There are at least two essentials for approaching him to these ends: (1) aliveness to the ranges and shifts of his oeuvre, which are functions of a radically evolving thought (there is no single, stable Foucault; thus, to depend on a single set of his texts for ultimate conclusions about his thought is risky). (2) awareness of his willingness to reverse himself, to turn his back on his own emotions and assumptions and even his magnificent thought edifices once their questionable foundations surface. Here are several examples. From having been the best of methodological hopes for the study of human beings, structuralism becomes a form of domination. Once a last refuge of freedom, sex, when understood as part of disciplinarity, becomes "boring" (Dreyfus and Rabinow 229). Care of the self, the latter an entity once scarcely mentionable, becomes paramount, once choosing self care comes to seem possibly a choice rather than a requirement ("I am going to take care of myself" [231]).

BY TITLE: DEVELOPING METHODOLOGIES, FOCI, RHETORICAL PERSPECTIVES

Supplanting what was to have been a history of psychiatry, *Madness*, Foucault's doctoral thesis and his first major work, traces the history of a definitive social practice shaping the modern West and developing into the burgeoning category systems, discourses, and practices that constitute contemporary psychology and psychiatry and literally create the objects they study. Rhetorics of humaneness claim for these disciplines an ever more refined humanity; rhetorics of scientificity, an ever closer faithfulness to what they find. Foucault shows via 943 thickly documented pages that neither humaneness nor science finally drives these human sciences but rather reason's sudden need for an object against which to define (and from which to distinguish) itself, as Enlightenment dawns. This work is prophetic in laying out in rudimentary and unthematized form three techniques that will characterize much of Foucault's work henceforth: (1) Historicizing the present, or genealogy, to some extent patterning every work but *Archaeology*, eschews explaining in favor of describing and, by piling up evidence of the historicity of given discourses and practices, disproves their claims to natural, necessary, noncontingent (here, humane or scientific) truth. (2) Archaeology discerns "discursive formations" (in this case, rhetorics of reason) that lie beyond the perception of consciousness *and* the unconscious and nonetheless determine what gets said and done in given periods and guarantee it a sense. Discursive formations are conditions of possibility for knowledges and inaccessible by their practitioners as these knowledges are developing. Only retrospectively can thought discern them. Having discerned the existence of discursive formations, Foucault can show three levels of rhetorics determining human being as it evolves in a given period: a surface level, an unthought but thinkable one (a preconscious of science, as it were), and a not-yet-thinkable level (that of discursive formations, which, in *Order*, are called "the positive unconscious of science"). Although it fades in Foucault's later thought, archaeology in some form characterizes every work henceforth. (3) Identifying discontinuities, a practice first encountered in the work of Canguilhem and Dumézil, reveals, in Foucault's hands, an added archaeological dimension. History becomes a story of disconnected periods whose character is determined more vertically, by the shifting discursive formations that ground them, than horizontally, in tracing a progressive course of reason.

Since they are not identified or explained, it is only in retrospect, after he has later named and refined them, that these techniques come to stand out, though Foucault was generally aware of his protomethodologies throughout *Madness*, as he was of his aim. For Canguilhem, in attempting to recruit him as thesis director, Foucault stated explicitly what in the work itself he presents only in a diffused way: that he would show their historical antecedents, and present-day psychology and psychiatry themselves, to have been manufacturers of their own objects.

Birth analyzes the discourses and practices of a medicine of the body in a way closely related to that used for the medicines of the mind in *Madness*. The rhetorics—in a way, pure mythologies—are similar—increasing humaneness and objectivity—as are their concrete results: increasing control and domination; incarceration; separation of subjects from one another and from their own bodies. The underlying discursive formation is a rhetoric of reason, which fails to recognize its own coercive character. Foucault's increasing control over his technique is marked here. Recognizing it in his title, Foucault emphasizes the growing significance of archaeology for his work.

Both *Birth* and *Madness*, as will *Discipline* and *Sexuality*, identify and emphasize what Foucault calls "dividing practices," the great modern divisions of subjects from one another and from themselves, in both body and mind, that are demonstrable results of certain enlightened rhetorics purporting to improve the lot of human beings but, more important, performing the demeanings and entrapments essential to the efficient and productive management of society.

With *Order* Foucault reaches the pinnacle of his analytical achievement. He also finds his voice. This work is his most splendid, from the point of view of its literary style, the rigor of its determining rhetoric—which Foucault does not yet think to analyze—its authoritative abandon, and, quite literally speaking, its depth—the discursive depths it operates at persistently. Every other work pales in comparison.

Foucault's voice and its eloquence are everywhere retained in the work; otherwise, the book splits into two distinct halves, their different character and insights and degrees of accessibility in part explainable across the fact that discursive formations, whose possibilities this work is the first to exploit fully, are inaccessible except in retrospect. Thus for the first two of the historical periods Foucault analyzes—Renaissance and Classical (Enlightenment)—which are behind him, the underlying discursive formations are identifiable, and they clarify the points he would make. For the third, the Modern (historical-organic), in which he still to an extent stands, they are unclear; the points they determine, elusive. In its brokenness, the work necessarily matches the radically discontinuous history it surveys.

Order is the work that has elicited the most controversy and is perhaps most notorious, since it makes much clearer than the two previous ones the questionableness, if not the emptiness, of a number of claims dear to humanism: the progress of reason in history and thus history's progressiveness, its relatively smooth linearity; its meaningfulness; the objectivity of the human sciences and the solid objectness of their objects; and any subjective function whatever, if by the phrase is meant human autonomy and self-determination. Foucault shows instead history's discontinuity, its chronologies composed of sudden and inexplicable shifts, or lurches, from one way of knowing to a quite different one, each determined by conditions of possibilities, or "laws," unperceivable by its inhabitants and making up "the positive unconscious of science." These determine what can be said and done in a given age by appearing to give it meaning. He shows "known" objects to have been constructed by a period's *ways* of knowing—shows subjects to be, like objects, products of discursive formations.

Rhetorics of reason, and thus of difference, again characterize the discursive formations of the central period, the Classical, Foucault's chief focus here and his target in all three major works to date, whereas rhetorics of sameness characterized those of the Renaissance. (Thus are explainable the "dividing," differentiating discourses and practices he has uncovered in the two earlier works and that, as he also shows here, appeared suddenly, as if out of nowhere: A lurch in history had occurred; a new, underlying discursive formation had replaced the old.)

Order is the work in which Foucault first operates across a rigorous near-structuralism. In demonstrating here the less autonomous than automatonous character of the human subject, Foucault also sets aside, sets out of consideration, the subject's rhetorics of truth and meaning. In bracketing both, he becomes more phenomenological than phenomenology. The loss of truth and meaning, and of the subject as well, has exercised Foucault's critics most.

To make his position and his methodology in *Order* clear, Foucault writes *Archaeology*, his only purely theoretical text. He writes it in the face of critics' puzzlement and incomprehension at *Order*, seeking to lay out the structuralist-inspired theory informing his thought. As incomparable in its austerity as is *Order* in its baroque splendor, the work theorizes the power of discursive formations, their unseeable controlling influence over all subjects, events, reality. No other work looks back to schematize its forerunner's methods in this way. The rhetoric that is its own condition of possibility, however, remains unspoken and apparently unseen as the book goes to press.

At some point during or after the composition of *Archaeology*, however, Foucault steps out of structuralism and, looking back, recognizes that the discursive formation he has allowed to determine his findings in *Order* and *Archaeology* much resembles the very one he had exposed as coercive in *Madness* and *Birth*. Its superobjectivity, he sees, is finally objectifying: It is a discourse of domination. It must be abandoned. This does not yet lead him to generate a quasi-unsubjectified subject, but it does lead him back to a reemphasis on genealogy as his method of choice—to working out a new and much expanded history of the present in *Discipline*, which exposes some of the modern West's most trusted discourses as rhetorics that in disciplining objectify, subjugate, and coerce human subjects. Exposure of these rhetorics' effects becomes an exposure of the larger society that employs them—as disciplinary, dividing, punitive, carceral.

In *Sexuality*, Foucault narrows his focus to a single, quintessentially modern discourse, that of sexuality, and the associated practices and discourses—many of the latter, pathologies—it has spawned, especially in the nineteenth and twentieth centuries. Thought to be the natural secret of every subject's identity, because, eventually, the certain source of her freedom, sexuality, as it is hounded by Foucault to its birthplaces, is exposed as a historical construct, a thick umbilical cord through which a host of social requirements are fed to a subject kept ravenous via alternating rhetorics of repression and incitement.

Extending his history of contemporaneity further back, in *Use* and *Care*, Foucault traces it to the practices of unremitting focus on the self organized around Christian confession—practices of persistent self-examination required by rhetorics of purity and undertaken for self-purification and its maintenance. These derive, Foucault discovers, from ancient "technologies of the self," techniques apparently freely applied to the self by male citizens (as opposed to women and slaves) of the ancient Greek world for purposes of self-mastery and government of others (the members of one's household and also the larger institutions of state if required). With the second of these works, attention to underlying discursive formations fades: Disciplinary societies seem but nightmares of the future.

In a final interview ("Freedom") Foucault, speaking out of his recent course work, outlines forms of power that characterize relations between self and other. Except for friendship, self-other relations are typically subject-object relations. Either side of the relationship may be individual or collective. Self-other relations may be either "relationships of power" or "states of domination." The differences between them have to do with reciprocity, with the relation's reversibility. Relationships of power permit reversibility of movement, are "variable and [allow the] different partners a strategy that alters them" ("Freedom" 3). States of domination are the reverse: "When an individual or a social group manages to block a field of relations of power, to render them impassive and invariable and to prevent all reversibility of movement . . . we are facing . . . a state of domination. It is certain that in such a state the practice of liberty does not exist" (3). One cannot both practice one's own and endanger the other's freedom at the same time. With this, Foucault turns the practice of freedom into an ethics, insisting that the practice of freedom must be first of all care of the self but that this must at the same time be care for the other. Thus his final formula: The practice of freedom is care for the self as an ethics (as care for the other).

Care, in emphasizing care of the self by the self, and the late courses, in suggesting possible subject-chosen ethical practices for consideration—truth telling and care for the other—also suggest the recovery of an uncompromised rhetoric of freedom for the subject that some rhetoricians may welcome in Foucault. But even these, as well as other rhetoricians now more cautionary than Foucault himself, will already have begun asking of rhetoric whether it will face down its own long history of involvement in manipulative discursivities, face down even the historical necessity that explains its own birth in objectifications of those it would persuade, in order to explore its potential role in furthering the possibilities for transforming states of domination into relationships of power.

INTERVIEWS

Foucault's numerous interviews are important sites of his thought-in-progress and of his assimilation and understanding of his earlier thought. Apart from their development of specific complexes of ideas, their importance lies in the succinct, straightforward, but also reinterpretive accounts they offer of Foucault's intents and achievements in given periods and works. Such accounts are available chiefly *in* the interviews (notably also in his summary of his work to date for admission to the Collège de France [Eribon 214–16]), most obviously because these elicit a brief, bare-boned directness atypical of his writing; equally important because his labors achieve their most explicit focus for Foucault in retrospect; also because a predominant theme from a present interview can metaleptically alter the identity of past works: A current thought becomes the real meaning of earlier discourses. Thus, a June 1976 interview recognizing the problem of power as Foucault's concern in *Discipline* (1975) can only retrospectively identify this idea as also the key to both *Madness* (1961) and *Birth* (1963): "I ask myself what else it was that I was talking about [in those works] but power. Yet . . . scarcely ever used the word and never had such a field of analyses at my disposal." And the late courses' focus (from 1981) on the problem of the subject and truth comes, in a January 1984 ("Truth and Power," in Foucault, *Power/Knowledge* 115) interview, to seem the unrecognized preoccupation of the entirety of Foucault's prior thought. Q: "[Is] your present philosophical research . . . still [as in 1981–1982] determined by the poles subjectivity and truth[?]" A: "In fact, that has always been my problem" ("Freedom" 1). Thus, in the interviews Foucault uncovers the unthought in his own thought. Additional examples abound. The interviews, indispensable as interpretive aids, are, then, not merely straightforward accounts. They also alter, and enrich, the written works by multiplying and layering, or transforming, their possibilities for interpretation. In so doing, the interviews emphasize for the rhetorician the crucial effects of new language (here, "naming") for bringing new, or latent, entities (here, new layers of thought) to light. As it is by viewing it from the point of view of power, or of truth, or of the subject, much of Foucault can be further illuminated by pointing to its fundamentally rhetorical consciousness.

BIBLIOGRAPHY

Primary Sources

Major Primary Works

Foucault, Michel. *The Archaeology of Knowledge.* 1969. New York: Harper, 1976.

————. *The Birth of the Clinic: An Archaeology of Medical Perception.* 1963. New York: Pantheon, 1973.

————. *The Care of the Self.* 1984. New York: Pantheon, 1986.

————. *Death and Labyrinth: The World of Raymond Roussel.* 1963. Trans. Charles Rues. Garden City, NY: Doubleday, 1986.

————. *Discipline and Punish: The Birth of the Prison.* 1975. New York: Pantheon, 1977.

————. *The History of Sexuality 1.* 1976. New York: Pantheon, 1978.

————. *Madness and Civilization.* 1961. New York: Pantheon, 1965.

————. *The Order of Things.* 1966. New York: Pantheon, 1971.

————. *Résumé des cours 1970–1982.* Paris: Julliard, 1989. (Course résumés, Collège de France.)

————. *The Use of Pleasure.* 1984. New York: Pantheon, 1985.

Essays and Interviews

Bernauer, James, and Thomas Keenan. "The Works of Michel Foucault 1954–1984." *The Final Foucault.* Ed. James William Bernauer and David M. Rasmussen. Cambridge, MA: MIT Press, 1988.

Foucault, Michel. "Dream, Imagination, and Existence." *Review of Existential Psychiatry* 19.1 (1984–1985): 29–78. Introduction to Ludwig Binswanger, *Le Rêve et L'Existence.* Trans. from the German by Jacqueline Verdeaux. Paris: Desclee de Brouwer, 1954.

————. "The Ethic of Care for the Self as a Practice of Freedom" (interview January 20, 1984). *The Final Foucault.* Ed. James William Bernauer and David M. Rasmussen. Cambridge, MA: MIT Press, 1988.

————. *Language, Counter-Memory, Practice: Selected Essays and Interviews.* Ithaca, NY: Cornell University Press, 1977.

————. *Power/Knowledge: Selected Interviews & Other Writings 1972–1977.* New York: Pantheon, 1980.

————. *Remarks on Marx.* New York: Semiotext(e), 1991.

————. "The Subject and Power" and "On the Genealogy of Ethics" (the latter edited from interviews and conversations of April 1983). *Michel Foucault: Beyond Structuralism and Hermeneutics.* 2nd ed. Ed. Hubert L. Dreyfus and Paul Rabinow. Chicago: University of Chicago Press, 1983. 208–26, 229–52.

Biography

Eribon, Didier. *Michel Foucault*. Cambridge, MA: Harvard University Press, 1991.
Macey, David. *The Lives of Michel Foucault*. New York: Pantheon, 1994.
Miller, James. *The Passion of Michel Foucault*. New York: Simon & Schuster, 1993.

Criticism

Clark, Michael. *Michel Foucault: An Annotated Bibliography*. New York: Garland, 1983.
Dreyfus, Hubert L., and Paul Rabinow, eds. *Michel Foucault: Beyond Structuralism and Hermeneutics*. 2nd ed. Chicago: University of Chicago Press, 1983.

ERNESTO GRASSI
(1902–1992)

Karen A. Foss

Ernesto Grassi was born in Milan, Italy, on May 2, 1902, the son of Giovanni Battista Grassi and Caterina Luce Grassi. He studied philosophy and literature at the University of Freiburg in Germany, earning his doctorate from the University of Milan in 1925. He married Elena Stigler in the same year. In 1929, Grassi became a lecturer in Italian literature at the University of Freiburg, a position he held until 1939, when he was named director of the Italian Institute for Humanist Studies in Berlin.

Grassi was advised to leave Germany during World War II and went first to Florence, Italy, and then to the University of Zurich, where he served as a visiting professor in philosophy from 1943 to 1946. Grassi returned to Germany in 1948 to become a professor and director of the Center for the Study of Philosophy and Humanism at the University of Munich. He also served as the president of the International Center for the Study of Humanism in Rome and held visiting appointments at the University of Buenos Aires, the University of San Paolo, and the University of Caracas. Upon his retirement, Grassi continued his association with the University of Munich as an emeritus professor, spending winters in Munich and summers at his home on the island of Ischia, Italy. He died on December 22, 1992, in Munich.

GRASSI'S RHETORICAL THEORY

Circumstances of birth and education largely were responsible for Grassi's rhetorical perspective, centered in the advocacy of Italian humanism as a philosophical and rhetorical movement of contemporary significance. Grassi's Italian heritage clashed with the assumptions of superiority accorded German philosophical thought. Italian humanism generally was rejected as without philo-

sophical importance; its significance was confined to the Renaissance rediscovery of the literature and civilization of ancient Greece and Rome. These
limited and largely negative assessments of the intellectual heritage of his home-
land led Grassi to devote himself to the study of Italian humanism, not simply
for its historical or literary value but as a philosophical movement concerned
with "the problem of words, of metaphoric thought, and of the philosophical
function of rhetorical thinking and speaking that was perfected as a new way
of philosophizing in the fifteenth century" (Grassi, "Remarks" 125).

Grassi's approach to rhetoric was inspired most directly by the work of Giambattista Vico, an eighteenth-century Italian philosopher, who Grassi believed
represented the thought of Italian humanism most fully. Grassi attached particular importance to Vico's discussion of ingenium, defined as nonrational insight
into similarities. Ingenium is the faculty of grasping what is common or similar
among objects, ideas, or experiences; it is the process of seeing relationships,
making connections, constructing interpretations, and choosing from among
them a path of action. The ability to interpret and to select among various
interpretations—the process of ingenium—is the basic process that distinguishes
humans from animals, confined as they are to instinctual responses. The capacity
ingenium offers for interpreting experience in a variety of ways thus results in
what Vico called the "humanization" or "historicization" of the world by
humans.

According to Vico and Grassi, ingenium manifests itself in three fundamental
human processes—imagination, work, and language. Imagination is a fundamentally and uniquely human process that enables humans to interpret sensory
experiences in order to understand and explain reality. In fact, however, this
process also creates reality because it fosters one interpretation over others. The
second manifestation of ingenium is work. While imagination allows humans to
conceptualize and interpret experience in various ways, work allows for the
realization of those interpretations in action. Finally, ingenium manifests itself
in language. In the process of naming something, humans create a symbolic
reality that stands apart from the world of sensory experience. Like work and
imagination, language also functions to separate humans from animals; language
is a humanizing process.

Grassi's approach to rhetoric consists of an entire system—from metaphor to
rhetorical speech to folly—grounded in the basic human process of ingenium.
Metaphor is the basic process of human thinking; it is a grasping, in language,
of similarities between two unrelated things. Metaphor is also the basic process
of language itself: To use language is to construct a symbol to stand for an
experience. Metaphor, then, provides the foundation for Grassi's rhetorical system because it encompasses the essential process of ingenium operationalized
in symbols.

After establishing the primacy of the metaphor in human thought and speech,
Grassi asserts the primacy of rhetorical language over rational speech. Rhetorical
speech is imagistic, inductive, and expressive and relies on making or seeing an

original connection, relationship, or insight. Rational speech, in contrast, is deductive and achieves its effect through logical demonstration. By design, rational speech is a closed system in which the starting premises are not questioned.

Grassi uses the example of a code to illustrate the differences between rational and rhetorical speech. As a system of signs, each element in a code receives its meaning from within the system; the code itself provides the tools by which to interpret the message. But such a code cannot move beyond itself to invent another code, to question the origins of the code, or to shift the particular meanings within the code. This task is left to rhetorical speech, which provides the means for understanding the initial ideas and impulses that gave rise to the premises upon which the code was based. For Grassi, then, rhetorical speech is superior to rational speech not only because it contains the fundamental human act of ingenium but because it necessarily precedes rational speech.

Grassi's notion of folly completes his rhetorical perspective, providing for an enactment of ingenium at the philosophical level. He analyzed the notion of folly through an examination of literary texts such as Cervantes's *Don Quixote* and Erasmus's *The Praise of Folly* to suggest that, in contrast to contemporary understandings, folly does not mean acting or speaking irrationally—a loss of contact with reality (Grassi and Lorch). Rather, folly is the ability to see what is possible in any situation.

The functions fools served in traditional societies is illustrative of how folly enacts ingenium. Fools managed times of transitions, when reality lost its usual structures and meanings—changes that could range from predictable seasonal cycles to death to catastrophic events such as plagues. Always a part of but also removed from a culture, fools offered insights into ways of managing these situations by pointing up the boundaries of the existing worldview and posing alternatives to it. These alternatives often were expressed under the guise of laughter, which allowed the unspeakable to be spoken and new possibilities to be offered in nonthreatening ways. Grounded in particular needs and experiences, the insights and ideas offered by fools were, in fact, the operationalization of ingenium; they made available a range of responses to new or fearful situations. Folly, then, is the process by which humans grapple with the fundamental questions of the nature of the human world, the possibilities for human existence, and the choices humans make in the creation of that world. Folly captures, for Grassi, the basic process of human life: "To live in folly is the profound reason for existence" (Grassi and Lorch 89). By constructing a rhetorical system that begins with the basic linguistic process of metaphor and moves through folly as a philosophical issue, Grassi demonstrated how ingenium is critical to all facets of human life.

Grassi's work is important for several reasons to contemporary rhetorical thought. First, his work revitalizes the ideas of the Italian humanists, recovering themes generally ignored in their work—ingenium, imagination, folly, the role of metaphor, and the primacy of human speech as constitutive of a social world. By returning to the Italian humanists' interest in language and rhetoric, Grassi suggests that Italian humanism was a precursor to contemporary interests in language as heuristic, epistemic, and inventive—rhetoric as the faculty by which humans construct their realities.

Grassi's attention to the significance of rhetoric as the means by which humans construct their worlds also suggests a reconceptualization of definitions of rhetoric and of the relationship between rhetoric and philosophy. Rhetoric, for Grassi, is not merely a stylistic addition to language or even the art of persuasion. Rather, rhetoric is "identified with the power of language and human speech to generate a basis for human thought" (Verene, Rev. 279). The power of any message, for Grassi, derives from its starting point in images that inspire wonder, admiration, engagement, and passion, and thus rhetoric deals with the fundamental questions of human existence, knowledge, and choice.

Grassi's definition of rhetoric, in turn, makes rhetoric the basis of philosophy rather than the reverse. Philosophy becomes possible only from a starting point in ingenium; it relies on the human power of ingenium to create metaphors from which humans then produce reasoning and other logical systems. Rhetoric, then, is not something added on to philosophical truth; it is the genesis of philosophical truth:

When we look at today's scientific panorama, philosophy hardly appears still to play a role, and rhetorical speech is recognized only outside the framework of scientific discourse as the superficial art of persuasion. . . . But let it be remembered that it is only within the limits of human communication and the tasks that arise from it that the problems of philosophy and the function of rhetoric can be discussed. (Grassi, *Rhetoric as Philosophy* 68)

As a result of his reversal of rhetoric and philosophy, Grassi also contributes a new perspective for understanding human action in the contemporary world. Grassi asserts the need to ground thought, speech, and action in an understanding of the nature of human beings and the processes by which that humanness emerges. In the contemporary privileging of logical, scientific thought, humans are disconnected from their basic, distinctive faculties of knowing. This divorce leaves them unable to realize the implications of their actions—for themselves and for the natural and social worlds. In response, Grassi asserts that the worldview of Italian humanism, grounded in the notion of ingenium as central to human interaction, can remind humans of the basic process of engagement by which they grasp, interpret, and give meaning to their realities. This worldview respects and celebrates the mystery, wonder, and creativity of human understanding and interaction. As Verene argues:

Grassi's thesis asks us to choose Vico over Descartes, the humanities over science as our master key to understanding the power of language. In an age in which philosophy is dominated by conceptual analysis, Grassi's view calls us back to remember what has been denied in the modern basing of philosophy and knowledge on logic and not on the imagination. He brings forth from his account of antiquity, the Renaissance, and Vico a whole world that has been lost. (Verene, Rev. 282)

BIBLIOGRAPHY

Primary Sources

Grassi, Ernesto. *Heidegger and the Question of Renaissance Humanism: Four Studies.* Trans. Ulrich Hemel and John Michael Krois. Binghamton, NY: Medieval & Renaissance Texts & Studies, 1983.

———. *The Primordial Metaphor.* Trans. Laura Pietropaolo and Manuela Scarci. Binghamton, NY: Medieval & Renaissance Texts & Studies, 1994.

———. "The Priority of Common Sense and Imagination: Vico's Philosophical Relevance Today." Trans. by Azizeh Azodi. *Social Research* 43.3 (1976): 553–75.

———. "Remarks on German Idealism, Humanism, and the Philosophical Function of Rhetoric." Trans. John Michael Krois. *Philosophy and Rhetoric* 19.2 (1986): 125–33.

———. *Renaissance Humanism: Studies in Philosophy and Poetics.* Binghamton, NY: Medieval & Renaissance Texts & Studies, 1988.

———. *Rhetoric as Philosophy: The Humanist Tradition.* Trans. John Michael Krois and Azizeh Azodi. University Park: Pennsylvania State University Press, 1980.

———. *Vico and Humanism: Essays on Vico, Heidegger, and Rhetoric.* New York: Peter Lang, 1990.

———. "Vico as Epochal Thinker." Trans. Roberta Piazza. *Differentia* 1.1 (1986): 73–90.

———. "Vico, Marx, and Heidegger." Trans. Joseph Vincenzo. *Vico and Marx: Affinities and Contrasts.* Ed. Giorgio Tagliacozzo. Atlantic Highlands, NJ: Humanities, 1983. 233–50.

———. "Why Rhetoric Is Philosophy." Trans. Kiaran O'Malley. *Philosophy and Rhetoric* 20.2 (1987): 68–78.

Grassi, Ernesto, and Maristella Lorch. *Folly and Insanity in Renaissance Literature.* Binghamton, NY: Medieval & Renaissance Texts & Studies, 1986.

Biography

Foss, Sonja K., Karen A. Foss, and Robert Trapp. *Contemporary Perspectives on Rhetoric.* 2nd ed. Prospect Heights, IL: Waveland, 1991.

Criticism

Fierz, Charles L. "Philosophical Implications of Ernesto Grassi: A New Foundation of Philosophy?" *Philosophy and Rhetoric* 27.2 (1994): 104–20.

Veit, Walter. "The Potency of Imagery—The Impotence of Rational Language: Ernesto Grassi's Contribution to Modern Epistemology." *Philosophy and Rhetoric* 17.4 (1984): 221–39.

Verene, Donald Phillip. "Philosophy, Argument, and Narration." *Philosophy and Rhetoric* 22.2 (1989): 141–44.

———. Rev. of *Die Macht der Phantasie* and *Rhetoric as Philosophy*, by Ernesto Grassi. *Philosophy and Rhetoric* 13.4 (1980): 279–82.

JÜRGEN HABERMAS
(1929–   )

Susan C. Jarratt

Jürgen Habermas is an influential contemporary exponent of critical theory, a twentieth-century philosophical approach that seeks "the self-emancipation of people from domination" through reason (Held 250).[1] Primary concerns of critical theory are the relationship between theory and practice after the failure of Marxist revolutions; an understanding of reason, science, and technology after the horrors of Nazism and the atomic bomb; and the functioning of cultural and social groups in a modern era of capitalist economies and administrative systems. Habermas's importance to rhetoric lies in his theorization of the centrality of communication to the project of critical theory. His historical account of various forms of publicity, particularly the eighteenth-century public sphere, and his articulation of a theory of communicative action constitute major contributions to twentieth-century rhetorical theory. He is an extremely prolific writer, one whose work has provoked abundant critical response.

Habermas was born in Düsseldorf in 1929 and raised in the small town of Gummersback. His father was head of the Bureau of Industry and Trade, and Jürgen belonged to the Hitler Youth before the war. He characterized his family's attitude toward the war as "bourgeois adaptation" ("Interview" 29), but Habermas himself as a teenager was dramatically marked by the revelation after the war of the "politically criminal" system of Nazism. Entering the university at Göttingen in 1949, he completed training at Bonn, receiving a doctorate in philosophy in 1954 with a dissertation on the philosopher F.W.J. Schelling. Martin Heidegger was an important early figure within this period, from whom Habermas gained a notion of hermeneutical understanding as a dialogue between the text and the interpreter.

During the course of his dissertation study, Habermas read Karl Marx and Georg Lukács, later focusing on the concept of ideology. The chief formative experience of his education was serving from 1956 to 1959 as assistant to Theodor W. Adorno at the Institute for Social Research in Frankfurt, founded in 1923. Work with the "Frankfurt School" critical theorists Max Horkheimer (author with Adorno of *Dialectic of Enlightenment*) and Herbert Marcuse (*One Dimensional Man, Eros and Civilization*) acquainted Habermas with critiques of positivist science, Freudian theories of the subject, and analyses of mass media and mass culture (*Theory* 2: 378–83). During this period Habermas wrote his first two books: *Student und Politik* (translated as *Toward a Rational Society* in 1970) and *The Structural Transformation of the Public Sphere* (1962), both strongly influenced by Marxism, sociology, and empirical social research. Habermas enthusiastically supported the student protest movement of the 1960s as efforts at radical democratization but later broke with major groups, believing they were falling short of their original goals (Held 250–51; "Interview" 33–39). His work since this early period has been largely theoretical.

Habermas became a professor of philosophy at Heidelberg in 1961, turning toward hermeneutics and American pragmatism. In 1964, he took Horkheimer's chair at Frankfurt and later became director of the Max Planck Institute for Research into the Living Conditions of the Scientific-Technical World (1971, Starnberg, Germany). In 1975, he returned to Frankfurt as professor of philosophy. From 1967 forward, Habermas has made frequent trips to the United States, holding visiting positions at the New School for Social Research, the University of California at Santa Barbara and at Berkeley, and elsewhere.

HABERMAS'S RHETORICAL THEORY

Jürgen Habermas might remind scholars in rhetoric of Aristotle or Ramus in the encyclopedic comprehensiveness of his vision.[2] His projects, however, are more often programs to be filled out rather than fully elaborated systems. Although Habermas's work can be approached in terms of its historical development (see Held; Hohendahl), the importance of communication runs throughout the corpus, orienting critical theory toward rhetoric. Like other critical theorists, Habermas participates in the philosophical project of turning a reasoned critique on Enlightenment itself. But he is far more ecumenical in method and systematic in approach than anyone working these fields today, and his approach to the Enlightenment far more positive, as he lays out a developmental account of rationality and a critical assessment of its institutionalization in social and political sites. A thoroughly interdisciplinary thinker, Habermas has drawn on the traditions of sociology (Weber, Mead, Parsons), psychology (Freud, Kohlberg, Piaget), economics and system theory, media studies, and pragmatic and linguistic philosophy (particularly speech act theory), among others. Habermas's characteristic scholarly impulses are incorporation and differentiation. Beginning with Marx's historical materialism, Habermas shifts from a "species subject" to a focus on societies undergoing evolutionary changes not simply in modes of production but in cognition, family structure, moral capacity, differentiated economic systems, and language use (*Communication* 130–78).

Most significant for rhetoric is Habermas's shifts to communication as an

analytic focus, hoping to "overcome the paradigm of production, without aban-
doning the intentions of Western Marxism in the process" ("Profile" 78). The
theory of communicative action "takes into account the fact that the symbolic
reproduction of the lifeworld and its material reproduction are internally interdependent" (*Philosophical Discourse* 322). This shift has implications for theories of the subject. As one of Habermas's best explicators puts it, he creates
"a notion of ego identity that centers around the ability to realize oneself under
conditions of communicatively shared intersubjectivity" (McCarthy, introduction
to *Theory* 1: xxii). Feminist philosopher Johanna Meehan likewise characterizes
Habermas's central concerns as "a discursive theory of ethics" and the intersubjective constitution of identity through communication (2). Habermas has
worked out the implications of this central theme in three critical arenas: public
sphere, communicative action, and modernity.

Public Sphere

The element of Habermas's work with most currency at present is, ironically,
the earliest in composition. *The Structural Transformation of the Public Sphere:
An Inquiry into a Category of Bourgeois Society*, written in 1962 but not translated into English until 1989, sets out a historical trajectory of forms of
"publicity" in Western European societies from ancient Greece to the mass-
mediated publicity of advanced capitalist nations. Hohendahl describes the work
as a critical response to *Dialectic of Enlightenment*, shifting from Horkheimer
and Adorno's intellectual history to a "socio-historical analysis" (*Transformation*
2) that "explain[s] the transformation of cultural institutions through change in
the political system, whose development in turn is conceived through changes
in the economic system" (243). Habermas sets out four forms or phases of
publicity, beginning with a view of ancient Greek public life that has had much
power in historical rhetoric studies. Following Aristotle, Habermas places the
public life of free citizens in a "realm of freedom and permanence," characterized by discussion, legal discourse, and common action (4). Habermas observes that this sense of the "classical" public carries a "peculiarly normative
power" (4).

After summarizing the "representative publicity" of the high feudal Middle
Ages, marked by the absence of discourse and the appearance or "aura" of
powerful lords and ladies, Habermas concentrates on the bourgeois public
sphere, a space between state power, family intimacy, and economic/civic
exchange wherein private citizens gather to engage in critical-rational discussion
about issues of general interest. The bourgeois subjects of this sphere leave
behind particularities and interests, convening in public spaces (such as coffee-
houses) to develop critiques of coercive state power. This public sphere is made
possible by the existence of a "private"—characterized by intimacy, voluntari-
ness, and community—wherein necessities of life are met and subjectivity is
constructed. Habermas's discussion of the private includes accounts of the literary products associated with it—letters, novels, diaries—and links it with

women and children. In his description, public and private are mutually constitutive: The public sphere is inhabited by private citizens, and the private is
constituted for public recognition (*Transformation* 27–56). Habermas's theorization of public and private spheres is compatible with feminist historical analyses, although it is criticized by some for ignoring the ways gender inequity
grounds the very constitution of separate spheres (Landes) and for implicitly
reinforcing such inequities by failing to critique their existence (Landes; Meehan
91–116). Habermas charts the erosion of a democratic public in the nineteenth-
century through the emergence of special interest groups and a merging of economic with more general interests through demands for redistribution. The mass
media of the twentieth-century further impede the realization of critical public
discourse in advanced capitalist societies.

Public sphere theory has gained a wide audience for Habermas among scholars in the humanities, blossoming into critical/analytic projects such as the journal *Public Culture*, the edited collection *The Phantom Public Sphere*, and
conferences (see Calhoun). Criticism has generated related formulations such as
counterpublic (Fraser) and proletarian public (Negt and Kluge). Critics note that
the project confuses descriptive and normative impulses, invests the public/pri-
vate distinction with too much power, and participates in elitist Frankfurt School
pessimism about mass media. Scholars in composition studies are beginning to
explore the potential of public sphere theory for writing classrooms and rhetorical analysis (see Wells, "Rogue Cops").

Communicative Action

Habermas consolidates his shift to language as an organizing paradigm
through the essays collected in *Communication and the Evolution of Society* and
the massive two-volume *The Theory of Communicative Action*. The former includes a key essay, "What Is Universal Pragmatics?" wherein Habermas both
critiques and borrows from speech act theory to arrive at a theory of communicative competence: "the ability of a speaker oriented to mutual understanding
to embed a well-formed sentence in relations to reality" (29). Habermas seeks
to set out the conditions under which any speaker, regardless of experiential or
epistemic specificities, can engage successfully in the functions of representation, expression, and interpersonal relation. Habermas's communicative action
differs from a classical definition of rhetoric as persuasion in that the former is
oriented to reaching understanding. "Rhetoric," in Habermas's lexicon, is treated
somewhat dismissively as self-interested manipulation, or "strategic action" (41),
referring to everyday exchanges geared toward achieving predetermined ends.
But when such action breaks down, participants move to communicative action:
an open and arduous process of intersubjective engagement. At the core of the
theory is Habermas's belief that the success of rhetorical interactions depends
on a mutually agreed-upon rationality and that language is a medium for inter-
relating external, social, and inner worlds (67).

The Theory of Communicative Action embeds communicative competence within the relation between "system" and "lifeworld." Advanced capitalism, Habermas argues (following Weber), is marked by increasing "rationalization," wherein "steering systems" (bureaucratic systems like markets and administrations) take over social functions formerly controlled by more experientially oriented structures of norm and value. One result of this process is the "colonization" of the lifeworld as it becomes subordinated to system imperatives of money and power: "As the private sphere is undermined and eroded by the economic system, so is the public sphere by the administrative system" (*Theory* 2: 480). People are changed from citizen to client, from worker to consumer. Particularly important in this process are "those domains of action which are specialized for the transmission of culture, social integration or socialization of the young" ("Profile" 94–95)—thus, the relevance of his work for education and especially the teaching of writing, reading, and communication. Habermas fosters a communicative rationality based on the "unconstrained, unifying, consensus-bringing force of argumentative speech, in which different participants . . . owing to the mutuality of rationally motivated conviction, assure themselves of both the unity of the objective world and the intersubjectivity of their lifeworld" (*Theory* 1: 10).

In a truly rational society, "clients" and "consumers" would become participants in communicative action. While the grammaticality of communications in each of these areas is controlled by linguistic competence, Habermas is more interested in communicative competence: the ability (or failure) of speakers to meet validity conditions for three primary kinds of speech acts—claims of truth, appropriateness of rules of exchange, and sincerity of avowals of expressive states (*Communication* 52–59). When validity conditions are met, the result is communicative action: "[T]he level on which validity claims are taken for granted and discourse is not necessary" (Foss, Foss, and Trap 234). But when truth or appropriateness is called into question, participants moved to "discourse," a term Habermas defines quite differently from Foucault and Bakhtin. Discourse requires that participants proffer arguments for the justification of problematized validity claims, differentiated according to the type of claim at issue. When truth claims are challenged, speakers engage in theoretic discourse; when rightness and appropriateness are at issue, the discourse is practical (*Theory* 1:8–43). The universality of such claims is not imposed or assumed by Habermas but rather is constituted by the participants as an implicit criterion of communication: A "discourse theory of truth claims to reconstruct an intuitive knowledge of the meaning of universal validity—claims which every competent speaker has at his or her disposal" ("Profile" 86).

Modernity/Postmodernism

In the process of spelling out his theory of communicative action, Habermas has taken a different route from poststructural language theorists and postmodern philosophers. His 1973 *Legitimation Crisis* (trans. 1975), although largely taken up with economic arguments against systems theory, brings universal pragmatics to bear on the question of legitimation of advanced capitalist governments in a rhetorically staged ideology critique: an account of democratic governments' failure to engage in rationally motivated recognitions of norms (*Crisis* 95–143). Jean-François Lyotard takes issue with Habermas in his 1984 *The Postmodern Condition*, characterizing the latter's project as the "unacceptable remnant of a 'totalizing' philosophical tradition" (Jameson x). Although both Habermas and Lyotard subscribe to pragmatics—an understanding of language as action—and are interested in rules of language practice, they come to different conclusions. Against Lyotard, who finds in postmodernity a rejection of the grand narrative of Enlightenment reason, Habermas believes that "[t]he discontents of modernity are not rooted in rationalization as such, but in the failure to develop and institutionalize all the different dimensions of reason in a balanced way" (McCarthy, introduction to *Theory* 1? xxxix). He tries to imagine conditions under which members of a social system could "collectively and bindingly interpret their needs . . . through discursive will-formation" (*Crisis* 113).

Philosophical Discourse of Modernity is a set of lectures given from 1980 to 1984 in various settings (University of Frankfurt, Collège de France, Cornell University, and Boston College) in which Habermas spells out more elaborately his differences with poststructuralist and postmodern theorists of the subject. Tracing a concept of modernity from Descartes, Kant, and Hegel, he determines that "[in] modernity . . . religious life, state, and society as well as science, morality, and art are transformed into just so many embodiments of the principle of subjectivity" (*Discourse* 18). The critique of a subject-centered reason has driven twentieth-century philosophers. After mapping the "performative paradox" of Horkheimer and Adorno, who see no way out of the dilemma that ideology critique is itself a form of rationality (*Discourse*, Lectures I and V) and the aesthetic anarchism of Nietzsche (and others), who confront subject-centered reason with its "absolute other," Habermas suggests a third way out by shifting from a paradigm of individual consciousness to one of shared language in use. He engages in "the defense of modernity in the light of the principle of public participation" (Benhabib 85). His aim is not to turn back the rationalizing force of modernity but to enable forms of communicative action through which a transformed lifeworld might contain or counteract systems in everyday practice at a higher level of differentiation.

RELEVANCE FOR RHETORIC AND COMPOSITION

The work of Jürgen Habermas is richly suggestive for scholars in rhetoric and composition interested in the ways language works in public spaces to realize more fully the goals of the Enlightenment. Within a materialist paradigm of communication, Habermas emphasizes procedure as a way of framing human interaction, an emphasis compatible with, but more formal than, theories of process in composition studies. He performs a persuasive critique of the "subject of a philosophy of consciousness" without giving up on the project of trying to understand how people act as linguistic agents in the world, exploring possibilities of communication under conditions of late capitalism rather than pointing out impossibilities of communication in a postmodern era. Scholars in rhetoric will benefit from a more detailed explication of three key concepts in Habermas's theory: the ideal speech situation, rationality, and the subject.

Ideal Speech Situation (ISS)

Habermas has described the ISS as "somewhat too concrete a term for the set of general and unavoidable communicative presuppositions which a subject capable of speech and action must make every time he or she wishes to participate seriously in argumentation" ("Profile" 86). Technically, Habermas's ideal speech situation involves a three-part "general symmetry requirement": that is, no constraints, unimpaired self-representation, a full complement of norms and expectations (that is, norms and expectations apply to all participants, not just some). Foss, Foss, and Trapp identify these three conditions as the "linguistic conceptualization of the ideas of truth, freedom, and justice" (236). A problem arises when readers jump to the conclusion that Habermas believes that these terms are frequently met in real life. Rather, he is pointing out the way they already exist, counterfactually, as a set of presuppositions for anyone who engages in speech. They are the terms of humans' fundamental desire for connection through language: "Our first sentence expresses unequivocally the intention of universal and unconstrained consensus" (*Knowledge*, qtd. in Held, *Habermas* 247).

The key to understanding the ISS is to see it as a condition of possibility for any communication rather than as an imposed homogeneity: "I do *not* regard the fully transparent— . . . or indeed a homogenized and unified—society as an ideal, nor do I wish to suggest any other ideal" ("Profile" 94). A similar but more justified critique has been made against Habermas's description of public sphere on the grounds of its "implicit normative gradient" (Calhoun 430). Whatever its shortcomings, there is a richness of analysis made possible by the heuristic Habermas has provided: a vision of material/discursive practices leveled against coercive state power shaped by specific historical limits, economic circumstances, spatial locations, discursive technologies and forms, and participatory regulations. Reading a whole range of materials in terms of "spheres" of various kinds—public, counterpublic, proletarian, plebian, private, intimate—has generated considerable interpretive energy.

The shadow of normativity over the public sphere lurks around Habermas's project in general, particularly from a postmodern perspective. The theory of communicative action presupposes a "universal, non-arbitrary, normative framework" as foundation for critical theory (Foss, Foss, and Trapp 236). For some theorists, any reference to normativity speaks of restriction, law, discipline—everything contrary to the playful exuberance of certain forms of postmodernism. But, as Habermas points out, the pretense of dispensing with norms only allows for the entrance of a "cryptonormativity" that was already the problem with a positivistic tradition of human sciences against which both critical theory and postmodernism contend. In a critique of Foucault, Habermas argues that although Foucault's genealogical historiography pretends to operate descriptively, it is actually a resistant discourse: "Foucault understands himself as a dissident who offers resistance to modern thought and humanistically disguised disciplinary power" (*Discourse* 282). But, Habermas points out, only through the introduction of normative notions could Foucault explain why struggle is preferable to submission.

Rationality

From a postmodern perspective, Habermas's resuscitation of rationality poses a problem. But unlike Aristotle, who systematized reasoning in Western intellectual history and designated which types of people were capable of using it, Habermas is not "speaking of decisions about postulates of values" but dealing rather "with unavoidable premises which we cannot dispose of as we wish" ("Interview" 42). The gendering of rationality as masculine and its racialization as white/European has a long history and has done considerable damage to people in groups other than those to whom this kind of reason is ascribed. Habermas offers a definition of "reason" at once more general and more specific. In his terms, something is rational if it is susceptible to criticism and grounding (9). Related to the ancient concept of *logos*, "communicative rationality" is based ultimately on the central experience of the unconstrained, unifying, consensus-bringing force of argumentative speech (*Theory* 1: 10). *Constraint*, in this sense, means coercion; thus, "reason" is the human action by which we free ourselves from domination.

Habermas in fact distinguishes his "universal pragmatics" from a traditional logic of science in part through a critique of its rational subject: This kind of rationality "starts from the model of the isolated, purposive-rational actor and thereby fails ... to reconstruct in an appropriate way the specific moment of mutuality in understanding ... or in the acknowledgment of intersubjective validity claims" (*Communication* 8). Rather than the instrumental reason against which Horkheimer and Adorno railed in *Dialectic of Enlightenment*, Habermas is interested in "the structure of a rationality which is immanent in everyday communicative practice, and which brings the stubbornness of life-forms into play against the functional demands of autonomized economic and administrative systems" ("Profile" 80). He starts from Max Weber's observation that three differentiated aspects of rationality have come into irreconcilable conflict in the modern era: cognitively instrumental, moral practical, and aesthetic expressive (*Theory* 1: 1–273). Habermas describes the contexts of these modes of reason and suggests how they might fit together: "What does this rationality context mean for the socialization of individuals who speak and work and, by doing those two things, can't help but reproduce their lives with the aid of that three-sided rationality?" ("Interview" 42). He seeks through a theory of communicative action to challenge the separation of inevitably differentiated aspects of life in modernity and through democratic politics to overcome the capitalist reduction of rationality into cognitive-instrumentality, driving everything else into irrationality.

Subjectivity

Rationality is connected with a redefined subjectivity. Habermas's theory of communicative action constitutes a paradigm shift away from a subject defined in relation to an object and as a victim of subjection or subjugation. And this transformation of objectivity changes the nature of knowledge:

"Rationality" refers in the first instance to the disposition of speaking and acting subjects to acquire and use fallible knowledge. As long as the basic concepts of the philosophy of consciousness lead us to understand knowledge exclusively as knowledge *of* something in the objective world, rationality is assessed by how the isolated subject orients himself to representational and propositional contents. . . . By contrast, as soon as we conceive of knowledge as communicatively mediated, rationality is assessed in terms of the capacity of responsible participants in interaction to orient themselves in relation to validity claims geared to intersubjective recognition. (*Discourse* 314; emphasis added)

It is toward precisely such capacities with language—nonarbitrary, context specific, grounded in lifeworlds, and aimed at recognition of others—that many are working in rhetoric and composition studies.

NOTES

1. I thank Susan Wells for expert commentary on this entry and Scott Lyons, Gwendolyn Pough, and Jill Swiencicki for research assistance and stimulating conversations about Habermas.

2. Habermas has had many interpreters, redactors, and synthesizers. Most helpful are Benhabib, Held, Ingram, McCarthy, and Outhwaite.

BIBLIOGRAPHY

Primary Sources

Habermas, Jürgen. *Between Facts and Norms: Contributions to a Discourse Theory of Law and Democracy*. Trans. William Rehg. Cambridge: MIT Press, 1996.
———. *Communication and the Evolution of Society*. Trans. Thomas McCarthy. Boston: Beacon, 1979.
———. *Inclusion of Difference. Studies in Political Theory*. Ed. Ciaran Cronin and Pablo De Greiff. Cambridge: MIT Press, 1998.

————. *Justification and Application. Remarks on Discourse Ethics.* Trans. Ciaran Cronin. Cambridge: MIT Press, 1993.

————. *Knowledge and Human Interests.* Trans. Jeremy J. Shapiro. London: Heinemann, 1972.

————. *Legitimation Crisis.* Trans. Thomas McCarthy. 1973. Boston: Beacon, 1975.

————. "Modernity—An Incomplete Project." Trans. Seyla Benhabib. *The Anti-Aesthetic: Essays on Postmodern Culture.* Ed. Hal Foster. Port Townsend, WA: Bay Press, 1983. 3–15.

————. "Modernity versus Postmodernity." *New German Critique* 22 (Winter 1981): 3–14.

————. *Moral Consciousness and Communicative Action.* Trans. Christian Lenhardt and Shierry Weber Nicholsen. Cambridge: MIT Press, 1991.

————. *The New Conservatism. Cultural Criticism and the Historian's Debate.* Ed. and trans. Shierry Weber Nicholsen. Cambridge: MIT Press, 1989.

————. *The Philosophical Discourse of Modernity: Twelve Lectures.* Trans. Frederick Lawrence. Cambridge: MIT Press, 1987.

————. *Postmetaphysical Thinking, Philosophical Essays.* Trans. William Mark Hohengarten. Cambridge: MIT Press, 1993.

————. *The Structural Transformation of the Public Sphere: An Inquiry into a Category of Bourgeois Society.* Trans. Thomas Burger, 1962. Cambridge: MIT Press, 1989.

————. *Theory and Practice.* Trans. John Viertel. Boston: Beacon, 1973.

————. *The Theory of Communicative Action.* 2 vols. Trans. Thomas McCarthy. Vol. 1, *Reason and the Rationalization of Society,* 1984; Vol. 2, *Lifeworld and System: A Critique of Functionalist Reason,* 1987. Boston: Beacon.

————. *Toward a Rational Society: Student Protest, Science, and Politics.* Trans. Jeremy J. Shapiro. Boston: Beacon, 1970.

Biography

Dews, Peter, ed. *Habermas: Autonomy and Solidarity. Interviews with Jürgen Habermas.* London: Verso, 1986.

Habermas, Jürgen. "Interview with J. H. Starnberg, March 23, 1979." Interviewers: Detlev Horster and Willem van Reijen. *New German Critique* 18 (Fall 1979): 29–43.

————. "A Philosophico-Political Profile." Interviewers: Perry Anderson and Peter Dews. *New Left Review* 151 (May–June 1985): 75–105.

Held, David. *Introduction to Critical Theory: Horkheimer to Habermas.* London: Hutchinson, 1980.

Criticism

Benhabib, Seyla. *Critique, Norm, and Utopia. A Study of the Foundations of Critical Theory.* New York: Columbia University Press, 1986.

Bernstein, Richard J., ed. *Habermas and Modernity.* Cambridge: MIT Press, 1985.

Black Public Sphere Collective. *The Black Public Sphere.* A Public Culture Book. Chicago: University of Chicago Press, 1995.

Bohman, James. "Emancipation and Rhetoric: The Perlocutions and Illocutions of the Social Critic." *Philosophy and Rhetoric* 21.3 (1988): 185–204.

Burleson, Brant R., and Susan L. Kline. "Habermas' Theory of Communication: A Critical Explication." *Quarterly Journal of Speech* 65.4 (1979): 412–28.

Calhoun, Craig, ed. *Habermas and the Public Sphere*. Cambridge: MIT Press, 1992.

Farrell, Thomas B. *Norms of Rhetorical Culture*. New Haven, CT: Yale University Press, 1993.

Fraser, Nancy. "Rethinking the Public Sphere." In *The Phanton Public Sphere*. Ed. Bruce Robbins. Minneapolis: University of Minnesota Press, 1993. 1–32.

Foss, Sonja K, Karen A. Foss, and Robert Trapp. "Jürgen Habermas." *Contemporary Perspectives on Rhetoric*. Prospect Heights, IL: Waveland Press, 1985.

Hansen, Miriam. "Unstable Mixtures, Dilated Spheres: Negt and Kluge's *Public Sphere and Experience*, Twenty Years Later." *Public Culture* 5.1 (1993): 179–212.

Held, David. *Habermas: The Critical Debates*. Cambridge: MIT Press, 1992.

Hohendahl, Peter. "Critical Theory, Public Sphere, and Culture: Jürgen Habermas and His Critics." *The Institution of Criticism*. Ithaca, NY: Cornell University Press, 1982.

Ingram, David. *Critical Theory and Philosophy*. New York: Paragon House, 1990.

Jacob, Margaret. "The Mental Landscape of the Public Sphere: A European Perspective." *Eighteenth-Century Studies* 28.1 (1994): 95–114.

Jameson, Fredric. Foreword. *The Postmodern Condition: A Report on Knowledge*, by Jean-François Lyotard. Trans. Geoff Bennington and Brian Massumi. Minneapolis: University of Minnesota Press, 1984. vi–xxi.

Kelly, Michael, ed. *Critique and Power: Recasting the Foucault/Habermas Debate*. Cambridge: MIT Press, 1994.

Kerber, Linda K. "Separate Spheres, Female Worlds, Woman's Place: The Rhetoric of Women's History." *Journal of American History* 75.1 (1988): 9–39.

Knodt, Eva. "Toward a Non-Foundationalist Epistemology: The Habermas/Luhmann Controversy Revisited." *New German Critique* 61 (Winter 1994): 77–100.

La Capra, Dominic. "Habermas and the Grounding of Critical Theory." *Rethinking Intellectual History: Texts, Contexts, Language*. Ithaca, NY: Cornell University Press, 1983. 145–83.

Landes, Joan B. *Women and the Public Sphere in the Age of the French Revolution*. Ithaca, NY: Cornell University Press, 1988.

McCarthy, Thomas. *The Critical Theory of Jürgen Habermas*. Cambridge: MIT Press, 1978.

Meehan, Johanna, ed. *Feminists Read Habermas: Gendering the Subject of Discourse*. New York: Routledge, 1995.

Mendelson, Jack. "The Habermas-Gadamer Debate." *New German Critique* 18 (Fall 1979): 44–73.

Negt, Oskar, and Alexander Kluge. *Public Sphere and Experience: Toward an Analysis of the Bourgeois and the Proletarian Public Sphere*. Trans. Peter Labanyi, Jamie Owen Daniel, and Assenka Oksiloff. Minneapolis: University of Minnesota Press, 1993.

Outhwaite, William. *Habermas. A Critical Introduction*. Stanford: Stanford University Press, 1994.

Pateman, Carole. *The Disorder of Women: Democracy, Feminism and Political Theory*. Stanford: Stanford University Press, 1989.

Robbins, Bruce, ed. *The Phantom Public Sphere*. Minneapolis: University of Minnesota Press, 1993.

Wells, Susan. "Rogue Cops and Health Care: What Do We Want from Public Writing?" *College Composition and Communication* 47.3 (1996): 325–41.

———. *Sweet Reason: Intersubjective Rhetoric and the Discourses of Modernity.* Chicago: University of Chicago Press, 1996.

Willard, Charles Arthur. "The Problem of the Public Sphere: Three Diagnoses." *Argumentation Theory and the Rhetoric of Assent.* Tuscaloosa: University of Alabama Press, 1990. 135–53.

WINIFRED HORNER
(1922–   )

Krista Ratcliffe

Winifred Bryan Horner was born on August 31, 1922, in St. Louis, Missouri, to Winifred Kinealy Bryan and Walter Bryan. Horner attributes her love of language to her mother, who read Dickens's novels aloud to Win and her three older brothers during their summers in a rustic Ozark cabin. Horner credits her brothers with helping her develop a competitive spirit, which enables her to feel "completely comfortable fighting with guys" (Personal Interview). In 1943 she earned her A.B. in English from Washington University in St. Louis, where she was the first woman to edit the school magazine, *Eliot*. She may be the first prominent rhetoric and composition scholar to earn an "F" in composition, too: In the mid-1950s while living in rural Missouri with her husband and four young children, she enrolled in a writing course via correspondence but let it lapse. During this time, however, her freelance career soared. Her essay "How Long Can We Stay on the Farm?" was published in *The Saturday Evening Post* and later read into the *Congressional Record*. Pieces in *The New Yorker* and *Farm Journal* followed. Her secret? According to Horner, " 'The story is I used to get into the playpen and write while the children ran around the house' " (Muccigrosso 2).

In 1960, when her youngest child entered kindergarten, Horner enrolled in graduate school at the University of Missouri at Columbia (UM-C), earning her M.A. in literature in 1961. There she began teaching writing and after one semester was named assistant director of composition. From 1960 to 1966 she was a part-time instructor at UM-C; from 1966 to 1975, a full-time one, receiving tenure in 1969. In 1973 she began commuting to Ann Arbor to pursue her doctorate in English language and literature and linguistics at the University of Michigan, graduating in 1975. Horner returned to UM-C as a tenured assistant professor and was promoted in 1980 to associate professor and in 1984 to full professor, the latter occurring only after she challenged institutional gender biases that deferred her nomination. In 1985 Horner moved to Texas Christian University (TCU) as the first Radford Chair of Rhetoric and Composition. She held this endowed chair until 1993 when she was named TCU's Cecil and Ida P. Green Distinguished Emerita Professor, a position she retained until 1996. Now "retired," she continues to publish and attend scholarly meetings.

Horner's contributions to rhetoric and composition studies are myriad. A founding member of the field, she began reading rhetorical theory early in her career when confronted with literature teaching assistants whom she had to train to teach writing. Convinced that rhetoric provides a theoretical grounding for composition pedagogy and literacy practices, Horner doggedly pursued avenues to revive rhetoric as a scholarly field within English studies: She championed archival research, helped establish professional societies, celebrated pedagogy as an intellectual endeavor, provoked conversations among areas within English studies, and served as a role model and mentor to young scholars, particularly women. In sum, Horner's influence is quite simply—and quite impressively—this: Her life lived in the field of rhetoric and composition studies has significantly shaped the field as well as the lives of those people who comprise the field.

HORNER'S CONTRIBUTIONS

A noted scholar of eighteenth- and nineteenth-century rhetoric, Horner forwarded the cause of classical rhetoric, a system whose basic principles, she believes, account for written, spoken, and electronic communication. Rhetoric, she insists, should be studied not as "pure history" but as applicable to what we are doing today—hence, her admiration for the scholarship of Kathleen Welch (Personal Interview). Ever an able collaborator, Horner conceived *The Present State of Scholarship* (1983/1990) because she wanted to know more about the history of rhetoric and figured working with period experts would afford her such knowledge. Hailed as "the most-used bibliography in our field" (Enos 3), this text will become even more useful with Horner's plans to take it online. Her chapter on eighteenth-century rhetoric, cowritten with Kerri Morris Barton, is perhaps the most-read bibliography on that period. It defends the study of traditional rhetorical texts but also urges investigations of popular discourses (139). Because this chapter evaluates existing scholarship and establishes parameters for future scholarship, Horner has defined the field of eighteenth-century rhetoric for a generation of scholars and continues to do so.

Horner's work on nineteenth-century Scottish rhetoric, which appeared in a series of *Rhetoric Society Quarterly* (1989, 1990) articles and in her *Nineteenth-Century Scottish Rhetoric: The American Connection* (1993), demonstrates that classical rhetoric's influence did not end in the eighteenth century, as had previously been thought. By uncovering Scottish rhetoricians and their influences on U.S. rhetorical theory and pedagogy, Horner's research charts new territory for rhetoric scholars and reflects her respect for archival research. She remembers visiting the National Library in Scotland and being told by the librarian that " 'rhetoric is a very old-fashioned topic with us' " (Personal Interview). Horner's scholarship quickly modernized the topic. Her method is disarmingly simple: "Start with the data, contextualize it, and always remain aware of your own critical lens" (Personal Interview).

As a leader in professional organizations, Horner helped define rhetoric and composition studies and make it more visible within academia. She helped found the National Council of Writing Program Administrators, serving as its first vice president; the Rhetoric Society of America, serving as its first president (although she jokes about winning by only two votes, not by a margin of two votes but by a total of two voters); and the Coalition of Women Scholars in Rhetoric and Composition, an organization designed to mentor and share research among women. Horner also held top offices in the International Society for the History of Rhetoric, the Modern Language Association, the Linguistic Society of America, and the National Council of Teachers of English, among others. Horner either refereed articles or served on editorial boards for major journals—for example, *College English, College Composition and Communication, Rhetoric Review, Rhetoric Society Quarterly, Rhetorica*, and the *Journal of Basic Writing*—and she reviewed manuscripts for major presses—for example, University of Chicago Press, University of Missouri Press, Southern Illinois University Press, and Modern Language Association. In addition, she lectured extensively in the United States as well as in Scotland, England, Italy, China, and France.

As a rhetoric scholar located within English departments, Horner endured turf wars for most of her career. Although her professional activities lent credibility to rhetoric and composition studies nationally, local conditions spurred her interest in the split between literature and composition. When colleagues disagreed on whether literature belongs in the composition classroom, Horner published a collection of essays, *Bridging the Gap* (1983), that put this question into play. Although agreeing with those arguing no, she recognized the need for dialogue and initiated one. Today the dialogue continues, with her text an oft-cited authority.

In terms of pedagogy, Horner championed connections between rhetorical theory and composition pedagogy as evidenced by her work on the Festschrift for James J. Murphy, *Rhetoric and Pedagogy: Its History, Philosophy and Practice* (1995) and by her composition textbook, *Rhetoric in the Classical Tradition* (1988). Whether training teaching assistants or giving workshops, Horner's message was the same: "I see the composition classroom as a place for learning how to use language and through language—both reading and writing—connecting to your culture and empowering yourself" (Gaillet and Aley 19). An early advocate of writing across the curriculum (WAC), Horner believes "it is the thing that's going to save the world" (Personal Interview). While chairing the task force that developed UM-C's long-running WAC program, Horner clarified her position: Make writing the responsibility of every professor and keep the program separate from the English Department. A discussion of pedagogy and Horner is not complete without accolades from her students who have used the term "master teacher" to describe her (Gaillet and Aley 15). Undergraduate writers included this dedication in their class's collection of essays: "Dedicated / to Dr. Winifred Horner / who gave us each two gifts: / the insight to know we have a story / and the power to tell it." Former graduate student Lynée Gaillet offered this praise:

> As my teacher and mentor, [Horner] not only introduced me to a fascinating field of study, Scottish rhetoric, but encouraged me at every turn to participate fully in the discipline. She afforded me opportunities for research and publication, which in turn strengthened my teaching. As a participant in her graduate seminars at TCU, I learned by example how to help my students not only listen critically but also enter into the academic conversations taking place around them. She maintains close relationships with many of her former students—and her students' students as well! . . . I have the deepest regard for my mentor and friend, Win Horner. (Letter to author)

Horner is proud of her pedagogical influences: "One of the joys of my life is to hold a book in my hand that comes from my students" (Personal Interview). She is also humble: "My students mentor me" (Personal Interview).

As a mentor, Horner has few peers. Recognizing from her own experience that "it is hard to go it alone," she takes this role seriously: "The minute you have a student you have a deep responsibility to help and guide that person as long as you're able, and it doesn't stop at graduation" (Personal Interview). Her best advice came from her husband, Dave, early in her career: "Don't let the bastards get you down." In more polite vernacular Horner wisely claims, " 'It's not what happens to you that matters, it's how you react to it' " (Muccigrosso 3). Horner believes women have special problems within academe: "[W]omen are inclined—I know this because I did it—to fuss up and down the halls and not take action. We should shut up and do our work. . . . When you make mistakes, you then pick yourself up and start over" (Gaillet and Aley 23). Although Horner notes improvement in institutional and individual gender biases, she recognizes their continued existence. The key to combating such biases, she tells beginning women scholars, is: "Publish, publish, publish."

During her distinguished career, Horner published 13 books and monographs, wrote 26 articles and book chapters, presented 57 lectures/papers in the United States and abroad, and ran innumerable workshops. In turn, she received numerous prestigious awards including a 1993 Festschrift, a 1996 Arts & Sciences Distinguished Alumna Award from UM-C, and recognition by the Young Rhetoricians Society as the 1997 Rhetorician of the Year. Horner attributes her success to aggressiveness, a willingness to work hard, and luck, which she defines as "listening and seizing the moment" (Personal Interview). Two strategies helped her succeed: (1) involving her children in her graduate studies (e.g., reading Milton to them as she prepared for exams); yet (2) when necessary keeping work and family separate (e.g., giving each in their turn her undivided attention) (Personal Interview). These strategies must work. Her children, her husband, and every other person whose life Horner has touched, both personally and professionally, sing her praises—as mother, wife, scholar, teacher, colleague, mentor, and friend.

BIBLIOGRAPHY

Primary Sources

Horner, Winifred B. "Eighteenth-Century Rhetoric." *Encyclopedia of Rhetoric and Composition: Communication from Ancient Times to the Present.* Ed. Theresa Enos. New York: Garland, 1996. 205–7.

———. "Nineteenth-Century Rhetoric at the Universities of Aberdeen and St. Andrews with an Annotated Bibliography of Archival Materials." *Rhetoric Society Quarterly* 20.3 (1990): 287–99.

———. "Nineteenth-Century Rhetoric at the University of Edinburgh with an Annotated Bibliography of Archival Materials." *Rhetoric Society Quarterly* 19.4 (1989): 365–75.

———. "Nineteenth-Century Rhetoric at the University of Glasgow with an Annotated Bibliography of Archival Materials." *Rhetoric Society Quarterly* 20.2 (1989): 173–85.

———. *Nineteenth-Century Scottish Rhetoric: The American Connection.* Carbondale: Southern Illinois University Press, 1993.

———. *Rhetoric in the Classical Tradition.* New York: St. Martin's Press, 1988.

———. "The Roots of Writing Instruction: Eighteenth- and Nineteenth-Century Britain." *Rhetoric Review* 8.2 (1990): 322–45.

———, ed. *Composition and Literature: Bridging the Gap.* Chicago: University of Chicago Press, 1983.

———. *Historical Rhetoric: An Annotated Bibliography of Selected Sources in English.* Boston: G. K. Hall, 1980.

———. *The Present State of Scholarship.* 1983. Rev. ed. Columbia: University of Missouri Press, 1990.

Horner, Winifred B., and Shelley Aley. "George Campbell." *Eighteenth-Century British and American Rhetorics and Rhetoricians: Critical Studies and Sources.* Ed. Michael G. Moran. Westport, CT: Greenwood Press, 1994. 52–64.

Horner, Winifred B., and Kerri Morris Barton. "The Eighteenth Century." *The Present State of Scholarship.* Rev. ed. Ed. Winifred Horner. Columbia: University of Missouri Press, 1990. 114–50.

Horner, Winifred, and Michael Leff, eds. *Rhetoric and Pedagogy: Its History, Philosophy, and Practice Essays in Honor of James J. Murphy.* Mahwah, NJ: Lawrence Erlbaum, 1995.

Horner, Winifred B., Suzanne Webb, and Robert Miller, eds. *Harbrace Handbook.* 13th ed. New York: Harcourt Brace, 1997.

Biography

Crowley, Sharon. "Three Heroines: An Oral History." *PRE/TEXT* 9.3–4 (1988): 202–6.

Gaillet, Lynée. Letter to author. March 24, 1998.

Gaillet, Lynée, and Shelley Aley. "Interview with Winifred Bryan Horner." *Composition Studies* 22.2 (1994): 15–29.

Horner, Winifred. Personal Interview. April 3, 1988.

Muccigrosso, Catherine. "Columbia Woman's Endeavors are Inspirational, Admirable." *PRIME TIME, Columbia Daily Tribune* (Columbia, MO), May 11, 1997: 2–3.

Criticism

Enos, Theresa, ed. *Learning from the Histories of Rhetoric: Essays in Honor of Winifred Bryan Horner*. Carbondale: Southern Illinois University Press, 1993.

JAMES L. KINNEAVY
(1920–1999)

Phillip Sipiora

James L. Kinneavy was the grandson of John Patrick Kinneavy, who emigrated in 1861 from County Mayo, Ireland, at the age of 16, and immediately joined the Union army as a drummer boy. His grandson, James L. Kinneavy, was born in Denver, Colorado, on June 26, 1920, the eldest of four sons and one daughter born to James Kinneavy and Mary Theresa Peila, who was of Italian descent. Young James attended a public school until he was 8 years old, at which time his mother unexpectedly died. Financial circumstances forced James Kinneavy to place his five children into St. Vincent's Orphanage, and young James attended St. Catherine's parochial school for grades seven and eight. At age 15, being a young man of deeply religious faith, James joined the Christian Brothers teaching order, founded in 1680 by French priests. In 1937, he entered the seminary at De LaSalle Normal School in Lafayette, Louisiana. During this period of meditation and religious training, he assumed the name Brother Cornelius Leo, and for many years afterward, he was known as "Brother Leo."

At the age of 21, Brother Leo was ready for his first teaching position. From 1943 to 1949, he enrolled in a number of summer courses at St. Mary's University in San Antonio, Texas, and earned an Intermediate degree in theology, certified by the Christian Brothers Central Office in Rome. In 1949, Brother Leo enrolled at Catholic University of America, where he taught freshman English, French, and sophomore literature. Brother Leo majored in English and minored in philosophy and American literature. At Catholic University he was equally attracted to English and philosophy, but he chose English and was fortunate to find that the English department contained some first-rate philosophers and practioners of literary theory and rhetoric, principally James Craig La Drière, who later accepted a position at Harvard, and Father William Joseph Rooney. Kinneavy was an excellent student, having been graduated with full honors, as one might expect. Brother Leo's incredible memory and ability to instantly switch intellectual channels was legendary at Catholic University and is perhaps best documented by his passing his qualifying examinations in French *and* German on the same day.

With the Master of Arts degree in hand by 1951, Brother Leo went to work on his doctorate. His dissertation, "A Study of Three Contemporary Theories of Lyric Poetry," was written under the supervision of La Drière. Brother Leo received the Ph.D. in 1956, and his dissertation was published the same year by Catholic University. Between 1953 and 1955, Brother Leo taught at De LaSalle High School in New Orleans. His writing classes were so successful that 20 of his students earned scholarships to Tulane University based on essays they had submitted for admission. It was during these critical two years that Brother Leo began the preliminary investigation of *A Theory of Discourse*. In characteristic Kinneavy modesty, *Theory* was originally conceived as a high school syllabus for the province, which included most of the southwestern portion of the country. Brother Leo structured the syllabus on the classical liberal arts tradition: the study of grammar (literature), rhetoric (persuasion), and logic/dialectic (scientific/referential discourse).

It was in early 1958 that Brother Leo began to experience a religious and intellectual crisis—a struggle to reconcile the existence of evil with his concept of a benevolent God. Brother Leo found it increasingly difficult intellectually to accept a fundamental theological doctrine that a human could be subjected to an infinite punishment in hell for a finite action. It was clear that his formal affiliation with the Christian Brothers was drawing to an end. After a year's leave of absence, during which Brother Leo fully reconsidered his reasoning and beliefs, he requested and was granted a full dispensation from the holy orders he had taken many years earlier. Brother Leo now became Professor James L. Kinneavy of the English Department at Western State College in Gunnison, Colorado. In 1959, he married Geraldine Weaver and had completed his reentry to secular life. Although Kinneavy would never return to a formal affiliation with the Church, he would always remain, in his words, "a cultural Catholic."

The literary theory most influential during this period was, of course, New Criticism. Kinneavy conceived the aims of discourse by applying New Critical techniques of analysis to nonliterary discourse. He had been troubled for some time that freshman textbooks included neither an explicit discussion of theory nor any reference to rhetoric, and he decided to write a textbook of his own that would include rhetoric and be structured upon a theoretical system. At the same time, Kinneavy developed a separate theory of modes, significantly distinct from Alexander Bain's six modes of discourse (narration, description, exposition, argumentation, persuasion, and poetry), which were influential in nineteenth- and twentieth-century composition theory. At this point he had neither considered a theory of expressive discourse, nor had he adopted the communications triangle as his master semiotic system of language.

Professor Kinneavy taught at Western State until 1963, another critical period in his life. He had divorced Geraldine Weaver in 1959, and in 1961 he married Gloria Mitchell of Chicago, Illinois. This union resulted in two daughters, Janice Lynn (1961) and Kathleen Diane (1963). During these years, Kinneavy led an active physical life, skiing during the winter and playing a vigorous tennis game during the summer, all the time maintaining good relations with the local "Bohemian crowd," demonstrating his lifelong interest in "nonacademic types," which, to his credit, he maintained to his last days. "Mr. Kinneavy" is the way James L. Kinneavy answered his phone at home. It often surprised students to hear him call himself by that title, for to many of them he was always Dr. Kinneavy. Few called him "Jim," although they commonly addressed other prominent faculty members by their first names, perhaps not so much in deference to his age or position but rather as a matter of fitness. *Doctor*, after all, means, in the original Latin, "teacher," and Kinneavy was clearly as much teacher as scholar.

In 1963, Kinneavy accepted a joint appointment in English and English Education at the University of Texas at Austin. During the late 1960s, Kinneavy continued to revise *A Theory of Discourse*, which would become his most important theoretical treatise. He refined the communication triangle, and by 1966 several of the earlier chapters had been written and copyrighted. It was during this time, 1965–1969, that he completed *Theory* and much of its companion theoretical volume, *Modes of Discourse*, which was copyrighted in 1968, although never published in its full theoretical scope. (It was published in a truncated version as *Writing—Basic Modes of Organization*.) By 1971, *Theory* was finally completed and published by Prentice-Hall. Following the publication of *Theory*, Kinneavy wrote nearly a dozen books and over 50 articles or chapters in books dealing with literary criticism, rhetorical history and criticism, and the teaching of composition. In 1983, the University of Texas honored Kinneavy for his distinguished career as a scholar and teacher by naming him the Blumberg Centennial Professor of English. In 1992 and 1995, respectively, two independent *Festschriften* were published in honor of Kinneavy.

Kinneavy traveled around the country, speaking at academic conferences and holding seminars and workshops for nearly 50 years, all the time emphasizing the message that rhetoric and composition are, indeed, respectable intellectual activities. He taught graduate courses in rhetoric at the University of Pennsylvania, the Pennsylvania State University, and other institutions. He consulted with nearly a hundred other colleges and universities across the country. Dozens of Kinneavy's former students hold positions at colleges and universities across the country, and many of them administrate large and small writing programs. There is no question that Kinneavy's influence looms large in diverse ways.

KINNEAVY'S RHETORICAL THEORY

Since the publication of *A Theory of Discourse* in 1971, Kinneavy has generally been recognized as one of America's major rhetorical theorists. In *Theory*

Kinneavy systematically investigates the historical and theoretical bases of what he calls the aims of discourse (referential, persuasive, literary, and expressive) through extensive analyses of discourse that includes a wide-ranging discussion of practical applications and implications. Kinneavy systematically analyzes representative examples of referential discourse ("Vitamins and Endurance"), persuasive discourse ("Franklin D. Roosevelt's 'First Inaugural Address' "), literary discourse (Gerard Manley Hopkins's poem "That Nature Is a Heraclitean Fire and of the Comfort of the Resurrection"), and expressive discourse (the "Declaration of Independence"). Each analysis examines the logic, organization, and style of the respective discourse and includes a discussion of critical attributes characteristic of members of that class of discourse.

Kinneavy's *Theory* contributes far more, however, than a reassessment of Bain's forms of discourse. Kinneavy is also the first rhetorician to systematically and comprehensively examine (1) self-expression, giving it a philosophical basis in existentialism and phenomenology, drawing upon seminal works of Jean-Paul Sartre, Maurice Merleau-Ponty, Georges Gusdorf, and Ernst Cassirer; (2) informative discourse, incorporating contemporary logical theory from Carnap and Bar-Hillel; and (3) exploratory discourse, by integrating concepts from the philosophy of science and various continental influences on rhetoric and composition. Many composition textbooks now contain chapters on self-expression and informative writing, which can be attributed directly to Kinneavy's articulation of these aims. Kinneavy is also the first modern rhetorician to revive the tradition of dialectic as exploratory discourse in rhetoric and composition studies, a significant contribution in itself. William Zeiger, drawing upon Kinneavy, points out how important exploratory discourse is to intellectual inquiry. Other writing specialists (Clifton, Emig, and Herrington) have investigated exploratory discourse under the umbrella of "writing to learn" in the writing across the curriculum movement. Kinneavy's revival of dialectic as exploration has, arguably, been partly responsible for the recent "respectability" of the study of rhetoric and composition. Yet Kinneavy's major contribution to contemporary discourse is the historical case *Theory* builds for the importance of rhetoric throughout Western history, specifically through his rearticulation of aims of discourse as a reassertion of the liberal arts tradition.

Three views or "meanings" of rhetoric—style, persuasion, effective communication—have characterized the long tradition of rhetoric since antiquity. Kinneavy's *Theory* is a systematic and comprehensive representation of this conflated tradition in a full range of discourse that maintains the legacy of the liberal arts. Although the bulk of each chapter is devoted to the logic of the discourse under consideration, *Theory* is explicitly concerned with style, yet the exposition is unique in that Kinneavy systematically differentiates "styles" according to discourse purpose; referential, persuasive, literary, and expressive discourse each requires its idiosyncratic stylistic expression. Historically, there has been relatively little analysis, rhetorical or otherwise, of scientific discourse and even less investigation into the nature or formal properties of expressive language. What makes Kinneavy's examination of discourse styles significant is his systematic, interdisciplinary approach to the nuances of style across discourse aims. His eclectic synthesis of semantics, grammar, and discourse features of expressive language, for example, are generically differentiated from those of referential discourse. Although Kinneavy subordinates style to discourse aim and situational context, style is no less a significant component of his theory. What Kinneavy achieves is a systematic recognition of discourse exigencies and contexts requiring a unique stylistic expression. (A development that would find its full flowering in his later work on *kairos*.)

Most commentaries on *Theory* acknowledge the looming presence of Aristotle; indeed, Aristotelian semiotics informs the structure of Kinneavy's entire theoretical taxonomy. The connection between Aristotle's generic distinctions based upon probability—as found in the *Organon, Rhetoric*, and *Poetics*—and Kinneavy's division of discourse determined by the stressed component of the communication process are both grounded upon probability theory. Yet there are other similarities between Aristotle and Kinneavy, including their common defense of the uses of persuasion. As Kinneavy repeatedly emphasizes in *Theory*, this justification seems even more urgent today. *Theory*, however, goes beyond mere derivation of proofs; Kinneavy takes the Aristotelian framework and modifies it according to twentieth-century circumstances, and every chapter considers the situational context of the discourse under examination. In his analyses of advertising, propaganda, modern political discourse, religious rhetoric, media components of persuasion, audience, and forms and stages of persuasion, Kinneavy modifies Aristotle's template in attempting to demonstrate the pervasiveness of persuasion in the modern world. In his detailed examples and explanations, Kinneavy brings classical rhetoric into modern *praxis*, calling attention to classes of discourse that reflect levels of probability, with scientific, informative, and exploratory language representing a higher level of probability than persuasion, self-expression, or "literature."

The third view of rhetoric, the communication perspective, is arguably Kinneavy's greatest contribution to maintaining the rhetorical tradition. A major purpose of *Theory* is to identify and analyze genres of language, always with attention to probability, and the reader is explicitly reminded that purposes of discourse can be differentiated by levels of probability. A scientific "proof" is still more acceptable to the populace and specialized communities than proofs deliberately incomplete or rhetorically constructed on emotional and personal appeals. Kinneavy's substantive treatment of scientific proof in the form of induction and deduction in the chapter on referential discourse explains the operation of various kinds of proofs. Rhetorical proof requires a necessarily limited form of induction and/or deduction and often involves the use of personal and emotional appeals. Expressive discourse, by its very nature, is characterized by the personal and emotive, a sometimes impenetrable form of language, which Kinneavy explores in the concluding chapter of *Theory*.

There is yet another parallel to Aristotle and one more reason underlying Kinneavy's importance as a modern rhetorician: the presence of a constitutive ethics in Kinneavy's *Theory*. In the beginning of the *Rhetoric*, Aristotle speaks of the rhetor as one who "ought not to persuade people to do what is wrong" (1355a). Kinneavy's ethical stance, however, is more explicit than Aristotle's (in the *Rhetoric*) as Kinneavy calls attention to the potential for ethical abuse in scientific and persuasive discourse in *Theory* and subsequently addresses pragmatic moral issues in detail, calling for the explicit emphasis on ethics in the writing class ("The Liberal Arts"). It is this dimension of Kinneavy's work that represents the tradition of liberal humanism. The success of Kinneavy's theory lies in its systematic analysis of the history and characteristics of purposes and uses of language, representing what the best of the rhetorical tradition has always striven to achieve.

RECEPTION OF KINNEAVY'S THEORY

It cannot be denied that Kinneavy's work has evoked its share of criticism, both theoretical and practical. Knoblauch and Brannon, for example, find Kinneavy's "spectra of ideal aims . . . a characterization of reader response and should not be mistaken for a description of types of writing or (still less) ways to write. . . . There is nothing intrinsically or identifiably 'persuasive' about one range of textual features as opposed to another and therefore no persuasion" (28). Their position denies the dominant form of rhetoric in antiquity—persuasion—and fails to acknowledge most political, legal, and religious discourse, propaganda, and advertising. Another objection to Kinneavy's theory addresses problems intrinsic to his semiotic approach to language. Walter H. Beale, for example, raises two objections to Kinneavy's semiotic structure in asking that the pragmatics of a theoretical exposition address the rhetorical situation: "[T]he 'ultimate aims' of discourse ought not to be classified by unitary criteria (as Kinneavy proposes), because they are not, after all, fixed natural or conceptual categories but complex historical developments; they need to be understood in terms that reflect the ways in which clusters of motives and traits come together in a discourse situation" (60). Beale raises the critical issue of the relationship between a rhetorical act and the circumstances that contextualize that act. However, Beale is incorrect in his assertion that Kinneavy ignores qualitative differences between "speech act" and "discourse act." Indeed, Kinneavy's Introduction to *Theory* explicitly acknowledges the importance of context to the rhetorical act.

Other critics of Kinneavy are more concerned with his practice of rhetoric. Richard Fulkerson, for example, argues that Kinneavy's evidence is insufficient and, therefore, unconvincing. He argues "that Kinneavy fails to provide compelling support for the theory and that a number of his specific assertions fail to hold up under examination" (43). This view—that Kinneavy argues for aims that operate independent of one another—is not an uncommon criticism, yet it cannot be reconciled with Kinneavy's explicit statement about the interrelationship of discourse aims: "[N]o one who has ever studied the matter of aims of discourse ever pretended that aims do not overlap. . . . We have to separate the aims in order to study them in a systematic manner. Any science has to make such abstractions when it studies anything, and the study of discourse is no exception. . . . In many cases in these overlaps, one of the aims is dominant and the other is a means" (*Theory* 61–62). Like Fulkerson, David Foster believes that Kinneavy's work is far too ambitious. He criticizes Kinneavy for his "inconsistent treatment accorded different kinds of discourse" (54), suggests that Kinneavy relies too heavily upon Aristotle, and bemoans the fact that Kinneavy "is unable to synthesize Burke with other rhetorical approaches or suggest how useful Burke might be, along with Aristotle, in a genuinely fresh approach to persuasive discourse" (54). Kinneavy, along with Edward Corbett, was chiefly responsible for the reinstatement of Aristotle into the writing classroom, and that contribution alone is significant and "fresh."

Some commentators have criticized Kinneavy's primary concern with discourse purpose rather than with process of composition (Beale, Knoblauch and Brannon, O'Banion, Odell), an interesting objection in that Kinneavy never intended to examine the production of discourse in *Theory*. Kinneavy's approach to the process of writing has been addressed in at least three different textbooks: *Writing—Basic Modes of Organization, Aims and Audiences in Writing*, and *Writing in the Liberal Arts Tradition*. Yet this is not to acknowledge that some of these theoretical objections do not serve a purpose in raising important questions; any attempt to taxonomize discourse as systematically and comprehensively as Kinneavy has attempted is certain to reach some level of inconsistency and limitation. Indeed, in "Theory, Theories, or Lack of Theory," Kinneavy himself has critiqued *A Theory of Discourse*, a rare and refreshing gesture in today's scholarly world.

Theoretical objections aside, however, the practical influence of Kinneavy's theory cannot be denied; his work has been the cornerstone of dozens of textbooks on composition, many university and college programs, and entire state language arts systems (for specific applications of Kinneavy to composition, including technical writing, see Hagaman; Harris; Polnac). Kinneavy has also written influential essays about writing across the curriculum and has been instrumental in the development of writing across the curriculum programs across the country (see Crusius' bibliographical essay for an extensive treatment of Kinneavy's work).

KINNEAVY'S CONTINUING LEGACY

Kinneavy's influence is by no means limited to *A Theory of Discourse*. In 1987 he published *Greek Rhetorical Origins of Christian Faith: An Inquiry*, a historical examination of the influence of Greek rhetoric, principally *pistis*, on the New Testament concept of faith. The treatise has been well received in theological studies and continues to draw scholarly attention to the theoretical relationships between the secular and the sectarian. Kinneavy's historical essays on situational context and timing, "*Kairos*: A Neglected Concept in Classical Rhetoric" and "*Kairos* in Aristotle's *Rhetoric*" (Kinneavy and Eskin), have generated significant scholarship and have laid the groundwork for a collection of historical and contemporary examinations and applications of this seminal concept in classical and contemporary rhetoric (Sipiora and Baumlin).

In the 1990s Kinneavy turned to writing about a subject that he had engaged professionally since 1941: the issue of ethics. In 1999 he coedited a collection of essays, *Ethical Issues in the Teaching of College Writing*, which includes essays from leading scholars on various perspectives of ethics and their relevance to the contemporary writing scene. Kinneavy's essay in this volume, "Ethics and Rhetoric: Forging a Moral Language for the English Classroom," probes the relationship of ethics to the English classroom. This essay is a crystallization of his book-length work on the formation of a common moral code that might be accepted by both religious and nonreligious individuals and could be taught in the public school system. Such a moral code, according to Kinneavy, must necessarily be undogmatic, an ethical system untethered (insofar as this is possible) by inherited sectarian dogma. Kinneavy continued to work on this book, *A Moral Code for Use in Public Schools and Colleges*, until his untimely death on August 10, 1999, following a brief illness.

In the first century A.D., Quintilian wrote a monumental 12-volume tract, *Institutio Oratoria*, which attempted to articulate the best possible education for the son of his friend, Marcus Victorius. The study of rhetoric was an integral component of Quintilian's concept of a classical education, and he defines the ideal rhetor as "a good man speaking well"—*vir bonus dicendi peritus*. Quintilian could easily have been speaking of James L. Kinneavy, a scholar, teacher, humanist, and beloved figure to hundreds of colleagues and students across the country. Kinneavy lived his life in the richness of the tradition Quintilian sought to define in his enduring treatise. It might be said that no other twentieth-century rhetorician, or scholar of any other discipline, is more deserving to be recognized as Quintilian's ideal than this kind, humble man of letters. As he approached his ninth decade, James L. Kinneavy continued to lecture, write, and remain actively involved in the profession he so loved.

BIBLIOGRAPHY

Primary Sources

Books

Kinneavy, James L. *The Design of Discourse*. Englewood Cliffs, NJ: Prentice-Hall, 1969.
———. *Greek Rhetorical Origins of Christian Faith: An Inquiry*. Oxford: Oxford University Press, 1987.
———. "A Moral Code for Use in Public Schools and Colleges." Unpublished work.
———. *A Study of Three Contemporary Theories of Lyric Poetry*. Washington DC: Catholic University of America Press, 1956.

———. *A Theory of Discourse: The Aims of Discourse.* Englewood Cliffs, NJ: Prentice-Hall, 1971.

Kinneavy, James L., John Q. Cope, and J. W. Campbell. *Aims and Audiences in Writing.* Dubuque, IA: Kendall/Hunt, 1976.

———. *Writing—Basic Modes of Organization.* Dubuque, IA: Kendall/Hunt, 1976.

Kinneavy, James L., Frederic G. Gale, and Phillip Sipiora, eds. *Ethical Issues in the Teaching of College Writing.* New York: Peter Lang, 1999.

Kinneavy, James L., William J. McLeary, and Neil Nakadate. *Writing in the Liberal Arts Tradition.* New York: Harper & Row, 1985.

Articles

Kinneavy, James L. "The Basic Aims of Discourse." *College Composition and Communication* 20.5 (1969): 297–304.

———. "Contemporary Rhetoric." *The Present State of Scholarship in Historical and Contemporary Rhetoric.* Ed. Winifred Byran Horner. Columbia: University of Missouri Press, 1983: 167–213.

———. "Deconstructing the Rhetoric/Poetic Distinction: The Platonizing of Rhetoric and Literature." *Dieciocho: Hispanic Enlightenment, Aesthetics, and Literary Theory* 8.1 (1985): 70–79.

———. "Ethics and Rhetoric: Forging a Moral Language for the English Classroom." *Ethical Issues in the Teaching of College Writing.* Ed. James L. Kinneavy, Frederic G. Gale, and Phillip Sipiora. New York: Peter Lang, 1999. 1–20.

———. "The Exile of Rhetoric from the Liberal Arts." *Journal of Advanced Composition* 8.1–2 (1988): 105–12.

———. "From Aristotle to Madison Avenue: *Ethos* and the Ethics of Argument." *Ethos: New Essays in Rhetorical and Critical Theory.* Ed. James S. Baumlin and Tita French Baumlin. Dallas: Southern Methodist University Press, 1994. 171–90.

———. "*Kairos*: A Neglected Concept in Classical Rhetoric." *Rhetoric and Praxis: The Rhetoric of Practical Reasoning.* Ed. Jean Dietz Moss. Washington, DC: Catholic University of America Press, 1985. 79–105.

———. "The Liberal Arts and the Current Moral and Political Crisis." Address to La Salle University. Oct. 30, 1987.

———. "The Process of Writing: A Philosophical Base in Hermeneutics." *Journal of Advanced Composition* 7.1–2 (1987): 1–9.

———. "Restoring the Humanities: The Return of Rhetoric from Exile." *The Rhetorical Tradition and Modern Writing.* Ed. James J. Murphy. New York: MLA, 1982. 19–28.

———. "Translating Theory into Practice in Teaching Composition: A Historical View and a Contemporary View." *Essays on Classical Rhetoric and Modern Discourse.* Ed. Robert J. Connors, Lisa S. Ede, and Andrea A. Lunsford. Carbondale: Southern Illinois University Press, 1984. 69–81.

———. "William Grimaldi: Reinterpreting Aristotle." *Rhetoric and Philosophy* 20.3 (1987): 183–200.

———. "Writing about Ethical or Political Issues: How to Be Moral without Being Dogmatic." *Teaching Composition in the '90s: Sites of Contention.* Ed. Christina G. Russell and Robert L. McDonald. New York: HarperCollins, 1994. 33–52.

———. "Writing across the Curriculum." *Profession 83.* Ed. Richard Brod and Phyllis Franklin. New York: MLA, 1983. 13–20.

————. "Writing across the Curriculum." *Teaching Composition: Twelve Bibliographical Essays*. 2nd ed. Ed. Gary Tate. Fort Worth: Texas Christian University Press, 1987. 353–77.
Kinneavy, James L., and Catherine R. Eskin. "*Kairos* in Aristotle's *Rhetoric*." *Written Communication* 11.1 (1994): 131–42.

Biography

Sipiora, Phillip, Valerie Balester, and Rosalind J. Gabin. "James Louis Kinneavy: *Vir Bonus Agendi Peritus*." *Discourse Studies in Honor of James L. Kinneavy*. Ed. Rosalind J. Gabin. Potomac. MD: Scripta Humanistica, 1995.

Criticism

Beale, Walter H. *A Pragmatic Theory of Rhetoric*. Carbondale: Southern Illinois University Press, 1987.
Clifton, Linda. "Bibliography." *Roots in the Sawdust: Writing to Learn across the Disciplines*. Ed. Anne Ruggles Gere. Urbana, IL: NCTE, 1985. 229–35.
Connors, Robert J. "The Rise and Fall of the Modes of Discourse." *College Composition and Communication* 23.4 (1981): 444–55.
Crusius, Timothy W. "James L. Kinneavy: A Bibliography Essay." *A Rhetoric of Doing*. Ed. Stephen P. Witte, Neil Nakadate, and Roger Dennis Cherry. Carbondale: Southern Illinois University Press, 1992. 351–70.
Emig, Janet. "Writing as a Mode of Learning." *College Composition and Communication* 28.2 (1977): 122–28.
Foster, David. *A Primer for Writing Teachers: Theories, Theorists, Issues, Problems*. Upper Montclair, NJ: Boynton/Cook, 1983.
Fulkerson, Richard P. "Kinneavy on Referential and Persuasive Discourse: A Critique." *College Composition and Communication* 35.1 (1984): 43–56.
Gabin, Rosalind J., ed. *Discourse Studies in Honor of James L. Kinneavy*. Potomac, MD: Scripta Humanistica, 1995.
Hagaman, John. "Encouraging Thoughtful Revision in a Kinneavy-Framed Advanced Composition Course." *Journal of Advanced Composition* 1.1 (1980): 79–85.
Harris, Elizabeth. "Applications of Kinneavy's *A Theory of Discourse* to Technical Writing." *College English* 40.6 (1979): 625–32.
Herrington, Anne J. "Writing to Learn: Writing across the Disciplines." *College English* 40.4 (1981): 379–87.
Hunter, P. "That-We-Have-Divided-in-Three-Our-Kingdom, the Communication Triangle and a 'Theory of Discourse.' " *College English* 48.3 (1986): 279–87.
Kinneavy, James L. "Theory, Theories, or Lack of Theory." *Composition Chronicle* 5.4 (1992): 5–6.
Knoblauch, C. H., and Lillian Brannon. *Rhetorical Traditions and the Teaching of Writing*. Upper Montclair, NJ: Boynton/Cook, 1984.
O'Banion, John D. "*A Theory of Discourse*: A Retrospective." *College Composition and Communication* 33.2 (1982): 196–201.
Odell, Lee. "Teachers of Composition and Needed Research in Discourse Theory." *College Composition and Communication* 30.1 (1979): 39–45.

Polnac, Lennis. "When Theory Meets Practice: Using Kinneavy's Aims in a Community College Program." *English in Texas* 14.1 (1983): 32–37.

Sipiora, Phillip. "Rearticulating the Rhetorical Tradition: The Influence of *A Theory of Discourse*." *Journal of Advanced Composition* 8.1–2 (1988): 123–36.

Sipiora, Philip, and James S. Baumlin, eds. *Kairos and Rhetoric*. Albany, NY: SUNY Press, 2000.

Witte, Stephen P., Neil Nakadate, and Roger Dennis Cherry, eds. *A Rhetoric of Doing: Essays on Written Discourse in Honor of James L. Kinneavy*. Carbondale: Southern Illinois University Press; 1992.

Zeiger, William. "The Exploratory Essay: Enfranchising the Spirit of Inquiry in College Composition." *College English* 47.5 (1985): 454–64.

ALBERT KITZHABER
(1915–   )

David Brauer

Albert Raymond Kitzhaber was born in 1915 in Cedar Rapids, Iowa. He attended Coe College and completed a B.A. degree there in 1939. Two years later, Kitzhaber had earned a master's degree at Washington State College. He then moved on to Iowa State College as an instructor. Kitzhaber eventually served in the U.S. Army in Europe until the end of World War II in 1945. After the war, he returned to Iowa State to teach for three terms. Spurred by a desire to study the teaching of composition and rhetoric more closely, he entered the Ph.D. program at the University of Washington in 1948, where he studied under Porter Perrin. At Washington, Kitzhaber took graduate courses in the history of rhetoric, current rhetorical theory, and style. Perrin taught most of these courses and would engage Kitzhaber and his classmates in the significance of psychological and social theories as they related to rhetoric and composition. Kitzhaber's dissertation director, Perrin, taught his student that rhetoric and composition at the collegiate level involved much more than correctness and delivery, that the discipline touched upon the essential activities whereby the human subject creates, accumulates, and organizes knowledge. Kitzhaber completed his dissertation, published in 1990 as *Rhetoric in American Colleges, 1850–1900*, in 1953. While working on the dissertation, Kitzhaber taught and directed freshman composition at Utah State College in Logan from 1950 to 1952, then became director of freshman and sophomore composition and literature at the University of Kansas in 1952.

Six years later, Kitzhaber resigned his position at Kansas, embarking on stints in the Portland, Oregon, high school system and Dartmouth College. In 1962, he accepted a tenure-track position at the University of Oregon, where he settled until his retirement in 1980. But those years proved vibrant with activity in the field of rhetoric and composition. In that time period, Kitzhaber directed two five-year projects under "Project English," a creation of the U.S. Office of Education, and produced and tested experimental curricula for primary and secondary schools. He also served, among other positions, as a panelist at the White House Conference on Education (1965), a consultant to the U.S. Office of Education (1962–1970), and a member of the English Program Advisory Committee of the Modern Language Association (1966–1970).

Although sometimes overlooked in much of the theory-laden contemporary discussion on rhetoric and composition, Kitzhaber proved a critical figure in both preserving and bolstering the field when it was gravely threatened by issuing calls for institutional streamlining during the 1960s. His dissertation, moreover, is gradually proving to be a seminal work in the historiography of the profession. In *Rhetoric in American Colleges, 1850–1900*, published by the Southern Methodist University Press in 1990, Kitzhaber reminded us of the importance of looking to the past to understand our current situation and thus anticipated Edward Corbett's *Classical Rhetoric for the Modern Student* of the following decade. Kitzhaber helped link historical American pedagogy to its Greco-Roman and Scottish Common Sense roots, placing contemporary expression within a rich intellectual history spanning several millennia. Above all, he reminded us that history makes a discipline, and for that discipline to prosper, that history must be known and understood.

KITZHABER'S INFLUENCE ON TWENTIETH-CENTURY RHETORIC AND COMPOSITION

Kitzhaber's apprenticeship under Porter Perrin, coupled with his commitment to the field of composition, prepared him for a critical role in the "renaissance of rhetoric," a phrase James Berlin coined in *Rhetoric and Reality*. This "renaissance" refers to the period between 1960 and 1975, when composition research became federally funded for the first time in American history (Berlin 120). Kitzhaber had chaired the Conference on College Composition and Communication meeting in 1959, and the next decade would find him defending composition from both internal conflicts and external antagonists. His attention to the field's importance both in the academy and in the larger political sphere also proved essential. For Kitzhaber was able to help ground the rapidly changing field, as well as communicate its aims to a wide audience, including the legislators who provided funding. He would offer up the voice of the practitioner and the historian, one who deeply valued the day-to-day practice of composition instruction and the broad influences and contexts from which that same practice had evolved.

Since the end of the nineteenth century, composition studies had suffered from a poor standing in the academy. The emphasis on superficial correctness fostered by the four Harvard Reports of the 1890s and a lack of vision in research both account for this denigration, as literary studies had overshadowed writing instruction. Kitzhaber sought to remind both critics and defenders of composition that though current practices were intellectually impoverished, things had not always been that way. Nineteenth-century rhetoric had arisen from a rich pedigree of both Scottish Common Sense Philosophy of the previous century and a Greco-Roman rhetoric more than 2,000 years old. Ironically, though, formalism and mechanics eroded this foundation, rendering composition almost irrelevant and the rhetorical tradition nearly forgotten.

With the exception of the famous dissertation originally published in 1953, *Themes, Theories, and Therapy* of the following decade, and a list of articles, most of them educational in content, Kitzhaber actually published little of great significance in the field. Although the dissertation was widely read, it was not published in book form until 1990. Indeed, an investigation of his life finds that he spent more time defending composition in the public forum than in writing research to be read merely by colleagues. Composition studies needed a spokesperson in the 1960s and found one in Kitzhaber. In the article "Reform in English," for instance, he exhorted researchers to use wisely the government funds awarded to the field in the National Defense Education Act of 1964. Kitzhaber recognized that in order to legitimate itself, composition studies needed to reach the same level of scholarly sophistication that had enabled the literary branch of English in higher education to flourish. Kitzhaber, then, concerned himself with the logical means to that end: educating the educators. Instead of theorizing, he was prescriptive. One of the first fruits of the government funding had been the creation of summer instructor seminars, where college and high school teachers would go for six weeks of intensive training in teaching composition. Kitzhaber encouraged the attendants to think of this experience as providing a stepping stone to move from practitioner to professional: "But if the summer's study is successful, the person's teaching should be more informed, his perspective broader, his tolerance toward new ideas greater, the intellectual tone of his class livelier" ("Reform in English" 340). He had the vision to see this window of opportunity as having critical significance for the field, and he knew that any transformation would not come without deliberate attention. Only with a broad and deep surge in research and discussion about composition would that field advance.

But Kitzhaber also concerned himself with the academy in more explicit terms. He sought not only change in composition but in all of English studies. For too long, he argued, the different parts of English instruction, literary analysis, writing instruction, rhetoric, and linguistics, had existed with almost no relationship to one another. He pointed out that "[o]ne of the noteworthy intellectual tendencies of our time is the growing awareness of cross-relations among disciplines once thought separate" (342), and he argued that a more sophisticated understanding of the relationships among the various branches of the English Department would help the field in general, not merely composition. But if resistance to such activity was imminent, he saw it coming from professors of literature. He even went so far as to list the "characteristics" of what he called the "college English department syndrome": "the endless nit-picking, the deep distrust of new ideas outside one's narrow specialty, the sweeping and indiscriminate contempt for outgroups such as linguists and professors of Education, the serene obliviousness to all the problems of education below the college level, and above all the unshakable conviction of virtue" (340). Kitzhaber recognized that many of the prejudices that might hinder fundamental changes in English came not from poor literacy or lack of government support but from insensitivity and folly within English itself. Composition studies certainly needed to help itself, but literary studies needed to make room for composition to become integral to English, and that would involve recognizing in composition studies the legitimate ties to education, linguistics, and most important, rhetoric. Only when literary studies and composition began to embrace one another as partners in humanities education would rhetoric be recovered as integral to the field.

Indeed, closely associated with his apprehension of intellectual prejudice as a detriment to his field was a deep conviction that college composition needed to recover its ties with rhetoric, both classical and contemporary. Yet he saw no benefit in introducing classical rhetoric to students for its own sake, merely a matter of teaching the forms of discourse or the Aristotelian triad of *ethos*, *pathos*, and *logos* as more college classroom information unconnected to practice. In *Themes, Theories, and Therapy* he explains: "What is recommended here is a systematic attempt to help students become actively aware of what goes on inside good expository prose so they may come to know a little more about the nature of the tools they themselves are using and thus perhaps learn to use them more intelligently" (139). He called for system but did not equate that system with rigidity. From his informed perspective, a rarity in the 1960s, rhetoric was not merely a set of rules devised in centuries past meant to be blindly followed by student and instructor alike. Instead, rhetoric was an active, vital educational and social practice. In "New Perspectives on Teaching Composition," he explained that "composition . . . is not just a practical skill, a mere bag of tricks, but instead an important way to order experience, to discover ideas and render them more precise, and to give them effective utterance. It is intimately related to thought itself" (441). Although he was not a theorist, his words here both echo his contemporaries Wayne Booth and Kenneth Burke and anticipate the "linguistic turn" in the humanities that has deeply affected contemporary research and pedagogy in the field by way of poststructuralism and postmodernism. Kitzhaber was a practitioner, a spokesperson, and a historian with a knowledge of the historical ways in which rhetoric had been conceived and practiced. Thus, he knew that to contract its bounds to mere educational drill was not only to lose the fecundity of the discipline but also to put American culture at risk. Like Janet Emig, Kitzhaber saw writing as a mode of learning, a mode necessary for a culture's understanding of its knowledge and its experience. And though seen often as a service course, composition at the university was the site where this cultural practice would receive its due attention.

Even with his concern for teaching at the highest levels, Kitzhaber never suffered from a narrow focus. In articles such as "Reform in English," he argued that for English to be taught and learned successfully in college, the subject must be taught well at every level. He encouraged close cooperation between universities and secondary and primary schools, as well as the establishment of reasonable, practical criteria for placement in courses. The 1950s had seen a rift beginning to separate high school teachers from college professors, with each side blaming the other for the poor quality of student writing. But Kitzhaber understood the necessity for solidarity, as both sets of teachers finally depended on one another to properly disseminate instruction in composition. He understood that writing was a holistic knowledge: What one learned before always influenced present understanding and comprehension of the various aspects of writing. Furthermore, it was not merely the students who were at stake. If the profession itself did not come together, it risked collapse. Just as we understand learning as a collaborative process in our day, Kitzhaber understood instruction as a collaborative process in his own.

The conclusion to the aforementioned article finds him calling for an intimate collaboration between the Modern Language Association and the National Council of Teachers of English, two organizations at odds with one another in their vision of the English Department's place in the academy. He saw the possibilities at hand in 1965 and did not want to lose them:

In the years just ahead we will have opportunities to make sweeping improvements in the teaching of English that, just as little as five years ago, would have been thought mere hopeful fantasy. Nothing, it seems to me, would be more profitless than a competitive relationship between the two organizations, with the resulting duplication of efforts and divided policies. There is too much at stake for us to allow narrower loyalties or ambitions to get in the way. (344)

Such urgency was nothing new in Kitzhaber's pronouncements; sometimes he seemed a proselyte as much as a practitioner. Indeed, he saw the connections between pedagogical and institutional issues in ways that most of his contemporaries did not. For writing instruction did not take place in an academic vacuum. Administrative concerns, professorial concerns, and social concerns were always intersecting and informing one another, and Kitzhaber hoped to bring some balance and perspective to the conversation. His combination of breadth and depth on the issues involved stemmed in large part from his exposure both to Washington administrators as part of Project English and his involvement with the Conference on College Composition and Communication during the same time period. Moreover, he had himself served as an instructor of composition for more than a decade before he began to represent his peers in those arenas. So he understood the concerns of the various parties involved, and he worked to keep the discussion open and civil, always instructing his audiences about the ramifications of different courses of action.

In fact, Kitzhaber's criticism of the practice of rhetoric and composition in the university represented his most lucent work. *Themes, Theories, and Therapy* (1963), his other major book-length publication apart from the dissertation, offered both cogent analysis and solutions for instructor and administrator alike. Here, he contrasts the apparent purposes and the long-term results of instruction in freshman composition. The purpose of freshman composition, Kitzhaber claims, is twofold: as a "therapy" for incoming students whose writing skills did not meet the level of sophistication made necessary by the university environment and the world of employment beyond it, and "to focus the student's attention on fundamental principles of clear thinking and the clear and effective written expression of that thinking and to give him disciplined practice in applying the principles" (3). He favors the latter as a more appropriate description of the goal of college rhetoric; nevertheless, he pointed out that the improvement gained by students in freshman composition may be nothing more than a "temporarily conditioned reflex" (4). The occasion for the book was Kitzhaber's observation of a growing dissonance between purpose and result in regard to freshman composition instruction. Having identified a larger concern, he then systematically identifies the sources of the contradiction and recommends various means to dispel it.

For Kitzhaber, the basic problem behind the ambivalent long-term success of the freshman composition course in giving students necessary writing skills lay in uncertainty about aims and methods. Symptoms include inadequate teacher preparation, a wide divergence in practices and standards from one teacher to another, and the general misconception that composition was a body of knowledge rather than a complex skill. Moreover, the confusion and contradiction extend beyond the individual instructors. Kitzhaber notes that improved writing abilities among those entering college following World War II might render the necessity of freshman composition moot (97). On institutional trends, meanwhile, he argues that the propensity to exempt a large number of freshmen from composition based upon entrance exams revealed another misunderstanding about writing instruction, that "mere correctness [was] all that one should try to teach in a composition course, as though correct writing were necessarily the same as good writing" (99). In order to avoid the "backsliding" that occurred among college students after freshman composition, exemplified by data that Kitzhaber collected from Dartmouth and verified by similar patterns in other institutions, he proposes a number of recommendations. These include the necessity for smaller class sizes and teaching loads, exemption of fewer students from freshman composition, all ranks of teachers to take part in composition instruction, clear and standardized policies, and clear, enforced strictness on misspellings and other "gross" errors. Most important, though, Kitzhaber argues that writing instruction be stressed throughout one's college career. *Themes, Theories, and Therapy* exemplifies Kitzhaber's ability not only to critique specific aspects of the English Department but also to decipher the philosophy and implications behind administrative policies that failed to understand the place of rhetoric and composition in both the freshman year and the years beyond.

Although many details about his active involvement in the field during the 1960s have been forgotten, Kitzhaber's dissertation remains a significant achievement in composition historiography. *Rhetoric in American Colleges, 1850–1900* had achieved cult status in the field long before its first printing in book form, 37 years after he had finished it in 1953. For the book was the first attempt by any American to offer a lengthy study on the history of rhetoric and composition in his country, and the time period chosen as the historical focus had been a time of considerable transition not only for education but for the country as a whole. While slavery ended with the Civil War, Reconstruction commenced, and technology began to profoundly influence American culture, the colleges responded by admitting more students from the middle class. Protestant clergy lost their exclusive hold on higher education, the elective system was introduced, and graduate schools were created. Although he acknowledges the importance of this historical background, Kitzhaber spends most of the time discussing the shifts in philosophy and pedagogy that eventually divorced American rhetoric from its heritage. Kitzhaber notes that rhetoric as a practice of composition instruction was largely absent from American colleges before 1850, as literary societies provided students with the best opportunities for writing and speaking. And though writing would become prominent in the curriculum after that time, the abandonment of classical literature in favor of modern literature in English, the elective system, and the move toward more scientific, less abstract education would eventually narrow the definition of rhetoric to "practical rules to guide written composition" (76). Figures like Barrett Wendell and John Franklin Genung would respond to the pressure for pedagogical simplification by honing rhetoric down to its most simplistic principles. The effects would fit well in a new educational milieu built upon scientism and efficiency, but writing would now be seen as merely an exercise in one of the forms of discourse, not as dynamic communication.

Many of the chapters in *Rhetoric in American Colleges, 1850–1900* covered the textbooks and teachers of the period, with philosophical musings by Kitzhaber appearing at the end of major sections. While the book does well to point out the various contradictory voices that tried to define rhetoric at the end of the nineteenth century, Kitzhaber's conclusions seem oversimplified. For Kitzhaber, the archvillains in this drama were the Harvard Reports and the pedagogy of mechanical correctness that issued from them, and he overlooks the possibility that other factors might have been involved in the impoverishment of college composition. He painstakingly covers the theories and textbooks that held sway at the end of the nineteenth century, but the question of pedagogy remains cloudy. After building a complex framework of various aspects of rhetoric, from style to paragraph formation to the modes of discourse, he states that all of these details were abandoned in favor of practical pedagogy that reduced rhetorical instruction to mechanical correctness. But the causalities at work in his history need further explanation, and he neglects sociopolitical influences that played a role in the changes in rhetorical pedagogy. Even with all of its shortcomings, though, the book modeled the kind of historiography that would enable rhetoric and composition to get a sense of its past, thus allowing for a reasoned critique of the present and a promising strategy for the future.

To say that Kitzhaber was a revolutionary for composition and rhetoric in the 1960s would not be overstating the case. One would not likely think of his politics as particularly radical, for he did not campaign for any one group or interest. His interest was education, and rhetoric and composition insofar as that field contributed to education in America. He was in many ways a product of his time, striving to bring order to a critical element of a society that would deal with the anguish of the Bay of Pigs invasion and the assassination of a president. In reading his pronouncements and prescriptions, one finds little shocking or novel. His rhetorical theory basically adapted the historical traditions of Aristotle and Cicero along with the Scottish Common Sense Philosophy of Campbell, Blair, and Whately for modern purposes, completing that perspective with a knowledge of the social-rhetorical issues that informed both Kenneth Burke and Wayne Booth. Kitzhaber subtly but skillfully found a locus wherein all of these various points of view might intersect for the betterment of pedagogy and of the discipline.

A look at the contemporary discussion on composition theory and practice finds Albert Kitzhaber's name conspicuously absent. The conversation has taken a decidedly philosophical turn, as Stephen North both hoped and anticipated in his 1987 book *The Making of Knowledge in Composition*. But with that shift has come a tendency to forget the history of the field, and Kitzhaber now stands largely as a silent partner in the success of the field over the last three decades. He provided composition practitioners with a sense of their historical and educational bearings. Once able to see more clearly their role and importance in the English Department and in the humanities more generally, they were able to move from the standing of practitioners to that of clinicians/problem solvers and philosophers. But without Albert Kitzhaber to legitimate the field rhetorically as it was being bolstered financially by administrations concerned with the space race and other political endeavors, rhetoric and composition might still be fighting for a place in the American academy. Although he was no philosopher in the way that Stephen North has explained the term to us, Kitzhaber still thought and communicated deeply about history, context, and the need to continually redefine the role of composition studies. For with his leadership, composition studies in America was transformed in the 1960s from a practice to a discipline.

BIBLIOGRAPHY

Primary Sources

Kitzhaber, Albert R. "Death or Transfiguration?" *College English* 21.7 (1960): 367–73.
———. "New Perspectives on Teaching Composition." *College English* 23.6 (1962): 440–44.
———. "Reform in English." *College English* 26.3 (1965): 337–44.
———. *Rhetoric in American Colleges, 1850–1900*. Dallas: Southern Methodist University Press, 1990.
———. *Themes, Theories, and Therapy: The Teaching of Writing in College*. New York: McGraw-Hill, 1963.

Biography

Gage, John T. "Introduction." *Rhetoric in American Colleges, 1850–1900*, by Albert R. Kitzhaber. Dallas: Southern Methodist University Press, 1990. vii–xxii.

Criticism

Berlin, James A. *Rhetoric and Reality: Writing Instruction in American Colleges, 1900–1985*. Carbondale: Southern Illinois University Press, 1987. 125–30.
North, Stephen. *The Making of Knowledge in Composition: Portrait of an Emerging Field*. Upper Montclair, NJ: Boynton/Cook, 1987.

RICHARD A. LANHAM
(1936–   )

Christy Desmet

Richard A. Lanham was born on April 26, 1936, in Washington, D.C. He attended Yale University on a Yale-Ford Scholarship, receiving the B.A. in 1956. Lanham then served with the U.S. Army Communications Agency in Fort Myer, Virginia, receiving an honorable discharge in 1962, and worked as a museum aide at the Smithsonian Institution (1958–1959). He returned to Yale for graduate study in English, receiving the M.A. degree in 1960 and the Ph.D. in 1963. Between 1962 and 1965, Lanham was an instructor and then an assistant professor at Dartmouth College. He took a position as an assistant professor at the University of California at Los Angeles (UCLA) in 1965 and remained there for the rest of his teaching career, being promoted to associate professor in 1969 and to full professor in 1972. Lanham became professor emeritus of English at UCLA in 1994.

Lanham began his career as a traditional scholar of Renaissance and medieval literature, focusing on Chaucer and Shakespeare. His intellectual turn toward the emerging field of rhetoric and composition, a field that Lanham helped to define, is marked by the publication of *Style: An Anti-Textbook* (1974) and *Revising Prose* (1979). His work in composition influenced, and was in turn influenced by, his administrative experience at UCLA. In 1979, with the support of Executive Vice-Chancellor William Schaeffer, Lanham developed the UCLA Writing Programs, serving as director from 1979 to 1982 and executive director from 1982 to 1986. Throughout his academic career, Lanham has received numerous fellowships and honors: He has held a Guggenheim Fellowship (1987–1988), a Senior Fellowship from the National Endowment for the Humanities (1973–1974), and a Senior Fellowship from the Society for the Humanities at Cornell University (1984); most recently, he was Andrew W. Mellon Professor at Tulane University (fall 1995). As a rhetorician, Lanham has interested himself in the practical as well as the theoretical arts of language. He has served as an expert witness and literary consultant for copyright cases that involve films and television shows, ranging from *Jaws* and *Falcon Crest* to *Animal House*. Lanham's own company is Rhetorica, Inc.

Lanham's greatest contribution to contemporary rhetorical theory is his rehabilitation of style as a category worthy of serious theoretical attention. Throughout his career, Lanham has worked to reverse the Ramist subordination of style to content by rewriting the history of prose style as a history of behavior. As the introduction to *Analyzing Prose* (1983) puts it:

> Prose style models human motive. Every statement about style is, if we know how to interpret it, a statement about behavior. Thus the study of style is not a peripheral or cosmetic accompaniment to the exposition of self-standing ideas but a choreography of the whole dance of human consciousness, a dance in which practical purpose and information form but one part. (9)

Style becomes substance in Lanham's sophistic view of the world, where rhetoric is not just verbal decoration but the very means by which the self is constructed and society maintained. Lanham's campaign against the Platonic preference for transparent language also informs his contributions to composition pedagogy. *Style: An Anti-Textbook* (1974) offers a critique of clarity, brevity, and sincerity—the "C-B-S" style—that finds practical expression in the "Paramedic Method" developed by *Revising Prose* (1st ed. 1979) and its spinoff volume *Revising Business Prose* (1st ed. 1981). Addressed to ordinary readers, as well as students, and drawing on *exempla* from many disciplines and social spheres, Lanham's "Paramedic Method" seeks not only to demystify writing but also to cultivate a readership of self-directed stylists whose command of prose style sharpens their ability to read self-consciously—to "know what kind of message a message is" (*Analyzing* 9). *The Electronic Word: Democracy, Technology, and the Arts* (1993) attends to the relationship between writing and the new media, identifying the digital revolution as the fulfillment, paradoxically, of a postmodern aesthetic and of ancient Greek rhetorical pedagogy. Arguing that the electronic text can democratize learning, Lanham also returns to an earlier interest in the liberal arts curriculum, imagining a restructuring of the university that might develop from the ascendence of the "electronic word."

THE COURTIER'S LEGACY: LANHAM AND LITERARY RHETORIC

In his early explorations of literary rhetoric, Lanham analyzes the relation between style and motive to develop a counterhistory of Western selfhood. Together, *The Old "Arcadia"* (1965), *Tristram Shandy: The Games of Pleasure* (1973), and *The Motives of Eloquence: Literary Rhetoric in the Renaissance* (1976) reconstruct what Lanham calls the "rhetorical ideal of life" (*Motives* 1).

In these three books, Lanham positions himself increasingly as a literary eth-
nographer in the style of Clifford Geertz, who has encountered an exotic world
of play, game, and verbal combat that is at once more attractive and more
volatile than the Platonic traditions of thought passed down through the Anglo-
American liberal arts curriculum. In these three books, we see as well the development of his characteristic critical method, a species of Renaissance *argu-
mentum ad partem utramque*—arguing from both sides of an issue—that
modulates into a defense of the rhetorical view of the self and reality. For this
reason, Lanham structures his anatomy of life and literature around binary oppositions, foregrounding and pleading for what he sees as the lost, suppressed,
and devalued side of the Western self.

The Motives of Eloquence contrasts most clearly and succinctly two paradigmatic worldviews, "serious" and "rhetorical," that Lanham believes structure
Western thought and writing. According to the "serious" perspective, "Every
man possesses a central self, an irreducible identity. These selves combine into
a single, homogeneously real society which constitutes a referent reality for the
men living in it" (1). Language, in this worldview, exists to communicate facts
and concepts as efficiently as possible: "The good style, for either ordinary or
literary utterance, will be the transparent style, the style which is looked through
rather than noticed" (1). The "rhetorical" ideal of life provides the antithesis—
and an antidote—to this repressively "serious" culture. The rhetorical perspective emerges in the Renaissance from an educational system that pursues re-
lentlessly the art of verbal ornament:

Start your student young. Teach him a minute concentration on the word, how to write
it, speak it, remember it. Stress memory in a massive, almost brutalizing way, develop
it far in advance of conceptual understanding. Let words come first as objects and sounds
long before they can, for a child, take on full meaning. They are looked *at* before they
can be looked *through*. (2)

Derived from the Greek sophistic tradition, this educational system promotes
facility over originality, performance over profound thought. Rhetorical man
therefore lacks a central core: "Rhetorical man is an actor; his reality public,
dramatic. His sense of identity, his self, depends on the reassurance of daily
histrionic reenactment" (4).

Rhetorical man may seem merely shallow, preoccupied with verbal competition and aimless play. Yet Lanham sees the rhetorical view of life as not only
more liberated but also more ethical than the serious view. The student of rhetoric recovers pleasure by indulging in verbal games, but he also learns, through
debate, to look at both sides of every issue. If rhetorical man "relinquishes the
luxury of a central self, a soul, he gains the tolerance, and usually the sense of
humor, that comes from knowing he—and others—not only may *think* differently, but may *be* differently" (5). In Lanham's thematic *chiasmus*, style and
substance change places so that rhetoric becomes the social glue that keeps
Western culture, in spite of itself, from collapsing into metaphysical crisis.

The Old "Arcadia," a revision of the dissertation written for Davis P. Harding, contrasts the "serious" plot of Sir Philip Sidney's *Old "Arcadia"* with a "rhetorical" plot structured through poetry and debate. The young hero Pyrocles, cross-dressed as an Amazon to win the woman of his dreams and referred to consistently by the narrator as "she," exemplifies the cardinal rules of romance: that character is created, not discovered, and that language can make or break reality. Romance, as a genre, and the Amazon, as a character type, epitomize for Lanham (and presumably for Sidney) the rhetorical ideal of life. *Tristram Shandy: The Games of Pleasure* explores more fully the ethos of Lanham's rhetorical ideal. Here for the first time, he contrasts play and game as pleasurable motives for behavior beyond practical purpose. Here for the first time as well, Lanham evokes Kenneth Burke explicitly as a theorist, characterizing Sterne's novel as an exercise in "perspective by incongruity," a term used first by Burke in *Counter-Statement*. Engaging the reader in an allegorical contest between the philosophical (or serious) and rhetorical views of reality, *Tristram Shandy* "does not tell us how to endure time and chance but how to play games with them, capitalize on them, make them our own" (166–67). Lanham's anatomy of literary pleasure without Freud becomes a species of reader-response criticism that cultivates irony, which Kenneth Burke calls the "perspective atop perspectives," without relinquishing more involved forms of literary affect.

In *The Old "Arcadia,"* serious and rhetorical reality are posed as alternative approaches to life; in *Tristram Shandy*, they compete actively with one another for precedence. *The Motives of Eloquence*, the culmination of Lanham's counterhistory of literary rhetoric, imagines a dynamic "alternation" between serious and rhetorical reality that makes them complementary rather than merely in conflict or subject to blending. In *Motives*, Plato and Ovid epitomize, respectively, the serious and rhetorical positions. Socrates, arguing on behalf of transcendence and a truth beyond language, is a hypocrite. Ovid, the rhetorical man par excellence, offers a more complete, if less coherent, view of human history, but his world has no center. Neither perspective is complete without the other. *Hamlet*, in which Laertes plays the revenge hero purposively while Hamlet just "plays," emblematizes the disastrous (modern) opposition between serious and rhetorical reality. While *Hamlet* is a cautionary tale about Western man's split reality, Baldassare Castiglione's *The Courtier* becomes the reader's guidebook to healing that rift. The Courtier's particular virtue is *sprezzatura*, "a certain carefully rehearsed and prepared spontaneous rehearsedness" (*Motives* 150). The paradox inherent in the concept of *sprezzatura* disappears, however, when the relation between spontaneity and effort is described as one of process. The Courtier creates himself by acting in the public sphere—in effect, by playing himself—to build an urbane identity from the outside in. Literature's job, like that of the Courtier and of *The Courtier*, is therefore "reality-maintenance. Literature maintains reality by continually rehearsing it" (155) and, in so doing, forms and firms up the self.

KNOWING WHERE YOU STAND: THE SPECTRUM OF
MOTIVES

The Motives of Eloquence is itself an eloquent document, pleading for the
rhetorical ideal of life and exhorting Western man to heal his bifurcated self.
To the extent that Lanham's later writing grows more utopian, his own rhetoric
becomes more insistent. In the first chapter of *The Motives of Eloquence*, he
comes close to reifying the two ideals of life as preverbal and prehistoric essences. In the essays collected in *Literacy and the Survival of Humanism* (1983),
Lanham ventures further beyond narratology for the self's theoretical foundation.

"Post-Darwinian Humanism" (*Literacy* 122–43) grounds the rhetorical self in
three fields of inquiry: social dramatism or role-playing, game and play theory,
and sociobiology (128). Writers from George Herbert Mead to Erving Goffman
describe a self created and maintained histrionically, through role-playing. Social
dramatism, like *Motives* itself, argues "that the self grows not from the inside
out but from the outside in, that it is created by society. Our felt sense of
selfhood, in such a view, comes from enacting a series of roles, building up a
self from layers of dramatic reenactment. Instead of possessing a fixed, static
self, we must every morning get our act together again" (129). Lanham finds
the explicitly theoretical work on play and game full of self-contradiction and
so partners dramatism with sociobiology to mark the extremes of human motive.
"The Chaucerian Biogrammar and the Takeover of Culture" (*Literacy* 41–57)
defines the amoral impulse toward spontaneous play as a species of evolutionary
"vacuum behavior": "If, sometimes or often, we too do things just because we
are programmed to do them, just because the behavioral muscle wants to work,
then we must account for a kind of behavior which lies altogether outside our
customary theories of motive" (44). "Post-Darwinian Humanism" identifies
more explicitly a genetic, biological source for the play and game motives.
Within the Anglo-American educational tradition, Lanham argues, the humanities are studiously nonpractical: "[A]s humanists we are concerned with behavior
for its own sake" (137). Lanham's defense of sociobiology, however, works
purely by negation: "If man has no genetic biogrammar, where does this behavior come from? A purely culturalist view cannot account for it. Behavior for
its own sake presupposes an inherited behavior repertoire, a human biogrammar.
No biogrammar, no behavior for its own sake. No behavior for its own sake,
and, as we have seen, no humanities either" (137). Lanham implies strongly that
the biogrammar is "real," yet his use of rhetorical questions and an argument
from probabilities that ends in *aporia* softens his rhetoric considerably.

"Aristotle and the Illusion of Purpose" (*Literacy* 15–23) illustrates most
clearly the way in which Lanham carefully—and perhaps sophistically—avoids
essentializing the biogrammar's contribution to human motive. In rehearsing the
familiar opposition between serious and rhetorical attitudes—now called "Edenic" and "Post-Darwinian"—this essay defines the "Edenic" frame of mind as
at once essentialized and "severely culturalist" (16). Plato and the Christian

fathers are Edenists, but so too is behaviorist B. F. Skinner. These unlikely bedfellows are united by a desire to stabilize the self and to maintain a traditional morality. By contrast, the "Post-Darwinians" believe at once in the self's radical instability and its bodily origins. As Lanham puts it, the post-Darwinians "come into the world, then, not nakedly innocent but wearing genes" (16). By the logic of metaphor, genes are both the irreducible biological foundation of the self and clothing that can be put on and taken off at will. Lanham also circumvents sociobiology's tendency toward determinism by stressing more energetically than before the perceiver's contribution to representation. From self-consciousness comes freedom, for then we not only know why we act as we do but can see both life and literature differently.

"*At* and *Through*: The Opaque Style and Its Uses" (*Literacy* 58–86) provides the most sophisticated account to this point of Lanham's theory of style. It crystallizes the development of his thoughts about the role of style in maintaining self and culture and complicates the binary oppositions that to this point have constrained his thinking. *The Old "Arcadia"* outlines a textual opposition between speech (the locus of rhetorical reality) and narrative (the locus of serious reality). By *The Motives of Eloquence*, this narratological binary has been exfoliated, so that the narrative-speech continuum intersects with a vertical axis that charts generic distinctions between epic (the serious version of literary life) and pastoral (the rhetorical version of life) (Figure 1). Style gets a spectrum of its own, in which Lanham plots the traditional Ciceronian categories for style—high, middle, and low—against the reader's response to those styles as either "transparent" or "opaque" (Figure 2). Style, identified as both a category and an effect, is now positioned to assume the critical role it will play in "*At* and *Through*" as the "trigger" that makes a text "oscillate" between the two poles of "transparent" and "opaque" and therefore trains the reader to be self-conscious.

"*At* and *Through*" imagines not one or two but four spectra: text, perceiver, motive, and reality. Lanham takes Augustine's four-level typological scheme for biblical meaning, transfers the taxonomy from content to form, and makes that model dynamic rather than static. In this fourfold spectrum, the text exists on a sliding scale between "transparent" and "opaque" and the perceiver between "at" and "through" vision. While the opposition between a transparent and opaque textual surface is a familiar feature of Lanham's stylistic taxonomy, the perceiver now has greater autonomy and can *choose* to read the text in one way or another. The spectrum of motive moves between competition and play, with ethical motive or "practical purpose" standing squarely at the center. Likewise, the spectrum of reality moves between primate biogrammar (which is hardwired at the genetic level) and drama (which builds a self from the outside in through role-playing). Ordinary life stands at the middle of this last spectrum (Figure 3).

Lanham's spectrum for prose style achieves a dynamic quality from the tension between schemas based on two and three elements. *Style* states most clearly the historical basis for this system of classification. Evaluative language about prose has always been binary: Writing is either good or bad. At least since Cicero, neutral descriptions of prose have been based on a tripartite division

Figure 1
Lanham's Narratological Schema

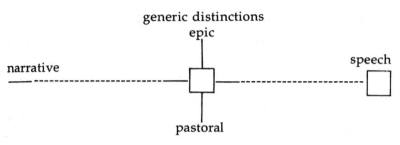

Source: *The Motives of Eloquence* 17. Used by permission.

Figure 2
Lanham's Spectrum of Style

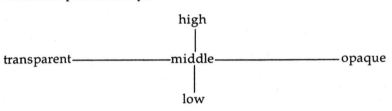

Source: *The Motives of Eloquence* 26. Used by permission.

into high, middle, and low styles. Mixing doubled terms with triplets goes one step toward complicating Lanham's model; it also helps to valorize the rhetorical ideal of life by making the ethical motive, or practical purpose, nothing more or less than a "radical mixture" of play and game. "Ordinary reality" turns out to be another radical mixture produced by the conjunction of genetic determinism and free play. By geometric sleight of hand, what seem to be our normal, referent reality and ordinary motives become empty categories. As *The Motives of Eloquence* makes clear in its discussion of *The Courtier*, "the mean is not an entity. It constitutes an empty category. It balances extremes, a moment of poise. It cannot be discussed except in terms of the extremes creating it" (159). In the most recent, streamlined version of Lanham's motival spectrum from *The Electronic Word*, the two middle terms, "ethical" motive or practical purpose and "ordinary reality," have vanished altogether, so that the center truly is empty.

At the same time, Lanham retains the satisfying simplicity of a binary rhetoric by drawing on gestalt theory, in particular from E. H. Gombrich's *Art and Illusion*. In "*At* and *Through*," the perceiver spectrum operates like the multistable illusions that Gombrich analyzes, which may look like a rabbit or a duck but never both at once (for an example, see *Analyzing* 203). In the same way,

Figure 3
Lanham's Four-Spectra Model for Prose Style

	1. TEXT	
Transparent		Opaque
(*behavioral trigger*)		(*symbolic trigger*)
(*stock response*)		(*metaphorical play*)
(*denotative clarity*)		(*stylistic excess*)

	2. PERCEIVER	
Through		At
(*common reader*)		(*critic as critic*)

	3. MOTIVE	
Competitive	Ethical	Dramatic
(*hierarchy*)	(*practical purpose*)	(*play*)
(*money*)		(*hobbies*)
(*game*)		(*honor*)
		(*form for its own sake*)

	4. REALITY	
Primate biogrammer	Ordinary life	Drama
(*dream*)	(*central,*	(*ritual*)
(*myth*)	*"serious"*	(*propaganda*)
	self)	(*naive allegory*)

Source: "*At* and *Through*" 68. Used by permission.

a text must, at any given moment, be either transparent or opaque. Its complexity comes from the perceiver's "oscillation" between attitudes. Lanham's desire to make the trigger both a biological necessity and a matter of free choice is evident in his shifting names for the trigger phenomenon, which an early draft of *Analyzing Prose* called the "on-off" rather than the "at-through" switch. It is unclear whether self-consciousness is a machine or a carefully cultivated habit. In fact, it is both. *Analyzing Prose* (1983) meditates at greater length on the paradoxical nature of Lanham's "at-through" switch. To look through a text, to treat it as transparent, is a "decision," for the simple reason that "perception is active, creative" (200, 217). Reading, on the other hand, is also a process, subject to motives beyond rational choice. Context, as when a teacher reads a student paper for grammatical errors, can trip the "at-through" switch. So can chance—a passage will simply strike us as eloquent, mannered, or downright funny. "At-through" vision therefore involves oscillation between two attitudes and two

Figure 4
"At-Through" Switch

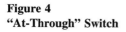

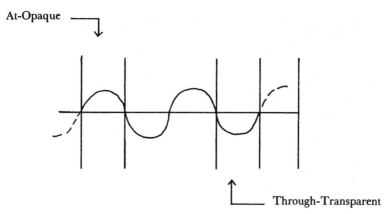

Source: Analyzing Prose 240. Used by permission.

types of vision. Lanham charts the process as shown in Figure 4. In *The Electronic Word*, finally, Lanham examines the instability of digital text, its particular susceptibility to alternations of attitude that may result either from random chance or from deliberate, even perverse, choices on the reader's part. Lanham sees the "electronic word" as offering new and exciting possibilities for stylistic self-consciousness.

Lanham resists the essentialism natural to binary thinking by redefining the either/or logic of gestalt theory as a both/and situation. "The Choice of Utopias: More or Castiglione?" (*Literacy* 24–40) sets up Sir Thomas More's *Utopia* as Lanham's representative of a "serious" vision of society that opposes ethics to pleasure. The result is a culture that is not so much repressive as incoherent, denying half of human motive and therefore splitting the self. Castiglione's *The Courtier*, by contrast, makes man whole by placing courtly games at the center of its chivalric society. Purpose, in Castiglione's utopia, is not banished but invigorated by the radical mix of motives allowed by courtly gamesmanship and play. Whatever Utopia does to better the human condition, Lanham concludes, the Courtier's world does better by addressing the whole range of human motive: "The choice of utopias comes down to this: more individualism or less, more self-consciousness or less, more style or less" (38). As an ideal society, Castiglione's Urbino is governed not by either/or but by both/and logic. It embraces both the serious and rhetorical ideals of life.

The most important development for Lanham's schema of stylistic self-consciousness is his notion of how the different spectra interact. In *Motives*, literary genre and style were locked into a two-dimensional relation as vertical and horizontal axes, with purpose and ordinary reality installed at their center. The stylistic spectrum offered in "*At* and *Through*," by contrast, is three-dimensional. (*The Electronic Word* says explicitly that the matrix could be rendered most logically by three-dimensional computer graphics.) The four spectra lie on top of one another, so that the reader or perceiver moves not only horizontally, between the poles of any one spectrum, but also vertically, among spectra. To give a specific example of how the spectrum charts stylistic attitude, a work such as Marcel Duchamp's urinal, when placed in a museum as a piece of sculpture, represents ordinary reality transparently; it is, after all, just a toilet (reality spectrum). But the "ready-made" artwork becomes "opaque" when spectators are provoked into looking "at" the urinal by the disparity between object and setting (perceiver spectrum). The motive in this case is quite mixed, evincing a sense of play but also the artist's desire for one-upmanship (motive spectrum). To arrive at a full understanding of this object and its significance, the critic must move from one spectrum to another and metaphorically change where he or she stands. As this example shows, Lanham's stylistic grid may also exploit the fourth dimension, time, which both hones the rhetor's skill at being self-conscious—*sprezzatura*—and allows for the liberating operations of chance. The more rapid the oscillation between "at" and "through" vision, the better the prose style, the more sophisticated the viewer, and the more interesting the reality being depicted.

PROSAICS AND PARAMEDICS: LANHAM AND COMPOSITION

Lanham began working in the field of rhetoric and composition precisely when his literary work was coming into sharp focus. *Style: An Anti-Textbook* and *Revising Prose* neatly frame *The Motives of Eloquence* as intellectual bookends. The "Introduction" to *Literacy and the Survival of Humanism* discusses the ironies of having a foot in two worlds, subject to the scorn of literary critics and the suspicion of composition scholars. Lanham's composition work, however, is remarkably optimistic and ambitious in its desire to reform institutions as well as students. He hopes not merely to heal the rift between English and rhetoric but to articulate a new relation between the theory and practice of writing based on the importance of style to self and culture. In so doing, Lanham argues for the restoration of rhetoric as an academic discipline and for rhetoric's return as the heart of the liberal arts curriculum.

Since for Lanham theory and practice go hand in hand, *Style: An Anti-Textbook, Revising Prose*, and *Analyzing Prose* form a trilogy of instruction for the well-tempered stylist. *Style*, in Lanham's own terms the most "serious" or "philosophical" of the three books, measures the lessons learned from Renaissance rhetoric against the institutional reality of freshman composition. Lanham targets as his opponent the "C-B-S" theory of style, which valorizes clarity, brevity, and sincerity without acknowledging the influence of context on these measures of rhetorical success. The moral language that governs composition textbooks, in particular, ties itself into logical knots by attributing moral valence to relative features of rhetorical performance. Clear prose, for instance, is good;

opaque—or obscure—prose is bad. But good prose, counters Lanham, is simply prose that succeeds, that defines a relation between self and other; it makes us "feel at home" (*Style* 32). To admonish students to "be clear" is, in effect, to tell them, satirically: "[B]e born again" (25). Although Lanham does not exactly say so, treating writing as opaque—a work of art—constitutes a first step toward revising a composition pedagogy based illegitimately on the C-B-S theory of style. To chart a student's writing along the same spectrum as the prose of Henry James or Ernest Hemingway attributes to it a sophisticated range of motive. To encourage students to engage in stylistic imitation, comparison, and translation in the style of Renaissance rhetorical pedagogy, as *Style* recommends, also confers on them a certain status as authors (see 66).

While *Style: An Anti-Textbook* exposes the follies of composition pedagogy, *Revising Prose* has no leisure for philosophical reflection. This book addresses itself to people in a hurry, people on the job, people in search of a quick fix for their prose style. It promises a utilitarian, no-nonsense approach to writing, then slyly courts a more thoughtful readership with wicked satire of the Official Style. The most successful of Lanham's books, *Revising Prose* has gone through four editions, each one substantially rewritten and updated in terms of its prose samples. The first edition (1979) addresses itself specifically to university students and professors and uses examples primarily from literary criticism. Intended "as a self-teaching text to accompany courses that require papers" ([1979] ix), *Revising Prose* emerged from the environment of writing across the curriculum and of the newly formed UCLA Writing Programs. The third and fourth editions of *Revising Prose* (1992) bring together a student audience with the professional audience targeted by *Revising Business Prose*.

Taking the sentence as its unit of observation, *Revising Prose* is formalistic and perhaps structuralist in orientation. "Get the basic architecture of the English sentence straight," the third edition proclaims, and "everything else will follow" ([1992] vii). (Not surprisingly, one of Lanham's last classes at UCLA was titled "The English Sentence" [Personal Interview]). Like fellow Yale graduate Stanley Fish, Lanham remains skeptical about formalism and stylistics, complaining that linguistics reduces language to mathematics and, therefore, ignores attitude or emotion, the crucial, if invisible, ingredient in any communication (*Style* 67).[1] Nevertheless, the "Paramedic Method," *Revising Prose*'s all-purpose diagnostic tool and rhetorical Band-Aid, begins and ends with the sentence.

Simple but effective, the Paramedic Method made *Revising Prose* a success in the textbook market for English composition. Lanham takes readers through an eight-step procedure based on identifying simple grammatical forms, fitting syntax to semantics, and then polishing sentences to give them shape and rhythm. The immediate goals of Lanham's Paramedic Method are simple: to trim unnecessary words (and so reduce prose's "lard factor"); to transform writer-based into reader-based prose (and so promote rhetorical relations); and to invest writing with a living voice (and so strengthen the writer's ethos or sense of personhood). Like Lanham's theoretical accounts of reading for style, the Paramedic Method also exploits time as an ally, both by staging and sequencing the steps for revision and by encouraging writers to practice the craft of revision regularly: The 1979 edition includes examples in the book itself, whereas the 1992 edition refers readers to *The Revising Prose Self-Teaching Exercise Book* (1987). *Revising Prose* also has larger political goals. The Paramedic Method, like the polemic in *Style*, combats the Official Style or "bureaucratese" by drawing attention to grammatical features that erase agency and responsibility (passive verbs, strings of prepositions, and long introductory phrases) and by satirizing directly examples of bombastic prose. The 1979 edition calls on students to fight the good fight against bureaucracy; more cautiously, the 1992 *Revising Prose* tells writers in the workplace that understanding professional jargon will help them negotiate, if not escape from, the bureaucracies they inhabit.

The third edition of *Revising Prose* recommends as its logical counterpart *Analyzing Prose* (1983), a primer in sophisticated reading, to complement the Paramedic Method's crash course in stylistic self-consciousness. *Revising Prose* has been criticized as a guide to editing rather than revision, encouraging an efficient focus on the prose surface that exposes but does not remedy defects of logic, imagination, or thought (Di Yanni 327). *Analyzing Prose* answers this charge by demonstrating repeatedly, through extensive close reading, that style is a synecdoche for structure and therefore illuminates invention as well as arrangement. *Analyzing Prose*, like *Revising Prose*, begins with the "English sentence." Lanham introduces novice stylists first to a basic repertoire of grammatical terms, identifying the verb and noun styles that *Revising Prose* offers as paradigms for the plain style and its flabby counterpart, the Official Style of bureaucracy. Then he teaches the difference between paratactic syntax (based on coordination) and hypotactic syntax (based on subordination) and between the periodic and running styles. Lanham starts with the sentence's basic building blocks, expands his frame of reference to whole sentences, and then to sentences in groups.

Analyzing Prose offers its readers extended practice in "perspective by incongruity." Reading closely a series of passages from sources literary and non-literary, Lanham demonstrates repeatedly that taxonomies depend on context. James stands opposite Hemingway, for instance, but only until you see both through the lens of Raymond Chandler. Such exercises cultivate in Lanham's readers a sense of irony that is sometimes gentle but often robust. Even the California state law against picking flowers on freeways provides a hilarious opportunity for prose anatomy (*Revising Prose* [1992] 74–78). Because he emphasizes context and encourages reading with an attitude, Lanham's pedagogy is not truly formalistic. Like the structuralists, Lanham dissects the text to see what makes it tick. Unlike the structuralists, however, he reads style consistently as an allegory for behavior, personifying the text and empowering the reader. In short, Lanham reintroduces to reading the element of drama, of histrionic engagement, that was endemic to ancient Greek rhetoric. The pleasures of the text, so analyzed, confer on the reader an aesthetic authority not available through most varieties of reader-response criticism. As a result, the style truly makes the man. In this case, he is a self-made gentleman, equally at home in the rarified realms of poetry and the prosaic world of business. He can speak or write in any stylistic register but maintains a skeptical distance from them all. *Analyzing Prose* therefore produces amateurs in the etymological sense, who through prose analysis achieve *sprezzatura* and, with it, true urbanity. That he is a "man" rather than a person is a problem that haunts Lanham's theory, based as it is on the agonistic model of the Renaissance educational system. Not until *The Electronic Word* does he complicate, if not revise completely, this masculine model of the Western self.

A Handlist of Rhetorical Terms (1st ed. 1968, 2nd ed. 1991) is a second companion piece to *Analyzing Prose*, serving as both dictionary and thesaurus for the aspiring prose stylists whose "intuitions" *Analyzing Prose* attempts to train. It avoids pedantic disputes over definitions but appeals to both the competitive and play motives by using tongue-twisting classical terms from Greek and Latin. A pronunciation guide guarantees, however, that budding sophists will speak the rhetorical terms trippingly on the tongue, so that anyone who buys the *Handlist* can achieve instant erudition. Lanham's willingness to see rhetoric as a tool, detached in sophistic fashion from highbrow philosophy, offers one way of mitigating the masculine slant of his theory: Practical rhetoric, for Lanham, is truly a lingua franca, an arcane art made available to one and all.

The most recent of Richard Lanham's books, *The Electronic Word: Democracy, Technology, and the Arts* (1993), analyzes the relation between style and technology within the context of postmodernism. Lanham is clear that technology follows culture and not the reverse: "[E]lectronic expression has come not to destroy the Western arts and letters, but to fulfill them" (xiii). "Digital Rhetoric and the Digital Arts" (*Electronic Word* 29–52) outlines the "convergence" between electronic textuality and postmodern art. Both are opaque, train the perceiver's attention, and valorize ornament—in short, both cultivate self-consciousness in the way that Renaissance literature and rhetorical training did. Lanham's explorations of postmodern art also make clearer than ever before just how much fun rhetoric can be. He discusses various exercises in ironic didacticism, from Jean Tinguely's clanking machines, which turn solemn art galleries into noisy play spaces, to Claes Oldenberg's epic *Batcolumn*, a gigantic comic book sculpture that rises up in the middle of downtown Chicago. The digital writer also has more fun than ever before. The power to play with colors, type, and shape allows for a wide range of stylistic choices, while the close relation between text and sound effects makes it easier to project voice into prose. The border between reading and writing is almost erased; in the world of hypertext, the reader exercises nearly total control over texts, so that all readers are creators.

Lanham sees these changes in textual relations as radically democratic, since the advent of digital text challenges the notion that texts can be "owned." The politics of quotation, as well, has changed. Lanham sees the digital text as bringing people together, so that communication is less a series of "orations" than a "continuing conversation," a metaphor used by George Herbert Mead for the social construction of selfhood. For the first time in Lanham's anatomy of motive, community predominates over competition, providing yet another way of resolving the problem posed by linking contemporary education at once to evolutionary vacuum behavior and to the ancient rhetorical *paideia*, both of which privilege ostensibly "masculine" behaviors. In "The Rhetorical Paideia: The Curriculum as a Work of Art," an essay that, as the concluding dialogue of *The Electronic Word* says wryly, "sank like a stone" ("Conversation with a Curmudgeon" 270), Lanham admits to the gender bias of rhetorical education but has no solution for it. In the postmodern utopia of his most recent book, however, the "electronic word" seems to transcend race, class, and gender. Digital text makes the kind of intellectual and stylistic modeling that produces latter-day courtiers available to everyone, not just to aristocratic males with enough time and money to attend contemporary versions of Plato's Academy.

In *The Electronic Word* and subsequent essays, Lanham examines in further detail the positive changes that the electronic word might bring to the contemporary university. Curriculum is a long-standing interest for Lanham. As the director of UCLA Writing Programs, he argued that freshman composition, the poor stepchild of the English Department, could be the center of a new core curriculum (*Literacy* 107–21). In a composition class, whose natural subject is writing itself, students can try on the "languages" they encounter in other courses but also achieve ironic distance from the competing professional discourses that clamor for their attention and loyalty. The freshman writing class therefore emerges not as a course without content but as the locus for radically mixed motives, a training ground in self-consciousness or that most Renaissance of social virtues, *sprezzatura*, a virtue much needed in the fragmented "supermarket" of the contemporary university, where students, when they "change classes, change worlds" (*Style* 77).

The Electronic Word, although a general cultural critique, remains deeply engaged with the undergraduate curriculum. Lanham sees the potential of electronic text to increase student efficiency (the goal of *Revising Prose*) and to provide opportunities for individualistic play (the goal of *Analyzing Prose*). Students in the post-Gutenberg university can access texts from anywhere and so shape their work habits to their 25-hour-a-week day jobs. They can also make those texts their own by annotating and even changing the text and by using multimedia to make language visible and audible (see "Electronic Textbooks," "Strange Lands," and "Extraordinary Convergence" in *The Electronic Word* and "A Computer-Based *Harvard Red Book*"). The electronic word democratizes the elite system of rhetorical education, both by providing access to texts and by orchestrating readers and writers in an academic community that is no longer fractured by disciplinary and departmental boundaries.

WHY BOTHER?: LANHAM AND THE REASONS FOR RHETORIC

Lanham once told a class of UCLA graduate students about studying rhetoric at Yale with Helge Kökeritz, who would bend excitedly over a text to exclaim, in the style of Gabriel Harvey reading *The Faerie Queene*, "Do you see this chiasmus?" "But Helge," the students responded, "what does it all mean?" Much of Lanham's intellectual energy has been devoted to explaining the meaning of rhetoric, how it works as a social, ethical, and political tool in an American democracy. But Lanham ultimately wants to galvanize readers, to make them care about language and, even more basically, to enjoy playing around with words. Virtually every one of his books ends with a peroration that addresses the question: "Why bother?"

The answers to that question vary. *Revising Prose*, predictably, is at once the most pragmatic and the most flippant in its tone. The book justifies itself in economic terms ("saves time and money when used as directed") and in terms of expedience ("useful in all jobs") ([1992] vii). *Style: An Anti-Textbook* sees the stylist's mission as political: to save society from its own linguistic habits. The final chapter of *Revising Prose* appeals as well to individual pride. We should "bother" not only because "*stylistic* judgment is, first and last, *political* judgment" ([1992] 96) but simply because we have to look at ourselves in the mirror every morning.

Analyzing Prose considers most fully the ethical questions that inform Lanham's theoretical work: "How do we make value judgments?" and "Why bother?" Value judgments, refined by training in "at-through" vision, become more sensitive to context. At his most extreme, Lanham suggests that there are no "bad" styles, only bad readers. He draws back from relativism, however, by basing value judgments on a measure of perceived self-consciousness. The analyst moves from an aesthetic judgment (how well a style allegorizes its content) to a social judgment (how worthy is the allegory). *The Electronic Word* considers even more broadly the relation between rhetoric and ethics by analyzing the "Q Question," Quintilian's circular argument that the eloquent man *must* be a good man, since without goodness eloquence cannot persuade (*Electronic Word* 155–94). For Lanham, as for the Renaissance authors he first studied, rhetoric is not intrinsically ethical but brings into focus moral questions and provides the verbal tools for making decisions. With Lanham, however, pleasure finally is the ultimate test of value. The first edition of *Revising Prose*, perhaps, offers the most stunningly simple answer to the question: " 'Why bother?' Because it's fun" ([1979] 115).

NOTE

1. Stanley Fish, "What Is Stylistics and Why Are They Saying Such Terrible Things about It?" *Is There a Text in This Class?* (Cambridge, MA: Harvard University Press, 1980), 68–96.

BIBLIOGRAPHY

Primary Sources

Books

Lanham, Richard A. *Analyzing Prose*. New York: Charles Scribner's Sons, 1983.

———. *The Electronic Word: Democracy, Technology, and the Arts*. Chicago: University of Chicago Press, 1993.

———. *A Handlist of Rhetorical Terms*. Berkeley: University of California Press, 1968; 2nd ed. Berkeley: University of California Press, 1991.

———. *Literacy and the Survival of Humanism*. New Haven: Yale University Press, 1983.

———. *The Motives of Eloquence: Literary Rhetoric in the Renaissance*. New Haven: Yale University Press, 1976.

———. *The "Old Arcadia."* Yale Studies in English 158. New Haven: Yale University Press, 1965. 183–405.

———. *Revising Business Prose*. New York: Charles Scribner's Sons, 1981; 2nd ed. New York: Macmillan, 1986; 3rd ed. New York: Macmillan, 1992; 4th ed. Boston: Allyn and Bacon, 2000.

———. *The Revising Business Prose Self-Teaching Exercise Book*. Paramus: Prentice-Hall, 1987.

———. *Revising Prose*. New York: Charles Scribner's Sons, 1979; 2nd ed. New York: Macmillan, 1986; 3rd ed. New York: Macmillan, 1992.

———. *The Revising Prose Self-Teaching Exercise Book*. Paramus: Prentice-Hall, 1987.

———. *Style: An Anti-Textbook*. New Haven: Yale University Press, 1974.

———. *Tristram Shandy: The Games of Pleasure*. Berkeley: University of California Press, 1973.

Essays

Lanham, Richard. "A Computer-Based *Harvard Red Book*: General Education in the Digital Age." *Gateways to Knowledge: The Role of Academic Libraries in Teaching, Learning, and Research*. Ed. Lawrence Dowler. Cambridge: MIT Press, 1997. 150–67.

———. "Convergent Pressures: Social, Technological, Theoretical." *The Future of Doctoral Studies in English*. Ed. Andrea Lunsford et al. New York: MLA, 1989. 73–78.

———. "The Implications of Electronic Information for the Sociology of Knowledge." *Technology, Scholarship, and the Humanities: The Implications of Electronic Information*. Summary of Proceedings (Irvine, CA, September 30–October 2, 1992). Santa Monica: The Program, 1992. 16–18. Available at: FTP://ftp.cni.org/CNI/documents/tech.schol.human/papers

———. "The Rhetorical Paideia: The Curriculum as a Work of Art." *College English* 48.2 (1986): 132–41.

Television Programs

Revising Business Prose. 3/4" U-Matic cassette, 1/2" VHS and Beta. New York: Charles Scribner's Sons, 1983. 30 minutes.

Revising Prose. 3/4" U-Matic cassette, 1/2" VHS and Beta. New York: Charles Scribner's
    Sons, 1982. 30 minutes.

Computer Programs

The Electronic Word: Democracy, Technology, and the Arts. Chicago: University of
    Chicago Press, 1993. Voyager "Expanded Book."
HOMER. Based on *Revising Prose.* Programming by Michael Cohen. New York: Charles
    Scribner's Sons, 1984.
The Hypertext Handlist of Rhetorical Terms: For Macintosh Computers. Based on *A
    Handlist of Rhetorical Terms.* 2nd ed. Berkeley: University of California Press,
    1996.

Biography

Desmet, Christy. Personal Interview. August 7, 1997.
Handa, Carolyn, and Gretchen Flesher. "An Interview with Richard Lanham: Learning
    by Going Along." *Writing on the Edge* 2.1 (1990): 6–22.

Criticism

Desmet, Christy. *Reading Shakespeare's Characters: Rhetoric, Ethics, and Identity.* Am-
    herst: University of Massachusetts Press, 1992.
Di Yanni, Robert. "The Return of Eloquence: Richard Lanham and the Teaching of
    Writing." *The Territory of Language: Linguistics, Stylistics, and the Teaching of
    Composition.* Ed. Donald McQuade. Carbondale: Southern Illinois University
    Press, 1986. 324–29.
Dowst, Kenneth. "The Stylist as Satirist: Richard A. Lanham." *Rhetoric Society Quarterly*
    9.1 (1979): 17–21A.
Ochsner, Robert S. *Physical Eloquence and the Biology of Writing.* Albany: State Uni-
    versity of New York Press, 1990.
Slevin, James F. "Learning the Language." *Liberal Education* 73.4 (1990): 14–17.

ANDREA A. LUNSFORD
(1942–   )

Roxanne Mountford

Andrea Abernethy Lunsford was born in Oklahoma on September 17, 1942. She spent her childhood in the foothills of the Smoky Mountains in eastern Tennessee, eventually moving with her family to St. Augustine, Florida, where she went to high school. Her father hoped that Lunsford would become a secretary after graduation, but she pursued a scholarship and attended the University of Florida instead, graduating magna cum laude with a degree in English in 1963. She graduated with an M.A. in 1965 from the same institution, writing her thesis on William Faulkner. Despite being told by a male adviser to "go home and have babies," Lunsford pursued a career in teaching, first as an instructor at Colonial High School in Orlando, Florida, from 1965 to 1968, and later at Hillsborough Community College in Tampa, Florida, from 1969 to 1972. In 1972 she entered the Ph.D. program in English at Ohio State University to study with Edward P. J. Corbett. She graduated in 1977. Lunsford's dissertation on basic writing helped found the Basic Writing Program at Ohio State, and her writing abilities even as a graduate student were legendary. One administrator recalls Lunsford turning over a trash can to use as a writing surface and completing a grant proposal in less than an hour. Corbett produced many distinguished students, but Lunsford is perhaps the most well known.

Lunsford's first position after the Ph.D. was in the English Department at the University of British Columbia (1977–1986); she directed the Writing Program there after receiving tenure in 1981. In 1986 she returned to the Ohio State University as a full professor to continue building the graduate program in Rhetoric and Composition. Under her leadership, the Rhetoric and Composition Program grew from 5 to 14 tenure-line faculty and received numerous large grants and awards for program excellence, including a multimillion-dollar grant from the Ohio Board of Regents. By 1998 she had directed the dissertations of more than 26 students, all of whom have gone on to careers in higher education.

She has received numerous awards from the profession, including the Richard Braddock Award for best article in *College Composition and Communication*, the Modern Language Association's Mina Shaughnessy Award for best book on the teaching of language and literature, and the Conference on College Composition and Communication's (CCCC's) Exemplar Award, the highest honor given to scholars in rhetoric and composition. She is the recipient of the YWCA Ohio Women of Achievement Award and is a University Distinguished Scholar at Ohio State University.

LUNSFORD'S RHETORICAL THEORY

Throughout her career, Lunsford has sought to join the Western rhetorical tradition with composition pedagogy, thus continuing Corbett's legacy. In 1984 she published an edited volume with Robert Connors and Lisa Ede, *Essays on Classical Rhetoric and Modern Discourse*, a book that continues to be one of the classics in the field. In their introduction, Connors, Ede, and Lunsford provide a historical overview of the rise and fall of instruction in classical rhetoric in America, from John Ward's *A System of Oratory* (1759) to Corbett's famous 1963 CCCC speech, "The Usefulness of Classical Rhetoric." They contend that "after a century of neglect a major revival of rhetoric—stimulated largely by a reawakening in classical rhetoric—is underway" (12). In the spirit of Corbett's *Classical Rhetoric for the Modern Student, Essays* makes explicit links between classical rhetorical theory and the composition classroom, arguing that while rhetoric in the early twentieth century could be faulted for a failure to consider praxis, composition, on the other hand, was undertheorized, "not an acceptable concern of 'serious' scholars" (13). They write, "The irony of this situation is only compounded when we note that one of the central characteristics of classical rhetoric was a unity of theory and practice" (13).

Lunsford, like Corbett before her, *most* closely aligns herself with Aristotle's theory of rhetoric, arguing for the relevance of classical rhetoric for the current period. She often begins her seminars in classical rhetoric with a diagram contrasting the legacies of Aristotle and Plato on the history of rhetoric, a diagram that of course favors Aristotle. For Lunsford, no theory of rhetoric has ever been as elegant and complete as Aristotle's *On Rhetoric*. For instance, in their essay "On Distinctions between Classical and Modern Rhetoric," Lunsford and coauthor Lisa Ede passionately reject the idea that there has ever been a "new rhetoric" distinct from classical rhetoric. As evidence, they posit three similarities between classical and modern rhetoric: (1) that both "view man as a language-using animal who unites reason and emotion in discourse with another," (2) that "[i]n both periods rhetoric provides a dynamic methodology whereby rhetor and audience may jointly have access to knowledge," and (3) that "[i]n both periods rhetoric has the potential to clarify and inform activities in numerous related fields" (45). Most damning, from their perspective, is the "whittling away of domain, a compartmentalization of its offices, and a frequent dramatic separation of theory and practice" in rhetoric after Quintilian. Using Aristotle as their exemplar, they end their essay with a call: "If rhetoric is to reach its full potential in the twentieth century as an informing framework for long-divorced disciplines and for instruction and conduct in reading, writing, and speaking, then we must define ourselves not in opposition to but in consonance with the classical model" (49).

However, Lunsford has been more at odds with the Western classical tradition in recent years. Along with Lisa Ede and Cheryl Glenn, Lunsford wrote one of the first feminist essays ever published in *Rhetorica*: "Border Crossings: Intersections of Rhetoric and Feminism" (1995), an essay that transforms Aristotle's five canons into a framework for a feminist theory of rhetoric. In this essay she acknowledges the association of the Western rhetorical tradition with hegemonic power. In 1996 she and Lisa Ede published an essay refiguring their Braddock award-winning essay "Audience Addressed/Audience Invoked" in light of cultural and feminist critiques of rhetoric ("Representing"). They suggest that like the rest of the field their early work identifies perhaps too closely with schooling and institutionalized rhetorics (172). They write: "We want now, at this disciplinary moment, to reaffirm [our commitments to the goals of schooling], while acknowledging the importance of inquiring into the nature of both teacher and student subjectivities, and of recognizing the implications of our cultural, political, economic, and institutional embeddedness" (173).

WRITING AS COLLABORATION

Lunsford is best known for challenging the romantic notion of the author that has been endemic to the humanities. All of her work in this area is coauthored with Lisa Ede, her Ohio State classmate and lifelong friend. Their work on this project began as they coauthored an essay for the 1984 *Essays* volume. They write, "Some in our field cautioned us . . . that we would never receive favorable tenure decisions or promotions if we insisted on publishing coauthored articles. Even those who did not caution us about the dangerous consequences of our habit professed amazement at our ability to write together, questioning us in detail as though we had just returned from a strange new country" (*Singular* 6). Their first essay on collaborative writing was published in 1983, in the second issue of *Rhetoric Review* ("Why Write . . . Together?"). Their work culminated in a major study of collaborative writing, *Singular Texts/Plural Authors*, published in 1990.

In *Singular Texts/Plural Authors*, a work that spans theory, empirical research, history, and pedagogy, Ede and Lunsford explore collaborative writing in the workplace and in the academy to uncover what constitutes "authorship" in these settings. Their study of writers in seven professional organizations establishes that "collaborative writing is a fact of life" (72) despite our culture's "deeply entrenched . . . assumption that authorship is inherently an individual enterprise" (73). The professionals Ede and Lunsford surveyed wrote with others in two primary modes: a "hierarchical" mode, whereby one author leads (and often takes primary credit for) the work of a group of writers, and a "dialogic" mode, whereby two or more authors share the credit and responsibility for their writing. But their review of the literature in many fields uncovers striking contradictions in the theory and practice of assigning authorship. For instance, they cite the case of the sociology of science, "where one method used in this research—counting the first author of studies and using this information to indicate the importance of a particular article or to derive maps of the structure of influence in disciplines—conflicts with one of this field's major theoretical assumptions: that modern science is inherently and necessarily a collaborative venture" (138). In addition, they note the paucity of work in pedagogy in English studies on collaborative writing, a field where work on the nature of the subject and the author is rich and suggestive of alternative classroom practices (138–39).

INTELLECTUAL PROPERTY

In the third chapter of *Singular Texts/Plural Authors*, Ede and Lunsford briefly explore the history of copyright law in order to show the youth of modern concepts of "authorship" (76–87). However, after the 1991 case of *Basic Books v. Kinkos*, Lunsford turned her attention to the implications of copyright law for students and teachers. In major addresses across the nation, Lunsford has informed educators of the dire consequences of a failure to speak out against increasingly restrictive and corporate-driven efforts to copyright ideas. In 1994 she founded the CCCC Caucus on Intellectual Property, a group that has been advising the National Council of Teachers of English (NCTE) and other organizations on issues of copyright. In 1996 she published with her student Susan West an article titled "Intellectual Property and Composition Studies," an essay that outlines the consequences of copyright law for writing teachers and their students. In it Lunsford and West argue "that a gradual tilting of America's intellectual property policies in the direction of information proprietors (not necessarily individual writers or creators . . .) and away from that of public users has led to the slippery slope we now cling to, a place where we have diminishing access as scholars, writers, teachers, and students to the materials necessary to enrich the cultural landscape for all" (387).

In the final analysis, Lunsford and West argue, scholars and academics are refusing to stop corporate efforts to close down fair use and extend copyright indefinitely because they are themselves ambivalent about issues of ownership over intellectual property. They write, "The academy's nearly compulsive scholarly and teacherly attention to hypercitation and endless listing of sources are driven, for the most part, by the need to own intellectual property and to turn it into commodities that can be traded like tangible property, a process of alienation that is at the heart of copyright doctrine based on the abstract concept of 'work' " (397). In her public addresses, Lunsford has suggested that scholars begin to refuse to turn over copyright of their work to journals and publishers and to allow free distribution of their work for educational use. In addition, she and West return to Aristotle's view of knowledge as constructed in collaboration with the audience to counteract the romantic sense of knowledge as "original" to the rhetor (or writer), urging teachers to imagine a world where ideas are public, not private property (402).

THE TEACHING OF WRITING

Lunsford returned to graduate school in 1972 because she did not feel prepared by her M.A. in literature to teach writing. Since her early work on basic writing, Lunsford has been motivated by the demands of the writing classroom. Her interests in pedagogy have led her to the study of audience ("Audience Addressed/Audience Invoked," with Ede, which received the Braddock Award in 1984) and student error (with Robert J. Connors) and to coauthorship of several major textbooks, including *The St. Martin's Handbook* (with Connors) and *The Presence of Others* (with John Ruszkiewicz). But most important for English studies, Lunsford has participated in major curriculum reform efforts that led to such publications as *The 1987 Coalition Conference: Democracy through Language* (with Richard Lloyd-Jones), *The Future of Doctoral Studies in English* (edited with Helene Moglen and James F. Slevin), and *The Right to Literacy* (also edited with Moglen and Slevin). Of the act of teaching, Lunsford has written:

[I]t seems to me that teaching at its best—the kind of teaching I can only aspire to—is . . . a form of gift-giving. When I think of my own experiences as a receiver of such gifts, I think most often of students who have been my teachers, and I find that what they have most often given me is the gift of a version—or a vision—of a teacher seen through their own best eyes. . . . [So many of my students] have been and continue to be exemplars for me, patterns that allow me to work the threads of my teaching and living into concert—sometimes harmonious, other times disharmonious—with others— and always a gift, whether it is accepted or not. ("Metaphors" 7–8)

In keeping with her overall view that ideas are formed in communities, Lunsford honors her students' work (and often publishes with them) and has been much loved in return.

Writing a biographical essay that honors Lunsford apart from her many collaborators is, of course, contradictory to the message of her own work. She is, as she has written, a "dialogic" collaborator, a writer who makes meaning in the company of others, even when composing by herself. She would want to be remembered for her motto: "No writer works alone."

BIBLIOGRAPHY

Primary Sources

Connors, Robert J., Lisa S. Ede, and Andrea A. Lunsford, eds. *Essays on Classical Rhetoric and Modern Discourse*. Carbondale: Southern Illinois University Press, 1984.

Connors, Robert J., and Andrea A. Lunsford. "Frequency of Formal Errors in Current College Writing, or Ma and Pa Kettle Do Research." *College Composition and Communication* 39.4 (1988): 395–409.

———. "Teachers' Rhetorical Comments on Student Papers." *College Composition and Communication* 44.2 (1993): 200–23.

Ede, Lisa S., Cheryl Glenn, and Andrea A. Lunsford. "Border Crossings: Intersections of Rhetoric and Feminism." *Rhetorica: A Journal of the History of Rhetoric* 13.4 (1995): 401–42.

Ede, Lisa S., and Andrea A. Lunsford. "Audience Addressed/Audience Invoked: The Concept of Audience in the Composing Process." *College Composition and Communication* 35.2 (1984): 155–72.

———. "Let Them Write—Together." *English Quarterly* 18.4 (1985): 119–27.

———. "On Distinctions between Classical and Modern Rhetoric." *Essays on Classical Rhetoric and Modern Discourse*. Ed. Robert J. Connors, Lisa S. Ede, and Andrea A. Lunsford. Carbondale: Southern Illinois University Press, 1984. 37–49.

———. *Singular Texts/Plural Authors: Perspectives on Collaborative Writing*. Carbondale: Southern Illinois University Press, 1990.

———. "Why Write . . . Together?" *Rhetoric Review* 1.1 (1983): 150–58.

Lloyd-Jones, Richard, and Andrea A. Lunsford. *The 1987 Coalition Conference: Democracy through Language*. New York and Urbana: MLA/National Council of Teachers of English, 1989.

Lunsford, Andrea A. "Aristotelian Rhetoric: Let's Get Back to the Classics." *Journal of Basic Writing* 2.1 (1978): 2–12.

———. "Composing Ourselves: Politics, Commitment, and the Teaching of Writing." *College Composition and Communication* 41.1 (1990): 71–82.

———. "The Content of Basic Writers' Essays." *College Composition and Communication* 31.3 (1980): 278–90.

———. "Intellectual Property, Concepts of Selfhood, and the Teaching of Writing." *Journal of Basic Writing* 11.2 (1992): 61–73.

———. "Metaphors to Teach By." Conference on College Composition and Communication, Washington, DC. March 24, 1995.

———. ed. *Reclaiming Rhetorica: Women in the Rhetorical Tradition*. Pittsburgh: University of Pittsburgh Press, 1995.

Lunsford, Andrea A., and Robert J. Connors. *The St. Martin's Handbook*. New York: St. Martin's, 1989. 2nd ed. 1992. 3rd ed. 1995.

Lunsford, Andrea A., and Lisa S. Ede. "Classical Rhetoric, Modern Rhetoric, and Contemporary Discourse Studies." *Written Communication* 1.1 (1984): 78–100.

———. "Representing Audience: 'Successful' Discourse and Disciplinary Critique." *College Composition and Communication* 47.2 (1996): 167–79.

———. "Rhetoric in a New Key: Women and Collaboration." *Rhetoric Review* 8.2 (1990): 234–41.

———. "Why Write Together: A Research Update." *Rhetoric Review* 5.1 (1986): 71–84.

Lunsford, Andrea A., and Sara Garnes. "Anatomy of a Basic Writing Program." *Journal of Basic Writing* 2.2 (1979): 38–51.

Lunsford, Andrea A., Helene Moglen, and James F. Slevin, eds. *The Future of Doctoral Studies in English*. New York: MLA, 1989.

———. *The Right to Literacy*. New York: MLA, 1990.

Lunsford, Andrea A., and John J. Ruszkiewicz. *The Presence of Others*. New York: St. Martin's, 1997.

Lunsford, Andrea A., and Susan West. "Intellectual Property and Composition Studies." *College Composition and Communication* 47.3 (1996): 383–411.

Criticism

Calderonello, Alice Heim, Donna Beth Nelson, and Sue Carter Simmons. "An Interview with Andrea Lunsford and Lisa Ede: Collaboration as a Subversive Activity." *Writing on the Edge* 2.2 (1991): 7–18.

Reiff, Mary Jo. "Rereading 'Invoked' and 'Addressed' Readers through a Social Lens: Toward a Recognition of Multiple Audiences." *JAC: A Journal of Composition Theory* 16.3 (1996): 407–24.

JEAN-FRANÇOIS LYOTARD (1924–1998)[1]

D. Diane Davis

Jean-François Lyotard was born in Versailles in 1924. He taught high school philosophy in Constantine, Algeria, from 1950 to 1952 and then at Prytanée Militaire, La Flèche, from 1952 to 1959 before eventually accepting a position at the University of Paris, Sorbonne (1959), beginning what would be a 39-year career of teaching and research in higher education. For 12 years (1954–1966), he was an active member of the militant leftist collective *Socialisme ou barbarie* (Either Socialism or Barbarism), and in 1955, he signed on as the Algerian commentator for the collective's journal, a "beat" he covered until Algeria won its war for independence in 1962. His columns expressed growing frustration with "The Party's" misinterpretations of the Algerian situation, arguing that Marxism's so-called universal categories did not account for this North American peasant society's empirical political reality (*Political Writings* 210). What Lyotard saw as the schism between abstract theory and the noncodifiable singularity of any "event" would later spark his renunciation of theory in *Libidinal Economy*—and his break from the collective in 1966. This is also the year Lyotard left Sorbonne for a position at Nanterre, which would become the heart of the 1968 student protests.

Lyotard helped organize these demonstrations and expressed frustration again about the Left's lack of support for them, declaring in "Nanterre, Here, Now" (*Political Writings* 57) that Marxism's "organization and discourse . . . are made of the same stuff as the objects of their criticism" (57). In 1970, he left Nanterre for the University of Paris VIII–Vincennes, and in 1971, he finished his doctorate and published *Discourse, Figure*, his first major philosophical work. Within two years, he had also published *Dérive à partir de Marx et Freud* (1973) and *Libidinal Economy* (1974). The latter, which Lyotard called his "evil book," an "honorable, sinful offering" (*Peregrinations* 13, 14), marked in "scandalous' fashion his turn from militant Marxist to post-Marxist cum postmodernist. In 1979, Lyotard published *Just Gaming* with Jean-Loup Thébaud and his most widely known work, *The Postmodern Condition: A Report on Knowledge*, which was commissioned by the Council of Universities in Quebec. In 1983, he co-founded the Collège Internationale de Philosophie and published *The Differend: Phrases in Dispute*, which examines justice in a world where "a universal rule of judgment between heterogenous genres is lacking in general" (xi). A "dif-ferend" is an injustice that is not litigable because the parties in conflict don't share the same rules of cognition, the same rules for linking phrases. Revisionary historian Robert Faurisson's claim that there were no gas chambers at Ausch-witz, Lyotard observes, recognizes "only the cognitive rules for the establish-ment of historical reality" (57); but "[p]hrases can obey regimens other than the logical and the cognitive" (65), and any judgment based solely on those regi-mens may be covertly smothering "unknown senses" (58). In the last section of the book, Lyotard acknowledges that "Marx tries to find the idiom which the suffering due to capital clamors for" (171), tries to bear witness to a differend—but, Lyotard notes, because Marxism forgets to listen for "what is not present-able under the rules of [its own] knowledge" (57) and does not recognize that "[e]very reality entails this exigency" (57), it remains complicit in what it strug-gles against. In *Heidegger and "the Jews"* (1988), Lyotard suggests that Hei-degger made a similar mistake: In attempting to bear witness to the occident's forgetting of Being, he forgot to listen carefully for what his own remembering had forgotten.

In the end, Lyotard had published more than 40 books, but, according to Lyotard scholar Geoffrey Bennington, he considered only three of them "real books": *Discourse, Figure; Libidinal Economy*; and *The Differend*.

POSTMODERNISM

In *The Postmodern Condition* (*PC*), Lyotard defines "the postmodern" as that state of crisis prompted by the recognition that the metanarratives that once presided over knowledge production and legitimation are themselves founded not on referential authority but on *more* narratives. The "postmodern condition" names that recognition that there are "many different language games—a het-erogeneity of elements" (xxiv), none more inherently legitimate than another. For Lyotard, however, the *post*modern does not come *after* modernism—he defines it as a *part* of the modern, modernism "in its nascent state" ("Answering the Question" 79). Modernism's condition of possibility is postmodernism's cri-sis: "a shattering of belief" and the "discovery of the 'lack of reality' of reality" (*PC* 77). This post/modern condition, which precedes the possibility of a mod-ernist response, is sparked in the experience of "the sublime sentiment," which Lyotard, after Immanuel Kant, defines as "an intrinsic combination of pleasure and pain: the pleasure that reason should exceed all presentation, the pain that imagination or sensibility should not be equal to the concept" (81). It's sparked, then, by the recognition that *there is the un(re)presentable*—which leaves us with this question: "Where, after the metanarratives, can legitimacy reside?" (xxiv–xxv). Modernist responses remain nostalgic for the unity that the experience of the unpresentable shatters and end up locating legitimacy in *another* metanarrative. Postmodern responses embrace the crisis, locating legitimacy precisely in the presentation of the unpresentable *as such*, in the striving "to impart a stronger sense of [it]" (81). This is the basis of the well-known Lyotard-Habermas debates. Jürgen Habermas locates legitimacy in "rational consensus," but Lyotard argues that the goal of consensus is itself founded on the grand narrative of emancipation (65) and that it sidesteps precisely what's at stake in the postmodern condition: "a sensitivity to differences" and a capacity "to tolerate the incommensurable" (xxv). Habermas's universal pragmatics, then, is a modernist response to "the postmodern condition."

PARALOGY

Lyotard offers paralogy as a postmodern response. Paralogy is the search for instabilities in any systematic theory, the appearance of which would defer consensus and cultivate *dissensus*. Paralogy is both a means of resistance to *homologia* (like-mindedness, totality) and the answer to Lyotard's original question: After the metanarratives, legitimacy resides in paralogy, which searches perpetually for new "moves," respecting both "the desire for justice and the desire for the unknown" (67). Paralogy "search[es] for and 'invent[s]' counterexamples, in other words, the unintelligible"; it "look[s] for a 'paradox' and legitimat[es] it with new rules in the games of reasoning" (54). The task of the postmodern writer is to present the "unintelligible" by working "without criteria in order to formulate the rules for what *will have been done*" (81)—and, in the process, to spawn the little narratives that attest to the polymorphous diversity of phrase regimens. The "only consensus" a postmodern writer should strive for, Lyotard says, "is one that would encourage this heterogeneity or 'dissensus' " (*Peregrinations* 44). For when one genre of discourse (linking system) gains the status of metadiscourse, the result is terror/totalitarianism (*Just Gaming* 44). The typical intellectual "helps forget differends, by advocating a given genre" (*Differend* 142), but Lyotard proposes that the scholar's responsibility is to "paralogize," to become pagan.

PAGANISM

In *Just Gaming*, Lyotard describes his pagan pragmatics, locating "the pagan" as one of three pragmatic poles: (1) the autonomous utterer, (2) the obligated addressee, and (3) the pagan/peasant addressee. In the first language game, the important thing is to speak, and in the second, the important thing is to listen to a knowing speaker (God). But in the third, the important thing is to "speak as a listener, and not as an author" (72): The author slot is emptied, leaving no autonomous utterer. All utterers—even the gods—are spoken to more than they speak: and though the gods may "signify," "they do not speak to [you], even when [you] consult them" (42). For Lyotard, paganism is "the game of the just" (72), in which no genre of discourse has ultimate authority. Because many language games operate simultaneously, addressees must listen "prudent[ly]," "negotiate," "ruse," "be on the lookout" for the unpresentable, for the differend.

LYOTARD AND WRITING/RHETORICAL THEORY

Lyotard consistently refutes rhetoric's traditional assumptions "that there is 'man,' that there is 'language,' that the former makes use of the latter for his own ends, and that if he does not succeed in attaining these ends, it is for want of good control over language 'by means' of a 'better' language" (*The Differend* xiii). Lyotard ignores the goal of "clarity" because clarity only further stabilizes established rules for linking and thinking. He calls instead for writing that links paratactically and without criteria, writing that hopes to inscribe *singularities—* "not 'innovations' (deducible from a body of axioms), but unprecedented things" (*Libidinal Economy* [*LE*] 255). He also disregards the goal of producing a reliable/responsible *ethos*, calling the process "a sham" (258) and arguing that "[t]he interests of that which is to be thought must unhesitatingly prevail over the concern to make a good impression, to construct one's authorial identity." Because "all thought conceals something of the unthought," he says, a writer's job is to "take it up, be it at the price of self-contradiction" ("Interview" 17). Lyotard mocks rhetoric's demand that a message be crafted according to careful audience and context analyses, calling instead for a writing that pitches itself to an undetermined audience without "bothering to try to control it," without fretting over how it is received (*LE* 255). Even the demand that one read critically is contested by Lyotard, who contends that the pagan reader's "overriding passion" is not "[t]o understand, to be intelligent"; it is "rather to be set in motion" (51). The stakes of writing and speaking, for Lyotard, have less to do with winning a point, communicating a message, or constructing identity than with "wag[ing] war on totality," bearing witness to "the unpresentable," "activating the differences [to] save the honor of the name" ("Answering" 82).

NOTE

1. As I was writing this entry, on April 20, 1998, Jean-François Lyotard lost his battle with leukemia. He was 73.

BIBLIOGRAPHY

Primary Sources

Lyotard, Jean-François. "Answering the Question: What Is Postmodernism?" *The Postmodern Condition: A Report on Knowledge.* Trans. Geoffrey Bennington and Baiah Massumi. Minneapolis: University of Minnesota Press, 1984. 71–82.

————. *Dérive à partir de Marx et Freud.* Paris: Union Générale d'Editions, 1973.

————. *The Differend: Phrases in Dispute.* Trans. Georges Van Den Abbeele. Minneapolis: University of Minnesota Press, 1988. Trans. of *Le Différend* (1983).

————. *Discours, Figure.* Paris: Klinckseick, 1971.

————. *Heidegger and "the Jews."* Trans. Andreas Michel and Mark Roberts. Minneapolis: University of Minnesota Press, 1990. Trans. of *Heidegger et "les juifs"* (1988).

————. *The Inhuman: Reflections on Time.* Trans. Geoffrey Bennington and Rachel Bowlby. Stanford: Stanford University Press, 1991. Trans. of *L'inhumain: Causeries sur le temps* (1988).

————. "Interview." With Georges Van Den Abbeele. *Diacritics* 14.3 (1984): 17–21.

————. *Just Gaming.* With Jean-Loup Thébaud. Trans. Wlad Godzich. Minneapolis: University of Minnesota Press, 1985. Trans. of *Au Juste* (1979).

————. *Lessons on the Analytic of the Sublime.* Trans. Elizabeth Rottenberg. Stanford: Stanford University Press, 1994. Trans. of *Leçons sur l'analytique du sublime* (1991).

————. *Libidinal Economy.* Trans. Iain Hamilton Grant. Bloomington: Indiana University Press, 1993. Trans. of *Économie libidinale* (1974).

————. *Political Writings.* Trans. Bill Readings and Kevin Paul Geiman. London: UCL Press, 1993. Trans. of *La Guerre des Algériens: Écrits 1956–63* (1988).

————. *The Postmodern Condition: A Report on Knowledge.* Trans. Geoffrey Bennington and Brian Massumi. Minneapolis: University of Minnesota Press, 1984. Trans. of *La Condition postmoderne* (1979).

Biography

Lyotard, Jean-François. *Peregrinations: Law, Event, Form.* New York: Columbia University Press, 1988.

Sim, Stuart, *Jean-François Lyotard.* New York: Prentice-Hall, 1996.

Criticism

Atwill, Janet M. "Contingencies of Historical Representation." *Writing Histories of Rhetoric.* Ed. Victor J. Vitanza. Carbondale: Southern Illinois University Press, 1994. 98–111.

Benjamin, Andrew, ed. *Judging Lyotard.* Warwick Studies in Philosophy & Literature Series. London and New York: Routledge, 1992.

Bennington, Geoffrey. *Lyotard: Writing the Event.* Manchester: Manchester University Press; New York: Columbia University Press; 1988.

Carroll, David. *Paraesthetics: Foucault, Lyotard, Derrida.* New York: Methuen, 1987.

Diacritics 14.3 (1984). Special Issue on Jean-François Lyotard.

Faigley, Lester. *Fragments of Rationality: Postmodernity and the Subject of Composition.* Pittsburgh: University of Pittsburgh Press, 1992.

Kent, Thomas. *Paralogic Rhetoric: A Theory of Communicative Interaction.* London: Bucknell University Press, 1993.

Olson, Gary. "Resisting a Discourse of Mastery: A Conversation with Jean-François Lyotard." *JAC* 15.3 (1995): 391–410.

Pefanis, Julian. *Heterology and the Postmodern: Bataille, Baudrillard, and Lyotard*. Post-Contemporary Interventions. Durham: Duke University Press, 1991.

Philosophy Today 36.1 (1992). Special issue on Jean-François Lyotard.

Readings, Bill. *Introducing Lyotard: Art and Politics*. Critics of the Twentieth Century. London and New York: Routledge, 1991.

Sutton, Jane. "Structuring the Narrative for the Canon of Rhetoric: The Principles of Traditional Historiography (an Essay) with the Dead's *Differend* (a Collage)." *Writing Histories of Rhetoric*. Ed. Victor J. Vitanza. Carbondale: Southern Illinois University Press, 1994. 156–79.

Vitanza, Victor J. "An After/word: Preparing to Meet the Faces that 'We' Will Have Met." *Writing Histories of Rhetoric*. Ed. Victor J. Vitanza. Carbondale: Southern Illinois University Press, 1994. 217–57.

———. "Critical Sub/Versions of the History of Philosophical Rhetoric." *Rhetoric Review* 6.1 (1987): 41–66.

———. *Negation, Subjectivity, and the History of Rhetoric*. Albany: State University of New York Press, 1997.

JAMES MOFFETT
(1929–1996)

John Warnock

James Moffett was born on May 23, 1929, in Cleveland, Ohio. He grew up in the South (Jackson, Mississippi, and Atlanta, Georgia) and attended DeVilbiss High School in Toledo, Ohio. He received his B.A. in English in 1952, and his A.M. in French in 1953, both from Harvard. He served in the U.S. Army from 1953 to 1955 and taught at Phillips Exeter Academy from 1955 to 1965. In 1965, he received a Carnegie Corporation grant to develop an innovative English curriculum and joined the Harvard Graduate School of Education as a research associate, where he worked until 1968. From that time on, he worked freelance as educational consultant, workshop leader, lecturer, and writer. Over the years, he taught at a number of institutions, including the University of California at Berkeley, San Diego State University, and the Bread Loaf School of English. He served as a member of the National Humanities Faculty of the National Endowment for the Humanities. He died on December 19, 1996.

Moffett was an educational theorist of "English"—by which he meant "all discourse in our native language—any verbalizing of any phenomena, whether thought, spoken, or written, whether literary or non-literary" (*Teaching* 9)—whose theorizing searched for the roots of learning and for fundamental relationships between the learner, what is learned, and the cultures and situations in which it is learned. From the beginning, he sought the unifying wholes of which particular educational theories and practices are a part. Though he is probably best known in the academy as a theorist, his first loyalty—from his position outside the establishment of those who teach teachers—has been to learners and teachers, not to other educational theorists. His theoretical and critical work has always derived from and sought its grounding in the concrete realities of educational practice—in curriculum and teaching materials.

In 1968, he published his first two books, *Teaching the Universe of Discourse* and *A Student-Centered Language Arts Curriculum, Grades K–13: A Handbook for Teachers. Teaching* became one of the founding works of theory for the newly reemerging field of rhetoric and composition. Moffett's aim in the book was to develop a theory that would have direct application to developing a curriculum for "English." Indeed the book comprises essays written while Moffett was preparing *A Student-Centered Language Arts Curriculum*, to which it is meant to be a companion volume. "These essays represent," wrote Moffett, "one teacher's efforts to theorize about discourse expressly for teaching purposes" (*Teaching* xi).

At the time Moffett was writing the essays collected in *Teaching*, he saw the curriculum for "English" as beset by a "failure to distinguish *kinds* and *orders* of knowledge," which he saw as a "crippling epistemological error built into the very heart of the overall curriculum" (*Teaching* 6). The error persisted, he argued, "partly because it is easier to tell somebody than it is truly to lead him, partly because we assimilate English, by false analogy, to such subjects as history and science" (*Teaching* 3).

Because of this error, the curriculum in English had failed to come to grips with how discourse *develops* in learners, failing even to recognize that learning how to discourse *is* a matter of mental growth, not just of learning in the narrow sense. The "backbone" of a sound curriculum for English, he argued, would be an account of "the sequence of psychological development," with "logical formulations of the subject" serving "only as aid in describing this natural growth" (*Teaching* 14). Development in English would be seen as a matter of changes in the *structure* of what is known, not just as a matter of accumulating knowledge.

Moffett acknowledged that "the chief difficulty with this strategy was the lack of information about how the thought and speech of children do in fact grow" (*Teaching* 15). Nevertheless, he thought it worthwhile to attempt to "piece together a theory of verbal and cognitive growth in terms of a school subject, basing it . . . on present knowledge, but definitely going beyond what can be proven" (*Teaching* 15). Once developed, this theory could be "tested in schools for efficacy" and offer assumptions that might be tested by other research. It would be, as he said, a theory "meant to be utilized, not believed" (*Teaching* 15). He was, he said, "after a strategic gain in concept" (*Teaching* 15).

Moffett's hope that his theory might be used to generate further research was realized in another seminal work for the field of rhetoric and composition—*The Development of Writing Abilities (11–18)*, by James Britton et al., published in 1975. This work took Moffett's spectrum of discourse as the point of departure for an elaborated developmental taxonomy used to ascertain what kinds and orders of writing students were actually doing in British schools. These researchers determined that students in the British schools surveyed were writing within a very narrow range indeed of the spectrum of discourse. Their work provided a happy example of how a theory like Moffett's could generate further helpful research.

Moffett's theory took as its point of departure the assumption that discourse at its most fundamental level is a matter of "somebody-talking-to-somebody-else-about-something." The elements of discourse, then, expressed grammatically, are "a first person, a second person, and a third person" (*Teaching* 10). To "get beyond the innocent look" of "this venerable trinity," he argued, we must engage in systematic "abstraction" (*Teaching* 10, 13, 18 ff.). It is just such feats of abstraction, he argued furthermore, that are in learners the foundation of growth in the abilities to discourse in English: "Abstraction, by selecting and ranking the elements of experience, reduces reality to manageable summaries. To abstract is to trade a loss of reality for a gain in control" (*Teaching* 23).

The two crucial relations among the elements ("persons") of discourse, Moffett argued, are the "I–you" relation, which he calls "dramatic" (or "rhetorical"), and the "I–it" relation, which he calls "abstractive" (or "referential"). Along these two axes of relation, Moffett proposed a developmental hierarchy of the "kinds and orders" of discourse that was based upon increasing distance in time and space. Along the referential axis (I–it relations), he proposed the developmental hierarchy of

what is happening—drama—recording

what has happened—narrative—reporting

what happens—exposition—generalizing

what may happen—logical argumentation—theorizing (*Teaching* 35)

Along the rhetorical axis (I–you relations), he proposed the developmental hierarchy of:

Reflection—Intrapersonal communication between two parts of one nervous system.

Conversation—Interpersonal communication between two people in vocal range.

Correspondence—Interpersonal communication between remote individuals or small groups with some personal knowledge of each other.

Publication—Impersonal communication to large anonymous groups extended over space and/or time. (*Teaching* 33)

In combination, these two arrays produced what he called "the spectrum of discourse."

Interior Dialogue (egocentric speech)			P
Vocal Dialogue (socialized speech)	*Recording, the drama of what is happening*	PLAYS	O
Correspondence			
Personal Journal			E

Autobiography		T
Memoir	*Reporting, the narrative of what happened*	FICTION
Biography		
Chronicle		
History	*Generalizing, the exposition of what happens*	ESSAY R
Science		
Metaphysics	*Theorizing, the argumentation of what will,*	Y
	may happen	

(*Teaching* 47)

Later chapters in *Teaching* developed complex and richly exemplified accounts of how the various kinds and orders of discourse appeared in literature and in the work of students in classrooms.

Moffett arrived at his formulation of the universe of discourse and its sequence of development "intuitively," he said. Later he found he could invoke the work of psycho- and sociolinguists like Piaget, Basil Bernstein, Vygotsky, and G. H. Mead to enhance the credibility of his proposals (Letter to the author, September 20, 1993). In the rich body of work that Moffett produced over his lifetime, this scheme of the "universe of discourse" remained fundamentally intact, although Moffett restated and refined it from time to time—noting, for example, that "poetry," and not just "science" and "metaphysics," addresses "what may happen."

"This whole theory of discourse," he wrote with characteristic diffidence, "is essentially an hallucination. Heaven forbid that it should be translated directly into syllabi and packages of serial textbooks" (*Teaching* 54). It was nonetheless clear that Moffett felt that his theory offered "a strategic gain in concept" for teachers, and he was committed to making concrete proposals about curriculum in "English" that teachers could find useful. Moffett realized that theories—especially taxonomies—tend to be translated into curriculum in rigid and over-simplified ways, and he urged his readers to cultivate a healthy understanding of the relation of such theory to actual development. It was apparent, he said, from his work with teachers who had used assignments generated from the theory, that he had discovered that "pupil capacity seems to vary as much horizontally throughout a population of one grade as it does vertically through the grades. . . . At every turn of the road we ran into the disconcerting fact that what a student could write seemed to depend more on his out-of-school language environment and previous school training than on his age" (*Teaching* 54–55). It followed that for the teacher "individualization" should always be the goal in the classroom. Furthermore, he claimed, it is "[t]hrough reading, writing, and discussing whole, authentic discourses—and using no textbooks—students can learn better everything that we consider of value in language and literature than they can by the current substantive and particle approach" (*Teaching* 7). Moffett's own curricular materials are models of how teachers may use theory to structure learning and development without vitiating the fundamental commitment to authentic discourse and to individual development.

Moffett's theory was criticized for neglecting context and situation, as other "personal growth" models had done. Personal growth is clearly the goal in his early proposals, and he did find support in biological models of cognitive development. But it is apparent from his teaching materials and other writings that he had a lively appreciation of how crucial social and cultural circumstances were to such personal development. He may not have seen the self as *only* the product of its circumstances, but neither did he assume that the self was simply a biological given, autonomous and integrated a priori, needing only to find a means of "expression."

Following the publication of his two important books in 1968, Moffett was senior editor for an extensive collection of pedagogical materials ("800 activity cards, dozens of games, 80 hours of recordings, and 175 paperback books of diverse reading material") for classrooms K–12, called *Interaction*, published by Houghton Mifflin in 1973. In 1974, Moffett's *Interaction* program was enveloped in "the most tumultuous and significant textbook controversy that North America has ever known" (*Harmonic Learning* 2). This controversy—which stemmed from a proposal to use these materials in a school district in West Virginia and which led to violence and assault—is the subject of Moffett's *Storm in the Mountains: A Case Study of Censorship, Conflict, and Consciousness* (1988), a book for which the National Council of Teachers of English awarded Moffett the David H. Russell Award for Research in the Teaching of English.

In 1981 Moffett published two books for which he was awarded the Distinguished Author Award by the California Association of Teachers of English in 1981: *Coming on Center: English Education in Evolution*, a collection of essays written by Moffett beginning in the 1970s on various topics, including the social and political contexts of schooling, ways of teaching literature, and meditation in teaching and learning; and *Active Voice: A Writing Program across the Curriculum*, which was a rewriting of assignments (with advice added about their use) developed while he was teaching at Phillips Exeter in the early 1960s. Six years later, Moffett published four coauthored anthologies of writing done from these assignments by students in elementary, middle, secondary, and college classes, *Active Voices: A Writer's Reader, I–IV*.

Moffett also edited (with Kenneth McElheny) *Points of View: An Anthology of Short Stories* (1966) and *Points of Departure: An Anthology of Nonfiction* (1985). Both of these books organize their selections according to the developmental spectrum of discourse set out in *Teaching*. In 1992, Moffett published *Detecting Growth in Language*, which is material extracted from *Student-Centered Language Arts* that shows teachers how to document growth for themselves, as an alternative to standardized testing.

In *Harmonic Learning: Keynoting School Reform* (1992), Moffett takes the controversy about the *Interaction* series as the point of departure in a book that explores the prospects of integrating the "learning fields" of "family, school, culture and nature." "Learning fields," he points out—returning to one of the basic distinctions he made in *Teaching*—are not the same thing as "subject fields," which are simply "expedient and logical classifications of content that do not take into account how individuals learn" (75). As was his wont, he sought in the tumult and particularities of life and learning a unifying structure, this time extending his range far beyond the domain of "English."

What I have tried to do here is go the whole holistic way in the sense of situating learning with "wholes" that include not only the totality of subject fields and of American society today but also "Western" culture and the pluralism of cultures past and present. This search across time and space for the biggest whole culminates in cosmology, which takes us back inward, as matter leads ultimately back to mind, to fields of consciousness that are coextensive with the fields of culture and cosmos. (vii–viii)

In 1994, two years before his death, Moffett's search for the "whole holistic way" produced *The Universal Schoolhouse: Spiritual Awakening through Education*. In this book, addressed both to "professional educators and to the public," Moffett argued against the governmental initiative for national assessment and a national curriculum and proposed instead that we "parlay school reform . . . into a totally individualized community learning network for all ages" and "merge most social services into education" (Letter to the author, September 20, 1993). In this far-reaching work, he explicitly asks his readers to suppose that the fundamental aim of living and of education is spiritual growth. In this vision,

[e]ach community should organize a totally individualized, far-flung learning network giving all people of all ages access to any learning resource at any time. Nothing is required, but everything is made available. Users make the decisions but avail themselves of constant counseling by a variety of parties. The very concept of schools, classes, courses, exams, and curriculum is superseded. Subjects and methods are reorganized around individual learners forging their personal curricula in interactions with others doing the same across a whole spectrum of learning sites, situations, and technologies. This is what I am calling the universal schoolhouse. (xvi)

His aim in the book, he says, is not to reform so much as to transform education and culture, a transformation that will have its origin in a personal transformation in which we come to realize the narcissistic self as a cosmopolitan Self. In this vision, life is "soul school" (331 ff.) and education is the "master social service" (295 ff.)

In his note about "The Author" in *Schoolhouse*, Moffett reveals that he spent 1973 to 1978 studying "yoga and spiritual discipline under Swami Sivalingam" (xxii). Moffett's later work has reflected a strong conviction that education should aim toward "human growth, which ultimately means spiritual development" (*Harmonic Learning* xi): "Finally, this fusion of idealism and realism embodies the perception that the truly practical way is the spiritual way. . . . By pushing holistic thinking all the way, to its basis in holiness, this proposal ultimately grounds educational and social transformation in spiritual evolution" (*Schoolhouse* xvii).

Moffett's early theoretical proposals concerning the nature of the universe of discourse and how to teach it had a profound and significant effect on early researchers and theorists in rhetoric and composition. His curricular materials have had a profound and significant effect on the practice of the teachers who have come to know them, notably the teachers who have come through the Bay Area and later the National Writing Project institutes. If his theory and curricular materials retain an extraordinary appeal and currency today, it may be because Moffett did locate the fundamental relationships he sought between the learner, what is learned, and the learning situation. His influence on the mainstream may have been limited by his skepticism about institutions and "[s]tate-set standardized learning programs" (*Schoolhouse* 340). He was not an academic careerist: While he did participate in professional academic conferences, he did not seek permanent academic employment or office. Nor was he an educational entrepreneur, hoping to profit from whatever political winds might be blowing through the educational establishment. He was governed always, it seems, by a deep desire to go "the whole holistic way," which led him later in his life to make explicit the connection he saw between the theory and practice he proposed and spiritual growth and to identify such growth as the ultimate goal of living and learning. The kind of spiritual growth he hoped for was not a kind likely to be welcomed by the powers that be.

In his insistence on occupying an intellectual and vocational position outside established institutions, in his transcendental impulse, and in his deep identification with the pragmatic realities of learners and teachers in schools and societies, he belonged to a distinguished intellectual and educational tradition of which he was a worthy representative.

NOTE

Deep thanks to Jan Moffett, Jim's widow, for help with the style and substance of this article. Thanks also to Tom Gage for helpful criticism and references. Mrs. Moffett is now working through the considerable body of unpublished writing her husband left at his death.

BIBLIOGRAPHY

Primary Sources

Britton, James, et al. *The Development of Writing Abilities (11–18).* London: Macmillan, 1975.

Moffet, James. *Active Voice: A Writing Program across the Curriculum.* 1981. 2nd ed. Portsmouth: Boynton/Cook, 1992.

———. *Coming on Center: English Education in Evolution.* Montclair, NJ: Boynton/ Cook, 1981.

———. *Coming on Center: Essays in English Education.* 1981. 2nd ed. Portsmouth: Boynton/Cook, 1988.

———. *Detecting Growth in Language.* Portsmouth: Heinemann, 1992.

———. *Harmonic Learning: Keynoting School Reform.* Portsmouth: Boynton/Cook, 1992.

———. *Storm in the Mountains: A Case Study of Censorship, Conflict, and Consciousness.* Carbondale: Southern Illinois University Press, 1988.

———. *Teaching the Universe of Discourse.* 1968. Portsmouth: Boynton/Cook, 1986.

———. *The Universal Schoolhouse: Spiritual Awakening through Education.* San Francisco: Jossey-Bass, 1994.

———, ed. *Points of Departure: An Anthology of Nonfiction.* New American Library Mentor Series. New York: Penguin USA, 1985.

———, senior ed./author. *Interaction: A Student-Centered Language Arts and Reading Program, K–12.* Boston: Houghton. 1973. Some of these materials are being republished in digital form by EDVantage. Available at: *http://www. EDVantage.com/*

Moffett, James, and Kenneth R. McElheny, eds. *Points of View: An Anthology of Short Stories.* New American Library Mentor Series. 1966. Rev. ed. New York: Penguin USA, 1995.

Moffett, James, and Betty Jane Wagner. *Student-Centered Language Arts, K-12.* 4th ed. Originally published as James Moffett, *A Student-Centered Language Arts Curriculum, Grades K–13: A Handbook for Teachers.* Boston: Houghton, 1968; reissued in 1976, with Betty Jane Wagner, as *Student-Centered Language Arts and Reading, K–13.* Portsmouth: Boynton/Cook, 1991.

Moffett, James, et al. *Active Voices: A Writer's Reader, I–IV* (I, grades 4–6, with Marie Carducci Bolchazy and Barbara Friedberg; II, grades 7–9, with Phyllis Tashlik; III, grades 10–12, with Patricia Wixon, Vincent Wixon, Sheridan Blau, and John Phreaner; IV, college, with Miriam Baker and Charles Cooper). 4 vols. Portsmouth: Boynton/Cook, 1987.

Criticism

Myers, Miles. *Changing our Minds: Negotiating English and Literacy.* Urbana: National Council of Teachers of English, 1996.

Smith, L.E.W. *Toward a New English Curriculum.* London: J. M. Den, 1972.

Zebroski, James Thomas. *Thinking through Theory: Vygotskian Perspectives on the Teaching of Writing.* Portsmouth: Boynton/Cook, 1994.

DONALD M. MURRAY
(1924–   )

Sherrie L. Gradin

Donald Morison Murray was born on September 16, 1924, in Boston, Massachusetts. He attended local Boston grammar and high schools. In spite of the fact that Murray has been consumed with reading and writing since his earliest memories, he found himself bored with school, dropping out of high school twice and finally flunking out in 1942. He attended Tilton School and took a degree there in 1943. As World War II gained momentum he was sent by the army to Durham, New Hampshire, and then overseas to Belgium and Germany as a paratrooper. His experience of the war has had a sharp and lasting power over Murray and his writing.

After the war, Murray returned to Durham and the University of New Hampshire to complete his college degree in English. In 1948 he returned to Boston as a copy boy at the *Boston Herald*. In 1951 he married his current wife (his confidant and inspiration), Minnie Mae. In 1954, a few short years after beginning his career as a copy boy, Murray was awarded the highly prestigious Pulitzer Prize for Journalism. In the same year, he left the *Herald* because he was under pressure to become an editor, but he wanted to continue to write. He worked at *Time* magazine until 1956 and then spent the years between 1956 and 1963 freelancing in New York and New Jersey. In 1963 Don and Minnie Mae returned to Durham and the University of New Hampshire, where Don was hired to renew a flagging journalism program housed in the English Department. While at the University of New Hampshire, Murray designed advanced composition courses and served as director of freshman English and as English Department chair. Before retiring in 1987, he helped create a successful doctoral program in composition studies. Murray has been honored with outstanding teacher awards and with honorary doctoral degrees from the University of New Hampshire (1990), Fitchburg State College (1992), and New Hampshire College

(1997). Most recently the Journalism Laboratory at the University of New Hampshire was named for him. Even as professor emeritus, Murray remains a prominent figure on campus.

Seven decades of Murray's writings, daybooks, and sketches have been collected by the Poynter Institute for Media Studies in St. Petersburg, Florida. Murray's published works include two novels, a book of nonfiction, 2 juvenile books, and numerous poems as well as countless newspaper articles. To date, his contributions to the craft of writing and the field of composition and rhetoric include 12 books and a number of articles.

MURRAY'S RHETORICAL THEORY

Clearly, Murray's influence has been forceful and long, spanning over 30 years during which he has continued to publish and lecture on writing and the teaching of writing. He has contributed a theoretical framework, for instance, that includes a focus on students as individuals and on personal voice. It is because of such theoretical notions as these that critics in the field have labeled him an expressivist or expressionist. Whatever one chooses to label Murray and his work, Murray remains a pioneer of the writing process movement that arose in the 1960s. His major contributions to the field also include the advocacy of a student-centered classroom, the conference method of teaching, writing as a form of discovery, the idea that content leads to form rather than the reverse, reading and writing for surprise, and the primacy of revision.

In his collection of essays *Learning by Teaching*, Murray states his belief that the writing classroom must be student and not teacher centered. He tells a revealing story about how he learned, finally, that students will write, discuss, and revise their writing if teachers get out of the way. He begins this story by relating a not-uncommon fear of a teacher—that if he doesn't lecture, doesn't tell his students exactly what writing is and what it ought to look like, if he doesn't place the spotlight on himself, his colleagues will consider him a fraud, not worthy of the title of "teacher." One day, as Murray tells the story, he was called away during class, and when he returned, the students he left passive and unengaged were busy discussing their own writing. Stunned, and momentarily hurt that his students didn't need him, Murray began his lifelong commitment to student-centered writing pedagogy (158). This epiphany led to Murray's conversion to the writing workshop, to students finding their own topics rather than being assigned topics, and to the conference method of teaching.

Both the writing workshop and the conference have become mainstays of the composition classroom nationwide. While Murray was not the only compositionist teaching through conferencing, he is the theorist who has most defined it for the field. He turned to the writing conference, preferred even over the writing workshop, because "[n]o class can move lockstep through a writing sequence which is meaningful. The students do not start at the same place and they do not end in the same place. They do not start at the same place and they do not follow the same path through the course" ("The Interior View," *Learning by Teaching* 12). Murray published a set of clear goals for conference pedagogy that included the following guidelines: The student writes; the student responds to the text or to the experience of producing it; the teacher listens to the student's response to the text and watches how it is presented; the teacher reads or listens to the text from the student's perspective; the teacher responds to the student's response (*Learning by Teaching* 163–64). Murray's writing conference empowers students by granting them control over their own writing, a notion alien to the teacher-controlled, current-traditional classroom.

Murray argues that teaching writing should mean teaching students that response is critical. He insists that the writer needs to listen not only to others about his or her text but to the writer's self as well. Murray champions the idea that writing and reading cannot be disconnected, and he believes firmly that details/planning/observations make writers see their processes.

Murray has argued passionately for a theory and practice that values the student as an individual who has a personal voice and unique experiences to discover through writing. His arguments have been transformative, directly responsible for helping shift the field from current-traditional rhetorics to process rhetorics. He has been soundly criticized, of course, in the 1980s and 1990s for these arguments. Postmodern and social-epistemic critics now consider Murray's theories limited by a romantic subjectivity that they regard as problematic. Murray's rhetoric does construct student writers as stable, determinant controllers of their own agency, clearly a problem for writing theorists who now understand individual agency as indeterminate, unstable, and socially constructed. While this critique of Murray's rhetoric is both necessary and important, Murray's theories on subjectivity and discovery should be remembered in appropriate context.

There are at least two ways in which to contextualize Murray's allegiance to individual experience, voice, and writing as discovery: one, through the way he chooses to identify himself, and, second, through a fuller explanation of the ways in which his beliefs arose in response to historical particulars in culture and education. Murray has always identified himself first and foremost as a writer who reads. He is certainly an academic, but his theories on composition arise out of his long career as a publishing writer; they are grounded in his experience as a writer and in the writing lives of the many students, writers, and editors he has worked with over the years. This is an identity Murray consciously chose during an era where writing teachers did little writing, hence the title of his influential text *A Writer Teaches Writing*, first published in 1968. Often the writer is at odds with the academic critic, and the tension between the two can take various forms. For instance, the "writer" tends to use his or her own knowledge about what happens in the act of composing as the guts of a theoretical position. The "academic critic" is inclined to mistrust the writer's perception as naive or solipsistic and, rather than trusting experience as a grounding point, takes the analytical reader's position—based on doubt and abstract theory. And while I distort and simplify the relationship between writer and academic "scholar" here, my point is that Murray's understanding of the composing process arises from the writer's perspective and that the perspective holds the individual, experience, and discovery as crucial tropes.

But Murray's theories do not reside in himself as writer unmoored from a historical context. As I have argued elsewhere (see *Romancing Rhetorics*), Murray found himself moved by the revolutionary spirit of the 1960s. His theories are directly responsive to current-traditional rhetorics that valued very little, if at all, the students' experience, ideas, or relationship to their subject. Much schooling centered on detached drill, skill, and memorization, and writing instruction usually followed suit. Teaching approaches did not center on invention or process but rather forced students to focus on the product and to write only in predetermined modes. Murray, as writer, understood that this model of teaching stymied student writing and thinking.

Murray's rhetorical theories, then, shifted the locus from the student without agency and as detached progenitor of a finished product to the student with agency, with control over his or her own version of reality and text. Rather than students trying to negotiate abstract, distant topics, Murray argued for the primacy of the students' own lives and experiences as the means and content of their writing.

Murray's popularizing of writing as discovery also worked directly against the notions of writing as somehow an intact product that moves swiftly and simply from the writer's head to the page. Murray's point is that writing is a way of seeing, a way of thinking as well as a way of communicating. His perspectives on writing as discovery have been crucial to the writing process movement and to writing across the curriculum movements that hold writing to learn as critical to their theoretical paradigm.

If writing is an act of discovery, then revision becomes a necessary part of the composing process. A major complaint against expressivists is that their theoretical stance too often jettisons concerns about audience and discourse communities. This is a misreading of most expressivists, however, and certainly a misreading of Murray. Throughout decades of writing and lecturing on the teaching of writing he has underscored the importance of communication to audiences of all kinds—thus his constant refrain, "A writer is an individual who uses language to discover meaning in experience and communicate it." And importantly, the key to moving from experience and discovery to communication is revision.

Murray's work, while both lauded and criticized over the past decade, remains influential in the field. He is the "academic sibling" or "father" to a generation(s) of scholars who have reimagined his theoretical contributions for the 1990s (Tom Newkirk, Patricia A. Sullivan, Robert J. Connors, Elizabeth Chiseri-Strater, Donna Qualley, Bruce Ballinger, Lad Tobin, Bonnie Sunstein, Don Jones, Cindy Gannett, and Robert Yagelski, to name just a few). Murray himself continues to learn and reshape his theories as they collide with new theoretical positions in the field. Likewise, there is a movement abroad to revisit expressivism from a postmodern point of view. Those of us who continue to read and listen to Murray, who critique and historicize his work, who are aware of the magnitude of his influence, continue to reimagine his theories through feminist, social-epistemic, poststructural, and postprocess perspectives. And students and teachers continue to find themselves inspired and empowered into language and committed teaching by Murray's work. His continues to be a forceful and influential legacy.

BIBLIOGRAPHY

Primary Sources

Murray, Donald M. *Crafting a Life in Essay, Story, Poem*. Portsmouth: Boynton/Cook, 1996.
————. *The Craft of Revision*. 3rd ed. New York: Harcourt Brace, 1998.
————. *Expecting the Unexpected*. Portsmouth: Boynton/Cook, 1998.
————. *Learning by Teaching*. 2nd ed. Portsmouth: Boynton/Cook, 1989.
————. *Read to Write*. 3rd ed. New York: Harcourt Brace, 1993.
————. *Shoptalk, Learning to Write with Writers*. Portsmouth: Boynton/Cook, 1990.
————. *A Writer Teaches Writing*. 1968. 2nd ed. New York: Houghton Mifflin, 1985.
————. *Write to Learn*. 5th ed. New York: Harcourt Brace, 1996.

Biography

Murray, Donald M. *Writer in the Newsroom*. The Poynter Papers. St. Petersburg, FL: The Poynter Institute, 1995.

Criticism

Berlin, James. "Rhetoric and Ideology in the Writing Class." *College English* 50.5 (1988): 477–91.
Gradin, Sherrie. *Romancing Rhetorics: Social Expressivist Perspectives on the Teaching of Writing*. Portsmouth: Boynton/Cook, 1995.
Jones, Donald C. "Beyond the Postmodern Impasse of Agency: The Resounding Relevance of John Dewey's Tacit Tradition." *JAC* 16.1 (1996): 81–102.
Yagelski, Robert. "Who's Afraid of Subjectivity? The Composing Process and Postmodernism or A Student of Donald Murray Enters the Age of Postmodernism." *Taking Stock: The Writing Process Movement in the '90s* Ed. Lad Tobin and Thomas Newkirk. Portsmouth: Boynton/Cook, 1994. 203–17.

RICHARD OHMANN
(1931–)

Nancy C. DeJoy

Richard Ohmann was born on July 11, 1931, in Cleveland, Ohio, the son of Oliver Arthur Ohmann (O. A. Ohmann) and Grace M. Ohmann. His father was a professor of psychology at Western Reserve and later worked in industrial relations at Standard Oil Company of Ohio. During the depression, Ohmann's parents were New Deal Democrats whose belief in the general ideal that all people should be treated equally was an integral part of Ohmann's home life. Richard Ohmann received his B.A. from Oberlin College (1952) and his M.A. (1954) and Ph.D. (1960) from Harvard University. From 1954 to 1958 he was a Teaching Fellow in General Education at Harvard University. In 1961 he took a position as assistant professor of English at Wesleyan University, where he remained for the next 33 years. Along with promotions to associate professor (1963) and professor (1966), Ohmann held the following administrative posts at Wesleyan: associate provost (1966–1969); acting provost (1969); chancellor pro tem (1969–1970); and director of the Center for the Humanities (1989–1994). In 1995 Ohmann was the Arnold Bernhard Visiting Professor of English at Williams College. He was named professor emeritus at Wesleyan in 1997. Professional honors awarded to Ohmann throughout his career include the Ruskin Prize for the best essay on John Ruskin (Harvard 1956), the Bowdoin Prize for the best essay in the Humanities (Harvard 1958), and the Conference on College Composition and Communication's third Annual Exemplar Award (1993).

Ohmann has not only published widely in the field, he has also been a professional activist involved in a variety of significant movements and professional organizations. He has been a member of many Modern Language Association (MLA) committees and was part of the Radical Caucus of 1968, which resulted in the election of radical professionals to high MLA offices and in many changes to the concerns and structure of the MLA. He was one of the founders of RESIST (1967), an organization that supported draft resistance and is now a funder of grassroots activist organizations. Ohmann is still a member of the board of RESIST. He was also a member of the original editorial group of *Radical Teacher (1975)*, a publication emerging from the Radical Caucus of 1968; he is currently a member of the board of that publication. Ohmann is also currently a member of his local school board. He has been an active member in the National Council of Teachers of English (NCTE), sitting on a number of their committees and holding the position of editor of *College English* from 1966 to 1978. Ohmann was president of the Society for Critical Exchange from 1990 to 1992. He has been an active reviewer of books important to the field throughout his career, often broadening both the scope of the field's discussion as well as bringing professional issues in rhetoric and composition to scholars in related areas of study (political science, education, fiction studies, and sociology).

Richard Ohmann's analysis of English studies in *English in America: A Radical View of the Profession* marked a turn from a traditional concern with syntax and style to a more radical concern with the structural and pedagogical issues confronting the profession. His analysis, and the ways he made room for comparative and contradictory responses during his tenure as the editor of *College English* (1966–1978), affected the focus of the profession more generally. Ohmann's analysis of the profession in *English in America* and his subsequent work as a teacher, scholar, administrator, and activist created not only new theoretical and practical approaches to a field of study; they also invited a profession to begin examining the conflicts and confrontations necessary for moving toward scholarly work based on integration across traditionally separated concerns.

OHMANN'S THEORY OF THE PROFESSION

As Ohmann states, *English in America: A Radical View of the Profession* "offers hypotheses about how this industrial society organizes the labor of people who work with their minds and whose work is anchored in bodies of knowledge and theory" (4). In fact, these "hypotheses" are the culmination of insights that stem from two main sources for Richard Ohmann: 16 years of active scholarship and study combined with critical reflection on his experiences as an academic during that time. The result is a text illustrating the challenges and promises that were to accompany subsequent attempts to reform English studies.

The critical rhetoric of reform posed in *English in America* is radically different from the traditional criticisms driving the "back-to-basics" and other conservative movements of its time. For instead of assuming that the standards for education were set and that schools were failing to meet those standards, Ohmann began with the assumption that the "facts [of economic, racial, gender and other social inequalities] suggest that there are unjust forces at work in our social process, not just bad theories about the teaching of eight-year olds" ("Graduate Students" 251). His radical view, then, asserted that "society needs help from the schools to justify its present divisions, including much inequality," inequalities that, as Ohmann illustrates, English has long supported (*English in America*; "Graduate Students"; Trimbur and Ohmann). Specifically, Ohmann analyzes Literature (the MLA, advanced placement, and the teaching of literature), English 101, English study's "professional ethos," and the past and future of university/society relations to identify how each illustrates "a reluctance to acknowledge any link between how we do our work and the way the larger society is run" (*English in America* 304).

Ohmann's critique of the MLA illustrates that its valorization of disinterested scholarship as the preferred product of English studies not only maintains social inequalities; it also offers rewards to those entering the profession who agree to do the same. Advanced placement practices combine College Entrance Examination Board (CEEB) and Educational Testing Services (ETS) exams to "endorse the idea of stratification" and to maintain a "competitive academic system and . . . a meritocracy based on individualistic ideas" (*English in America* 53). The teaching of literature through the New Critical ideology dominant at the time is critiqued for its tendency to make assumptions that affirm the idea that truth can best be found by distancing one's self from the "real," "unordered," "unorganized" world (73–76), thereby honoring a split between thinking and action that rationalizes economic inequalities between those who do the physical labor and those who do the intellectual labor of a culture (89). "In this last task," Ohmann states, "the American literary profession has cooperated, in part by insisting that the means to personal well-being and wholeness is through withdrawal from social action and the achievement of all-embracing states of mind" (89). Ohmann's connected critique of first-year writing gives significant insight into the recent history of composition studies, despite the fact that it is grounded on assumptions seriously challenged by the rise of modern process-model composition theories, movements, and practices (e.g., everyone in English studies would rather teach literature than writing; composition studies is the physical labor of English studies; etc.). Analyzing the "important subterranean links" between the values of freshman composition and those of industrial society (94), Ohmann identifies the ways in which both position students as "docile and limited" even in classrooms where teachers are asking them to be "free, critical, and creative" (142). The professional ethos of English studies is critiqued for its similarities both to other social hierarchies that create castes within classes (e.g., high school faculty versus faculty at elite institutions) and to those that act as gatekeepers of the status quo (e.g., "Standard English" enforcement). In the final chapter of the book, Ohmann states: "Much of what is wrong in the profession reflects the needs of advanced capitalism and is remediable only through deep social change" (304–5), and he posits "politics" as the source of that change (304).

The nature of the politic asserted here combines activism outside the academy with a kind of activist interpretation as the foundation for English studies within the academy. Ohmann's rhetoric, then, endorses an approach to English studies that positions culture and critique at the center of the discipline, and not only for students but, perhaps more important, for those teaching in and administering the profession.

OHMANN'S RHETORICAL THEORY

Ohmann's rhetorical theory is informed by Marxist critical strategies that foreground "the circumstances within which practitioners actually work, or . . . functions that their practices might have for *them*" (*Politics* 3). Convinced by history (see, for example, *Selling Culture*) and present conditions, Ohmann's rhetoric questions assertions about the humanizing effects of the humanities in general and literary studies specifically. Using counterexamples and historical evidence, Ohmann's rhetoric begins by acknowledging that literary studies has not changed the structural inequalities of society since its institutionalization in American higher education. Composition has fared no better here, valorizing practices that do more to fuel capitalism than anything else (*English in America, Politics*, "Graduate Students"). What Ohmann suggests is a pedagogical rhetoric that acknowledges the importance of understanding the forms and structures of language ("Literature as Sentences," "In Lieu of a New Rhetoric," and "Writing and Empowerment" and "Reflections on Class and Language" in *Politics*). Firmly grounded in an approach to style and linguistics worked out by Ohmann in earlier texts ("Born to Set It Right," "In Lieu," "Literature as Sentences," *Shaw*), the later rhetoric also addresses Marxist concerns more directly as analytic and generative activities necessary to an empowering literacy education. In Ohmann's rhetoric, the Marxist concepts of use value, exchange value, production, commodity, and alienated and unalienated labor become analytic concepts necessary for understanding and explaining the activity of professing literacy at the present time. Such understanding and explanation are necessarily informed by historical perspectives that reveal contradictions at the heart of our practices (*English in America, Politics*). These professional contradictions—Why isn't criticism "entirely satisfying to those who practice and consume it? Why doesn't criticism appear to us as an area of freedom—both a free exercise of our creative labor and a freely chosen collaboration with others in the exchange and development of ideas?"—have parallels when in writing instruction. "The writer's situation is heavy with contradictions," states Ohmann (*Politics* 252). He continues:

She is eighteen years old, a newcomer to college, where she is invited both to assume responsibility for her education and to trust the college's plan for it; . . . to see herself as an autonomous individual and to be incessantly judged.

The writing class heightens these tensions. Writing. The word whispers of creativity and freedom; yet there is usage, there are assignments and deadlines, there is the model of The Theme, there are grades. We tell students to find their own voices, yet most feel subtly and not-so-subtly pressed to submerge their identities in academic styles and purposes not their own. (*Politics* 252)

Because professors and students experience parallel contradictions, both groups need the concepts of use value, exchange value, production, commodity, and alienated and unalienated labor to understand the self/other relationships that constitute, and are constituted by, literacy. Mass culture and the forms of literacy it prefers are primary resources for moving these analytic concepts to the level of practice within English studies (208). Mass culture is not just something to "write *about*" in the classroom. The forms of mass culture are necessarily also objects of critique both for Marxism and within the larger historical frame of higher education in America. For this reason, Ohmann's rhetoric invites students to reproduce forms of mass culture, such as the interview, knowing that doing so will invite critical reflection on the "forms and limitations" of that culture (253).

Scholars have offered serious alternatives to the history of rhetoric put forth in Ohmann's work. Most serious are those histories that acknowledge and address the rise of process-model approaches to composition studies in the mid- to late part of the century. These histories note and explore rhetorics of empowerment, such as expressive and epistemic methods, not mentioned by Ohmann. However, as James A. Berlin notes in *Rhetoric and Reality*, Ohmann was one of the *College English* editors who "continued to keep rhetoric and writing at the center of the concern of English departments" (131) and whose attempts (with Harold Martin) to construct a "synthesis" of contemporary rhetorics "presents some of the spadework for an epistemic rhetoric" (168).

Despite, or perhaps because of, its lack of attention to the more dominant process approaches of his time, Ohmann's rhetoric invites English studies— teachers and students alike—to rethink the role of analysis in general, and Marxist analysis in particular, in relation to the teaching and study of literature, writing, and literacy by centering historical and cultural studies as vital to that profession. He does so by analyzing and generating texts and trends that lie at the foundation of the profession and through his professional and political activism (see also Trimbur and Ohmann). His insistence that professing English studies is a matter of integrating scholarship, teaching, and an engaged political life created an approach that the profession continues to explore, one that continues to have serious and major impacts on how we think about not only what we do but also how we do it and upon the limitations and possibilities of those practices for human lives.

BIBLIOGRAPHY

Primary Sources

Ohmann, Richard. "Born to Set It Right: The Roots of Shaw's Style." *G. B. Shaw: A Collection of Critical Essays*. Ed. Ralph James Kaufman. Englewood Cliffs, NJ: Prentice-Hall, 1965. 26–41.

———. "English Departments and the Professional Ethos." *New Literary History* 5 (1974): 565–93.

———. *English in America: A Radical View of the Profession.* New York: Oxford University Press, 1976.

———. "Graduate Students, Professionals, Intellectuals." *College English* 52.3 (1990): 247–57.

———. "History and Literary History." *Poetics Today* 9.2 (1988): 357–75.

———. "An Informal and Perhaps Unreliable Account of the Modern Language Association of America." *The Antioch Review* 29.2 (1969): 329–47.

———. "In Lieu of a New Rhetoric." *Professing the New Rhetorics: A Sourcebook.* Ed. Theresa Enos and Stuart C. Brown. Englewood Cliffs, NJ: Prentice-Hall, 1994. 298–306.

———. "Literature as Sentences." *Contemporary Rhetoric: A Conceptual Background with Readings.* New York: Harcourt Brace Jovanovich, 1975. 296–304.

———. "The MLA and the Politics of Inadvertence." *Publications of the Modern Language Association of America* 83.4 (1968): 988–90.

———. *Politics of Letters.* Middletown, CT: Wesleyan University Press, 1987.

———. "Reflections on Class and Language." *College English* 44.1 (1982): 1–17.

———. *Selling Culture: Magazines, Markets, and Class at the Turn of the Century.* New York: Verso, 1996.

———. *Shaw: The Style and the Man.* Middletown, CT: Wesleyan University Press, 1962.

———. "Teaching as Critical Practice." *Critical Theory and the Teaching of Literature* 3.1 (1985): 59–85.

———. "Use Definite, Specific, Concrete Language." *College English* 41.4 (1979): 390–97.

———. "What is Criticism?" *Radical Teacher: A Newsjournal of Socialist Theory and Practice* 18.1 (1980): 29–32.

Ohmann, Richard, and Harold C. Martin. *The Logic and Rhetoric of Exposition.* New York: Holt, Rinehart and Winston, 1957.

Ohmann, Richard, ed. *Making and Selling Culture.* Middletown, CT: Wesleyan University Press, 1996.

Criticism

Berlin, James A. *Rhetoric and Reality: Writing Instruction in American Colleges, 1900–1985.* Carbondale: Southern Illinois University Press, 1987.

Brereton, John C. *The Origins of Composition Studies in the American College, 1875–1925.* Pittsburgh: University of Pittsburgh Press, 1995.

Cline, Andy. "The Textbook Sucks: Considering Freshmen Rhetorics 20 Years after Ohmann's Critique in *English in America*" (August 10, 1997) [cited April 23, 1998]. Available at: http://cctr.umck.edu.88/userx/acline/index.html

Court, Franklin E. *Institutionalizing English Literature: The Culture and Politics of English Study, 1750–1900.* Stanford: Stanford University Press, 1992.

Hasegawa, Tsuyoshi. "Ohmann and Fish: The End of Generative Stylistics." *Language Studies* 65.1 (1998): 73–109.

Lindemann, Erika, and Gary Tate. *An Introduction to Composition Studies.* New York: Oxford University Press, 1991.

Murphy, James J. *A Short History of Writing Instruction from Ancient Greece to Twentieth Century America*. Davis, CA: Hermagoras Press, 1990.

Trimbur, John, and Richard Ohmann. " 'In the Beginning Was the Sixties': A Conversation with Richard Ohmann and John Trimbur." PRE/TEXT 13.1–2 (1992): 134–47.

Unsworth, John. "Orchestrating Reception: The Hierarchy of Readers in Post-modern American Fiction." *Centennial Review* 34.3 (1990): 413–32.

WALTER J. ONG
(1912-   )

C. Jan Swearingen and Martin M. Jacobsen

Walter Jackson Ong was born in Kansas City, Missouri, in 1912, during a period of "intellectual slumber" in American Catholicism that followed papal encyclicals condemning Americanism and Modernism (Farrell, "Introduction"). As a result, his Jesuit education at St. Louis University in the 1930s and early 1940s coincided with a moment of awakening within American Catholic intellectual circles. Ong's biographers (Farrell, "Introduction," "Overview"; Lumpp) are recovering this milieu and aligning it to the rich convergence of theories and theorists, secular and religious, that mingle throughout Ong's works: Etienne Gilson, Jacques Maritain, William F. Lynch, George Herbert Mead, Marshall McLuhan, Perry Miller; and later: Bernard Lonergan, Eric Havelock, Alexander Luria, Albert Lord, and Milman Parry, among many others.

Ong completed a degree in classics in 1933 at Rockhurst College, in Kansas City, Missouri. He proceeded to St. Louis University for M.A. work from 1938 to 1941, where Marshall McLuhan directed his M.A. thesis on Gerard Manley Hopkins's use of sprung rhythm. McLuhan also introduced Ong to the history of rhetoric in general and in particular to a figure who would occupy much of his Ph.D. work at Harvard: Peter Ramus. McLuhan had become familiar with Ramus during his work at Cambridge and had by the time he worked with Ong come to know Perry Miller's work on Ramus and other Renaissance and Puritan rhetorical systems. Under Miller's direction at Harvard, Ong completed a dissertation that distilled extended study in Paris and other European locations where Ramus's works can be consulted firsthand. While in Paris, Ong encountered for the first time the work of another figure who would inform his investigations of the evolution of human consciousness: Pierre Teilhard de Chardin. Harvard University Press published Ong's two-volume study of Ramus in 1958. Volume 1, *Ramus, Method, and the Decay of Dialogue*, remains a model of scholarship in the history of rhetoric, and a magisterial study of late Renaissance and early modern textual and rhetorical cultures, both inside and outside of university cultures. In this work can be observed themes that are developed in Ong's later work: orality, agonism, classroom rhetorical cultures, and concepts of self, author, context, and audience that are created in the teaching of oral and written language: rhetoric and literature.

From 1959 to 1970 Ong was professor of English at St. Louis University. Beginning in 1970, with Charles Hofling, he cofounded and codirected a joint program both for M.D.s who were residents in psychiatry and for invited Ph.D. students in English (Farrell, "Overview"). With the success of this program, Ong was appointed professor of humanities and psychiatry, a position he held until his retirement. During the 1970s and early 1980s Ong produced many works on psychiatric approaches to language and culture. He addressed colonialism, racism, and male antifeminism in "Truth in Conrad's Darkness," written after a series of "26 lectures delivered throughout Africa (April–May 1974) sponsored by the U.S. Board of Foreign Scholarships in commemoration of the (25th) anniversary of the Fulbright academic foreign exchange program" (Lumpp 17; also see Farrell, "Overview"). Although Ong's use of a contrastive model of oral and literate consciousness and culture became a subject of many debates concerning Eurocentrism and "essentialism" (Daniell, "Orality"), Ong's work on these topics was among the first to define links among cognitive studies in language and culture and historical studies in rhetoric. Most scholars working in the areas of literacy studies, language and cognition, and the history of rhetoric acknowledge the pioneering work of Ong in all of these fields during the 1960s, 1970s, and 1980s.

Ong coedited *The Quarterly Journal of Speech* from 1960 to 1977. He was elected in 1978 as president of the Modern Language Association; the adaptation of his presidential address, "Literacy and Orality in Our Times," has been reprinted in 10 different publications. Its themes were further developed in *Orality and Literacy*, the most widely translated and hotly debated among Ong's works. Throughout his professorial career Ong worked in inner-city tutoring programs sponsored by St. Louis University and as a tutor at North House, the Jesuit residence in St. Louis's inner city. After his retirement, Ong continued to teach regularly at St. Louis University.

Walter Ong's contributions to rhetorical history and theory, discourse studies, literary history, and literacy-orality studies are extensive and well known in more than 15 languages. Beginning with *Ramus, Method, and the Decay of Dialogue*, and continuing with *The Presence of the Word, Rhetoric, Romance, and Technology, Interfaces of the Word, Fighting for Life*, and *Orality and Literacy*, Ong consistently focuses on the technologies of the word alongside the degrees of separation that each technology imparts, or is believed to impart. Rhetoric receives able attention in Ong's scholarship as the one mode of oral discourse in antiquity that assumed singular importance as it began to shape Western rhetoric, literacy, and educational curricula. Ong emphasizes that both rhetorical practice and rhetoric's form as a curriculum subject have undergone recurrent phases of renewal and technification within different periods: from the viva voce presence of the spoken word to the technologies of written communication and print, from inventively composed speeches and interlocution to memorized declamations and classroom writing exercises, from voice to text and textbook. Consistently linking the history of rhetoric with the history of literacy sustains the visibility of vernacular rhetoric as an oral genre continually interacting with— and often reinvigorating—formalized rhetorical instruction in different periods. The attention given to vernacular versus Latin traditions in rhetorical practice and curriculum provides especially useful information concerning contact and border rhetorics such as those that emerged during the Renaissance with the first vernacular prose writers. The vernacular—the constantly evolving spoken variants of language that gradually develop written forms—in time after time and place after place has given new life to ossified practices of rhetoric and its classroom teaching.

Ong's work on Ramus emphasizes a paradox: Ramus was among the first to indict the list-style logics that accompanied the first generation of print textbooks as a reductive technologizing of the word but then turned out a number of list-and-chart-structured textbooks in "practical" argumentation himself. Ong's studies of classroom instruction and textbooks in the sixteenth century provide an extensive analysis of the different rhetorical systems that were converging in the Gutenberg era, shaping and being shaped by the entirely new print culture. Protestantism, with its emphasis on vernacular translations of the Bible and mass reading education, was one impetus for Gutenberg. Ong's work traces a number of cultural and religious beliefs about language upon language practice: rhetoric, literary genres, orality, and literacy in different times and places. In advancing the study of rhetoric as conveying a system of beliefs about language, thought, culture, and what it is to be human, Ong locates the practice, study, and teaching of rhetoric in ethical as well as epistemological contexts. Scholars and teachers in literary studies, linguistics, rhetoric, and contrastive studies of oral and written language continue to draw on his work. Debates about the validity of the orality-literacy contrast continue to be revived (Daniell, "Narratives").

Because many studies of rhetoric are necessarily recursive, they have readily drawn upon the back-to-the-future pattern that Ong's work has championed ("McLuhan"). Ong illuminates a diversity of oral and literate paradigms in antiquity and provides a number of models for cross-cultural comparisons of genres: agonistic rhetoric, epic narrative plots and genres, the structure and rhetoric of diverse literary genres from antiquity to the present. A constant theme is how the presence of the word animates the presence of persons, one to another. Only through persons speaking to one another does the word become present. The orality of rhetoric provides Ong with many examples of presence. Argumentation receives special attention as a mode of viva voce and written rhetoric that has long presented agonistic paradigms for imitation and emulation, especially to educated males in Western European cultures. Ong provides several ways of understanding the resulting tensions, oppositionalisms, and absolutisms. Because he locates his enquiries within the concept of the global village, his numerous treatments of the Western agonistic literate heritage link and compare not only past and present but Western with other world cultures: oral and literate alike. Agonism emerges from Ong's analysis as a quintessentially Western mode, bearing vestiges of its origins in epic and in rhetorical ceremonial display—a paradigm that is part bluff and part fighting for life. In contesting Ong's claims for the distinctiveness of Western agonistic argument, important advances in understanding different cultural practices of argument, negotiation, and logic have developed (Daniell, "Against"). Although he often speaks of differences—oral versus literate, romance versus technology—Ong consistently looks at differences in order to find common grounds, common places, and common meanings. Whether speaking of gender, or of the contrast between literate and oral cultures and consciousness, Ong emphasizes again and again the importance of identifying difference in order to maximize agreement and understanding ("American"). The cross-cultural understanding that orality-literacy studies provide facilitates greater understanding between different peoples and far greater understanding of the intimacy with which technologies relate to human life ("Orality-Literacy" 217–18). Openly emphasizing the redemptive, reconciliatory potential of the study of difference is a hallmark of Ong's thought; it has received mixed reactions within academic discourses dominated by an emphasis on difference and alterity as an end in itself.

Ong's contributions to the theorizing of presence and absence have been prodigious. In a series of diverse works, he has constructed a "model of orality that can stand alongside the Derridean constellation of qualities and attitudes associated with writing in its explicitness and comprehensiveness" (Sussman 215). His sustained exposition of the value of orality, the vernacular, the mother tongue, and the mother as the first voice provides a harmonic counterpart to deconstruction's powerful dismantlings of textuality and presence. In a dialectical appraisal of orality and literacy as complementary and mutually defining, Ong proposes that we can only say "language speaks us" in the ongoing and self-perpetuating activity "we speak language." Interwoven with analyses of textuality and difference, Ong's appraisals of orality and presence span from examinations of media to models of identity, speaking, writing, and reading that are aligned to one another. The healthy—in some ways—alienation of the individual from the inner self through the interiorization of the word, according to Ong, creates a productive space in which interpretation for the first time is possible as a conscious act. However, interpretation brings with it choices, and the requirement of methods, purposes, and values that have yet to catch up with the alienated self who, especially in the modern era, Ong argues, is overwhelmed by anxiety ("American").

Ong defends literacy and its modes of alienation as psychically valuable not because they are inevitable—as decreed in postulates of illusoriness and absence propounded by deconstructionist theorists—but because they form the basis for new, evolving, spoken, living discourses, for change and growth in models of identity, and for the freedom to interpret, to find and make meanings in new contexts (e.g., *Faith and Contexts*). Ong's phenomenology of literacy illuminates the sense in which the freedoms and choices opened up by the spaces of distanciation of exterior and interior, media and self, create moral and cultural conundra that do not exist in communal, homogeneous, oral societies. With literacy comes diversity of self and culture, because with literacy comes access to other cultures and individualities, other inner selves that are also other possible selves (e.g., Bruner). Ong proposes that, paradoxically, it is the process of exteriorization of media, mass media today, that has brought about some of the crisis of the interior self. "The media have become detached from the human person to a degree, externalized, depersonalized, made into 'things.' So we are told, and so we feel" ("American" 121).

Although not always named as such, rhetoric is rarely absent from Ong's portrait of literacy, orality, and consciousness. Since classical times, the communication arts, the medieval *artes sermocinales*, consisting of grammar, rhetoric, and dialectic, or logic, were "our first secular possessions to receive full development." So secular were these communication arts that in several different periods the Church sought to restrict or eliminate them. "Early Christians regarded these arts with the same misgivings which some Christians today manifest toward technology and science—grammar, rhetoric, and logic were things too much of this world. Some early church fathers saw the study of grammar and rhetoric as a capitulation to secularism" ("American" 121). Ong reminds us how very recently it was that most communication was wholly oral, and most communication instruction largely rhetorical, with writing regarded as subordinate to oratory, or primarily as a rehearsal for speech. This world is gone, replaced by multiple media that overwhelm us with images and deluge us with information and input (Palmeri). The personalized voice of rhetoric conveyed by training in ethos and the presence of the speaker-audience relationship have waned in a manner parallel to that described by Ong for the era of Ramus: Dialogue has decayed. When the word is technologized, as it was by Ramus, and is again now by mass media, the processes of speaking, reading, and interpreting tend to decay as dialogue and be recast as formulas. The technologizing of the word is often signaled by a waning understanding of interpretation; dialogue decays, and the belief that communication and interpretation are dialogues is supplanted by things, not persons: outlines and schematizations of arguments, the notion that when we control the technology of language we have the power to control other people as well. Rhetorical history and practice are invited by Ong's work to reclaim their historical roles as reformers and revivers of dialogue, of the viva voce, by addressing the ambivalence toward pluralism and the depersonalization effected by mass media in our current cultural environment.

Rhetoricians can be instructed by Ong's insights into oral and literate conceptions of culture and consciousness (e.g., Sreberny-Mohammadi). Ong's double historical vision views rhetoric as at times one of the technologizings of the word, in a figure like Ramus, and at others as a liberatory vehicle. We are enjoined to look for those points at which rhetoric has been restored to its dialogical roots and for points where dialogue has restored rhetoric to its role within and among the liberal arts as a whole. The rhetorics of reading and interpretation come into play as well with the distancings of voice inherent in textuality. Texts teach us to ask questions different from those we ask in a viva voce dialogue. "Can a person mean more than he or she is fully aware of? Of course. Can Sophocles in writing Oedipus Rex know about what Freud was later to style the Oedipus complex?" ("God's Known" 223). The interiorization of consciousness that is brought about by writing and the concomitant diversification of identities and meanings within literate human cultures create precisely this situation, in Ong's analysis. "We have to enter into dialogue with writers, but we have to bring into the dialogue with them what we know that they did not know. There is no other way to read a text than to enter into some sort of dialogue. To understand, you have to bring what the writer wrote into relationship with the fullness of your own knowledge and the fullness of your own knowledge into relationship with the writer's" (223). Efforts to revive, or redefine, universal values of the human, human rights, and humanism, a global vision of shared human identity, can be informed by Ong's long-standing attentions to the evolution of human consciousness and the responsibilities of the interiorized self within that evolution. Through the distanciation imposed by literacy and interiorization, through the capacity for self-scrutiny, self evaluation, moral choice, and moral self-definition, the stranger and barbarian within are chastened as the first and paradigmatic act of becoming human ("Orality-Literacy").

Ong's best-known and most translated work treats the technological basis of media-centered cultural change. *Orality and Literacy: The Technologizing of the Word* (1982) compares orality and literacy not merely as methods of textual production and reception but as distinct worldviews that may be compared within as well as across cultures. Ong proposes, heuristically, that primary oral cultures tend toward an "aggregative, paratactic, oral-style thinking" that is "evanescent" (32), disappearing as soon as it is produced and requiring a communal, empathic, embodied environment (27–57). He characterizes literacy as the "abstract, analytic, visual coding" (28) of alphabetic literacy, which leads to "text-formed thought" (55), which he characterizes as "structured, directly or indirectly by the technology of writing" (78) and underlies abstractions such as readership (74), private reading (131), and the "ownership of words" (131).

Ong may seem at first glance to focus on the orality/literacy question as if orality and literacy exist in an eternally fixed and static binary relationship; however, an equally accurate reading of this work may find his categorizations of orality and literacy as representative of conceptual centers that are constantly shifting and changing. His representation of these centers often looks outward toward the borders between orality and literacy, finding crucial concepts such as oral literature and preliteracy, which require and receive criticism, and secondary orality, which has extended his theoretical enterprise and led to further scholarship. In discussing the notion of "oral literature" (11), a concept he calls both "monstrous" (11) and "self-contradictory" (13), Ong points out that the term not only lacks accuracy but also reflects both the "pre-emptive and imperialist activity" of writing and the "state of awareness of an earlier generation of scholars" (11–12). He moves, then, to an analysis of the term "preliterate" as depicting "orality—the 'primary modeling system'—as an anachronistic deviant from the 'secondary modeling system' that followed it" (13). Thus, while Ong at some points reduces orality and literacy to a few seemingly antipodal principles, he also cites the misconceptions that exist at the margins of these cultural systems and places responsibility for any final reductiveness on the sources of these misunderstandings. In a 1997 response to a reviewer, Ong once again defined his views of orality by way of correcting an attribution of, "(without any quotations), an interpretation of the relationship between the oral and the textual word which I have never proposed, namely, that 'the emergence of literacy necessarily entails the extinction . . . of an inferior mode (orality).' I have never stated that orality is 'inferior.' In *Orality and Literacy* (the only one of my works which Reynolds mentions), I decry the tendency to identify orality with the 'primitive' or 'savage' and state that 'orality is not despicable. It can produce works beyond the work of literates, for example, the *Odyssey*' (175)" ("Letter to the Editor").

Perhaps the most innovative and prescient of Ong's border sightings is secondary orality, which, he argues, emerges when speech is the primary medium but in a form that can be recorded, such as radio, television, and innumerable recording devices. Two differences separate primary and secondary orality. The first is technological. In recording a spoken product, the "evanescence" of primary orality exists no longer. The oral product, by taking on the durability and reproducibility of literate products, becomes textual. The second difference separating primary and secondary orality lies in the literacy-based construction of oral products. Nearly all of the channels mentioned here rely on scripts, or at least the hierarchical, analytic speech products speakers in literate cultures have trouble escaping (135–38). Before and after the production of orality in most modern cultures stands the indelible stamp of literacy. This provocative concept led scholars to examine the margins of orality and literacy and to extend Ong's system as a foundation for the concept of secondary literacy (Killingsworth). In part, secondary literacy encodes secondary orality. That is, the pervasiveness of secondary orality has relegated those immersed therein to conceive of writing as a skill of secondary importance. Again, an important orality/literacy issue emerges at the edges of Ong's phenomenological characterization of media-centered lifeworlds.

Ong's work on the role played by agonism in psychosocial gender development and self definition has been widely and repeatedly charged with essentialism, sexism, Eurocentrism, and other crimes. Binaries such as oral-literate and masculine-feminine that Ong presents as heuristic have been read literally by some critics as claims about the inherent nature of the oral, the literate, masculine, feminine. Ong is first and foremost an interpreter, an observer, and a widely renowned popular scholar who is able to present literary and rhetorical history to a wide popular audience. When he employs categorizations, by his own definition, they function as sketches, heuristic paradigms, and hypotheses and are illustrated with literary and cultural as well as statistical sociological examples. The canons of positivism and scientific fact that much poststructural and postmodern theory purports to deconstruct have entered through the back door of the contemporary critical toolshed and are now being used to dismantle the kind of nuanced interpretive cultural essay that has long been the hallmark of the liberal arts and modern humanities. Regardless of whether one is speaking of religion, or gender, or orality "you cannot argue the existence of anything from what you do not know. One can prove nothing from the absence of knowledge" ("American" 119). Ironically, many of the critics who have challenged Ong on scientific grounds as being biased or lacking support for scientific claims are also antipositivists. The now-well-known claim that Ong, along with Eric Havelock, is a propounder of a "great leap" theory (Daniell "Against," "Narratives," "Orality") has invited further examination and clarification of the claims made for orality and literacy. In lumping Ong and Havelock together, great leap theorists have obscured important differences between Ong and Havelock, differences that are important to defining Ong's contributions to rhetorical as well as oral-literate studies.

Havelock's work is primarily that of a classical philologist; at times, it delves into sociobiology. A self-proclaimed secular intellectual, Havelock seeks evidence of changes in cognitive hard wiring that might have been effected by literacy in the ancient world. Havelock's interest in the cognitive consequences of literacy is neurological and textual: In the ancient Near East, how did the shift from the ear to the eye affect syntax and genre? Ong is a literary and rhetorical historian with an extensive knowledge of psychiatry and therapeutic discourses in different religions and cultures. While Ong's work touches on neurology, it is also focused on how cultural belief systems encoded in different forms of language are transmitted by different media. What are the effects of these changes in language forms—genres and media—upon human consciousness and self-concept? Even a cursory glance at Ong's titles traces these lines of interest, including numerous studies of oralism within different periods in Western Europe: medieval, Tudor, romantic, the "ear" that is necessary to an understanding of Hopkin's sprung rhythm, the telling difference between Spenser's use of epithets and Milton's avoidance of them. Ong's treatment of the individualism and interiority created by some forms and practices of literacy is a valuable and compassionate appraisal of what most teachers of rhetoric, composition, and reading experience: Leading students to the creation of an inner self, a private self, through reading and writing, is an ethically complex act. It provides, or even imposes, a supplement to the home and cultural milieu of students that may feel to students like a replacement, an invasion, or a rebuke. Ong's appraisals of rhetorical agonism in Western educational curricula continue to inform the classroom teaching of rhetoric and argumentation by making pedagogy more responsible to cultural diversity. Not all cultures argue, and even among those who do, agonistic, adversarial argument is relatively rare. Ong has much to say about the mixed blessing of Western European adversativeness. It may be that Ong will forever be remembered, erroneously, as a defender of the superiority of Western literate culture. However, those tempted to rest with this definition would find instructive a thorough review of Ong's work, especially on Conrad, and one of his first titles: *The Barbarian Within*.

BIBLIOGRAPHY

Primary Sources

Ong, Walter J. "Agonistic Structures in Academia, Past to Present." *Interchange: A Journal of Education* 5.4 (1974): 1–12.
———. *American Catholic Crossroads*. Westport, CT: Greenwood Press, 1981.
———. "American Culture and Morality (1963)." *Faith and Contexts*. Vol. 1. Ed. Thomas J. Farrell and Paul A. Soukup. Atlanta, GA: Scholars Press, 1992.
———. *The Barbarian Within, and Other Fugitive Essays and Studies*. New York: Macmillan, 1968.
———. "Comment." *College English* 40.8 (1979): 871–73.
———. *Faith and Contexts*. 4 vols. Vol. 1, *Selected Essays and Studies 1952–1991* (1992). Vol. 2, *Supplementary Studies 1946–1989* (1992). Vol. 3, *Further Essays 1952–1990* (1995). Vol. 4, *Additional Essays and Studies* (forthcoming). Ed. Thomas J. Farrell and Paul A. Soukup. Atlanta, GA: Scholars Press, 1999.
———. *Fighting for Life: Contest, Sexuality, and Consciousness*. Amherst: University of Massachusetts Press, 1989.
———. *Frontiers in American Catholicism*. New York: Macmillan, 1961.
———. "God's Known Universe and Christian Faith." *Faith and Contexts*. Vol. 1. Ed. Thomas J. Farrell and Paul A. Soukup. Atlanta, GA: Scholars Press, 1992.
———. *Hopkins, the Self, and God*. Toronto: University of Toronto Press, 1993.
———. *Interfaces of the Word: Studies in the Evolution of Consciousness and Culture*. Ithaca, NY, and London: Cornell University Press, 1982.
———. *In the Human Grain*. New York: Macmillan, 1967.
———. "Letter to the Editor." *TLS*, 15 (August 1997): 17.
———. "Literacy and Orality." *ADE Bulletin* 58 (November 1978): 1–7.
———. "McLuhan as Teacher: The Future Is a Thing of the Past." *Journal of Communication* 31.2 (1981): 129–35.
———. *Orality and Literacy: The Technologizing of the Word*. New Accents. London: Routledge, 1982.
———. "Orality-Literacy Studies and the Unity of the Human Race." *Faith in Contexts*. Vol. 1. Ed. Thomas J. Farrell and Paul A. Soukup. Newbury Park: Sage, 1992.
———. *The Presence of the Word: Some Prolegomena for Cultural and Religious History*. Minneapolis: University of Minnesota Press, 1991.

————. *Ramus and Talon Inventory: A Short-Title Inventory of the Published Works of Peter Ramus (1515–1572) and of Omer Talon (ca. 1510–1562) in Their Original and in Their Variously Altered Forms, with Related Material: 1. The Ramist Controversies: A Descriptive Catalogue. 2. Agricola Check List: A Short-Title Inventory of Printed Editions and Printed Compendia of Rudolph Agricola's Dialectical Invention (De Inventione Dialectica).* Cambridge: Harvard University Press, 1958. Distributed in Great Britain by London: Oxford University Press. Facsimile rpt. Folcroft, PA: Folcroft Press, 1969.

————. *Ramus, Method, and the Decay of Dialogue: From the Art of Discourse to the Art of Reason.* Cambridge: Harvard University Press, 1983.

————. *Rhetoric, Romance, and Technology: Studies in the Interaction of Expression and Culture.* Ithaca and London: Cornell University Press, 1990.

————. "Text as Interpretation: Mark and After." *Semeia* 39.1 (1987): 7–26.

————. "Voice as a Summons to Belief." *The Barbarian Within, and Other Fugitive Essays and Stories.* New York: Macmillan, 1962.

————. *Why Talk? A Conversation about Language.* National Humanities Faculty Why Series. San Francisco: Chandler and Sharp, 1973.

————, ed. *Collecιaneae praefationes, epistolae, orationes,* by Petrus Ramus and Audomarus Talaeus. A facsimile of the 1599 Marburg edition. Hildesheim: Georg Olms Verlagsbuchhandlung, 1969.

———— *Darwin's Vision and Christian Perspectives.* (Coauthor and editor.) New York: Macmillan, 1960.

————. *Knowledge and the Future of Man.* New York: Holt, Rinehart and Winston, 1968.

————. *Scholae in liberales artes,* by Petrus Ramus. A facsimile of the 1569 Basel edition. Hildesheim: Georg Olms Verlagsbuchhandlung, 1970.

Ong, Walter J., and Charles J. Ermatinger, eds. and trans. *Logic,* by John Milton. *Complete Prose Works of John Milton.* Vol. 8. New Haven and London: Yale University Press, 1982.

Biography

Bibliography of Works by Walter J. Ong. Comp. Betty Youngkin. (August 5, 1998). University of Dayton. Available at: http://homepages.udayton.edu/~youngkin/

Farrell, Thomas J. "An Introduction to Ong's Work." *Faith and Contexts.* Vol. 1. Ed. Thomas J. Farrell and Paul A. Soukup. Atlanta, GA: Scholars Press, 1992. xi–lv.

————. "An Overview of Walter J. Ong's Work." *Media, Consciousness, and Culture.* Ed. Bruce E. Gronbeck, Thomas J. Farrell, and Paul A. Soukup. Newbury Park, CA: Sage, 1991. 25–46.

Gronbeck, Bruce. "Ong, Walter J." *Encyclopedia of Rhetoric and Composition.* Ed. Theresa Enos. New York: Garland, 1996. 479–480.

Lumpp, R. F. "A Biographical Portrait of Walter Jackson Ong." *Oral Tradition* 2.1 (1987): 13–18.

Criticism

Bizzell, Patricia. "Arguing about Literacy." *College English* 50.2 (1988): 141–53.

Daniell, Beth. "Against the Great Leap Theory of Literacy." *PRE/TEXT* 7.3–4 (1986): 181–93.

———. "Narratives of Literacy: Connecting Composition to Culture." *College Composition and Communication* 50.3 (1999): 393–410.

———. "Orality." *Encyclopedia of Rhetoric and Composition.* Ed. Theresa Enos. New York: Garland, 1996. 480–484.

Farrell, Thomas J. *Walter Ong's Contributions to Cultural Studies: The Phenomenology of the Word and I–Thou Communication.* Cresskill, NJ: Hampton Press, 1999.

Goody, Jack, and Ian Watt. "The Consequences of Literacy." *Comparative Studies in Society and History* 5.3 (1963): 304–45.

Heath, Shirley Brice. "Protean Shapes: Ever-Shifting Oral and Literate Traditions." *Spoken and Written Language: Exploring Orality and Literacy.* Ed. Deborah Tannen. Norwood, NJ: Ablex, 1982. 91–117.

Killingsworth, Jimmie. "Product and Process, Literacy and Orality: An Essay on Composition and Culture." *College Composition and Communication* 44.1 (1993): 26–39.

Lakers, John Joseph. *Christian Ethics: An Ethics of Intimacy.* Quincy, IL: Franciscan, 1996.

Lazere, Donald. "Orality, Literacy, and Standard English." *Journal of Basic Writing* 10.2 (1991): 87–98.

Ogbu, John U. "Literacy and Schooling in Subordinate Cultures: The Case of Black Americans." *Literacy in Historical Perspectives.* Ed. Daniel Resnick. Washington, DC: Library of Congress, 1983. 129–53.

Olson, David R. "From Utterance to Text: The Bias of Language in Speech and Writing." *Harvard Educational Review* 47.3 (1977): 257–81.

Palmeri, Anthony. "Ramism, Ong, and Modern Rhetoric." *Media, Consciousness, and Culture.* Ed. Bruce Gronbeck, Thomas J. Farrell, and Paul A. Soukup. Newbury Park, CA: Sage, 1991. 50–63.

Sreberny-Mohammadi, Annabelle. "Media Integration in the Third World: An Ongian Look at Irony." *Media, Consciousness, and Culture.* Ed. Bruce Gronbeck, Thomas J. Farrell, and Paul A. Soukup. Newbury Park, CA: Sage, 1991. 133–146.

Sussman, Henry. *High Resolution: Critical Theory and the Problem of Literacy.* New York: Oxford University Press, 1989.

Swearingen, C. Jan. "Discourse, Difference, and Gender: Walter J. Ong's Contributions to Feminist Language Studies." *Media, Consciousness, and Culture.* Ed. Bruce E. Gronbeck, Thomas J. Farrell, and Paul A. Soukup. Newbury Park, CA: Sage, 1991. 210–22.

———, ed. *The Literacy/Orality Wars.* Special Issue. *PRE/TEXT* 7.3–4 (1986): 115–218.

Tannen, Deborah, ed. *Spoken and Written Language: Exploring Orality and Literacy.* Norwood, NJ: Ablex, 1982.

Walters, Keith. "Language, Logic, and Literacy." *The Right to Literacy.* Ed. Andrea A. Lunsford, Helene Moglen, and James F. Slevin. New York: MLA, 1990. 173–88.

Ze, David. "Walter Ong's Paradigm and Chinese Literacy." *Canadian Journal of Communication* 20.4 (1995): 523–40.

CHAÏM PERELMAN
(1912–1984)

Ray D. Dearin

Chaïm Perelman was born on May 20, 1912, in Warsaw, Poland, the son of Abraham and Lea (Garbownik) Perelman. He moved with his family to Belgium in 1925, where he remained, except for several stints abroad as a visiting professor, for the rest of his life. Perelman received a doctorate in law in 1934 and another in philosophy in 1938, both from the Free University of Brussels. He became a professor of logic and metaphysics and dean of the faculty of philosophy and letters at the same institution. After serving as a leader in the Belgian resistance movement during World War II, Perelman became the director of the Center for the Philosophy of Law and the National Center for Logical Research. As a consequence of the renown his attainments had brought to his adopted country, the king of Belgium proclaimed him Baron Perelman in December 1983, shortly before he died suddenly and unexpectedly of a heart attack on January 22, 1984.

The contributions of Chaïm Perelman to modern rhetorical thought emanated directly from an intellectual quest he undertook early in his career. As expressed by Max Loreau, that mission was *"to produce an instrument capable of achieving in the realm of values results exactly analogous to those pursued by analytical reasoning in the domain of the exact sciences"* (Loreau 456). Perelman's first essay, "Esquisse d'une logistique des valeurs" (1931), reflected the assumptions of logical positivism, which stressed the futility of arguing about values. The resolution of various logical paradoxes occupied his attention throughout the 1930s, and in an article entitled "Une conception de la philosophie" (1940), Perelman pointed out certain resemblances between the scientific method and philosophy. "The philosophical method has the same logical structure as that of science," he wrote. "It consists of deducing from certain principles and from certain definitions . . . a set of consequences, and of comparing, as far as possible, these consequences with the facts" (46). Perelman's faith in positivism and science as instruments for creating a "logic of value judgments" was shattered, however, as a result of his investigations during the 1940s, and his quest for a nonformal logic led him to "rediscover" the rhetorical and dialectical writings of the ancient Greeks and Romans and to elaborate the most comprehensive theory of rhetoric as argumentative discourse since Richard Whately published *The Elements of Rhetoric* in 1828.

PERELMAN'S PHILOSOPHICAL ASSUMPTIONS

Four aspects of Perelman's thought are foundational to his philosophical goal and must be explicated before one approaches his theory of rhetoric.

The Nature and Importance of Philosophy

For Perelman, philosophy plays a primary role in the resolution of human problems, one that science can never usurp. In a critique of Auguste Comte's positivism, he wrote:

It cannot be denied that Comte's analysis is correct regarding certain areas of knowledge where scientific answers have completely replaced theological or philosophical concepts. But that is quite another thing from saying that *all* human problems can be solved by calling on the experimental or deductive methods of science alone. The study not of what is but of what ought to be, what has the greater value, what is preferable, and what should determine our choices and our conduct can be abandoned to scientific methods only when we are dealing with purely technical problems. But that is far from being the case. Not only does the solution of our fundamental problems elude science and technology; the very hypothesis that philosophy can be dispensed with is itself a philosophical hypothesis. (*Historical Introduction* 5–6)

Perelman's conception of philosophy differs markedly from the systems of earlier philosophers based on necessary or self-evident theses. Instead of seeking eternal and immutable principles, he believed, philosophy should "elaborate principles of being, thought and action that are humanly *reasonable*" ("On Self Evidence" 5–6). Moreover, philosophy cannot rely upon the methods of formal logic; its goal "is to influence the mind and win its agreement, rather than to perform purely formal transformations of propositions" (*Historical Introduction* 101). From such axioms, Perelman deduced that every metaphysician is forced to rely upon the processes of rhetorical argumentation in order to defend a particular worldview or "propose to humanity objective principles of action that will be valid for the will of all reasonable [persons]" (*Justice* 78).

A Modern Epistemology

Not surprisingly, Perelman's conception of philosophy engendered a distinctive theory of knowledge. The rationalists, positivists, and empiricists all failed to grasp that, unlike physical phenomena, mental phenomena are not susceptible to quantification. Nor could the Cartesian model of an eternal and unchanging reason account for changes in historical and social conditions. Perelman exposed these and other shortcomings in the traditional philosophies as he began his search for a working logic adequate for the needs of the modern world.

While rejecting the classical rationalist idea that certain axioms are self-evident, Perelman nonetheless refused to veer to the opposite extreme embraced by nominalism and accept the view that the selection of fundamental postulates is entirely arbitrary. Instead, he conceived an epistemology in which the dubious distinction between knowledge and opinion is blurred. "I shall grant the status of knowledge," he said, "to a tested opinion, to an opinion, that is, which has survived all objections and criticisms and with regard to which we have a certain confidence, though no certainty, that it will resist all such future attacks" (*Idea of Justice* 117). The effect of Perelman's theory of knowledge, as can be seen, is to highlight the role of *reason* and, by extension, the *techniques of reasoning* that are actually used in human decision making.

The Judicial Model of Reason

From the beginning of his professional life, the study of law animated Perelman, guided his thoughts, supplied conundrums as grist for his intellectual mill, and constituted an alternative career that paralleled his work as a logician, ethicist, and rhetorician. His search for a "logic of value judgments" gained impetus in the early 1940s as a result of his systematic analysis of the core legal concept, *justice*. Seeking to clear away the confusion surrounding the multiplicity of meanings that had become encrusted around the idea of justice throughout history, the Belgian philosopher arrived at "a kind of nucleus of justice, . . . independent of varying usage-associations, and of the ideological implications of such usage" (Stone 302). Perelman found a single, abstract principle running beneath the various systems of concrete justice. "Formal justice," as he called this notion, "consists of *a principle of action in accordance with which beings of one and the same essential category must be treated in the same way*" (*Idea of Justice* 16). Although formal justice is always flouted to some extent by arbitrary elements in all normative systems of justice, this general principle allowed Perelman to broaden the scope of his inquiry beyond the field of ethics to cover the problem of *justification* in general.

Perelman's conception of justification, which is suffused throughout his writings rather than contained within a single book or monograph, is based upon two rhetorical considerations: (1) Justification is a matter of audience adherence, not logical validity; and (2) arguments are not used to justify propositions but behaviors. "If we justify an individual," wrote Perelman, "we either justify his conduct or show that he is not responsible for it, but then we provide an excuse, not a justification" (*The New Rhetoric and the Humanities* 127). One does not justify statements or individuals but their choices, actions, intentions, and decisions.

For a model of the kind of nonformal reasoning he had in mind, Perelman turned to jurisprudence. He believed that the investigation of proofs used in law could, "more than any other study, acquaint us with the relations existing between thought and action" (*Idea of Justice* 108). Courtroom reasoning, as Perelman saw it, closely parallels the kind of everyday decision making one is faced with on a daily basis. Judges are required to render decisions and offer reasons, usually in the absence of standards that would be recognized by the canons of formal logic. Moreover, legal reasoning ordinarily recognizes that presumption favors the status quo, a principle closely allied with the importance of following precedent in human reasoning and conduct. Here Perelman's "formal justice," the idea that beings of the same essential category should be treated alike, comes into play. This principle is generalized by Perelman into a "rule of justice" and plays a key role in his theory of rational argumentation.

An Enlarged View of Rationality

In place of the narrow conception of reason inspired by the Cartesian rationalists and modern mathematical logicians, Chaïm Perelman held the broader, rhetorical view that reason not only discovers truth and error but also justifies and argues. "This broadening of our concept of reason, which no longer limits the rational to the analytical," he said, "opens a new field of study to the investigations of the logicians; it is the field of those reasons which, according to Pascal and according to contemporary logicians, reason does not know" ("How Do We Apply Reason to Values?" 802). A significant effect of this enlarged view of reason is to dissolve the conviction-persuasion dichotomy that has plagued rhetorical theory for centuries. This distinction can perhaps be traced back to the types of reasoning contrasted by Aristotle in his *Topics* and his *Rhetoric*. In any case, philosophers following Descartes have tended to fall into the same error. Pascal opposed will to understanding, insight to geometry, the heart to reason, and persuasion to conviction. Kant opposed faith to science, and Bergson opposed intuition to reason. Perelman believed that these philosophies were based upon the erroneous idea that the human mind is made up of completely separated faculties. The conviction-persuasion opposition, reminiscent of faculty psychology, could not suffice, Perelman believed, "when one leaves the bounds of a strict rationalism and examines the diverse means of obtaining the adherence of minds" ("Logique et rhétorique" 7; translation mine).

By expanding the scope of reason, Perelman sought to provide a rational basis for law, philosophy, ethics, political debate, and other fields of endeavor that could not be considered relevant to the strict, formalistic logic embraced by most twentieth-century philosophers. He believed that only a reason broad enough to manifest itself in all the areas of human activity where justifications have to be made can be a truly practical reason.

PERELMAN'S RHETORICAL THEORY

In his pursuit of a logic capable of dealing with values, Perelman adopted the practice of the nineteenth-century logician Gottlob Frege, who conducted a systematic study of the patterns of reasoning used by mathematicians. To assist him with the exhaustive investigation he had in mind, Perelman selected Mme. Lucie Olbrechts-Tyteca (1899–1988), a woman whose education in literature and sociology complemented his own philosophical and legal training. Starting in the late 1940s, the two researchers undertook a comprehensive survey and analysis of the kinds of arguments actually used by jurists, moralists, politicians, and others who try to "make a rule prevail" in circumstances where neither formal logic nor empirical science can settle the matter.

During the course of their investigations, Perelman and Olbrechts-Tyteca "rediscovered" the rhetorical and dialectical writings of classical antiquity, including Aristotle's *Rhetoric* and *Topics*. From his philosophical perspective, Perelman conceived of rhetoric and dialectic as a unified whole in which dialectic serves as the theoretical basis for argumentation; rhetoric, on the other hand, constitutes a practical discipline that utilizes dialectical techniques in order to convince or to persuade.

Perelman and Olbrechts-Tyteca's decade-long collaboration resulted in several publications, including a collection of essays entitled *Rhétorique et philosophie: Pour une théorie de l'argumentation en philosophie* (1952). Individual studies in this volume focused on the relationships between logic and rhetoric, freedom and responsibility, act and person in argumentation, and other topics of concern to philosophers grappling with the nature of "proof" or the problem of what constitutes the "good choice" in philosophical debates. As the subtitle of the book suggests, these essays were intended merely as preliminary probes, or initial attempts that the authors hoped would lead to a satisfactory theory of philosophical argumentation.

The culmination of the Belgian authors' joint research program came in 1958 when the Presses Universitaires de France published their two-volume treatise, *La nouvelle rhétorique: Traité de l'argumentation*. Translated into English as *The New Rhetoric: A Treatise on Argumentation* (1969), the title showed that Perelman's interest had expanded well beyond the scope of philosophical deliberation; it now embraced the entire field of rhetorical discourse.

Perelman's Conception of Rhetoric

For Perelman, *"rhetoric is the study of the means of argumentation which allow us to obtain and to increase the assent of people to specific theses pre-*

sented to them" ("Proof in Philosophy" 356). In effect, he defined rhetoric as the theory of argumentation and recognized that all argument is a function of the audience to whom it is addressed. The term *audience* embraced readers as well as listeners; all modes of verbal expression that make up the discursive means of argument, whether oral or written, were brought within his theory. The Ciceronian canons of memory and delivery were omitted from consideration, however, resulting in a paradoxical narrowing of the scope of rhetoric from its classical origins.

The scope of the "new rhetoric" was broad enough to encompass an endless variety of audiences. Rhetorical activity occurs in an intimate deliberation with oneself or a single auditor, or when we attempt to persuade others, or even when we reason *in abstracto* and try to convince everybody. The decision to include within the purview of rhetoric all cases where argumentative techniques are used to address audiences is consistent with Perelman's enlarged view of reason and with his refusal to accept the conviction-persuasion duality.

Like the classical writers, Perelman and Olbrechts-Tyteca restricted rhetoric to the domain of the likely, the plausible, the probable (to the degree, that is, that probability escapes mathematical certitude). Unlike a formal demonstration, an argument is neither correct and compulsory nor incorrect and totally without worth but is strong or weak, relevant or irrelevant, depending upon the reasons that justify its usage under the circumstances. In argumentation there are no contradictions, only incompatibilities; one is left with "the obligation of choosing between two beings, two rules, two solutions, two actions" ("De la temporalité" 127; translation mine). Rhetoric and argumentation, in sum, deal only with the contingent and the probable. In Perelman's view, rhetoric differs from logic primarily in that "it is occupied not with hypothetical, categorical, or abstract truth, but with adhesion. Its goal is to produce or increase the adhesion of a definite audience to certain theses, and its point of departure will be the adhesion of this audience to other theses" ("Logique et rhétorique" 14–15). Another difference is that "while in logic one always reasons at the interior of a postulated system, considered as taken for granted, in a rhetorical argument anything can at any time be called into question; one can at any time withdraw his adherence" (21). Operating within a fixed system with predetermined instruments of reasoning, logic is not subject to the temporal influences that beset rhetoric. Further, whereas in logic the reasoning is constraining, according to Perelman and his coauthor, there is no constraint in rhetoric: "Rhetorical argumentation is not constraining because it does not unfold inside a system whose premises and rules of deduction are univocal and fixed in a invariable manner" (21–22).

The contrasts just noted between rhetoric and logic, it must be emphasized, relate only to the modern formalistic sense of the term *logic*. At times, Perelman calls rhetoric itself a "logic"—sometimes, as we have seen, a "logic of value judgments" or a "logic of the preferable." In these instances, rhetoric is asserted to play a methodological role in the structuration of human knowledge analogous to the function performed by logic in the more inclusive sense.

Underlying all of Perelman's rhetorical thought is the idea that rhetoric is a method, not a subject. In a letter to the present author, on May 27, 1969, Perelman wrote that rhetoric presupposes the existence of some matter of substance but has no subject matter of its own. Concerning the conditions necessary for rhetoric, Perelman and Olbrechts-Tyteca held that "rhetoric, as a discipline, presupposes the existence of facts appropriate to it. These are audiences, arguments, and adherences" ("Act and Person in Argument" 252).

Basic Features of the "New Rhetoric"

Perelman and Olbrechts-Tyteca's *New Rhetoric* is comprehensive in scope, tediously analytical in method, and thoroughly eclectic in its choice of source materials. The treatise purports to describe the processes and techniques of non-formal reasoning that can be found in many different situations in daily and professional life (8). The authors seek to analyze the forms that these arguments take and to study minutely the vital principles of argumentation used in a wide variety of settings.

Under the heading "The Framework of Argumentation," Perelman and his colleague discuss the nature and scope of argumentation. Two concepts in this part of the treatise involve significant departures from traditional rhetorical doctrine.

First, the concept of audience, which was central in all the ancient theories of rhetoric, is greatly enlarged. Perelman's concern as a philosopher in search of a logic of value judgments led him to ask which audience a philosopher is trying to reach. The answer could not be that a philosopher is satisfied to persuade a particular audience, whose individual biases and emotional susceptibilities render it inadequate as a standard of rationality. "Whoever develops a philosophical system," he insists, "undertakes to address everyone and to convince everyone," and, "If such a thing as a philosopher's mission exists, it is that he be the advocate of reason and the defender of universal values deemed to be valid for [everyone]" (*Historical Introduction* 99; *Justice* 72). Unlike other rhetors, who are content to persuade particular audiences, a philosopher must seek to convince a *universal audience*.

No aspect of Perelman's philosophical or rhetorical thought has generated as much controversy as has the idea of the universal audience. Philosophers, legal theorists, and rhetorical critics have responded with detailed critiques (see, for example, Johnstone, Natanson, Zaner, Ray. For Perelman's responses, see: "Reply to Henry W. Johnstone, Jr.," "Reply to Mr. Zaner," and "The New Rhetoric and the Rhetoricians"). These critics have objected that the universal audience cannot exist in actuality, and, if it did, no one could convince it of any thesis having real content. Perelman acknowledges that such an audience is a mental conception of the one who appeals to it, a construct of the speaker's imagination, and that the audience varies not only from one conception of it to another but is conditioned also by historical, cultural, and sociological factors. As to the impossibility of convincing everyone, Perelman and Olbrechts-Tyteca recognize that philosophers cannot convince every listener to accept their positions, so they address a universal audience on the grounds that all who accept their reasons must also accept their conclusions. *"The agreement of a universal audience the authors argue, is thus a matter, not of fact, but of right"* (*The New Rhetoric* 31). Viewed from a sociological standpoint, the universal audience becomes the rational conscience of an epoch or civilization (*Rhétorique et philosophie* 120). The study of various conceptions of this audience, suggest Perelman and Olbrechts-Tyteca, would prove useful because they would teach us what people in different periods have considered as *"real, true, and objectively valid"* (*The New Rhetoric* 33). Although the concept of the universal audience is but a relatively minor part of the comprehensive theory of rhetoric espoused by Perelman, its uniqueness and controversiality make it easily the most striking element in his treatment of the framework of argumentation.

Another noteworthy feature of the "new rhetoric" is the treatment given to epideictic oratory. Although this genre of discourse seemed to have more connection to literature than to argumentation in the classical theories, Perelman considered it to be a central part of the art of persuasion. The function of epideictic rhetoric is to intensify the adherence to certain values already held by an audience, thus establishing bases upon which deliberative and forensic orators can rest their appeals (*The New Rhetoric* 51–52).

The Starting Point of Argument

Part Two of *The New Rhetoric* is devoted to an analysis of the starting points or premises that serve as the foundations of arguments. To begin with, persuaders must find "agreements" already acknowledged by an audience upon which to base their arguments; in effect, the adherence of minds is the starting point as well as the end of argumentation. In Perelman's view, "All argumentation depends for its premises—as indeed for its entire development—on that which is accepted, that which is acknowledged as true, as normal and probable, as valid" (*Idea of Justice* 156). Whether the theses granted are derived from common sense (as conceived by the audience) or from a particular scientific, juridical, philosophical, or theological discipline, these arguments must be known and understood if the argumentation is to be efficacious.

Agreements occur at varying levels of generality and are held with variable intensity. Beginning with the most specific, concrete objects of agreement and moving to the most general, abstract ones, Perelman and Olbrechts-Tyteca deal with facts and truths, presumptions, values, hierarchies of values, and *loci*, or "commonplaces." Facts are "objects of precise, limited agreement," whereas truths involve the complicated relationships among facts (*The New Rhetoric* 68–69). Presumptions enjoy universal agreement, but adherence to these presumptions is not absolute, and audiences expect their adherence to be strengthened at key points by other strategies (70). For example, the idea that the quality of an act reveals the quality of the person responsible for it is a widespread presumption, but it may require additional support when adduced in a specific case. Values, defined as "objects of agreement which do not claim the adherence of the universal audience," range from abstract concepts such as the *True*, the *Good*, and the *Beautiful* to concrete values "attaching to a living being, a specific group, or a particular object" (75–76).

Loci, or "commonplaces," which Perelman associates with "common values, common notions, and common rules of conduct, borrowed from common language," are the most general starting points of argument. Perelman and Olbrechts-Tyteca do not provide an exhaustive list of *loci*. They simply classify them under a few general headings: *loci* of quantity, quality, order, the existing, essence, and the person. These categories, they believe, are of utmost importance in actual argumentation. *Loci* are not preconstructed arguments to be inserted at will but are premises of a general nature that serve as foundations for values and hierarchies. As such, these elements serve as a necessary source of persuasion that one has no choice but to use (84).

The agreements held by the audience cannot function as starting points for argumentation until they are chosen and adapted for the purposes of the speaker. Some latent agreements may remain unexploited by the arguer, whereas others are magnified in importance simply by being invoked. The act of selecting some elements and applying them in an argument, Perelman and Olbrechts-Tyteca claim, makes them important. Using these elements gives them "presence," a central factor in argument that is often ignored in highly rational systems (116). Although Cicero and other rhetoricians had advanced similar ideas, *presence* is clearly a psychological datum in Perelman's theory, and his treatment of this concept is clearly influenced by modern psychologists such as Jean Piaget and Jean Paulhan.

Besides the selection of data, the persuader is faced with another problem, that of interpretation. For insights into linguistic interpretation, Perelman and Olbrechts-Tyteca draw upon the work of I. A. Richards. However, instead of looking upon rhetoric as a "study of misunderstanding and its remedies," as Richards did in *The Philosophy of Rhetoric*, the Belgian authors rule out the idea that clarity or univocity is a goal for all language functions: "Language is not only a means of communication: it is also an instrument for acting on minds, a means of persuasion" (132). The ambiguity of language contributes to a certain plasticity of ideas that often serves the purpose of argument.

In addition to the starting points that concern the selection and adaptation of argumentative data, Perelman and Olbrechts-Tyteca discuss others relating to the presentation of data and form of the discourse. They devote a separate chapter of their treatise to devices such as verbal forms, modalities in the expression of thought, and rhetorical figures of speech. All these elements are treated only in terms of their implications for argumentation.

Techniques of Argumentation

The bulk of *The New Rhetoric* is devoted to a systematic analysis of the schemes of argumentation that are actually used in nonformal reasoning. For specimens of such arguments, Perelman and Olbrechts-Tyteca turn to novels, academic articles, speeches, philosophical tracts, and other sources, including humor magazines. They classify the argumentative processes they discover into two broad categories: structures involving either the *association* or *dissociation* of ideas. Since Perelman maintained that psychological theories as such fall outside the realm of rhetoric, it should be emphasized that the "associationism" of John Locke, David Hartley, Joseph Priestley, and John Stuart Mill had no bearing on his thinking at this point. He simply appropriated the term "association" as a convenient instrument for explaining how certain structures of argument can be related to other structures in order to bring about an adherence of minds.

According to Perelman and Olbrechts-Tyteca, the schemes of association are three: (1) "quasi-logical" arguments; (2) arguments based on the structure of reality; and (3) arguments that aim at *establishing* the structure of the real.

Quasi-logical arguments convince a listener because they share a similarity with "formal reasoning of logic or mathematics." But these arguments are not formal in character: Submitting them to analysis shows right away that they differ from "formal demonstrations, for only an effort of reduction makes it possible for these arguments to appear demonstrative" (193). Some quasi-logical arguments depend on logical relations—contradiction, total or partial identity, and transitivity; others depend on mathematical relations—the connection between the part and the whole, the smaller and the larger, and frequency. In Perelman's way of conceiving the distinctions between logic and rhetoric, the terms *enthymeme* and *epicheirema* used by the ancient rhetoricians "correspond roughly to quasi-logical arguments presented in syllogistic form" (230).

To clarify Perelman's thinking about quasi-logical arguments, a simple example of reasoning drawn from Aristotle should suffice: "All men do wrong from one of three motives: *A, B,* or *C*; in my case *A* and *B* are out of the question, and even the accusers do not allege *C*" (234). Based upon the mathematical relation that the whole is the sum of its parts, this argument is not purely formal; it requires a knowledge of the actual relations that the parts have with the particular case being considered. The argument is quasi-logical because one's interlocutor might fail to agree that all the possible motives for wrongdoing have been exhausted. When such an argument is not by itself convincing, other forms of argumentation besides quasi-logical ones must be used.

A second category of associative techniques includes arguments that make use of the structure of reality "to establish a solidarity between accepted judgments and others which one wishes to promote" (261). The links between the accepted judgments and those desired by the persuader will be established by invoking either sequential relations or relations of coexistence. Arguments based on sequential relations correspond closely to the area of traditional logic termed "causal reasoning." As a case in point, consider the argument of "direction" that warns against pursuing a certain course of action indefinitely. This kind of argument prevents the application of "the device of stages." If a person gives in once, the argument goes, he will have to give in again, and who knows when the process will conclude? This strategy often appears in labor and diplomatic negotiations (282). In this argument the structure of reality is pictured as a series of stages leading to a disastrous end. Moreover, the argument assumes a point of no return, after which the end becomes inevitable. The argument thus achieves its effect, but only if one's interlocutor assents to this view of reality.

A type of argumentation based on relations of coexistence presumes that definite relationships exist between an act and the person who acts. Perelman and Olbrechts-Tyteca explain that a person appears to be a stable entity that provides coherence to the qualities, acts, and judgments associated with him (295). In a lengthy essay analyzing these relationships, Perelman and his colleague write:

[T]he stability of the person is never completely assured, though certain linguistic techniques help to emphasize the impression of stability. The use of proper names allows the continuity of the person to be presumed; other ways of speaking manifest a permanent trait of the person. Thus the insertion of a typical category ("your stingy father"), the use of an epithet ("Charlemagne of the flowery beard") or the hypostasis ("his generosity has contributed . . .")—each of these reinforces the impression of the stability of the whole person by emphasizing a characteristic of the person which is regarded as permanent. ("Act and Person in Argument" 254)

These examples illustrate the argumentative role of figures of speech. Far from being mere verbal adornment, such devices bring about the adherence of minds by limiting the attention to a presumed characteristic of the person.

The last associative devices discussed in *The New Rhetoric*, techniques designed to *establish* the structure of reality, correspond to what has traditionally been called inductive and analogical reasoning. Arguments utilizing examples, illustrations, and models that seek to construct a notion of reality in the minds of an audience are treated rather perfunctorily. Because of its primary place in argumentation, however, Perelman and Olbrechts-Tyteca treat analogy more fully as an element of proof, as "a resemblance of structures, the most general formulation of which is: A is to B as C is to D" (372). To explicate the argumentative processes at work, the authors take a typical analogy used by Aristotle: "For as the eyes of bats are to the blaze of day, so is the reason in our soul to the things which are by nature most evident of all." This argument is then elucidated:

A and B together, the terms of which the conclusion relates (reason in the soul, obviousness) we shall call the *theme*, and C and D together, the terms that buttress the argument (eyes of bats, blaze of day), we shall call the *phoros*: . . .

For an analogy to exist, it is also necessary that the theme and the phoros belong to different spheres. When the two relations encountered belong to the same sphere, and can be subsumed under a common structure, we have not analogy but argument by example or illustration, in which the theme and the phoros represent two particular cases of a single rule. (373)

Analogy is not simply a mathematical proportion. The value of the terms of the theme is enhanced or depreciated as a result of the interaction that occurs when *A* and *C* and *B* and *D* are brought closer together. Moreover, the action is sometimes in the opposite direction as the terms of the phoros undergo a change in value. Because they develop and extend thought, analogies are vital in argumentation as devices that establish the structure of reality. Likewise, metaphor, "a condensed analogy, resulting from the fusion of an element from the phoros with an element from the theme," is not simply a technique of embellishment—it is an inventional technique of considerable importance in Perelman's theory.

Besides employing associative schemes, arguers sometimes seek to separate elements that have been thought to be connected or interdependent. This process, called the "dissociation of concepts" by Perelman and Olbrechts-Tyteca, results in a restructuring of the elements themselves. The prototype of all conceptual dissociation is the "appearance-reality" dichotomy used widely in philosophical discussion (415). Other "philosophical pairs" resulting from a series of dissociations include dualities such as "means/end," "act/person," "accident/essence," "relative/absolute," "theory/practice," "letter/spirit," and so forth. In each case, a particular philosophical doctrine specifies a criterion of value (the second term) and asserts that the other idea (the first term) fails to satisfy the established criterion.

Philosophical pairs are not merely rejected links of association but represent an attempt to fashion (or refashion) the reality recognized by an interlocutor, their ultimate aim being to secure his or her adherence to a proposed thesis. Other techniques, such as certain kinds of definitions, are also means of dissociation. For example, a definition is dissociative "whenever it claims to furnish the real, true meaning of the concept as opposed to its customary or apparent usage" (444).

Since all the techniques of argumentation, whether associative or dissociative, are conditioned by factors such as their order and relative emphasis, Perelman and Olbrechts-Tyteca devote a final chapter to the interaction of arguments. They recognize that certain techniques seem to lend weight to the argumentation. For instance, figures of speech such as *insinuation, reticence,* and *litotes* are "techniques of restraint" that strengthen the effect of arguments by presenting the speaker as a moderate person of sincerity and balanced judgment (467). As to the most effective ordering of arguments, the proponents of the new rhetoric emphasize the placement of argumentative elements in terms of the audience's adherence to them, the necessity for using the introduction as a device for conditioning the audience, and the strategic sequencing of the arguments so as to maximize their psychological impact. In brief, the treatment of the interaction of arguments, like the discussion of the techniques of association and dissociation, is designed to elaborate a consistent point of view about rhetoric as the study of efficacious argument.

PERELMAN'S THEORY IN PERSPECTIVE

Chaïm Perelman never intended to make original contributions to rhetorical theory. In a highly revealing essay, published five years after the appearance of *The New Rhetoric*, Olbrechts-Tyteca explained that, for her and Perelman, rhetoric was "neither by profession nor by taste" dear to them. She confessed that at the beginning of their investigation they were "about as ignorant of rhetoric as an honest man can be in the twentieth century" ("Rencontre" 3; translation mine). It was almost by accident, she went on to say, that they encountered rhetoric.

Perelman can best be located in modern rhetorical thought by reference to his philosophical goals and training as a logician. It is significant that the two principal theorists who inspired Perelman—Aristotle and Whately—both developed logics as well as rhetorics ("Rencontre" 9). Perelman's concept of argumentation, however, bears only a superficial resemblance to Whately's. Perelman's disregard of the subject of delivery, his integration of epideictic discourse (so distasteful to Whately) into argumentation, and his association of rhetoric with the philosophical problem of gaining adherence all indicate that the Belgian logician desired mainly to understand the workings of arguments, whereas the English archbishop had the practical problems of speakers in mind.

In 1977 Perelman published a condensed version of the treatise on argumentation under the title *L'Empire rhétorique: Rhétorique et argumentation*, which was translated into English as *The Realm of Rhetoric* (1982). His ideas on rhetoric can also be found scattered throughout more than 20 books and 300 articles that he wrote on philosophy, logic, sociology, and law. As one of the leading apostles of a new rhetoric, Perelman wielded enormous influence over the field of rhetorical studies during the last half of the twentieth century. His reactions to the reception of his ideas by rhetorical scholars appear in his own words in "The New Rhetoric and the Rhetoricians: Remembrances and Comments," a posthumously published essay in the *Quarterly Journal of Speech*.

BIBLIOGRAPHY

Primary Sources

Perelman, Chaïm. "Une conception de la philosophie." *Revue de l'institut de Sociologie* 20.1 (1940): 39–50.

———. "Esquisse d'une logistique des valeurs." *Revue de l'Université de Bruxelles* (1931): 486–96.

———. *An Historical Introduction to Philosophical Thinking*. Trans. Kenneth A. Brown. New York: Random, 1965.

302 Twentieth-Century Rhetorics and Rhetoricians

———. "How Do We Apply Reason to Values?" *Journal of Philosophy* 52.26 (1955): 797–802.

———. *The Idea of Justice and the Problem of Argument.* Trans. John Petrie. London: Routledge and Kegan Paul, 1963.

———. *Justice.* New York: Random, 1967.

———. *The New Rhetoric and the Humanities.* Dordrecht: D. Reidel, 1979.

———. "The New Rhetoric and the Rhetoricians: Remembrances and Comments." Trans. Ray D. Dearin. *Quarterly Journal of Speech* 702 (1984): 188–96.

———. "On Self-Evidence in Metaphysics." *International Philosophical Quarterly* 4.1 (1964): 5–19.

———. Personal letter to Ray D. Dearin. May 27, 1969.

———. "Proof in Philosophy." *Hibbert Journal* 52 (1953–54): 354–59.

———. *The Realm of Rhetoric.* Notre Dame, IN: University of Notre Dame Press, 1982.

———. "Reply to Henry W. Johnstone, Jr." *Philosophy and Phenomenological Research* 16.2 (1955): 245–47.

———. "Reply to Mr. Zaner." *Philosophy and Rhetoric* 1.3 (1968): 168–70.

Perelman, Ch., and L. Olbrechts-Tyteca. "Act and Person in Argument." *Ethics* 61 (1951): 251–69.

———. "De la temporalité comme caractère de l'argumentation." *Il Tempo: Archivio di Filosofia* (1958): 115–33.

———. "Logique et rhétorique." *Revue philosophique* 140.1 (1950): 1–35.

———. *The New Rhetoric: A Treatise on Argumentation.* Trans. John Wilkinson and Purcell Weaver. Notre Dame, IN: University of Notre Dame Press, 1969.

———. *Rhétorique et philosophie: Pour une théorie de l'argumentation en philosophie.* Paris: Universitaires de France, 1952.

Biography

Dearin, Ray D. "Chaïm Perelman." *Encyclopedia of Rhetoric and Composition.* Ed. Theresa Enos. New York: Garland, 1996. 501–502.

Frank, David A. "The New Rhetoric, Judaism, and Post-enlightenment Thought: The Cultural Origins of Perelmanian Philosophy." *Quarterly Journal of Speech* 83.3 (1997): 311–42.

Criticism

Dearin, Ray D. *The New Rhetoric of Chaïm Perelman: Statement and Response.* Lanham, MD: University Press of America, 1989.

Johnstone, Henry W, Jr. *Philosophy and Argument.* University Park: Pennsylvania State University Press, 1959.

Loreau, Max. "Rhetoric as the Logic of the Behavioral Sciences." Trans. Lloyd I. Watkins and Paul D. Brandes. *Quarterly Journal of Speech* 51.4 (1965): 455–63.

Natanson, Maurice. "Rhetoric and Philosophical Argumentation." *Quarterly Journal of Speech* 48.1 (1962): 24–30.

Olbrechts-Tyteca, L. "Rencontre avec la rhétorique." *Logique et analyse* 6.1 (1963): 3–18.

Ray, John W. "Perelman's Universal Audience." *Quarterly Journal of Speech* 64.4
      (1978): 361–75.
Richards, I. A. *The Philosophy of Rhetoric*. New York: Oxford University Press, 1936.
Stone, Julius. *Human Law and Human Justice*. Stanford, CA: Stanford University Press,
      1965.
Zaner, Richard M. "Philosophy and Rhetoric: A Critical Discussion." *Philosophy and
      Rhetoric* 1.2 (1968): 61–77.

I. A. RICHARDS
(1893–1979)

Stephen H. Browne

Few thinkers in our century have left their imprint so visibly on the scenes of literary and rhetorical criticism as Ivor Armstrong Richards. A thinker of eclectic interests, an educator of unusual range and ambition, and an author of works in critical theory, applied criticism, pedagogy, poetry, and drama, Richards remains at once a highly influential and yet clusive figure in the history of British and American letters. Widely considered the "father" of American New Criticism, Richards brought to the study of literary texts a combination of insights from psychology, philosophy, and linguistics; together, these modes of inquiry in turn fashioned a type of analysis that was to reign without competition for nearly half a century. Richards's attempt to reconceive rhetoric as the "study of mis-understanding and its remedies" was an extension of his more general program for reforming literary analysis. This reconception is most fully presented in *The Philosophy of Rhetoric*. A collection of lectures published in 1936, Richards's brief volume marks an important early contribution to the "New Rhetoric."

The virtues of Richards's approach to the analysis of literature and rhetoric in his time may well account for his obscurity in our own. Reacting against the historicism of late nineteenth- and early twentieth-century literary study, he sought to refocus the text as an object worthy of systematic and rigorous inter-pretation; dismayed by the state of undergraduate learning, he sought to delineate good criticism from bad; frustrated by a rhetorical tradition that seemed unable to get beyond broad and superficial rules, he sought to accord the subject a seriousness of mission heretofore unrealized. Late twentieth-century criticism, for good or ill, has defined itself against many of the assumptions and practices at work in Richards's thought; still, his insistence that rhetoric serve purposes beyond teaching the young how to score debating points remains a position ignored only at peril to rhetoric's growth and vitality.

The following survey of Richards's career locates his work on rhetoric within the contours of his critical project generally. Although *The Philosophy of Rhetoric* may profitably be read on its own terms, the treatise is best understood, to use one of Richards's foundational terms, in context. To this end, I will briefly summarize relevant features of the author's life; identify important influences at work in the conception and delivery of his ideas; examine key concepts as they are developed in the central works of the 1920s; treat in greater detail the six essays making up *The Philosophy of Rhetoric*; and conclude with observations on Richards's legacy as it bears on current rhetorical theory and criticism.

The ecumenical range of Richards's thought became evident early in his personal development. Son to a Welsh engineer, Ivor was born in Sandbach, England, on February 26, 1893. Tuberculosis kept him out of World War I and prompted a lifelong enthusiasm for mountain climbing, a sport that, however unlikely, seems to have animated his poetical imagination as well as his lungs. In 1915 Richards graduated in "moral sciences" from Magdalen College, Cambridge, and undertook premedical studies. That path proved a short one, and after a year he returned to Cambridge to lecture in its new English School. By the late 1920s, he had established himself both as a critic of international reputation and as a lecturer of extraordinary popularity. After a year lecturing at Tsing Hua University (Peking), Richards paid his first visit to Harvard; a Rockefeller grant kept him there from 1939 to 1944; and permanent appointment as professor of English cemented his relations to the university until his retirement in 1963. With most of his interests in critical theory well behind him, Richards spent his remaining years very active in writing poetry and drama and in promoting his longtime project for an international "Basic English."

To have come of age on both sides of the Great War was to have reckoned with more than the usual challenges of early adulthood; to have done so in England, as a precocious student of both the sciences and the arts, is to have engaged a world of unprecedented change and moral urgency. The academic climate of the period, no less than that of the political, was at once formidable and stimulating, and it lent to Richards's development its peculiar blend of uninhibited intellectualism and anxiety over the loss of cultural standards. Both these traits show themselves unmistakably in Richards's work, especially during the 1920s. In this, his period of greatest success as a critic and theorist of the language arts, we find a thinker at the very top of his craft, didactic, self-confident, straining for effect and usually producing it. There is, in short, a conspicuous rhetoric to Richards's writing, and that is no small part of his legacy. He was among the most vocal of those insisting that the idea and its expression could not be separated; it is appropriate here, then, to take him at his word and identify the theoretical forces giving shape, color, and purpose to his writing.

Eclectic as Richards certainly was, we can still characterize an essential dimension of his thought, and that was, above all, a will to clarify. Readers then and now have found in this no little irony, given the sometimes exasperating quality of his prose. But the intention itself was never anything less than sincere, and in it we can trace intellectual affinities and influences directly to several sources. At the forefront of those to whom Richards was most indebted was his mentor, the renowned Cambridge realist G. E. Moore. From Moore the student learned if not the full range of subtleties for which that philosopher is justly known then the habitual impatience with thinkers-in-the-large, the romantics, the aestheticists, the older rhetoricians who seemed incapable of attending to the elemental properties and functions of language. For Richards as for Moore, the prize of knowledge was to be glimpsed not through the telescope but the microscope. First analysis, then synthesis: Anything else, Richards would come to argue, was at best foolishness, at worst a barrier to the ultimate betterment and liberation of humankind.

Richards's degree in the "moral sciences" is nicely suggestive of another prominent strain in his work. He never purported to be a "scientist," of course, but he was deeply impressed by work first in psychology and then in linguistics. Fusing the two fledgling disciplines, Richards found that he could productively integrate accounts of mental function with the functions of language as such; the result was something like a science of criticism with a moralistic twist. At a rather early date he was pointing to domains of inquiry, among them psycholinguistics and cognitive rhetoric, that would bear rich fruit several decades later. In practical terms, this emphasis on the relationship between the structure of language and mind, and of both to the world, allowed Richards to develop an approach to interpretation that was, if not entirely unique, distinctive and so forcefully expressed as to shape generations of literary critics.

Richards's thought was, through and through, instrumentalist. This perspective is manifested in a variety of ways in all of the theoretical and critical writings; most prominently, it is evident in his abiding emphasis on the several functions of language and in the detection and correction of errors in language use. In 1923, Richards published with C. K. Ogden *The Meaning of Meaning*, a work of extraordinary range and influence. In it, the authors display with great ingenuity how such a view can shape our understanding of language and its uses. Among the principles advanced in *The Meaning of Meaning* that will continue to undergird Richards's later work are *context*, the "Triangle of Interpretation," and the uses of language as either "referential" or "emotive." As we shall see below in reviewing *The Philosophy of Rhetoric*, context is taken to be the governing term for the analysis of meaning; all words, the authors argue, take on their function and hence their meaning by virtue of the context of their usage. The point may seem obvious to us now, but at the time Richards and Ogden saw themselves battling a centuries-old habit of mistaking the word for the thing and of assuming that words contain one and only one proper meaning. By way of illustrating their argument, the authors propose a triangulated diagram, the corners of which designate the (1) symbol, or word whose task it is to signify; (2) reference, or the cluster of mental images, feelings, ideas, and experiences invoked by the symbol; and (3) referent, or object and events in the world to which this reference points. The key to understanding the triangle rests in the relational dynamics that obtain between and among each of the terms. Above all, the interpretation of any given symbol or word is to be understood as determined by its context and by the uses to which it is being put. These functions may be delineated further as referential (object or fact in the world); emotive; relative to one's audience; relative to subject; and intentional.

The Meaning of Meaning continued to makes its influence felt in Richards's ensuing projects, notably *Principles of Literary Criticism* (1924), *Practical Criticism* (1929), and *The Philosophy of Rhetoric* (1936). In addition to elaborating upon the several functions of language and the preeminence of value to the production and interpretation of literature, the former is important to students of rhetoric for its definition of communication. In view of Richards's effort more than a decade later to reconceive the study of rhetoric as a study in misunderstanding and its causes, the position taken here is highly suggestive. We should start with the premise, Richards remarks, that humans are by nature separated: "Their experience at the best, under the most favourable circumstances, can be but similar. Communication, we shall say, takes place when one mind so acts upon its environment that another mind is influenced, and in that other mind an experience occurs which is like the experience in the first mind, and is caused in part by that experience" (*Meaning* 177). *Practical Criticism*, considered by many to be among his best and most influential works, details and comments upon his famous experiment with Cambridge undergraduates. Asked to read and interpret a set of poems without benefit of contextual information, students unwittingly provided their teacher with a rich storehouse of examples of (mostly bad) critical habits. Again, this imaginative, often cranky and frequently witty study in the pitfalls of interpretation is made finally to underscore a theme that will carry itself directly into *The Philosophy of Rhetoric*. "We must make ourselves more aware of how the language we so much depend upon works," Richards concludes. The confusions so dramatically illustrated in the experiment were based in approaches to poetical writing, he reasons, "but prose, the prose of discussion, reflection and research, the prose by which we try to grapple intellectually with a too bewildering world, suffers quite as much from other confusions" (319).

In 1936 Richards traveled to Bryn Mawr College on an invitation to deliver the year's Mary Flexnor Lectures. He chose as his subject what must have seemed the unpromising topic of rhetoric, by his own reasoning "the dreariest and least profitable part of the waste that the unfortunate travel through in Freshman English!" (3). The claim was hyperbolic, of course, a rhetorical move designed specifically to announce the speaker's intentions to recover gold from dross. That rhetoric as a discipline had in fact sunk so low "that we would do better just to dismiss it to Limbo than to trouble ourselves with it" (3) is of course arguable. He was apparently unaware, for example, that a young but robust academic organization, now called the National Communication Association, had been formed a decade previously in a breakaway from English departments for the purposes of revitalizing the subject as an object of serious research. On the scene, too, was a critic by the name of Kenneth Burke, who was to revolutionize rhetorical studies in ways that Richards could not have predicted.

In any case, from his perspective rhetoric was sorely in need of a complete overhaul, and he aimed to undertake such a task. The result was a singular reconception of the art and its first principles, unlike anything imagined before and startling in its implications. The collected essays, published a year later under the title *The Philosophy of Rhetoric*, thus represent a major development in twentieth-century efforts to rethink the function and scope of rhetoric.

However distinctive Richards's offering may seem now, the basic argument is almost entirely subsumable under the aegis of his work in the 1920s. In its general outline, the "philosophy" adheres closely to principles laid out in the major texts noted above. In particular, we find in its 138 pages the familiar tones of lament and rally, the out-with-the-old, in-with-the-new rhetoric that so flavors virtually all his work. There is, in addition, the overriding concern to reformulate the study of language from the ground up, to look "microscopically" at the base units of language and to examine the interaction between words as producers of meaning. The central and controlling principle is context, the importance of which is illustrated not through its novelty but through its utility in explaining the rhetorical function of words. *The Philosophy of Rhetoric* is thus an elaboration of its author's thinking and not a departure from it; in its treatment of metaphor, however, the work offered up a lasting and influential account of how words "interinanimate" each other to create meaning. Each of these several components to what Richards called his "context theorem of meaning" will be examined in turn.

For Richards, the prospects for a "New Rhetoric" entailed displacing the Old. It was to be founded on principles definitively *other* than those associated with a 2,000-year-old tradition of theorizing the art. A substantial part of his first lecture is thus devoted to a highly stylized but devastating critique of rhetorical lore, the chief fault of which was its tendency always to "stir the fire from the top" (6). By this Richards meant to criticize a way of approaching rhetoric, epitomized by the eighteenth-century rhetorician and logician Richard Whately, as a set of prudential rules, devolving finally into "the usual post-card's worth of crude common sense" (8). The reason for this, Richards argues, has everything to do with how rhetoric was ultimately conceived: not, as he would have it, as "a discipline aiming at mastery of the fundamental laws of language" but merely as "a set of dodges that will be found to work sometimes" (7). By failing to attend to the dynamics of language itself, "microscopically," according to Richards, rhetoricians remanded themselves to such a level of generality as to reduce their subject to largely useless, always superficial, prescriptions for the invention, disposition, and delivery of arguments.

The critique is not without merit. At least as it was frequently taught in the classroom, rhetoric had by Richards's time been reduced to such an exercise in the obvious. That the rhetorical tradition as it was handed down from antiquity was the source of the problem is less clear. Certainly Richards may be faulted for misconstruing his own rhetorical purposes, a body of theory that in fact had much of value to say about civic affairs and democratic polity. In part this oversight is owing to Richards's own distaste for disputation—at least among others—and in part to an authentic grievance against those who would diminish the prospects of rhetoric by relegating it to the orator's platform alone. He did not, however, wish to define rhetoric out of existence: On the contrary, he sought to reframe the study of rhetoric in such a way as to make it an effective instrument for the diagnosis and remedy of faulty communication.

Why rhetoric should be thus seized upon as especially suited to this end is an important question, and in answering it, Richards advances toward the positive phase of his argument. The reason is that rhetoric, of all modes of analysis, is predicated on the assumption that ideas cannot be separated from words; together, the thought and its expression provide a basis on which questions of meaning may be most productively analyzed. And it is this problem, *how meaning is created and how it ought to be interpreted*, that grounds Richards's attempt to reformulate the study of rhetoric. In order to get at a set of answers worth considering, the student of rhetoric must therefore eschew such generalities as trafficked in by most theorists and enter into the very vitals of language itself. Here, at the level of words and their interplay, may be discovered the real generating principles of meaning, communication, hence of understanding and of misunderstanding. The remainder of *The Philosophy of Rhetoric* takes us to this level and insists that we remain just there.

But the way, Richards will contend, is not clear. Among the multiple barriers posed by the Old Rhetoric is its conviction not only that words contain meaning but that each word embodies within itself only one proper meaning. As long as this presumption holds, the analysis can go no further because it must deflect attention from the most important, most fundamental question of all: how context, not the word itself, determines meaning. This "Proper Meaning Superstition," as Richard dubs it, in effect "forgets (as it frequently does) that the stability of the meaning of a word comes from the constancy of the contexts that give it its meaning" (11). In various ways throughout his lectures, Richards will assail this "Superstition" as a fundamental cause of misunderstanding, miscommunication, and much that he finds unsavory about dispute. Indeed, the preoccupation of the Old Rhetoric with "the battle of words" (24) might be owing to just this error: It purports to be an art of disputation, the cause of which was in part the result of its own misguided conception of how meaning was created. Along the way toward dismantling such "superstitions," Richards himself will need to battle several competing theories, including associationist and other eighteenth-century epistemologies. As these barriers are systematically eliminated, he will arrive always at his favored principle, the "context theorem of meaning," the chief value of which is to "prevent our making hundreds of baseless and disabling assumptions that we commonly make about meanings, over-simplifications that create false problems interfering with closer comparisons—and that," Richards concludes, is the theory's "main service" (38).

What, then, is the nature of this "context"? What does it *mean*? More accurately, what does it *do*? For the answer, we must remind ourselves of Richards's general aim, that is, to so grasp the dynamics of meaning as to grasp how and thus why people come to understanding. And to this end we must take the line of inquiry all the way back to its source in human nature itself. Thus another question: What, ultimately, is the relationship between mind and world? Humans, Richards notes, are of all other animals most responsive to such stimuli as the world generates. The character, pattern, and range of response are not arbitrary but governed, which is to say determined by contexts. Contexts shape responses by allowing our perceptive capacities to sort out from among an indefinite number of stimuli those that are relevant and related; these sorted perceptions, the result of the mind's ability to move from the abstract to the particular, are the basis of meaning.

The point to be drawn from all this is in fact a fairly simple one, at least for readers on the other end of the twentieth century. Words do not obtain their meaning in isolation, nor can they be said to own a meaning, proper or otherwise. Meaning is relative to the context of its usage; and thus as contexts change, so will meaning. Any accurate account of meaning will accordingly be an account of the contexts in which the word was used. Bearing this in mind, the critic, indeed all users of language systems, can avoid the innumerable pitfalls always confronting those who hang on the one word, one meaning fallacy. As is typical of Richards's thinking generally, the context theory of meaning he proposes winds up in a set of didactic and diagnostic prescriptions. For Richards, to understand the basic functions of language is to avoid its misuse and misinterpretation.

Unquestionably the most influential discussion in *The Philosophy of Rhetoric*, as we noted above, bears on the source and function of metaphor. For students of rhetoric, Richards's treatment of the subject has been of particular interest, and it continues to be widely cited as among the most important, if frequently challenged, accounts in the twentieth century. But if Richards's theory of metaphor may be considered independently, and it usually is, we are reminded that it is fully explicable only when integrated into the analysis represented above. The most explicit linkage to the "context theorem of meaning" comes in the form of a principle nearly as familiar and referred to by Richards as the "interinanimation of words." It may be explained by taking as a given context the unit of the sentence. The theorem holds, again, that words take on their meaning by virtue of the context that delegates them as efficacious representations. Now, as sentences are composed of other words, the meaning of any one will be the function of its interaction with others in it. That one word will be conditioned by its specific relation to the sense, feeling, tone, and other functions imparted by the sentence taken as a whole. Taken together, they are "the resultants which we arrive at only through the interplay of the interpretive possibilities of the whole utterance" (55). This process holds as well for words only implied but not stated, background meanings latent in the contextual elements being represented. Through their "interinanimation," their breathing of life into each other, words come to *mean*.

In Richards's formulation, metaphor is exemplary of this very process. That is, metaphor rightly understood: The ancients and their followers erred in this regard as they had in others, especially as they assumed such tropes to be merely dressing on the body of sense. For Richards, conversely, metaphor is nothing less that "the omnipresent principle of language" (92), indeed constitutive of thought itself. Put simply, explains Richards, "when we use metaphor we have two thoughts of different things active together and supported by a single word, or phrase, whose meaning is a resultant of their interaction." Metaphor, like all words, achieves its meaning by effecting "a transaction between contexts" (94). The Old Rhetoric, encumbered as it was by its macroscopic habits, had been unable to arrive at a level of specificity required for the analysis of metaphor; it could only think in terms of one word, one idea, onto which a figure was imposed for stylistic effect. In this conception, neither the one nor the other really changed in meaning; they merely coinhabited the same semantic space. As a corrective, Richards proposes that we think rather in terms of "tenor," by which he designates "the underlying idea or principle subject" (97), and "vehicle," by which he designates the figure with which the tenor cooperates to create meaning. A third term, "ground," refers then to what it is that the two words, however disparate, may be said to have in common. Understood in this sense, "the copresence of the vehicle and tenor results in a meaning (to be clearly distinguished from the tenor) which is not attainable without their interaction." Similarly, Richards insists, "the vehicle is not normally a mere embellishment of a tenor which is otherwise unchanged by it but . . . a vehicle and tenor in cooperation give a meaning of more varied powers than can be ascribed to either" (100).

It is perhaps a measure of the distance between Richards's milieu and ours that a conception of metaphor so untroubling as this would then be promoted as a radical departure from traditional views of the subject. Then, too, we might register that fact as evidence of how successful Richards was in reimagining the very logics of inquiry against which he struggled and, in some cases, prevailed. Either way, we have in Richards a unique and provocative voice of reform in twentieth-century thinking about the theory, practice, and analysis of rhetoric. Much that he exemplified has since passed from our interest, favor, and recognition: The historicism that he so adamantly repudiated has returned in a different guise to occupy a great deal of critical work in our time; his relentless pursuit of meaning-in-the-text, with all its attendant protocols and principles of discrimination for protecting against inappropriate readings, must seem authoritarian. But in addition to his lasting contributions to the theory of metaphor,

Richards ought to command our attention for what he thought the study of rhetoric was ultimately capable of. In the end, he confided to his Bryn Mawr audience, he hoped that

a patient persistence with the problems of Rhetoric may, while exposing the causes and modes of the misinterpretation of words, also throw light upon and suggest a remedial discipline for deeper and more grevious disorders; that, as the small and local errors in our everyday misunderstandings with language are models in miniature of the greater errors which disturb the development of our personalities, their study may also show us more about how these large scale disasters may be avoided. (136–37)

The New Rhetoric, for Richards at least, had found a context of its own.

BIBLIOGRAPHY

Primary Sources

Richards, I. A. *Interpretation in Teaching*. New York: Harcourt, Brace, 1938.
———. *Mencius on the Mind: Experiments in Multiple Definition*. London: Kegan Paul, Trench, Trubner, 1932.
———. *The Philosophy of Rhetoric*. 1936. New York: Oxford University Press, 1965.
———. *Poetries and Sciences*. London: Routledge and Kegan Paul, 1970.
———. *Practical Criticism*. 1929. New York: Harcourt, Brace & World, 1956.
———. *Principles of Literary Criticism*. 1924. New York: Harcourt, Brace, 1956
Richards, I. A., and C. K. Ogden. *The Meaning of Meaning: A Study of the Influence of Language upon Thought and of the Science of Symbolism*. London: Routledge, Kegan Paul, Trench, Trubner, 1923.

Biography

Russo, John Paul. *I. A. Richards: His Life and Work*. Baltimore: Johns Hopkins University Press, 1989.

Criticism

Brower, Ruben, Helen Vendler, and John Hollander, eds. *I. A. Richards: Essays in His Honor*. New York: Oxford University Press, 1973.
Constable, John, ed. *Selected Letters of I. A. Richards*. Oxford: Oxford University Press, 1990.
Hotoph, W.H.N. *Language. Thought and Comprehension: A Case Study in the Writings of I. A. Richards*. London: Routledge and Kegan Paul, 1965.
Needham, John. *"The Completest Mode": I. A. Richards and the Continuity of English Criticism*. Edinburgh: Edinburgh University Press, 1982.
Schiller, Jerome P. *I. A. Richards' Theory of Literature*. New Haven, CT: Yale University Press, 1969.

FRED NEWTON SCOTT
(1860–1931)

Christine Ross

In 1953, in his now widely read dissertation *Rhetoric in American Colleges: 1850–1900*, Albert Kitzhaber presents Fred Newton Scott as the only nineteenth-century rhetorician who might be called "an original theorist" (57). Scott's work nevertheless remained largely unknown until the wider reception of Donald C. Stewart's scholarship in the late 1970s and early 1980s. In the wake of that reception, Scott has emerged as a major figure in the history of modern rhetoric. James Berlin's *Writing Instruction in Nineteenth-Century American Colleges* presents Scott as the author of a "new pedagogical paradigm" and a rhetorical theory that is distinctively "democratic" (77–78). More recently, Robert Connors's *Composition-Rhetoric* locates Scott's work as a point of transition from speech-based to print-based rhetorical theory. In *The Life and Legacy of Fred Newton Scott*, Donald and Patricia Stewart narrate much of Scott's work in relation to the twentieth-century emergence of writing instruction as a scholarly discipline.

Fred Newton Scott was born in 1860 to Mary Bannister and Harvey David Scott, an Indiana lawyer and member of Congress. He entered the University of Michigan as a freshman and was awarded Michigan's Ph.D. in June of 1889. That fall, Scott was hired as an instructor in writing. By 1903, Scott had developed an international reputation; he had created and become head of the Department of Rhetoric at Michigan; and he had attracted to his department some of the nation's most well-prepared and talented graduate students. In addition to his participation in a large number of other professional organizations, Scott became president of the Modern Language Association (MLA) in 1907 and served as the first president of the National Council of Teacher of English (NCTE) from 1911 to 1913. He retired from Michigan in 1926 and died in San Diego in 1931.

SCOTT'S RHETORICAL THEORY

The breadth of Scott's learning would be unusual in the specialist world of the late twentieth century. Scott prepared himself to do work in comparative literature and linguistics, acquiring seven languages in five of the eight subdivisions of Indo-European.[1] Scott wrote a dissertation on the reception of Italian criticism during the English Renaissance; he published articles composed in German, translations of Russian poetry and drama, articles on English style, and research grounded in comparative linguistics (Stewart and Stewart [cited hereafter as SS] 10, 13, 131, 221–225). Scott was also an expert in nineteenth-century aesthetics and the history of rhetoric; he wrote and lectured extensively on the teaching of English; and he was well read in the human sciences. Stewart and Stewart's *Life and Legacy* offers a rich portrait of a scholar who published, lectured, and traveled widely; who was in many respects a public intellectual; and who was valued by colleagues for his judgment and leadership. Erudite in many disciplines, Scott enjoyed teaching, and reading the compositions of, beginning writers ("The Teacher and His Training" 327–28). He defined his discipline as rhetoric.

Judging from Stewart and Stewart's chronological list of "Works by Fred Newton Scott," Scott's publication history falls into rough periods.[2] He wrote on literature and linguistics in bursts: 1890–1895; 1904–1909; 1913–1915, 1920–1924. Early in his career, he prepared scholarly editions of texts in the history of rhetoric (1891–1895) and collaborated in writing eight textbooks (1893–1907). *Paragraph-Writing*, written with Joseph Denney, was the first and most successful. Scott also edited a series of "Contributions to Rhetorical Theory," published by Ann Arbor Press (1895[3]–1918). After his reputation was established, Scott published articles on rhetorical theory and the teaching of English, as well as reviews (1903–1927). In 1926, Scott collected some of his articles in *The Standard of American Speech and Other Papers* (cited hereafter as *SAS*). This anthology is the text most frequently cited when scholars discuss Scott's theories of rhetoric.

Scott's work is situated between the nineteenth and twentieth centuries and their two different worlds of rhetorical theory and practice. In that sense, Scott worked without a model of the discipline in rhetoric he inaugurated and appears to have understood his work as speculative and propaedeutic in relation to a science-yet-to-be. Although his rhetorical theory transforms considerably over time, Scott increasingly understands his scholarship to fall short of the "science of rhetoric" he argued for. His own style is often intuitive and literary.[4]

In 1890, Scott changed the name of his course in "Rhetoric" to "Science of Rhetoric" (SS 15), and he published *The Principles of Style* (cited hereafter as *PS*), a text to be used by students in a second course of that title. In this textbook, Scott presents the pedagogy through which he organized his first courses and the conception of rhetoric he revised throughout his career. This initial rhetoric organizes four developmental methods of study, the first of which is behaviorist.

The student learns apparently "abstract and arbitrary rules—'Thou shalt' do this or avoid that," which "must be worked into the student's raw and wincing memory by main strength" until "the habit of using them [is] reduced to automatism" (*PS* 1–2). Proper habits are organized by rational principles. Therefore, the second method of study proceeds as a metacritical "search for some fundamental principle[s]," which could hold no interest until fluency had prompted intuition of practical unity (2). Behaviorist inculcation of rule-governed practice therefore provided the basis for recursive reasoning in relation to the unity and coherence of literate performance. The pupil who mastered these two methods had mastered a "science of rhetoric" (PS 1–3), Scott's first course in 1890.

The third method of study inculcates by main force the rules and exemplars of literary expression and completes instruction in "the Lower Rhetoric" (4). Scott's student would then proceed to a fourth and final method: "the exercise of certain mental functions in higher degree," including "Imagination and Feeling" (5). Study of this "Higher Rhetoric" produces a romantic recursivity and lifelong dialectic of affect and reason through which "personality" is created and expressed. Habit becomes animated and an organic part of personality: "[T]he new sap of feeling and imagination . . . flow[s] back into the hard abstractions of the Lower to give them richness and ease," infusing "dry bones" with "life" (7). Scott's course on *The Principles of Style* was an introduction to this "Higher Rhetoric."

The rote training and recursive romanticism of *The Principles of Style* would seem antithetical to the socially oriented rhetorical theory that has been Scott's signature in modern criticism. Scott's focus on a more classically social rhetoric of modern print literacy is indicated by an essay topic offered to students in *The Principles of Style*: "General changes in the scope and character of Rhetoric due to (a) the invention of printing, (b) the rise in importance of the newspaper" (40). A student-centered pedagogy is suggested by the "personal research" and written essays he required (9). The increasing importance of audience and science in Scott's theory is suggested by his publication of new editions of George Lewes's *Principles of Success in Literature* (ca. 1891) and Herbert Spencer's *Philosophy of Style* (ca. 1892). Scott takes pains to demonstrate that Spencer locates the study of literature within "Sociology" and "psychological phenomena determined by social conditions" (xvi).

Thirteen years after *The Principles of Style*, Scott's article on "Rhetoric" in *The New International Encyclopaedia* states that a "truly scientific exposition [of rhetoric] would demonstrate that the peculiar forms and qualities of any piece of discourse are the natural outcome of the interaction of the individual and society in the process of communication" (1021). Rhetoric is a human science like sociology and studies the social forces that organize all language use, including literature. In a 1909 talk titled "Rhetoric Rediviva," Scott argues that rhetoric is a "genuine science" because it includes: (1) a distinct subject matter; (2) a method based in observation, experiment, and generalization; (3) an organized body of "interlocking principles, laws and classifications" (414).

Rhetoric is now more empirical than rationalist in method and is supported by "the contributions of sociology and psychology" (417). However, when Scott became active in the NCTE in 1912, he argued against an exclusively science-based discipline of rhetoric. He does so in response to the use of data-driven empirical methods to norm teachers and students on a bell-shaped curve (*SAS*, "Our Problems"; see also "Efficiency for Efficiency's Sake"). Scott's disquiet over the new role of science in education is perhaps reflected by a 1913 review, where he states that rhetoric needs "its Kant or its Hume" to "clear away" inconsistent traditions and "bring to light the permanent, underlying principles" of rhetoric (cited in SS 142).

Scott never produced a synthetic work organized by the "interlocking principles, laws and classifications" necessary to science in "Rhetoric Rediviva." He rather draws on two different models of research: (1) empirical investigation in the human sciences and (2) the hermeneutic traditions of literary criticism and speculative, systematic critique. In many respects, these two models are at odds, depending upon which disciplinary tradition one engages. In any case, Scott draws concrete examples from literature or the natural sciences, but his principles of argument are speculative, rationalist, and reflective. He generally uses examples to critique received opinions and to support speculation on the origins of speech, rhetoric, and linguistic form. But the difficulty—and perhaps the impossibility—of Scott's having developed either a critical or empirical synthesis is suggested by *The Standard of American Speech*.

The Standard of American Speech collects essays that Scott wrote from 1904 to 1923. The collection is apparently designed to suggest a theoretical whole as opposed to offering a representative sample of Scott's work. Scott does not include early work that made his reputation, for example. Nor does he present essays in anything like chronological order. The collection, rather, proceeds as a disciplinary "ascent" from present practical issues of general concern—the degree of standardization one can expect of a living language—to the most speculative, theoretically ambitious essay that Scott ever wrote: "The Origin of Speech." The collection can also be read as a genealogical "descent" from Scott's often-mentioned Platonic ideal of using rhetoric for civic purposes to its historical ground in practical activity at the anthropological dawn of "human nature."

Scott's speculations reveal his command of the new sciences of origin, such as biology, anthropology, psychology, sociology, and linguistics, as well as idealist genetic narratives derived from Hegel. However, Scott's *telos* or sense of an ending is not, as it is for pure science or philosophical discipline, knowledge per se. The ideal end of rhetorical study and research is an ability to perform as a linguistic being, through an integration of knowing, doing, and being. Nor does Scott understand the origin in terms of the immediacy of a subject's knowing an object independent of social relations, as do Hegel and the empirical and speculative traditions descended from Locke. For Scott, the immediacy of human being-knowing is praxic, social, and rhetorical. Implied in Scott's conception of rhetoric is an integration of theory and practice for which there is no model in the intellectual traditions Scott knew. In the 1920s, Scott suggests that he cannot supply a synthesis that would organize the field of rhetorical study (*SAS* 29–30).

Scott's speculations lead him, over time, to shift his attention from the formality of text to the rhetorical being of the learner and teacher. Throughout his later essays, Scott evokes the elusive form of an event-centered and performative understanding of language. This sensitivity to a rhetorical experience of language is evoked, increasingly, to argue for pedagogical change. In "Composition as a Mode of Behavior," children are presented as linguistic beings whose scrambled schoolroom sentences are "the outward sign of an inward lesion" (*SAS* 28), which is produced when the inert formality of school language disrupts the immediate rhetoricity of their habitual modes of speaking. While Scott expects students to internalize the forms of discourse and grammar that school teaches and that well-trained literates require, he argues, increasingly, for ameliorating the violence of first learning as much as possible (26–27).

Virtually all modern readers of Scott understand his textbooks to be conservative or less forward looking than his theoretical statements.[5] However, Scott's textbooks enact his distinctive blend of empirical and formalist study of language. In his 1903 *Encyclopaedia* article, for example, the "formal problems" to be addressed by a science of rhetoric include: "the structure and morphology of discourse in (a) its minuter forms (words, phrases, sentences, paragraphs, figures, rhythms), (b) its larger forms (whole compositions), (c) its typical modes (description, narrative, exposition, argument, persuasion)" (1021). "[S]tructure and morphology" reflect Scott's training in comparative linguistics and the axiomatic, ideal structure of language and its fundamental units: vowels, consonants, phonemes, morphemes, words. Scott would seem to understand units of discourse as similarly axiomatic. Like vowels and consonants, the modes of discourse would be a priori structures rather than historically and socially contingent. Such a view of discourse would not ultimately be static, but Scott's treatment is, for lack of a principle of transformation. Scott is not unaware of this formism. But he understands formism as preparatory. Empirical studies would ultimately supply the psychosocial principles of discursive transformation over time.

Scott and Denney's textbook *Paragraph-Writing* has been maligned by late twentieth-century readers because it performs such a systematic, formal analysis. The first third of the text offers a theoretical justification for, and structural analysis of, a variety of paragraph forms, situating them in relation to the modes of discourse. It is inaccurate to say, however, that Scott is conservative in defending continued use of the modes of discourse. Scott doesn't defend their continued use any more than a linguist would defend continued use of consonants. *Paragraph-Writing* is, rather, doing what Scott understands to be appropriately theorized instruction. In his view, scholars should identify forms of discursive unity so that students can learn to manipulate them effectively. As

Scott argues in "Two Ideals of Composition," teaching formality per se is not pedagogically unsound. Indeed, teachers must teach it if they are to teach at all. But teaching form for its own sake *is* a problem. Effective teaching is determined most significantly by a teacher's sense of the rhetorical purpose of instruction in rhetoric. Redundantly, then, effective pedagogy in rhetoric is rhetoric itself (*SAS*).

The mark of Scott's comparativist training and speculative bent appears throughout his textbooks in the new forms of study he requires. Nineteenth-century textbook questions appear at the close or foot of the lesson as tests of comprehension or memory (Connors 72–79). Scott's questions are generative, speculative, and integral to the lesson and the discipline (e.g., *Lessons in English* and *Elementary English Composition*). In Scott's *An Introduction to the Methods and Materials of Literary Criticism*, to know literary criticism is to know the questions literary critics ask. Scott's earliest courses in *The Principles of Style* and *The Interpretation of Art* often require speculative "personal research" and practical comparison of two texts or two authors. Increasingly, Scott's textbooks offer doubled-columned, comparativist problem-posing, which engages students in generative manipulation of language that, at its best, teaches some principle of form. To judge from his textbooks, Scott increasingly understood comparativist manipulation of language to be a primary mode of learning. Finally, the elusive generativity of his comparativist approach may have contributed to Scott's understanding of rhetorical force as an event irreducible to form.

Research to date has defined Scott as a major figure through the narratives of larger histories of writing instruction and rhetorical theory. For that reason, however, the distinctiveness of Scott's work has been somewhat obscured. Scott's career traversed the growing break between literature and rhetoric, philosophy and science, as language studies and the modern disciplines continued to fragment in the early twentieth century. The complex interaction of multiple emergent disciplines and the evolving tension between empirical and speculative models in Scott's rhetorical theory remain to be studied and would provide the basis for a rich genealogy of modern language studies and discipline.

NOTES

1. Scott studied (1) Sanskirt, (2) Latin, Italian, and French, (3) Greek, (4) German, and (5) Russian—which are, respectively, of the Indic, Italic, Hellenic, Teutonic, and Balto-Slavonic subfamilies of Indo-European. In an essay in *The Standard of American Speech*, Scott represents himself as fluent in modern and old Dutch (110). He also knew Old English. His claim that anyone who knew English, Latin, and German could easily learn Old English would be based in his knowledge that English, German, and Old English are all Teutonic ("The Teacher and His Training" 313). Dutch is as well. Stewart and Stewart report that although they have not been able to verify it, those who knew Scott believed him to have considerable command of 14 languages (n3, 215).

2. See prefatory note to the Bibliography below.

3. Apparently Stewart and Stewart could not verify the date of the first text in this series.

4. Some of the more literary essays in *The Standard of American Speech* are: "A Substitute for the Classics," "Poetry in a Commercial Age," "A Fable of Bidpai," "The Congress of Letters," and sections of "A Note on Walt Whitman's Prosody." Discussion of these essays would require more extended analysis than this entry permits.

5. For example, in *The Methodical Memory*, Sharon Crowley includes Scott in a list of those who wrote textbooks that taught "current-traditional rhetoric," which makes Scott conservative (70). James Berlin claims that the market for textbooks required Scott to be more conservative in his textbooks than he really was (77). Stewart and Stewart argue that "it is important to keep in mind the dichotomy between Scott's conservative presence in the textbooks and the more innovative thinking in his theoretical papers" (131). Robert Connors's study is an exception.

BIBLIOGRAPHY

In *The Life and Legacy of Fred Newton Scott*, Stewart and Stewart offer a comprehensive bibliography of Scott's publications. They do not include Scott's syllabi. Although research for this entry did not include a comprehensive search for syllabi, it did surface a quite interesting syllabus entitled "The Interpretation of Art" for a course Scott taught at Michigan in the early 1890s. Stewart and Stewart also provide extensive bibliography on secondary literature and criticism. The bibliography below is confined to works cited in this entry.

Primary Sources

Carpenter, George R., Franklin T. Baker, and Fred Newton Scott. "The Teacher and His Training." Section II. *The Teaching of English in the Elementary and Secondary Schools.* London and Bombay: Longmans, Green, and Co., 1903. 305–41.

Gayley, Charles Mills, and Fred Newton Scott. *An Introduction to the Methods and Materials of Literary Criticism.* Boston: Ginn and Company, 1899.

Scott, Fred Newton. *The Interpretation of Art, with Special References to Leonardo Da Vinci and Michael Angelo.* Ann Arbor, MI: Inland Press, 1892.

———. "Introduction and Notes." *George Henry Lewes; Principles of Success in Literature.* Ed. Fred Newton Scott. 3rd ed. Boston: Allyn and Bacon, 1917.

———. "Introduction and Notes." *Herbert Spencer: Philosophy of Style.* Ed. Fred Newton Scott. 2nd ed. Boston: Allyn and Bacon, 1917.

———. *The Principles of Style.* Ann Arbor, MI: Inland Press, 1890.

———. "Rhetoric." *The New International Encyclopaedia.* Vol. 14. Ed. David Coit Giliman, Harry Thurston Peck, and Frank Moore Colby. New York: Dodd, Mead and Company, 1903. 1020–22.

———. "Rhetoric Rediviva." Ed. Donald C. Stewart. *College Composition and Communication* 31.4 (1980): 413–19.

———. *The Standard of American Speech and Other Papers.* Boston: Allyn & Bacon, 1926.

Scott, Fred Newton, and Joseph Villers Denney. *Elementary English Composition.* Boston: Allyn and Bacon, 1908.

———. *Paragraph-Writing*. 2nd ed. Boston: Allyn & Bacon, 1894.

———. *Paragraph-Writing*. New Edition. Boston: Allyn & Bacon, 1909.

Scott, Fred Newton, and Gordon A. Southworth. *Lessons in English*. Book One. Boston: Benj. H. Sanborn & Co., 1906.

Biography

Stewart, Donald C., and Patricia L. Stewart. *The Life and Legacy of Fred Newton Scott*. Pittsburgh. University of Pittsburgh Press, 1997.

Criticism

Berlin, James. *Writing Instruction in Nineteenth-Century American Colleges*. Carbondale: Southern Illinois University Press, 1984.

Connors, Robert J. *Composition-Rhetoric: Backgrounds, Theory, and Pedagogy*. Pittsburgh: University of Pittsburgh Press, 1997.

Crowley, Sharon. *The Methodical Memory: Invention in Current-Traditional Rhetoric*. Carbondale: Southern Illinois University Press, 1990.

Kitzhaber, Alfred R. *Rhetoric in American Colleges, 1850–1900*. 1953. Dallas: Southern Methodist University Press, 1990.

Stewart, Donald. "Rediscovering Fred Newton Scott." *College English* 40.5 (1979): 539–47.

MINA SHAUGHNESSY
(1924–1978)

Mary Hurley Moran

Born on March 13, 1924, to Ruby Alma Johnson Pendo, a former teacher, and Albert Pendo, a miner, Mina Pendo Shaughnessy grew up in the small coal-mining town of Leeds, South Dakota. She attended Northwestern University, where she concentrated in speech and theater, and upon graduation in 1946, she moved to New York City to become an actress. Within a year, however, Shaughnessy abandoned this plan in favor of an academic career.

In 1947 she enrolled in a Bible Studies program at Wheaton College in Illinois (raised in a devout Lutheran home, Shaughnessy remained strongly religious throughout her life, converting to Catholicism on her deathbed); but after a year she decided to switch to literature and so returned to New York to enter a Master's program in English at Columbia. While working toward her degree, she taught part-time at the National Bible Institute (later named Shelton College) and earned a reputation as an outstanding teacher.

Lacking a doctorate, however, Shaughnessy was unable to obtain a full-time academic position (she hoped eventually to return to graduate school for a Ph.D., but for a number of reasons, among them financial straits and the particular demands of her husband's career [she married Donald Shaughnessy in 1953], she never managed to). Instead, she spent the next 10 years working a variety of jobs, which, although not constituting the conventional path to an academic career, would prove to be excellent training for her eventual role as an expert in the fields of writing and education. These included helping with the research and writing of a biography of John D. Rockefeller, Jr., and of a study of black schools in the South; revising for publication a memoir about New York's Riverside Church; and working as an editor at McGraw-Hill from 1956 to 1961.

Shaughnessy finally decided to take a part-time academic position in 1961, teaching in the General Studies division at Hunter College, an experience that first introduced her to underprepared students. Although at Hunter (1961–1964) and later in a full-time position at Hofstra University (1964–1967) she taught the usual generalist mixture of composition and literature courses and wrote literary criticism, she was becoming increasingly interested in remedial writing. Consequently, when offered a position in 1967 in the City College of New York's (CCNY's) recently inaugurated open admissions program, she accepted.

It was here that Shaughnessy found her true niche. Over the course of the next 11 years, she taught in and directed CCNY's basic writing program; trained teachers in the program; founded the field's first major periodical, the *Journal of Basic Writing*; served as first director of the City University of New York's Instructional Resources Center; was appointed an associate dean of the City University of New York (CUNY); wrote a groundbreaking book on basic writing; and delivered numerous conference addresses on behalf of the causes of open admissions and remediation. As a result of her activism, she quickly became known as the nation's foremost authority in the new field of basic writing.

This prominence is reflected in the large number of national committees and boards that Shaughnessy was invited to join (among them the Board of Advisors of the Fund for the Improvement of Post-Secondary Education, the Conference on College Composition and Communication [CCCC] Committee on Teaching and Its Evaluation in Composition, the Modern Language Association [MLA] Committee on Teaching and Related Professional Activities, and the National Humanities Faculty) and by her being honored with a National Endowment for the Humanities proclamation, signed by President Jimmy Carter, in recognition of her work on behalf of literacy. This award was presented in October 1978. A month later, on November 16, 1978, Shaughnessy died of the cancer that she had battled for the previous year and a half; she was 54 years old.

Shaughnessy's significance to twentieth-century rhetoric is that she defined and validated—and even provided the name for—the field of basic writing (prior to this time referred to as "remedial" or "developmental" or even "bonehead" English); she revolutionized the way we regard basic writers, showing that they are educable students whose errors are due to lack of practice with written discourse rather than to stupidity or laziness; and she provided basic writing teachers with desperately needed guidance grounded in current developments in linguistics, psychology, sociology, and the then-fledgling field of composition theory.

SHAUGHNESSY'S RHETORICAL THEORY

The main tenet of Shaughnessy's rhetorical theory is that there is a logic and an intelligent purpose behind the errors that basic writing students make, much as there is with second-language learners trying to master the rules of an unfamiliar linguistic code, and that the teacher's job is to explore this reasoning and use it to develop effective, individualized instruction. It is this message that is expressed in nearly all of the essays and speeches Shaughnessy produced but most comprehensively in her landmark 1977 work *Errors and Expectations*.

This book almost single-handedly transformed basic writing into a respectable, legitimate field. With its rigorous content and lapidary prose style, *Errors and Expectations* went a long way toward converting skeptics who regarded basic writing as the bastard child of composition, and composition in turn as the bastard child of the traditional English Department. Shaughnessy showed that the etiology of student writing problems is as worthy a scholarly endeavor as the analysis of literary texts (so convincing was her argument that, according to E. D. Hirsch, many traditionally trained English professors who attended her MLA talk on the subject were inspired to switch into composition ["Opening Remarks" 96]). This effect, though, was secondary; Shaughnessy's primary purpose in writing the book was to provide a guideline and resource for those like herself, who, with no training and no body of scholarship to turn to, suddenly found themselves required to teach students whose writing "was so stunningly unskilled that [one could] not begin to define the task nor even sort out the difficulties" (*Errors* vii).

With this need in mind, Shaughnessy created a guidebook that attempts to give a true picture of the kinds and extent of errors typical of BW (her abbreviation for "basic writing") students and to suggest instructional methods tailored to such errors. Accordingly, she presents example after example of actual BW student writing—excerpts taken from the 4,000 or so placement essays she analyzed as part of her research for the book. Whereas some proponents of open admissions were alarmed at her exposing to public view the "dirty little secret" (Lyons, "Mina Shaughnesy and the Teaching of Writing" 5) of basic writing programs (that is, the near-illiterate nature of BW prose), fearing such exposure would confirm the skeptics' hunch that these students do not belong in college, Shaughnessy believed that the only way to address the problems effectively was to be armed with a comprehensive, accurate understanding of them. Her teaching experience told her that the kinds of tidy, discrete errors presented as examples in conventional textbooks—a lack of subject-verb agreement or a dangling participle, say, in a sentence that is otherwise lucid and syntactically correct—are a far cry from the labyrinthine, error-encrusted sentences, such as the following, that BW students typically produce: "In my opinion I believe that you there is no field that cannot be effected some sort of advancement that one maybe need a college degree to make it" (*Errors* 62).

Not only the examples she includes but also the kinds of errors she focuses on distinguish Shaughnessy's approach from that of conventional grammar/composition textbooks. Her scrutiny of BW prose and her interviews with BW students led her to isolate six broad categories—what she calls "territories of difficulty"—that present problems for such students. She devotes a chapter to each in *Errors and Expectations*, and a glance at these chapter titles—"Handwriting and Punctuation," "Syntax," "Common Errors," "Spelling," "Vocabulary," "Beyond the Sentence"—reveals the unconventionality of Shaughnessy's approach. For example, handwriting is normally regarded as a superficial skill, extraneous to a student's ability to compose syntactically correct sentences or well-developed paragraphs, but Shaughnessy shows that students who have done little writing can be so preoccupied with the motor-mental coordination of hand-writing that they cannot concentrate on sentence structure or meaning. Spelling, too, is an area either overlooked or given short shrift in composition courses, and yet poor spelling is one of the main obstacles to clear writing for BW students. One more example is vocabulary. Composition handbooks and teachers tend to be leery of teaching vocabulary for fear it will result in awkward or inflated prose—that is, students' use of contextually inappropriate synonyms or of "five-dollar" words. Shaughnessy, however, points out that for BW students a limited vocabulary is frequently the cause of sentence structure problems, in that the lack of an apt word can cause a student struggling to express a particular concept to create a tangled or bloated syntactical mess.

Shaughnessy arranges each body chapter the same way: First she describes the error, providing an abundance of examples; then she explores the possible reasons why BW students make the error; and then she suggests instructional methods for helping them master it. Shaughnessy's most original, most impressive contribution is her analysis of the reasoning behind BW students' errors. Stepping imaginatively into the minds of basic writers, she exposes the very legitimate reasons for their confusion and mistakes. She points out that what teachers have traditionally considered "simple" rules are not in fact so simple. One example is the requirement of the *s* inflection on present-tense indicative verbs used with third-person singular subjects. Although speakers of standard English unconsciously follow this rule when they write, BW students whose dialect allows the *s* to be dropped (as in "The boy hear birds") must try consciously to master the rule. But what can confuse them is that they frequently hear correct constructions in which the *s* on a present-tense verb following a third-person singular noun is omitted, as, for example, in "Does *he want* a course in biology?" "Can *she run* as fast as her brother?" and "She makes the *student laugh*." Such students must not only combat their instinctive, dialect-driven tendency to drop the *s* but try to master abstract grammatical points such as mood and modals. It is therefore entirely understandable that many BW students run into problems concerning *s* inflections. Shaughnessy applies this same kind of detailed exploration to all categories of BW errors, showing that the students' difficulties stem not from stupidity but from a variety of other causes, including dialect interference, perceptual problems, habitual use of verbal rather than written patterns of discourse, and ineffective prior instruction.

Much of Shaughnessy's approach grew out of her research into current theory in the fields of linguistics and TESL (teaching English as a second language) Shaughnessy points out that BW students, like ESL students, are attempting to master a new code and that often an indication of this attempt is a temporary increase in error. Teachers should therefore bear in mind that as students begin to use more complex structures, they will make proportionally more errors; conversely, students who play it safe and stick to relatively simple structures that they are confident about will commit fewer errors but will not be developing as writers.

Another way Shaughnessy reveals the influence of TESL theory is in her assertion that the same error may be made by different students for different reasons and that therefore pedagogy must focus on causes rather than rules and must be individually tailored, to the extent that this is possible. For example, one student may fail to use a capital letter where required because of ignorance of the conventions governing capitalization, whereas another may commit the same error because of handwriting difficulties that make formation of the lowercase easier than formation of the capital. Instruction for the former should involve exposure to the conventions, for the latter practice in handwriting. Similarly, punctuation errors on one student's paper could reflect weak proofreading skills (the student simply does not notice the errors when reading over the paper), whereas the same errors on another student's paper could reflect the student's confusion about how phrase, clause, and sentence boundaries are marked. The solution for the former student might be perceptual discrimination exercises and for the latter instruction and practice in expanding kernel sentences using embedding and linking and the punctuation marks these entail.

An important effect of this kind of cause-oriented approach to error is that it brings to light a pattern to an individual student's errors. Once this pattern is revealed, the task of addressing these errors seems less daunting for both the teacher and the student. For example, although a paper may appear on the surface to contain, say, 15 errors, these errors may actually grow out of only three sources of difficulty or confusion that the teacher needs to help the student master. The student feels less overwhelmed by the prospect of learning 3 rules rather than 15 and, more important, feels empowered by the knowledge that his or her errors grow out of legitimate confusion rather than stupidity.

Shaughnessy's talks and published essays generally cover the same points that she presents in *Errors and Expectations*, but many (e.g., "Open Admissions and the Disadvantaged Teacher," "The Miserable Truth," and "Speaking and Doublespeaking about Standards") also make more direct pleas for continuing the policy of open admissions and for taking seriously the field of basic writing. Although opponents of remediation claim to be fighting for standards, Shaughnessy argues that their real goal is the perpetuation of the traditional elitist role of universities, whereas in a democracy the true goal of universities should be to educate all people, even the most disadvantaged members of society. She also points out that achieving this goal requires university professors to rethink their established methods of teaching: When children of privilege were their students, professors were assured success, for the students were in a sense already educated; but with disadvantaged students, professors must develop *real* teaching standards. In a sense, then, she turns the tables on her opponents by pointing out that teachers of remedial students have higher standards than teachers of advantaged students.

In a famous *College Composition and Communication (CCC)* article entitled "Diving In," Shaughnessy outlines the stages the traditionally trained English professor usually goes through when assigned a basic writing course: from reliance on conventional methods of teaching to the realization that these methods don't work with such students and ultimately to the realization that one needs to remediate oneself—"to become a student of new disciplines [composition research, linguistics, psychology, and so on] and of his students themselves" (238)—in order to meet the challenge of educating such students. Here and elsewhere Shaughnessy tries to combat the entrenched resistance on the part of English Departments to composition in general and basic writing in particular by arguing for the need for scholarship and training in these fields. In another *CCC* article, "Some Needed Research on Writing," she discusses some of the directions this research might take, including investigations into the cognitive abilities of young adults whose verbal development has been delayed and into ways of systematically and intensively instilling in BW students those writing subskills—such as an adequate vocabulary—that more privileged college freshmen have absorbed naturally over the previous 18 years. Shaughnessy was an enthusiastic supporter of the then-new work being done on the writing process and on sentence combining, and in many talks and articles she called for continued research in these areas, particularly as they concern basic writers.

RECEPTION OF SHAUGHNESSY'S WORK, THEN AND NOW

As has been pointed out, Shaughnessy's work was instrumental in changing the way a great many in the English profession regarded composition and basic writing. According to accounts by several who heard her speak at conferences, this conversion was due as much to Shaughnessy's style—her eloquence and graceful bearing (the result of years of training in public speaking and acting), the compelling "moral authority" (Hirsch, "Opening Remarks" 96) and almost religious zeal she exhibited, and her universally acknowledged physical beauty— as to the substance of her talks. Some who were skeptical of her ideas, however, pointed out that perhaps her effectiveness as a teacher was a product of these personal qualities rather than of her theories and methods—in other words, her effectiveness could not be replicated by those who lacked her charisma. These critics were also skeptical of the adulation with which Shaughnessy was regarded by her colleagues in CCNY's basic writing program and mockingly referred to them as "Mina's minions" (Maher 90).

The more serious and more widespread criticism, though, was leveled at Shaughnessy's politics—that is, at what the Old Guard in the academy considered her dangerously liberal embrace of open admissions. In works with such titles as *The End of Education* (Wagner) and *The Death of the American University* (Neller), these critics decried the abandonment of standards and the worthlessness of a college degree that this abandonment would result in. While it is true that Shaughnessy was an outspoken advocate of open admissions, it seems ludicrous to call her a radical. Indeed, by today's standards there was much that was conservative in her views about the teaching of English. She did not call for a dismantling of the canon but, on the contrary, was outspoken in her admiration of, in today's jargon, "dead white European male" writers, especially Milton, Bacon, and Henry James (she once said that her ideal teaching schedule would be one course in basic writing and one course on Milton [Lyons, "Mina Shaughnessy and the Teaching of Writing" 7]). While she did include some works by minorities in her otherwise traditional reading lists and did welcome new perspectives, she was very much an upholder of the classics as the culmination of the best that has been thought and written. To her mind, a major goal of open admissions was to equip the disadvantaged with the ability to read and appreciate the canon, not to question it (these views prompted E. D. Hirsch to praise her as a modern-day Matthew Arnold ["Culture and Literacy" 27]— that is, as a bearer of civilization and literacy). Similarly, she wanted open admissions to empower students by giving them proficiency in standard English, not by giving them "the right to their own language," as the more liberal in the composition profession were advocating at the time.

Although Shaughnessy was sensitive to the conflicts minority students could feel between their home dialect and standard English and although she encouraged pride in the former, she nonetheless emphasized the importance of mastering standard written English. To do so, she knew, students would need to get control of their errors—and hence the emphasis on error in *Errors and Expectations*. Aware that there was a movement afoot to ignore error altogether and to concentrate instead on what students had to say, Shaughnessy addressed this issue head-on in her introduction. She agreed that the old emphasis in composition courses on product and absolute correctness is misguided but pointed out that error mastery must be a focus—albeit not the only or the central focus—of such courses because BW students' writing is so filled with errors that meaning is lost and communication is impossible. She points out, however, that while teachers need to spend a great deal of time analyzing and finding patterns to their students' errors so as to instruct the students most effectively, error discussion need not and should not take up most of the classroom time.

Today, two decades after her death, Shaughnessy's views continue to dominate the field of basic writing, and *Errors and Expectations* remains an important resource for BW teachers. The spring 1994 issue of the *Journal of Basic Writing* commemorated Shaughnessy by reprinting some of her essays and a number of eulogistic pieces by colleagues, and every year a Mina Shaughnessy Award is presented to a scholar in the field of composition who has produced outstanding work. Inevitably, though, there has been some backlash. One form this takes is an undermining of Shaughnessy's idealism about the educability of open admissions students. Andrea Lunsford has called into question Shaughnessy's assertion that BW students are not cognitively lacking, merely unpracticed in academic discourse. And journalist James Traub did a longitudinal study of CCNY's basic writing program in the 1990s and discovered that the majority of BW students he followed ultimately failed academically. Traub believes that Shaughnessy exaggerated the success of her approach and minimized the daunting nature of the remedial task (116–20).

The other type of criticism comes from those on the Left who fault Shaughnessy with not having been radical enough. Foremost among these critics are Min-zhan Lu and Pamela Gay, who, in articles published in the early 1990s, accuse Shaughnessy of racism and imperialism in her upholding of academic discourse as the standard to be attained. Lu ("Conflict and Struggle") and Gay believe that the BW teacher should help students explore and express the conflicts they feel between their home dialects and standard English and should make them aware of the ways standard English can be used by those in power to keep down the powerless. Lu also takes issue with Shaughnessy's notion that language is essentially innocent, that is, that expressing one's meaning in standard English does not essentially change one's meaning, indeed that it even helps one more effectively articulate it. Such a view, argues Lu, is not only elitist but also naive; it is based on the essentialist assumption that meaning precedes and is independent of language ("Redefining the Legacy of Mina Shaughnessy").

A number of composition experts have rushed to Shaughnessy's defense in the wake of Lu's and other cultural critics' criticism. Patricia Laurence and others argue that one must take into account the historical and political context in which Shaughnessy was working: the volatile early 1970s period of open admissions, student protests, and administration backlashes. What was needed at the time was appeasement and compromise; for Shaughnessy to have fostered conflict in the classroom would have been irresponsible and counterproductive. Lu's charge about Shaughnessy's politics of linguistic innocence is also rebutted on the grounds of historicism. Barbara Gleason points out that Shaughnessy "was working within the dominant paradigm of her day, a time when transformational generative grammar was as intellectually forceful as poststructuralist theory is today," and hence her premise that linguistic form is separate from meaning was neither naive nor conservative for her time (887).

Although Shaughnessy has been subject to attacks from critics on both the Right and the Left, the majority of those in the field of composition hold her in high esteem. Her legacy is the thriving state of research being conducted into the causes of basic writing students' difficulties and the widespread practice on the part of basic writing teachers to discover the logic and the patterns behind their students' error making.

BIBLIOGRAPHY

Primary Sources

Shaughnessy, Mina P. "Basic Writing." *Teaching Composition: Twelve Bibliographical Essays*. Ed. Gary Tate. Fort Worth: Texas Christian University Press, 1987. 177–206.

———. "Diving In: An Introduction to Basic Writing." *College Composition and Communication* 27.3 (1976): 234–39. Rpt. in Maher 255–62.

———. "The English Professor's Malady." *Journal of Basic Writing* 3.1 (1980): 91–97. Rpt. in *Journal of Basic Writing* 13.1 1994: 117–24; and in Maher 291–98.

———. *Errors and Expectations: A Guide for the Teacher of Basic Writing*. New York: Oxford University Press, 1977.

———. "The Miserable Truth." *The Congressional Record* (September 9, 1976): E4955–56. Rpt. in *Journal of Basic Writing* 3.1 (1980): 109–14; and in Maher 263–69.

———. "Open Admissions and the Disadvantaged Teacher." *College Composition and Communication* 24.5 (1973): 401–4. Rpt. in *Journal of Basic Writing* 3.1 (1980): 104–8; and in Maher 249–54.

———. "Some Needed Research on Writing." *College Composition and Communication* 28.4 (1977): 317–20. Rpt. in *Journal of Basic Writing* 3.1 (1980): 98–103; and in Maher 284–90.

———. "Speaking and Doublespeaking about Standards." *Mina P. Shaughnessy: Maher. Her Life and Work*, by Jane Maher. Urbana, IL: NCTE, 1997. 270–78.

———. "Statement on Criteria for Writing Proficiency." *Journal of Basic Writing* 3.1 (1980): 115–19. Rpt. in Maher 279–83.

———. "Teaching Basic Writing." *Journal of Basic Writing* 13.1 (1994): 103–16.

Biography

Maher, Jane. *Mina P. Shaughnessy: Her Life and Work*. Urbana, IL: NCTE, 1997.

Criticism

Bartholomae, David. "Released into Language: Errors, Expectations, and the Legacy of Mina Shaughnessy." *The Territory of Language: Linguistics, Stylistics, and the Teaching of Composition*. Ed. Donald A. McQuade. Carbondale, Southern Illinois University Press, 1986. 65–88.

Gay, Pamela. "Reading Shaughnessy from a Postcolonial Perspective." *Journal of Basic Writing* 12.2 (1993): 29–40.

Gleason, Barbara. Contribution to "Symposium on Basic Writing, Conflict and Struggle, and the Legacy of Mina Shaughnessy." *College English* 55.8 (1993): 886–89.

Heller, L[ouis] G. *The Death of the American University*. New Rochelle, NY: Arlington House, 1973.

Hirsch, E. D., Jr. "Culture and Literacy." *Journal of Basic Writing* 3.1 (1980): 27–47.

———. "Opening Remarks at an MLA Session in Memory of Mina Shaughnessy, December 28, 1979." *Journal of Basic Writing* 13.1 (1994): 95–98.

Hunter, Paul. " 'Waiting for an Aristotle': A Moment in the History of the Basic Writing Movement." *College English* 54.8 (1992): 914–27.

Laurence, Patricia. "A Comment on the Symposium on Basic Writing." *College English* 57.1 (1995): 104–5.

———. "The Vanishing Site of Mina Shaughnessy's *Errors and Expectations*." *Journal of Basic Writing* 12.2 (1993): 18–28.

Lu, Min-zhan. "Conflict and Struggle: The Enemies or Preconditions of Basic Writing?" *College English* 54.8 (1992): 887–913.

———. "Redefining the Legacy of Mina Shaughnessy: A Critique of the Politics of Linguistic Innocence." *Journal of Basic Writing* 10.1 (1991): 26–40.

Lunsford, Andrea A. "Cognitive Development and the Basic Writer." *College English* 41.1 (1979): 38–46. Rpt. in *A Sourcebook for Basic Writing Teachers*. Ed. Theresa Enos. New York: Random House, 1987. 449–59.

Lyons, Robert. "Mina Shaughnessy." *Traditions of Enquiry*. Ed. John Brereton. New York: Oxford University Press, 1985. 171–89.

———. "Mina Shaughnessy and the Teaching of Writing." *Journal of Basic Writing* 3.1 (1980): 3–12.

McAlexander, Patricia J. "Mina Shaughnessy and K. Patricia Cross: The Forgotten Debate Over Postsecondary Education." *Rhetoric Review*. In press.

Smith, Virginia. "Keynote Address [at the First Shaughnessy Memorial Conference, April 3, 1980]." *Journal of Basic Writing* 3.1 (1980): 19–26.

Traub, James. *City on a Hill: Testing the American Dream at City College*. Reading, MA: Addison-Wesley, 1994.

Wagner, Geoffrey. *The End of Education*. South Brunswick, NJ: A. S. Barnes, 1976.

STEPHEN E. TOULMIN
(1922–   )

Lisa L. Hill

Stephen Edelson Toulmin was born on March 25, 1922, in London, England. He attended King's College, where he received a Bachelor of Arts Degree in mathematics and physics in 1942. He served the British government as a junior scientific officer during World War II and returned to Cambridge after the war, where he earned a Master of Arts Degree in 1946 and a Doctor of Philosophy Degree in 1948 (Foss, Foss, and Trapp 78). During his studies at Cambridge he was taught and influenced by Ludwig Wittgenstein and began what has become a lifelong project—an inquiry into the nature of rationality.

This inquiry has taken Toulmin to numerous university positions and has inspired several highly influential publications. After completing his dissertation, "Reason in Ethics," Toulmin began the first of many teaching appointments— visiting and full-time—that have sent him from England to Australia and across the United States. He was appointed lecturer in philosophy at Oxford in 1949, where he stayed until 1954. From 1954 to 1955 he served as visiting lecturer at the University of Melbourne, and from 1955 to 1959 he taught philosophy and headed the department at the University of Leeds in England. During his tenure there, Toulmin published *The Uses of Argument*, a book that questioned the strict use of formal logic in practical argumentation and contributed to the revival of the study of rhetoric.

Toulmin's 40-year "intellectual odyssey" (Wartofsky) took him to New York University and Columbia University in 1959 where he served as visiting professor. In 1960 he returned to England to direct the unit for the history of ideas of the Nuffield Foundation. From 1965 to 1969 he was professor of history and the philosophy of ideas at Brandeis University and professor of philosophy at Michigan State University from 1969 to 1972. He served as professor of humanities at the University of Santa Cruz from 1972 to 1973, and from 1973 to

1986, he became professor of philosophy and social thought at the University of Chicago. In 1978, he published *An Introduction to Reasoning*, with Richard Rieke and Alan Janik. This book, more explicitly rhetorical than *The Uses of Argument*, works to explicate the layout of practical argument introduced in the earlier book (*Who's Who 1998* 4356).

In 1982 Toulmin began what has become an ongoing affiliation with the University of Chicago's Center for Clinical Medical Ethics, "a pioneering group of physicians and lay people dedicated to resolving moral quandaries that arise in medical practice, especially those raised by the use of emerging medical technologies" (Sullivan). Following his appointment at the University of Chicago, Toulmin served as Avalon Professor of Humanities at Northwestern University from 1986 to 1992 (*Who's Who 1998* 4356).

In 1990, he published his most recent book, *Cosmopolis*, and was named Henry R. Luce Professor at the Center for Multiethnic and Transnational Studies at the University of Southern California (USC), where he holds a joint appointment in the Department of Anthropology. He has been named Jefferson Lecturer in March 1998 by the National Endowment for the Humanities, the highest honor conferred by the federal government for achievement in the humanities (Sullivan; Wartofsky). Toulmin currently lives on the USC campus, where he and his wife serve as faculty masters who "act as mentors to the undergraduate residents, planning activities and outings designed to foster community between the students . . . and faculty" (Sullivan). These living arrangements suit Toulmin, who maintains, "Students get only part of their education from formal classwork" (Sullivan). Indeed, Toulmin's present living circumstances bear out the pragmatic philosophy that informs his rhetoric: Situation is everything.

TOULMIN'S RHETORICAL THEORY

Although Toulmin has situated *himself* on the philosophy side of the rhetoric/philosophy divide, his *writing* makes two important contributions to rhetoric. First, his oeuvre has attempted to bridge the gap between philosophy and rhetoric, and it has done so to some degree on rhetoric's own terms by questioning the emphasis placed on formal logic by philosophers. Toulmin places *his* emphasis on a kind of "reasonableness" that reincludes the context or situation in which any given argument takes place, the historical, even anthropological variables that are not accounted for because they do not count in systematic logic. Like Aristotle, Toulmin is interested in the pragmatics of argument. Thus, his second contribution to rhetoric is a model that serves as a tool for argument analysis and as a heuristic for the invention of new arguments.

Toulmin's work has taken a circuitous path toward rhetoric that was cleared by American speech-communications scholars Wayne Brockreide and Douglas Ehninger, who read his book *The Uses of Argument* for what they describe as the "dynamic" Toulmin "model" (Brockreide and Ehninger 46). This model consists of six interrelated elements: claim, data, warrant, qualifier, backing, and

rebuttal. Toulmin's motives for writing the book, however, were connected neither to a desire to create an argument model nor to resurrect the study of rhetoric
but rather to a desire to call into question the philosopher's reliance on formal
logic as the sole arbiter of argument. For Toulmin's purposes, the book is a
critique of philosophic reasoning that relies on the search for the ideal and the
absolute—what is certain—rather than on what is practical, uncertain, and contingent.

To escape the bonds of narrow formal logic that philosophers have previously
enforced, *The Uses of Argument* revalues the modal terms in an argument's
claim—words that suggest possibility or certainty such as "may," "might," "possibly," "necessarily," and even "cannot." Toulmin underscores the complex
rhetorical nature of modals with a joke from *Punch*: "*Steward of Cross-Channel
Packet*: 'You can't be sick in here, Sir.' *Afflicted Passenger*: 'Can't I?' " (*Uses*
11). This example allows Toulmin to establish the existence of argument features
that are field-dependent and those that are field-invariant. Thus, he is able to
argue that the *force* of the modals remains field-invariant, whereas the *criteria*
that back and help to establish the validity of the modals are field-dependent;
for example, it is *physically possible* for the afflicted passenger to be sick in a
socially unacceptable location. He concludes, "[T]he meaning of the term 'possible' is field-invariant. The criteria of possibility, on the other hand, are field-
dependent" (37).

In another rhetorical move to avoid the narrow syllogistic argument of formal
logic that decontextualizes the argument structure, Toulmin uses his discussion
of "field" to emphasize the importance of context or situation. He asserts that
the field determines the way in which assertions that are made within it must
be supported: The standards of proof or evidence are field-dependent. For Toulmin, "A man who makes an assertion puts forward a claim—a claim on our
attention and our belief" (11), and he will be believed depending on the nature
of his character and his reputation. But his audience can challenge that claim
and demand an argument in support of it; thus the primary purpose of argument
for Toulmin is "justificatory arguments brought forward in support of assertions,
in the structures they may be expected to have, the merits they can claim and
the ways in which we set about grading, assessing, and criticising them" (12).
These justificatory arguments and our methods of critiquing them, he argues,
are inevitably field-dependent.

Toulmin's justificatory argument requires three primary elements: *claim,
grounds* (or data), and *warrants*. The data or grounds are the evidence that
support the assertion or claim, whereas the warrant makes possible the connection of grounds to assertion or claim. Each of these elements must be grounded
in a specific situation, since, he maintains, "[t]he conclusions we come to, the
assertions we put forward, will be of very different kinds, according to the nature
of the problem we are pronouncing judgement about" (13).

Toulmin explains grounds and warrants by way of questions asked of the
claim. *Grounds* (*Uses* 97) or *data* (Toulmin, Ríeke, and Janik 26) answer the

question "What have you got to go on?" (13), and these facts or evidence may in turn be challenged if we are asked to indicate the "bearing of our conclusion on the data already produced" (*Uses* 99). The question, "How do you get there?" insists that there must be a connection, a *warrant*, between our claim and our grounds. This connection must be made explicit, according to Toulmin, by way of "general, hypothetical statements, which can act as bridges, and authorize the sort of step to which our particular argument commits us" (99).

Three more elements of argument, *qualifier, rebuttal*, and *backing*, arise from the interconnection among claim, grounds, and warrant. "Some warrants," Toulmin tells us, "authorize us to accept a claim unequivocally, given the appropriate data. . . . [O]thers authorize us to make the step from data to conclusion . . . subject to conditions" (100). An unequivocal claim, for example, might use the modal "necessarily," whereas an equivocal claim might use modal *qualifiers* like "probably" or "presumably" (100; emphasis added). So, too, arguments may need an element to address "conditions of exception or *rebuttal*" (101; emphasis added). Finally, if our warrant does not seem sufficiently strong to carry the data or grounds to the claim, we may need to add *backing* to strengthen the warrant. Backing will answer the question, "Why do you think that?" (103).

Reviews of *The Uses of Argument* in England called it an antilogic book and dismissed it, yet it continued to sell well, largely due to the influence of theorists of communication in the United States. In 1960, in their article "Toulmin on Argument," Wayne Brockreide and Douglas Ehninger found in Toulmin's book a structural model of argumentation and "a system for classifying artistic proofs [ethos, pathos, and logos] which employs argument as a central and unifying construct" (44). Ehninger and Brockreide may be credited with popularizing the model through their textbook *Decision by Debate* (1965). In 1978 Charles Kneupper introduced the Toulmin model to composition studies as a heuristic for writing in his article "Teaching Argument." In the 1990s, the Toulmin model informs two widely used argument textbooks, Rottenberg's *Elements of Argument* and Ramage and Bean's *Writing Arguments*.

If *The Uses of Argument* provides us with one of Toulmin's earliest attempts to explain the work of rationality, *Cosmopolis* provides us with one of the latest. In *Cosmopolis*, Toulmin argues that from Descartes on philosophy has concerned itself with a search for foundations. Toulmin would return to an understanding of rationality before Cartesian foundations, taking as his model Montaigne and his essays. For Toulmin, Montaigne's essays attempt to explain the writer's thoughts in relation to his own experience rather than to that of some absolute preexistent criteria outside himself. Calling for a return to the heterogeneity and uncertainty that characterized sixteenth-century philosophical thought, Toulmin recommends leaving the ruins of the temple of rationalism constructed by Descartes and advocates returning to the town in which the temple was built to see how we lived "before the rationalist dream seized hold of people's minds" (304).

From his earliest work to his latest, Toulmin has tried to give ear to that which has been excluded from philosophy, and he has named this exclusion "situation," a term excluded by philosophers invested in the dream of rationality. This effort has made of the philosopher a rhetorician. We are fortunate that we have yet to hear what will have been Toulmin's final words on his lifelong project.

BIBLIOGRAPHY

Primary Sources

Olson, Gary A. "Literary Theory, Philosophy of Science, and Persuasive Discourse: Thoughts from a Neo-premodernist." *Journal of Advanced Composition* 13.2 (1993): 283–309.

Toulmin, Stephen E. *Cosmopolis: The Hidden Agenda of Modernity*. Chicago: University of Chicago Press, 1990.

———. *The Uses of Argument*. Cambridge: Cambridge University Press, 1959.

Toulmin, Stephen, Richard Rieke, and Alan Janik. *An Introduction to Reasoning*. New York: Macmillan, 1978.

Biography

Foss, Sonja K, Karen A. Foss, and Robert Trapp. *Contemporary Perspectives on Rhetoric*. Prospect Heights, IL: Waveland Press, 1985.

Sulliven, Meg. "Philosopher–Scholar Receives Highest Honor from NEH." Available at: http://www.usc.edu/ext-relations/news_service/chronicle_html/1997.02.7.html/ Philosopher_Scholar_Recei.html. Accessed 1/9/00.

Wartofsky, Marx W. "Stephen Toulmin: An Intellectual Odyssey." Available at: http:// www.neh.gov/publications/magazine/97–03/wartofsky.html. Accessed 1/9/00.

Who's Who in America 1998. 52nd ed. Vol. 2. New Providence, NJ: Marquis Who's Who, 1997.

Criticism

Brockreide, Wayne, and Douglas Ehninger. "Toulmin on Argument: An Interpretation and Application." *Quarterly Journal of Speech* 46.1 (1960): 44–53.

Ehninger, Douglas, and Wayne Brockreide. *Decision by Debate*. New York: Dodd, Mead, 1963.

Kneupper, Charles W. "Teaching Argument: An Introduction to the Toulmin Model." *College Composition and Communication* 29.3 (1978): 237–41.

Ramage, John D., and John C. Bean. *Writing Arguments*. 3rd ed. New York: Macmillan, 1995.

Rottenberg, Annette P. *Elements of Argument*. 5th ed. New York: St. Martin's, 1996.

———. *The Structure of Argument*. 5th ed. Boston: Bedford, 1996.

VICTOR J. VITANZA
(1940–   )

Michelle Ballif

Born on December 17, 1940, in Houston, Texas, to Pauline Ditta and Joseph Vitanza, Victor Joseph Vitanza was delivered by Dr. G. Suttle Ham; his first word was "pasta"; his first "sentence" was "Some more." These seemingly insignificant biographical details foreground Vitanza's contribution to twentieth-century rhetoric. Delivered by a Ham, Vitanza has played the "ham" to "*new* audiences . . . those people and ideas . . . 'excluded' " by philosophy and philosophic rhetoric ("Retrospective" xiii). Vitanza came to play this role because of his love of pasta and Socrates's attack on cookery in the *Gorgias*: "I guess I responded personally because my family, specifically my maternal grandparents, were from a long line of very proud Sicilian cooks. . . . And so in brief, this is how I came to know rhetoric—through . . . its counterpart, through cookery" ("Rhetoric" 205, 206). But just as Plato's talk about "cookery" is a pretext to condemn sophistry, Vitanza's talk about "pasta" is a pretext to talk about "some more" (208). For Vitanza, "some more" is that which has been excluded by the logic of negative dialectics; "some more" is that which is beyond one/two; thesis/antithesis thinking. Thus, by "hamming" it up, Vitanza attempts to disrupt philosophic rhetoric's systematic exlusions and to open the space (the Third Sophistic) for that which has been excluded (the Third Man).

BIOGRAPHY

A self-proclaimed "accidental academic," Vitanza was raised by a family "who could not even claim to be blue collar" and who certainly weren't involved in academe. He claims he went to the "serious" high school only because his friends went. He was, however, serious about performing, and so he attended the Berklee School of Music in Boston, where he studied "composition." As a drummer, he traveled with various bands, playing jazz in nightclubs as well as playing an extended gig for the Shamrock Hilton, where he performed with such stars as Rosemary Clooney. Eventually tiring of life on the road, Vitanza enrolled in the University of Houston as an English major only because his friends did, remained enrolled only because he did not want to be drafted and sent to Vietnam, and finally graduated in 1967. Because the war continued, Vitanza continued in school, receiving an M.A. in 1970, and then enrolled in Northern Illinois University's doctoral program. Still enrolled, after completing course work, he taught at the University of Nantes (1972–1973). Finally the war was over, and Vitanza had to decide about academic life. He returned to Illinois, completed his exams and dissertation, "The Dialectic of Perverseness in the Major Fiction of Edgar Allan Poe," graduated in 1975, and accepted a tenure-track position at Eastern Illinois University, where this "accidental" academic taught American literature until 1982 (personal email).

Vitanza's turn to rhetoric was equally serendipitous. In 1978, as a National Endowment for the Humanities Fellow-in-Residence at Carnegie Mellon, he studied "Rhetorical Invention and the Composing Process" under the direction of Richard E. Young. During this time, Vitanza and seminar fellows (including James Berlin, Lisa Ede, and Charles Kneupper) read contemporary poststructuralist texts, "which were not getting any play . . . in the journals of our field" and, therefore, conceived of a journal, which would allow these new ideas to play ("Retrospective" xvi). Soon thereafter, Vitanza inaugurated *PRE/TEXT: A Journal of Rhetorical Theory* (1980), which continues to "commission and publish manuscripts that other journals in the field did not or would not (think of) publish(ing)" ("Retrospective" xiii).

In 1982, Vitanza accepted a position at the University of Texas at Arlington, where he established a graduate program in rhetoric, composition, and criticism; helped coordinate the freshman composition program; founded and directed (1987–1994) the Center for Rhetorical and Critical Theory; and organized a national conference, "Writing Histories of Rhetoric" (1989). Currently he is a full professor there. He continues to publish *PRE/TEXT*, although without institutional support, and founded in 1997 (with Cynthia Haynes) an electronic supplement to the journal: *PRE/TEXT: Electra(Lite)*.

Vitanza's early publications addressed issues in American literature, focusing on authors such as Poe, Melville, Emerson, and John Barths. As his research and teaching interests shifted to rhetoric and composition, so did his conference presentations and publications, specifically to issues in historiography, including *Writing Histories of Rhetoric* (1994) and *Negation, Subjectivity, and the History of Rhetoric* (1997). Although still writing about histories of rhetoric, Vitanza's publications have gone virtual with *Writing for the World Wide Web* (1998) and *CyberReader* (1996).

VITANZA'S CONTRIBUTIONS TO TWENTIETH-CENTURY RHETORIC

Vitanza's work attends to the problem of the "Third Man," to that which must be excluded in order for communication (or community) to take place. According to Michel Serres, "To hold a dialogue is to suppose a third man and to seek to exclude him; a successful communication is the exclusion of the third man . . . the prosopopoeia of noise" (qtd. in *Negation* 44). The problem of the "Third Man" is symptomatic of the logic of the dialectic: *the* epistemic motor of Western thought, which establishes some *positive* ("The Good," "The True," "The Beautiful") through a *negation* of the Other and an *exclusion* of all that can't be *synthesized*. The resulting "positive" is thus bought at too high a price: For "Dialectics by negation led, Adorno more pointedly argues, quite logically to Auschwitz" ("Threes" 199). Countering the dialectic, Vitanza offers the Third— the term that resists being synthesized—in an attempt to lend an ear to the "noise," which he has variously called a "counter" rhetoric, an "antibody rhetoric," a "pararhetoric," a *"dissoi paralogoi,"* and "Third Sophistic."

Vitanza's contribution to historiography is his insistent call that we attend to (in Foucault's terms) the "counter-memory" of any given history of rhetoric ("Some Rudiments" 196). In *Negation, Subjectivity, and the History of Rhetoric*, "Some Rudiments of Histories of Rhetorics and Rhetorics of Histories," and " 'Notes' towards Historiographies of Rhetorics," Vitanza argues that this exclusion is accomplished not only via "Traditional Historiography" (written as a narrative of the "Great Man") but also via "Revisionary Historiography" (written to revise or redeem the history of rhetoric). Contrariwise, Vitanza offers " 'sub/ versive' *hysteriography*" as a "nonfascistic, nontotalitarian hermeneutic" ("Some Rudiments" 232), which seeks to counter and disrupt traditional rhetoric (and the politics and ethics such rhetoric sustains), thereby to "dis/locate *The* dominant discourse" ("Threes" 198). Vitanza's contribution to composition studies, likewise, is his critique of traditional as well as critical writing pedagogies. Vitanza argues these practices create writing subjects who are subjected to the dominant discourse ("Three Countertheses" and "Concerning a Post-Classical Ethos").

This "dominant discourse" hails us as humanist subjects, subjecting us to the Enlightenment's Grand Narrative, which promises emancipation in/through *reason*. But this emancipation is illusory, as theorists such as Michel Foucault have argued, for one can only be a subject insofar as one has been subjected to reason (to the violence of negative dialectics) and insofar as one has been disciplined and thus legitimated by the State (*polis*). Vitanza calls this double bind of subjectivity "social bondage": "[T]he means of being an individual via the species, the means of deliberation, and the means of reaching consensus are always already coded—that is, predetermined by both Kapitalist and Socialist modes of production. . . . What is wanted, then, is dissensus (*heterologia* or *paralogia*)" ("Concerning" 401). *Dissensus*, for Vitanza, is the way to resist the *synthesis* required by reason and power, for the logic of dialectics *is* the logic of power: Both require purgations; both operate according to a restrictive economy. Plato's *Republic* required the purgation of all sophists and poets; traditional rhetoric requires the purgation of sophistic (spurious and deceptive) language. In short, Vitanza argues, what traditional rhetoric has excluded is *desire* ("Three Countertheses" 142). Thus Vitanza's counter rhetoric is "rhetoric + *eros*" or "rherotics" (rhetorics of "unfettered desire") (*Negation* 24, 3), fueled by a desire for societies, subjectivities, and rhetorics without reserve.

Vitanza's "counter" rhetoric is not, however, merely the dialectical Other of traditional (Platonic, Aristotelian) rhetoric. As "Third Man," it is Other than the Other. Vitanza resists the binary logic of either/or (Aristotle's law of noncontradiction) by dealing only thirds: "[I]nstead of traditional and/or revisionary history, I have written of sub/versive hystery; instead of dialectic and/or dissoi logoi, I have enacted dissoi paralogoi (polylectics); instead of philosophy and/or philosophical rhetoric, or First and/or Second Sophistics, I have described/enacted Third Sophistic (para)rhetorics" ("Threes" 208). His counter rhetoric is a third, which is (un)accounted for by way of "one, two, and some more," thus calling attention to the way a pararhetoric would avoid being accounted for by traditional, logical, metonymical methods. This "some more" is thus radical multiplicity, "nonpositive affirmation," and a "nonsynthesized, nonsynecdochic" term, which has no relation to the negative or negative dialectics (*Negation* 58; "Threes" 198, 202). Rather, it "denegate[s] the negative" (*Negation* 13) and thereby disrupts the stranglehold of the Negative as well as avoids the trap offered by negative deconstruction, whereby the binary is simply reversed, newly privileging the previously negated term, such as privileging Woman over Man (*Negation* 67).

This third term as a Third Sophistic would be "an 'art' of 'resisting and disrupting' the available means (that is, the cultural codes) that allow for persuasion and identification: the 'art' of not only refusing the available (capitalistic/socialist) codes but also of refusing altogether to recode, or to reterritorialize, power relations" ("Some More" 133). A Third Sophistic is thus a "some more" that would disrupt the dominant discourse of traditional rhetoric (with its principle of exclusion). Although this Third Sophistic can be historically located in the nineteenth and twentieth centuries, following the second sophistic (second century A.D.) and the first sophistic (fifth century B.C.E.), Vitanza's use of the term resists traditional notions of temporality; his histories of rhetoric are composed not of the past but of the *future anterior*—a tense that addresses *what will have been* (*Negation* 238). Vitanza's Third Sophistic seeks "to create the conditions of the possibilities" beyond the dialectic (post-Plato; post-Freud; post-Marx; postmodern), to create a space (post*polis*) that does not require exclusions but is what "Lyotard calls the *pagus* (the savage place, 'a border zone where genres of discourse enter into [perpetual] conflict over the mode of linking' " (*Negation* 317).

Whereas Aristotle's art of rhetorical invention is generated by *topoi*, Vitanza's sophistic art engages "*atopoi*" as "*de/conceptual*" points of departure ("Threes" 205), including "mis-representative an*ti*dotes," "dissoi-*para*logoi," and "thea-*tricks*" (*Writing Histories* 250). These *atopoi* serve to construct histories (or "hysteries") in the future anterior, which "wage perpetual war" against Grand Narratives, the dialectic, and the Truth (250). Thus, a Third Sophistic practice has "de/conceptual" beginnings but no end: It is continual argumentation, continual critique. It is an "excursion in search of 'the excluded third man' "; yet it is an excursion that will never conclude (*Negation* 311). For if the Third Man is "found" and included, it "will make everyone's task more difficult" (312), for then one would have to seek for the *new* Third Man—that which was excluded in order for *this* Third Man (or woman) to appear.

While Vitanza searches for the "excluded third man" in the History of Rhetoric, he simultaneously introduces various Third Men (and Women) into the discipline of composition studies: "I 'inappropriate' outsiders such as Deleuze and Guattari, Cixous and Clément . . . in ways that might shake the very incipient foundations of composition-as-canonized studies" ("Interview" 54). These foundations, Vitanza argues in "Three Countertheses," are established by contemporary compositionists only by denying the postmodern crisis of legitimation, as this crisis places in "aporia the very value, or even possibility, of community itself, which traditionally has been the end of rhetoric" (140).

But, of course, this is precisely what Vitanza is after: placing in aporia the foundations of rhetoric. He attempts this further by *performing* the Third Man. Through his writing and speaking style, characterized by puns, allusions, and "unhinged sentences," he "would be that third, forever interrupting the conversations. . . . When the field of composition studies carries on a conversation and, consequently, excludes, I will be there babbling. . . . I would be the eternal return of the 'counter-memory' " ("Interview" 58).

Predictably, Vitanza's performance of the Third Man has rendered him odd man out, subject to criticism. George Kennedy, for example, has characterized Vitanza's style as "Vitanzan Vitalism" as "a form of *letteraturizzazione*, a kind of linguistic herpes that comes and goes" (231). James Murphy writes: "Vitanza's style is probably exalting for some, frustrating for others. He seems to have a pathological fear of completing a thought" (268). Both Kennedy and Murphy see Vitanza's style as an *unnecessary* excess—one that privileges style over substance and that leaves us, according to Kennedy, "flesh without muscle" (231). In other words, Vitanza is criticized for not offering *substantial* history (Scott 236) nor substantial solutions for all that he problematizes (Murphy 268). Even sympathetic readers such as J.D.H. Amador wonder if Vitanza's critique of power and subjectivity doesn't leave us without a substantial and empowered subject (par. 14). These criticisms, strangely, are asking Vitanza to do precisely what he is resisting: to propose "final solutions." Vitanza as well as his journal *PRE/TEXT* is, according to James Berlin, dedicated to the "continual disruption of all complacency" ("Introduction: Another View" xxv). This will have been Vitanza's contribution to twentieth-century rhetorics.

BIBLIOGRAPHY

Primary Sources

Vitanza, Victor. "Cackling with Tears in My Eyes; or, Some Responses to 'The Gang of Three': Scott-Leff-Kennedy." *Rhetoric Review* 7.1 (1988): 214–18.

———. "Concerning a Post-Classical Ethos, as Para/Rhetorical Ethics, the 'Selphs,' and the Excluded Third." *Ethos: New Essays in Rhetorical and Critical Theory.* Ed. James S. Baumlin and Tita French Baumlin. Dallas: Southern Methodist University Press, 1994. 389–431.

———. "Critical Sub/Versions of the History of Philosophical Rhetoric." *Rhetoric Review* 6.1 (1987): 41–66.

———. *Negation, Subjectivity, and the History of Rhetoric.* Albany, New York: State University of New York, 1997.

———. " 'Notes' towards Historiographies of Rhetorics; or, The Rhetorics of the Histories of Rhetorics: Traditional, Revisionary, and Sub/Versive." *PRE/TEXT* 8.1–2 (1987): 63–125.

———. "Of MOOs, Folds, and Non-reactionary Virtual Communities." *High Wired: On the Design, Use, and Theory of Educational MOOs.* Ed. Cynthia Haynes and Jan Rune Holmevik. Ann Arbor: University of Michigan Press, 1998. 286–310.

———. "An Open Letter to my 'Colligs': On Paraethics, Pararhetorics, and the Hysterical Turn." *PRE/TEXT* 11.3–4 (1990): 237–87.

———. " 'Some More' Notes, Toward a Third Sophistic." *Argumentation* 5 (1991): 117–39.

———. "Some Rudiments of Histories of Rhetorics and Rhetorics of Histories." *Rethinking the History of Rhetoric: Multidisciplinary Essays on the Rhetorical Tradition.* Ed. Takis Poulakos. Boulder, CO: Westview Press, 1993. 193–239.

———. "Taking A-Count of a (Future-Anterior) History of Rhetoric as 'Libidinalized Marxism' (A PM Pastiche)." *Writing Histories of Rhetoric.* Carbondale: Southern Illinois University Press, 1994. 180–216.

———. "Three Countertheses: Or, A Critical In(ter)vention into Composition Theories and Pedagogies." *Contending with Words: Composition and Rhetoric in a Postmodern Age.* Ed. Patricia Harkin and John Schilb. New York: MLA, 1991. 139–72.

———. "Threes." *Composition in Context.* Ed. W. Ross Winterowd and Vincent Gillespie. Carbondale: Southern Illinois University Press, 1994. 196–218.

———. *Writing for the World Wide Web.* Boston: Allyn & Bacon, 1998.

———. ed. *CyberReader.* 1996. 2nd ed. Boston: Allyn & Bacon, 1998.

———. *Writing Histories of Rhetoric.* Carbondale: Southern Illinois University Press, 1994.

Biography

Haynes-Burton, Cynthia. "Interview with Victor J. Vitanza." *Composition Studies* 21.1 (1993): 49–65.

Vitanza, Victor. Personal email. June 23, 1998; September 29, 1998.

———. " 'A Retrospective and Two Prospectives." *PRE/TEXT: The First Decade*. Pittsburgh: University of Pittsburgh Press, 1993. xi–xxiii.

———. " 'Rhetoric, Cookery, and Recipes': Preface 2." *PRE/TEXT* 1.1–2 (1980): 205–14.

Criticism

Amador, J.D.H. Rev. of *Negation, Subjectivity, and the History of Rhetoric. H-Net Book Review* (September 1997). Available at: http://www.h-net.msu.edu/reviews/rhetor@msu.edu

Berlin, James. "Introduction: Another View." *PRE/TEXT: The First Decade*. Ed. Victor Vitanza. Pittsburgh: University of Pittsburgh Press, 1993. xxiii–xxviii.

Kennedy, George. "Some Reflections on Neomodernism." *Rhetoric Review* 6.2 (1988): 230–33.

Leff, Michael. "Serious Comedy: The Strange Case History of Dr. Vitanza." *Rhetoric Review* 6.2 (1988): 237–45.

Murphy, James J. Rev. of *Writing Histories of Rhetoric. Quarterly Journal of Speech* (May 1997): 267–68.

Scott, Robert. "Non-discipline as a Remedy for Rhetoric? A Reply to Victor Vitanza." *Rhetoric Review* 6.2 (1988): 233–37.

Richard M. Weaver
(1911–1963)

Martin J. Jacobi and Bernard K. Duffy

Richard Weaver, born in North Carolina, earned a B.A. at the University of Kentucky, an M.A. in English at Vanderbilt University, and a Ph.D. at Louisiana State University. After his schooling he emigrated from his beloved South to teach rhetoric and composition at the University of Chicago's undergraduate college, where he spent his entire career. A bachelor who lived austerely and privately in a rented room, Weaver's teaching and his often-controversial scholarly writing consumed his entire adult life. For one who passionately believed that "the purpose of life is not contemplation, but action," Weaver's vocation as professor and self-avowed "practicing humanist" constituted a mode of action in the world. He turned out several books and a score of carefully crafted essays before his untimely death from a heart attack at the age of 53.

During his lifetime he published three scholarly books, *Ideas Have Consequences* (1948), *The Ethics of Rhetoric* (1953), and *Visions of Order* (1964), with chapters ranging from literary history and criticism to rhetorical theory and southern history but all somehow suggesting his philosophical and cultural conservatism and many underscoring the vital role of rhetoric in the understanding and maintenance of traditional culture. Among his works, the most important to rhetoric is *The Ethics of Rhetoric* and, secondarily, a collection of essays assembled posthumously and published under the title *Language Is Sermonic* (1970). After his death, admirers of Weaver also published his dissertation, *The Southern Tradition at Bay* (1968); another collection of essays, *Life without Prejudice* (1965); and a volume of his essays on southern themes, *The Southern Essays of Richard M. Weaver* (1987). In addition, Weaver published a textbook for freshman composition, *Rhetoric and Composition: A Course in Reading and Writing* (1957).

Richard Weaver was, by predisposition, a staid, conservative southerner. He returned to the family farm each summer to plow a field behind two mules, and he bemoaned the leveling process that created a national instead of regional identity. Philosophically, he supported the southern agrarian movement, writing numerous articles in praise not only of Ransom's and Tate's literary critical acumen but also in praise of the stand they and the other southern Agrarians took against modernism, corporatism, mechanization, and progressivism in educational and societal practices and values. His identification with the southern agrarians also bespoke a cultural conservatism and a suspicion of what his society called "progress." In numerous essays (collected in *The Southern Essays of Richard M. Weaver*), he extolled the Southern Agrarians' resistance to the encroachments of northern industrialism, business enterprise, and commercial culture, and he also extolled their support for the values he felt were part of the southern tradition and heritage. When, for example, Weaver wrote an essay on the rhetoric of the Scopes trial, which is in fact a thinly veiled defense of the right of Tennessee to secede from the modern scientific world by enacting the antievolutionist Butler Act, he wrote Donald Davidson, his mentor at Vanderbilt and lifelong friend, to declare that this essay would show his southern friends where he really stood. He felt he had to atone for another essay in which he had spoken approvingly of Abraham Lincoln's rhetoric, which he believed manifested the conservative habit of arguing from first principles. Despite Lincoln's prosecution of the Civil War, Weaver believed that his rhetoric placed him in the sphere of intellectual conservatives. To judge from the wide-ranging topics of his book chapters and essays, Weaver filtered the world through his rhetorical conceptions. He was a man of words, not a man of action, but his words helped influence a generation of conservatives at a time when conservatives felt as misunderstood as liberals do in our own day.

Historically, Weaver claimed high status for the antebellum Southern society, because he approved of its feudal system, its code of chivalry, its gentleman class, and its religiousness. Thus, he claimed that the plantation system allowed for a stable society in which all societal members could know—and therefore be content with—their places and roles in the society: The rich landowners were responsible for training themselves to administer the society fairly and effectively and for maintaining the social structure and moral values; others were responsible for performing their roles as merchants, artisans, laborers, and so on. He even intimates that slaves were not ill served by the "peculiar institution" when it was operating justly. His cultural yardstick, then, is the agrarian South as it existed before being engulfed by the insurgent forces of modern mass culture—urbanization, industrialism, commercialism, and the mass media.

Intellectually, however, Weaver was at one and the same time a cultural and social conservative and an iconoclast. He was an outspoken reactionary against modernism, armed with a neo-Platonic philosophy, a sophisticated understanding of classical rhetorical theory, and the zeal of one confident in the truth. His approval of the antebellum Southern social system is mirrored in his belief that in many ways medieval Europe expressed what is best about human society and in his charge that the West's rejection of this social system and its philosophical underpinnings led to industrial capitalism and an immoral, materialistic culture. His position is contrary to the modernist presuppositions of many of his contemporaries and contrary to the postmodern presuppositions of many today: He asks readers to believe that there are abiding truths and values that comport with the truths and values that have always been praised by Western cultures.

Professionally Weaver was a knowledgeable and adroit teacher and rhetorician, capable of explaining the subtleties of Plato, richly expounding upon classical principles of rhetoric, and employing rhetorical precepts to dissect discourse that interested him—whether the rhetoric of political luminaries such as Abraham Lincoln, Edmund Burke, Daniel Webster, and Robert Hayne, or the speeches of nineteenth-century orators, or the deceptively objective prose of social scientists of his own generation. His professional publications address not only aspects of classical philosophy and rhetoric but also rhetoric's application in the everyday world. Further, Weaver spoke often to groups in the Chicago area and elsewhere and published spirited political opinion pieces in such journals of popular opinion as *Modern Age* and the *National Review*.

He is most controversial in his role as cultural critic. Weaver provides a brief and incisively argued overview of the cultural decline of the West in the opening of his *Ideas Have Consequences*. He identifies the beginnings of the fall in the early fourteenth century, in the triumph of Occarn's nominalism over the Platonic realism that had before then held sway. This triumph, in effect the denial of the transcendent realm, means that nature is no longer an imperfect imitation but something that contains the principles of its own constitution and behavior. Nominalism, then, contended Weaver, leads quickly to the development of science as the tool for closely examining and understanding nature. The cultural decline continues, Weaver argued, as the scientific emphasis on nature as a self-operating mechanism and humans as rational animals itself leads to a philosophic materialism and psychological behaviorism that assumes biological necessity and environmental determinism: Human beings are unable to control their own lives or to overcome the environmental pressures on their cultural and social institutions. Individual freedom and individual responsibility are lost, and we become the lost souls of the modern materialist state.

The targets of his criticisms of modernism are varied: the mass media, business culture, social science, "equalitarianism," liberal attitudes toward criminality, the blurring of sexual distinctions and hierarchy, educational relativism, and jazz music, to name a few. Those who benefit from the status quo see these liberal forces as socially and culturally dangerous and demonize them. For Plato, it is the sophists who are to be demonized; for Weaver, it is what today we call relativists, social and other constructionists and deconstructionists, and postmodernists or poststructuralists. He opposes social scientists who emphasize determinism and behaviorism, educational theorists who promote education for democracy and other "progressive" agenda items, and politicians who do not demand responsibility of citizens but instead pander to citizens' greed, selfishness, and laziness. He opposes those who use rhetoric to manipulate people, whether through capitalist advertising or through government propaganda (and he notes the areas of overlap). For example, in "The Great Stereopticon," an essay about the mass media of newspapers, radio, and film that appears in *Ideas Have Consequences* (92–112), Weaver trenchantly complains about the media's focus on the sensory world, about its propaganda for modern thought and manners, and about its trivialization and fragmentation of life. A culture shaped by the modern mass media is remote from a culture that admires the aesthetics and cultural presumptions of nineteenth-century oratory. Such oratory appeals to a firmly held set of common values that Weaver thinks the modern world has atomized. For Weaver the modern perception that the old oratory was anachronistic demonstrates more than a change in literary standards. At root it shows how the presumptive, incontestable truths of a homogenous society to which the old orator had appealed are now replaced by moral relativism, on one hand, and a scientific notion of truth as empirical fact, on the other. The anachronism of old oratory was merely suggestive of the much larger problem of social anomie. According to Weaver, modern society under the influence of a pervasive scientific and scientistic orientation prefers fact to proposition and empirical reality to ideas as essences and therefore values individual rather than cultural perception. The modern sophists had left neo-Platonists like Weaver with little influence.

Weaver's conservatism includes a strong belief in the value of cultural traditions, and he concerns himself with the loss of place for what has guided the culture in its practices, its beliefs, and its values. Because "tradition" is for Weaver an absolute good, its antithesis is "progress," which replaces traditions with change—and usually in favor of what is larger, more mechanized, and more bureaucratized. The emphasis on progress comes from the belief that we are always evolving, growing, accumulating wisdom, that every day in every way things are getting better. Traditions are important to the culture and its societies, Weaver maintains, because they serve as reminders of our origins and supports for our daily lives. They are valuable because truth is stable, not something that transmogrifies with time, not something that progresses as humankind progresses. The stability of truth requires that we conserve our knowledge and wisdom rather than assume its frequent and inevitable obsolescence. However, despite the importance of stable truths, Weaver offers no explicitly identified truths, nor a clear lineage and methodology for obtaining those truths, so he cannot clearly delineate the range of traditional values and practices. He sketches instead a culture that includes competing beliefs and values, with those appreciated by Weaver and those detested by him both having good claims as the culture's tradition, since, after all, the triumph of a nominalist philosophy dates to the Medieval Age.

One way to state matters is to say that current cultural theory cannot allow Weaver's assumptions regarding traditional beliefs and values to pass unchallenged. The beliefs, practices, and values that Weaver thought he could assume of his reading public—and it should be mentioned that the decade of his greatest productivity was the 1950s—are today problematized by the counterstatements of Marxists, feminists, African Americanists, queer theorists, and others. Quite clearly, Weaver operates much like the nineteenth-century practitioners of "spacious rhetoric," who assumed that they and their audiences shared a culture and so shared its beliefs, practices, and values. To articulate those beliefs, much less to argue for them, would have been perceived by those rhetors, and apparently by Weaver, as superfluous if not insulting to the audiences' intelligence. In short, although Weaver asserts that there are certain truths and values that would militate against much of what we believe and do as base, and although he often in his more political writing corrects the errors in various modern, liberal positions, he fails to identify those certain truths, let alone provide compelling reasons why we should accept them as certain. An unstated assumption, then, in Weaver's writing seems to be that while we may not be able to define the Good, we all know it when we see it.

We can know, for instance, what is good and bad in American life. The very taxonomy Weaver uses for his "god terms" and "devil terms" indicates his political conservatism, as do his comments and critiques concerning American education, big business, and social movements. Although his apologists like to point out that Weaver was not involved in any partisan causes, his arguments on behalf of a political and cultural credo won him conservative friends and admirers, including Willmore Kendall, described by Garry Wills, the popular historian, as "suicidally frank" for his criticism of Lincoln's argument in the Gettysburg Address that the nation was founded upon the principle of equality; William F. Buckley, editor of the right-wing *National Review*, to which Weaver contributed book reviews and opinion pieces; and Henry Regnery, whose Regnery Press published conservatives such as Buckley and Weaver. In many ways, Weaver's thoughts and stated positions do compare with the conservatism currently represented in the American political sphere. He is suspicious of big government, preferring smaller government that reflects regional interests, needs, and values. (For instance, he supports the traditional states' rights argument of the South.) He is opposed to what today is sometimes called identity politics. He attacks the liberalizing of the woman's place in society and culture, he is suspicious of claims that black people are the equal of whites, and he sneers often and extensively at the "equalitarianism" of liberal education policies and other attempts to level the playing field for all members of the community. He maintains that people should be judged on their merits and accomplishments, although he does not question the assumptions behind the hierarchy of merits, nor does he concern himself with the relative inequality of opportunity. Although he reveres traditional beliefs and values, one of his biggest shortcomings is that he refuses or is unable to clarify what they may be and, therefore, who may be helped and who hurt in a society governed by them. By dismissing race, class, and gender issues, Weaver in effect preserves the status quo, which of course can be construed as conservative.

However, in one important area, that of economics, Weaver is not at all like present-day political conservatives. In fact, he sees the economic realm as a prime agent for a good deal of the corruption of the society. Most notably, Weaver is no friend of industrial capitalism, supporting, rather, an economic system that emphasizes small farms and other small businesses. What Weaver particularly dislikes in the business world is that it is the latest and most pernicious manifestation of the degradation brought about by the decline of Platonic realism and the values it espouses. He excoriates the corporatist mentality, an orientation that reveres progress and profits, that looks for economic benefit and not honor or justice or humanitarianism, and that treats workers immorally by taking away initiative and personal responsibility. He describes the plight of the modern American—beset by loss of traditional values through multiculturalism, commodified by materialists, and asked to ignore the natural hierarchy that exists in the species as well as the hierarchy that must exist in any well-maintained society.

Capitalism, Weaver contends, cannot be a force for the maintenance of traditional beliefs and values, because it relies on industrialism, which unsettles establishments and initiates the endless innovations of technological "progress," and because it destroys the attitude of leisure needed for philosophic speculation and artistic creation. Furthermore, capitalists ought never to be public leaders, Weaver asserts, because they do not stand on principle but rather rely on expediency to generate profits. Weaver claims as an indisputable truth that their commercial success relies on shiftiness and opportunism and that they exploit artists and idealists but also distrust and even hate them. Further, they dehumanize their workers by forcing a method of production that requires workers to relinquish freedom, initiative, even thinking. Perhaps this lengthy quotation can stand for Weaver's position on business:

There are always those with a negative understanding of the good, that is to say, with a perception of how the good attracts the masses of the people, but without any impulsion toward it. These may well be the most evil members of society[:] while applying decorum to themselves, they bring the good into disrepute, they exhaust its power for meretricious ends, and so diminish the power of the ordinary man to distinguish between good and bad. Commercial men are usually of this [group]. (Goodnight 389–90)

On the other side of the debate, one is reminded of an earlier "businessman" and forerunner of social Darwinism, Callicles, who ironically admonished Socrates in the *Gorgias* to avoid the "abysses of philosophy" and "take up the Fine Art of Business"—by which he meant rhetorical pragmatism—so that Socrates could at least defend himself if falsely accused.

To reinform society about its traditional base and to coalesce, preserve, and reanimate cultural values, Weaver supports the use of "noble rhetoric." His notion of rhetoric's place in society grows out of Isocrates's conviction that in learning rhetoric one also learns the values of society and out of Cicero's belief in the centrality of rhetoric and his notion that in rhetorical discourse all knowledge passes in review. Weaver sees rhetoric as a bridge between abstract philosophy and historical reality. The orator takes philosophical propositions and applies them to real situations in the practical world. Without rhetoric, such philosophical propositions would remain merely powerful ideas, and Weaver believes fervently that the purpose of life is to act upon the world. "The purpose of life," he says, "is action, not contemplation," and he sees rhetoric as the individual's chief mode of action. This positioning seems odd for one as contemplative as Weaver, although his emphasis upon action does seem appropriate within the framework of a Christian morality in which good works demonstrate moral purpose.

Based upon his reading of the *Phaedrus*, Weaver argues that the work of the ethical rhetor is to give guidance to souls, as opposed to the sophist Gorgias's belief that the orator is a *psychagogos*, an enchanter of souls. For both Plato and Weaver, there is no chance of moving souls in the right direction without first using dialectic to inquire into the truth. Weaver interprets Plato as saying not only that dialectic must precede rhetoric but that rhetoric must fulfill the implications of the dialectic by making the logical analogical, that is, by embodying a line of reasoning in language, which Weaver, like I. A. Richards, sees as composed of metaphor. Rhetorical discourse, though not the ideal truth itself, offers a resemblance of the truth, which, if crafted to match the psychology of the audience, renders this truth persuasive.

While Weaver understands dialectic to be a necessary part of rhetoric, he also sees it to be subversive without rhetoric's influence, because while it can expose errors and show weaknesses in received beliefs, it can give us no reasons to believe; it is a methodology, without any motive force of its own. It can undermine received beliefs and so can lead to social agnosticism. When used "alone," it is, as Weaver claims, "essentially revolutionary and without commitment to practical realities" (*Visions of Order* 70). Dialectic comes the closest to appearing on its own, Weaver intimates, in the scientific realm. Science is analogous to the role that dialectic plays more generally in Weaver's rhetorical theory in that it too emphasizes dialectic and eschews nondemonstrable truths as irrelevant. And science, of course, plays a large part in the change in Western society for the worse. By itself, like dialectic, it is subversive and has proven itself, to Weaver's satisfaction, to be so by undermining the Western world's cultural practices, beliefs, and values. The rise of science meant a decline in the practice of a full rhetoric. Weaver notes that scientists go beyond dialectic when they attempt to persuade readers of the validity of their positions, and he argues thereby that the reasoning of dialectic is to be complemented with inspiration and emotion to construct a full rhetoric. In his analysis of the *Phaedrus*, Weaver also complains about what he calls "semantically purified speech," a false ideal of "pure notation" that has no rhetorical evocation (*Ethics of Rhetoric* 7). According to Weaver, this distinctly nonrhetorical view of language again reflects the scientistic impulses of the culture. Elsewhere he speaks derisively about the

General Semanticists' desire to "plane the tropes off of language" to create an objective discourse, free of ambiguity, subjective expressiveness, or persuasive appeal. Rhetoric, then, must necessarily provide feeling and motion, a sense of direction and a goal, so that Weaver's rhetoric becomes (to paraphrase Weaver's own definition) the process of securing truth and presenting that truth artfully.

Weaver takes the position that "language is sermonic," that discourse is a carrier of tendency and thus attempts persuasion. Since language is sermonic, its use always involves ethical action. Like Plato, Weaver believes that he must battle forces that call into question society's assumptions and accepted ways of thinking, acting, and judging. As Weaver defends rhetoric from the charge that it is merely propaganda, he argues that discourse can be both persuasive and ethical. Thus, Daniel Webster prosecuting the Knapp/White murder cause uses a rich rhetorical language, as well as his enormous prestige, to craft a narrative that leads the jury to a just decision. Rhetorical language exceeds the facts and offers reasons for a decision beyond logical. A meanly deceptive rhetoric appeals only to the emotions and exists as the counter image of objective, purely rational discourse. But Aristotle did not say that rhetoric exists at some nexus between emotions and logic but between politics and ethics; rhetors must appeal to a cultural common ground, which embodies ethical precepts as well as logical presuppositions. All rhetoric is ethically involved, but Weaver insists that the best rhetoric urges audiences to right thought and conduct.

Consistent with Weaver's neo-Platonism are his preferences among argument types: definition or principle, analogy or similitude, cause and effect, circumstance, and argument from authority. Weaver holds that argument from definition is a philosophically preferable form of argument because when not simply sententious, it requires the determination of essences. Lincoln is his example of a rhetor who rather consistently argued from a priori principles and whose definitions were both original and educative, not only for his day but for posterity. Argument from analogy is second in Weaver's ranking because it also relies upon definition. Concerning cause and effect argument, Weaver has less to say, nor does he quibble with the argument from consequence, which could be used by conservatives and liberals alike. But he disdains the so-called argument from circumstance, which effectively says that one must act because impelled to by the status quo. Such arguments he sees as the stuff of liberal rhetoric and as short-circuiting of all arguments to the contrary. Arguments from authority he treats equivocally, because moral authority cannot be spurned by any conservative, but he cautions against the modern genuflection to authority based purely upon specialized knowledge, that is, the authority of the scientist or technologist.

Weaver's rhetorical theory indicates an obvious debt to Kenneth Burke, whose discussion of positive, dialectical, and ultimate terms in *Grammar of Motives* predated Weaver's discussion of it in *The Ethics of Rhetoric*. More generally, Weaver has assimilated many of Burke's ideas (he even attended a weeklong seminar Burke gave at the University of Chicago), and his emphasis on the ethics of rhetoric is quite Burkean in its flavor. What Weaver might have taken from the portion of Burke's purely oral presentation cannot be known, but to-

ward the close of his life Burke ruminated that he would have written a book
on the ethics of rhetoric, were it not for Weaver's book of this title. But despite
similarities in some areas of their rhetorical theory, Weaver and Burke stood
poles apart politically.

Weaver's knowledge of rhetorical history and theory served him well as a
teacher of composition, and he was, in fact, a significant early voice in the
discipline who brought to bear upon the teaching of writing his wide knowledge
of rhetorical principles and practices. As early as 1948 he published "To Write
the Truth" (*Language Is Sermonic* 187–200) in the leading composition journal
College English, he authored or coauthored a number of other articles on composition theory and practice, and he wrote the textbook *Rhetoric and Composition*, which went through two editions. In his writing he encourages the
centrality of argument, he argues for the importance of the classical *topoi* and
other tools of invention, and he provides sound advice on organizational and
stylistic matters. And, significantly, he emphasizes the ethical implications of
composition, thereby presaging the current turn to this topic in the journals of
the discipline.

Whatever one thinks of Weaver's cultural and political theories, his contributions to rhetorical studies have been extraordinarily valuable. He wrote about
rhetoric long before the time when English and speech professors decided that
a renaissance in rhetoric was under way, and he wrote with unusual grace and
insight about the importance of rhetoric to human life.

BIBLIOGRAPHY

Primary Sources

Weaver, Richard M. *The Ethics of Rhetoric*. Chicago: Henry Regnery, 1953.
———. *Ideas Have Consequences*. Chicago: University of Chicago Press, 1948.
———. *Language Is Sermonic: Richard M. Weaver on the Nature of Rhetoric*. Ed.
   Richard L. Johannesen, Rennard Strickland, and Ralph T. Eubanks. Baton Rouge:
   Louisiana State University Press, 1970.
———. *Life without Prejudice and Other Essays*. Chicago: Henry Regnery, 1965.
———. *Rhetoric and Composition: A Course in Reading and Writing*. New York: Holt,
   Rinehart, 1957.
———. *The Southern Essays of Richard M. Weaver*. Ed. George M. Curtis III and James
   J. Thompson, Jr. Indianapolis, IN: Liberty Press, 1987.
———. *The Southern Tradition at Bay: A History of Postbellum Thought*. Ed. George
   Core and M. E. Bradford. New Rochelle, NY: Arlington, 1968.
———. *Visions of Order: The Cultural Crisis of Our Time*. 1960. Baton Rouge: Loui-
   siana State University Press, 1964.

Biography

Young, Fred Douglas. *Richard Weaver, 1910–1963: A Life of the Mind*. Columbus:
   University of Missouri Press, 1995.

Criticism

Beale, Walter H. "Richard M. Weaver: Philosophical Rhetoric, Cultural Criticism, and the First Rhetorical Awakening." *College English* 52.6 (1990): 626–40.

Bliese, John R. E. "Richard M. Weaver and the Rhetoric of the Lost Cause." *Rhetoric Society Quarterly* 19.4 (1989): 313–25.

———. "Richard Weaver's Axiology of Argument." *Southern Speech Communication Journal* 44.3 (1979): 275–88.

Bradford, M. E. "The Agrarianism of Richard Weaver: Beginnings and Completions." *Modern Age* 14.3–4 (1970): 249–56.

Duffy, Bernard, and Martin Jacobi. "A Comprehensive Bibliography of Works by and about Richard M. Weaver." *Rhetoric Society Quarterly* 25 (1995): 258–73.

———. *The Politics of Rhetoric: Richard M. Weaver and the Conservative Tradition.* Westport, CT: Greenwood Press, 1993.

Goodnight, Gerald Thomas. "Rhetoric and Culture: A Critical Edition of Richard M. Weaver's Unpublished Works." Diss., University of Kansas, 1978.

Johannessen, Richard L. "Conflicting Philosophies of Rhetoric/Communication: Richard M. Weaver versus S. I. Hayakawa." *Communication* 7 (1983): 289–315.

———. "A Reconsideration of Richard Weaver's Platonic Idealism." *Rhetoric Society Quarterly* 21.2 (1991): 1–10.

———. "Richard M. Weaver's Use of Kenneth Burke." *Southern Speech Communication Journal* 52.3 (1987): 312–30.

Kendall, Willmoore. "How to Read Richard Weaver: Philosopher of We the (Virtuous) People." *Intercollegiate Review* 2.1 (1965): 77–86.

Sproule, J. Michael. "Using Public Rhetoric to Assess Private Philosophy: Richard M. Weaver and Beyond." *Southern Speech Communication Journal* 44.3 (1979): 289–308.

W. ROSS WINTEROWD
(1930–   )

Kathy M. Houff

W. Ross Winterowd was born on January 24, 1930, in Salt Lake City, Utah. In his autobiographical writings, he describes his working-class upbringing with affection and establishes some of the key elements of his pedagogical history. He grew up in White Pine County, Nevada, in an apartment above a J. C. Penney store. Winterowd writes, "The town I grew up in was not, then, one of the world's great centers of culture" (*Culture* 140). Despite this cultural scarcity, Winterowd became "an omnivorous reader—largely because [his] father shared his passion for books with [him]" (142). This passion encompassed both classic texts and "doggerel" verse, and his father, who tended bar, dealt roulette, and quoted poetry, was Winterowd's first literary mentor, one who taught his son to value a wide range of texts. Winterowd states, "Though purists might deplore my father's taste for florid or ribald verse, nonetheless poetry became a part of my experience" (145). The necessity of "experiencing" literature plays an important part in Winterowd's contribution to literary and rhetorical studies, and he returns to this idea throughout his career. He comments that from early adolescence he viewed poetry not as something "strange" and inaccessible but as something enjoyable (*Department* 28). This joy in literature and a commitment to sharing it with a wide range of readers and writers is another project to which Winterowd has been devoted.

Although neither of Winterowd's parents graduated from high school, by his account "they were idiosyncratic autodidacts and ardent readers" (24). Winterowd's mother was less influential in shaping her son's "literary" mind, but he mentions her reading tastes and activism: "Mother's literary taste was more pragmatic; she read mainly political books" (24). His mother's political practicality, along with his working-class upbringing, may have influenced Winterowd's approach to pedagogy, a student-centered approach compatible with the liberatory education embraced by Paulo Freire. Winterowd's assertion that "the study of literature should be an applied field, asking and trying to answer questions about the uses of literature" ("Learning" 310–11), also reflects his mother's practical influence.

In *The English Department*, Winterowd's "personal and institutional history," he provides additional insight into his development as a rhetorician and teacher, using two of his high school teachers as exempla. He evokes his teacher during his junior year of high school as the model grammarian of her period. He writes, "We were so busy learning 'grammar' that we had no time to write poems, stories, or essays" (33). Although he seems to have been fond of Miss Hayes, Winterowd questions her methods and training. She represented the typical high school English teacher of this period who "had never considered composition-rhetoric as a problematic and an art, as she had literature" (76–77). Reestablishing composition-rhetoric as both problematic and art has been one of Winterowd's primary goals.

Winterowd recalls his "beloved high school teacher Glen A. 'Dunc' Duncan" (102) in a chapter entitled "Romantic Agonies," wherein he explores both his fascination with and rejection of the Romantic philosophy of literature. This philosophy played a significant role in the marginalization of composition and rhetoric. As literary studies focused increasingly on the world inside the poet's mind, the role of rhetoric, which always remains connected to the public arena, dwindled to insignificance within English departments. In addition, more quotidian texts, those that could not be classified as "art," became devalued. Winterowd asserts that "one reason for the marginalization of composition within the establishment (e.g., MLA) comes about partially through the devaluation of the empirical-pragmatic-applied" (134). Beginning with his reclamation of Aristotle as a practical empiricist first and foremost, Winterowd's career has been a scholarly and teacherly quest to revalue these things.

Winterowd's account of his earliest experiences with academia suggests that although he took great pleasure in literature, he was initially puzzled by literary criticism. He writes, "[P]atients etherized on tables and woman talking of Michelangelo had great meaning, I was certain, if I could just dig it out, but regardless of my efforts, I was unable to get through the overburden of words to the lode of meaning" (29). Even after the mysteries of poetry had been explained to him, he valued understanding less than "the resonances evoked" (29). Winterowd gravitated, fortunately, toward the study of rhetoric, a field where readers' and listeners' responses to words is paramount. Literature, like all discourse, should communicate ideas and not be studied as merely a beautiful artifact. He writes, "Language means. Always. Therefore we must consider the nature of meaning" (*Culture* 30). Language, all language, should resonate and communicate. In the spirit of Kenneth Burke, Winterowd writes, "[W]orks of art [should] engender attitudes which are preparations for action" (*Department* 157). For Winterowd the study of rhetoric helps us understand how, why, and what language does and allows us to explore "the nature of meaning." Winterowd continued to study and appreciate literature, but he did so through the lens of rhetoric.

Winterowd comments on how he accepted his "Romantic Agonies" and moved beyond them. He writes:

Immersed in this institutionalized, purified view of literature, I was trying, in my own terms, to make sense of Plato's *Phaedrus*, Aristotle's *Rhetoric*, Cicero's *De Oratore*, Quintilian's *Institutio*, and *On the Sublime*. Since I had been a student of Albert R. Kitzhaber . . . I became aware that rhetoric was a possible, if not totally respectable, subject of research . . . and then I began to read Kenneth Burke, who asked not what literature *is* but what it *does*. ("Learning" 308)

Winterowd discovered in rhetoric a subject that "provides the unifying theory that we need" (*Composition/Rhetoric* 334). He has never excluded literature, but he asserts unequivocally that English departments need to be "departments of reading *and writing*" (332) (emphasis added). He asks, "How many departments that you know of encourage the exploration of the whole world of writing?" (334). His appreciation of language and of a range of texts never faltered, but he found in rhetoric a more satisfying way to approach these subjects. As he writes in his first book,

[R]hetoric proffers the hope of meaningful and humane courses in high school and college. . . . Furthermore, rhetoric does synthesize; it is the ecumenical umbrella under which grammar, poetry, logic, composition, and public speaking can find shelter. One might say that rhetoric is a metasubject that can serve to unify the diverse aspects of the study of discourse of all kinds. (*Synthesis* vii)

After attending the University of Nevada at Reno, Winterowd completed his B.S. at the Utah State University in 1952. That same year he married Norma Graham of Fairview, Utah. His undergraduate degree was followed by time in the military. While completing his graduate education, he was an instructor of English at Carbon College during 1955–1956, spent a year at Kansas University as a graduate student and teaching assistant, and then transferred to the University of Utah. Winterowd received his Ph.D. from Utah in 1965. He then spent four years as an instructor and as an assistant professor at the University of Montana before joining the faculty at the University of Southern California. In 1972, Winterowd founded the doctoral program in Rhetoric, Linguistics, and Literature (RLL) at the University of Southern California. He directed this program from 1972 to 1982 and again beginning in 1987. The RLL program emphasized the synthetic nature of Winterowd's conception of rhetoric. Although the program is defunct, it produced 56 Ph.D.s and 3 M.A.s, all trained under rhetoric's "ecumenical umbrella."

W. Ross Winterowd is an unabashed, enthusiastic champion of rhetorical studies, which he claims "at present are simply more interesting than literary studies" (*Composition/Rhetoric* 334). He suggests, "[W]ell, just for fun, try rhetoric. You'll like it" (335).

WINTEROWD'S CONTRIBUTIONS TO CONTEMPORARY RHETORIC AND COMPOSITION

In a 1995 interview, Winterowd remarked, "For our purposes, the early sixties was the starting point. Rhetoric then began to gain definition" (Bannister and O'Connor 35). During this exciting period for rhetorical studies, and throughout his career, Winterowd helped redefine and reclaim rhetoric in four significant, interrelated ways. He has explored the historical marginalization of rhetoric, helped to reclaim invention, reexpanded rhetoric's scope, and revalued composition and pedagogy. In Winterowd's first book, *Rhetoric: A Synthesis*, published in 1968, he begins by addressing a pressing problem. How has rhetoric become the Cinderella of the English Department? Why has she been left to sweep the hearth while her overdressed stepsisters cavort at the Prince's ball? He writes, "With only a few notable exceptions, the art of rhetoric has been static for two hundred years" (v). In order to help prepare the way for a "new rhetoric," he explores its past. He writes, "[I]n the eighteenth century . . . for the first time, the manifold possibilities of rhetoric in all their richness and complexity fully emerged" (46). The richness of neoclassical rhetoric resulted from the convergence of "three diverse and popular movements": the "rediscovery" of Longinus, the burgeoning elocutionary movement, and The Royal Society's obsession with "the doctrine of perspecuity" (46). Unfortunately, the diversity of eighteenth-century rhetoric was also divisive. These varied movements focused, however differently, on style, and thereby contributed to the reduction of rhetoric in the nineteenth and twentieth centuries. Winterowd remarks, "[B]y the time English departments came into being . . . rhetoric had pretty much been pared down to stylistics" (Bannister and O'Connor 36). This emphasis on stylistics, joined with the impact of the Enlightenment, valued rationalism and denied the importance of "eloquence" (*Department* 43). When these elements were added to the methodization of composition studies, engendered by neoclassical rhetoricians' interest in faculty psychology, the result was a radically reduced rhetoric. Unfortunately, the lasting, practical legacy of eighteenth-century rhetoric was current-traditional rhetoric that prevailed in public schools for the next 200 years. In *The English Department*, Winterowd analyzes popular English (language arts) textbooks from the eighteenth century on and considers the largely undisputed hegemony of the current-traditional approach in them. He faults this approach because it replaces invention with method, focuses unproductively on correctness, and supports an unchallenged elitism. While Winterowd directs us toward an understanding of "the forces and counterforces of the neoclassical tradition" that will enable us "to understand the rhetorical problems of our age" (*Synthesis* 76), and acknowledges the richness of eighteenth-century rhetoric, he also explores the lasting influence of current-traditional rhetoric in order to replace it with a contemporary rhetoric, less hampered by method and obsessed with style.

Although Winterowd traces the rise of current-traditional rhetoric to the neoclassical rhetoricians, he claims that the primary force methodizing and marginalizing rhetoric, since the eighteenth century, has been Romanticism. Winterowd stops short of demonizing Samuel Taylor Coleridge but claims that the poet expressed the "questionable Romantic doctrines," that continue to influence current pedagogy (*Department* 115). These doctrines help explain rhetoric's decline in English departments. That "[t]he poet is more human and of more worth than the nonpoet" (115) demotes the rhetorician. Coleridge's theory of the primary and secondary imagination "allows one to hierarchize products of the imagination" (115) to the detriment of all expository writing. Romanticism also asserts that "the ideal is so superior to the empirical that the empirical is below serious consideration" (115). These doctrines, embraced wholeheartedly or unconsciously, dealt a dangerous blow to rhetorical studies. Winterowd writes, "Romanticism invented the autonomous inspired-imaginative-genius author, split the canon, and did away with invention" (43). He "detail[s] the manifestations and ravages of Romanticism in literary studies, such as the marked tendency to make empirical work taboo and the degradation of 'applied' knowledge such as studies of teaching" (9). However, his contribution to contemporary rhetoric goes beyond locating a reason for its declining status in the humanities. He has worked to reform rhetoric in three specific ways, by reclaiming invention, reexpanding rhetoric's scope, and revaluing pedagogy.

Winterowd and Invention

As a rhetorician and compositionist "outsider," one of Winterowd's contributions to contemporary rhetoric has come in the form of the questions he has asked himself and his colleagues. How did rhetoric come to be "merely" the study of style and organization? How might we redefine and reclaim rhetoric in the twentieth century? Who has contributed to the "new" rhetoric? What other disciplines have and will contribute to the revitalization of rhetoric and writing instruction? His work, both as theorist and teacher, foregrounds the value of interrogation as a heuristic device. The introduction to his second book concludes: "If *Contemporary Rhetoric* brings up the important questions regarding composition, then it will have served its purpose, for it will have acted as a heuristic" (37). In his earlier work, *Rhetoric: A Synthesis*, Winterowd reclaims the pragmatic emphasis in Aristotelian rhetoric and focuses on his methods of invention. From reconsidering Aristotle's *topoi*, to advocating the use of Kenneth Burke's "Five Key Terms of Dramatism," to exploring the "Tagmemic Contribution" of Young, Becker, and Pike, Winterowd sees heuristics as essential to reclaiming rhetoric's vitality and value. He writes, "One of the most interesting (and certainly one of the most neglected) aspects of rhetoric is the notion of topics or places of invention" (*Contemporary* 39). The triumph of

Platonic (or neo-Platonic) thought over Aristotelian within English departments led to this neglect. Winterowd writes, "Platonic invention would be directed inward, and terms such as 'inspiration' and 'creation' are virtually synonymous for invention. Aristotelian invention would be directed outward and can be associated with 'discovery' " (*Teacher's* 11). In both *Contemporary Rhetoric* and *Composition/Rhetoric: A Synthesis*, Winterowd devotes substantial chapters to topical invention. He classifies all possible topics into four major groups (*Contemporary* 45) and then considers the pedagogical applications of each. Ultimately his goal in revitalizing invention is a practical one. He writes, "[O]ne of the most intransigent problems for inexperienced (and experienced!) writers is invention . . . [and] topics as they have developed and as they are developing provide the best devices of invention" (47).

Expanding the Scope of Rhetoric

Winterowd expands the new rhetoric by allowing it to consider a tradition other than the more generally accepted Aristotelian or Platonic. In the opening chapters of *Rhetoric: A Synthesis*, he considers the advantages of reclaiming the skeptical or sophistic perspective. In *The English Department*, he writes, "[O]ne hope for the future is the emergence of a skepticism not unlike that expressed by Isocrates" (8). The two most productive tenets of Isocrates's skeptical and sophistic perspective are, according to Winterowd, "his stress on eloquence in the service of persuading others" (*Teacher's* 15) and "his denial that there is a foundation, an ultimate truth" (16). This antifoundationalism puts the rhetorical focus not on "the search for an absolute, but [on] the ability to cope with the events in an ever-changing, uncertain world" (16). Winterowd embraces these elements of Isocrates because they are "more of this world than the arguments that we find in the Platonic dialogues" (17). Winterowd's view of rhetoric insists upon its "worldliness."

Winterowd also calls attention to the short shrift Aristotle gives to style. Although reducing rhetoric to "mere stylistics" is damaging, eliminating the range of stylistic choice from contemporary rhetoric has equally hazardous repercussions. By "tell[ing] us that style ought to be clear, that its ideal is a vehicle that will carry reason without arousing either pleasure or pain" (*Synthesis* 41), Aristotle lays the groundwork for a rhetoric that can be purely logical and methodical. Such a radically reduced rhetoric risks becoming obsessed with correctness and method. Aristotle also lays the groundwork for a rhetoric divorced from literature. Winterowd writes, "What Aristotle fails to realize is the nexus between rhetoric and esthetics" (41). Aristotle further creates a schism between rhetoric and literature because "he fails to discuss epideictic rhetoric in detail, and hence his treatise is weighted toward disputation" (29). Winterowd argues that "rhetoric also has its moments of repose . . . when the only action it hopes to bring about is that of the audience's gift of sympathy and understanding" (26). He expands the definition of rhetoric beyond the merely persuasive and claims that "the purposes of rhetoric are in accord with the purposes of art" (26). The connection between rhetoric and art is integral to Winterowd's application of rhetorical analysis to literature.

Kenneth Burke, "whose genius lies primarily in showing the relevance of rhetoric in literature" (78–79), provides Winterowd with a model in this regard. He champions Burke and includes his "Five Key Terms of Dramatism" in *Contemporary Rhetoric*, asserting that the terms are "the most widely known and influential set of topics since Aristotle and Cicero" (155). Burke's definition of form, the "arousing and fulfillment of desires" (qtd. in *Contemporary* 183), is, according to Winterowd, "endlessly useful" (183). He states, "Well, clearly, Burke for years was devalued. You know, that book I did years and years ago [*Contemporary Rhetoric*] I think it was the first time Burke ever came into a freshman composition class. I was very proud of that" (Bannister and O'Connor 38). One of Burke's chief values for Winterowd is the way in which he shows how art, like rhetoric, can, should, and does persuade. More important, he revalues language and insists that it do something.

Along with Burke, Winterowd credits, among others, Francis Christensen, Marshall McLuhan, and Noam Chomsky with providing some of the elements of thought necessary for a new rhetoric to truly come into being. This diverse range of thinkers illustrates another of Winterowd's contributions to contemporary rhetoric: his willingness to incorporate a wide range of thought. The new rhetoric he envisions will cast a wide theoretical net in the service of practical ends. It will provide means of analyzing and judging style systematically and will with the help of linguistics "provide a system of analysis and a viable taxonomy" (*Synthesis* 82). The new rhetoric will be and is clearly a public and populist rhetoric. Winterowd writes, "This new rhetoric, now fragmented and awaiting synthesis, is emanating in part from ad agencies, governments, the political fringe" (78).

In addition to exploring the history of rhetoric, Winterowd has considered linguistics, neuroscience, cognitive science, literary criticism, and politics in his wide-ranging published work. One might even say of Winterowd that he is the great synthesizer. An expansive view of rhetoric also allows Winterowd to question the definition of "literature." His impassioned reclamation of "creative nonfiction," in *The Rhetoric of the "Other" Literature*, as a genre worthy of and suited to literary analysis reflects Winterowd's ongoing commitment to expanding the scope and range of "literary" studies.

Winterowd and Composition and Pedagogy

In his first book Winterowd introduces one of his most insistent themes. He bewails the position of rhetoric in English departments. He writes:

Not only are rhetoricians suspect; they are downright unwelcome. Of course, most English departments do tolerate a kind of mugwump rhetorician, the kind who organizes and administers freshman courses in composition . . . courses typically based on writing literary analysis and taught by people who do not have the faintest idea of what rhetoric really is. (153–54)

Winterowd asserts "that composition/rhetoric is not only a body of theory, but also an art; theory often arises from practice; pedagogy has always been an essential part of the field" (*Teacher's* 89). Over time, his work became increasingly practical and pedagogically oriented. In *Synthesis* he foresaw the need for "a space age Quintilian" (83) who would help organize and bring to the classroom the "new rhetoric." Winterowd became, at least in part, his own Quintilian. His *Contemporary Rhetoric: A Conceptual Background with Readings* arguably functions as a modest, modern *Institutes of Oratory*, Quintilian's major project that synthesized the best of classical rhetoric. While Winterowd's other works are less "synthetic," his *Contemporary Rhetoric* collects numerous contemporary rhetoricians and comments on their works. The book is divided into sections on invention, style, and form and is balanced between theory and practice. Like the *Institutes*, it "is a book for students as well as teachers" (x).

Winterowd has actively studied the teaching of rhetoric/writing both at the college and high school level. It can be said of him as it was of Quintilian that "he was a successful and experienced schoolmaster, accustomed to think in terms of the classroom" (Gwynn 189). From biographical reminiscences to his founding of the RLL program and particularly in his *A Teacher's Introduction to Composition in the Rhetorical Tradition* (with Jack Blum), Winterowd has focused on pedagogy. His interest in rhetorical theory, linguistics, and cognitive science always finds its way back to the composition classroom.

His early educational experiences led to his research on English textbooks. Winterowd critiques several texts that enjoyed massive and prolonged popularity and writes, "[L]anguage arts textbooks, such as *English in Action*, became possible—became inevitable!—when rhetorical invention ceased to be discovery and became creation" (*Department* 34). Texts such as these emphasized style and form, methodical forms of instruction, correctness, and grammar (38). The popularity of these texts puzzles and troubles Winterowd, who states that "massive evidence leads one to conclude that systematic grammatical study of any kind does not improve one's writing or speaking ability" (43).

By considering basic problems in literacy, and by reaching out to "everyone who has a child in grade school or high school, acquiring the basics of reading and writing and then moving onward to a 'higher' literacy that allows him or her to participate fully in the culture and economy of our society" (*Culture* xi), Winterowd has committed himself to an egalitarian view of rhetorical studies. This populist view reaches far beyond the halls of academe. He writes, of learning to read, "This last step is perhaps the most important. In it reading becomes its own reward, a pleasure and a way of life. If the child does not take this step, he or she will forever be a handicapped reader or a nonreader" (89). With regard to the composing process, he makes a similar claim. He writes, "[W]e have . . .

forgotten that the best reason for writing is the pleasure which the writer derives from the act" (123).

Quintilian's remarks in his preface to the *Institutes* describe with depressing accuracy the struggles Winterowd has encountered in trying to reestablish the importance of rhetoric and composition pedagogy in literature-centered English studies. Quintilian writes:

Perhaps [instructors] despised the preparatory studies as less important; or perhaps they considered them to be outside their proper work, now that the professions are divided; or most probably they saw no prospect of popularity for good work on a subject which is very necessary, but unostentatious: men usually admire the roof of a building, and forget the foundations. (Qtd. in Gwynn 185)

As a teacher and scholar, Winterowd has consistently championed rhetoric's power and potential, has struggled to move rhetorical studies from the margins to the center of legitimate academic pursuits, and has contributed to the growth of rhetoric and composition studies both practically and theoretically. As part of a generation of rhetoricians who helped create dramatic changes in the way composition is taught and the way rhetoric as an academic field is viewed, Winterowd has been forced to consider his and rhetoric's position within traditional English studies. Unfortunately, unlike Quintilian, who was arguably "a man of high social standing" (Gwynn 184), Winterowd exists at the margins of the English Department. Commenting on his position both as a young student and as a seasoned rhetorician, he writes, "I am at ease with my colleagues who represent the Kultur of literature, am even fond of most of them . . . yet I am still as much outside as I was in the 1947 freshman English class at the University of Nevada" (*Department* 29). Winterowd has paradoxically embraced his outsider status while continuing to struggle against it. And even from the margins, he extends an invitation to all who would join him, sustained by his belief that "[t]he symbol of rhetoric is the open hand, beckoning to understanding" (*Synthesis* 85).

BIBLIOGRAPHY

Primary Sources

Winterowd, W. Ross. *Composition/Rhetoric: A Synthesis*. Carbondale: Southern Illinois University Press, 1986.
————. *Contemporary Rhetoric: A Conceptual Background with Readings*. New York: Harcourt Brace Jovanovitch, 1975.
————. *The Culture and Politics of Literacy*. New York: Oxford University Press, 1989.
————. *The English Department: A Personal and Institutional History*. Carbondale: Southern Illinois University Press, 1998.
————. "Learning to Live with Your Past and Liking It." *Writing Theory and Critical Theory*. Ed. John Clifford and John Schilb. New York: MLA, 1994. 306–12.

———. *Rhetoric: A Synthesis.* New York: Holt, Rinehart and Winston, 1968.

———. *The Rhetoric of the "Other" Literature.* Carbondale: Southern Illinois University Press, 1990.

Winterowd, W. Ross, and Jack Blum. *A Teacher's Introduction to Composition in the Rhetorical Tradition.* Urbana, IL: NCTE, 1994.

Biography

Bannister, Linda, and Kevin O'Connor. "Interview with W. Ross Winterowd." *Writing Instructor* 16.1 (1996): 35–41.

Criticism

Covino, William A. "Winterowd, W. Ross." *Encyclopedia of Rhetoric and Composition: Communication from Ancient Times to the Information Age.* Ed. Theresa Enos. New York: Garland, 1996. 767.

Gwyn, Aubrey Osborn. *Roman Education from Cicero to Quintilian.* New York: Teacher's College Press, 1966.

BIBLIOGRAPHICAL ESSAY

Scholars looking for a wealth of research on twentieth-century rhetoric and rhetorical theory will find that the area has not yet been fully explored, nor have many of the new critical methodologies—such as semiotics, deconstruction, and cultural studies—been brought fully to bear on the material (although that is rapidly changing). As the bibliographies on the individual entries in this volume suggest, while the major figures of the period—such as Kenneth Burke, Jacques Derrida, and Michel Foucault—have been discussed in detail, many of the secondary figures have received scant attention, as their bibliographies confirm. Fortunately, the reader interested in studying the rhetoric of the century in more depth will find important works to consult. We will limit our discussion to these more general works and refer interested readers to the entries in the volume on individual rhetoricians for more focused bibliographical information.

CURRENT-TRADITIONAL RHETORIC

Most research on current-traditional rhetoric has been conducted by its skeptics, those who desire to point out the limitations of a system that has dominated academic rhetoric from the nineteenth century through at least the first half of the twentieth century. Since this volume, due to space limitations, has not emphasized current-traditionalism and its proponents, we offer here only a brief discussion of the major research on this school.

In 1978 Richard Young discussed current-traditional rhetoric in "Paradigms and Problems," offering the following famous definition:

> The overt features [of current-traditionalism] . . . are obvious enough. The emphasis on the composed product rather than the composing process; the analysis of discourse into words, sentences, and paragraphs; the classification of discourse into description, narration, exposition, and argument; the strong concern with usage (syntax, spelling, punctuation) and with style (economy, clarity, emphasis); the preoccupation with the informal essay and research paper; and so on. (31)

Current-traditionalism grew out of the nineteenth century (although its roots go back at least to the eighteenth (see Thomas P. Miller's *The Formation of College English* [1997]), and several important books have examined that development. The oldest is by Albert R. Kitzhaber, *Rhetoric in American Colleges, 1850–1900* (1990), which is the published version of his 1953 dissertation. Kitzhaber's critical approach examined unsympathetically the assumptions of nineteenth-century rhetoric and identified the four major rhetoricians of the period: Adams Sherman Hill, John Franklin Genung, Barrett Wendell, and Fred Newton Scott. Kitzhaber's critical stance influenced the work of Robert J. Connors, who wrote a series of important essays on current-traditionalism that have been collected in his recent book *Composition-Rhetoric* (1997). (See the Connors entry for a fuller bibliography of his essays.) The sixth chapter in James A. Berlin's *Writing Instruction in Nineteenth-Century American Colleges* (1984) examines critically the rise and consequences to American education of current-traditionalism, and Berlin continues that critique in *Rhetoric and Reality* (1987), which traces current-traditionalism in the twentieth century, and in essays such as "Current-Traditional Rhetoric" (1980) (with Robert P. Inkster), "Contemporary Composition: The Major Pedagogical Theories" (1982), and "Rhetoric and Ideology in the Writing Class" (1988). Sharon Crowley has conducted a detailed study of the weakness of current-tradition invention in *The Methodical Memory* (1990). Other studies have offered more neutral analyses of the rise of current-traditionalism. Arthur N. Appelbee's *Tradition and Reform in the Teaching of English* (1974), Nan Johnson's *Nineteenth-Century Rhetoric in North America* (1991), and David R. Russell's *Writing in the Academic Disciplines, 1870–1990* (1991) all in part offer interpretations of the rise of current-traditional theory and practice during the nineteenth and twentieth centuries. John C. Bereton's *The Origins of Composition Studies in the American College, 1875–1925* (1995) is particularly useful because it provides key source material on the rise of current-traditional rhetoric, especially at Harvard, as well as some responses to it.

EXPRESSIVE RHETORIC

One of the first sustained critiques of the current-traditional approach was expressive rhetoric. Although this school is now associated with recent theorists and scholars such as James Britton, Donald Murray, Ken Macrorie, Janet Emig, and Peter Elbow, expressivism and the expressive essay, as Chris Anderson argues in "Late Night Thoughts on Writing and Teaching Essays" (1990), have a long history. Expressivism follows in the tradition of Montaigne, Thoreau, E. B. White, and George Orwell and is important for inexperienced writers to use because it allows them "to dramatize the process of their thinking" (88). In fact, according to William Zeiger in "The Personal Essay and Egalitarian Rhetoric" (1989), the personal, expressive essay, because it lacks the rigid logic of the formal essay, allows for "a rambling, capricious structure . . . [that exhibits] the idiosyncratic thoughts and feelings of the author" (235). But often teachers have ignored the expressive tradition. As Priscilla A. Abrahamson argues in "Between a Rock and a Soft Spot" (1993), many writing teachers, especially on the high school level, have emphasized hard, analytical writing at the expense of the "softer" expressive tradition that encourages the "development of the self" (17). Joyce Honeychurch in "Language, Cognition, and Learning: Expressive Writing in the Classroom" (1990) offers a short history of the British school of expressionism that centered around James Britton and the London Association for the Teaching of English (LATE). Christopher C. Burnham in "Expressive Rhetoric" (1993) provides another history that emphasizes the American expressivists such as Donald Murray, William Coles, and Peter Elbow, among others.

Discourse theorists have established expressivism as a distinct kind of discourse. Perhaps the most influential theorist is James Britton. With colleagues Tony Burgess, Nancy Martin, Alex McLeod, and Harold Rosen in *The Development of Writing Abilities (11–18)* (1975), he researched the kind of writing that children produced in British schools during the 1960s and early 1970s and developed his influential taxonomy of discourse based on the function categories of transactional, expressive, and poetic. Most school writing, he discovered, was transactional, which included informative and conative (regulative and persuasive) writing. Students had little chance to produce expressive writing, the kind of writing, Britton and his colleagues argued, that was the relatively unstructured, not highly explicit writing that reveals the writer's self and personality to a sympathetic audience. The second major theorist is James Kinneavy, who in his important *A Theory of Discourse* (1971) identified expressive discourse as one of the four major aims of discourse, along with reference, persuasive, and literary. Expressive discourse, which is a component in all other kinds of discourse, Kinneavy argues, "gives all discourse a personal significance to the speaker and listener" (396).

Two book-length studies have appeared recently that justify and extend expressive theory. The first is Jeanette Harris's *Expressive Discourse* (1990), which, as the title suggests, examines expressive writing as a distinct form of discourse. Expanding on Britton's and Kinneavy's assumptions that expressive discourse forms the basis of all other writing, Harris builds a complex and valuable model of text construction and interpretation based on expressive assumptions. She posits the existence of a writer's interior text—a fragmentary, "embryonic" version of the text that begins in the writer's mind—and a generative text, which consists of all the stages of the writing process as the text moves toward completion. Once the text is complete, the reader experiences the process in reverse, first reconstructing a generative and then an interior text. The second book is Sherrie L. Gradin's *Romancing Rhetorics* (1995). Gradin explores the parallels between Romanticism and expressive composition theory, arguing that both must be viewed more positively due to their emphasis on educational freedom and reform, and the role of imagination in learning and composing. She also argues that the view that expressive rhetoric assumes an isolated writer needs rethinking and advocates for a theory of social-expressivism recognizing that "[t]he romantic subject is defined only through the connections to other objects, subjects, and . . . through language" (101).

Much of the recent scholarship on expressivism has been critical of its assumptions and methods. One such critic is David R. Russell, who in "Romantics on Writing" (1988) argues that expressive pedagogy leads to undemocratic and oppressive practice because it encourages the view that writing results from inspiration, not application. Henry A. Giroux in *Theory and Resistance in Education* (1983) argues that the expressive view, by emphasizing the individual, ignores the function of writing in the world and the social nature of language in general (219). Lester Faigley in "Competing Theories of Process" (1986) makes a similar argument: Expressivism privileges the self and tends to lead to solipsism (531). In "Teaching Expressive Writing as Narrative Fiction" (1996), Candace Spigelman presents a different criticism. When writing expressively, students subvert the expectations of honest writing by fictionalizing their texts. But perhaps the most influential critic has been James Berlin, who, in a series of articles and books, has criticized expressive rhetoric for being apolitical and too fixated on the individual apart from social and political contexts. In his influential article "Contemporary Composition: The Major Pedagogical Theories" (1982), Berlin traces the American roots of expressivism to Emerson and Transcendentalism. The "ultimate source," however, is Plato with his emphasis on the personal search for truth (768). Like Plato, the expressionist theorists emphasize the need for dialectic in the form of interaction among individuals in the class as writers attempt to formulate and clarify their private visions, but this interaction lacks the political commitment to change that Berlin values. In a related article, "Rhetoric and Ideology in the Writing Class" (1988), Berlin examines the ideology of expressive rhetorics and concludes they grew out of the elitist rhetoric of liberal culture that assumed that writing was a gift of genius. Expressivism, however, became democratized and idealized by emphasizing the innate goodness of the individual. Since individual exploration and expression became the heart of this school, expressivists such as Peter Elbow and Donald Murray were not particularly interested in questions of political action. Resistance was always conceived in individualistic, not social, terms (487). In *Rhetoric and Reality* (1987), Berlin traces in more detail the development of expressivism in the twentieth century, emphasizing its connections with Freudianism, early writing process methodologies, and creative writing.

Other scholars have attempted to reconceive expressive rhetoric in relation to other theories. Reed Way Dasenbrock, for instance, in "The Myths of the Subjective and the Subject in Composition Studies" (1993), attempts to reconcile expressive and social constructivism. Expressivism is problematic because of its radical individualism and its tendency to deemphasize mastery of linguistic codes. The social constructivist view also has problems in that it assumes that writers are created entirely by the discourses that surround them. Dasenbrock turns to the work of Donald Davidson to enunciate a position that allows for private thought that is also public in the sense that it is similar to the thought of others (28). Stephen M. Fishman and Lucille Parkinson McCarthy in "Is Expressivism Dead?" (1992) reject the assumption that expressivism, unlike social constructivism, emphasizes the romantic isolation of the individual. Instead, Peter Elbow's expressivism, they argue, is in the tradition of German romantics such as Gottfried Herder, who advocated an expressivism that makes possible the "restructuring" of "community" (649). Furthermore, expressivism's goal of helping students connect with their own experience is not inconsistent with helping them master "the rules of a disciplinary language" (656). Such an approach is necessary because it connects a disciplinary method with the students' "lived experience" (654). In a second article, "Explicating Our Tacit Tradition" (1993), Fishman again rejects the position that Elbow is a naive romantic by placing him in the tradition of John Dewey, who had a deep commitment to community and, like Elbow, was not "narrowly focused on individual self discovery" (316). Mark Wiley in "Writing in the American Grain" (1989–1990) argues that both Peter Elbow's expressivism and David Bartholomae's social construction are in the Emersonian tradition because both emphasize the importance of voice. For Elbow, it's "real" voice; for Bartholomae, it's the voice of one's discourse community (58). Finally, Janine Reed in "Self-Orientation in 'Expressive Writing' Instruction" (1994) questions the position that expressivism must emphasize a limited, "authentic" self. She argues that expressive discourse should emphasize a dynamic self that constructs meanings as it changes.

One practical criticism of expressivism has been that it does not prepare students to write academic prose. The classic discussion of this issue took place at the 1989 and 1991 Conferences on College Composition and Communication between David Bartholomae and Peter Elbow and was published in the February 1995 issue of *College Com-*

position and Communication. In "Writing with Teachers" (1995), Bartholomae argues for the importance of academic writing, claiming that it is the real work of the academy. Such writing reveals to students the "traces of power, tradition, and authority" (64) that are reenacted whenever writing takes place. In "Being a Writer vs. Being an Academic" (1995), Elbow answers by arguing that he does not want to make first-year students into academics; instead, he wants them to come to view themselves as writers who enjoy the act of self-expression. Not all researchers accept Elbow's position. Matthew Wilson in "Research, Expressivism, and Silence" (1995), for instance, argues with Bartholomae that expressive writing, while promising to empower students, "actually disempowers them" by impeding the transition to academic discourse, especially the research paper (251). Expressive writing offers students insights into their personal lives, but it prevents them from connecting those personal narratives to more public discourses (251). Not all researchers agree. Elizabeth Robertson in "Moving from Expressive Writing to Academic Discourse" (1988) reports on a student who used journal writing to move from purely expressive exploration to a more demanding academic discourse, and Christopher Burnham in "Expressive Rhetoric" (1993) argues that this kind of rhetoric functions epistemically—that it is a form of writing that emphasizes "both individual and social identity and value" (154).

COGNITIVE RHETORIC

Cognitive rhetoric uses the findings of cognitive psychology to develop a rhetorical theory that views writing as a problem-solving process. Because it is viewed as a form of problem solving, writing becomes a goal-directed procedure in which writers consciously select strategies to reach those goals and then use methods by which to test whether or not those goals were achieved. In short, cognitive rhetoric attempts to make much of the writing process a controlled, conscious process rather than primarily an unconscious, messy one. Cognitive rhetoric was developed largely through the work of Linda Flower (who often collaborated with the cognitive psychologist John Hayes), in works such as her textbook *Problem-Solving Strategies for Writing* (4th ed. 1993), her edited *Making Thinking Visible* (1994), and *The Construction of Negotiated Meaning* (1994), and through the work of Carl Bereiter and Marlene Scardamalia in *The Psychology of Written Composition* (1987), one of the most thorough statements of the cognitivist position. Other books also advance this position. Gregg and Steinberg's early edited volume *Cognitive Processes in Writing* (1980) collects important early work, Penrose and Sitko's edited collection *Hearing Ourselves Think* (1993) reports on classroom research from the cognitive perspective, and Ronald T. Kellogg's *The Psychology of Writing* (1994) (which expands his "Observations in the Psychology of Thinking and Writing" [1993]) analyzes the rich experimental tradition in cognitive science as it applies to writing. Good overviews of research on the cognitivist position include Andrea A. Lunsford's "Cognitive Studies and Teaching Writing" (1985) and Donna Haisty Winchell's "Developmental Psychology and Basic Writers" (1990).

The cognitivist position was originally articulated in the 1970s and 1980s. In "Lessons from the Language Teacher" (1973), James W. Ney called for the use of cognitive learning in controlled writing exercises and assignments, and in "Composing: A Cognitive Process Theory" (1976), Charles Stallard argues for a task analysis method of teaching composition to make the steps in the cognition of writing apparent to students. In an early seminal essay, "Writing as a Mode of Learning" (1977), Janet Emig argues that writing is a unique medium to facilitate "higher cognitive functions" (122), and in "Heuristics and Composition" (1970) Janice Lauer surveys work in cognitive psychology useful for teaching invention strategies in rhetoric. (She was accused of positivism by Ann E. Berthoff in "The Problem with Problem Solving" [1971] and answered her in "Counterstatement" [1972].) Richard Larson had earlier provided problem-solving procedures useful for invention in "Discovery through Questioning" (1968) and in "Problem-Solving, Composing, and Liberal Education" (1972). In "The Process of Writing and the Process of Learning" (1980), Lee Odell argues that writing helps students master a subject matter and develop sophisticated cognitive strategies, and in "Teaching Writing by Teaching the Process of Discovery" (1980), Odell argues that cognitive processes can help students see writing as a discovery process. Carl Bereiter in "Development in Writing" (1980) sketches an early form of the developmental cognitive model for rhetoric, Collins and Gentner in "A Framework for a Cognitive Theory of Writing" (1980) provide a general framework for discussing the cognitive elements of the writing process, and Kenneth Dowst in "Cognition and Composition" (1983) examines the usefulness of contemporary cognitive theory to teaching writing. Karen Spear in "Thinking and Writing" (1983) argues that Benjamin S. Bloom's taxonomy of cognitive modes offers the best system for developing a cognitive-based series of writing assignments. In a more recent essay, Collins, Brown, and Holum in "Cognitive Apprenticeship" (1991) argue that writing can be taught using the cognitive apprenticeship method that makes sophisticated writing skills based on problem solving visible to students.

Cognitive rhetoric has received its share of criticism. Ann E. Berthoff in "From Problem-solving to a Theory of the Imagination" (1972) rejects the tendency of cognitivists to separate thinking and feeling and argues for the epistemic position that language does not merely name; it also transforms (647). In his chapter entitled "The Formalists" in *The Making of Knowledge in Composition* (1987), Stephen M. North, following the lead of Marilyn Cooper and Michael Holzman in "Talking about Protocols" (1983), criticizes Flower and Hayes for confusing their formalist model of the composing process with empirical reality. Joseph Harris in "Rethinking the Pedagogy of Problem-Solving" (1988) critiques cognitive rhetoric as articulated in Flower's textbook *Problem-Solving Strategies for Writing* as presenting an oversimplified version of the communication process. In another criticism of Flower, Robert Brooke in "Control in Writing" (1989) deconstructs her notion of control, arguing that the writing process is by definition complex and out of control. Cooper and Holzman in "Talking about Protocols" (1983) attack the use of protocols as a method of data collection on the grounds that it leads to a partial picture of the writing process. (Flower and Hayes respond in "Response to Marilyn Cooper and Michael Holzman" [1983] by arguing that protocols, while not perfect, are the best source of data for their goals to explore the planning and generation of ideas in writing [97].) James A. Berlin in "Rhetoric and Ideology in the Writing Class" (1988) takes Flower to task on the grounds that her rhetoric prepares students "for the world of corporate capitalism" (482) and ignores notions of social responsibility. (Berlin provides a less critical evaluation in *Rhetoric and Reality* [1987].) In "Cognition, Convention, and Certainty" (1982), Patricia Bizzell attacks cognitive rhetoric for ignoring the important role that social context plays in conditioning thought. In fact, one of the major criticisms of cognitive rhetoric is that it does not place enough emphasis on social contexts of writing, as Judith Langer argues in "Musings" (1985).

The criticism, often from social constructivists, that cognitive rhetoric ignores social contexts has been answered by cognitivists and their sympathizers. Carolyn L. Piazza in "Identifying Context Variables in Research on Writing" (1987) argues that cognitive rhetoric assumes a complex theory of context. Carol Berkenkotter in "Paradigm Debates, Turf Wars, and the Conduct of Sociocognitive Inquiry in Composition" (1991) argues that the field of composition should recognize the importance of both the cognitive and the social research traditions. Michael Carter in "The Idea of Expertise" (1990) argues that while cognitive rhetoric emphasizes general knowledge and social constructivist rhetoric stresses more particular social knowledge, both systems are important. Beginning writers find the general heuristic and writing strategies of cognitive rhetoric useful; expert writers, on the other hand, find the intuitive, local knowledge based on their experience with particular schemata and social contexts necessary. Stuart Greene in "Toward a Dialectical Theory of Composing" (1990) defends cognitive rhetoric from the attack of the "strong social constructivist view" by calling for a cognitive-social epistemic. This position recognizes both "the power of social and ideological forces that can circumscribe thought and action" and "the critical role that individuals play in the construction of meaning" (152–53). Linda Flower in *The Construction of Negotiated Meaning* (1994) presents her own modified view of cognitive rhetoric in the form of a social cognitive theory. Like Greene, she recognizes that social and ideological forces shape the writer and the text, but writing is still the product of the individual writer functioning within larger contexts.

Much early work on cognition and writing was applied to basic writers. Andrea A. Lunsford's classic argument in "Cognitive Development and the Basic Writer" (1979) stakes out the position that many basic writers have not reached the level of cognitive development necessary "to form abstractions and conceptions" (38). Marilyn S. Sternglass in "Assessing Reading, Writing, and Reasoning" (1981) argues that writing programs should use the Wilkinson instrument for evaluating student writing to determine the writers' cognitive level for placement purposes. Karen Spear in "Building Cognitive Skills in Basic Writers" (1983) makes an argument for using Benjamin Bloom's six-stage taxonomy of cognitive development to measure growth in a basic writing class. The classic critique of these positions is "Narrowing the Mind and Page" (1988) in which Mike Rose questions the application of research in cognition—especially notions of cognitive styles, hemisphericity, and cognitive development—to remedial writers. These theories too often ignore individual differences, remove attention from the students' actual writing, and encourage cultural stereotyping.

One new area of research is the influence of affect or emotion on cognition. Alice G. Brand in "Hot Cognition" (1985–1986) argues that cognitive rhetoric has neglected the importance of affect in the composing process, and Susan McLeod in "Some Thoughts about Feelings" (1987) argues that researchers should study affect and its relationship to cognition in the writing process and suggests three areas that deserve attention: writing anxiety, beliefs, and motivation. Brand in "The Why of Cognition" (1987) calls for the development of an adequate theory of emotion to explain what motivates the writer to make rhetorical and linguistic choices. In "The Affective Domain and the Writing Process" (1991), McLeod offers definitions of such key terms as *emotions, feelings, beliefs*, and *moods*. Kristie S. Fleckenstein in "Defining Affect in Relation to Cognition" (1991) responds to McLeod by offering an affective continuum to suggest the range of affect as it relates to cognition. In "Social Cognition, Emotions, and the Psychology of Writing" (1991) Brand shows that while contemporary social cognitive psychologists have integrated emotions into their theories, cognitive rhetoricians have lagged behind.

Some work has appeared on "social cognition," a formal term for audience awareness. Donald L. Rubin in "Social Cognition and Written Communication" (1984) examines the many complex elements that make written communication dependent on social cognition. Burleson and Rowan in "Are Social-Cognitive Ability and Narrative Writing Skill Related?" (1985) question Rubin's position and conclude that there is no relationship between social cognitive ability and the quality of narrative essays. Piche and Roen conclude in "Social Cognition and Writing" (1987) that they found a high correlation between "interpersonal cognitive complexity" and the abstractness and overall quality of persuasive discourse. In "Social-Cognitive Ability and Writing Performance" (1985), Barry M. Kroll found the highest correlation between social cognition and narrative writing and a lower correlation with persuasive essays. He concludes that the correlation was high in the first because the narrative mode was less cognitively demanding than the persuasive.

Mike Rose has examined writing anxiety from the cognitive point of view. In the classic study "Rigid Rules, Inflexible Plans, and the Stifling of Language" (1980), Rose argues that writing is a "complex problem-solving process" (390) that can be disrupted by the application of rigid, ineffective rules or planning strategies. These problems can lead to blocked writers. While nonblockers also use rules and plans, these are not rigid enough to block writing. Rose expands his argument in *Writer's Block* (1984) in which he explores the complex cognitive variables that prevent otherwise competent writers from writing.

A number of empirical studies have been conducted that determine the importance of cognition to writing. Russell K. Durst in "Cognitive and Linguistic Demands of Analytic Writing" (1987), for instance, compared summary and analytical writing and found that students writing analytically "employed more varied and complex thinking operations than summary writing" (347). Freedman and Pringle in "Writing in the College Years" (1980) found that when they studied the writing of high school and college students in terms of cognitive sophistication, teachers graded primarily for details and specifics, not for a high level of abstraction and complex thought. The researchers conclude that teachers need to be retrained to appreciate cognitive complexity. Dillworth, Reising, and Wolfe, however, reach a different conclusion in "Language Structure and Thought in Written Composition" (1978). They found that readers value student papers that combine cognitive and syntactic complexity. Collette Daiwte in "Physical and Cognitive Factors in Revising" (1986) found that students revised more effectively when given "the direct cognitive aids of a revision prompting program" (141). Michael Kearns in "Topical Knowledge and Revising" (1990) reaches a different conclusion on the importance of cognition and revision. He finds that the students' knowledge of the topic more than the students' cognitive development was the most important factor in effective revision. Sheridan Blau in "Invisible Writing" (1983) reaches a similar conclusion. He had students write papers with empty ball point pens on carbon paper. He found that no matter how abstract the writing task, writers wrote effectively using this method, probably because they were forced to concentrate more fully on the writing task and its topic. In a more general study, Benton, Kraft, Glover, and Plake in "Cognitive Capacity Difference among Writers" (1984) examined the ability of writers to manipulate information in their short-term memories and concluded that good writers manipulated that information "more rapidly than poor writers do" (829).

RECLAMATION OF THE CLASSICAL TRADITION/ HISTORIOGRAPHIES OF RHETORIC

Composition studies' renewed interest in classical rhetoric could be marked by Edward P. J. Corbett's landmark essay "The Usefulness of Classical Rhetoric," published in 1963, and his textbook *Classical Rhetoric for the Modern Student*, which first appeared in 1965. Because classical rhetoric has been seen as a way to challenge current-traditional rhetoric, the last part of the century witnessed an explosion of publications, professing not only the usefulness of classical rhetorical principles (namely, invention) but also the usefulness of classical rhetorical pedagogical practices (especially sophistic). Such publications, which situated contemporary writing issues alongside the rhetorical tradition, include C. H. Knoblauch and Lillian Brannon's *Rhetorical Traditions and the Teaching of Writing* (1984), Robert Connors, Lisa Ede, and Andrea Lunsford's edited volume *Essays on Classical Rhetoric and Modern Discourse* (1984), Sharon Crowley's *Ancient Rhetorics for Contemporary Students* (1994), and Theresa Enos's Festschrift to Winifred Bryan Horner, *Learning from the Histories of Rhetoric* (1993), Kathleen Welch's *The Contemporary Reception of Classical Rhetoric* (1990), Winifred Horner and Michael Leff's Festschrift to James J. Murphy, *Rhetoric and Pedagogy: Its History, Philosophy, and Practice* (1995), and Marjorie Woods's "Among Men—Not Boys: Histories of Rhetoric and the Exclusion of Pedagogy" (1992).

Rhetorical studies also, in its newly found enthusiasm for historical antecedents, produced a number of anthologies, collecting rhetors throughout the centuries. While some anthologies, such as James L. Golden, Goodwin F. Bergquist, and William E. Coleman's *The Rhetoric of Western Thought* (1989), emphasize rhetorics of argumentation, others, such as Patricia Bizzell and Bruce Herzberg's *The Rhetorical Tradition* (1990), intend to represent rhetoric in its "broadest" role as a "force in society and a factor in the creation of knowledge" (v). Another popular anthology is Thomas M. Conley's *Rhetoric in the European Tradition* (1994), which features extensive introductory remarks prefacing each rhetorical period.

In addition to anthologizing the rhetorical tradition, rhetorical scholars have been constructing various histories and studies of classical rhetoric. Two brief histories include Edward Corbett's "A Survey of Rhetoric" (included in *Classical Rhetoric for the Modern Student*) and Roland Barthes's "The Old Rhetoric: An *Aide-mémoire*" (1988). Corbett's survey intends to introduce the student to the "key figures" and "significant developments" of rhetoric (539). Barthes composes his narrative not only diachronically but also synchronically, attempting to display rhetoric as a "kind of artifact . . . destined to produce discourse" (14). Both authors preface their reconstructions with an acknowledgment of the lack of a full-scale history of rhetoric. This echoes James J. Murphy's claim of 1983, in "The Historiography of Rhetoric: Challenges and Opportunities," that there is "no single accepted history of rhetoric in any language" (3). Murphy notes that George Kennedy's *Classical Rhetoric and Its Christian and Secular Traditions from Ancient to Modern Times* (1980) is a "step in the direction of a universal history" (3). Stepping in another direction is C. Jan Swearingen's *Rhetoric and Irony: Western Literacy and Western Lies* (1991), a study beginning with the Preplatonics and traversing the centuries, which historicizes the conception of rhetoric as a manipulation of language. Brian Vickers's *In Defence of Rhetoric* (1988) offers another such history.

Murphy, with Richard A. Katula, subsequently published *A Synoptic History of Classical Rhetoric* (1994), an edited collection of six topical essays on the origins of rhetoric and on key figures and movements. The collection also includes a bibliography on the history of rhetoric, compiled by Michael Leff. Murphy also has edited the collection *A Short History of Writing Instruction from Ancient Greece to Twentieth Century America* (1990), featuring essays detailing pedagogical practices in each major period of the history of rhetoric, in addition to *The Rhetorical Tradition and Modern Writing* (1982). George Kennedy has published a number of standard studies on various periods of classical rhetoric: *The Art of Persuasion in Greece* (1963) and *The Art of Rhetoric in the Roman World* (1972).

More recently, Thomas Cole, in *The Origins of Rhetoric in Ancient Greece* (1991), has challenged the standard histories of classical rhetoric by distinguishing rhetoric from what he calls neorhetoric and protorhetoric, arguing that discourse prior to Plato was largely arhetorical. Edward Schiappa advances a similar argument in "Did Plato Coin *Rhetorike*?" (1990), suggesting that our histories of rhetoric have mistakenly attributed rhetoric's origin to Corax and Tisias. Richard Enos argues, however, in *Greek Rhetoric before Aristotle* (1993) that "[r]hetoric did not originate at a single moment in history. Rather it was an evolving, developing consciousness about the relationship between thought and expression" that manifested itself in a variety of ways (ix). Additional work by Enos has enriched the discipline's understanding of classical rhetoric. His works include *Roman Rhetoric: Revolution and the Greek Influence* (1995) and *The Literate Mode of Cicero's Legal Rhetoric* (1988).

The revival of classical rhetoric, and the interest in historicizing rhetorical practice, has led to the publication of various studies of other periods. These include: Michael G. Moran's *Eighteenth-Century British and American Rhetorics and Rhetoricians* (1994) and Nan Johnson's *Nineteenth-Century Rhetoric in North America* (1991), which identifies three approaches to rhetoric during this period: classical, belletristic, and epistemological. Winifred Bryan Horner's *Nineteenth-Century Scottish Rhetoric: The American Connection* (1993), as the title suggests, presents archival work to demonstrate how Scottish rhetoric contributed to contemporary composition practices. Gregory Clark and S. Michael Halloran's edited *Oratorical Culture in Nineteenth-Century America* (1993) analyzes the decay of civic discourse, as does Halloran's article "Rhetoric in the American College Curriculum: The Decline of Public Discourse" (1982). James Berlin's *Writing Instruction in Nineteenth-Century American Colleges* (1984) and *Rhetoric and Reality: Writing Instruction in American Colleges, 1900–1985* (1987) both trace the major pedagogical movements and reveal ideological undercurrents. Miriam Brody's *Manly Writing: Gender, Rhetoric, and the Rise of Composition* (1993) traces—from the age of Enlightenment to the present day—how writing instruction has perpetuated the ideology and ideal of manliness. Robert Connors's *Composition-Rhetoric: Backgrounds, Theory, and Pedagogy* (1997) details the history of nineteenth-century composition practice. Sharon Crowley's *Composition in the University: Historical and Polemical Essays* (1998) traces the history of the required freshman composition course and makes the groundbreaking call (what she calls "a modest proposal" [241]) for abolishing this requirement. Winifred Bryan Horner's edited *Historical Rhetoric: An Annotated Bibliography of Selected Sources in English*, published in 1980, begs for a new edition.

Alongside this proliferation of new histories is a concern for revising the historical tradition, for exposing its prejudices and its blindspots, and for composing more inclusive histories. Historians are asking us to reexamine and reconstruct the rhetorical tradition.

James Kastely, for example, rethinks rhetoric as Socratic refutation, *elenchus*, rather than as persuasion (*Rethinking the Rhetorical Tradition: From Plato to Postmodernism* [1997]), and Janet Atwill restores a "neglected tradition of rhetoric, embodied . . . in Protagoras's political *techne* and Isocrates' *logon techne* and preserved, in a somewhat modified form, in Aristotle's *Rhetoric*" (*Rhetoric Reclaimed: Aristotle and the Liberal Arts Tradition* [1998] 1). Historians have questioned the tradition's racism (Martin Bernal, *Black Athena: The Afroasiatic Roots of Classical Civilization* [1989]; Jasper Neel, *Aristotle's Voice* [1994]; Sonja Foss, Karen Foss, and Robert Trapp, "Challenges to the Rhetorical Tradition" [1991]), and a very prolific group has questioned the tradition's sexism.

Patricia Bizzell, as have others, has made a call for a feminist examination of the tradition ("Opportunities for Feminist Research in the History of Rhetoric" [1992–1993]). Part of that reexamination, she argues, is to recover and to include female rhetorics within the canon. In *The Rhetorical Tradition*, the anthology she prepared with Bruce Herzberg, Bizzell includes women alongside the traditionally canonized males, including Christine de Pisan, Laura Cereta, Martha Fell, Sarah Grimké, Hélène Cixous, and Julia Kristeva. Karlyn Kohrs Campbell's *Man Cannot Speak for Her* (1989), which analyzes first-wave feminists as rhetors, is another example of revisionary work, as is Krista Ratcliffe's *Anglo-American Feminist Challenges to the Rhetorical Traditions: Virginia Woolf, Mary Daly, Adrienne Rich* (1996). Andrea Lunsford's edited collection *Reclaiming Rhetorica: Women in the Rhetorical Tradition* (1995), through discussions of women such as Diotima, Aspasia, Margery Kempe, and Mary Wollstonecraft, challenges the tradition by redefining rhetoric. Lunsford writes: "The realm of rhetoric has been almost exclusively male not because women were not practicing rhetoric—the arts of language are after all at the source of human communication—but because the tradition has never recognized the forms, strategies, and goals used by many women as 'rhetorical' " (6). Cheryl Glenn's work, particularly *Rhetoric Retold: Regendering the Tradition from Antiquity through the Renaissance* (1997), is another example of an attempt to "map the silences"—that is, not only to put excluded, and therefore silenced, women back on the historical map but also to map "silence" itself as a rhetorical form.

This recovery work has been challenged by other feminists, particularly Michelle Ballif ("Re/Dressing Histories" [1992]) and Barbara Biesecker ("Coming to Terms with Recent Attempts to Write Women into the History of Rhetoric" [1992]). Biesecker, specifically critiquing the work of Kohrs Campbell, argues that "mere inclusion of women's texts in the rhetorical canon" (142) does not challenge the ideology of the canon—the ideology that dispenses the power "to affirm certain voices and to discount others" (143). Biesecker asks us to question the canonization process itself. Susan C. Jarratt begins this questioning in a guest-edited issue of *Rhetoric Society Quarterly* (1992), where she has assembled essays that "ask not 'Who are the neglected women rhetoricians?' but rather 'How does gender give meaning to the organization and reception of historical knowledge?' Our task here is looking again, listening again with different ears to the canonical, male-authored texts in rhetoric's history" ("Performing Feminisms" 1). Andrea Nye's *Words of Power: A Feminist Reading of the History of Logic* (1990) is an example of how Jarratt's task can be fulfilled on a large scale.

Another concern of historiographers of the rhetorical tradition is a reclamation of sophistry, which the tradition has—since Plato's condemnation of it—effectively excluded. The renewed interest in sophistry is no doubt influenced by the poststructuralist deconstruction of Truth and Jacques Derrida's deconstruction of Plato in "Plato's Pharmacy" (1981), for example. John Poulakos, in "Toward a Sophistic Definition of Rhetoric" (1983) and "Gorgias' *Encomium to Helen* and the Defense of Rhetoric" (1983), offers us a useful, alternative rhetoric to Platonic and Aristotelian rhetorics. In an analogical reading of Gorgias' *Encomium*, Poulakos argues that Gorgias chose Helen as a "personification of rhetoric" due to their marked similarities: "Both are attractive, both are unfaithful, and both have a bad reputation" (6). As did Helen, rhetoric has the disruptive power to challenge cultural hegemony. Susan Jarratt, in *Rereading the Sophists* (1991), argues that sophistic rhetoric has the power to reinterpret "elements of mythic history" (22); in this way, she links sophistic rhetoric with liberatory pedagogy, where sophistic rhetorical practices offer students a method to examine and to negotiate the cultural myths that perpetuate injustice. Her insistence that rhetorical practice "must be able to move from critique to reconstruction" (27) and to social action makes Jarratt's sophistic pedagogy akin to philosophic pragmatism. The link between sophistry and pragmatism is further explored in Steven Mailloux's edited collection *Rhetoric, Sophistry, Pragmatism* (1995). Sophistry has been also advanced by Jasper Neel's *Plato, Derrida, and Writing* (1988), by Sharon Crowley's "A Plea for the Revival of Sophistry" (1989), and by Roger Moss's "The Case for Sophistry" (1982).

Edward Schiappa characterizes this fascination with sophistry (as a necessary alternative to Platonic and Aristotelian rhetorics) as a useless fiction. In fact, he argues the "sophists" are a "mirage" and such appropriations of them anachronistic and historically inaccurate ("Sophistic Rhetoric" [1991] 5). John Poulakos, however, responds to Schiappa, identifying his methodology as an advancement of "an untenable view of interpretation. Specifically, he suggests that the interpreter can escape his/her present horizon and retrieve the past as it was," which Poulakos maintains is impossible ("Interpreting Sophistical Rhetoric" [1990] 220–21).

The Poulakos/Schiappa debate as well as the Campbell/Biesecker debate discussed above raises the historiographical issues that contemporary rhetorical theorists have been concerning themselves with since the mid-1980s: What are facts? What does it mean to "recover" or "reread" facts, facts that are themselves, unavoidably, rhetorical? And what is at stake in any given history? Kathleen Welch suggests that historians from "the Heritage School," including Knoblauch and Brannon, write nostalgic and elitist histories of the "golden age of rhetoric" ("A Critique of Classical Rhetoric" [1987]). Carole Blair argues that traditional histories based on patterns of continuity and discontinuity "defeat the principal goal of historical inquiry in rhetorical theory" ("Contested Histories of Rhetoric" [1992] 404). The Octalog among James Berlin, Robert Connors, Sharon Crowley, Richard Enos, Victor Vitanza, Susan Jarratt, Nan Johnson, and Jan Swearingen on "The Politics of Historiography" (1988) furthered this conversation by examining the methodologies and implications within any given history. Two special issues of *PRE/TEXT* (1987 and 1990) feature essays on the topic, as does Vitanza's edited *Writing Histories of Rhetoric* (1994) and Takis Poulakos's edited *Rethinking the History of Rhetoric* (1993).

Vitanza, in a series of articles, argues that there are three approaches to writing histories of rhetoric. He identifies them as traditional, revisionary, and sub/versive. The first methodology presumes that "data are representations of manifest reality" and that history is "relatively value neutral and without any rhetorical or ideological dimensions" ("Some Rudiments" 201). Revisionary historiographies are produced as either "full disclosure" of previously excluded facts or interpretations or "self-conscious critical practices," where histories are produced in order to do something, to effect some political goal (210). Sub/

versive "hysteriography," however, has no intention of redeeming the past, or of finally reinterpreting it. "What the Third Sophistic hyster(y)ias of the antibody rhetoric are, then, are *plasma* transfusions/transumptions into the diseased body of the history (suppressed/repressed hysteria) of philosophical rhetoric" (237). Vitanza performs this "hyster(y)ia" in his book *Negation, Subjectivity, and the History of Rhetoric* (1997).

SOCIAL-EPISTEMIC RHETORIC

In 1967, Robert Scott published "On Viewing Rhetoric as Epistemic," introducing a term that gained wide use and acceptance in the spirit of the New Rhetorics. To view rhetoric as epistemic was to side against Plato in suggesting that rhetoric is no mere handmaiden to truth but that is itself a way of knowing, a way of creating truth. The work of James Berlin expounds on epistemic rhetoric, tracing its usage in *Rhetoric and Reality* (1987) (165–77), claiming that in "studying rhetoric—the ways discourse is generated—we are studying the ways in which knowledge comes into existence. Knowledge, after all, is an historically bound social fabrication rather than an eternal and invariable phenomenon located in some uncomplicated repository" ("Rhetoric and Ideology" [1988] 493). Berlin adds the prefix "social" to the term to distinguish his work from the cognitivists or "psychological-epistemic" theorists. For social-epistemic theorists, not only is knowledge a social construct, but so is the knowing subject, which "emerges through the linguistically-circumscribed interaction of the individual, the community, and the material world. There is no universal, eternal, and authentic self" (493).

According to Kenneth Bruffee, writing in the mid-1980s, a social-epistemic "assumes that there is no such thing as a universal foundation, ground, framework, or structure of knowledge. There is only an agreement, a consensus arrived at for the time being by communities of knowledgeable peers" ("Social Construction, Language, and the Authority of Knowledge: A Bibliographical Essay" [1986] 776). Bruffee makes this claim following his reading of Thomas Kuhn's *The Structure of Scientific Revolutions* (1970), wherein Kuhn argues that scientists do not objectively discover the "truth" of the universe but rather conduct research with paradigms of thought that govern and predetermine their so-called discoveries. Thus to construct knowledge is to "justify . . . a certain kind of relationship among ourselves and among the things we say" ("Liberal Education and the Social Justification of Belief" [1982] 105). Justification is relational and contextual and takes place through social discourse.

Bruffee's appropriation of Kuhn has greatly influenced composition studies. Maxine Hairston, in "The Winds of Change: Thomas Kuhn and the Revolution in the Teaching of Writing" (1982), claims that the field has undergone a paradigm shift. Patricia Bizzell, in "Thomas Kuhn, Scientism, and English Studies" (1979), advocates that English studies embrace social-constructionist presuppositions and methodologies. She writes: "Under the new paradigm, the domain of English studies can be the study of the ways in which a language community's methods of argumentation establish standards for thinking and acting together that are [quoting Chaïm Perelman and Madame Olbrechts-Tyteca, *The New Rhetoric*] 'neither compelling nor arbitrary,' but reasonable—in other words, the domain of rhetoric" (769–70). Bizzell's comments echo the rhetorical theories of Kenneth Burke and Wayne Booth.

A predominant composition strategy practiced by social-epistemic pedagogues is "collaborative writing." Bruffee, in "Collaborative Learning and 'The Conversation of Mankind' " (1984), argues that the purpose is to help students engage in the consensual intellectual negotiation that leads to collective consensus. Using Stanely Fish's idea of "interpretive communities" (*Is There a Text in This Class?* [1980]), Bruffee foresees collaborative writing as constructing "discourse communities" of knowledgeable peers. Karen Burke LeFevre's *Invention as a Social Act* (1987) and Andrea Lunsford and Lisa Ede's *Singular Texts/Plural Authors* (1990) challenge the assumption that writing is a solitary act and encourages students to acknowledge their own social construction by engaging in writing assignments specifically created to demand group interaction, research, and dialogue. The social constructivist emphasis on consensus has attracted criticism, namely from Greg Myers's "Reality, Consensus, and Reform in the Rhetoric of Composition Teaching" (1986) and John Trimbur's "Consensus and Difference in Collaborative Learning" (1989). Gregory Clark's *Dialogue, Dialectic, and Conversation: A Social Perspective on the Function of Writing* (1990) acknowledges the dangers of consensus but maintains they can be thwarted by adopting a rhetorical process of continual "critical evaluation and exchange" (61).

A number of feminist composition theorists have claimed that social constructivist ideals represent a "feminization" of composition pedagogy and offer the possibility of reconstructing the classroom as a site of social cooperation, connectedness, and nurturance. Catherine E. Lamb, in "Beyond Argument in Feminist Composition" (1991), argues that the feminist composition classroom would foster negotiation, mediation, and resolution. Elizabeth Flynn, in "Composing as a Woman" (1988), characterizes the "emerging field of composition studies as a feminization of our previous conceptions of how writers write and how writers should be taught" (423). Jan Zlotnik Schmidt's edited collection *Women/Writing/Teaching* (1998), Louise Wetherbee Phelps and Janet Emig's edited *Feminine Principles and Women's Experience in American Composition and Rhetoric* (1995), and Cynthia L. Caywood and Gillian R. Overing's edited *Teaching Writing: Pedagogy, Gender, and Equity* (1987) address these issues. Although supportive of feminist goals, Susan Jarratt has critiqued this so-called feminization of the classroom. She writes: "For some composition teachers, creating a supportive climate in the classroom and validating student experience leads them to avoid conflict [and] . . . leaves them insufficiently prepared to negotiate the oppressive discourses of racism, sexism, and classism" ("Feminism and Composition: A Case for Conflict" [1991] 106). Evelyn Ashton-Jones, in "Collaboration, Conversation, and the Politics of Gender" (1995), offers this criticism: "My aim is not only to argue that the ideology of gender is indeed reproduced in the interactional dynamics of writing groups but also to suggest the extent to which the feminist valorization of collaborative learning in composition leads away from such analysis and, thus, unwittingly colludes in the reproduction of gender structure that feminists seek to disrupt" (7). Susan Jarratt and Lynn Worsham's edited *Feminism and Composition Studies: In Other Words* (1998) seeks to address "questions of difference" by "exploring the productive intersections and tensions" between the discourses of feminism and composition theory (1).

Another manifestation of social-epistemic rhetoric is in the practice of critical pedagogy, informed by neo-Marxist thought, specifically the critical theory advanced by the Frankfurt School and articulated by Paulo Freire (*Pedagogy of the Oppressed* [1989]) and Stanley Aronowitz and Henry Giroux (*Education Still Under Siege* [1985]). The assumption is that because knowledge is a social construct, it can never be ideologically innocent. Further, according to Berlin, to teach writing is to compose writing subjects who will serve a particular ideology. In *Rhetoric and Reality* (1987), Berlin reveals the ideologies advanced by current-traditional, expressivist, and cognitive rhetorics. Social-epistemic rhetoric, as Berlin explains in "Rhetoric and Ideology in the Writing Class" (1988), "offers an explicit critique of economic, political, and social arrangements," with the express purpose of—in Ira Shor's words—teaching students "to be their own agents for social change, their own creators of democratic culture" (48). Shor, in *Critical Teaching and Everyday Life* (1980), argues that "the most breathlessly utopian aspect [of critical pedagogy] is the conviction that critical thought and the practice of freedom are foundations for exorcising mass culture, purging sexism and racism, evoking class solidarity, and initiating social reconstruction" (269–70). John Clifford and John Schilb's edited collection *Writing Theory and Critical Theory* (1994) and Patricia A. Sullivan and Donna J. Qualley's edited *Pedagogy in the Age of Politics: Writing and Reading (in) the Academy* (1994) address such possibilities, as does Karen Fitts and Alan W. France's edited *Left Margins: Cultural Studies and Composition Pedagogy* (1995), which includes contributors such as Henry Giroux, Mas'ud Zavarzadeh, Gerald Graff, Richard Ohmann, and Gary Tate. The editors explain that the purpose of the volume is the "actualization of theory into practice" (x). They write: "Although we are convinced that there is no politically neutral . . . way to teach . . . we realized we were failing to make manifest for many of our students the linkage between writing and cultural reproduction that recent theoretical work in rhetoric and composition has exposed" (ix).

Social-epistemic's focus on issues of race and class has also fueled discussion regarding literacy, specifically multicultural literacy. Work on literacy issues includes *Perspectives on Literacy* (1988), edited by Eugene R. Kintgen, Barry M. Kroll, and Mike Rose, which analyzes literacy from various positions and which includes contributions by famous literacy scholars such as Jack Goody, Ian Watt, Walter J. Ong, Eric A. Havelock, and Shirley Brice Heath. Donaldo Macedo's *Literacies of Power: What Americans Are Not Allowed to Know* (1994), Victor Villanueva's *Bootstraps: From an American Academic of Color* (1993), and David Schaafsma's *Eating on the Street: Teaching Literacy in a Multicultural Society* (1993) focus on issues of multicultural literacy. According to Schaafsma, because "literacy is social action and not simply the encoding of language, it is important for those that are interested in the teaching of literacy to understand how teachers' values shape their instruction" (xix). Other discussions include C. H. Knoblauch and Lillian Brannon's *Critical Teaching and the Idea of Literacy* (1993) and Carol Severino, Juan C. Guerra, and Johnnella E. Butler's edited *Writing in Multicultural Settings* (1997). One essay in the collection, " 'Better Than What People Told Me I Was': What Students of Color Tell Us about the Multicultural Composition Classroom," by Carol A. Miller, articulates the basic issue: "Most broadly, teachers and students must find ways to reconcile the contending demands of educational systems and community forces, since to adopt unequivocally the language and values of the dominant culture means for many students to risk identity and the sense of belonging" (297). Mary Louise Pratt's "Arts of the Contact Zone" (1991) attempts to suggest a way in which such a reconciliation can take place. She defines "Contact Zone" as the "social spaces where cultures meet, clash, and grapple with each other, often in contexts of highly asymmetrical relations of power, such as colonialism, slavery, or their aftermaths as they are lived out in many parts of the world today" (34). Teachers can negotiate these Contact Zones if they stop thinking of their jobs as teaching a universal literacy and begin thinking of their jobs as understanding literacy as a "gathering of people each of whom [speaks] two languages and [understands] a third and [holds] only one language in common with any of the others" (38).

The Right to Literacy (1990), edited by Andrea Lunsford, Helene Moglen, and James Slevin, begins with the assumption that literacy is a right and not a privilege (2). But the editors—ever critical—recognize that "literacy is not in itself a panacea for social inequity; it does, in fact, guarantee little. It will not effect the redistribution of this nation's wealth," power, or privilege. Further, "because as [Paulo] Freire says, both illiteracy and literacy education are inevitably political, literacy workers in all contexts do well to refrain from jumping on the literacy bandwagon without first questioning the motives of both those who are driving it and those who are funding its operations" (2).

Critics of social-epistemic rhetoric are of two major kinds: those who think it is too liberal, advancing politics instead of writing instruction (Maxine Hairston, "Diversity, Ideology, and Teaching Writing" [1997]), or too conservative, refusing to be suspicious enough of the ideology of critical thought (Marshall Alcorn, "Changing the Subject" [1995]; Victor Vitanza, "A Feminist Sophistic?" [1995]).

POSTSTRUCTURALIST AND POSTMODERN RHETORICS

The poststructuralist challenge to the foundations of philosophic thought is, in effect, a demonstration of the rhetorical nature of those foundations. Poststructuralism questions the stability of the sign and the efficacy of the sign to represent or make present Reality, arguing rather that signs point to other signs, not to Reality, and that signifieds (such as Truth) exist by virtue of unstable signifying practices not as preexisting givens. This claim echoes Friedrich Nietzsche's infamous definition of Truth as a "mobile army of metaphors, metonyms, and anthropomorphisms" ("On Truth and Lying in an Extra-Moral Sense" [1989] 250). Hence Truth is a rhetorical construct, a claim that shatters the age-old distinctions between philosophy and rhetoric, word and thing, and challenges the precept that ideas are merely dressed in rhetorical garb, that figures and tropes are mere ornaments to adorn Truth.

In 1966, Jacques Derrida delivered "Structure, Sign, and Play in the Human Sciences" at the International Colloquium on Critical Languages and the Sciences of Man at The Johns Hopkins University, one of the first statements made in the name of "poststructuralism," a term coined specifically for this conference (Payne 436). In that address, later published (1978), Derrida deconstructs the foundation of structuralism and argues that structure has been evoked as an origin in order to limit the free play of its signification. He suggests an alternate approach to interpretation, which affirms "play and tries to pass beyond man and humanism, the name of man being the name of that being who, throughout [its] history . . . has dreamed of full presence, the reassuring foundation" (93).

This dream of presence, as the Western tradition's "reassuring foundation," is then repeatedly challenged throughout the rest of the century. Roland Barthes publishes "The Death of the Author" (1986), and although he's referring there to authors of literary texts, his challenge to the classical notion of the author as the one who gives voice or presence to the word certainly has felt its effect in rhetorical theory, heralding the death of the rhetor. Barthes argues that writing begins with the death of the author, as writing is "the destruction of every voice, every origin" (49).

The speaking/writing subject is no longer taken to be the origin of language. Poststructuralists suggest, alternately, that language is the subject's condition of possibility. Michel Foucault's "The Discourse on Language" (1972), delivered as an address in 1970, challenges the belief that it is "we alone, who give [language] its power" (216). Rather, language has its "devilish features," which institutions attempt to control (215) in order to "avert its powers and its dangers" (216). These powers and dangers are those that Plato warned us against when he attacked sophistic rhetoric. For Plato, discourse could lead us to Truth or away from Truth. This distinction between philosophic and sophistic rhetoric—or in other words, between literal meaning and figural meaning—is deconstructed by Paul de Man in "Semiology and Rhetoric" (1979), where he argues that language's power is evident "not when we have, on the one hand, a literal meaning and on the other hand a figural meaning, but when it is impossible to decide . . . which of the two meanings (that can be entirely incompatible) prevails. Rhetoric radically suspends logic and opens up vertiginous possibilities of referential aberration" (10).

Poststructuralist thought has influenced rhetorical studies and the theorization of the composition classroom. Sharon Crowley, for example, in *A Teacher's Introduction to Deconstruction* (1989), acknowledges that a deconstructive pedagogy is impossible to realize as "the term itself is an oxymoron" (45). Nevertheless, she outlines its possible characteristics, including a rejection of the traditional model of authority, a reinforcement of writing as a process, and a continual revision of the syllabus (46). Rejecting the traditional model of authority includes teacher as authority and writer as author/ity of the text, acknowledging that subjectivity is a construct of discourse, materialized in race, gender, and class distinctions. Accordingly, theorists such as David Bartholomae in "Inventing the University" (1988) demonstrate how "academic discourse" is constituted, as Foucault suggested, in order to regulate social order. Theorists have also asked how writing teachers are complicit with this regulation by professing the discourses of privilege and thereby constituting writing subjects that will perpetuate injustice. Linda Brodkey in "On the Subjects of Class and Gender in 'The Literacy Letters' " (1997) writes: "The discursive subject is of particular interest to those of us who teach writing because language and discourse are understood to be complicit in the representation of self and others, rather than the neutral or arbitrary tools of thought and expression. . . . Among other things, this means that since writers cannot avoid constructing a social and political reality in their texts, as teachers we need to learn how to 'read' the various relationships between writer, reader, and reality that language and discourse supposedly produce" (640).

Reading these relationships and teaching students how to be "active interpreters of their own experience" (Trimbur 127) is the role of cultural studies, according to John Trimbur in "Composition Studies: Postmodern or Popular" (1993). The construction of such interpreters is a way to "fill in the gap left vacant by the postmodern death of the subject with a nonessentialized self that allows for agency and utopian aspirations" (130). James Berlin's *Rhetorics, Poetics, and Cultures* (1996) makes a similar claim.

Rhetorical studies have predictably wrestled with the poststructuralist deconstruction of the subject. Anne Ruggles Gere's edited *Into the Field: Sites of Composition Studies* (1993) devotes an entire section to "Postmodern Subjectivities." Lester Faigley, in *Fragments of Rationality: Postmodernity and the Subject of Composition* (1993), states that "ways of theorizing subjectivity are needed that neither hold out for liberal humanism, collapse subjectivity in vague notions of community, nor reject the idea of a subject altogether" (239). The project, then, as Susan Miller's title suggests, is *Rescuing the Subject* (1989) from poststructuralist thought and postmodern conditions.

A thick collection of essays in James S. Baumlin and Tita French Baumlin's *Ethos: New Essays in Rhetorical and Critical Theory* (1994) takes the problem of the subject as an opportunity to revisit and refigure classical rhetoric's concept of *ethos*. The book, which includes a bibliography of research on *ethos*, features contributors such as Marshall W. Alcorn, Susan C. Jarratt and Nedra Reynolds, Victor J. Vitanza, and C. Jan Swearingen. Coeditor James Baumlin introduces the issue: "Evidently, a post-Cartesian *ethos* needs to explore a different model of mind than one that defines ego as a mode of self-presence and self possession (that is, as a unified consciousness in control of its meaning)" (xxii–xxiii). Contributors Susan Jarratt and Nedra Reynolds ("Splitting Image" [1994]) attempt to do just this through an examination of two classical rhetorical notions: *ethos* and *nomos*. Tracing the etymology of *ethos* leads to *ethea*, meaning "haunts" (48). Their argument is that this etymology suggests that one's *ethos* is formed in the places in which one "hangs out" (48). Additionally, *nomos*, or cultural practices and beliefs, also haunt our ethos (48), thereby establishing a subjectivity that is positioned and constructed through current cultural practices.

Such attempts to rescue the subject have met with criticism. One example is Michelle Ballif's "Seducing Composition: A Challenge to Identity-Disclosing Pedagogies" (1997), wherein she questions compositionists' abiding faith in representation and challenges the motivation behind that faith and behind our will to produce subjects. Another critique is Marshall Alcorn's "Changing the Subject of Postmodernist Theory" (1995). Specifically addressing Berlin, claiming that Berlin's pedagogy awkwardly grafts Humanism onto postmodernism in an attempt to offer an agent of change, Alcorn argues: "The postmodernist subject, unlike the humanist subject, is *essentially* a structure of discourse conflict; it has no mechanism or motivation for being anything *other* than such a structure of conflict" (339–40). Alcorn, working out of Lacanian psychoanalytic theory, further suggests that Berlin's pedagogical hope overlooks the libidinal power of language. The realized tension here is between conceptualizing rhetoric as essentially epistemic or as libidinal. According to Geoffrey Sirc, in "Writing Classroom as A & P Parking Lot" (1993), "Desire remains the key component lacking in most composition theory" (36).

Lynn Worsham, in "Writing against Writing: The Predicament of *Écriture Féminine* in Composition Studies" (1991), examines several attempts to appropriate the French feminist notion of "*écriture féminine*" (roughly defined as a writing of/through pre-Oedipal bodily desires) into composition theory and claims that it "cannot be freely imported into the writing classroom to work alongside academic discourse toward the goal of literacy—that is, to the extent that literacy and the literate mind are governed by the epistemological attitude and its positioning of the speaker or writer in a phallic position of mastery over discourse . . . aligned with the ideology of the clear and the distinct, the transparency of communication, the overriding need for consensus and communication" (93).

This echoes the infamous debate between Jean-François Lyotard and Jürgen Habermas. Lyotard claims that Habermas's notion of "communicative action" as a rhetorical practice of consensual negotiation "does violence to the heterogeneity of language games" (*The Postmodern Condition* [1984] xxv). A postmodern rhetoric would advance the heterogeneity of discourse, not homology, would "wage a war on totality" and consensus (*The Postmodern Condition* 82), just as a feminine text, according to Hélène Cixous in "The Laugh of the Medusa" (1980), cannot fail to be more than subversive . . . to smash everything, to shatter the framework of institutions, to blow up the law, to break up the 'truth' with laughter" (258).

There have been several books addressing the intersections between postmodern theory and composition pedagogy, including Dennis J. Ciesielski's *Between Philosophy and Rhetoric: Aesthetics and Meaning in the Postmodern Composition Classroom* (1998),

Derek Owens's *Resisting Writings (and the Boundaries of Composition)* (1994), Thomas Kent's *Paralogic Rhetoric* (1993), and Gary A. Olson and Sidney I. Dobrin's coedited *Composition Theory for the Postmodern Classroom* (1994) with contributors such as Jacqueline Jones Royster, James Kinneavy, Thomas Kent, and Henry Giroux. Jasper Neel, in *Plato, Derrida, and Writing* (1988), argues that although we should resist Platonic notions of rhetoric, we should also resist Derridean practices. He writes: "Writers who give in to Plato in effect cease to be writers and become philosophers. . . . Writers who give in to Derrida become philosophers who never finish unworking all those discourses that conceal or remain ignorant of their own written rhetoricity" (203).

An additional important collection is Patricia Harkin and John Schilb's *Contending with Words: Composition and Rhetoric in a Postmodern Age* (1991). In their introduction, Harkin and Schilb remind us of the Foucauldian principle of how ideology is institutionalized. Therefore, to challenge ideology requires challenging our institutional practices as rhetoricians in a postmodern age (6). Sharon Crowley, in an afterword ("Reimagining the Writing Scene" [1991]), writes: "These authors expect composition teachers . . . to reject much of what now passes for composition theory . . . and to learn to tolerate ambiguity, variety, and conflict instead of valuing clarity, identity, and harmony" (190–91). Victor J. Vitanza's "Three Countertheses: Or, A Critical In(ter)vention into Composition Theories and Pedagogies" (1991) asks practitioners and theorists to rethink the very foundations of composition studies, which he identifies as: "(1) the will to systematize (the) language (of composing), (2) the will to be its author(ity), and (3) the will to teach it to students" (140). Vitanza counters these foundations, arguing countertheses that suggest we "paralogize" "the university so that it might become a (polymorphous) perversity" (159).

Resistance to just such a radical postmodern rhetoric is evident in Michael Bernard-Donals and Richard Glejzer's coedited *Rhetoric in an Antifoundational World* (1998), Patricia Bizzell's "Beyond Anti-Foundationalism" (1993), and Elizabeth A. Flynn's "Rescuing Postmodernism" (1997), where provisional foundations are advanced, where objectivity and subjectivity are reconstructed, and where composition studies is rescued from postmodernism.

ELECTRONIC AND COMPUTER-ASSISTED RHETORICS

Recent interest in electronic rhetorics and computer-aided composition has resulted in a number of publications as well as the creation of new journals such as *Computers and Composition* and, appropriately, a number of new online journals devoted to the issue of technology and writing, including *Kairos, CWRL, RhetNet,* and *PRE/TEXT: Electra(Lite)*. Early publications tend to uncritically and unabashedly tout the revolutionary potential of computer technology and networked classrooms. Claims are made that word-processing capabilities encourage revision, reinforcing the process—not product—paradigm, and that computer-assisted writing improves student productivity, as demonstrated by Thomas Barker's "Studies in Word Processing and Writing" (1986). Likewise, Leslie D. Harris and Cynthia A. Wambeam, in "The Internet-Based Composition Classroom: A Study in Pedagogy" (1996), report that online writers are more productive, enjoy writing more, and are better writers than their traditional counterparts. The further claim is that internetworked writing "facilitates liberation from traditional instutional learning disablers such as the proscenium classroom, the presentational mode, and academic language," thereby facilitating students, particularly those who are traditionally marginalized or silenced by institutions and academic language (Romano, "The Egalitarianism Narrative" [1993] 5). Although more recent scholarship tends to be more critical and less utopian in scope, researchers continue to argue the benefits of electronic and computer-assisted rhetorics.

Thomas T. Barker's "Computers and the Instructional Context" (1990) addresses how computers in the classroom enhance collaboration not only between the students but also between students and teacher in constructive and productive ways. Deborah Holdstein and Cynthia Selfe's edited collection *Computers and Writing: Theory, Research, Practice* (1990) and Carolyn Handa's edited *Computers and Community: Teaching Composition in the Twenty-first Century* (1990) are useful resources exploring how computers foster collaboration and enhance a more student-centered writing classroom.

Other researchers focus on how electronic rhetorics affect literacy—its acquisition and its characteristics. Myron C. Tuman's edited *Literacy Online: The Promise (and Peril) of Reading and Writing with Computers* (1992) challenges the literacy debates of the 1980s, which he argues overlooked how computers "will reshape not just how we read and write and, by extension, how we teach these skills but our very understanding of basic terms such as *reading, writing,* and *text*" (8). Susan C. Herring's edited *Computer-Mediated Communication: Linguistic, Social and Cross-Cultural Perspectives* (1996) foregrounds the unique characteristics of online discourse, termed *computer-mediated communication*—its written nature yet oral quality and its lack of extralinguistic "cues as to the gender, identity, personality, or mood of their interlocutors" (4)—and speculates on the implications for literacy. Cynthia L. Selfe and Susan Hilligoss's edited *Literacy and Computers: The Complications of Teaching and Learning with Technology* (1994) explores changing contexts and definitions of literacy.

Christina Haas, in *Writing Technology: Studies on the Materiality of Literacy* (1996), argues that the "tendency is to look through computer technology to the economic, practical, political, or pedagogical goals that the technology might serve" (xi). By looking at the technology as transparent, she suggests, we overlook the materiality of technology, "the place where culture and cognition meet. . . . For better or worse, writers do not reinvent the tools of literacy; they come with a history and a whole set of cultural ways of thinking inherent in them" (229). This attention to the ways technology materializes cultural relations shifts attention from how writers use technologies to how technologies constitute writers. Tharon Howard, in *A Rhetoric of Electronic Communities* (1997), argues that electronic discourse is "often neither liberated nor liberating. . . . Thus my examination of electronic communities is firmly situated in the Althusserian observation that no discourse is free of ideology; . . . [but rather in James Berlin's words] 'all discourse has designs on us' " (23). Howard, then, asks What designs, then, does electronic literacy have on us? Joseph Janangelo's "Technopower and Technoppression: Some Abuses of Power and Control in Computer-Assisted Writing Environments" (1991) suggests that one such design is evidenced by the "monitoring and control that can take place in computer-assisted learning environments [making] students and teachers vulnerable in ways that we never were before" (47).

Such claims complicate earlier utopian visions as presented by Lester Faigley's *Fragments of Rationality* (1993) and Cynthia Selfe and Paul Meyer's "Testing Claims for Online Conferences" (1991), which suggest "egalitarian classrooms." These claims have been challenged by research that demonstrates that "[g]ender asymmetries [for example] have been found to carry over wholesale from face-to-face interaction, and even to be exaggerated" in computer-mediated communication (Herring 4). Cynthia Selfe in "Lest We Think the Revolution Is a Revolution" (1999) examines contemporary cultural narratives about technology—narratives that reassert the status quo rather than revolutionize it. Gail Hawisher and Cynthia Selfe's edited *Passions, Pedagogies, and 21st Century Technologies* (1999) confronts these complicated issues.

Whether electronic rhetorics can herald global literacies or democratic communities (Howard Rheingold, *The Virtual Community* [1993]) or, as Beth Kolko argues, construct virtual identities for political purposes ("Bodies in Place" [1998]) continues to be debated and foregrounds a distinction between virtual reality and "real life." D. Diane Davis challenges this binary in her essay "(Non)Fiction('s) Addiction(s)" (1998) by drawing on the poststructuralist critique of truth and representation and the postmodern loss of the real. Within virtual spaces and through electronic rhetorics, according to theorists such as Jay Bolter (*Writing Space* [1991]), Michael Joyce (*Of Two Minds* [1995]), and George Landow (*Hypertext* [1992]), writing will cease to pretend platonically to refer to reality but will paralogically engage the free play of signification and thereby disrupt dominant discourses. This new model for language, according to Stuart Moulthrop in "The Politics of Hypertext" (1991), is "not as a hierarchy but as a network of relationships: the model for written discourse is no longer a linear chain of reference but a recursive, allusive web of correspondences" (255). Greg Ulmer's "Grammatology (in the Stacks) of Hypermedia: A Simulation" (1992) and Johndan Johnson-Eilola's *Nostalgic Angels: Rearticulating Hyptertext Writing* (1997) explore the possibilities.

Thomas T. Barker and Fred O. Kemp's "Network Theory: A Postmodern Pedagogy for the Writing Classroom" (1990) argues that although the new technologies facilitate postmodern composition, the instructional environment seems oblivious to the need to do so (26). Henrietta Nickels Shirks predicts that the environment will change as will "the theoretical foundations of composition studies as the notion of the writer as communicator is augmented by that of the writer as architect of information. As creators of multiple pathways through information, today's writers will undoubtedly abandon linear written communication as they begin to further develop the multidimensional realm of hyptertextual communication" ("Hypertext and Composition Studies" [1991] 200). Geoffrey Sirc and Tom Reynolds, in "The Face of Collaboration in the Networked Writing Classroom" (1990), for example, demonstrate how the social-constructivist theoretical foundations of invention as a social act need to be rethought and rearticulated for an electronic environment. Cynthia Haynes and Jan Rune Holmevik's edited *High Wired: On the Design, Use, and Theory of Educational MOOs* (1998) offers practical and theoretical means to effect these changes.

A continuing critique of electronic and computer-assisted rhetorics is that of computer access and how, according to Charles Moran, "emerging technologies are increasing the wealth-gap that now exists in our society" ("Access" [1999] 220). Moran's essay, after reviewing the literature, offers an agenda for a technologically enhanced pedagogy that doesn't contribute to class inequity (218–19). Lester Faigley's "Beyond Imagination" (1999), likewise, addresses this issue. Moran and Faigley require us to ask difficult political questions. James E. Porter raises ethical questions in his *Rhetorical Ethics and Internetworked Writing* (1998). In the face of the postmodern critique of ethical principles, Porter asks the kinds of difficult questions raised at century's end: How should we participate as writers and publishers of electronic discourse, as listowners, as participants in lists, and as teachers in networked environments? What are the ethical problems endemic to these roles and situations? What principles will we use to make choices?

SELECTED BIBLIOGRAPHY

Abrahamson, Priscilla A. "Between a Rock and a Soft Spot: Re-viewing College Preparatory Writing." *English Journal* 82.6 (1993): 14–20.

Alcorn, Marshall W., Jr. "Changing the Subject of Postmodernist Theory: Discourse, Ideology, and Therapy in the Classroom." *Rhetoric Review* 13.2 (1995): 331–49.

Anderson, Chris. "Late Night Thoughts on Writing and Teaching Essays." *PRE/TEXT* 11.1–2 (1990): 85–93.

Appelbee, Arthur N. *Tradition and Reform in the Teaching of English.* Urbana, IL: National Council of Teachers of English, 1974.

Aronowitz, Stanley, and Henry A. Giroux. *Education Still under Siege: The Conservative, Liberal, and Radical Debate over Schooling.* South Hadley, MA: Bergin & Garvey, 1985.

Ashton-Jones, Evelyn. "Collaboration, Conversation, and the Politics of Gender." *Feminine Principles and Women's Experience in American Composition and Rhetoric.* Ed. Louis Wetherbee Phelps and Janet Emig. Pittsburgh: University of Pittsburgh Press, 1995. 5–26.

Atwill, Janet M. *Rhetoric Reclaimed: Aristotle and the Liberal Arts Tradition.* Ithaca: Cornell University Press, 1998.

Ballif, Michelle. "Re/Dressing Histories; Or, On Re/Covering Figures Who Have Been Laid Bare by Our Gaze." *Rhetoric Society Quarterly* 22.1 (1992): 91–98.

———. "Seducing Composition: A Challenge to Identity-Disclosing Pedagogies." *Rhetoric Review* 16.1 (1997): 76–91.

Barker, Thomas T. "Computers and Instructional Context." *Computers and Writing.* Ed. Deborah Holdstein and Cynthia Selfe. New York: MLA, 1990. 7–17.

———. "Studies in Word Processing and Writing." *Computers in the Schools* 4.1 (1986): 109–21.

Barker, Thomas T., and Fred O. Kemp. "Network Theory: A Postmodern Pedagogy for the Writing Classroom." *Computers and Community: Teaching Composition in the Twenty-first Century.* Ed. Carolyn Handa. Portsmouth, NH: Boynton/Cook, 1990. 1–27.

Barthes, Roland. "The Death of the Author." *The Rustle of Language.* Trans. Richard Howard. New York: Hill and Wang, 1986. 49–55.

———. "The Old Rhetoric: An *Aide-mémoire.*" *The Semiotic Challenge.* Trans. Richard Howard. New York: Hill and Wang, 1988. 11–94.

Bartholomae, David. "Inventing the University." *Perspectives on Literacy.* Ed. Eugene R. Kintgen, Barry M. Kroll, and Mike Rose. Carbondale: Southern Illinois University Press, 1988. 134–65.

———. "Writing with Teachers: A Conversation with Peter Elbow." *College Composition and Communication* 46.1 (1995): 62–71.

Baumlin, James S., and Tita French Baumlin, eds. *Ethos: New Essays in Rhetorical and Critical Theory.* Dallas: Southern Methodist University Press, 1994.

Benton, Stephen L., Robert G. Kraft, John H. Glover, and Barbara S. Plake. "Cognitive Capacity Difference among Writers." *Journal of Educational Psychology* 76.5 (1984): 820–34.

Bereiter, Carl. "Development in Writing." *Cognitive Processes in Writing.* Ed. Lee W. Gregg and Erwin R. Steinberg. Hillsdale, NJ: Erlbaum, 1980. 73–93.

Bereiter, Carl, and Marlene Scardamalia. *The Psychology of Written Composition.* Hillsdale, NJ: Erlbaum, 1987.

Bereton, John C., ed. *The Origins of Composition Studies in the American College, 1875–1925.* Pittsburgh: University of Pittsburgh Press, 1995.

Berkenkotter, Carol. "Paradigm Debates, Turf Wars, and the Conduct of Sociocognitive Inquiry in Composition." *College Composition and Communication* 42.2 (1991): 151–69.

Berlin, James A. "Contemporary Composition: The Major Pedagogical Theories." *College English* 44.8 (1982): 765–77.

———. "Rhetoric and Ideology in the Writing Class." *College English* 50.5 (1988): 477–94.

———. *Rhetoric and Reality: Writing Instruction in American Colleges, 1900–1985.* Carbondale: Southern Illinois University Press, 1987.

———. *Rhetorics, Poetics, and Cultures: Refiguring College English Studies.* Urbana, IL: NCTE, 1996.

———. *Writing Instruction in Nineteenth-Century American Colleges.* Carbondale: Southern Illinois University Press, 1984.

Berlin, James A., Robert J. Connors, Sharon Crowley, Richard Leo Enos, Victor J. Vitanza, Susan C. Jarratt, Nan Johnson, and Jan Swearingen, with James J. Murphy. "The Politics of Historiography." *Rhetoric Review* 7.1 (Fall 1988): 5–49.

Berlin, James A., and Robert P. Inkster. "Current-Traditional Rhetoric: Paradigm and Practice." *Freshman English News* 8.3 (1980): 1–4, 13–14.

Bernal, Martin. *Black Athena: The Afroasiatic Roots of Classical Civilization.* Piscataway, NJ: Rutgers University Press, 1989.

Bernard-Donals, Michael, and Richard Glejzer, eds. *Rhetoric in an Antifoundational World.* New Haven: Yale University Press, 1998.

Berthoff, Ann E. "From Problem-solving to a Theory of the Imagination." *College English* 33.6 (1972): 636–49.

———. "The Problem of Problem Solving." *College Composition and Communication* 22.3 (1971): 237–42.

Biesecker, Barbara. "Coming to Terms with Recent Attempts to Write Women into the History of Rhetoric." *Philosophy & Rhetoric* 25.2 (1992): 140–61.

Bizzell, Patricia. "Beyond Anti-Foundationalism to Rhetorical Authority: Problems Defining 'Cultural Literacy.' " *Academic Discourse and Critical Consciousness.* Pittsburgh: University of Pittsburgh Press, 1993. 256–76.

———. "Cognition, Convention, and Certainty." *PRE/TEXT* 3.3 (1982): 213–43.

———. "Opportunities for Feminist Research in the History of Rhetoric." *Rhetoric Review* 11.1 (1992–1993): 50–58.

———. "Thomas Kuhn, Scientism, and English Studies." *College English* 40.7 (1979): 764–71.

Bizzell, Patricia, and Bruce Herzberg, eds. *The Rhetorical Tradition.* Boston: Bedford/ St. Martin's, 1990.

Blair, Carole. "Contested Histories of Rhetoric: The Politics of Preservation, Progress, and Change." *Quarterly Journal of Speech* 78.4 (1992): 403–28.

Blau, Sheridan. "Invisible Writing: Investigating Cognitive Processes in Composition." *College Composition and Communication* 34.3 (1983): 297–312.

Bolter, Jay David. *Writing Space: The Computer, Hypertext, and the History of Writing.* Hillside, NJ: Lawrence Erlbaum, 1991.

Brand, Alice G. "Hot Cognition: Emotions and Writing Behavior." *Journal of Advanced Composition* 6.1 (1985–1986): 6–15.

———. "Social Cognition, Emotions, and the Psychology of Writing." *Journal of Advanced Composition* 11.2 (1991): 395–407.

———. "The Why of Cognition: Emotion in the Writing Process." *College Composition and Communication* 38.4 (1987): 436–43.

Britton, James, Tony Burgess, Nancy Martin, Alex McLeod, and Harold Rosen. *The Development of Writing Abilities (11–18).* London: Macmillan Education, 1975.

Brodkey, Linda. "On the Subjects of Class and Gender in 'The Literacy Letters.' " *Cross-Talk in Comp Theory.* Ed. Victor Villanueva, Jr. Urbana, IL: NCTE, 1997. 639–58.

Brody, Miriam. *Manly Writing: Gender, Rhetoric, and the Rise of Composition.* Carbondale: Southern Illinois University Press, 1993.

Brooke, Robert. "Control in Writing: Flower, Derrida, and Images of the Writer." *College English* 51.4 (1989): 405–17.

Bruffee, Kenneth A. "Collaborative Learning and 'The Conversation of Mankind.' " *College English* 46.7 (1984): 635–52.

———. "Liberal Education and the Social Justification of Belief." *Liberal Education* 68.2 (1982): 95–114.

———. "Social Construction, Language, and the Authority of Knowledge: A Bibliographical Essay." *College English* 48.8 (1986): 773–90.

Burleson, Brant R., and Katherine E. Rowan. "Are Social-Cognitive Ability and Narrative Writing Skill Related?" *Written Communication* 2.1 (1985): 25–43.

Burnham, Christopher C. "Expressive Rhetoric: A Source Study." *Defining the New Rhetorics.* Ed. Theresa Enos and Stuart C. Brown. Newbury Park, CA: Sage, 1993. 154–70.

Campbell, Karlyn Kohrs. *Man Cannot Speak for Her.* 2 vols. Westport, CT: Greenwood Press, 1989.

Carter, Michael. "The Idea of Expertise: An Exploration of Cognitive and Social Dimensions of Writing." *College Composition and Communication* 41.3 (1990): 265–86.

Caywood, Cynthia L., and Gillian R. Overing, eds. *Teaching Writing: Pedagogy, Gender, and Equity.* Albany: SUNY Press, 1987.

Ciesielski, Dennis J. *Between Philosophy and Rhetoric: Aesthetics and Meaning in the Postmodern Composition Classroom.* New York: Peter Lang, 1998.

Cixous, Hélène. "The Laugh of the Medusa." Trans. Keith Cohen and Paula Cohen. *New French Feminims.* Ed. Elaine Marks and Isabelle de Courtivron. New York: Schocken Books, 1980. 245–64.

Clark, Gregory. *Dialogue, Dialectic, and Conversation: A Social Perspective on the Function of Writing.* Carbondale: Southern Illinois University Press, 1990.

Clark, Gregory, and S. Michael Halloran, eds. *Oratorical Culture in Nineteenth-Century America: Transformations in the Theory and Practice of Rhetoric.* Carbondale: Southern Illinois University Press, 1993.

Clifford, John, and John Schilb, eds. *Writing Theory and Critical Theory.* New York: MLA, 1994.

Cole, Thomas. *The Origins of Rhetoric in Ancient Greece.* Baltimore: Johns Hopkins University Press, 1991.

Collins, Allan, John Seely Brown, and Ann Holum. "Cognitive Apprenticeship: Making Thinking Visible." *American Educator* 15.3 (1991): 6–11, 38–48.

Collins, Allan, and Dedre Gentner. "A Framework for a Cognitive Theory of Writing." *Cognitive Processes in Writing.* Ed. Lee W. Gregg and Erwin R. Steinberg. Hillsdale, NJ: Erlbaum, 1980. 51–72.

Conley, Thomas M. *Rhetoric in the European Tradition.* Chicago: University of Chicago Press, 1994.

Connors, Robert J. *Composition-Rhetoric: Backgrounds, Theory, and Pedagogy.* Pittsburgh: University of Pittsburgh Press, 1997.

Connors, Robert J., Lisa S. Ede, and Andrea A. Lunsford, eds. *Essays on Classical Rhetoric and Modern Discourse.* Carbondale: Southern Illinois University Press, 1984.

Cooper, Marilyn, and Michael Holzman. "Talking about Protocols." *College Composition and Communication* 34.3 (1983): 284–93.

Corbett, Edward P. J. *Classical Rhetoric for the Modern Student.* 3rd ed. Oxford: Oxford University Press, 1990.

———. "The Usefulness of Classical Rhetoric." *College Composition and Communication* 14.3 (1963): 162–64.

Crowley, Sharon. *Ancient Rhetorics for Contemporary Students.* New York: Macmillan, 1994.

———. *Composition in the University: Historical and Polemical Essays.* Pittsburgh: University of Pittsburgh Press, 1998.

———. *The Methodical Memory: Invention in Current-Traditional Rhetoric.* Carbondale: Southern Illinois University Press, 1990.

———. "A Plea for the Revival of Sophistry." *Rhetoric Review* 7.2 (1989): 318–34.

———. "Reimagining the Writing Scene." *Contending with Words.* Ed. Patricia Harkin and John Schilb. New York: MLA, 1991. 189–97.

———. *A Teacher's Introduction to Deconstruction.* Urbana, IL: NCTE, 1989.

Daiwte, Collette. "Physical and Cognitive Factors in Revising: Thoughts from Studies with Computers." *Research in the Teaching of English* 20.2 (1986): 141–59.

Dasenbrock, Reed Way. "The Myths of the Subjective and the Subject in Composition Studies." *JAC* 13.1 (1993): 21–32.

Davis, D. Diane. "(Non)Fiction('s) Addiction(s)." *High Wired: On the Design, Use, and Theory of Educational MOOs.* Ed. Cynthia Haynes and Jan Rune Holmevik. Ann Arbor: University of Michigan Press, 1998. 267–85.

de Man, Paul. "Semiology and Rhetoric." *Allegories of Reading: Figural Language in Rousseau, Nietzsche, Rilke and Proust.* New Haven, CT: Yale University Press, 1979. 3–19.

Derrida, Jacques. "Plato's Pharmacy." *Disseminations.* Trans. Barbara Johnson. Chicago: University of Chicago Press, 1981. 61–172.

———. "Structure, Sign, and Play in the Discourse of the Human Sciences." *Writing and Difference.* Trans. Alan Bass. Chicago: University of Chicago Press, 1978.

Dillworth, Collett B., Jr., Robert W. Reising, and Denny T. Wolfe. "Language Structure and Thought in Written Composition: Certain Relationships." *Research in the Teaching of English* 12.2 (1978): 97–106.

Dowst, Kenneth. "Cognition and Composition." *Freshman English News* 11.2–3 (1983): 1–14.

Durst, Russell K. "Cognitive and Linguistic Demands of Analytic Writing." *Research in the Teaching of English* 21.4 (1978): 347–76.

Elbow, Peter. "Being a Writer vs. Being an Academic: A Conflict in Goals." *College Composition and Communication* 46.1 (1995): 72–83.

Emig, Janet. "Writing as a Mode of Learning." *College Composition and Communication* 282 (1977): 122–28.

Enos, Richard Leo. *Greek Rhetoric before Aristotle.* Prospect Heights, IL: Waveland Press, 1993.

———. *The Literate Mode of Cicero's Legal Rhetoric.* Carbondale: Southern Illinois University Press, 1988.

———. *Roman Rhetoric: Revolution and the Greek Influence.* Prospect Heights, IL: Waveland Press, 1995.

Enos, Theresa, ed. *Learning from the Histories of Rhetoric: Essays in Honor of Winifred Bryan Horner.* Carbondale: Southern Illinois University Press, 1993.

Faigley, Lester. "Beyond Imagination: The Internet and Global Digital Literacy." *Passions, Pedagogies, and 21st Century Technologies.* Ed. Gail E. Hawisher and Cynthia L. Selfe. Logan: Utah State University Press, 1999. 129–39.

———. "Competing Theories of Process: A Critique and a Proposal." *College English* 48.6 (1986): 527–62.

———. *Fragments of Rationality: Postmodernity and the Subject of Composition.* Pittsburgh: University of Pittsburgh Press, 1992.

Fish, Stanley. *Is There a Text in This Class?* Cambridge, MA: Harvard University Press, 1980.

Fishman, Stephen M. "Explicating Our Tacit Tradition: John Dewey and Composition Studies." *College Composition and Communication* 44.3 (1993): 315–30.

Fishman, Stephen M., and Lucille Parkinson McCarthy. "Is Expressivism Dead? Reconsidering Its Romantic Roots and Its Relation to Social Construction." *College English* 54.6 (1992): 647–61.

Fitts, Karen, and Alan W. France, eds. *Left Margins: Cultural Studies and Composition Pedagogy.* Albany: SUNY Press, 1995.

Fleckenstein, Kristie S. "Defining Affect in Relation to Cognition: A Response to Susan McLeod." *Journal of Advanced Composition* 11.2 (1991): 447–53.

Flower, Linda. *The Construction of Negotiated Meaning: A Social Cognitive Theory of Writing*. Carbondale: Southern Illinois University Press, 1994.

———. *Problem-Solving Strategies for Writing*. 4th ed. Fort Worth, TX: Harcourt Brace, 1993.

———, ed. *Making Thinking Visible: Writing, Collaborative Planning, and Classroom Inquiry*. Urbana, IL: National Council of Teachers of English, 1994.

Flower, Linda, and John R. Hayes. "Response to Marilyn Cooper and Michael Holzman, 'Talking about Protocols.' " *College Composition and Communication* 34.1 (1983): 284–93.

Flynn, Elizabeth A. "Composing as a Woman." *College Composition and Communication* 39.4 (1988): 423–35.

———. "Rescuing Postmodernism." *College Composition and Communication* 48.4 (1997): 540–55.

Foss, Sonja K., Karen A. Foss, and Robert Trapp. "Challenges to the Rhetorical Tradition." *Contemporary Perspectives on Rhetoric*. 2nd ed. Prospect Heights, IL: Waveland Press, 1991. 273–314.

Foucault, Michel. "The Discourse on Language." *Archaeology of Knowledge & The Discourse on Language*. Trans. A. M. Sheridan Smith. New York: Pantheon, 1972.

Freedman, Aviva, and Ian Pringle. "Writing in the College Years: Some Indices of Growth." *College Composition and Communication* 31.3 (1980): 311–24.

Freire, Paulo. *Pedagogy of the Oppressed*. Trans. Myra Bergman Ramos. New York: Continuum, 1989.

Gere, Anne Ruggles, ed. *Into the Field: Sites of Composition Studies*. New York: MLA, 1993.

Giroux, Henry A. *Theory and Resistance in Education*. South Hadley, MA: Bergin, 1983.

Glenn, Cheryl. *Rhetoric Retold: Regendering the Tradition from Antiquity through the Renaissance*. Carbondale: Southern Illinois University Press, 1997.

Golden, James L., Goodwin F. Bergquist, and William E. Coleman, eds. *The Rhetoric of Western Thought*. Dubuque, IA: Kendall/Hunt, 1989.

Gradin, Sherrie L. *Romancing Rhetorics: Social Expressivist Perspectives on the Teaching of Writing*. Portsmouth, NH: Boynton/Cook, 1995.

Greene, Stuart. "Toward a Dialectical Theory of Composing." *Rhetoric Review* 9.1 (1990): 149–72.

Gregg, Lee W., and Erwin R. Steinberg, eds. *Cognitive Processes in Writing*. Hillsdale, NJ: Erlbaum, 1980.

Haas, Christina. *Writing Technology: Studies on the Materiality of Literacy*. Mahwah, NJ: Lawrence Erlbaum, 1996.

Hairston, Maxine. "Diversity, Ideology, and Teaching Writing." *Cross-Talk in Comp Theory*. Ed. Victor Villanueva, Jr. Urbana, IL: NCTE, 1997. 659–75.

———. "The Winds of Change: Thomas Kuhn and the Revolution in the Teaching of Writing." *College Composition and Communication* 33.1 (1982): 76–88.

Halloran, S. Michael. "Rhetoric in the American College Curriculum: The Decline of Public Discourse." *PRE/TEXT* 3.3 (1982): 245–64.

Handa, Carolyn, ed. *Computers and Community: Teaching Composition in the Twenty-first Century*. Portsmouth, NH: Boynton/Cook, 1990.

Harkin, Patricia, and John Schilb, eds. *Contending with Words: Composition and Rhetoric in a Postmodern Age*. New York: MLA, 1991.

Harris, Jeanette. *Expressive Discourse*. Dallas, TX: Southern Methodist University Press, 1990.

Harris, Joseph. "Rethinking the Pedagogy of Problem-Solving." *Journal of Teaching Writing* 7.2 (1988): 157–65.

Harris, Leslie D., and Cynthia A. Wambeam. "The Internet-Based Composition Classroom: A Study in Pedagogy." *Computers and Composition* 13.3 (1996): 353–71.

Hawisher, Gail E., and Cynthia L. Selfe, eds. *Passions, Pedagogies, and 21st Century Technologies*. Logan: Utah State University Press, 1999.

Haynes, Cynthia, and Jan Rune Holmevik, eds. *High Wired: On the Design, Use, and Theory of Educational MOOs*. Ann Arbor: University of Michigan Press, 1998.

Herring, Susan C., ed. *Computer-Mediated Communication: Linguistic, Social and Cross-Cultural Perspectives*. Amsterdam: John Benjamins, 1996.

Holdstein, Deborah H., and Cynthia L. Selfe, eds. *Computers and Writing: Theory, Research, Practice*. New York: MLA, 1990.

Honeychurch, Joyce. "Language, Cognition, and Learning: Expressive Writing in the Classroom." *Journal of Curriculum and Supervision* 5.4 (1990): 328–37.

Horner, Winifred Bryan. *Nineteenth-Century Scottish Rhetoric: The American Connection*. Carbondale: Southern Illinois University Press, 1993.

———, ed. *Historical Rhetoric: An Annotated Bibliography of Selected Sources in English*. Boston: G. K. Hall, 1980.

Horner, Winifred Bryan, and Michael Leff, eds. *Rhetoric and Pedagogy: Its History, Philosophy and Practice. Essays in Honor of James J. Murphy*. Mahwah, NJ: Lawrence Erlbaum, 1995.

Howard, Tharon. *A Rhetoric of Electronic Communities*. Greenwich, CT: Ablex, 1997.

Janangelo, Joseph. "Technopower and Technoppression: Some Abuses of Power and Control in Computer-Assisted Writing Environments." *Computers and Composition* 9.1 (1991): 47–64.

Jarratt, Susan C. "Feminism and Composition: The Case for Conflict." *Contending with Words: Composition and Rhetoric in a Postmodern Age*. Ed. Patricia Harkin and John Schilb. New York: MLA, 1991. 105–23.

———. "Performing Feminisms, Histories, Rhetorics." *Rhetoric Society Quarterly* 22.1 (1992): 1–5.

———. *Rereading the Sophists: Classical Rhetoric Refigured*. Carbondale: Southern Illinois University Press, 1991.

Jarratt, Susan C., and Nedra Reynolds. "The Splitting Image: Contemporary Feminisms and the Ethics of *Ethos*." *Ethos: New Essays in Rhetorical and Critical Theory*. Ed. James S. Baumlin and Tita French Baumlin. Dallas: Southern Methodist University Press, 1994. 37–63.

Jarratt, Susan C., and Lynn Worsham, eds. *Feminism and Composition Studies: In Other Words*. New York: MLA, 1998.

Johnson, Nan. *Nineteenth-Century Rhetoric in North America*. Carbondale: Southern Illinois University Press, 1991.

Johnson-Eilola, Johndan. *Nostalgic Angels: Rearticulating Hypertext Writing*. Norwood, NJ: Ablex Press, 1997.

Joyce, Michael. *Of Two Minds: Hypertext, Pedagogy, and Politics*. Ann Arbor: University of Michigan Press, 1995.

Kastely, James L. *Rethinking the Rhetorical Tradition: From Plato to Postmodernism.* New Haven: Yale University Press, 1997.

Kearns, Michael. "Topical Knowledge and Revising." *Journal of Teaching Writing* 9.2 (1990): 195–207.

Kellogg, Ronald T. "Observations in the Psychology of Thinking and Writing." *Composition Studies/Freshman English News* 21.1 (1993): 3–41.

———. *The Psychology of Writing.* New York: Oxford University Press, 1994.

Kennedy, George A. *The Art of Persuasion in Greece.* Princeton, NJ: Princeton University Press, 1963.

———. *The Art of Rhetoric in the Roman World (300 BC–300 AD).* Princeton, NJ: Princeton University Press, 1972.

———. *Classical Rhetoric and Its Christian and Secular Traditions from Ancient to Modern Times.* Chapel Hill: University of North Carolina Press, 1980.

Kent, Thomas. *Paralogic Rhetoric: A Theory of Communicative Interaction.* Lewisburg: Bucknell University Press, 1993.

Kinneavy, James L. *A Theory of Discourse: The Aims of Discourse.* 1971. New York: Norton. 1980.

Kintgen, Eugene R., Barry M. Kroll, and Mike Rose, eds. *Perspectives on Literacy.* Carbondale: Southern Illinois University Press, 1988.

Kitzhaber, Albert R. *Rhetoric in American Colleges, 1850–1900.* 1953. Dallas: Southern Methodist University Press, 1990.

Knoblauch, C. H., and Lillian Brannon. *Critical Teaching and the Idea of Literacy.* Portsmouth, NH: Heinemann, Boynton/Cook, 1993.

———. *Rhetorical Traditions and the Teaching of Writing.* Upper Montclair, NY: Boynton/Cook, 1984.

Kolko, Beth. "Bodies in Place." *High Wired: On the Design, Use, and Theory of Educational MOOs.* Ed. Cynthia Haynes and Jan Rune Holmevik. Ann Arbor: University or Michigan Press, 1998. 253–65.

Kroll, Barry M. "Social-Cognitive Ability and Writing Performance." *Written Communication* 2.3 (1985): 293–305.

Kuhn, Thomas S. *The Structure of Scientific Revolutions.* 2nd ed. Chicago: University of Chicago Press, 1970.

Lamb, Catherine E. "Beyond Argument in Feminist Composition." *College Composition and Communication* 42.1 (1991): 11–24.

Landow, George P. *Hypertext.* Baltimore: Johns Hopkins University Press, 1992.

Langer, Judith. "Musings . . . A Sociocognitive View of Language Learning." *Research in the Teaching of English* 19.4 (1985): 325–27.

Lanham, Richard A. *The Electronic Word: Democracy, Technology, and the Arts.* Chicago: University of Chicago Press, 1993.

Larson, Richard. "Discovery through Questioning: A Plan for Teaching Rhetorical Invention." *College English* 30.2 (1968): 126–34.

———. "Problem-Solving, Composing, and Liberal Education." *College English* 33.6 (1972): 628–35.

Lauer, Janice. "Counterstatement: Response to Ann E. Berthoff." *College Composition and Communication* 23.2 (1972): 208–10.

———. "Hearistics and Composition." *College Composition and Communication* 21.3 (1970): 396–404.

LeFevre, Karen Burke. *Invention as a Social Act*. Carbondale: Southern Illinois University Press, 1987.

Lunsford, Andrea A. "Cognitive Development and the Basic Writer." *College English* 41.1 (1979): 38–46.

———. "Cognitive Studies and Teaching Writing." *Perspectives on Research and Scholarship in Composition*. Ed. Ben W. McClelland and Timothy R. Donovan. New York: MLA, 1985. 145–61.

———. "Intellectual Property in an Age of Information: What Is at Stake for Composition Studies?" *Composition in the Twenty-first Century: Crisis and Change*. Ed. Lynn Z. Bloom, Donald A. Daiker, and Edward M. White. Carbondale: Southern Illinois University Press, 1996. 261–72.

———, ed. *Reclaiming Rhetorica: Women in the Rhetorical Tradition*. Pittsburgh: University of Pittsburgh Press, 1995.

Lunsford, Andrea A., and Lisa Ede. *Singular Texts/Plural Authors: Perspectives on Collaborative Writing*. Carbondale: Southern Illinois University Press, 1990.

Lunsford, Andrea A., Helene Moglen, and James F. Slevin, eds. *The Right to Literacy*. New York: MLA, 1990.

Lyotard, Jean-François. *The Postmodern Condition: A Report on Knowledge*. Trans. Geoff Bennington and Brian Massumi. Minneapolis: University of Minnesota Press 1984.

Macedo, Donaldo. *Literacies of Power: What Americans Are Not Allowed to Know*. Boulder, CO: Westview Press, 1994.

McLeod, Susan. "The Affective Domain and the Writing Process: Working Definitions." *Journal of Advanced Composition* 11.1 (1991): 95–105.

———. "Some Thoughts about Feelings: The Affective Domain and the Writing Process." *College Composition and Communication* 38.4 (1987): 426–35.

Mailloux, Steven, ed. *Rhetoric, Sophistry, Pragmatism*. Cambridge: Cambridge University Press, 1995.

Miller, Carol A. " 'Better Than What People Told Me I Was': What Students of Color Tell Us about the Multicultural Composition Classroom." *Writing in Multicultural Settings*. Ed. Carol Severino, Juan C. Guerra, and Johnnella E. Butler. New York: MLA, 1997. 287–97.

Miller, Susan. *Rescuing the Subject*. Carbondale: Southern Illinois University Press, 1989.

Miller, Thomas P. *The Formation of College English: Rhetoric and Belles Lettres in the British Cultural Provinces*. Pittsburgh: University of Pittsburgh Press, 1997.

Moran, Charles. "Access: The A-Word in Technology Studies." *Passions, Pedagogies, and 21st Century Technologies*. Ed. Gail E. Hawisher and Cynthia Selfe. Logan: Utah State University Press, 1999. 205–20.

Moran, Michael G. *Eighteenth-Century British and American Rhetorics and Rhetoricians: Critical Studies and Sources*. Westport, CT: Greenwood Press, 1994.

Moss, Roger. "The Case for Sophistry." *Rhetoric Revalued*. Ed. Brian Vickers. Binghamton, NY: Center for Medieval and Early Renaissance Studies, 1982. 207–24.

Moulthrop, Stuart. "The Politics of Hypertext." *Evolving Perspectives on Computers and Composition Studies*. Ed. Gail Hawisher and Cynthia Selfe. Urbana, IL: NCTE, 1991. 253–71.

Murphy, James J. "The Historiography of Rhetoric: Challenges and Opportunities." *Rhetorica* 1.1 (1983): 1–8.

———, ed. *The Rhetorical Tradition and Modern Writing*. New York: MLA, 1982.

————. *A Short History of Writing Instruction from Ancient Greece to Twentieth Century America*, Davis, CA: Hermagoras, 1990.

Murphy, James J., and Richard A. Katula, eds. *A Synoptic History of Classical Rhetoric*. 2nd ed. Davis, CA: Hermagoras Press, 1994.

Myers, Greg. "Reality, Consensus, and Reform in the Rhetoric of Composition Teaching." *College English* 48.2 (1986): 154–73.

Neel, Jasper. *Aristotle's Voice*. Carbondale: Southern Illinois University Press, 1994.

————. *Plato, Derrida, and Writing*. Carbondale: Southern Illinois University Press, 1988.

Ney, James W. "Lessons from the Language Teacher: Cognition, Conditioning, and Controlled Composition." *College Composition and Communication* 24.2 (1973): 182–87.

Nietzsche, Friedrich. "On Truth and Lying in an Extra-Moral Sense." *Friedrich Nietzsche on Rhetoric and Language*. Ed. and trans. Sander L. Gilman, Carole Blair, and David J. Parent. Oxford: Oxford University Press, 1989. 246–57.

North, Stephen M. *The Making of Knowledge in Composition: Portrait of an Emerging Field*. Upper Monclair, NJ: Boynton/Cook, 1987.

Nye, Andrea. *Words of Power: A Feminist Reading of the History of Logic*. New York: Routledge, 1990.

Odell, Lee. "The Process of Writing and the Process of Learning." *College Composition and Communication* 31.1 (1980): 42–50.

————. "Teaching Writing by Teaching the Process of Discovery: An Interdisciplinary Enterprise." *Cognitive Processes in Writing*. Ed. Lee W. Gregg and Erwin R. Steinberg. Hillsdale, NJ: Erlbaum, 1980. 139–54.

Olson, Gary A., and Sidney I. Dobrin, eds. *Composition Theory for the Postmodern Classroom*. New York: SUNY Press, 1994.

Owens, Derek. *Resisting Writings (and the Boundaries of Composition)*. Dallas, TX: Southern Methodist University Press, 1994.

Payne, Michael, ed. *A Dictionary of Cultural and Critical Theory*. Malden, MA: Blackwell, 1998.

Penrose, Ann M., and Barbara M. Sitko, eds. *Hearing Ourselves Think: Cognitive Research in the College Writing Classroom*. New York: Oxford University Press, 1993.

Phelps, Louise Wetherbee, and Janet Emig, eds. *Feminine Principles and Women's Experience in American Composition and Rhetoric*. Pittsburgh: University of Pittsburgh Press, 1995.

Piazza, Carolyn L. "Identifying Context Variables in Research on Writing." *Written Communication* 4.2 (1987): 107–37.

Piche, Gene L., and Duane Roen. "Social Cognition and Writing: Interpersonal Cognitive Complexity and Abstractness and the Quality of Students' Persuasive Writing." *Written Communication* 4.1 (1987): 68–89.

Porter, James E. *Rhetorical Ethics and Internetworked Writing*. Greenwich, CT: Ablex Press, 1998.

Poulakos, John. "Gorgias' *Encomium to Helen* and the Defense of Rhetoric." *Rhetorica* 1.2 (1983): 1–16.

————. "Interpreting Sophistical Rhetoric: A Response to Schiappa." *Philosophy and Rhetoric* 23.3 (1990): 218–28.

———. *Sophistical Rhetoric in Classical Greece*. Columbia: University of South Carolina Press, 1995.

———. "Toward a Sophistic Definition of Rhetoric." *Philosophy and Rhetoric* 16 (1983): 35–48.

Poulakos, Takis, ed. *Rethinking the History of Rhetoric: Multidisciplinary Essays on the Rhetorical Tradition*. Boulder, CO: Westview Press, 1993.

Pratt, Mary Louise. "Arts of the Contact Zone." *Profession 91*. New York: MLA, 1991. 33–40.

Ratcliffe, Krista. *Anglo-American Feminist Challenges to the Rhetorical Traditions: Virginia Woolf, Mary Daly, Adrienne Rich*. Carbondale: Southern Illinois University Press, 1996.

Reed, Janine. "Self-Orientation in 'Expressive Writing' Instruction." *Journal of Teaching Writing* 13.1–2 (1994): 108–26.

Rheingold, Howard. *The Virtual Community*. Reading, MA: Addison-Wesley, 1993.

Robertson, Elizabeth. "Moving from Expressive Writing to Academic Discourse." *Writing Center Journal* 9.1 (1988): 21–28.

Romano, Susan. "The Egalitarianism Narrative: Whose Story? Which Yardstick?" *Computers and Composition* 10.1 (1993): 5–28.

Rose, Mike. "Narrowing the Mind and Page: Remedial Writers and Cognitive Reductionism." *College Composition and Communication* 35.3 (1988): 267–302.

———. "Rigid Rules, Inflexible Plans, and the Stifling of Language: A Cognitivist Analysis of Writing Block." *College Composition and Communication* 31.4 (1980): 389–400.

———. *Writer's Block: The Cognitive Dimension*. Carbondale: Southern Illinois University Press, 1984.

Rubin, Donald L. "Social Cognition and Written Communication." *Written Communication* 1.2 (1984): 211–45.

Russell, David R. "Romantics on Writing: Liberal Culture and the Absolution on Composition Courses." *Rhetoric Review* 6.2 (1988): 132–48.

———. *Writing in the Academic Disciplines, 1870–1990: A Curricular History*. Carbondale: Southern Illinois University Press, 1991.

Schaafsma, David. *Eating on the Street: Teaching Literacy in a Multicultural Society*. Pittsburgh: University of Pittsburgh Press, 1993.

Schiappa, Edward. "Did Plato Coin *Rhetorike?*" *American Journal of Philology* 111.4 (1990): 457–70.

———. "Neo-Sophistic Rhetorical Criticism or the Historical Reconstruction of Sophistic Doctrines." *Philosophy and Rhetoric* 23.3 (1990): 192–217.

———. "Sophistic Rhetoric: Oasis or Mirage?" *Rhetoric Review* 10.1 (1991): 5–18.

Schmidt, Jan Zlotnik. *Women/Writing/Teaching*. Albany: State University of New York Press, 1998.

Scott, Robert L. "On Viewing Rhetoric as Epistemic." *Central States Speech Journal* 18.1 (1967): 9–17.

Selfe, Cynthia L. "Lest We Think the Revolution Is a Revolution." *Passions, Pedagogies, and 21st Century Technologies*. Ed. Gail E. Hawisher and Cynthia L. Selfe. Logan: Utah State University Press, 1999. 292–322.

Selfe, Cynthia L., and Susan Hilligoss, eds. *Literacy and Computers: The Complications of Teaching and Learning with Technology*. New York: MLA, 1994.

Selfe, Cynthia L., and Paul Meyer. "Testing Claims for Online Conferences." *Written Communication* 8.2 (1991): 163–92.

Severino, Carol, Juan C. Guerra, and Johnnella E. Butler, eds. *Writing in Multicultural Settings*. New York: MLA, 1997.

Shirks, Henrietta Nickels. "Hypertext and Composition Studies." *Evolving Perspectives on Computers and Composition Studies*. Ed. Gail Hawisher and Cynthia Selfe. Urbana, IL: NCTE, 1991. 177–202.

Shor, Ira. *Critical Teaching and Everyday Life*. Boston: South End Press, 1980.

Sirc, Geoffrey. "Writing Classroom as A & P Parking Lot." *PRE/TEXT* 14.1–2 (1993): 27–72.

Sirc, Geoffrey, and Tom Reynolds. "The Face of Collaboration in the Networked Writing Classroom." *Computers and Composition* 7.1 (1990): 53–70.

Spear, Karen. "Building Cognitive Skills in Basic Writers." *Teaching English in the Two-Year College* 9.2 (1983): 91–98.

———. "Thinking and Writing: A Sequential Curriculum for Composition." *Journal of Advanced Composition* 4.1 (1983): 47–63.

Spigelman, Candace. "Teaching Expressive Writing as Narrative Fiction." *JAC* 16.1 (1996): 119–40.

Stallard, Charles. "Composing: A Cognitive Process Theory." *College Composition and Communication* 27.2 (1976): 181–84.

Sternglass, Marilyn S. "Assessing Reading, Writing, and Reasoning." *College English* 43.3 (1981): 269–75.

Sullivan, Patricia A., and Donna J. Qualley, eds. *Pedagogy in the Age of Politics: Writing and Reading (in) the Academy*. Urbana, IL: NCTE, 1994.

Swearingen, C. Jan. *Rhetoric and Irony: Western Literacy and Western Lies*. New York: Oxford University Press, 1991.

Trimbur, John. "Composition Studies: Postmodern or Popular." *Into the Field: Sites of Composition Studies*. Ed. Anne Ruggles Gere. New York: MLA, 1993. 117–32.

———. "Consensus and Difference in Collaborative Learning." *College English* 51.6 (1989): 602–16.

Tuman, Myron C., ed. *Literacy Online: The Promise (and Peril) of Reading and Writing with Computers*. Pittsburgh: University of Pittsburgh Press, 1992.

Ulmer, Greg. "Grammatology (in the Stacks) of Hypermedia: A Simulation." *Literacy Online: The Promise (and Peril) of Reading and Writing with Computers*. Ed. Myron C. Tuman. Pittsburgh: University of Pittsburgh Press, 1992. 135–54.

Vickers, Brian. *In Defence of Rhetoric*. Oxford: Clarendon Press, 1988.

Villaneuva, Victor, Jr. *Bootstraps: From an American Academic of Color*. Urbana, IL: NCTE, 1993.

Vitanza, Victor J. "A Feminist Sophistic?" *JAC* 15.2 (1995): 321–49.

———. *Negation, Subjectivity, and the History of Rhetoric*. Albany: State University of New York Press, 1997.

———. "Some Rudiments of Histories of Rhetorics and Rhetorics of Histories." *Rethinking the History of Rhetoric*. Ed. Takis Poulakos. Boulder, CO: Westview Press, 1993. 193–239.

———. "Three Countertheses: Or, A Critical In(ter)vention into Composition Theories and Pedagogies." *Contending with Words*. Ed. Patricia Harkin and John Schilb. New York: MLA, 1991. 139–72.

———, ed. *Writing Histories of Rhetoric*. Carbondale: Southern Illinois University Press, 1994.

Welch, Kathleen E. *The Contemporary Reception of Classical Rhetoric: Appropriations of Ancient Discourse*. Hillsdale, NJ: Erlbaum, 1990.

———. "A Critique of Classical Rhetoric." *Rhetoric Review* 6.1 (1987): 79–86.

Wiley, Mark. "Writing in the American Grain: Peter Elbow's and David Bartholomae's Emersonian Pedagogies of Empowerment." *The Writing Instructor* 9.1–2 (1989–1990): 57–66.

Wilson, Matthew. "Research, Expressivism, and Silence." *JAC* 15.2 (1995): 241–60.

Winchell, Donna Haisty. "Developmental Psychology and Basic Writers." *Research in Basic Writing*. Ed. Michael G. Moran and Martin J. Jacobi. Westport, CT: Greenwood Press, 1990. 31–47.

Woods, Marjorie. "Among Men—Not Boys: Histories of Rhetoric and the Exclusion of Pedagogy." *Rhetoric Society Quarterly* 22.1 (1992): 18–26.

Worsham, Lynn. "Writing against Writing: The Predicament of *Écriture Féminine* in Composition Studies." *Contending with Words: Composition and Rhetoric in a Postmodern Age*. Ed. Patricia Harkin and John Schilb. New York: MLA, 1991. 82–104.

Young, Richard. "Paradigms and Problems: Needed Research in Rhetorical Invention." *Research on Composing: Points of Departure*. Ed. Charles R. Cooper and Lee Odell. Urbana, IL: National Council of Teachers of English, 1978. 29–47.

Zeiger, William. "The Personal Essay and Egalitarian Rhetoric." *Literary Nonfiction: Theory, Criticism, Pedagogy*. Ed. Chris Anderson. Carbondale: Southern Illinois University Press, 1989. 235–44.

INDEX

ABOUT THE EDITORS AND CONTRIBUTORS

MICHELLE BALLIF is Assistant Professor of English at the University of Georgia, where she teaches courses in rhetoric, composition, and critical and literary theory. Her research focus is the intersection between classical rhetoric(s) and postmodern theories. She has published in *PRE/TEXT, JAC, Rhetoric Review, Rhetoric Society Quarterly*, and *Studies in Psychoanalytic Theory*. Her book *Seduction, Sophistry, and the Woman with the Rhetorical Figure* is forthcoming from Southern Illinois University Press.

DAVID BRAUER is Assistant Professor of English at Lander University, where he teaches freshman English, advanced writing courses and rhetorical theory. His research interests include the intersection between composition and literature.

STEPHEN H. BROWNE is Professor of Speech Communication at The Pennsylvania State University. He is the author of *Edmund Burke and the Discourse of Virtue* (1993) and *Angelina Grimke: Rhetoric, Identity, and the Radical Imagination* (1999). He teaches courses in rhetorical theory and criticism, and currently serves as editor of *Philosophy and Rhetoric*.

CHRISTOPHER C. BURNHAM, Professor of English and Academic Department Head, has been teaching university-level writing since 1972. He joined the English faculty at New Mexico State University in 1981. His expertise covers rhetoric and the teaching of writing; program assessment and evaluation; writing and learning, especially academic and personal uses of journals; and the nonfiction prose essay. He is currently working on a National Science Foundation–supported grant, "Science Literacy in Non-SMET Majors," developing materials to be used within a first-year writing course to enhance science literacy among nonscience majors. The materials include readings, writing assignments, and critical thinking exercises investigating how science-based thinking and methodology permeate current culture and politics. This follows earlier work published in *Investigating Astronomy: Model-Building and Critical Thinking* (1997) with B. McNamara, B. Bridges, and M. French, that offered a writing-based approach to teaching introductory astronomy with minority and female students as the primary audience. He is also working on the rhetoric of Thomas Merton, monk, mystic, and peace activist of the 1960s.

GREGORY CLARK is Professor of English at Brigham Young University, where he currently directs the American Studies program. He teaches courses in rhetoric, writing, and American literature and culture. His research and writing examine matters of rhetorical theory and the history of rhetorical practice in the United States. He is author of numerous articles and chapters, of *Dialogue, Dialectic, and Conversation* (1990), and coeditor, with S. Michael Halloran, of *Oratorical Culture in Nineteentnth-Century America* (1993). He is also Editor of *Rhetoric Society Quarterly*.

D. DIANE DAVIS is an Assistant Professor of Rhetoric at the University of Iowa. Her research and teaching interests include rhetoric and writing theory, cybercommunications, and posthumanist rhetorics of community. Her first book, *Breaking Up [at] Totality: A Rhetoric of Laughter* (2000), is the second volume in Southern Illinois University Press's New Rhetorical Philosophy series, and her essays have appeared in such journals as *PRE/TEXT, JAC, Rhetoric Review, Rhetoric Society Quarterly*, and *Studies in Psychoanalytic Theory*.

RAY D. DEARIN is Professor of English, Speech Communication, and Political Science at Iowa State University, where he teaches courses in rhetorical theory, public address, and political communication. He has edited *The New Rhetoric of Chaim Perelman: Statement and Response* (1989) and has published essays in journals such as the *Quarterly Journal of Speech, Communication Education, Central States Speech Journal*, and the *Presidential Studies Quarterly*.

NANCY C. DEJOY is Associate Professor of English at Millikin University, where she directs First-Year Writing Programs and holds the Professorship for Excellence in Teaching. She teaches first-year writing, writing seminars, rhetorical theory, feminism, and science fiction. Her research interests include literacy-based service learning, the history of modern composition studies, and revising the process model to accommodate critical discursive practices in rich ways. She is Director of the Summer Seminar in Rhetoric and Composition and Editor of *Composition Chronicle*. Her work has been published in a variety of journals and anthologies. Her most recent essay, "I Was a Process-Model Baby," appears in the Southern Illinois University Press collection *Post-Process Theory: Beyond the Writing-Process Paradigm* (edited by Thomas Kent, 1999).

CHRISTY DESMET, an Associate Professor of English at the University of Georgia, is the author of *Reading Shakespeare's Characters: Rhetoric, Ethics, and Identity* (1992) and coeditor of *Shakespeare and Appropriation* (1999). She has published essays on rhetoric in early modern drama and on contemporary rhetoric and composition, including "Equivalent Students, Equitable Classrooms" in *Feminism and Composition Studies: In Other Words* (edited by Susan Jarratt and Lynn Worsham, 1998).

RONDA LEATHERS DIVELY is Assistant Professor of Composition and Rhetoric, the Area Head for English Education, and the recently appointed Director of Writing Studies at Southern Illinois University at Carbondale. In addition to teaching graduate seminars in the composition and rhetoric program, she teaches English methods, young adult literature, and various undergraduate writing courses. Her research focuses primarily on matters of invention and on various aspects of religious discourse. She has presented several papers at the Conference on College Composition and Communication and has published in *Composition Studies, Kansas English*, the *Illinois English Bulletin, Composition Forum, Readerly/Writerly Texts*, and *Writing on the Edge*.

BERNARD K. DUFFY is Professor and former Chair of the Speech Communication Department at California Polytechnic State University in San Luis Obispo. He teaches classical and contemporary rhetorical theory and the history of American public address, subjects about which he has published articles, essays, and books. He is coeditor, with Halford Ryan, of *American Orators before 1990* (1987); coeditor, with Lorraine Jackson, of *Health Communication Research* (1998); coauthor, with Martin Jacobi, of *The Politics of Rhetoric: Richard Weaver and the Conservative Tradition* (1993); and coauthor, with Ronald Carpenter, of *Douglas MacArthur: Warrior and Wordsmith* (1997). He is also coeditor for Greenwood Press of a series of 28 books on individual American orators.

THERESA ENOS is Professor of English and Director of the Rhetoric, Composition, and the Teaching of English Graduate Program at the University of Arizona. Founder and Editor of *Rhetoric Review*, she teaches both graduate and undergraduate courses in writing and rhetoric. Her research interests include the history and theory of rhetoric and the intellectual work and politics of rhetoric and composition studies. She has edited or coedited seven books, including the *Encyclopedia of Rhetoric and Composition: Communication from Ancient Times to the Information Age* (1995), and has published numerous chapters and articles on rhetorical theory and issues in writing. She is the author of *Gender Roles and Faculty Lives in Rhetoric and Composition* (1996) and immediate past president of the National Council of Writing Program Administrators.

KAREN A. FOSS is Professor and Chair of Communication and Journalism at the University of New Mexico, where she teaches courses in rhetorical theory, rhetorical criticism, feminist rhetorical theories, and gender and communication. Her research interests include contemporary rhetorical theory, especially feminist perspectives on rhetoric; the discourse of marginalized groups; and contemporary social movements. She is the coauthor of *Contemporary Perspectives on Rhetoric* (1991), *Women Speak: The Eloquence of Women's Lives* (1991), *Inviting Transformation: Presentational Speaking for a Changing World* (1994), and *Feminist Rhetorical Theories* (1999).

LUANNE FRANK is Associate Professor of English at the University of Texas at Arlington, where she teaches courses in contemporary thought (poststructuralist theory and its antecedents), psychoanalysis, semiotics, and hermeneutics. Her research interests include eighteenth-century German thought (Hamann, Herder), Heidegger, and the clandestine suppression of femaleness in world culture. She has edited *Literature and the Occult* (1977), coedited *Husbanding the Golden Grain* (1973) with Emory George, cotranslated and coedited with Marianne Burkhart, introduced Emil Staiger's *Basic Concepts of Poetics* (1991) (a Heideggerian poetics), and published on eighteenth-century aesthetic and semiotic theories.

SHERRIE L. GRADIN is Professor of English and Director of the Writing across the Curriculum Program at Ohio University. She teaches courses in rhetorical theory and writing. Her research interests include writing program administration, history of rhetoric, and gender studies. Gradin has published articles on writing program administration and a book on expressivist rhetorics, *Romancing Rhetorics* (1995). She has a composition textbook cowritten with Duncan Carter forthcoming.

RUSSELL GREER is Assistant Professor of English at Texas Woman's University, where he teaches modern rhetoric and nineteenth- and twentieth-century English literature. His research interests include editorial theory, composition, and Bakhtin studies.

CYNTHIA HAYNES is Assistant Professor in the School of Arts & Humanities and Director of Rhetoric and Writing at the University of Texas at Dallas, where she teaches both graduate and undergraduate rhetoric, composition, digital culture, informatics, and electronic expression. Her articles have appeared in *PRE/TEXT, Composition Studies, Works & Days, The Writing Center Journal, Kairos*, and *CWRL*, as well as in several recently published collections of essays. She is coeditor (with Victor Vitanza) of *PRE/TEXT: Electra(Lite)*, an electronic journal publishing innovative scholarship in/on digital rhetorics. With Jan Rune Holmevik, she is cofounder of Lingua MOO, coeditor of their collection of essays, *High Wired: On the Design, Use, and Theory of Educational MOOs* (1998), and coauthor of *MOOniversity: A Guide to Virtual Learning Environments*, forthcoming from Allyn and Bacon.

LISA L. HILL is Assistant Professor at Southeastern Oklahoma State University, where she teaches courses in rhetoric, writing, critical theory, and ancient humanities. She is the Coordinator of the Southeastern Honors Program and is active in Honors at the regional and national levels. With interests in composition, rhetoric, psychoanalysis, gender studies, critical theory, and the phenomenon of postmodernism, she has published essays in *Keywords in Composition Studies* and a review article in the journal *Composition Studies*. Work in progress includes an article linking rhetorics, poetics, aesthetics, and subjectivity and a book-length project that rereads the writing of Virginia Woolf for rhetorical theory and composition pedagogy.

KATHY M. HOUFF teaches English at the University of Georgia. Her teaching and research interests include composition and rhetoric, creative writing, American nineteenth- and twentieth-century writing, and feminist pedagogy.

MARTIN J. JACOBI is Professor and Chair of the English Department at Clemson University, where he teaches classical and contemporary rhetoric and composition. In addition to a number of articles on rhetoric and composition, he is coeditor, with Michael G. Moran, of *Research in Basic Writing* (1990) and coauthor, with Bernard Duffy, of *The Politics of Rhetoric: Richard M. Weaver and the Conservative Tradition* (1993). He is currently at work on a book on Wayne C. Booth for SUNY Press.

MARTIN M. JACOBSEN is Assistant Professor at West Texas A&M University, where he directs the Writing Center and teaches English. He is also associate editor/Webmaster of the LINGUIST List. He earned his Ph.D. in Discourse Studies at Texas A&M University. An active Web designer, he has published and presented on nonlinearity and hypertext.

SUSAN C. JARRATT is Professor of English and Affiliate of the Women's Studies Program at Miami University in Oxford. Her 1991 book *Rereading the Sophists: Classical Rhetoric Refigured* won Honorable Mention for the Modern Language Association's Mina Shaughnessy Prize and has recently been rereleased in paperback. She coedited *Feminism and Composition Studies: In Other Words* (1998) with Lynn Worsham and is currently working on a book about rhetoric, critical theory, and public space with the assistance of a National Endowment for the Humanities Fellowship.

HANS KELLNER is Professor of English at the University of Texas at Arlington, where he teaches courses in rhetorical theory and historical discourse. He is the author of *Language and Historical Representation: Getting the Story Crooked* (1989) and numerous essays; he has also edited with F. R. Ankersmit *A New Philosophy of History* (1995).

PATRICIA J. McALEXANDER is an Associate Professor in the English component of the University of Georgia's Division of Academic Assistance. She has published a number of articles on teaching composition and has coauthored a book, *Beyond the "SP" Label* (1992) and a grammar text, *Correct Writing* (6th ed., 1995).

MARY HURLEY MORAN is Associate Professor in the Division of Academic Assistance at the University of Georgia, where she teaches basic writing, composition for nonnative speakers, and grammar. She has published books on contemporary British novelists Margaret Drabble and Penelope Lively, as well as articles on modern British fiction, composition, basic writing, and technical communication.

MICHAEL G. MORAN is Associate Professor of English at the University of Georgia, where he teaches courses in eighteenth-century British literature, rhetorical theory, and writing. His research interests include the history of rhetoric and the history of technical communication. He has edited and coedited books in rhetoric and technical communication, including, with Debra Journet, *Research in Technical Communication* (1986), which won a National Council of Teachers of English Award. More recent books include *Eighteenth-Century British and American Rhetorics and Rhetoricians* (1994) and, with Teresa Kynell, *Three Keys to the Past: The History of Technical Communication* (1999).

ROXANNE MOUNTFORD is Assistant Professor of English at the University of Arizona, where she teaches courses in contemporary rhetorical theory and criticism, research methods, and composition. Her research interests include gender and communication, religious rhetoric, and new methodologies for the study of rhetoric. She has published in *Rhetoric Review, College English, JAC*, and other journals and has chapters in several books, including Peter Mortensen and Gesa Kirsch's *Ethics and Representation in Qualitative Studies of Literacy* (1997). She is working on a book about women preachers.

GERALD P. MULDERIG is Associate Professor of English and Director of First-Year Writing at DePaul University in Chicago, Illinois. He is the author of *The Heath Handbook* (1990) and of articles on rhetorical criticism, the teaching of writing, and the history of rhetoric and composition in the nineteenth and twentieth centuries.

GERALD NELMS is Associate Professor of English at Southern Illinois University at Carbondale. He was Acting Chair of his department for 1998–1999 and is currently Assistant to the Chair. He teaches courses in composition history, theory, and practice and in technical communication. His research interests include the history and theory of composition and rhetoric, oral history, invention theory, writing across the curriculum, and technical communication. He has published in *Rhetoric Review, Rhetoric Society Quarterly*, and *Written Communication* and is currently at work on a historical introduction to composition theory and a composition textbook, informed by social cognitive theories of writing. Professor Nelms also hosts *Music from Beyond the Lakes*, a weekly New Age and world music radio show.

DEBORAH A. NOEL is completing a Ph.D. in rhetoric and literacy studies at the University of Georgia. Her research interests include rhetoric and composition, poststructuralism, feminist theory, historiography, and American fiction. Her forthcoming dissertation examines the relationship between writing and death, with a focus on the epitaph in American novels.

KRISTA RATCLIFFE is Associate Professor of English at Marquette University in Milwaukee, Wisconsin. She teaches writing, rhetorical theory, and women's literature. Her scholarly work emerges at the intersections of rhetorical theory, feminist theory, and reading/writing pedagogy, as evidenced by her book *Anglo-American Feminist Challenges to the Rhetorical Traditions: Virginia Woolf, Mary Daly, Adrienne Rich* (1996) and by her articles in *CCC, Rhetoric Review, Studies in the Literary Imagination*, and *The Writing Instructor*. Her current book-length study, *Rhetorical Listening*, explores how rhetoric and composition studies may recover listening in theory and praxis in ways that promote a feminist literacy—a literacy in which awareness of gender is complicated by other cultural categories, such as "race" (including whiteness). The purpose of such literacy is to facilitate cross-cultural dialogues in the classroom and beyond.

NEDRA REYNOLDS is an Associate Professor of English at the University of Rhode Island, where she teaches courses in writing and rhetorical theory. Her recent publications include an article in *CCC* on "Composition's Imagined Geographies" and a chapter in *Feminism and Composition Studies: In Other Words* (1998) on feminist cultural studies and composition. *Portfolio Keeping: A Guide for Students* (2000) and *Portfolio Teaching: A Guide for Teachers* (2000) were published by Bedford Books, and she has recently coedited the fifth edition of *The Bedford Bibliography for Teachers of Writing* (2000).

CLAIRE ROCHE is a Ph.D. candidate in Rhetoric and Composition and teaching assistant in the College Writing Program at the University of Rhode Island.

CHRISTINE ROSS is an Assistant Professor in the Department of English and Comparative Literature at the University of California, Irvine, and Course Director for Writing 39B, the entry-level freshman course in composition. She has given papers at the Conference on College Composition and Communication, the International Society for the History of Rhetoric, and does interdisciplinary research on Standard English in the history of composition-rhetoric and nineteenth-century U.S. literature.

PHILLIP SIPIORA is Associate Professor and Associate Chair of English at the University of South Florida, where he teaches courses in the history of rhetoric, American literature, and film. He has published essays on classical and modern rhetoric, as well as on twentieth-century literature. He has coedited two books on rhetoric, including *Ethical Issues in College Writing* (edited by Fredric G. Gale, Phillip Sipiora, and James L. Kinneavy, 1999) and *Rhetoric and Kairos: Essays in History, Theory, and Praxis* (edited by Phillip Sipiora and James S. Baumlin, 2000). A second volume in the *Kairos* series is under contract with

Edwin Mellen, *Kairos in Translation: Twentieth-Century Essays on the Temporal Dimensions of Rhetoric* (edited by James S. Baumlin and Phillip Sipiora).

JO SUZUKI is Assistant Professor of English at The Master's College in Santa Clarita, California. He teaches courses in rhetoric and composition, contemporary critical theory, English linguistics, and world literature. His current research projects include capitalism and pedagogy and schizoanalytic cultural criticism.

C. JAN SWEARINGEN is Professor of English at Texas A&M University and has also served in the English Departments of the University of Texas at Arlington, Texas Christian University, and the University of Arizona. Her book *Rhetoric and Irony: Western Literacy and Western Lies* shared the 1991 W. Ross Winterowd Award from *JAC* for the best book published that year in composition theory. She has published numerous chapters and articles on the history of rhetoric, feminist approaches to rhetoric, women rhetoricians, discourse analysis of speech genres, rhetoric and religion, and the rhetoric of human rights in emerging democracies. She is the 1998–2000 President of the Rhetoric Society of America and editor of *Rhetoric, the Polis, and the Global Village*, papers from the 1998 Rhetoric Society of America meetings.

REX L. VEEDER is Associate Professor of English at St. Cloud State University, where he teaches rhetoric, composition, and the teaching of English. He is the Composition Director as well as the Director of the American Indian Center. His research interests include cross-cultural rhetoric, teaching and learning methods, and the history of romantic rhetoric. He has been the Editor for the *Rhetoric Society Quarterly* and has published in *Rhetoric Review* and the *Rhetoric Society Quarterly*. He is currently finishing a textbook that focuses on rhetoric, genre, and incubation.

VICTOR J. VITANZA is Professor of English at the University of Texas at Arlington, where he teaches a variety of courses in literacy and electracy. He is the Editor of the journal *PRE/TEXT*, the Coeditor of *PRE/TEXT: Electra(Lite)*, and the moderator of the *PRE/TEXT List* (www.pre-text.com). His most recent book is *Negation, Subjectivity, and the History of Rhetoric* (1997). He is completing a book tentatively titled *Canonicity, Rape Narratives, and the History of Rhetoric* and has begun another book titled *James Berlin and Cultural Studies*.

JOHN WARNOCK teaches rhetoric at the University of Arizona.

TILLY WARNOCK is Associate Professor of English at the University of Arizona, where she directs the Composition Program and is a member of the Rhetoric, Composition, and Teaching of English faculty. Her research focuses primarily on the teaching of writing, on writing program administration, and on Kenneth Burke and contemporary rhetorical theory. She has published articles on rhetoric, composition, writing centers, and Kenneth Burke. She published a composition textbook, *Writing Is Critical Action* (1988), and with Joe Trimmer she edited *Understanding Others: Cultural and Cross-Cultural Studies and the Teaching of English* (1992).

JAMES P. ZAPPEN is Associate Professor in the Department of Language, Literature, and Communication at Rensselaer Polytechnic Institute, where he teaches courses in rhetorical theory and Web design. He has research interests in dialogical rhetoric, cyberhetoric, and electronic community networking and has published articles in *Philosophy and Rhetoric, Rhetoric Review, Rhetoric Society Quarterly, Rhetorica*, and other journals.

SHANNON ZIMMERMAN is a Ph.D. candidate in English at the University of Georgia, where he specializes in British Romanticism, literary theory, and rhetoric. His dissertation "The Terror of the Text" (1999) examines the psychology of canonization. He has presented papers at numerous conferences and currently works as a Web designer in Alexandria, Virginia.

ISBN 0-313-30391-6

90000>

EAN

9 780313 303913

HARDCOVER BAR CODE